Burma—From Kingdom to Republic

BURMA
FROM KINGDOM
TO REPUBLIC

A Historical and Political Analysis

FRANK N. TRAGER

FREDERICK A. PRAEGER, *Publishers*
New York · Washington · London

FREDERICK A. PRAEGER, PUBLISHERS
111 Fourth Avenue, New York, N.Y. 10003, U.S.A.
77–79 Charlotte Street, London, W.1, England

Published in the United States of America in 1966
by Frederick A. Praeger, Inc., Publishers

Library of Congress Catalog Card Number: 65–24936

Printed in the United States of America

To

My Wife, Helen

*Who from the beginning shared in the satisfactions
and the labors of our Burmese experience and
who contributed to, while living
through, the preparation of this book*

PREFACE

ON THE FOURTH DAY of each January, the people of Burma celebrate the occasion that marks the re-establishment of their independence as a nation-state. The transfer of power from a British colonial regime to a republic took place at 4:20 A.M., January 4, 1948. This, according to Burmese authority, was the "auspicious" time to proclaim the event which had already been assured by agreement with London. The Burmese Declaration of Independence reviewed the past and called attention "once more" to "the complete freedom that is our birthright." It and the accompanying ten-point "Pledge to the Union" paid homage to one named person, Bogyoke (a special affectionate term for General, used sparingly) Aung San, whose principles and unremitting labor "brought us the coveted crown of complete freedom."

The events that this declaration and pledge symbolize brought me and my wife to Burma. For the U.S. Government quickly exchanged instruments of recognition, and, in 1950, signed the first aid agreement with the Union of Burma. We arrived in Burma in 1951—and have returned repeatedly.

The idea for this study grew out of the need for some such work, for material on Burma by Americans was in very short supply. Once, in the middle 1950's, I undertook the task of editing and co-authoring what became a twenty-man effort on Burma. The three volumes we produced were destined for governmental agencies. I decided then that I would someday do my own study, and this is it.

The more I have learned about Burma and the Burmese, the more I have become convinced that central to an understanding of its 1,500 years of recorded history are the ideas of independence and unity of the several ethnic groups who people the "golden land." The hundreds of square miles of ripening rice before the harvest, matching the color of the innumerable gold-leaf–covered pagodas, prompted the name of the "golden land," which Burmese have adopted for their country. And quietly, but fiercely, they love their land. Few—very few—leave it permanently.

The basic theme of this study is the independence of Burma: how it was lost and regained and retained. A secondary theme, implicit in the first, is Burma's relations to the major powers whose roles in Asia affect her international conduct. These are, of course, the People's Republic of China, the U.S.S.R., and the United States.

The book is designed to help the reader, especially the Western reader, gain an understanding of a too-little-known country. It may come as a surprise, but Americans, through missionaries, actually have had contact with Burma longer than with any other Asian nation. From the time that Adoniram and Ann Judson arrived in Rangoon as Baptist missionaries in July, 1813, some Americans have been in continuous residence in that country. Despite this, Burma remained relatively unknown to the United States. For with the exception of the missionary writings, few American scholars had devoted themselves to its study before World War II. Only two scholarly books on Burma by Americans were published in the U.S. between the two World Wars—one in 1922, the other in 1942. Since then, this deficiency has been slowly remedied.

The patterns of Burma's history are examined here less for their own sake than for the light they shed on the development of an inviting land and the outlook of its attractive people. The records, both past and present, have been, I trust, objectively searched and amply presented. However, the reader will easily discover that the weight of the argument in this study favors Burma's long-held goal of independence and unity, without which her chance for survival in a difficult world would easily disappear.

Not all her difficulties are externally stimulated. Burma's civilian and military leaders since independence have been generally socialist, or, to use Nehru's word to describe himself and close colleagues, socialistic. But they have not yet been able to combine this brand of socialism with full freedom. That remains the major domestic task as Burma approaches the close of the second decade as an independent republic. All friends of Burma expect an early and generous resolution of the problems involved in this task.

FRANK N. TRAGER

Salem Center, New York
August, 1965

ACKNOWLEDGMENTS

The list would be very long if I were to name the Burmese who, always with friendly patience, transmitted to me some knowledge and insight. In Burmese fashion they would prefer to be unnamed. But if by chance they read these pages, they will recognize my debt and accept my gratitude.

Of the several times we revisited Burma, twice I was the fortunate recipient of travel and research grants. I am indebted to the Council on Foreign Relations for its Carnegie Fellowship and to the Relm Foundation. Once I was a "guest of state" of the Burma Government.

F.N.T.

CONTENTS

Burma—From Kingdom to Republic

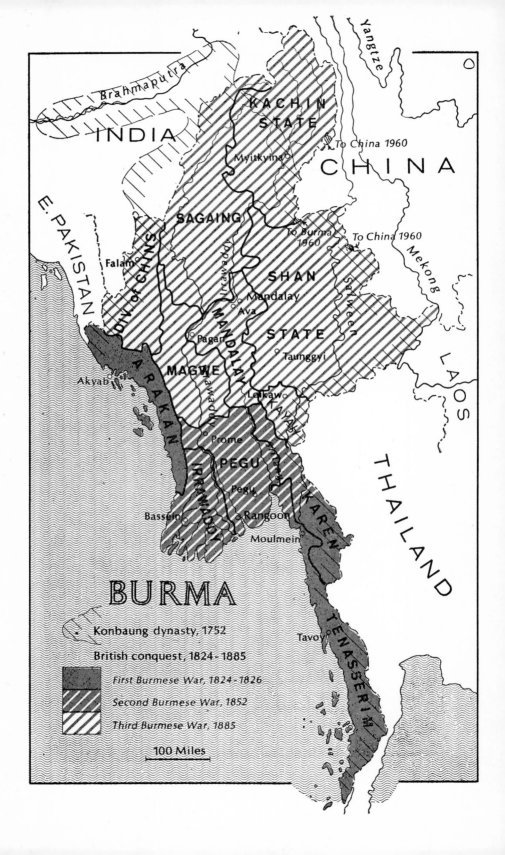

Yangtze

Brahmaputra

INDIA

E. PAKISTAN

KACHIN STATE

Myitkyina

To China 1960

CHINA

SAGAING

To Burma 1960

To China 1960

Mekong

Salween

LAOS

Falam

UNION OF CHINS

SHAN

MANDALAY

Mandalay

Ava

Pagan

STATE

Taunggyi

MAGWE

Akyab

Loikaw

ARAKAN

Prome

Irrawaddy

Salween

THAILAND

PEGU

Pegu

KAREN

Bassein

Rangoon

Moulmein

BURMA

Konbaung dynasty, 1752

British conquest, 1824-1885

First Burmese War, 1824-1826

Second Burmese War, 1852

Third Burmese War, 1885

TENASSERIM

Tavoy

100 Miles

PART I · THE RISE OF MODERN BURMA

WHEN SPAIN AND PORTUGAL divided the world between them at the end of the fifteenth century, Southern Asia, including Burma, was awarded to the Portuguese. Adventurers in search of profits and missionaries in search of souls invaded the area, but in the century that followed, Burma beckoned to Portuguese and other foreign commercial interests far less than did India and the East Indies. This was partly because of Burma's remoteness from the chief shipping lanes. The main reason for the absence of European encroachment, however, was the renaissance that sixteenth-century Burma was experiencing under the strong Toungoo dynasty, founded by Minkyinyo (1486-1531) and his son, Tabinshwehti (1531-50). These Burman kings extended their rule to the other major ethnic groups, the Shans and the Mons, unifying Burma for the second time in its history. The first consolidation had taken place under the Pagan dynasty, which ruled from the middle of the eleventh century to the end of the thirteenth, when Burma was defeated by the Mongols. The Toungoo kings, especially Bayinnaung (1551-81), celebrated in European song and story as Braginoco, successfully defended Burma against Portuguese encroachments, and for a time they extended its boundaries to include Chittagong, Manipur, and Assam in the west, and Laos and Siam in the east.

Throughout the sixteenth century, Burma's capital, Pegu—whose famous jars for storing rice and water are still being made—was praised in the reports of European visitors, from Ludovico di Varthema, who reached Burma in 1503, to Caesar Fredericke, who reported on its commerce and customs in the 1560's. Ralph Fitch, the first Englishman to visit the country, described Pegu in the late 1580's as "a citie very great, strong, and very faire, with walles of stone, and great ditches round about it . . . whose streets are the fairest that ever I saw, as straight as a line from one gate to the other, and so broad that tenne or twelve men may ride a front thorow them." [1]

Burma's local trade and external commerce in precious and other metals, jewels, rice, shellac, Pegu or Martaban jars, and teak were conducted with "business-like methods and honesty [which] won the esteem of European merchants." [2] Portuguese freebooters were employed as business and administrative agents and especially as mercenaries in the wars against Burma's neighbors, but the missionizing efforts of her Roman Catholic priests were rejected by the Buddhist population.[3]

The connection between the Englishman Ralph Fitch and Burma had both actual and symbolic effects—not the least of which was that one of his descendants, Lieutenant-General Albert Fytche, served in Burma as Chief Commissioner from 1867 to 1871. When Ralph Fitch returned home, in 1591, English maritime and trading interests had been stimulated by the defeat of the Spanish Armada. Fitch and his companions had journeyed eastward on behalf of one of the several chartered trading companies interested in the Middle East. His account of lucrative trading possibilities with India and Burma, buttressed by that of Caesar Fredericke, which had been translated and published just prior to his return, fed the growing demand among London merchants for the right to some of the rich rewards of commerce with the Indies.[4] At the turn of the century, two events further roused the fighting spirit of the British merchants: the death in 1598 of Philip II of Spain and Portugal, foe of England; and the alleged sudden monopolistic combine forged by the Dutch and Portuguese pepper traders in Antwerp, which forced the price of that essential commodity from 3 to 8 shillings a pound. Meetings in London in 1599 led the next year to the formation and chartering of the East India Company.[5] And it was this "Honorable Company," as it was called by those who served it, and its successor companies that in the seventeenth and eighteenth centuries gradually made their way into Burma.

To Burma by Way of India and Siam

The Governor (or chief officer) and Company of Merchants Trading to the East Indies—the original name of the East India Company—received their charter from Queen Elizabeth, who gave them virtual sovereign power abroad and exclusive trading rights against "interlopers," or other private English traders. In return, the Company eventually acquired an Asian empire for the Crown, which it ruled until 1858. In 1602, the Dutch East India Company was organized as a unit by six existing Dutch companies. It was managed by the *Heeren XVII*, seventeen delegates chosen from among the organizing companies or chambers. In time, the two rival British and Dutch companies displaced the Portuguese, although even today remnants of old Portuguese possessions exist, and individuals of Portuguese-Asian ancestry continue to live and work in these Asian lands.

There is no need to detail here the changing alliances and wars among the European powers that sought to gain commercial advantage and wield imperial power over the various peoples who inhabit the huge area stretching from Afghanistan to the Pacific Ocean. Invariably, their armed conflicts, piracy, and competition in Asia reflected their political rivalries in Europe.[6] But it is necessary to note the consequences of these policies, which brought the rival powers to Burma by way of India and Siam. The decline of Portuguese power was followed by the strengthened hold of the Dutch. Eventually, the Dutch established their major base in the thousands of islands, including the Spiceries (as they were called), that make up Indonesia. The British followed, gradually ousting the Dutch from India, Ceylon, Burma, and Malaya in alternating periods of war and peace, but ultimately defending and restoring to the Dutch, after the Napoleonic Wars, their stake in Indonesia.

As a result of separate voyages begun in 1601, the British East India Company established factories and settlements at Surat on India's west coast, which by 1630 had become "the most important English factory in the East," and at Masultipatam on the Coromandel coast, between 1611 and 1630. It founded Fort St. George at Madras in 1640, and secured footholds in Bengal, erecting a factory on the Hugli River in 1642 and a fort, Fort William, in Calcutta, in 1696. When, in 1661, Catherine of Braganza brought the territory of Bombay to Charles II as part of her dowry, that city area replaced Surat in importance.[7] The evolution of the Company's three Indian "presidencies"—Bombay, Madras, and Calcutta—in the second half of the seventeenth century led its officers in London to make a bid for territorial, in addition to commercial, supremacy in the Bay of Bengal and the Indian Ocean. "In memorable and prophetic words," the Company announced in 1687 that it intended to " 'establish such a polity of civil and military power, and create and secure such a large revenue . . . as may be the foundation of a large-well-grounded sure English dominion in India for all time to come!' " [8]

The "sure English dominion" of India heralded in the 1680's was delayed by several factors at home and in Asia. The Stuarts were displaced by the bloodless revolution of 1688. Whiggery and Protestantism triumphed in England and broke the long-standing royal-chartered monopoly of the East India Company. For twenty years, various commercial and political factions vied for "free trading" shares in the profitable East Indian trade. Finally, in 1708, Parliament decreed the organization of the several competing merchant factions and their supporters into the United Company of Merchants of England Trading to the East Indies. The Honorable Company was restored and, if anything, became more powerful than it had been. In the interim, the Company in India had become aware of competition from a relatively new quarter—France. Beginning in 1604, the French made several unsuccessful attempts to copy the Dutch and English pattern for securing a portion of the East India trade, and in 1664 they launched the Compagnie Royale des Indes Orientales.[9]

Organized by Colbert, with sponsorship and investment from Louis XIV, the French East India Company located factories at Surat and Masultipatam in 1668-69 and at Pondicherry in 1674. Its efforts in India were somewhat interrupted by the wars of Louis against the Anglo-Dutch combination, but French missionaries after 1660 and factors of the Company after 1680 secured a strong foothold in Ayuthia, the capital of Siam. Ayuthia at the time has been described as "the strong great city, seated upon an island round which flowed a river three times the size of the Seine. There rode ships from France, England, Holland, China and Japan." [10]

The Honorable Company was displeased not only with the growth of French influence in Siam, but also with its share of Siam's trade gained by interloping English merchants.

In the latter part of the seventeenth century, Siam provided entrepôt facilities at Ayuthia for a varied trade, including that, much coveted, from China and Japan. It then possessed the Tenasserim port of Mergui, which had formerly belonged to Burma, as it does today. This harbor, strategically located on the eastern shores of the Bay of Bengal, shortened the route from India to Ayuthia, avoiding the longer voyage around Malaya, and to its China-Japan trade. It also furnished a profitable anchorage for those engaged in coastal trade, while providing a base to wait out the shifting winds in the alternating cycles of the southwest and northeast monsoons so important to the sailing ships of the time.[11] Mergui had become a major port for the interlopers, freewheeling, free-trading merchants and sea captains who flouted and helped to break the original monopoly on trade held by the British East India Company.

There was a second type of interloper, who frequently received overt or tacit permission from the company to ship and trade in the coastal ports and who, as frequently, carried cargoes for the private benefit of the Company's Asian staff. Such (at least for a time) was Samuel White, *shahbandar* or chief officer of the port of Mergui, in the employ of King Narai of Siam (1657-88), who had received his appointment through the powerful office of the King's chief adviser, the fabulous Constant Phaulkon.[12] Before Phaulkon was executed by Narai's successor, he initiated a policy that then and later served Siam well. Since the Dutch company, which had established a factory at Ayuthia in 1604, appeared to have a virtual monopoly of Siam's trade, Phaulkon, who had entered the King's employ in 1678 and soon became the Superintendent of Foreign Trade, arranged to diversify Siam's trading partners. He first attempted to enlist against the Dutch the support of the English at Ayuthia and other officials sent out from Madras, but they were either too weak or too uncomprehending of his design. Phaulkon then turned to the French, and twice between 1684 and 1687 succeeded in arranging for an exchange of embassies. The French East India Company and French missionaries benefited by a convention signed on December 19, 1685, and the Siamese in turn were provided with some 600 French troops, 300 artificers, three men-of-war, and four other ships. These arrived in September, 1687.[13]

Thus, at the very time when the British East India Company resolved to become a "nation in India"[14] and to expand its trade with Siam, it faced serious competition from the French and from English interlopers. The Stuarts were reluctant to clash with Louis XIV, their ally in the war with Holland (1672-74). But a proclamation by James II "recalling his subjects from the service of his majesty of Siam" served as the springboard for action by the Company. In 1687, it sent Captain Anthony Weltden, master of the man-of-war *Curtana*, to execute the new policy. The King's proclamation served its purpose against the interlopers at Mergui, but it did not allay the concern of the Company over the rising power of the French in Siam. Since the Company was sovereign in its Asian operations, it decided "to make war upon the said king [of Siam] and his subjects in order to reprize ourselves for damages sustained through him and them."[15] The London Court of Committees of the Company, its ruling body, issued secret instructions to this effect in 1686,[16] and also decided—with disastrous results—to attack the Grand Mughal, Aurangzebe, of India, because his governors, particularly those in Bengal, were hospitable to interlopers and not particularly impressed by the Company's role in Calcutta.

Events in Siam—sometimes referred to there as the revolution of 1688—thwarted the plans of both the English and Siam's allies, the French. In March, 1688, King Narai fell ill; his favorite, Phaulkon, was executed in June by the regent, Phra Petraja. The latter represented a Siamese faction determined to get rid of the English, as well as the French, whose missionary priests had thoroughly alarmed Buddhist monks. The King died in July, and the regent was crowned as King Ramesuen in October. Under the terms of an earlier agreement, the French were permitted to withdraw to Pondicherry.[17] They left in November, ending their experience in Siam and closing the country to European trade and other contacts for a century. Some sixty Englishmen were killed in a Siamese attack on the Europeans at Mergui in July, 1687. Siam retained this port until Burma recaptured it in the eighteenth century. The company's war with Siam was ended.[18] At the same time, in India, the Company had to accept a "humiliating peace" (the phrase is from *The Imperial Gazetteer of India*) from Aurangzebe, and it paid a considerable fine in order to be allowed back into Bengal and Calcutta.

For the time being, the Company's bellicose policy in India and Siam had failed. Especially after the deposition of James II, its royal monopolist charter was attacked at home and successfully challenged in the ports and factories around the Bay of Bengal.[19] As a result, the Company exercised caution in repairing its fortunes in Asia, while it awaited the outcome of various moves that eventually led to its reorganization in 1708. Nevertheless, the Company continued to seek an alternative, East Bay of Bengal harbor, for refitting its ships and handling its trade in the changing monsoon cycle. After the disaster at Mergui, Captain Anthony Weltden of the *Curtana* put in at the Burmese island of Negrais, at the mouth of the Bassein River, a debouchment of the Irrawaddy Delta. He surveyed the island and found its advantages so persuasive "that he took possession thereof for them [the Company] in the King of England's name." [20]

In time, the reorganized United Company of Merchants of England Trading to the East Indies repaired the disasters of the closing decades of the seventeenth century. It became strong enough to execute successfully the commercial and territorial policy initiated in the 1680's.[21]

This led to the next and more aggressive stage of Anglo-French rivalry in Asia, which was to continue throughout the eighteenth and nineteenth centuries. The interests of the two clashed in India and later in Burma. After the death of Aurangzebe in 1707, the Mughal Empire that had been controlled from Delhi began to disintegrate. By interfering in the affairs and quarrels of the Indian states during the next fifty years, the European powers sought and secured their own advantages. The prize, which was not only the commerce but also the territory of India, was won by the English in the long years of war from the beginning of the War of the Austrian Succession in 1740 to the end of the Seven Years' War in 1763. The Company proceeded to consolidate its power from three major bases—Bombay, Madras, and especially Calcutta—while it permitted an ever-widening range of financial manipulation and corruption. Englishmen competed for appointments to India in order "to make the maximum of money in the minimum of time." [22]

The last decades of the eighteenth century also saw the founding of studies in the Indic languages and arts at Western universities, thereby enriching the West with knowledge and appreciation of an ancient civilization comparable to its Judeo-Christian and Greco-Roman heritage.

British India now abutted on the Kingdom of Burma.

The Company and the Kingdom

It was in this context that Burma continued to encounter Western advances in Asia. The growing power of the British East India Company coincided with the decline of the fortunes of the Toungoo dynasty in Burma. The outer reaches of the empire established by Bayinnaung in the sixteenth century were held weakly by two of his successors, Anaukpetlun (1605-28) and Thalun (1629-48), whose reigns were marked by a period of devastating and debilitating domestic and foreign conflicts, precursors of a century of decline. The capital had remained at Pegu until 1635, symbolizing the unity of the Burmans and the Mons. Then Thalun withdrew it to Ava, a traditional heartland capital founded in 1364 by a Shan chieftain. There, or near there, 400 miles from the sea, in the vicinity of the last capital of the kingdom at Mandalay, the Burmese court remained until the end of Burmese independence in 1885.

Although we do not know the exact reasons for the Burmese withdrawal from Pegu to Ava, we can dismiss the charges made by D. G. E. Hall that its removal came about because of Burmese "intransigence and xenophobia," and the lack of desire for Western trade "on any satisfactory scale." [23] No doubt there were several reasons for the move to Ava. Pegu's value as a seaport was declining because of silting, and the majority ethnic group, the Burmans, were not ocean-going sailors. The Delta area of Lower Burma had not yet become the productive countryside of later days. The Burmans had long made use of irrigation and other water-saving devices to farm the central dry zone, their granary, which receives 20 to 30 inches of rain during the monsoon season. Siam, the major traditional enemy on the east, could perhaps have been more easily threatened or attacked from the north via the Burmese-held province of Chiengmai (now a province of Thailand) than from Pegu. The Burman court may also have felt insecure among the numerous more or less subdued Mons of that region. To this must be added traditional Burman satisfaction with the part of the country that they knew best. Finally, a growing concern over the dangers that threatened Burma from Portuguese, Dutch, French, and English trade rivalries may have been a factor in the withdrawal from Pegu, with its easy access from the sea.[24] Ava provided better protection for the Burmese kings, although, except in times of strong rulers, the move left their power weakened in the Delta area.

Meanwhile, the first formal contact had been established between Burma and the British East India Company. In 1611, the Company had established a factory at Masultipatam on the Indian Coromandel coast, and from that outpost it sent to Siam two factors or agents, who made the trek north from Ayuthia to Chiengmai. One of them, Thomas Samuel, was taken prisoner by King Anaukpetlun of Burma, when he captured Chiengmai from Siam in 1615. The prisoner was treated well at Pegu, and was permitted to carry on trade until his death in the same year. In 1617, the Company sent two agents to the Burmese capital to recover his goods. They remained for two years, acquired somewhat questionable reputations, and returned to Masultipatam in 1620 bearing gifts from the King to the Company and a letter "signifying his desire to give free Trade and entertainment to the English nation, if they would with their shipping repair unto his Country." Nothing came of this.[25]

After negotiations with King Thalun at Ava, the Dutch company established its first factory in Burma at Syriam, near Rangoon, in 1635. Twelve years later, the British followed suit. Both companies were operating from factories on the western side of the Bay of Bengal. On the eastern side of the bay, Syriam, or any of the Burmese ports in the delta or on the Arakan coast, afforded the companies a base for their ships while they waited for the alternating winds at each turn of the six-month monsoon cycle. Thus Burma was strategically located for any power that sought to dominate the Bay of Bengal and the Indian Ocean lanes in the days when sailing ships were subject to the vagaries of the monsoons. However, after the Burmese kings had withdrawn from Pegu to Ava and their fortunes had declined in the Delta area, Lower Burma became less secure. Further, it became more difficult to transact business with the king in his inland capital, some 400 miles up the Irrawaddy River. (According to one account, it took thirty days to cross from Madras to Syriam, and an additional forty-two days to go upriver from Syriam to Ava.[26])

Dutch naval superiority in the war of 1652 led to the expulsion of the English from Syriam in 1657, but the Dutch left in 1679 because of new uncertainties that beset the Burmese trade. The King had prohibited the export of saltpeter, essential in making gunpowder, and had refused to allow the Dutch to maintain a trading station near China's Yunnan border because of difficulties with marauding remnants of the defeated Ming Chinese forces not yet (1658-62) completely vanquished by the Manchus.[27] (This situation is analogous to that after 1949 when the Communist and Kuomintang Chinese contested on Burmese soil.)

The departure of the Dutch and the defeat of the British Company by Siam led its officers to give renewed attention to the ports of the Burmese Delta. During the long, relatively peaceful and unenterprising reign of King Minrekyawdin (1673-98), the British tried twice (in 1680 and 1684) to reopen a factory at Syriam[28] and, for a time, used Syriam as a repairing station, as did the French. Captain Weltden's claim of the island of Negrais was another of these moves. In 1695, Nathaniel Higginson, Governor of the Company at Fort St. George, sent a mission headed by Edward Fleetwood to Ava, to inquire about two vessels and their crews, apparently being detained there, and to ask the King to authorize "a factor next Monsoon to reside at Syriam." According to Fleetwood, the Burmese wanted the English to trade at Syriam, and also to use that port for repairing ships and building new ones, and as a place of continuing residence for a Company factor. Two years later, Thomas Bowyear was appointed as "Chief at Syriam." [29]

The Kingdom of Ava, as Burma was then called, clearly welcomed the opportunity to trade with the British, and it extended similar privileges to the French. The Company does not appear to have capitalized on the Fleetwood and Bowyear missions, perhaps because it was reorganizing its affairs in London and was determined first to make its position in India more secure. However, in 1709, a year after the United Company was formed in London, Roger Alison was sent to Ava and, apparently, his mission succeeded in winning greater freedom for British trade.[30] From then until 1743, when the English factory at Syriam burned down, the Company's affairs at that port continued to be managed by a succession of chiefs or residents.[31]

England and the Rise of the Konbaung Dynasty

Because of Anglo-French rivalry in Siam and India, it was inevitable that when a new war broke out in Europe it would engulf their Asian interests. It was essential to any power that sought full domination of the Bay of Bengal to control Burmese ports on the eastern side of the bay. Thus, the British Company was quick to counter any attempt by the French to seek Burmese favor. The Company had cause for concern. The rivalry, which outlasted the eighteenth-century struggle for India, accounts in part for the final British thrust against the remains of the Kingdom of Burma in 1885; one of the effects was to expel French influence from the western flank of mainland Southeast Asia.

In 1729, the Mons, seeking to enlist the aid of the French in their bid for power against the weakening Burman dynasty at Ava, offered to cede some territory to them. At this time, however, the French appeared to be content with their position at Syriam, where they had a factory and shipbuilding facilities.[32] In the period of renewed Anglo-French conflict (especially after 1740), Mahadammayaza-Dipati (1733-52), last and weakest king of the Toungoo dynasty, occupied the throne at Ava. While Upper Burma was defending itself against a former vassal state, Manipur (1740-49), the Mons succeeded briefly in restoring their power in Lower Burma. After besieging and taking Pegu in 1740, they crowned one of their chiefs, took Syriam, and in 1752 destroyed Ava. At first they allowed the British and French East India companies to retain their factories at Syriam, but in 1743 they burned out the English factory in the belief that the Company was supporting the Burmans. Expelled from Syriam, the English re-established their main trading base at Negrais, which Captain Weltden had claimed for the Crown as early as 1687. In this phase of the struggle within Burma, the French—carrying out the policy formulated by Dupleix in India—now gave their support to the Mons (also called Peguers, or Peguans, or Talaings). Thus, by the 1740's and 1750's, the British and French had become involved in Burma's internal strife, as they had previously in India, and both companies sought what Michael Symes called "their separate interests," with each supporting an opposing contestant in the civil war.[33]

The course of events was changed, however, when the Mon rebellion was suppressed by a new Burman dynasty founded by Alaungpaya, a leader from Shwebo, about 40 miles northwest of Ava, who began his campaign in 1752. In the eight remaining years of his life—he died from wounds received at the siege of Siam's capital, Ayuthia—Alaungpaya succeeded in establishing the Konbaung dynasty and in reuniting Burma for the third time in its history. He also reduced outlying provinces in India, Laos, and Siam to vassalage, as had his illustrious sixteenth-century predecessor, King Bayinnaung.

Once victorious, Alaungpaya notified the British Company of his conquest of Pegu and indicated his desire for a conference. In June, 1757, the Company appointed Ensign Robert Lester as "Embassador Extraordinary to the Buraghmah King." [34] Their encounter fittingly reveals and, in effect, sums up the relationship between Burma and the West in the preceding years. Lester set out by schooner from Negrais, bearing a treaty of friendship and alliance between Burma and the Company for the King's approval, together with gifts of guns, gunpowder, China carpets, silk cloth, and handkerchiefs. He met Alaungpaya's guides at Bassein and was conducted to the King some days upriver, after having had the treaty translated into Burmese via Portuguese. Lester complained of the "very impertinent language" used by an English employee of the translator, Antonio, and added that "I meet with many things amongst these People that would try the most patient Man ever existed, but as I hope it is for the good of the Gentlemen I serve, I shall put up with them and proceed." The meeting with King Alaungpaya took place on July 23. The King cited a letter he had sent to the King of England "written on a leaf of Virgin Gold," and a second one "on Paper, to the Company, sent from Ava in 1757." [35] The letter to the King of England referred to the earlier and friendly commerce between the two countries, which had been stopped by "the revolution in Pegue." It also called attention to the fact that the English had settled at Negrais without Burmese approval, but, the King continued, "tho' jealousy naturally reigns in kings, yet we were greatly pleased and rejoiced at the news." Having made his point, the King then gave his approval to the Company's settlement at Negrais and a new one at Bassein.[36]

Lester quickly bypassed this delicate subject, calling the King's attention to the new treaty now being offered, saying "it would be a means of uniting the two nations together for ages to come."

There followed a delightful exchange between the King and the Ambassador. Discomfited by the requirement of kneeling in the royal presence, Lester sat down on "a small stool." As he explained, "This caused laughter among the great men about me." The King joined in the laughter and asked "what was the reason that Englishmen Could not kneel?" Lester replied that they were not accustomed to it. The King then asked several questions: "Does your king go to the wars and expose his person as I do? Do you understand the use of ordnance? Could you point a gun to kill a man at a great distance? Is there as much rain in your country as in this? . . . How much money does the Company pay you per month? Why don't you black [tattoo] your bodies and thighs as we do (at the same time rising up and showing me his thigh)?"

The royal questions were answered by Lester in a manner "which seemed to please them." They then discussed the reasons for retaining the Negrais settlement instead of locating up the river at Bassein. The Ambassador indicated that the English would be glad to have both places but wanted specifically to deny Negrais to the French, "who . . . we were now at war with" and who might try to take it. Lester continued, "He [the King] then asked me, if we were afraid of the French; I told him that the English and the French had no great liking for each other but there never was that Englishman born, that was afraid of a Frenchman."

Ambassador Lester got his treaty, but not before the King warned him against offering support to the "stragling Peguers." Alaungpaya "had been informed" that such support had occurred at Negrais, "which had hindered them [Peguers] from being subject to his laws, and that . . . nothing of that kind must be done for the future."

The Treaty of Friendship and Alliance of July 28, 1757, was the first formal agreement negotiated between Burma and a Western power.[37] Its nine articles "absolutely" granted to the Honorable United Company the island of Negrais and a tract of land at Bassein for factories which the Company would fortify. The King allowed the Company—but not private parties—to trade "throughout all his dominions, without let or hindrance and free of all duties and customs whatsoever." Similar trading courtesies were extended to the Burmese in English-held Indian ports. The Company pledged itself to turn over to the King annually "one piece of ordnance to carry a twelve pound shot" and "200 Viss [about 700 pounds] of good gunpowder, as an acknowledgement, that they bear in remembrance the King's friendship." The Company also agreed "to aid, assist and defend, the King of Ava and Pegu, and his successors against all their enemies by sea and land, and for that purpose to furnish such a number of troops, with proper warlike stores as the occasion may necessarily require, and the said Company can conveniently spare . . . upon consideration, nevertheless that the King shall defray . . . all charges whatsoever." Since the King anticipated some trouble at Tavoy, in the Tenasserim, an article was devoted to this, in the spirit of the foregoing.

The treaty succeeded in promoting neither friendship nor alliance. The Anglo-French struggle in India during the Seven Years

War occupied the major attention of the two competing powers. The Company decided to withdraw from the settlement at Negrais, except for its interest in maintaining there a supply of teak, and in the spring of 1759, removed some thirty-five Europeans and seventy "Black people" (Indians) from the island. During the summer, the Company "dispatched the *Victoria*, Snow, Captain Walter Alves, to carry Mr. Southby to Negrais" to take care of the teak. Alves and his passenger arrived in early October. But Alaungpaya, it was reported, had already become suspicious of the English. He had been advised by an Armenian, Gregory (Awas), in his service as collector of customs at Rangoon, that the Negrais settlement had furnished muskets, powder, and shot to the Mons, who had not yet been completely suppressed. The rumor recalled a similar episode at Syriam in 1755 against which the King had warned Ambassador Lester when he signed the treaty. In addition, members of the Armenian community long resident in Burma were said to feel that the English at Negrais both interfered with the King's trade and "undersold" them, and "spoiled the market." "Everything that in the least be made to serve as an argument against the English, was always aggravated and put up in the worst light possible, by Gregory to the Buraghama King." It is possible that the King was also disturbed by reports of British activity and advancing control on the Coromandel coast and in Bengal, and, fearing that an attempt might be made "to bring the Country [Burma] under subjection," decided to put an end to such difficulties by taking command of the Negrais settlement and making prisoners of the English officials there. Whatever his reasons, Alaungpaya sent a detachment of 60 soldiers commanded by a Frenchman (previously a prisoner) in his service to seize Negrais.

On October 6, 1759, Captain Alves' passenger, Captain William H. Southby, several other Englishmen, their servants and Indian employees—in all, about 100 individuals—were massacred; 4 Englishmen were taken captive to show the king; and the settlement was burned down. The *Victoria* and a second ship, the *Shaftsbury*, which had been in the harbor when the former arrived, escaped with 60 men, 3 women, and a child.[38] Alves returned to Bengal on November 10, 1759.

Symes later explained that the "tragical catastrophe" at Negrais came at a time when the English in India were not "in circumstances to revenge the murder of their servants, and exact retribution for the insult to their flag." [39] In 1760, however, they secured the release of the captives through a second visit by Captain Alves, but "policy also rendered it expedient to avoid an irreconcilable breach with the Birmans, as tending to give the French interests an ascendancy in that quarter, and enable them to gain a firmer footing in a country whose maritime advantages, and contiguity to our possessions, might afford them opportunities to disturb our tranquility and molest our trade." The breach between the Honorable

Company and Burma was not an irreconcilable one, but thirty-five years elapsed before the Company sent another official mission to that country.

Despite the earlier policy of the French in support of the Mon rebellion, Alaungpaya's son, King Hsinbyushin, was prepared (circa 1766) to allow them to re-establish their commerce. In a letter addressed to the French authorities at Pondicherry, he acknowledged the presents of their ambassador, Feraud, and offered them a site below Rangoon for a factory; he granted them permission to conduct their business exempt from duties but forbade them to sell war materials without his permission.[40]

Alaungpaya died in May, 1760.[41] He had revived a strong national spirit in Burma, had begun to fill out the main lines of her former boundaries, and had extended them in the northwest and the east. At the same time, he had effectively checked the intrigues and adventures of the English and French contestants for empire. Two of his sons who succeeded him, Hsinbyushin (1763-76) and Bodawpaya (1782-1819), defended and advanced the fortunes of the Konbaung dynasty and the Burman Empire. But eventually, when English power was securely anchored in India, after France had been decisively vanquished there (although she still remained a threat elsewhere in Asia), the Honorable Company again turned its attention to Burma. This time, some two hundred years after Ralph Fitch, the first Englishman to visit *Suvannabhumi*, the "Golden Land," British persistence and skills triumphed over Burma's kings, who failed to keep pace with the times.

All the conditions for a clash between the English and the Burmese had appeared by the end of the eighteenth century. The Burmese had mastered the arts of eighteenth-century warfare. They had successfully repulsed the armies of the great Manchu emperor, Ch'ien Lung (see below) in 1765-69, destroyed Ayuthia, the capital of Siam, and added parts of Siam, Laos, Manipur, Assam, and Chittagong to their possessions. In the previous century, the Burmese had ousted the Dutch and had vanquished or absorbed other Europeans who had come to their shores in the first waves of European exploration. Among these were the Portuguese and some Armenians. They had parried the French and the English during the eighteenth century without, however, fully appreciating the magnitude of the struggle between the two powers. Certainly, the Konbaung kings failed to understand the significance to Burma of the Indian policy pursued victoriously by the British governors-general from the time of Warren Hastings (1774-86), the Marquess Cornwallis (1786-93), Sir John Shore, afterward Lord Teignmouth (1793-98), and especially the Marquess Wellesley (1798-1805). It was Wellesley who formulated what had become and would remain as policy: "The British must be the one paramount in India, and . . . the native princes could only retain the personal insignia of sovereignty by surrendering their political independence." [42] And when the Company once more turned its attention to Burma, this was the policy put into practice there by Wellesley and his successors. The Company and the Court of Ava approached each other's domains at the headlands of the Bay of Bengal.

Under weak and strong kings, whether Burman or Mon, the Burmese insisted throughout the period of their first contacts with the West—that is, from the beginning of the sixteenth through the eighteenth century—that the customs and traditions of their court and their culture be observed by foreigners. The English bridled at these and were in this period largely indifferent to Burmese culture. The humor in the exchange between King Alaungpaya and Ambassador Lester over the question of kneeling or sitting before the Burmese throne was an early example of what became a more serious issue as the Company sent subsequent missions to Ava. Governor-General Cornwallis was the first nobleman appointed to that post by the Company. He and his successors acted as if they were royalty—they were in fact Oriental potentates in India. They therefore insisted that their officers, whether military or civilian, be received as ambassadors and not as business representatives or traders. The Burmese, however, persisted in regarding the Company as a trading institution.[43] Though they were prepared, as we have seen, to negotiate treaties of friendship and alliance with Westerners, they expected strict adherence to their terms of reference. More important, they demanded that any commercial enterprise which they were willing to admit to their ports should have its sanction in a relationship of equal sovereigns, and not in one between their king and a trading company.

The Burmese were usually willing to grant commercial and related privileges to foreigners in their ports, but when their rulers were strong, they refused to tolerate any interference in their domestic affairs. Nor would they grant exclusive rights to any one foreign company. Inevitably, this attitude had an adverse effect on Burmese-European relations. For each of the great East Indian trading companies—Dutch, French, and English—in conformity with the mercantilist theories of the day, sought a monopoly for itself, and none of them hesitated to interfere in domestic politics in furthering its own plans. More than once, the clash of policies resulted in disaster. The Siamese massacre of the English at Mergui, which helped to turn English and French attention to Burma, the Burmese massacre of the English at Negrais, and similar treatment accorded the Portuguese and French at Syriam were merely extreme responses in the contemporary mode to prevalent Western policies and practices.

Throughout the first two centuries of its contact with the West, Burma remained a quasi-feudal state. The authority of the king was in principle complete and personal. Loyalty to him and to his appointees, who governed directly, and fealty from subordinate princes, who retained only the powers that the throne delegated or left to them, provided the foundations of administration. Customary law and royal edict guided the administrators, who were, for the most part, linked by common adherence to the Buddhist religion and culture. Under strong kings, Burma was unified; at other times, it disintegrated into a collection of petty and warring principalities. Because Burma, like most of mainland Southeast Asia, lay outside the main lanes of European mercantilist interest, it escaped for a time the fate of the Indian subcontinent and the Indonesian archipelago. But at the same time, this persistent isolation meant that Burma was dependent largely on its own resources for whatever growth and cultural advances its people achieved.

After Warren Hastings became the first Governor-General of India in 1774, a contest between the Company and Burma became inevitable. Bengal, then the richest province of India, arched around the bay that bears its name, and its hinterland in Assam and Chittagong met and clashed with Burmese expansion under the vigorous and aggressive Konbaung dynasty. Equally important to British interests was the latent threat of French influence and expansion. Both threats, the Company believed, had to be fought. In the eighteenth century, Britain had achieved supremacy in India by diplomacy where feasible, by war when necessary. During the nineteenth century, British rule was extended to Burma in the same way. The challenge was one that the Konbaung kings were ill-equipped to meet.

T HE STRONG THIRTY-SEVEN year reign of King Bodawpaya (1782-
1819), the third son of Alaungpaya, set the stage for the inescapable collision with the advancing course of the British Empire in
India. He rounded out the borders of Burma by conquering in
1784 the *Raja* of Arakan, again, as in the sixteenth century, incorporating that province into Burma; he continued, fruitlessly, the
wars against Siam; in 1812-13 he added Manipur and in 1816, Assam to his dependencies. (Assam was then converted into a Burmese province.) He exchanged missions with the Chinese that
only subsequent Western error and Chinese traditional historical
pride chose to call "tributary." According to Sangermano, he expected at one time to make the emperor of China "his tributary"
and to "possess himself of the British colonies, attack the Great
Mogul in his empire, and in time make himself undisputed master
of the whole of the southern island." [1] Sangermano's portrait of
Bodawpaya is one of unrelieved "barbarity and pride, that whoso
but hears it [the King's name] must shudder with horror." [2]
Phayre, usually objective on such matters, remarked that this description of the King "when compared with other evidence . . .
does not appear to be too severely drawn"; but, he adds, "he was a
man of ability and, except in the great folly of heading an invasion
of Siam, carried out his plans, for what he considered the glory of
his kingdom, with prudence and perseverance." [3] This King built a
new capital at Amarapura; constructed many pagodas, including
the unfinished one at Mingun, a mass of bricks reputedly 500 feet
high; engaged in notable public works; sent diplomatic and religious missions to India and Ceylon; fostered a literary renaissance;

shrewdly manipulated the power of his throne; provided for a successor (his grandson, Bagyidaw, 1819-37); and is "considered by the Burmese to have been the ablest statesman of his line." [4] In all, a "masterful man who never hesitated to punish." [5]

The Resumption of British-Burma Relations

In 1795, Sir John Shore, then Governor-General in India, decided to reopen formal negotiations with the Burmese. Though, in the interim, English traders had continued relations with Burma at Rangoon Port, not since Captain Walter Alves concluded his mission to Ava in 1760 had the Honorable Company determined to send an official envoy to the Burma Kingdom. [6] Michael Symes, then a captain in His Majesty's Seventy-Sixth Regiment, was sent on this, his first, embassy to King Bodawpaya. Symes was followed in 1796 by Captain Hiram Cox, who was recalled in 1798 after serving as the Company's Resident at Rangoon and visiting the Burmese capital at Amarapura for "nine weary months" (the phrase is Henry Yule's). (Actually Cox left Rangoon for Amarapura on December 5, 1796, and returned on November 1, 1797.) Symes, now a lieutenant colonel, was again sent to Burma in 1802, this time by Marquis Wellesley, who had replaced Sir John Shore in India in 1798 and had already committed himself to a forward policy that called for British paramountcy over the "native princes," along with an unrelenting struggle against the French. In 1803, a young lieutenant, John Canning, who had been a member of the second Symes mission, was named as agent to Rangoon. Because of the "insolent violence" of the Burmese deputy governor, then temporarily in charge at Rangoon, he left after seven months. However, Governor-General Lord Minto (1807-13) twice reassigned Captain Canning to Burma, in 1809 and again in 1811. Canning was recalled in 1812. "This was the last mission up to the breaking out of war in 1824." [7]

A fact of importance must here be noted: From the end of the eighteenth century there begins to appear, chiefly in English, a steady, ever-increasing stream of published and archival material about Burma. These are participant and secondary accounts by the British East India Company's soldiers and civilians, by Roman Catholic and, chiefly, American Protestant missionaries in Burma, among others. In addition, the "general fulness" of official Burmese-language records and chronicles "is remarkable." [8] As Cady has pointed out in noting the abundance of English-language sources, "the principal problem in interpreting Burma's history since 1800 arises from the one-sided character of these English language sources which inevitably portray the foreigners' version of events and reflect basic assumptions often at variance with the Burmese point of view. Both detachment and imagination are required in dealing with them." [9] No modern or contemporary Burmese scholar has written a detailed history of Burma during the period prior to the establishment of the British connection in 1824-26.*

The reasons for the various missions to Burma are not difficult to discover. We learn that "it was possible to buy goods for £3,000 in Calcutta and sell them for £8,000 in Burma." The Burmese Government prohibited the export of any gold and silver acquired in this trade; "from this developed the shipbuilding industry of Rangoon. . . . So important did this industry become, that at one time there were 3,000 men employed in the shipyards, the average pay being eight annas a day for carpenters." [10] Teak from Burma was essential to the Company's shipyards at Madras and Calcutta, as was her market for cotton and woolen goods from England.

However, trade and shipping were not the only objects of the successive missions. As the British Empire in India and Bodawpaya's Burma acquired contiguous boundaries, border troubles erupted both at the Arakan-Chittagong frontier and in the area of Assam and Manipur. Rights of pursuit, apprehension, and punishment of dissident factions that crossed the border after raiding expeditions into Burma became the subject of acrimonious debate and local police actions between the Company and the Court. Burmese incursions into Assam and Manipur and the possibility that they might advance farther west into India proper also gave the British cause for alarm.[11]

"The vain dream of an extensive overland trade to China through Rangoon which continued to haunt the minds of English merchants for the next hundred years was another reason for promoting friendly relations with Burma." But above all, the British were concerned about French influence in Burma. After the outbreak of war in 1793, which, except for the brief interlude of the 1802 Peace of Amiens, continued to Waterloo, they wished to prevent the French from using Burma's ports as bases from which to attack Indian and the Company's shipping in the Indian seas. This situation at the turn of the eighteenth century was not dissimilar to that a hundred years earlier at Mergui. "Hence the appearance in the Rangoon River on the 19th March 1795 of Captain Michael Symes, who had been deputed by the Company's government to negotiate an understanding relating to these matters." [12]

The published records prepared by Symes (and others) during his two missions to Burma provide most of the data necessary to understand the eventual outbreak of war between the Company and the Kingdom. War was most probably contemplated by Wellesley, but he was deterred by events in India and elsewhere. Both

---

* Several contemporary Burmese, including Professor Kyaw Thet and Dr. Than Tun, and Dr. Yi Yi, are presently working on some of this material for the Burma Historical Commission. See Dr. Than Tun, "Historiography in Burma," *Working People's Daily Supplement on the Union Day 1965* (Rangoon), February 12, 1965, and Htin Aung, *The Stricken Peacock, Anglo-Burmese Relations, 1752-1948* (The Hague: Nijoff, 1965).

parties to the dispute contributed to the security of the Arakan-Chittagong border between 1801 and 1811, thereby alleviating tension. But similar problems erupted after that as the Company diminished the strength of its border guard. And other issues as suggested above were to arise, bringing about the inevitable conflict between the imperialist Company and the imperious Court of Ava.

Symes returned from his first mission with an agreement in the form of a "Letter from the King of Ava to Sir John Shore, Governor-General," in which the King directed that

> English merchants are to be permitted to go to whatever part of the Burman dominions they think proper, either to buy or to sell . . . and should the English Company think proper to depute a person to reside at Rangoon, to superintend mercantile affairs, maintain friendly intercourse, and forward letters to the Presence [King], it is ordered that such person shall have a right of residence . . . shall be allowed to come to the Golden Presence [King] for that purpose.

The King consented to the policing of the Arakan-Chittagong border, and agreed that "enemies of England, as well European as Indian . . . should not be assisted at our ports with warlike implements" or provisions but that "when merchants come to trade, they will be allowed to carry away their commodities, agreeably to the usage of merchants." Obviously, Symes achieved only part of his mission. Though Burma would refuse "all nations" the right to purchase warlike weapons or provisions, she would welcome friendly commercial relations with England, would willingly allow a resident at Rangoon, but would not deny other merchants (i.e., the French) similar courtesies. The Arakan border question would be presumably handled by the establishment of proper policing on the frontiers and by the extradition of "criminals" or "delinquents of this description" who crossed the borders.[13]

Symes was sensitive, as subsequent envoys and Residents frequently were not, to the fact that the Burmese viewed him "in the capacity of an agent, from a subordinate and commercial settlement, rather than the delegate of a great and sovereign state."[14] Repeatedly, the King referred to the governor-general of India not as the sovereign Company but as the representative of the King of England. In that sense, the governor-general was in Burmese eyes a mere provincial officer, a *myosa*, "eater of a province." As in the time of Alaungpaya, Bodawpaya and his successors insisted on treating with their equals, the kings of England. Shore (1793-98), Wellesley (1798-1805), and Minto (1807-13), during whose regimes in India the missions of Symes, Cox, and Canning were dispatched to Burma, might regard themselves, and were regarded by the conquered Indian princes, as sovereigns in India. To the Burmese kings, they remained minor political officials. However correctly the Konbaung kings may have understood this status relationship, they completely failed to understand the power relationship. For this they were constantly charged by the British with arrogance, insolence, and rudeness, and for this they undoubtedly suffered, though in any event they would have been unable to stem the course of empire.

The 1795 mission of Michael Symes is notable in another respect. It led to his report, *An Account of an Embassy to the Kingdom of Ava,* published in 1800 in a beautiful quarto volume of more than 500 pages with splendid engraved plates and maps. His book—the first major account of Burma in a Western language—contains a historical memoir chiefly devoted to eighteenth-century Burma, including a description of the land and the people, an account of the kingdom's government, religion, economy, social customs, education, and even a discussion of the types of entertainment, partially derived from Siam after the conquest of Ayuthia. On this mission, which lasted from February 21 to December 22, 1795, Symes was accompanied by his assistant and secretary, Ensign Thomas Wood, as well as by Dr. Francis Buchanan, surgeon, a "professor of Hindoo learning" and "a Mussulman [Muslim] professor of language." Including sepoy guards and servants, his entourage numbered "more than seventy persons." Dr. Buchanan added to Symes's volume a section on "rare and curious plants," and separately he also published the first long account in English "On the Religion and Literature of the Burmas." [15] Symes and, to a slightly lesser extent, Buchanan recognized that to deal with Burma it was necessary to have some appreciation of the history and culture of the country and its people.

In a significant statement of his views at the end of his first mission, Symes concluded that the "interest" and "national security" of British India required promotion of the teak trade and discouragement of shipbuilding in Rangoon lest, urged on by the French, a "formidable navy" rise on the banks of the Irrawaddy. "We require and should seek for nothing more than a mart for our manufactured goods, and, in return, to bring back their unwrought materials; interference in any other shape appears to be impolitic, and likely, in the end to prove prejudicial to ourselves." He particularly commended the use of the harbors at Negrais, Rangoon, and Mergui. He felt that Burma's "advantages arising from situation, extent, produce, and climate" were "second in importance to China alone, whilst, from its contiguity to British India, it becomes to us, of much greater consequence."

[The] characteristic pride and unbounded arrogance which govern their [the Burmese] conduct towards other states, may lead them to offer indignity . . . which we shall be obliged to repel [yet] steadiness and temper in our negotiations, and a reasonable allowance for their mistaken principles, will go far, to avert the ill consequences that might arise from their haughty and weak assumption. . . . [The nations east of Bengal] compose a body in extent and number of inhabitants more than equal to all Europe. . . . [They] are connected by a striking similarity of manners and political maxims, to which, as they cannot be suddenly changed, we ought to assimilate, in our intercourse with their governments, as far as the dignity of our own will permit. To preserve a correspondence and a good understanding with the court of Ava, is essentially expedient for our own prosperity; but . . . that connection should not be too intimate. A limited trade and a preponderating influence, sufficient to counteract the machinations of our enemies, are the utmost length that we should go; by not interfering farther, the Burmans will be convinced of the moderation and justice of our principles, and learn from them to repel the insidious advances of any other power. . . . It is our interest to maintain their independence, and to guard it from foreign encroachment, whilst a knowledge of this truth cannot fail, in the end, to unite the Burman government to ours in bonds of reciprocal amity and confidence.[16]

The sobriety of Symes's report and his concluding advice to the Company undoubtedly influenced or confirmed the thinking and policy adopted by Sir John Shore, the Governor-General. The latter was a servant of the Company elevated to this high post by his previous chief, Lord Cornwallis (1786-93), who had been sent to India shortly after his defeat at Yorktown (1781) in the American Revolution. Shore was a cautious official, conscious that his abilities did not measure up to his situation.[17] His five years as Governor-General were marked by a continuing Indian battle against the Company as well as by insubordination on the part of the Company's own army officers. He could not afford to risk the physical and financial cost of aggressive operations in Burma. Hence, when he decided to implement the agreement brought back by Symes in the "Letter from the King of Ava to Sir John Shore," he determined to send to Rangoon a resident instructed to abide strictly by the terms of the agreement.

Between Symes's first (1795) and second (1802-3) missions, Captain Hiram Cox was chosen to be Resident in Burma (1796-98). Whereas, unlike Symes, his conduct there seems to have been offensive to the Burmese, his almost completely unrelieved antagonistic views about them and about Symes deeply colored much subsequent British opinion.[18] He regarded his stay in Burma as one continuous affront to British dignity and power; in his eyes, Symes was to blame because he had accepted many affronts and yet wrote about Burma and the Burmese in friendly fashion. Cox had been instructed to allow the commerce between the two countries to develop "its natural course," to concern himself with such complaints as arose, to be on the watch for "intemperance and misconduct of British subjects," and to give "particular attention" to counteracting the "French influence in the ports or dominions of Ava." He was to proceed in the manner outlined by Symes, acquainting the Burmese with the "pacific principles" of the "British power in India" and by "hinting" at the desirability of an exchange of envoys. He was not to press his own position as an envoy but rather was to act in behalf of the Company's commercial interests and anti-French policy.[19]

There is little doubt that Cox had a fine appreciation of the possibilities inherent in commerce with Ava. His material on this subject presented by William Francklin in *Tracts* (pp. 26-122), clearly exceeds any prior known description. But his inability to understand either his role as an agent or his cautious political instructions is everywhere evident. Not only did he attempt to persuade the King to let him organize a private, non-Company monopoly in three commodities, the profits of which would be shared by the Throne, Cox, and a Burmese partner,[20] he also insisted, contrary to his instructions, that he be treated as "the Representative of the Bengal Government" (i.e., an ambassador).[21] The Company recalled him in 1798, but under Wellesley he was again used on the Chittagong frontier with Burma.[22] The Burmese charged Cox with "ill-humor" and "rusticity," and closed the matter by writing, "Whatever has passed I [the King's ministers speaking for him] regard as the sole act of Hiram Cox and not of the Governor-General." [23]

The Honorable Company's Forward Policy and the Search for a "Crisis of Affairs"

The immediate occasion for Symes's second mission to Ava in 1802 was a revival of border trouble at the frontier between the Burmese province of Arakan and the British Bengal district of Chittagong. After King Bodawpaya had reincorporated Arakan into Burma, dissident Arakanese and a mixed racial group of Indians and Burmese Muslims known as Mughs (or Maghs)—among whose descendants are the present dissident Mujahids—fled over the ill-defined border of the Naaf estuary. From this vantage point they raided Burma and were in turn unsuccessfully pursued by the King's men. Neither the Burmese nor the English were then willing or prepared for hostilities. Marquis Wellesley, appointed as Governor-General in 1798, and King Bodawpaya, both preoccupied with other matters, attempted to settle the border issue and the extradition of offending migrants by an exchange of letters between June, 1799, and June, 1800. They failed because the Company would not or could not spare men for a border guard to restrain the émigrés, and would not surrender any but criminal elements. A further, more threatening letter sent by the Burmese late in 1801 resulted in prompt action. Wellesley sent a frontier guard to the border to keep the peace and dispatched Symes to Burma to negotiate a full settlement.[24]

If the immediate reason for Symes's second mission to Burma was the obvious matter of the border troubles—a recurring issue that was eventually and conventionally to serve as the "cause" of the First Anglo-Burmese War of 1824-26—there were other and more profound explanations for this none-too-successful event.

Though the evidence for the selection of Symes, as Hall points out,[25] cannot be conclusive, it is clear that once Wellesley decided to send a mission to Ava, Colonel Symes was an ideal choice for the Governor-General's purpose. He had already established good relations with the Burmese, had published an impressive study of the country, and was a reliable and cultivated officer with many years of military experience. We are told that the Governor-General thought that Symes was qualified "in a peculiar degree for the situation of envoy"; and that he had "verbally communicated" to Symes "the motives which rendered it [the mission] expedient." [26]

Wellesley's motives are not difficult to discern. From the beginning of his term in May, 1798, five years after the war with France had again broken out, until his recall in 1805, he pursued a well-advertised, aggressive policy of annexing Indian states and of placing others under a system of subsidiary alliances. Arms and intervention in the affairs of these states were the twin procedures that led to the aggrandizement of British rule, direct and indirect, in India. His second major ambition was to thwart the French. In pursuit of this goal he confirmed the retention of Ceylon as a Crown Colony in 1798; authorized the use of the Company's English and sepoy troops to fight the French in Egypt in 1801, and looked acquisitively at Java, a Dutch colony in quondam alliance with Napoleon. British sea power had won a resounding victory over the French in the 1798 Battle of the Nile where Nelson defeated Napoleon and, as the copybooks say, "saved India." But the battle on land and in Asian waters continued. The uneasy Peace of Amiens, 1802, which provided for a partial restoration of French-Dutch possessions in India and the Indies, not only did not last, its provisions were flouted by Wellesley even before the war broke out again in 1803. As one British historian remarked,

> . . . the implications of this [Wellesley's] policy, which could in the end have no geographic boundary [in India] save the Himalayas and the sea, were little liked by the cautious East India Company at home and were only half liked by Pitt and his Cabinet. But all attempts to call a halt to the British advance, though seriously made after Wellesley's retirement, proved nugatory in the face of inexorable facts.[27]

Whatever the views of Pitt and the Company, there is no doubt that Wellesley pursued his expansionist policy in India and elsewhere in Asia. He added most of south India to territory held by England; he weakened the Maratha Confederacy, which eventually led to the acquisition of central India in 1818; and he pushed out north and west from Bengal, beyond Delhi. By 1802, he had already achieved a considerable measure of success in his Indian campaigns. The border incident between Chittagong and Burma served as an appropriate occasion to examine the forward policy possibilities in Burma, across the Bay of Bengal. It is here suggested that the second Symes mission was part of a large-scale intelligence operation which Wellesley planned to develop in accordance with the findings and the opportunities. That this is not mere surmise may be gathered from a careful examination of his instructions to Symes and of Symes's written reports and journal.[28] (Symes also delivered an oral report of which there does not appear to be any written record.)

Though the Company had been irritated by the refugee-border problem and was affronted by the communications received from the Burmese provincial governor in Arakan, other "considerations . . . render the mission of an envoy to Ava for the purpose of defining and improving our commercial and political relations with the Burman Government." Such considerations were impediments to trade, including harassment of British merchants and traders; disaffection of Ava toward British interests; protection afforded in Burmese ports to French privateers based at Mauritius and nearby islands, who preyed on British shipping; "the manifest disposition of the Court of Ava to favour the cause of France" and the potential danger to English Indian interests if France acquired a secure base "on the eastern side of the Bay of Bengal," a continuing preoccupation of the British since the fiasco and massacre at Mergui[29] at the end of the seventeenth century.

Symes's written instructions, dated March 30, 1802, amplify these considerations while iterating the high opinion of the envoy held by the Governor-General. He was to seek an "amicable accommodation" on the border-refugee issue and effect an agreement to install an ambassador at the Court and a resident in Rangoon. But, more important, he was told that the "ultimate object" of the mission was "to establish an improved system of alliance between the British Government and that state, with a view to secure to the Company the political and commercial advantages of which such an alliance is susceptible." The alliance was to have two major objectives. At a minimum, it was to renew "those [commercial] privileges and immunities" that Symes had obtained in 1795 and, if possible, extend them. He was authorized to bargain the shadowy claim that the Company held to the Burmese island of Negrais "as an equivalent for some concessions." Second, he was to seek "the exclusion of the subjects of France from any establishment within the Dominions of Ava, and the supersession of their influence in the concerns of that state . . . it is this consideration which principally constitutes the political importance to the Company of an improved alliance with the State of Ava" (pp. 100-109).

Four weeks later, Symes received a second set of instructions based on an intelligence report to the effect that King Bodawpaya contemplated abdicating and naming his eldest son as successor; allegedly, a second son, aided by the Siamese, planned to contest the succession. Symes was given power and authority to command troops that could be put in the service of the heir apparent. He was advised "that such a state of events would precisely constitute that crisis of affairs which is most to be desired for the purpose of establishing British influence and of promoting British interests in the Burmese empire." The Governor-General permitted Symes to exercise his judgment as to whether the heir apparent, in return for this military aid, should "subsidize permanently the British force." Wellesley was prepared not only to waive the subsidy, but also to allow Symes wide discretionary powers if he could conclude an arrangement even for the "temporary employment of the British forces for the settlement of the Government" (pp. 115-16).[30]

The "crisis of affairs" that Wellesley sought as a pretext for advancing into Burma was only incidentally related to the casual and in this instance erroneous intelligence concerning Bodawpaya's proposed successors. The expression of Wellesley's policy, as in the two sets of instructions given to Symes, can be matched in the paper prepared for the Governor-General the previous year by Major William Francklin.[31] Here also are the references to the desirability of expelling the French, the need for displaying British power, "the offering the assistance of our troops to support and protect them [the Ava government] against all opposition, whether foreign or domestic," and the establishment of commercial factories at Rangoon, Mergui, and Bassein (Negrais).

Wellesley's far-reaching ambitions in the Indian Ocean area—extending from Mauritius on the west to Java on the east—clearly included Burma. For these ambitions "he had spent money with profusion and had scorned to take even sums of the nature of prize money to which he was entitled." Though recalled in 1805, subsequently "the Company then bestowed the rare honour of erecting his statue in his lifetime and . . . presented him with £20,000." [32]

Symes kept a journal of his mission which, together with several appendixes, including a commercial (not political) agreement with the Burmese, he submitted to Wellesley on his return to India in February, 1803. In the journal, Symes does not substantially alter his earlier views of King Bodawpaya. He describes the King as "eccentric," with an "ill regulated mind. . . . He is a child in his ideas, a tyrant in his principles, and a mad man in his actions" (p. 230). "Patience" and "forbearance" were required in dealing with the Court, but not at the sacrifice of dignity (p. 158). As in the earlier mission, "our principal inconveniences arise from the malevolence of foreigners [French, Armenians, Portuguese] rather than any ill disposition on the part of the Burmans" (p. 125). But this time he found the country less prosperous: "we have come here in a season of scarcity" (p. 125); there had been a "rapid decline . . . indicated by the decay of towns, neglect of cultivation and the complete desertion of entire villages," which he ascribed to recent wars and to the oppressive behavior of "its own governors" (pp. 136-37). Even the splendor of the Court had "faded," its power had "diminished" but not so its "pride" (p.

191). Symes charged the King with allowing Burma, "one of the fairest regions, and in local advantages one of the most important sovereignties on the globe, to decay under a system of administration the most unjust, impolitic and ruinous that human folly ever contrived or the cowardice of man submitted to" (p. 185).

Symes began the journal by promising "a dull diary" (though it is anything but dull) rather than risking "suppression of any point of intelligence or matter of fact which may be important . . . and have weight in influencing the decision which your Lordship will now come to on the momentous question of peace or war." Obviously, Wellesley was not averse to war as a means of annexing further territory,[33] for Symes referred to this possibility more than once. Despite his promise of fullness of intelligence, he later indicated that he would reserve certain political and military matters for "personal communication." Though we do not know what this personal report contained, it would appear that Symes carefully went about building up an English-sympathizing faction in Burma (p. 232) that might cooperate with Wellesley, who was described by Symes as one who "possesses sovereign power over all the British possessions in India, and who in his relation to all potentates of the East is himself a Sovereign" (p. 127).

Symes certainly continued his good personal relations with the Burmese. On his departure, the Governor of Pegu gave him a private letter for the Governor-General, praising his "wisdom and prudence" and urging that Symes be considered for future deputations to Burma "if there be occasion to send a person for the managing of business" (pp. 258-59). But in effect the Burmese agreed to no more than the conditions that Symes had obtained in 1795 (pp. 245, 253-57). He summed up the agreement as follows: "his Majesty [of Burma] was displeased at the conduct of Captain Cox and irritated because his agent was not allowed to purchase firearms and military stores in Calcutta; but he is now pleased to be reconciled, declares his disposition to be friendly, and his ports free to us as usual." But then Symes added, revealing a sharper pen, that the King did not treat the specific purposes of the mission; "it seems he will treat with no power on earth as an equal . . . he will grant a boon but will not make a treaty. . . . His Majesty was angry, but is now in good humour; he was offended and now forgives. With such a monarch and such a Court it is impossible to maintain an intercourse on the relation of equal states" (pp. 228-29).

Symes concluded his report (pp. 231-34) by belittling the errors of his antagonist and immediate predecessor, Cox; he asserted that the King's displeasure in Cox originated not in the latter's faults but in the King's concern over English "superiority." "It was fear operating on pride and these together engendered hatred."

Throughout the journal, he had studiously commented on the attitudes held by the Court toward the French and the English.[34]

He concluded that the King had become "convinced that nothing is to be expected from such representatives [French] or from the nation they belong to" (p. 198); and that the King's "anger and antipathy to the English were caused by a sense of their superiority . . . his partiality to the French arises from a persuasion that he has nothing to apprehend from their power," and that they are useful as a "counterpoise" to the English. Symes believed that French influence had been diminished if not eradicated "even in his Majesty's mind"; and "an alliance between the Burmese and the French has been prevented" (p. 232).

On the other hand, Symes considered that the position of the English, despite the objectionable conduct of private English traders and others in the country, had considerably improved. Letters dispatched to Bengal from Rangoon on June 4 and July 12 give an account of such persons (about sixty in number) "some of whom (but, I am sorry to add, very few) are men of respectable conduct." He indicated also that "a powerful party has been formed in favour of the English, which, let the result be peace or war, cannot fail to give us an advantage, either a preponderating weight in their counsels, or (if such aid were necessary to our success) an easy conquest in the field." He believed that the Burmese were open to a "change," which would not be violently opposed or reluctantly received; "and that by his conduct of his mission he had enabled the Governor-General to adopt a suitable policy toward Burma." On the issue of whether it shall be "peace or war," he planned to express himself in a "personal conference."

> I have quitted Ava with sufficient provocation to justify war, and with civility enough to continue at peace; nor do I apprehend that much advantage will accrue to our rivals [the French] in either event. At the same time where there is a choice there may be a preference; and I am decidedly of opinion that a paramount influence in the Government and administration of Ava, obtain it how we may, is now become indispensably necessary to the interest and security of the British possessions in the East.

Thus Symes substantially altered his recommendation as to the Company's policy toward Burma between his first and second missions. He returned to Bengal in February, 1803, at a time when Wellesley was preparing for a series of major advances against his formidable Indian adversaries, the chiefs of the Maratha Confederation of central and northern India. Since war with France had again broken out and since the French were aiding the Indians, the successes that Wellesley and his generals, Arthur Wellesley (his brother, later Duke of Wellington) and Lord Lake, won in 1803 were doubly welcomed. But Burma, therefore, could not be on Wellesley's agenda. The years 1804 and early 1805 proved to be less good for Wellesley's forward policy; he was recalled. In the interim, the Company did not officially act on the agreement that

Symes brought back. As a preliminary measure, it authorized Symes to depute Lieutenant John Canning, who had accompanied him, as his "private agent" to Rangoon. The latter received his instructions from Symes (pp. 262-66) dated May 7, 1803. Canning was to serve as an intelligence officer on "the progress of French interests in that quarter." This was the "primary object" of his mission, which was to be so conducted as not to "excite suspicion." He was told explicitly that he was not to put himself forward as an envoy; he was to correspond with Symes or the Secretary of the Secret and Political Department, using "cypher" if necessary; he could return at his own discretion if he found the "Burmese Government so hostile as to render your residence there irksome and unavailing." Canning precipitously left Rangoon in November of the same year.

Whatever may have been the reception of Symes's first *Account*, certainly those in authority who received and read his second could not help but be impressed with it. Symes had succeeded in winning Burmese personal approval while clearly and impressively standing up for his rights as an envoy—not a business agent. Despite his unfavorable opinion of the King, he secured royal authority to send Company envoys and residents to Burma (though, except for the assignment of Canning as his private agent in 1803 and Canning's service under Lord Minto in 1809 and 1811, the Company did not avail itself of his device until after the First Anglo-Burmese War). The arrangements that he negotiated for the security of the Arakan border kept the peace as long as the British kept their part of the bargain. Though neither Symes nor any British successor ever secured dynastic Burmese consent for the expulsion of the French—this was among the causes of the Third Anglo-Burmese War in 1885—Symes correctly reported that the French were not so severe a threat to British interests in Burma as had been expected. Symes believed that he had won several Burmese friends in high places and among the Roman Catholic missionaries, who certainly cooperated with him both in 1795 and 1802, and there is evidence to corroborate this. However much he incorrectly predicted that the Burmese would "change" their King (Bodawpaya reigned until his death in 1819), the grandson who succeeded him, Bagyidaw (1819-37), had in fact been on friendly terms with Symes.

"How Wars Are Got Up in India; The Origin of the Burmese War[s]"

What Symes told Wellesley privately about a policy for war or peace we do not know, but the authority that Wellesley permitted Symes to exercise in the deputation of Canning in 1803 surely indicates that the Governor-General responded favorably to his envoy. In any event, conditions other than those directly related to Burma determined the immediate outcome. Wellesley's 1804-5 setbacks in India and his recall meant that the Company and the British Cabinet wished to follow a more cautious policy in that arena of the global Napoleonic Wars. Wellesley was succeeded by Lord Cornwallis, who died en route to India, and by Sir George Barlow (1805-7). But it was Lord Minto (1807-13), who picked up the threads of the earlier "sovereign" Governor-General. During Minto's regime, the French islands in the West Indian Ocean and Java (returned later to the Dutch) were added to the advancing British Indian colonial dominions. He was followed by Lord Hastings (1813-23) who completed Wellesley's acquisitive design and aggressive policy in India, and also added Nepal and Sikkim—and Singapore. During this time British paramountcy over almost all the "native states" was effectively established. In the west, British India abutted on Sind, Punjab, and Afghanistan; in the east on Manipur and Assam, at that time Burmese dependencies again. Through the Arakan princes, the Burmese also put forward shadowy feudal claims to Chittagong and Dacca, which only added fuel to the smoldering fire. Hastings resigned in January, 1823; there was a short interregnum by a senior civilian, John Adams, followed by the appointment of Lord Amherst in August, 1823, who pressed the issue with Burma until war was declared.

Scattered frays in the Arakan with advance posts of Burmese soldiers began in September, 1823, and in Manipur in January, 1824. War was formally declared by the Company against the Kingdom on March 5, 1824. It was concluded by the punitive Treaty of Yandabo, signed on February 24, 1826. Two American Baptist missionaries to Burma who had been imprisoned during the war along with some other Westerners, Dr. Jonathan Price and Adoniram Judson (whose imprisonment so deeply outraged American Protestant opinion in the nineteenth century), served as translators and intermediaries during the British-Burmese negotiations for the treaty and a stipulated but postponed commercial agreement. The treaty provided that Burma pay a large indemnity of 10 million rupees (£1 million), yield her suzerainty over Manipur and Assam, cede the Burmese provinces of the Arakan and Tenasserim, and permit the exchange and residence of "accredited Ministers." Siam, Burma's traditional enemy and a British ally in the war, was to receive an unspecified reward. The second treaty between Burma and the Company was far different from the one Ensign Lester had easily obtained from King Alaungpaya in 1757. And the Company secured an objective which it had been pursuing for 150 years. It now possessed safe ports on the east side of the Bay of Bengal.[35]

During the war,[36] dynastic Burma lost her last great general, Maha Bandula, and the Konbaung kings suffered their first major military defeat since the rise of Alaungpaya. The dynasty never fully recovered from these. Its earlier successes in defense against Chinese imperialism (see below), in imperialist victories on the Southeast Asian mainland and between the trans-Chindwin and

Brahmaputra river basins on the northwest, had fed the kings and their councils, the Hlutdaw (an advisory cabinet without departmental portfolios), with illusions of supremacy if not invincibility. The Burmese fought an effective but doomed eighteenth-century battle at the end of the first quarter of the nineteenth century. Their equipment, despite superior jungle-fighting ability, was no match for advancing British military power. They were absolutely ignorant of the significance and the technological implications of the *Diana,* a 60-horsepower steamship which made a first appearance in Asian waters as part of the British fleet that attacked Rangoon in May, 1824. Not even the loss of 15,000 out of a force of 40,000—mostly through disease and inefficient logistical supply—could stop the British at this time. The Burmese could never have held Manipur and Assam once British Indian power moved in that direction. But the mountainous jungle area that separates Burma from India—the area about which the Chindits and the Marauders of World War II were to learn at dire cost—might have served as a boundary between British India and dynastic Burma. Such a boundary, and its related counterpart of the Naaf estuary between Burma and Chittagong, might have sustained a border peace as in the first decade of the nineteenth century.

Such a border peace might have prevailed had Burma agreed to exclude the relatively unimportant French interests, to give British commercial interests predominance, and, above all, to recognize the paramount Company as if it were the British Throne. Burmese national conceptions, advanced and held by bad and good, weak and strong kings, before, during, and after the First and Second Anglo-Burmese wars, never yielded on these fairly constant demands from the Company. When the British Empire took over from the British Company there was no basic change in British imperialist policy. And by this time, the desire to control the Irrawaddy River road to China added incentive to the policy-makers. Since there was little power left in royal Burma, she succumbed after a fourteen-day contest in November, 1885, the so-called Third Anglo-Burmese War. This Company policy toward Burma anteceded Symes's second mission if not his first, though he became, because of Wellesley, its most carefully instructed bearer. He and several of his successors who had been sent on missions to, or residencies in, Ava (among them John Crawfurd, Henry Burney, Arthur P. Phayre, and Henry Yule) left us the richer through their written concern, inevitably partisan, for "matters Burmese." [37]

Any assessment today of the First and Second Anglo-Burmese wars cannot avoid the conclusion that both the kings and the governors-general moved ineluctably to them. To write, as D. G. E. Hall has, that "no Machiavellian policy of expansion was involved," that the British sought "to avoid war" and search "for ways and means of establishing peaceable relations" [38] is to bedevil the issue in the adjectival use of Machiavelli's name. The published records from the end of the seventeenth century onward clearly indicate that the Company believed in the need for a foothold in Burma and in the commercial gains that could be made once such a foothold was established. Imperialist political motivation strongly and clearly supplied by Wellesley, as we have seen, was liberally added to the economic drive. Force was merely an instrument of politics and economics, to be used as required. It needed an occasion to explode, which it found in 1824. That the British and British Indian forces endured severe casualties in a very costly war, badly mismanaged from the start, did not change the policy of expansion.

Estimates of the cost of the war to the Company range from £5 to £14 million—either sum being high for those days. The Company first attempted to send high-caste Bengali troops across the bay. For religious-caste reasons the troops refused to go by sea. This led to what the English have called the "Mutiny" of the Forty-Seventh Native Infantry at Barrackpur (above Fort William, Calcutta). The recalcitrant troops were ordered out on parade and then shot "by two British regiments"; some were tried and hanged. The Indians call this the "massacre" at Barrackpur. Following this event Amherst used Indian troops from Madras who had no such inhibitions. But the cost in money and men did not change the policy; it merely altered the schedule of its application. The lessons of the First Anglo-Burmese War were well learned when in 1852 Governor-General Dalhousie coolly and opportunistically initiated the second. He sent Bengali troops by land to Burma and built a road across the Arakan Yoma to make connections with the Irrawaddy River Valley. He also used Madras troops, who did not hesitate to cross by sea, and he made prominent use of the British Navy. He also provided ample supplies and medical protection for his troops. Even so, the war lasted almost a year and the pacification after it took about four years. The Burmese did not yield easily. The Company, Dalhousie excepted, continued to insist on political treaties, commercial agreements, and the accompanying signs of formal relationships implied by "accredited Ministers." Dalhousie, in December, 1852, merely proclaimed the annexation of the Burmese province of Pegu, which thus land-linked the earlier acquisitions of the Arakan and Tenasserim provinces. The three provinces were separately ruled by Company officials until, with the expiry of the Company, they became, in 1862, a single province of British India, ruled by a chief-commissioner.

On the other side, Burmese royalty, puffed up beyond its capabilities and its knowledge of the world beyond, did not seek to escape from the first war and could not escape from the second and the third. John Crawfurd is the first to report how the Burmese recorded the First Anglo-Burmese War. In an entry for November 2, 1827, in *Journal of an Embassy . . . to the Court of Ava*, he writes:

I learnt last night, from good authority, that the Court Historiographer had recorded in the National Chronicle his account of the war with the English. It was to the following purport:— In the years 1186 and 87, the Kula-pyu, or white strangers of the West, fastened a quarrel upon the Lord of the Golden Palace. They landed at Rangoon, took that place and Prome, and were permitted to advance as far as Yandabo; for the King from motives of piety and regard to life, made no effort whatever to oppose them. The strangers had spent vast sums of money in their enterprise; and by the time they reached Yandabo, their resources were exhausted, and they were in great distress. They petitioned the King, who, in his clemency and generosity, sent them large sums of money to pay their expenses back, and ordered them out of the country.[39]

Parenthetically, it may be remarked that it is understandable when such alleged Burmese historical self-deception was reported (for Burmese scholars have searched in vain to find Crawfurd's source) with relish by British participants and early arrivals on the nineteenth-century scene. But it is also repeated by such contemporary British historians of Burma as Harvey and Hall, the latter comparing the item to a choice bit of "Dr. Goebbels' propaganda."

The three Burmese kings who reigned between strong King Bodawpaya and wise King Mindon contributed to the unfolding disaster. After his defeat in 1824-26, Bagyidaw agreed to and initially profited by the Crawfurd agreement for the exchange of ministers. He sent Burmese envoys to Calcutta in 1827 and 1830, seeking to diminish the severity of the imposts of the Treaty of Yandabo. He accepted in friendly fashion Major, later Colonel, Burney as the Company's resident minister from 1830 onward; and Burney successfully intervened with the Company to restore to Burma the Kabaw Valley, a part of her northwest frontier with Manipur. But Bagyidaw otherwise failed to regain the lost Burmese provinces; gradually he slipped into unrelieved melancholia said to have been caused by the humiliation that he felt over his defeat. He was replaced by his brother, King Tharrawaddy (1837-46), who decided to repudiate the Treaty of Yandabo—a meaningless gesture since the Burmese had already paid in coin and realm for its provisions. Despite earlier and friendly relations with Burney, he also refused to recognize the Company Resident Minister, thereby forcing the latter to deal with a provincial governor in Rangoon instead of with the Throne. Burney withdrew in 1837, and by 1840 his two successors had also yielded. From then until the arrival of the Phayre mission at the capital in 1855, there was no diplomatic recognition of a Company representative by the throne. The Company's business in Burma had to be conducted in and through Rangoon—and with increasing difficulty.[40]

Tharrawaddy may have contemplated military action to rid the country of the British while the Company was engaged in its disastrous First Afghan War, 1839-42. What deterred him—as with so many other tantalizing questions about Burmese events—we do not know. He deployed a considerable force in Lower Burma and in the fall of 1841 staged an unusual and impressive entry into Rangoon with 15,000 men, ostensibly to build a new city safely removed from the guns of a hostile naval force at port-side. He is alleged to have tried to persuade the Company to return the ceded provinces of Arakan and Tenasserim. The Company regarded the Tenasserim as a losing proposition and therefore not worth retaining. However, the London government rejected the idea of restoring the province to Burma. Tharrawaddy returned empty-handed to his capital at Amarapura in early 1842. He, too, then went into mental eclipse, was deposed by his son the Pagan Min in 1845, and died the next year.[41] It was during the Pagan Min's reign (1846-53)—given over to "gambling and cockfighting"[42]—that Lord Dalhousie, one of the great proconsuls among the rulers of India, was appointed to the governor-generalship (1848-56). The Burmese could not have had a more formidable opponent at one of the weakest moments in their history.

Burmese informed opinion today clearly acknowledges the fallen state of the Kingdom during the reign of these three monarchs, but it is also inclined to quote with approval the text of Richard Cobden on "How Wars are Got up in India; The Origin of the Burmese War."[43] Cobden indicts British policy, the Company, and Dalhousie in a brilliantly argued brief based almost exclusively on official British documents and translations of Burmese documents supplied to Houses of Parliament in June, 1852, and March, 1853. He described how the British show of naval force was sent to Rangoon to collect an alleged debt of less than 10,000 rupees; and how subsequently the Governor-General, "to enforce his rights and vindicate his power" (pp. 95-96), issued an ultimatum in which he raised his demands to 1 million rupees (£100,000) and threatened "immediate war" unless the King acceded to his incredible demands. Cobden emphasized his argument in one instance by changing the locus from Rangoon to Charleston, South Carolina, and then asked rhetorically whether English conscience would have allowed such an event to happen (pp. 67-69). His closing statement (pp. 104-5) not only summarized the main events of the war but also expressed an opinion easy to share today.

> Lord Dalhousie begins with a claim on the Burmese for less than a thousand pounds; which is followed by the additional demand of an apology from the Governor of Rangoon for the insult offered to our officers; next, his terms are raised to one hundred thousand pounds, and an apology from the King's ministers; then follows the invasion of the Burmese territory; when, suddenly, all demands for pecuniary compensation and apologies cease, and his Lordship is willing to accept the cession of Pegu as a "compensation" and "reparation" for the past, whilst at the same time he pens long minutes to prove how calamitous it will be to us to annex that province to our Indian

empire! Conceding, I say, the *bona fides* of all this—ought not we to advertise in the *Times*, for a Governor-General of India who can collect a debt of a thousand pounds without annexing a territory which will be ruinous to our finances?

But the fact is, and the sooner we all know it the better, nobody gives us credit for sincerity when we protest our reluctance to acquire more territory, whilst our actions are thus falsifying all our professions. Nor, speaking nationally, are we entitled to such credit.

Dalhousie continued hostilities until December, 1852, at which time he apparently determined to end the war and absorb his gains —the richest province of lower Burma.

Mindon's Valiant Failure and the End of the Kingdom

After the annexation of Pegu, to the latitude 6 miles north of Myede, Burma became a small kingdom, completely landlocked, referred to most frequently as Upper Burma, wedged between English and French territory of the Indochina Peninsula and the eroding empire of the Manchus to the north. A palace revolution displaced the Pagan Min and brought his half-brother, Mindon, to the throne (1853-78). The British could not quarrel with him, for he was genuinely a man of peace[44] who vainly tried to restore to the Kingdom some of its losses. He sent an envoy to Calcutta in 1854 and in return received Commissioner Phayre the following year on a mission for a treaty to document the annexations of the 1852 war. But though the King refused the treaty, Dalhousie, Phayre, and Yule, who separately have written about the mission, were entirely satisfied "that peace with Burma is to the full as secure as any written Treaty could have made it." [45]

Throughout his reign, Mindon made efforts to bring Burma into fruitful contact with the nineteenth-century world. He built a new and substantial capital at Mandalay; sent missions (and students) to London, Paris, and Rome to enlist support for the restoration and preservation of Burma, and even sent Burma's first official message to the President of the United States. He willingly cooperated with arrangements suggested by Phayre whereby a British citizen, Thomas Spears, would serve as a Company correspondent at the capital, and after Phayre's second visit in 1862, he agreed to the reopening of the British residency. In 1871, he convened the Fifth Great Buddhist Council—not to be repeated until 1954-56—seeking through a revivification of Buddhist teaching to rebuild Burmese morale. But this gifted Burman King, the last but one in the dynasty, at best delayed the end. As Fytche, Phayre's successor in 1867 as Chief Commissioner in British Burma, wrote,

. . . the second Burmese war of 1852-1853 was more effective than that of 1824-1826; but was unfortunately brought to a premature close. On neither occasion did we take due advantage of our conquest . . . it would have been an easy task to have reduced the King of Burma to the condition of a feudatory prince, maintained by a subsidiary alliance, like the Prince of India. Of late years the British Government seems to have awaked to a sense of their omission.[46]

Mindon died in October, 1878.[47] His successor, King Thibaw (1878-85), a weakling dominated by his queen and her mother, provided the easy excuse for the British Government to correct the earlier "omission." Thibaw began his reign with the "murder of the kinsmen," a brutal disposal of possible royal competitors. This not unusual dynastic practice, well-known in England from the days of the War of Roses, aroused British opinion and led indirectly to the closing of the residency after the death of the last Resident, R. B. Shaw.[48] For a brief time, British India flirted with the possibility of deposing Thibaw in favor of another, friendlier prince, but the idea was abandoned when British India again became involved in a none-too-successful war with the Afghans (1878-80). Thibaw, or at least his ministers, further complicated the situation by reopening negotiations with the French; in the British view, this threatened English passage to the China trade via the Irrawaddy system and Yunnan.

However, the immediate cause of the war was a Burmese attempt to levy a fine on the Bombay Burmah Trading Corporation of 2.3 million rupees payable to the King, and 500,000 rupees payable to his foresters for the illegal extraction of teak from the royal preserves. The fine was excessive and uncollectable, but as the *Gazetteer* authors remark, "there is little doubt that the Burmese had some causes of complaint." In answer, the British Government of India sent an "ultimatum" to the King. This called for a settlement of the matter on the basis of negotiation between the Crown and an envoy from the Viceroy; it also included a demand that a diplomatic agent should be allowed to reside in Mandalay—ignoring, of course, the fact that after 1879 the British themselves had chosen not to appoint a successor to Shaw. Finally, the ultimatum contained a stipulation that the Burmese were to provide "facilities for opening up British trade with China" and that the Burmese Government "would in future be required to regulate the external relations of the country in accordance with the advice of the Government of India." [49]

These terms were dispatched to Mandalay on October 22, 1885; a reply was demanded by November 11. On November 9, the Burmese Government replied, pointing out that the fine was justified on the evidence and not negotiable; that the British had withdrawn their representative and could appoint a new one; that the Burmese would be glad to facilitate British-China trade along with similar ventures of others; and that no sovereign nation could agree to having its external affairs managed by another. The *Gazetteer* authors, seemingly oblivious to their incorrigible arrogance, refer to the Burmese reply as amounting to "an unconditional refusal," which the British India Government had anticipated by readying

10,000 soldiers. On November 14, this military force proceeded north from Rangoon. On November 28, King Thibaw surrendered in Mandalay to General Harry Prendergast. He was exiled to India in 1886, just as the last Mughal emperor of Delhi had been exiled to Burma in 1857. On January 1, 1886, Lord Dufferin (1884-88), a strong Viceroy in the Wellesley tradition, proclaimed the annexation of the remnant Kingdom of Burma.[50] The annexation was quickly engineered by the adroit Conservative political leadership of Lord Randolph Churchill, the Secretary of State for India. Although the Indian Viceroy, Lord Dufferin, announced the annexation on January 1, 1886, debate in Parliament did not take place until the next month, after the Liberal Party victory of Prime Minister Gladstone. The new government sustained the action, and Gladstone cynically referred to the war as a "defensive" one in the interests of securing India.[51] The "omission" was rectified. British Burma was absorbed in three bites, 1824-26, 1852, 1885.

Though each of the Anglo-Burmese wars was undertaken for specific reasons, a more basic cause for the engulfing of Burma is to be found in the expansionist policies of western European nations which, especially after the downfall of Napoleon, turned their restless commercial energies to the East. In Britain, the dissolution of the British East India Company's monopoly of the China trade in 1834 stimulated a wide range of new and growing commercial interests in the East, and the opening of the Suez Canal in 1869 tremendously shrank the distance between Europe and the East. From the end of the eighteenth century, Britain as well as other European nations stepped up efforts to open the closed ports of China and penetrate the river highways to the far interior, which hitherto could be reached only by difficult and dangerous overland routes. In the years when missions were being sent to the Burmese kings, other missions traveled the long way to Peking (where parallel difficulties in gaining their ends followed upon the Englishmen's refusal to perform ceremonial bows before the Ch'ing emperor). In these years, while British administrators were taking over control of Lower Burma, enlarging their areas of paramountcy in India, and less successfully in Afghanistan, Lord Napier and his successors were struggling to break down the rigid monopoly of the Hong merchants in their dealings with the European factories at Canton, attempts that ended in the first Anglo-Chinese war (the so-called Opium War, 1839-42), the cession of Hong Kong to the British, and the opening of the first five treaty ports of China.[52] Chief among the rivals of the British in the power struggle in this area were the French, for though the British pushed the French out of India and eventually out of Burma, they were no less ambitious than the British in seeking power and territory in Asia.

In the early nineteenth century, this rivalry was played out on the Indochinese Peninsula, the northern peripheries of which touch both on India and China. At the beginning of the century,

Burma, Thailand, and the countries that later became French Indochina were still free, but in the years that followed the French and the British moved in parallel directions, and both eyed keenly the potentialities of the southwest China trade. As the English advanced into Burma, so the French moved into Cochin-China; they came into complete control of Indochina shortly after the time that the British annexed the whole of Burma.

In Burma, the river system seemed to provide possibilities for access to the China trade that would either reinforce those who had entry into China from the Chinese seaports and rivers, or make it available for those who had been denied such access. Mountain passes linking Yunnan and northeastern Burma, connecting the river valleys, had been from time immemorial the routes by which peoples had drifted south and, in historic times, by which Chinese traders carried Burmese silver, tin, and jade back to Yunnan. The key to trade with interior China seemed to be control of the Irrawaddy River—the "road to Mandalay"—and the overland route from Bhamo and Lashio to Yunnanfu (Kunming) —the "Burma Road." John Crawfurd, in his *Journal of an Embassy . . . to the Court of Ava*,[53] reported that Burmese cotton valued at £228,000, not an inconsiderable sum in those days, was exported to Yunnan and Szechwan in 1826, and that the total value of the Sino-Burmese trade ranged from £400,000 to £700,-000 per annum. English interest in some route into southwestern China was kept alive through a notable series of reports, surveys, and missions that followed closely upon each other from the period following the First Anglo-Burmese War until after the Third.[54] When the British annexed Upper Burma and incorporated the entire country into the Indian provinces, they immediately tried to come to terms with the Chinese, partly because they were concerned lest the Chinese in Yunnan take advantage of the disturbances of the annexation period to carve out a piece of Burma for themselves before the British could establish authority over the border areas, but mainly because the French already had access to China from the vantage of the Red River Valley and, in addition, had a growing commercial and political interest in Thailand.[55]

The immediate interests of the British and French were served in gaining control of the peoples and resources of Burma and the countries of French Indochina. Their keenness to do so cannot be separated altogether from the international struggle for the Chinese prize. In this struggle, Thailand, unlike Burma and the rest of the Indochinese peninsula, managed to maintain a precarious independence as a buffer state between the always-active rival imperialisms. It is interesting to note that the U.S. Minister to Bangkok, John Halderman, predicted, correctly, in 1883 that the British Viceroy in India would "incorporate" the remaining independent kingdom of Burma in "Her Britannic Majesty's Indian Empire."[56]

At the beginning of this account, reference was made to the

richness of resource material on nineteenth-century Burma. Symes, Buchanan, Cox, Sangermano, Crawfurd, Burney, Bayfield, Gouger, Phayre, Yule, Fytche, the writers on the wars, and the long line of missionaries beginning with the Americans, Ann and Adoniram Judson, and many others described Burma's people, form of government, religion, festivals, and customs. On the other hand, these writers seldom, if ever, doubted the righteousness of Britain's imperial purpose, and seldom, if ever, sympathized with Burma's desire to retain her independence.

The white Westerner, whatever his faults, is in these writings accorded relatively undiluted partisanship, while the other race is described as the victim of "despotic" monarchy, attached to a non-Western, "heathen" religion. For the nineteenth-century European, knowledge of another people's way of life—particularly if an "exotic," non-Christian culture was involved—carried with it no enjoinders to adapt himself to or to show respect for their modes of behavior. On the contrary, it seemed doubly incumbent upon the European visitor to maintain his own proper customs and etiquette and to flout the other's. So in the history of Anglo-Burmese relations one reads at length about the difficult "shoe question"—the Burmese insistence upon the removal of shoes in sacred places and on ceremonial occasions, and the British insistence upon remaining correctly shod. W. S. Desai, in his *History of the British Residency in Burma* (p. 129), offers an apt summary of this cultural conflict. He quotes a Burmese minister somewhat plaintively talking to Major Burney: "Your and our customs are so completely opposite in so many points. You write on white, we on black paper [*parabeiks*]. You stand up, we sit down [kneel or bend down]; you uncover your head, we our feet [no shoes] in token of respect." Even as late as 1875, the British Government of India with a "new pride in empire . . . issued instructions that in the future the British Resident at Mandalay was not to take off his shoes on going into the royal presence." [57] Since the Burmese, for their part, would not permit the insult, the British resident "could no longer be received in audience. The loss of direct personal contact with the king was disastrous for both sides." Consequently, in Burma as elsewhere, contact resulted only in limited communication. What remained were unequal competing interests on Burmese soil. In time, the corroding effects of an antiquated and weakening monarchy yielded to the advancing power of the British Raj. The monarchy disappeared, unlamented; the Burmese survived and learned to fight with new weapons acquired under the British Administration. It had taken them approximately as long—some sixty years— to lose their freedom as it was to take them to win it back.

The End of the Kingdom and the Beginnings of Nationalism

A BRASS PLAQUE at the southern garden gate of the palace at Mandalay read: "King Thibaw sat at this opening with his two queens and the queen mother when he gave himself up to General Prendergast on the 30th of November, 1885." * (Other records indicate that it was November 29, 1885, a little before 3:30 P.M.) So ended the third and last Anglo-Burmese War. Burma became "part of Her Majesty's Dominions" and would "during Her Majesty's pleasure be administered by such officers as the Viceroy and Governor-General of India may from time to time appoint." [1] For sixty-two years, from the end of the monarchy until independence was regained, Burmese patriots and nationalists never ceased waging an anti-British, anticolonial struggle in some form. Over several decades, however, their weapons, their sources of inspiration, and the scope of their political ambitions changed.[2]

For at least eight years after the war ended, pockets of armed resistance held out against British attempts at pacification. The banner of national aspiration was then taken up by Buddhist lay organizations, first in the countryside and later in Rangoon. Subsequently, after World War I, the Burmese took advantage of the Montagu-Chelmsford reforms in India to agitate—in the end, successfully—for their application to Burma. In this way, minor forms of home rule were introduced, political parties were organized, and elections were held under various nationalist slogans. Buddhism and Western democratic forms of political and organizational maneuver were adapted to the Burmese scene. In the mid-1930's, a second

* The plaque was destroyed in the post-independence period by a mayor of Mandalay.

generation of nationalist leaders emerged, and unhesitatingly agitated for full independence. They grafted onto the nationalist program of their elders new techniques and slogans, borrowed from a Marxism they absorbed chiefly through English sources. It was this second group, the Thakins, that finally led Burma to independence on January 4, 1948.

The fourteen-day war in 1885 ended with the annexation of Upper Burma and the consolidation of British control over the whole country. In 1901, John Nisbet, who had been a chief forest officer in Burma, could write: "The ultimate annexation of Ava on 1st January, 1886, completely settled all political and commercial grievances, and added to the British Empire in India vast territories rich in material wealth, and far richer still in future possibilities." [3] But, in fact, some five years passed and at least 30,000 troops were engaged before the British pacified the new territories. Even after 1890, guerrilla activities and dacoity, or group banditry, continued to disturb the peace.[4] This resistance created its own legends, and one of its leaders, Bo Min Yaung, who gained more than local fame, was the maternal grandfather of the hero of Burma's independence movement, Aung San.

As guerrilla resistance was brought under control, Burmese patriots found new ways to express their spirit of national pride. They began to observe a Padawmu Day in commemoration of the dethronement of King Thibaw, in spite of the fact that they regarded his reign as calamitous for Burma. At first the celebrations were nonpolitical, but as they grew in fervor, they came to serve as the vehicle for a "British quit Burma at once" campaign.[5]

With the military struggle hopelessly lost and organized political activity forbidden, educated Burmese made use of a traditional type of Buddhist laymen's society to develop new forms of opposition to the British Raj. At least as early as 1897, the year in which Burma was made a province of India, new Burmese Buddhist societies began to appear in Moulmein, Myingyan, Mandalay, and Bassein. In keeping with tradition, their purpose was to foster Buddhist education and social improvement. But a new dimension was added: the study of Burmese history and discussions of the example offered by the growing Indian nationalist movement. By 1904, students at Rangoon College were organized along similar lines. In 1906, the first Young Men's Buddhist Association (YMBA) was formed, which rivaled as it also imitated the missionary-created Young Men's Christian Association. Within a decade, the YMBA had become a national organization with branches throughout Burma. When, in 1919, India acquired some modest aspects of home rule under the Montagu-Chelmsford dyarchy reforms, from which the province of Burma was pointedly excepted, Burmese leaders within and outside of the YMBA intensified their nationalist activities and presented demands similar to those of the Indian National Congress. For this purpose, in 1919-20, they organized the General Council of Burmese Associations (GCBA), embracing many of the earlier Buddhist groups. The GCBA was the matrix out of which all later nationalist political parties and groups were formed.

In Burma, as elsewhere in Southeast Asia in the early decades of the twentieth century, religion inspired indigenous national sentiment and gave a focus to a nationalist movement. Burmese Buddhists had been aroused by what they regarded as Western denigration of their religious and social institutions and by attitudes of superiority revealed in the conduct of the Europeans. They responded by forming organizations from which came, in time, both rebellious religious leaders (like U Ottoma, U Wisara, and Saya San) and irreconcilable nationalist politicians.[6]

The desire to restore Buddhism to pre-eminence in British Burma was a moving force not only for Buddhist monks and teachers, but also for the new elite who were acquiring "the not unmixed blessing of a Western education." In a speech in 1908 (from which the preceding quotation was taken), U May Oung, B.A., LL.B., president of the Rangoon YMBA, described the situation in which "modern Burmans" found themselves: "On all sides they saw the ceaseless, ebbless tide of foreign civilization and learning steadily creeping over the land. . . . Unless they prepared themselves to meet it, to overcome it, and to apply it to their own needs, their national character, their institutions, their very existence as a distinct nationality would be swept away, submerged, irretrievably lost." [7] The Western-educated Burmese, U May Oung declared, was in danger of becoming deracinated; he needed to recover his "Burmanity" as well as to acquire "ambition, a spirit of emulation, and new openings for his labour . . . at a time when there was a spirit of reform in the air, a gradually increasing demand for improvement accompanied by unmistakable signs of social and religious activity."

In 1950, Furnivall described U May Oung's speech as a "distant echo from the Nationalist dawn," [8] but, although restrained, it was not an isolated summons to Burmese nationalism. Simple literacy —the ability to read and write a letter in Burmese—maintained and extended by the widespread *pongyikyaung* (monastic school), was "thrice as widespread [in Burma] as in India, no fewer than 72 per cent of the men, 22 per cent of the women" had acquired such skill. "It has been like this for centuries." Under the British a second system of education developed alongside this traditional monastic one. By the end of World War I, the high-water mark of government-aided schools in Burma, some 250 middle and high schools in which English was taught attracted ever-increasing numbers of Burmese students who recognized that Western education opened the way to opportunity and preferment in British Burma. Foremost among men with modern education were the very few

Burmese who could afford the luxury of a degree from Oxford or
Cambridge, and those who could obtain a degree from an Indian
university. Harvey (the source for the statistics above) states that
before the University of Rangoon was founded in 1920, "Burma
had accumulated 400 graduates with an Indian degree," but he
gives no figures for Burmese with English or continental European
degrees.[9]

Burmese leaders increasingly recognized education—whether it
came exclusively from the *pongyikyaung* or from the Anglo-
vernacular and English-language schools—as a means for carrying
on their nationalist campaigns and for acquiring patriotic followers
among the less literate masses. From 1920 onward, the student
strike, together with the organization of the first "national
schools," was increasingly employed as a nationalist tool. The student strike of that year served as the springboard for an all-
Burmese national school movement, independent of British colonial support; and the student strike was again instrumental in the
second or Thakin phase of the struggle for independence. "The
spirit of reform" thrived among the educated, who raised their
voices in a "gradually increasing demand for improvement." However, the lieutenant-governors who ruled Burma autocratically up
to Dyarchy (1923) were unaware of or unresponsive to the new
spirit of national pride and the rising demands for reform.

Nationalism and Dyarchy

Until the end of World War I, Burma was described as "the
most placid province in India," [10] and its people were regarded as
politically apathetic.[11] Consequently, when the Montagu-Chelmsford Report of 1918 expressly excluded Burma from the reforms
awarded to India under the Act of 1919, the protest "which suddenly arose in Burma . . . took everybody by surprise." [12] The report stated that "Burma is not India. Its people belong to another
race in another stage of political development . . . the desire for
elective institutions has not developed in Burma. . . . We therefore set aside the problem of Burma's political evolution for separate and future consideration." [13]

Though the events that followed took the British "by surprise,"
the objection of the Burmese to having their country's problems
"set aside" marked not the beginning but the climax to a series of
Burmese protests. The colonial government misread or overlooked
evidence that was readily available, as shown by Furnivall in his
analysis of the *Annual Reports on the Administration in Burma,*
and other official documents.[14] These reports indicated, for example, that some Burmese were aware of the significance of the Japanese victory over Russia in 1905; that some Burmese were looking to
the example set by the Indian National Congress; that Burmese
had participated in insurrections against the British after each of
the Anglo-Burmese wars; that "petty local risings every few years"

had continued into the twentieth century; and that Burmese sang such songs as "It is not fit . . . that foreigners should rule the royal Golden Land." As Furnivall remarked, "Their sympathies were clearly apparent to anyone whose official position allowed him to move inconspicuously among them."

The influence of Buddhism and the nationalist role of the Buddhist societies had been apparent for many years. The speech by U May Oung, a well-known member of one of these societies, had received prominent attention in the British-owned English-language newspaper in Rangoon. Nor was there any doubt why the Burmans had demanded during World War I that they be allowed to organize a Burmese regiment, the first since 1885. It was, in the words of a Burman Subadar Major, "a duty to our country, to our self-respect." [15] Finally, the Burmese delegates who appeared before the British Joint Select Committee in Calcutta and London during 1919 to urge extension of constitutional reforms to Burma were men who had been thoroughly schooled in Western political ways.

Burmese nationalism did not spring up suddenly in 1919. What changed was the mode of expression. Where Buddhism and Buddhist organizations had formerly been its fulcrum, after World War I the expression of nationalism became openly political. Significantly, it was the educated members of the YMBA and the GCBA who led the new nationalist movement. In September, 1920, they supported the first of the student strikes, which, with the use of the boycott as a political weapon, began as a factitious protest against measures in regard to matriculation requirements and tuition costs in the Rangoon University Act of 1920. (The act provided Burma with its first resident university, replacing two colleges that had been previously subordinated to the University of Calcutta.) As one result of the strike, a Council of National Education was formed as a Burmese body "to control and direct education designed to be in accordance with the wishes of the Burmese people," and one of the founders of the YMBA, U (later Sir) Maung Gyee, was elected president.[16] By this time, however, nationalist aims went far beyond a desire to have a voice in the development of educational policy. Burmese political leaders called for separation from India, for home rule and self-rule, and, still in a small voice, for independence. Their campaign was partially successful. In 1921, the colonial government was persuaded to extend to Burma the limited privileges of the Montagu-Chelmsford dyarchal reforms, known as the Government of India Act of 1919. This step became operative in 1923.

The British conceived of Dyarchy as a ten-year experiment for India, and, accordingly, for Burma. The act called for an exploratory statutory commission to consider further changes at the end of this period. In fact, the Simon Commission, as it came to be known, was appointed ahead of schedule, on November 26, 1927. Thus the Burmese, no less than the Indians, became fully aware that they were engaged in a continuing political struggle to achieve some larger nationalist aims. This phase in Burma's history lasted until the British Parliament passed the India and Burma acts of 1935, which became effective on April 1, 1937, and finally ended Burma's status as a "province" of British India.

Dyarchy was the name given to the reforms of 1919-23. In principle, it extended a measure of home rule to the province of Burma, under a British governor and his Executive Council. The council consisted of the governor, two appointed members (one of whom was usually a Burmese), and two ministers, who represented and were responsible to a unicameral Legislative Council. The governor, advised by the two appointed members (first, U Maung Kin, followed by U May Oung, both founding members of the YMBA), exercised power over "reserved subjects": finance and revenue, police, justice, and the maintenance of law and order. The representative ministers were in principle charged with responsibility for "transferred subjects": local self-government and the provincial departments of agriculture, forests, education, health, public works, and excise. Of the 103 members of the Legislative Council, 58 were elected in general constituencies, that is, by the Burman majority. The other 45 members were either elected by communal (Europeans, Indians, and Chinese) and business groups or appointed directly by the governor. As before the establishment of Dyarchy, the governor exercised direct rule over the Shan, Kareni, Kachin, Chin, and Hill tribal areas, which constituted more than 40 per cent of Burma's total area, and included between 10 and 15 per cent of its population. Formerly called the "Excluded Areas," these parts of Burma were now named the "Scheduled Areas," in contrast to "Burma Proper." [17]

The home-rule gains acquired under Dyarchy were more apparent than real. Burmese leaders were acutely conscious of the fact that the governor could legally "dissent," or, in effect, veto the advice of any of his council members or ministers. Through his control of finances, he could nullify recommendations of the ministers, and in any event, the "reserved subjects" had first lien on annual revenues, to the disadvantages of social and economic welfare measures. In addition, the senior civil servants, members of the Indian Civil Service, an almost exclusively British bureaucracy, had direct access to the governor, socially and politically. They could and did circumvent the wishes of the appointed and elected Burmese ministers.[18] The Burmese were also aware of the dangers inherent in providing separate communal and appointive representation in the Legislative Council. This continued, they rightly felt, the divisive British policy of emphasizing ethnic and communal differences. It also effectively prevented the Burmese from securing a true majority in the Council unless virtually all the fifty-eight general constituencies returned a single-party group.[19] Finally, the British Government of Burma was still subordinate to the British

Government of India. And in India, as in Burma, opposition moves could be nullified since the viceroy, too, could legally ignore the advice of the partially elective Indian legislature. This body had 145 seats. Of these, 5 were assigned to the province of Burma, but 2 of the 5 were always filled by the Government of Burma and the European community there.

Nationalists in Burma understood the meager nature of these reforms as well as did nationalists in India—where Mahatma Gandhi had launched his 1920-21 campaign of noncooperation with Dyarchy. This understanding conditioned and determined Burmese political responses throughout the period from the enactment of the Montagu-Chelmsford reforms to the establishment of a new Constitution in 1937, following the act of 1935. Western writers have not infrequently echoed John L. Christian's judgment that this nationalist response to Dyarchy brought about a complex and "kaleidoscopic" movement of "programs, platforms, leaders and party names." [20] But despite the ferment and the diversity of the movement, the nationalist issues of the time were basically two: whether or not to cooperate with British power in carrying out the dyarchical reforms, and whether or not to campaign for the separation of Burma from India as a proper step toward achieving effective self-government and home rule. These issues developed successively, with a considerable amount of overlapping, between the time of the Simon Commission and the national elections of 1932.

To cooperate or not to cooperate was the question which in the early 1920's divided Burmese nationalists who had previously been relatively united in the YMBA and the GCBA. They split into two major factions which, despite changes in name, persisted for more than a decade. These factions did not form stable party structures resembling either the British or American party system; they were more like the multiparty arrangements in France, where individual leadership frequently has more weight than organizational commitment. They retained their roles in and won support from various groups and leaders among the *pongyis*, the Buddhist lay organizations, and the Buddhist masses. Though the nationalist struggle became overtly political once the Montagu-Chelmsford reforms had been broached, it did not become divorced from its origin in Burmese Buddhism. On domestic issues other than cooperation and separation, members of the various factions frequently united to take a nationalist stand. In such matters as antitax agitation; the relief of peasants from the ubiquitous *chettyars* (an Indian caste of moneylenders); the legal defense of aggressive and rebellious personalities, including U Ottama and U Wisara, *pongyis* who were imprisoned by the British authorities; or legal and other support for student strikes, national schools, and peasant rebellions, including the bizarre one of Saya San—in these and kindred issues, the two main factions took first a nationalist and only secondarily, if at all, a factionalist stand.

The first of these two main factions, largely inspired by the *pongyi* U Ottama, and led by the ardent nationalist lawyer, U Chit Hlaing, favored home rule, opposed Dyarchy as offering too little, and probably favored independence (though in the early 1920's this was unclear). Its members were most commonly known as the Chit Hlaing–GCBA–Boycott nationalists. Other leaders of the group were Tharrawaddy U Pu and the martyred *pongyi*, U Wisara. These were the noncooperators, the irreconcilable nationalists. To a considerable extent they were influenced through U Ottama by the Indian National Congress and particularly by Gandhi's views on noncooperation and civil disobedience. They boycotted the elections and apparently succeeded in influencing a considerable majority of the voting public to refrain from going to the polls in the elections of 1922, 1925, and 1928. After the Simon Commission recommended the separation of India and Burma, this opposition group became antiseparationist. They announced their support of attachment to India, believing they could thereby gain for Burma the more immediate benefits of home rule, which the Indian National Congress seemed to be winning rapidly. (At this time the alternative, dominion status for Burma, appeared a most unlikely prospect.) They now decided to discontinue their earlier political strategy, the electoral boycott, and together with a smaller group led by Dr. Ba Maw—who was to play an increasingly important role to the end of World War II—they contested the 1932 elections as the Anti-Separationist League. However, they were resolved not to accept ministerial office in the event of an electoral victory. The issue of cooperation versus noncooperation formally disappeared in this electoral contest.

The second main faction, a minority group of the GCBA, was prepared to cooperate with the dyarchical reforms in order either to press forward, through elections and other means, to genuine home rule, or to expose the weaknesses of the system. It was known at first as the "21 Party" because of its twenty-one prominent leaders, including U Maung Gyee and U Pu, who later became ministers, U Thein Maung, the first Chief Justice of the Supreme Court in independent Burma, and U Ba Pe, one of the most prominent journalists of the day. Ba Pe and Maung Gyee had been founding members of the YMBA. Members of this faction regularly formed the opposition to the governments under Dyarchy. In successive elections, the "21 Party" group campaigned as the "Home Rule," "Nationalist," and "People's" Party. In the elections of 1922, it captured twenty-eight of the fifty-eight general constituency seats; by 1928, it held forty seats. But because of the peculiar constitution of the 103-member Legislative Council, it was never able to win more than one of the two elective ministerial posts in the governor's Executive Council. In 1932, this faction decided to campaign for a separationist policy. The decision was based not on confidence in the Simon Commission Report, but on the belief that by this tactic Burma would more rapidly achieve full representative government, free of Indian influence.

In 1933, the Joint Committee of the British Parliament on Indian Constitutional Reform heeded both the Burmese cooperators and noncooperators, the separationists and the antiseparationists, and concluded with some insight that "the difference between them . . . has, we think, been mainly one of tactics." [21] Suspicion of any British offers and varying attitudes toward dyarchy as a desirable or practical form of government were among the factors that maintained the organizational differences in Burmese nationalist outlook and party.

In addition to the two major nationalist factions, there was a third group that was politically prominent in the period of Dyarchy. Its members were supporters of the British Government, and to a large extent they enjoyed British confidence and rewards during the trying years before Burma was finally separated from India. Unlike the nationalist groups, which were predominantly Burman and Buddhist, this group represented the powerful minorities in Burma: the British, Indian, and Chinese business communities, Christian (and other) Karens, and Eurasians. There were, however, also some Burmans. Among the leaders were Sir J. A. Maung Gyi (a Burman), Sir (and also Dr.) San C. Po, Sir Lee Ah Yain, Sir P. P. Ginwala, J. E. Dubern, Sir Oscar de Glanville, and Dr. Alan Murray. Their British honors reveal both their merit and the closeness of their British connection. The group was known first as the Progressive Party, and later as the Independent Party; popularly, it became best known as the Golden Valley Party—named for a wealthy suburban residential area on the outskirts of Rangoon. Its members were usually less successful in elections than their nationalist opponents, but they received high government posts because they were conservative and pro-British. They supported separation in 1932, which prompted one Burmese journalist to comment that as soon as the people discovered what the Golden Valley Party was for, they "put their weight on the other side." [22] The party was virtually eliminated as a political force in the 1936 elections, but not before its Burman leader, Sir J. A. Maung Gyi, served for a short period in 1930 as acting Governor, the only time a Burman attained this high post.

Antiseparationist nationalists won the elections in 1932 but could not command a majority in the Legislative Council of December, 1932, and June, 1933, especially since the government had virtually determined on separation. Since the Burmese who favored the Indian connection clearly did so because they thought it was tactically useful, it soon became evident that all factions among the nationalists, however much they debated its merits, would accept a new political arrangement that would take Burma out of the Indian Empire. The issue then became when and under what conditions of responsible self-government the change should take place.

It was resolved in 1935, when the British Parliament passed the Acts of India and Burma. A new constitution for a separated Burma went into effect after the elections of 1936, on April 1, 1937.

The nature and extent of Burmese home rule under the new 1935 Constitution have been vigorously debated. John L. Christian, writing at the beginning of World War II, took the view that the "new constitution is intended to be a Moses leading the Burmese into the promised land of national liberty." [23] Furnivall, writing in the 1942-45 period, was somewhat less exuberant and more aware of its "defects." [24] That the Constitution brought Burma a "larger installment of autonomy and parliamentary government" [25] is beyond dispute.

The new government was headed by a governor appointed by the Crown, and a council of ten ministers (instead of four) selected from the legislature. In addition, the governor could appoint three counselors who represented him in the legislature. As before, the Scheduled, or Excluded, Areas remained under the governor's direct authority. A chief minister, selected by the governor from among the elected representatives, was to organize and distribute the remaining portfolios. A bicameral legislature, consisting of a Senate and House of Representatives, meeting annually, could enact local legislation and set up committees to inquire into a wide variety of matters, such as agrarian distress, taxation, corruption, or village administration, which could then lead to the enactment of new laws. Of the 36 members of the Senate, one-half were appointed by the governor and one-half elected by the House of Representatives. The House was composed of 132 members, of whom 92 were elected from territorial constituencies, 12 were communally designated and elected separately by the Karens, 8 by the Indians, 2 by the Anglo-Burmans, 3 by the Europeans, 11 by special commercial interests including the predominantly non-Burmese chambers of commerce, 2 by Indian labor (trade unions), and 1 each by Burman labor and the university. Since one chamber of commerce was Burmese and since the university representative was expected to be Burmese, it was possible for the Burman ethnic majority to win a total of 95 out of the 132 House seats. [26]

But Burmese nationalists soon became cynical about their new powers. They rightly regarded the Constitution as perhaps even more dyarchical than its predecessor. The governor retained an impressive reservation of both subjects and powers. He had sole control over the reserved subjects of defense, external affairs, ecclesiastical (i.e., Christian) affairs, the Excluded Areas, monetary policy, currency, and coinage. Without necessarily seeking ministerial advice, he could exercise "his individual judgment" on and had "special responsibility" for eight enumerated types of domestic concern. Leach remarked that "all these special powers may sound formidable," but that practice would ameliorate their severity. [27]

Christian banked on the good judgment of the governor to consult with his ministers so as to diminish the "excessive" charter of power assigned to him by the Constitution.[28] The Burmese were not long in expressing their dissatisfaction about their self-governing powers under the new Constitution. As Dr. Maung Maung remarked, though Burma was legally separated from India, she was still "an appendage to India." [29]

Because of the ethnic composition of the new legislature, a party could command a majority of the 132-member House only if it won 67 of the 95 Burmese seats. In practice, however, a Burmese chief or prime minister could form a government only by making concessions to the European and non-Burmese groups that controlled the other 37 seats. This limited the range of performance for the Burmese ministers, even in respect to those subjects over which, in principle, they exercised departmental authority. It also sharply increased the competition among the Burmese politicians for the perquisites of highly paid office.

None of the four Cabinets or Councils of Ministers formed between 1937 and 1942 was based on a stable parliamentary majority. The Chief Ministers were Dr. Ba Maw (April, 1937-February, 1939), U Pu (February, 1939-September, 1940), U Saw (September, 1940-January, 1942), and Sir Paw Tun, who went into exile with the British Governor in 1942 when the speedy victory of the Japanese in Burma doomed any future development for the Constitution of 1937. In the single national election held in preparation for this Constitution, in 1936, the nationalist factions, still retaining support from various *pongyi*-influenced sections of the old GCBA, again divided the Burmese electorate. U Ba Pe's coalition People's Party won the largest bloc of seats, forty-six; U Chit Hlaing won twelve; and Ba Maw, campaigning under a new, somewhat socialistic label, the Sinyetha, or Poor Man's Party, captured fourteen to sixteen seats. One new grouping of young nationalists, running for office for the first time, won four seats. This was an alliance of young nationalists and socialists who came to be known collectively as the Thakins.

Shortly after his appointment as prime minister of a coalition Cabinet, Dr. Ba Maw, in a speech on December 17, 1937, before old school friends, said:

My political struggle . . . revolves around a clock. I, and indeed all Burmans, are determined to order our own progress according to our own clock, or at least according to a world clock, but it so happens that the British Government wants to order our progress according to a British clock. The argument for the British clock is, of course, that it has regulated British progress and, therefore, it must be good enough to regulate Burmese progress. It has taken Britain several centuries to achieve her own progress and it must, according to the British clock theory, take the same number of centuries or slightly more for Burma or, for that matter, any other country, to do the same thing. . . . Needless to say, I have never been able to accept this theory which makes the British clock set my time.[30]

His statement aptly summarized the position of the nationalists, including those who fought Ba Maw, as they struggled to set their own timetable and character up to World War II. In a sense, it also confirms an observation made by Sir Harcourt Butler when he was Governor of Burma, that Dyarchy "has almost become a term of abuse. I have heard of one man saying of another, 'You are a Dyarchy.' " [31]

The Burmese nationalists did not like what they got under Dyarchy.

Nationalism and the Thakins

The Burmese nationalists who achieved top rank during the 1920's and 1930's were in the main reformers. Although they may have contemplated the idea of independence outside of the British Empire, in practice they worked for full home rule or self-rule, to be attained by evolutionary and parliamentary means. While they were preoccupied with the strategy and tactics of national reform and with the considerable monetary and other advantages of holding office under the British, a new generation of radical nationalists, most of whom were born in the period of World War I, began to emerge. These men, Thakins, were entirely committed to independence. They developd an ideology that prepared for "a general political and economic revolution in the country by armed conflict if necessary." [32]

The Thakins, too, had "the not unmixed blessing of a Western education." As ardent, combative nationalists gathering strength in the late 1930's, they had inevitably become exposed, through their education and their knowledge of events, to the doctrines then fashionable. Theirs was the time of Fascism, Nazism, anti-Western Asian imperialism (led by Japan), and—following the seventh meeting of the Comintern in 1935—the Marxist mixture of socialism and Communism known as People's Frontism. In the years immediately preceding World War II, the ideas associated with the People's Front and anti-imperialism increasingly colored Thakin policies and programs. Burmese nationalism, now dogmatically associated with sloganeering Marxism derived almost exclusively from English and Indian sources, captured their imagination. They grafted onto their indigenous roots a simplified version of Marxist philosophy that identified the arrival of the British as imperialism; attacked the British, Indian, and Chinese exploitation of Burmese human and natural resources as capitalism; and justified unrelenting opposition to both in slogans, agitation, propaganda, and forms of political and economic organization drawn in large part from Marxist socialist and Communist models.

These new nationalists have been known by various names. During the Saya San peasant rebellion of 1930-32, they began to call themselves the Dohbama Asiayone, the We-Burmans Association. In the 1936 elections, they joined forces with some older nationalists who had founded groups known as Ko Min Ko Chin (One's Own King, One's Own Kind), and as "Fabians" (for Fabian Socialists); together they elected four members to the lower House. After 1939, they joined with Ba Maw's Sinyetha to form the Freedom Bloc. Their opponents usually called them extremists. But they are best known by the name they chose for themselves—Thakins. "*Thakin*" in Burmese, like "*sahib*" in Hindi, means "master." The Burmese were required to use this form of address with an Englishman unless a more elevated title was indicated. In the mid-1930's, these nationalists took the title for themselves in derision of the British when they resolved to become masters in their own country. The Thakins, the Thakin Party, or the Thakin movement are imprecise but effective ways of referring to them. They gave a new dimension to Burmese nationalism, and in the 1940's they led their country to independence outside the Commonwealth.

The Thakin movement crystallized around the second student strike begun by the Rangoon University Students' Union (RUSU) on February 25, 1936. It was led by a twenty-nine-year-old law student, a former educator who had taken his bachelor's degree in 1929, known then as Thakin Nu, and later, after the first postindependence national elections of 1951, as U Nu (Mr. Tender). Thakin Nu was then president of the RUSU and a founder of the Nagani (Red Dragon) Publishing House and Book Club, which had been modeled after the Left Book Club in London. He had translated both Dale Carnegie and Karl Marx into Burmese. But though he was an outstanding member of the cadre that made the revolution in Burma, and became Burma's first prime minister after independence, it was the secretary of the RUSU, Aung San, who in the critical decade following the strike and boycott movement of 1936 achieved the undisputed leadership of the struggle for independence. On Aung San the Burmese nationalists later conferred for the first time the title "Bogyoke," "Great General."

The issues of the student strike were merely incidental to the anti-British campaign, though in a later demonstration at the British Secretariat it gave them their first martyr, the student Aung Gyaw. Nominally there was a demand for a more democratic academic administration and a more suitable curriculum. Students Nu and Aung San were suspended for making critical speeches and writing or editing derogatory articles in the student journal, *Oway*, which Aung San edited. But if these issues had not been found, there would have been others. The country responded to the students and supported them. Eventually those expelled were readmitted to the university, but this did not end the contest. This group of students included many of the dramatis personae—and they were joined by others—who occupied the center of the nationalist political stage from this time forward.[33]

A student movement, even when led by determined nationalists like Thakins Aung San and Nu, does not usually make a revolution. So the Thakins early turned their attention to the feeble organizations of labor and peasant groups that had been formed just before the depression years of 1929-31. They gave nationalist political direction to these groups, and at the same time supported the more immediate demands of the workers and peasants. In numerous memorials they called for higher wages and improved working conditions, better housing and welfare, using these appeals as instruments in the struggle against British rule and capitalism. Despite government suppression and arrests, the strike was used with increasing effectiveness as a political and economic weapon. In an effort to bridge the gap between Burmese and Indian labor, and especially to heal the wounds caused by Burmese anti-Indian riots in the 1930's, the Thakins organized All-Burma Labor Conferences to which they invited guest speakers from India's National Congress. These conferences also reflected their continuing interest in and connection with leading Indian nationalists.

The Thakins added to their strength and to their popularity in the countryside in other ways. They emphasized wearing national dress, and the clack-clack of their wooden slippers through the streets of Rangoon and Mandalay became a familiar sound of the nationalist movement. As always, they enlisted support from the Sangha, the Buddhist *pongyi* brotherhood. Seventeen of them, including seven *pongyis*, were mortally wounded when the police fired on a huge demonstration in Mandalay, in 1939. So they had more martyrs. Their Nagani Book Club published and distributed widely a variety of translated and original stories and pamphlets designed to fan nationalist and revolutionary ardor. In the House of Representatives, their leading spokesman, Thakin Mya, vigorously criticized the new Constitution. He and his colleagues were pledged to "wreck" it rather than make it "work." They refused to draw their salaries as members. Outside the House, Thakin Nu and others "burnt the Union Jack and a copy of the Government Act in a gesture of contempt." The Burmese-language press and a Burmese-owned English-language triweekly, *The New Burma*, fully chronicled their doings and otherwise "helped to keep nationalism aflame." [34]

In brief, the Thakins succeeded in doing what the preceding generation of nationalist leaders had failed to do: they brought together, organized, and led a mass base of workers and peasants. They felt themselves to be an integral part of this group, and were its articulate spokesmen. In this they drew upon the strong nationalist sentiment existing in the country and won the support of the Buddhist *pongyis*. To indigenous nationalism they added the ideas and methods acquired through their reading of Marxist philosophy. More or less consciously, they were forging a nationalist-Marxist amalgam which, with few deviations, carried them to their goal.[35]

The Thakins, much more than earlier nationalists, were clearly aware of their goal. As early as 1938, when socialist Thakin Mya organized the Peasants' and Workers' Party, he and other Thakins recognized that they stood for independence. This party was reorganized the following year as the Burma Revolutionary Party (BRP), or National or People's Revolutionary Party, with an underground section. In September, 1939, the BRP published a nine-point program, offering its cooperation to any other nationalist formation that would support a new election for a constituent assembly charged with the responsibility "to frame a constitution for an independent Burma." On this basis the BRP, in the same month, joined forces with Dr. Ba Maw and others, including Buddhist groups, to form the Freedom Bloc, a name taken in obvious imitation of Subhas Chandra Bose's Forward Bloc in India. Ba Maw became its president-dictator ("Ahnashin"), and Aung San its secretary.[36]

The coming of the war in 1939 did not stop the Thakins. Unlike their fathers, who had been willing to support Britain in 1914-18, they accelerated their nationalist campaign after the new war broke out. Their movement was declared illegal under the Defense of Burma Act in 1940. A number of members, including Dr. Thein Maung, Dr. Ba Maw, Thakins Nu, Ba Hein, Soe, Ba Sein, together with three Japanese agents, were arrested and sentenced to terms of imprisonment or detention. In March, after serving seventeen days in prison, Aung San headed a Thakin delegation that attended the Ramgarh Indian National Congress, at which the Burmese met Gandhi, S. C. Bose, and Nehru. On his return to Burma, a warrant for his arrest precipitated his flight across Thailand to Amoy, whence he was taken to Tokyo. Nor was Aung San alone. In all, "Thirty Comrades," later called the "Thirty Heroes," were aided on their way to Japan where, subsequently, at Hainan Island, they received a course of military instruction in preparation for launching the Burma Independence Army (BIA). Many of these thirty had been smuggled out of Burma in February-March, 1941, when the Japanese clandestinely returned Aung San for a week of meetings with the BRP.[37] Among them were Thakins Shu Maung (Bo Ne Win), Tun Ok, Hla Pe (Bo Let Ya), Aung Than (Bo Set Ya), San Hlaing (Bo Hmu Aung), Hla Maung (Bo Zeya), Tun Shein (Bo Yan Naing), Shwe (Bo Kyaw Zaw), Aung Thein (Bo Ye Htut), Kyaw Sein (Bo Mo Nyo), and Saw Lwin (Bo Min Gaung), men who later became army officers, cabinet ministers, political leaders, ambassadors—and some of whom became Communists.

Although, according to some accounts, Aung San's escape to Japan was accidental (that is, it is said that he was to escape to China to look at the developments of the Communist Eighth Route Army), it was probably planned. The Thakins had been approached by Japanese agents, as had others in Burma—for example, U Saw, a prewar premier and the leader of the Myochit (Patriots') Party, and Dr. Thein Maung, publisher of the English language triweekly *New Burma*. Sometime in 1939 or early 1940, the Thakins reached an agreement with Japanese agents, later reinforced by Colonel Minami (whom the Burmese called "Bo Mogyo" ["Thunderbolt"] and who was also known as Colonel Suzuki). Accordingly, the Burma Revolutionary Party, with its underground counterpart, agreed to recruit the men to be trained by the Japanese as officers for a future independent Burma and a Burma Independence Army. These moves in Burma were planned by the Japanese as part of their "southern-advance policy" (*Nanshin Seisaku*), which was designed as a holy war (*Seisen*) to liberate the 130 million tropical peoples from the colonial domination of the white peoples.[38]

Parenthetically, it may be useful to point out that Burmese nationalists had not taken a clear stand on Japan's invasion of China, even after the Marco Polo Bridge incident in July, 1937. Thakin Nu, Deedok Ba Choe (the well-known journalist, frequently called the Fabian [Socialist]), U Ba Lwin (the head of a national school), U Ba (an educator), Daw Mya Sein (U May Oung's daughter), and several others visited China on goodwill missions in 1939-40. But in general, the Burmese were (and still are) suspicious and fearful of China and the Chinese. When Deedok Ba Choe translated *San-Min Chu-I* (*Three Principles of the People*) into Burmese, his countrymen noted that Dr. Sun Yat-sen claimed Burma as having "formerly belonged to China." Burmese nationalists did not look with favor either on the opening of the Burma Road in 1937 or on Churchill's temporary concession to the Japanese when he ordered the road closed in the summer and early fall of 1940. They regarded Sino-British policy on that famous 800-mile stretch as a threat to Burmese security. Thakin Nu, writing in late 1945, says somewhat plaintively that "everyone in Burma . . . knew that in China the Japanese were committing murder and robbery and rape [but] they refused really to believe all these things." As he explained, Japan's defeat of Russia in 1905 and her leadership as an Oriental nation against Western imperialism gave hope of independence to other Oriental peoples.[39]

Early in the war, Burmese nationalists made three attempts to gain their ends by peaceful, cooperative means. In the fall of 1940, Prime Minister U Saw asked for a constitution that would grant Burma dominion status as defined by the Statute of Westminster of 1931; the request was refused. A second attempt was made after the Atlantic Charter of August, 1941, had aroused Burmese hopes for dominion status. Point Three of the Charter stated that the signatories "respect the right of all peoples to choose the form of government under which they will live." However, in an address to the House of Commons on September 9, Prime Minister Churchill declared: "Burma is covered by our considered policy of establishing Burmese self-government and by measures already in progress" —a statement no Burmese nationalist could accept. In spite of this, U Saw, accompanied by U Tin Tut, a leading civil servant, went to London in October, 1941, to transmit a new request for dominion status at the end of the war. U Saw met with Churchill twice, but came away empty-handed.[40] On his way home, he was arrested by the British on suspicion of treasonable contacts with the Japanese, and was detained in Uganda until 1946. This strange, self-educated, uncouth leader, who had won a following among the peasant masses, had now made his greatest effort for Burma. His last actions, after the war, brought tragedy to his country. He was of the stuff out of which Fascists had been made in the 1930's.

A third effort was made, this time by the Thakins after Japan had surprised the British by entering Burma from the Tenasserim at the end of 1941. General Aung San and his thirty comrades had raised a small army on the Thai side of the border, and re-entered Burma shortly after the first air raids on Victoria Point, Mergui, and Tavoy. En route to Rangoon, which fell to the Japanese in early March, 1942, Aung San added several thousand men to his Burma Independence Army, only a portion of whom were adequately armed. The Burma Independence Army, one of them wrote, "was a motley crowd . . . of teachers, students, politicians, professional men, farmers and workers [and] bad hats." It eventually grew from "a mere handful to 50,000 strong." [41] Its troops fought with the Japanese against British forces "with some bravery and exercised a moral effect . . . quite out of proportion to its numbers." [42] Perhaps the most trying battle in this early period was at Shwedaung, on the Japanese march to Prome, where the army was "reported to have fought with fanaticism and were killed in large numbers." [43]

Late in April, 1942, some weeks after these events, when the Japanese armed forces were poised for the attack on Mandalay, the last British stronghold in Burma and one of the last in all of Southeast Asia, the Allies made a belated attempt to win the support of the Thakins. Thakin Nu, who had been in prison for eighteen months, was then held in the filthy, cholera-ridden, overcrowded Mandalay jail, where he was visited by a Chinese delegation led by a General Wang (otherwise unidentified) whom he had met previously while on a goodwill mission to Chungking. General Wang, apparently an emissary from the Allied forces, had the power to free the Thakins if they would agree to take part in turning the Japanese out of Burma—at that moment a most forlorn hope. The Communist leaders in the group of Thakins in the Mandalay jail (Soe, Kyaw Sein, and Ba Hein) were prepared, now that the Soviet

Union was a Western ally, to accept the offer. They were willing to fight "the Fascists." However, Thakin Nu imposed conditions, incorporated in a resolution prepared by him and his Thakin fellow prisoners, which General Wang agreed to transmit to the British Governor, Sir Reginald Dorman-Smith: "Proclaim our independence now or promise it as soon as the war is over. Proclaim it and we will help you, and if you don't proclaim it we will worry you." [44]

Optimistically, Thakin Nu thought that it was not yet too late, that a British proclamation or promise of Burmese independence would rouse the whole country and turn the Burmese against the Japanese. There is no public record of a British reply, but it mattered little either way, for the Japanese could not then have been stopped. By the end of May, 1942, they had cut the Burma Road, the British had evacuated Mandalay, and Allied troops were withdrawing to India and to China. The Japanese were in full control of Burma. The political prisoners at Mandalay, at Monywa (led by Thakin Than Tun), and at Mogok (led by Dr. Ba Maw) were left to free themselves. The British Burma Government withdrew to Simla to await the end of the war and its return to what would, in its opinion, remain for a number of years British Burma.

The government-in-exile at Simla, headed by Sir Reginald Dorman-Smith, included Prime Minister Sir Paw Tun, Finance Minister Sir Htoon Aung Gyaw, several British and Burmese civil servants, including U Tin Tut, U Kyaw Min, U Hpu, and Daw Mya Sein—and a group of prewar moderate Burmese nationalists. The exiled government was not especially successful in winning political support from London. But it prepared for the future reconstruction of Burma under a dyarchical government limited to a postwar period of five to seven years.[45] Its program was never acceptable to the Thakins.

The Thakins and the War

The war and the occupation accelerated Burmese nationalist developments. For, although the residual power always remained in Japanese hands, the Burmese nationalists were accorded the façade and some of the tangible aspects of sovereignty. Administratively subject to ultimate Japanese veto-power, they ran the country after August, 1942. "Independence" was granted to Burma in August, 1943, and Ba Maw's government declared war on the United Kingdom. At all times the manpower of the Burmese army, whether it was called the Burma Independence Army (BIA), the Burma Defense Army (BDA), or the Burma National Army (BNA), remained under the effective control of General Aung San and other Burmese officers loyal to him. There is no doubt that with few exceptions—chiefly Communists like Thein Pe, Soe, and Tin Shwe, and the Fabian Deedok Ba Choe—Burmese nationalist, socialist, and Communist leadership initially collaborated with the Japanese. When, in February, 1945, at the request of the British

Special Operations Executive Force 136 (the British equivalent in Burma of the American Office of Strategic Services Detachment 101) Mountbatten reviewed and upset a subordinate order denying further distribution of arms to the Burma Defense Army then readying itself for an attack on the Japanese army, he insisted that the leaders of the BDA were to be informed that "their past offences" (they "were known to be guilty of treason in the past by collaborating with the Japanese") "were not forgotten . . . though any service to the Allied cause would be taken into account." [46] The Burmese never saw their collaboration with the Japanese as treasonable. For them, it was a means to a goal—the goal of independence. But they came to realize that the Japanese had no intention of granting them genuine freedom.

Thakin reaction against the Japanese began in late 1942,[47] as Thakin Mya (whom Furnivall called "the wisest among the nationalist leaders") became aware that the Japanese "train up pupils, but they remain the masters." [48] Even Dr. Ba Maw, the chief administrator for the Japanese, had resolved to prevent them from "cheating us." [49] According to Thakin Nu, Ba Maw, who knew of the various plans made by what Thakin Nu calls the "Inner Circle" of the Thakins, never betrayed them to the Japanese, but instead "would say just what he liked and do just what he liked. . . . Moreover we were well aware that we had no one among us to match Dr. Ba Maw in resisting Japanese pretensions." [50] There is little doubt that the relationship between Dr. Ba Maw and the Japanese provided a cover for the Thakins in their drive toward independence. After the Japanese set up a subordinate Burmese administration in August, 1942, the Thakin Inner Circle decided that certain ones among their number "would be more useful inside the Government while the Army leaders [General Aung San and Colonel Ne Win] recognizing that the Japanese had cheated us, urged Ba Maw as Chief Administrator to station the whole Burmese army together in one place." [51] Months later, in March, 1943, Aung San met Colonel Suzuki in Tokyo, where he had been recalled because it was said he was too friendly to the Burmese; reputedly, he told Aung San that he was in disgrace. This incident reinforced Aung San's growing conviction that the Japanese were insincere in promising independence for Burma.

Having recognized the realities of the situation, the Thakins took what clandestine steps they could to alter it. The Burma Defense Army included a battalion of Karens commanded by a Sandhurst-trained Karen officer, Hanson Kya Doe. Through these Karen channels, the Thakins communicated with one of the British officers, Major H. P. Seagrim, who had stayed behind after the evacuation and had re-established radio contact with the British forces in India in mid-October, 1943. In November, 1943, his Karen assistant, Po Hla, an officer in the Burma Rifles who had been an honors graduate from the University of Rangoon in 1939, brought word from the Karens in the Burma Defense Army that the Burmese leaders "were already plotting revolt against the Japanese." [52] Force 136 had already established liaison with several Communist Thakins who, as Thakin Nu reported, had gone underground in the spring of 1942 but who had consistently maintained contact with the Thakins in the government. [53]

There has never been any dispute as to when some Burmese Communists began to resist the Japanese. The authenticity of the BDA-Seagrim 1943 contact has also been established and accepted. [54] What has remained an issue is why the Burmese turned against the Japanese. The Burmese were neither pro-Japanese nor anti-British, as such. They supported the Japanese because at the time they had good reason to doubt that the British would give them independence. They wanted freedom and independence for their country—a simple, clear proposition for which they were willing to fight. Therefore, when the Burmese realized that the Japanese were denying them the reality of independence, they felt no hesitation in turning against them. It took them much less time to recognize the reality of the situation with respect to Japan than it had in the case of England.

The Burmese Resistance Movement took formal political shape as a typical People's Front in August and September 1944. Secret meetings were held at various homes (Nu's, Than Tun's) during which the leadership of the Burma Defense Army, the Burma Revolutionary Party (socialists), the newly formed Burma Communist Party, and other groups organized the Anti-Fascist Organization, or Burmese Patriotic Front, subsequently better known as the Anti-Fascist People's Freedom League, the AFPFL. [55]

However, though British leaders accepted the aid of the Burmese Resistance, they could barely conceal their disdain and distrust. Their interests were opposed. The BIA had killed British soldiers and Burma Karens who had remained loyal to the British connection, and it had aided the enemy, Japan. Therefore, for example, the Chief Civil Affairs Officer, Major General C. F. B Pearce, an Indian civilian from Burma, regarded the recognition accorded the Resistance in September, 1944, "and its leaders, particularly Aung San, with the gravest suspicion and was disinclined to enter into any arrangements for cooperation with them." [56] As Cady remarks, with some understatement, "such persons, with occasional exceptions, usually lacked sympathy for the Burmese point of view." [57]

This is not the place to detail the progress of the war in the Burma theater. On May 25, 1942, General Stilwell had said: "I claim we got a hell of a beating. We got run out of Burma and it is humiliating as hell. I think we ought to find out what caused it, go back and retake it." [58] In time, the Allies succeeded in regaining Burma. In March, 1945, they retook Mandalay. On the southward campaign toward Rangoon they were openly joined, on March 27, by General Aung San and his troops (the date has become a national holiday in Burma, where it is known as Resistance Day). Rangoon fell on May 2. On May 17, the British issued a White Paper defining policy for the returning Burma government-in-exile administration. Japan surrendered on August 12. Civilian government was restored in Burma on October 16, 1945.

The White Paper authorized the governor to carry out his task with "direct responsibility to His Majesty's Government" under Section 139 of the 1935 Act for "three years more, that is till 9th December, 1948." [59] Only then would the prewar parliamentary provisions and electoral processes of the act be restored. During this period of "controlled government," the governor would have the means and the power "to associate with himself representatives of Burmese opinion in executive and legislative capacities." According to this schedule, the British would return to Burma under conditions of control antecedent to the degree of Dyarchy actually operative under the 1935 Act and Constitution. Only after the restoration of these prewar arrangements would consideration be given to the possibility of "full self-government within the British Commonwealth . . . in Burma proper." But even then the Excluded Areas—43 per cent of the total area of Burma—would be subject to a "special regime" until such time as their inhabitants signified "a desire for amalgamation with Burma proper."

It was clear in 1945 that the British Government had postponed to an indefinite future any possible agreement with the Burmese nationalists about self-government or dominion status within the Commonwealth. It did not or would not take seriously General Aung San's view, as reported by Field Marshal Sir William Slim, that he "did not want British or Japanese or any other foreigners to rule his country." [60]

Bogyoke Aung San

Throughout the war the stature of Aung San as a political and military leader had grown. From the beginning he seemed never to have doubted his direction: opposition to colonialism, whether British or Japanese; positive determination to help win freedom for Burma. Highly intelligent and bluntly forthright in speech and conduct, he was a leader whose uncomplicated outlook won the support of an ever-growing following. Born on February 13, 1915, he was a student when he began his political activities in the mid-1930's, but his influence spread steadily beyond his own Thakin group. The Burmese people, with the exception of Communists and the older politicians who followed the British into retreat in India, never hesitated in their loyalty to him. Unknown abroad before the war, and called by Churchill the "traitor rebel leader" of a "quisling army" when he became known,[61] Aung San won the respect of British military leaders with whom he had direct contact, and impressed them with the strength of his position. Field Marshal Sir William Slim, reporting his conversations with Aung San in May, 1945, wrote: "He was not the ambitious, unscrupulous guerrilla leader I had expected. . . . I judged him to be a genuine patriot and a well-balanced realist—characters which are not always combined. . . . The greatest impression he made on me was one of honesty. . . . I have always felt that with proper treatment, Aung San would have proved a Burmese Smuts." [62]

Aung San exerted leadership because he possessed the qualities of a leader. He did not overlook political realities and the need to build organizations through which policy could be carried into practice. During the war he built up an army that he led first against the British and later against the Japanese, but he also looked to the future. While the war was still going on, he tried to mitigate the animosities between Burmans and Karens, which had been intensified by conflicts between the Burma Independence Army and the Delta Karens who had supported the British. Although Aung San was only partially successful in his conciliatory efforts, Thakin Nu considered that "all the Karens that he met trusted him implicitly, and came to respect him." [63] In much the same way Aung San, in the years immediately after the war, set about winning the confidence of the Shans, Kachins, Chins, and other peoples of the Hill and Frontier Areas as a necessary first step toward the unification of Burma in the ongoing contest for independence.

Equally important were the efforts he made to bring together into one organization the existing parties and factions that made up the wartime coalition, the Anti-Fascist People's Freedom League. This typical People's Front group originally included the Socialist (formerly the Burma Revolutionary Party) and Communist parties as well as various non-Marxist parties, and also trade unions and a number of women's, youth, ethnic, veterans', and Buddhist organizations. (Later, in November, 1946, Aung San and Thakin Nu determined on the exclusion of the Burma Communist Party, then and since led by Aung San's brother-in-law, Thakin Than Tun.) Knowing that he had to have the backing of the people if his avowed aim of independence was to be achieved, Aung San worked to create a coalition broad enough to indicate that he had national support, and strong enough to withstand the inevitable strains. From the beginning of his renewed contacts with the British, he made his purpose clear. When, in May, 1945, he met with Field Marshal Slim, he asserted that he was the representative of the new provisional government of Burma, created by the AFPFL in August, 1944, and asked for the status of an ally. He stated that even though he was willing to subordinate his command to the Allied strategy, it was the intention of the AFPFL to establish an independent republic.[64]

On this central issue, the plans of the AFPFL were in direct conflict with those of the British Government for the immediate future of Burma. In 1942, the British Government had sent Sir Stafford Cripps to India with a limited proposal concerning India's possible independence after the war (which the Indians rejected). No such policy of self-government was either promised or announced for Burma; this colony, in the words of the White Paper, would attain self-government only "as circumstances permitted." Collis tells us that during a December, 1944, House of Commons debate on a "Blueprint for Burma," it was proposed that dominion status be awarded to Burma six years after the return of a civilian government; in the interim Burma would be ruled by the extraordinary powers conferred on the governor by Section 139 of the Act of 1935. In effect, this blueprint, if adopted, would have meant that the British had at least set a definite timetable for Burmese self-government within the Commonwealth. However, as noted above, the White Paper of May, 1945, dropped this provision. In his published account of the debate, Collis added that he did not then expect the Burmese to accept these views even if the British Government approved them. He commented also that at that time neither he nor the debaters had "heard of Aung San, General of the Burma Defence Army . . . of the AFPFL, and had no conception of what had been happening inside Burma." [65]

But Vice Admiral Mountbatten was better informed. In May, 1945, he urged the British Chiefs of Staff to treat Aung San's army and proposed rising against the Japanese quite seriously.

> I felt [he wrote] that it would be unrealistic not to treat the AFPFL as what it was: a coalition of the political parties commanding the largest following in the territory. . . . I therefore suggested to Sir Reginald Dorman-Smith [the Governor of Burma] that Lieutenant-General Slim might be allowed to tell Major-General Aung San that his excellency would consider the eventual inclusion of members of the AFPFL in his Executive Council, when Civil Government was restored; but Sir Reginald telegraphed that he could not for a moment contemplate giving an undertaking to consider this.[66]

Dorman-Smith did, however, want to "build a contented Burma, which will have no wish whatsoever to contract out of the Empire." To him this meant dominion status at some stipulated but deferred postwar time.[67]

Until the end of the war, British policy for Burma was based on purely military considerations determined by Mountbatten and his staff. Mountbatten, one of the few men who clearly perceived the force of Burmese nationalism—of Aung San and the AFPFL—was successful in his dealing with Aung San on military problems. Beyond this, he was convinced that the goodwill of the Burmese could—and would—be retained if, at an early return of civil government, responsibility were transferred to the nationalist leaders. Discussing the situation, Collis wrote that "Lord Mountbatten has told me that he believes that if it had been left to him at this stage, from June 1945 onward . . . if a man sharing his opinions had been appointed as Governor, his hope would have been realized." [68] But the Civil Affairs Service, headed by Major General C. F. B. Pearce, with Colonel F. S. V. Donnison as his deputy, opposed Mountbatten's views. They "disputed the representative character of the nationalist fronts," counseled the returning powers to be firm against those fronts, and thereby "re-establish themselves" with the aid of "the moderates" or "respectable elements" who opposed the "extremists." [69]

The Churchill government supported Mountbatten only in the military phase of his operations. When the time came for the government to declare its postwar civilian policy for Burma,[70] it rejected both Dorman-Smith's proposal that Burma be permitted to attain full self-government within five to seven years[71] and the sagacious advice of Mountbatten. Its declared policy was retrogressive on the issues of self-government, including the relation of Burma Proper to the Excluded or Scheduled Areas. The White Paper restored Burma to "predyarchy days." [72] Sir Reginald Dorman-Smith who, as Governor of Burma, was responsible for carrying out its provisions, called it "infuriatingly vague." [73] To the Burmese it was more infuriating than vague. To Bogyoke Aung San it was the signal for a new phase of the battle for independence.

Civil government was restored to Burma in mid-October, 1945. At this time Aung San made his last bid for official recognition as representative of the wartime AFPFL provisional government. He requested the governor to appoint seven of the eleven members of the Governor's planned Executive Council (or eleven if the council was to have fifteen members) from a list submitted by the AFPFL's Supreme Council. It seems clear that at this time Dorman-Smith had no desire to conciliate the AFPFL, nor did the recently elected Labour government at home advise him to do so. Dorman-Smith offered the AFPFL two places on the Executive Council—an offer that was promptly refused.

The relationship between the government and Aung San's party continued to reflect the British dislike and distrust of the nationalist leaders. But if to the British Aung San was a traitor, a collaborator with the enemy, and a quisling,[74] to the Burmese he was unmistakably a hero and a great leader.[75] He had deeply impressed a few of the military leaders whom he met: Lord Mountbatten, Field Marshal Sir William Slim, and Major General Sir Hubert Rance, among others. Despite the conflict between them, he "also cast his spell over Dorman-Smith," who wrote to the new Labour Secretary of State for India and Burma, Pethwick-Lawrence, "We must, I think, accept it as a fact that Aung San is the most important figure in Burma today. Everyone appears to trust and admire him. . . . His troops adore him and will do anything he says. . . . He has no ambition. . . . If there was an election in Burma now and Aung San were to head a party he would sweep the country." [76] Increasingly, in London as well as at home, Aung San was recognized as the true national leader of the Burmese. Dorman-Smith to the contrary, he did have an ambition—to free Burma. To that end he set his course. When it became clear that the policies of the White Paper were to be carried out, the struggle for power between the nationalists and the British Government entered the final phase.

I N THE BRIEF interval between the end of hostilities and the return of the British Burma Government from Simla in October, 1945, Aung San and the AFPFL carried out a vigorous drive for recognition. Though the favor they won from the British military leadership ultimately contributed to their success, their initial attempt failed. The provisions of the White Paper were put into effect. From November, 1945, to January, 1947, when Prime Minister Attlee held the conversations with Aung San[1] that led directly to independence twelve months later, there ensued a political conflict from which a threat of armed struggle was never absent. Aung San, the AFPFL, and their nationalist allies throughout the country conducted an amazingly adroit campaign, well worth study by students of political science.[2]

The AFPFL Contests the White Paper

The basic policy followed by Aung San and the Thakins was settled in the August, 1944, meetings that gave birth to the AFPFL. The "Manifesto"[3] issued at that time not only called for armed resistance against "the Japanese Fascists," but also provided a fifteen-point outline of a democratic constitution for "independent Burma" that would determine the character of the "People's Government." The "Manifesto" also provided guidelines concerning social insurance and welfare and such administrative areas as "progressive" education, agriculture, industry, and the judiciary. However, it was silent as to the future of the Burmese armed force, now called the Burma National Army (BNA). This issue loomed large in the minds of the Burmese and the British after Aung San marched his troops to join the Allies in March, 1945.

As the British advanced down the Irrawaddy valley in the spring of 1945, they observed "everywhere" the display of the AFPFL red-and-white-starred flag (described in the "Manifesto" as the "Victory Flag") and the activity at local AFPFL headquarters.[4] In the words of Sir William Slim, the problem was "how to treat the Burmese National Army, originally Japanese sponsored, but now in arms against them." The British could not afford to gain a new enemy in the rear by declaring the BNA an illegal organization.

In the second half of May, 1945, British policy was announced. Politically, the White Paper refused recognition to General Aung San's provisional government. Militarily, the Southeast Asian Command, under Lord Louis Mountbatten and later Sir William Slim, was empowered to incorporate a portion of the BNA in the regular Burma Army and to disband the rest. On May 16, General Aung San met with General Slim, and, on June 10, with Admiral Mountbatten, to work out the details of this policy. Disbanding of the old army and re-enlistment in the new, now renamed the Patriotic Burmese Forces (PBF), began at the end of June. The changeover did not proceed smoothly. The British wished to re-enlist the PBF members on an individual basis; the Burmese wanted to maintain their re-enlistments on a unit basis. Additional conferences held in July and August led up to the major one, convened by Admiral Mountbatten at Kandy, on September 6. Here grievances were amicably adjusted by Mountbatten and Aung San. By the end of 1945, about 10,000 men of the PBF had been processed through the disbandment centers, and a "surprising quantity of arms . . . was handed in." Nevertheless, it was clear that a substantial difference over the issue of individual versus unit re-enlistment remained, and at least 3,500 armed BNA soldiers never appeared at any disbandment center.[5] These men constituted the nucleus of Bogyoke Aung San's military threat in the political struggle ahead.

In the meantime, as the Japanese were forced to retreat, the AFPFL began to operate openly. From March 27, 1945, until the Japanese surrender on August 12, the League's leaders were primarily involved in carrying out military and guerrilla activities, but they did not neglect their organizational needs. As resistance groups emerged from the underground, the Supreme Council of the AFPFL was enlarged from nine to sixteen and then to thirty-six members; ultimately, it became the Council of Fifty, providing places for up-country leaders who would join the others as conditions became more secure.[6]

On May 25, 1945, the AFPFL Council, in its first policy statement, rejected the terms of the White Paper and reaffirmed the positions taken in the 1944 "Manifesto." To gain Burmese public support, the council organized mass meetings throughout the country, the most important of which was held at Naythuyein Hall in Rangoon on August 19. There, Aung San condemned Fascist ideology, supported the Atlantic Charter, and called for unified support for a provisional national government until elections could be held that would mark the beginning of responsible self-government in Burma. He called upon those of his troops who had not yet proceeded to disbandment centers, as well as various guerrilla-type forces, to volunteer their services to the country. This was the beginning of the People's Volunteer Organization (PVO), ostensibly an ex-servicemen's association for reconstruction in war-devastated Burma. Actually, the PVO was the League's army, under Aung San's command, in the final struggle for independence. (Subsequently, after the assassination of Aung San, it was to become a major source of trouble to the fledgling government of independent Burma.)

Strongly backed throughout the countryside, Aung San met the returning government on October 17, 1945, as the representative of the AFPFL provisional government, and requested the governor to appoint seven of the eleven members of the new Executive Council (or eleven, if the Council was to have fifteen members) from a list of names submitted by the AFPFL Supreme Council. Despite the changeover from the Churchill government to the Labour government headed by Clement Attlee, Dorman-Smith had no new instructions to deal in a more conciliatory fashion with Aung San. He offered the AFPFL two places on the Executive Council—an offer which was promptly refused. In response, Aung San and the Council intensified the campaign against the government.

On November 18, at the "biggest mass meeting ever held in Burma"—at the Shwedagon Pagoda—Aung San openly challenged the government.[7] He told his huge audience that the proposals put forward by the AFPFL had been rejected. But, he continued, since the governor had declared (in an address at the time of his return) that his program was neither rigid nor inelastic, the Supreme Council of the AFPFL would "henceforth concentrate all its efforts to get the programme changed." [8] Aung San's blandly threatening speech led to a series of resolutions. One called for the mobilization of the Burmese people; another offered "practical service" to the people; still another demanded that the world and the British people be told how the British Government had returned to re-establish monopolistic rule. The governor had said that, despite his rule under Section 139, "Burma's battle for freedom is over." Aung San replied that the battle had just begun.

The strains of political tension were multiplied by the stress of postwar suffering. Commenting on the effects of total warfare, the *Military Administration's Handing Over Report* stated that "no British possession has suffered so much damage." [9] The civil administration had great difficulty in restoring law and order and in getting reconstruction under way in the ravaged countryside. Though the price of paddy, the most important index in Burma's economy, was fixed at 50 per cent above the prewar level, the overall cost of living had risen several hundred per cent. The inevitable demonetization of Japanese currency contributed further to the hardships of the people.[10] Early in the war, the departure from

Burma of the Indian *chettyars* had freed cultivators from their heavy indebtedness, and the Japanese had allowed them to take possession of the land. In Burmese eyes, it now appeared that the people would again be landless and debt-ridden.[11] The government rejected an AFPFL proposal that ex-soldiers, including those in the newly formed PVO, be used for land-reclamation work because of the high war loss of work cattle. Instead, the government reinstituted the detested policy of bringing in low-paid ("coolie") labor from India. Finally, it was apparent that the government intended "to assist in re-establishing the prewar British firms" and their British administrative personnel "notoriously inimical to Burma's political aspirations." [12]

As the pace of unrest quickened, each new incident added to the strength of Aung San and his followers. When Dorman-Smith appointed his Executive and Legislative Councils without including representatives of the AFPFL, he brought into the government Burmese of the older generation and others who had no standing among the nationalists—men such as Sir Paw Tun, who joined forces with ex-Premier U Saw when he was released from custody in February, 1946, and Tun Ok, a former Thakin, whom both the Thakins and the Japanese had dropped from leadership in the summer of 1942. These were the men who, together with prominent civil servants—including the former Chief Civil Affairs Service Officer, Sir C. F. B. Pearce, and Judge Sir John Wise—advised the governor in March, 1946, to arrest Aung San on a charge of murder. (During the war, Aung San had presided over a court-martial and sentenced to death a headman who had organized villagers against the Burma Independence Army.) The affair was widely reported in Rangoon and London. The Commander in Chief of the Burma Command, General Sir Harold Briggs, warned that mutiny in the countryside would follow Aung San's arrest; in spite of this, the Labour government, in April, ordered a warrant to be issued. Fortunately, the order was rescinded before it could be executed. There can be little doubt that Sir Harold's judgment was correct; as it was, the incident vastly enhanced Aung San's reputation.[13]

As one Burmese authority commented:

> The Governor himself was not in an enviable position. Loyalty to the older politicians who had followed him into exile in India, and for those who waited for him through the war in Burma, lack of a correct appraisal of the strange and fluid situation . . . and the need to take instructions from London, which was still further away from the heart of affairs, on matters of policy, made his task and position extremely difficult.

There was "frustration" in the Executive and Legislative Councils. "The Councillors meant well, and did their best to serve, but they enjoyed no real powers but what the Governor granted them, and the Governor had no real powers in the country, for the people did not obey his writs any more, but followed Aung San and the AFPFL." [14]

Another incident occurred after the governor had criticized the Burmese press for describing him as an "imperialist" and a "capitalistic expansionist," and for its general antigovernment attitude. He issued "a stern warning" to "certain elements . . . spreading sedition and disturbing the minds of the people." He also sharply questioned the "wearing [of] military uniforms and the performance of military drill by non-military personnel." [15] Aung San immediately came to the defense of the PVO. PVO members wore uniforms, he declared, because there was not enough other clothing; they drilled because they might later join the Burma army; they were instructed to help farmers with cultivation. If some of them overstepped the law, they should be arrested and speedily tried, instead of being detained for an indefinite time without trial.[16]

Demonstrations in favor of the AFPFL continued all over Burma. Usually they were reported—in the British and the Burmese-owned press alike—as "orderly," "quiet," and "earnest." Some, however, ended in incidents of violence, which heightened anti-British feeling and were used to good purpose by Aung San and his followers. For example, on May 18, 1946, the police attempted to break up a demonstration at Tantabin, in the Insein district, protesting the arrest of PVO members. They fired on the crowd, killing three peasants and wounding eight others. The government feared that a new Saya San peasant rebellion might break out; instead, Aung San organized a great public funeral. A Burmese newspaper account of the event—and the Dorman-Smith papers—show clearly Aung San's capacity to control a potentially explosive situation:

> The funeral of the three victims of the shooting by the police in connection with anti-repressive-measures demonstrations in the Insein District took place at Tantabin last Saturday when over twenty thousand people from Rangoon, Hmawbi, Tharrawaddy and even from the Delta were present. About 230 buses went from Rangoon and about 100 buses came from Tharrawaddy side to Tantabin. Many came by motor boats and motor-sampans from the Delta towns also. President Aung San addressed the gathering at the funeral.
>
> Over twenty thousand lunch packets were distributed free at Shwe-Hlay-Gyi Village while tea and cold drinks were freely served by residents of Hmawbi and Insein. Those who could not return to Rangoon after the funeral were brought over to Hmawbi, where they were fed and given shelter for the night by the hospitable town-folks of Hmawbi. Special arrangements were made for the pongyis.
>
> Like all previous gatherings organized by the Anti-Fascist Peo-

ple's Freedom League, the whole funeral-procession was a spontane-
ous, peaceful and well-disciplined affair.[17]

In mid-May, Aung San forcefully restated the position of the
nationalists, in a lengthy "Presidential address" at the opening of
the second session of the AFPFL Supreme Council.[18]

The AFPFL, he said, was ready to negotiate: "We still offer our
hand of friendship, we still do desire to come to peaceful settlement on the questions both immediate and long term. Meanwhile
we remain in 'prepared peace.'" On the other hand, the AFPFL
was also ready to engage in an "extra-legal struggle for freedom if
that should become necessary." Though Aung San did not regard
such a struggle as inevitable, he said that "it rests with the British
side whether they choose to have it or not." His proposals to the
government remained essentially unchanged: The nationalist leaders wanted recognition of "the full right of our nation to independence." On this occasion—the only one for which there is no explanation—he suggested that if the AFPFL program was accepted,
Burma might "elect to enter the British Commonwealth of Nations." The Council "unanimously" approved Aung San's position.[19]

The Supreme Council left the way open for conciliation—on
Aung San's terms. The All-Burma Peasants' Organization (ABPO)
conference held at Henzada a week earlier (May 9-12) had made a
less peaceable impression, for its resolutions made pointed reference to the 1930-32 Saya San "uprising against the British imperialists." However, the conference also endorsed in advance the resolutions of the AFPFL Supreme Council. The tactical competence of
the AFPFL leaders—and their alternating emphasis on the possibilities of negotiation and violence—is suggested by the fact that
although the tougher ABPO resolutions were passed before the Supreme Council met, they were reported in the press several days
after those of the Council, at the same time at which the Tantabin
funeral demonstration was reported.[20]

A full year had passed since Aung San had first stated his position to the British military leaders at General Slim's headquarters,
and it now appeared that the British community in Rangoon and
the government in London recognized the strength and intransigence of Bogyoke Aung San and his party. The London *Times*
commented on May 15 that "the British cannot afford to allow the
Burmese to lose heart" and pointed to the need for associating the
"more vigorous in the Burmese political life" with the "present
administration." The same article urged that "a date should be
fixed without delay for the general elections which will restore responsible government as a stage in the progress towards full authority." At the very least this meant a restoration of the 1935 dyarchical Constitution. On May 19, an editorial in the *New Times of
Burma* called for a meeting between Aung San and the governor so

that the "two hands of friendship outstretched" might clasp "in a friendship . . . which will set Burma onto its feet again."

Thus, within a few days, each of the main participants in the political struggle voiced a response to the events of the preceding months. Meanwhile, on April 22, Dorman-Smith, in a message to Arthur Henderson, Parliamentary Under Secretary of State for India and Burma, had advised that "it is very difficult to see how anything short of handing over complete power to a provisional Government could ease [the tension]." He therefore proposed early elections for a constituent assembly, to be held in 1947, to prepare for a constitution and a Burmese government in 1948. He also offered his resignation.[21]

There is no public record of Henderson's reply to Dorman-Smith, but two things become clear. At the end of May, 1946, the Conservative Party requested a debate on the situation in Burma. On June 7, a full debate took place in the House of Commons. Henderson's statements during the course of the debate suggested that the Labour government had not yet come to a final decision about Burma, though it accepted the governor's resignation. He described the proposed elections as an expression of the government's "intention to press on without delay with the remaining stages of the White Paper," thereby ignoring for the time the AFPFL's rejection of that "infuriatingly vague" policy statement. He called the AFPFL a "promising party," which had "strong support and very great possibilities," and urged the AFPFL leaders to join the existing Executive Council, presumably in the minority status previously offered. He did not go beyond this.[22]

Meanwhile, it was announced in Rangoon that the governor was "suffering from a severe attack of amoebic dysentery" and had asked to be relieved from duty. Sir Henry F. Knight was appointed acting governor until, on July 31, Sir Hubert Rance, who had been Mountbatten's original candidate for the office in 1945, and who was favorably regarded by Aung San, was named to succeed Dorman-Smith. On June 6, just before his departure, Dorman-Smith held a last conference with Aung San and four others. He again urged them to join the Executive Council, and they again put forward their views, which he promised to convey in person to his government; he also expressed the hope that they would continue conversations with the acting governor.[23] He wrote to Sir Henry that Aung San "is Burma's popular hero and without any shadow of doubt he has the biggest personal following of any man in the country. . . . I look upon him as a very sincere man. . . . His League does possess the only nation-wide organization. . . . I think he is out for peace and tranquility. He has enough sense to realize that an uprising can only mean added misery." [24]

The change of governors did not change AFPFL policy. By repeated demonstrations and strikes of organized labor, Aung San sought to impress upon the British the necessity of recognizing the

AFPFL and its policies. Demonstrators continued to protest the police action at Tantabin and to pay homage to the dead, whom they considered martyrs. On July 24 and 25, the AFPFL held meetings to celebrate the arrival of Suresh Bose, brother of the Indian independence leader Subhas C. Bose, who had made Rangoon a base of operations during the war. These meetings were a prelude to a new campaign against "repressive measures." This was timed to begin at the end of August, just before Sir Hubert Rance was expected to arrive. In July, also, the smoldering quarrel between the Communists and the Socialists in the AFPFL broke into the open. Aung San publicly announced that the AFPFL would not participate in demonstrations planned by the Communists—foreshadowing the expulsion of the Burma Communist Party (BCP) from the League. He also brought about the replacement of Communist Than Tun by Socialist Kyaw Nyein as secretary of the League; the Communist candidate, Thein Pe, was defeated. Having led in the criticism of the Communists, Aung San now made his most Marxist speech—perhaps to demonstrate that the current differences between the Socialists and the Communists had to do only with internal issues and did not affect the over-all political position of the AFPFL. In a record five-hour address to the AFPFL's third Supreme Council meeting,[25] he presented a standard variant of the two-camp theory of "old democracies and new democracies." He described capitalism as a "necessary step" on the way to socialism. Imperialism, in his view, though greatly weakened, still persisted, but "its Day of Judgment is coming." He did not expect a third (imperialist) world war to break out and therefore expressed the belief that by "work, work, work, action, action, action, self-reliance, self-reliance, self-reliance," success could be achieved in Burma.

Sir Hubert Rance, the new governor, arrived in Rangoon on August 30 to face a month of carefully planned, crippling strikes: by the police on September 5, the postal workers on September 15, the government press on September 16, and, finally, a general strike on September 23. While these were going on, Rance interviewed leaders in the AFPFL coalition, as well as two prewar premiers—Dr. Ba Maw, who, having broken with the AFPFL, had revived his wartime Mahabama (Great Burma) Party, and U Saw, who had revived his prewar Myochit (Patriot) Party. Rance also talked with Thakin Ba Sein, an early nonsocialist, right-wing leader of the Thakin movement.

Finally, on September 26, the governor was authorized by London to announce that on his recommendation His Majesty's Government had agreed to accept the AFPFL's proposal in regard to the Executive Council originally made to Dorman-Smith in October, 1945.

In the reorganized Executive Council, of which the governor was to be chairman, ministers or councillors would have the same powers as in 1937-42; in addition, it was agreed that the ministers of defense and external affairs would be Burmese nationals, and the minister of finance would have the right and duty to consider fiscal affairs and forward his recommendations to London. Though the Frontier Areas were still excluded from its jurisdiction, the new Executive Council was to be kept informed about matters concerning their governance. Rance invited the AFPFL to name six of the eleven members of the new council. The portfolios of Defense and External Affairs went to Aung San, who was named deputy chairman of the Council—in actuality, prime minister.[26] Thus the White Paper was scrapped; the AFPFL had won recognition in place of the wartime Simla regime.

The AFPFL Enters the Executive Council

The AFPFL leaders immediately accepted Governor Rance's solution. Their public announcement on September 26 described the new council as an Interim Government, which could break the "prolonged political deadlock" resulting from "the breakdown of political negotiations between the AFPFL and the British Government." They welcomed the acquisition of the two ministries—defense and external affairs—as an advance over 1935, and were willing to postpone "making an issue" over finance and the Frontier Areas. Nevertheless, they also indicated that the "Interim Government . . . does not yet satisfy the complete requirements of a National Government as we have envisaged [it] and is certainly not yet a provisional Government which could lead us straight to the establishment of a free, independent Burma." [27]

A few days before the governor took his decisive step, the AFPFL had called for nationwide "anti-White Paper demonstrations." [28] Held on schedule on September 29, these were now turned into victory celebrations. Yet when Aung San addressed the demonstrators, he told them he was speaking "with a heavy heart." His experience as a minister under the Japanese "had taught him to be careful and wary. It remained to be seen what it would be like to be a Councillor with the British." [29]

Aung San faced his greatest challenge. From the days of the resistance to October, 1946, the AFPFL leaders had been in the opposition as agitators, propagandists, and organizers of the "freedom struggle." Now Aung San, as Chief Minister, and his party had to demonstrate their ability to represent and lead the country. It was necessary for the AFPFL not only to end the strikes and restore law and order, but also to preserve the essential unity of Burmese nationalism while executing a positive program.

The first step toward restoring order was taken at once. On October 2, Aung San announced that a "full settlement had been reached between the strike leaders representing the various unions and the Government." But in the interim the rift between the AFPFL and the Communists had been widening. Though the

Communist Party had participated in AFPFL acceptance of the new Executive Council, its journal, *Pyithuahna* (literally, "people's power," but called *The Thunderer* in English), soon attacked Aung San and the Council for the way they had ended the general strike. This, in addition to previous Communist tactics, persuaded Aung San, as president of the AFPFL, that he could no longer work with the Communists, either as individual members of the League or as a party. On October 10, 1946, the Executive Committee of the AFPFL voted to expel the Communist Party from the League and forced its member, Thein Pe, to resign from the Executive Council of the government. The decision, announced by Thakin Nu on October 13, was ratified by the AFPFL Supreme Council at its November 1-3 meeting.[30] Thein Pe, speaking for the two factions of the Communist movement, one led by Thakin Soe and the other by Thakin Than Tun, gave notice on October 28 that "the Communist Party will appeal to the country in the forthcoming elections to endeavor to rescue the national movement and achieve Burma's complete freedom." [31] He denounced Aung San and the Executive Council as "tools of the policy of repression . . . collaborating with imperialism [who] have become reformist [and have] surrendered to British duplicity." He also declared that until the elections took place, the Communists intended to sponsor mass political strikes and promote workers' and peasants' movements against imperialism and capitalism. Thus, as soon as it was in power, the new government faced a new opposition.

The AFPFL now adopted and publicized a one-year timetable that it desired to negotiate with the British Government. It called for the transformation of the Interim Government into a Provisional Government by January 31, 1947; for the holding of national elections (not for a new legislature, as specified in the Act and Constitution of 1935, but for a Constituent Assembly to draft a new constitution); and for a declaration of intent by the British Government, looking toward Burma's freedom within one year from January, 1947.[32] The importance that the AFPFL attached to the timetable was emphasized by the headline under which its terms were announced: "AFPFL Executive Councillors to resign if demands not met by January 31, 1947." [33]

The extraordinary fact is that after a little more than a year of indecision, the British Labour Government calmly and graciously accepted the timetable. On December 3, Governor Rance chose the Orient Club of Rangoon—a club started by Burmese because they had been excluded from the British Pegu Club—to announce that he had the task of "leading Burma to full self-government in what must be relatively speaking a short period" and that "His Majesty's Government does not wish to stand in the way of Burma's freedom." [34] On December 20, Prime Minister Attlee invited Aung San and a delegation for talks in London.

The talks began on January 13, 1947. Councillors Thakin Mya,

U Tin Tut, and U Ba Pe, together with U Kyaw Nyein and U Aung Than (Bo Set Ya), were Aung San's AFPFL colleagues in the negotiations. U Saw, representing the Myochit Party, and Thakin Ba Sein, representing the Dohbama Asiayone (We Burmans Association), with their advisers, U Ba Yin and Thakin Chit, were also part of the delegation, but refused to concur in the final agreement. Daw Than E (later a member of the United Nations Secretariat) was the delegation's highly competent and politically astute hostess.

The agreement that resulted, entitled *Conclusions Reached in the Conversations Between His Majesty's Government and the Delegation From the Executive Council of the Governor of Burma*, was initialed by the Prime Minister and Bogyoke Aung San on January 27.[35] It provided for elections in April for a Constituent Assembly that would be completely free to determine Burma's future course, and for recognition of the Executive Council as an Interim Government comparable to that in India. In addition, the powers of the Councillors for Defense and External Affairs were increased, since, at long last, the government could determine how to raise and spend its revenues through the authority now conferred on the Finance Minister. A key provision, Number 8, referred to the Frontier Areas. The British conceded that this territory, excluded from Burma Proper since the annexation in 1886, was a legitimate subject for discussion, and it was agreed that a special conference should be held at Panglong in February, 1947, on the issue of its future relationship to Burma Proper. At this conference, His Majesty's Government and the Interim Government would seek "to achieve the early unification of the Frontier Areas and Ministerial Burma with the free consent of the inhabitants of those areas [and] a Committee of Enquiry shall be set up forthwith as to the best method of associating the Frontier peoples with the working out of the new constitution for Burma." Both the opening and closing paragraphs of the *Conclusions* referred to the future of independent Burma "within or without the British Commonwealth of Nations."

Aung San returned home in triumph. His battle was won.

The majority of the Burmese rallied to Aung San and to the AFPFL. There was, however, opposition from the Communists and from prewar politicians who thought that they might displace Aung San by charging that he had settled for too little. Three ex-premiers, Sir Paw Tun, Dr. Ba Maw, and U Saw, together with Thakin Ba Sein, formed the Nationalist Opposition Front. U Saw and Thakin Ba Sein resigned from their ministerial posts in the Interim Government; they were speedily replaced by two highly regarded nationalists, the journalist Deedok Ba Choe, and Abdul Razak, a Muslim leader who, since the days of the 1920 National School strike, had served the nationalist cause in Mandalay as a prominent *sayagyi* (a respected schoolteacher). Though the opposition groups were vocal, they could not affect the outcome either through agitation or Communist-sponsored strikes. On February 5, the AFPFL overwhelmingly ratified the Attlee-Aung San agreement. Burma's timetable for independence was set.

Toward Ethnic Unity and Federal Union

One hurdle remained before the Interim Government could proceed with the elections for the Constituent Assembly: to find a formula to unite Burmans with the principal minority groups, the Shans, the Kachins, the Chins, the Karens, and the Kareni. These culturally diverse peoples had been in various stages of political and governmental separation since 1826. In order to understand the nature of the task, and the difficulties that had to be surmounted, it is necessary to look back at British rule in Burma.

After the first two Anglo-Burmese wars, the British East India Company directly administered the conquered and ceded provinces: Arakan and Tenasserim after 1826; Pegu, later divided into Pegu and Irrawaddy, after 1852. In 1862, these four provinces were combined and ruled directly as one under the Crown by a chief commissioner responsible to the British governor-general of India. The former provinces now became administrative units, and the area as a whole was called Lower or British Burma to differentiate it from the remaining Kingdom of Burma. After the Third Anglo-Burmese War in 1885, the kingdom was annexed to British Burma. The direct rule of the chief commissioner and his deputies was extended to that part of the former kingdom now constituted as four additional British divisions: Sagaing, Mandalay, Minbu, and Meiktila. The rest of the kingdom, the mountainous north and the plains and river valleys south of the saucerlike rim of the Himalayas, was "excluded" from direct rule. These four additional divisions and some contiguous areas came to be called, loosely, Upper Burma.[36]

In 1897, the office of the chief commissioner was elevated to that of lieutenant governor, still responsible to the British Government of India; associated with him was an appointive Legislative Council of nine.[37] This system of direct gubernatorial rule with some kind of legislature representing the eight divisions was continued until 1947, except for the war years 1942-45. Dyarchy in its 1923 and 1935 variations was adjusted to allow the continuance of this system of separate rule. All of Lower Burma and most of Upper Burma, the area of the eight divisions, came to be called Burma Proper—an indication that the British wished to confine "Burma" to the territory largely inhabited by the majority Burman group. As the Legislative Council gradually increased in size and acquired more authority. Burma Proper was also referred to as Parliamentary or Ministerial Burma.

The Excluded Area, some 113,000 square miles (about 43 per cent of Burma's territory), is inhabited by ethnic minorities constituting some 15 per cent of Burma's total population. They are principally the Shans, ethnic and linguistic cousins of the Lao and Thai peoples, in central and northeast Burma; the Kachins in the north, the Chins in the northwest, both subgroups of the Tibeto-Burman majority; and the Karens and a subgroup, the Kareni, probably related to the Shans, in the lower reaches of the Shan Plateau and along the Salween River. There are also numerous other tribal or hill peoples who are related ethnically to these major groups. In periods of strong Burman rule during the Pagan, Toungoo, and Konbaung dynasties, these peoples were under the suzerainty of the Burman kings, who permitted them to retain their ancestral ways and their internal forms of government, provided they remained loyal to the throne and contributed military levies and other forms of support. It is significant that the Chins and Kachins held out against British pacification as late as 1894-95, while the Shan feudal overlords—*sawbwas*, or *saophas*—vainly attempted to rally to the support of a Burman prince after King Thibaw, a half-Shan, had been defeated and deposed.

British administration of this area after 1886 continued the Burmese practice of indirect rule. The Shan and Kareni states were permitted to retain their feudal hereditary sawbwas, who were advised by British superintendents. The three Kareni states (the present Kayah state) were not formally included in British Burma. By virtue of an 1875 agreement between the British and the Kingdom of Burma, this area was declared to be "independent." However, after 1886, these states became a protectorate under the British Crown. In 1922, the northern and southern Shan states were federated under a Shan State Council in which a British commissioner served as president. Though the Sagaing and Mandalay divisions were under direct rule, Chin and Kachin country came within their boundaries, and here, especially in the hills, the tribal and clan chiefs, or *duwas*, were left in control as long as their administration was fairly competent and just.[38] The British created the Burma Frontier Service for these areas, distinct from the Indian Civil Service whose members made up the senior bureaucracy of Burma Proper. Its operation as a separate organization served to widen the gap between the two parts of Burma.

The regions of indirect rule came to be known by various names, such as the Frontier, Excluded, or Scheduled Areas. Some less populated portions of this territory were named Hill Tracts; others, for example the northeast Wa border or the northwest Naga border, were called Backward Areas. The Shans, Kachins, Chins, and Kareni occupied fairly well-defined regions. The Karens, however, while they occupied a large part of the Salween River district south of the Kareni states, were also widely dispersed—as were the Mons, who had finally been conquered by the Burmans in the eighteenth century—through the delta region of Lower Burma.

They were both a hill and a plains people, some as backward and others as advanced as any in Burma. This was a factor in the later Karen rebellion. Under the Act of 1935, which separated the province of Burma from India, the Scheduled or Excluded Areas were assigned either to Part I, the less politically advanced regions, or to Part II, the more politically advanced regions, which included some districts entitled to representation in the legislature. In theory, a Part I region could advance to Part II and could eventually merge with Ministerial Burma, but none had done so by 1939.

Communication between the Burmans of Ministerial Burma and the Frontier peoples declined sharply after annexation. As Furnivall remarks, "British rule did nothing to foster national unity. On the contrary, both directly and indirectly, it stimulated sectional particularism." [39] It was divisive within both Burma Proper and the Frontier Areas. Consequently, the nationalist spirit of the Burmans moved toward the frontier very slowly.

When the British returned after World War II, the White Paper (Part II, Section 7) maintained the prewar division. The Kareni states were still bound by treaty and the Federated Shan States and the Frontier Areas were excluded from the administration of Burma Proper. They would have "a special regime under the Governor until such time as their inhabitants signify their desire for some suitable form of amalgamation of their territories with Burma Proper."

It was this fact of exclusion that Aung San, as *de facto* prime minister of the Interim Government, sought to alter. The Attlee-Aung San *Conclusions* of January, 1947, afforded him the opportunity of ultimate success. During the war, the British had called attention to a Burmese demand for "the inclusion of the 'Excluded Areas' in political Burma" and to the partial fulfillment of that demand by a formal treaty between Japan and the "independent" Burma Government. They also had taken note of the mixed levies of Kachin, Burman, and Shan troops, some of whom wore the nationalist insignia colors.[40] The Kachin *duwa* from Sama, Sinwa Nawng, helped to organize these levies and joined forces with the Thakins. This was the beginning of his friendship with Aung San, which led to later political agreements concerning the emergence of a Kachin state in a united Burma.

The wartime Thakin cultivation of Burma's minorities[41] has been rewarded with additional alliances among those Chins, Kachins, Shans, and Karens who, while remaining loyal (or neutral) to the British connection during the war, were nonetheless willing to further the cause of nationalism and independence at the end of the war. Among their leaders were U Vum Ko Hau (Chin), Sao Shwe Thaike, Sao Hkun Hkio, and, especially, Sao Sam Htun (Shans), Duwas Zau Lawn and Zau Rip (Kachins). Karens were at this time already divided between those who supported the

AFPFL (such as Mahn Ba Khaing and Mahn Win Maung), and those who basically were Karen separatists (Saw Sankey and Saw Ba U Gyi).

In 1946, the Thakins stepped up their efforts to win over the Frontier peoples. In October-November, Aung San and Thakin Nu toured the upcountry areas and urged the formation of a Supreme Council of the United Hill Peoples (SCOUHP) to include Chins, Kachins, and Shans. A preliminary meeting of SCOUHP, attended by Thakin Nu on behalf of the AFPFL, was held in November, 1946, at Panglong, in the Shan states. Sao Shwe Thaike, later to become the first president of independent Burma, was named president of SCOUHP.[42] The success of these preliminary efforts, the smooth preparations for the main Panglong Conference of February, 1947, and the subsequent sittings of the Frontier Areas Committee of Enquiry, heralded by Item Number 8 in the Attlee-Aung San *Conclusions,* enabled Aung San to face the outcome with confidence.[43]

Bogyoke Aung San and U Tin Tut, accompanied by A. G. Bottomley, British Under Secretary of State for Dominion Affairs, met with representatives of the Shans, Kachins, and Chins, at Panglong, February 7-12, 1947. According to the agreement that resulted, a representative of SCOUHP "shall be appointed a Counsellor to the Governor to deal with the Frontier Areas"; the subject of the Frontier Areas was to be "brought within the purview of the Executive Council"; there were to be two deputy councillors representing the groups of which the appointed councillor was not a member; "full autonomy in internal administration for the Frontier Areas [was] accepted in principle"; the creation of a Kachin state was found to be "desirable," and steps to that end were to be taken at the Constituent Assembly; and, finally, arrangements providing for financial aid from revenues and other sources "similar to those between Burma and the Federated Shan States" were, if feasible, to be applied to the Kachin and Chin areas. The Karenni states would decide whether they would accede to the Union. The agreement left open the question of a possible Chin state. The Federated Shan States already existed.[44]

Thus, for the first time since 1826, all parts and peoples of Burma could function together legally under the then existing Burma Executive Council, of which Aung San was chief councillor and architect. Though the Panglong Agreement did not yet commit the Shans, Kachins, Chins, and others to a permanent union with the Burmans, it provided a basis on which such a commitment could be made at the constituent assembly. The signing of the agreement on February 12, 1947, is now celebrated officially in Burma as a national holiday, Union Day.

At the conclusion of the conference, Aung San had immeasurably advanced his timetable of "independence within one year." It was now necessary for London to ascertain whether this settlement was acceptable to all parties, while making preparations for the forthcoming elections to the Constituent Assembly. This was the task of the Frontier Areas Committee of Enquiry, a binational committee headed by Lieutenant Colonel D. R. Rees-Williams, which began its meetings about March 7 and concluded them on April 24, 1947.[45] There was little doubt about the basic recommendation that this committee would make. Its members were instructed to seek early and voluntary unification of the Frontier Areas and Ministerial Burma. They were aware of the success of the Panglong Conference and the favorable report about it tendered to Governor Rance by Under Secretary of State Bottomley. After holding twenty-four formal and informal meetings in various localities, the committee reported that "all witnesses before us expressed without hesitation the desire that representatives of their States and local areas should take part in the work of the Constituent Assembly." To carry out its recommendation to this effect, the committee proposed that the Frontier Areas be allotted forty-five seats in the Assembly (ten more than their proportion of the population warranted) in order to insure a "satisfactory division" within the geographical units: Shans, 26; Kachins, 7; Chins and other, 6; Karenni, 2; Karens of the Salween district, 2; others, 2. Safeguards were provided to insure that the decisions of a majority of the Assembly concerning the mode of government for all of Burma would be ratified by a majority in each Frontier Areas delegation.

The Committee of Enquiry cautioned against granting any area an excess of "internal autonomy" at the expense of the future central government. The report alluded to the request by witnesses "for the right of secession," which subsequently was written, in limited fashion, into the Burma Constitution.[46] The committee also heard the views of various groups of Karens, some of whose representatives favored complete separation from Burma (a form of "Karenistan" within the British Commonwealth); while others favored a federal Karen state similar in character to the proposed Kachin state; and still others recommended the inclusion of predominantly Karen areas, such as the Salween district, in ministerial Burma, while retaining administrative posts and cultural autonomy for Karens.[47] The report which, by omission, rejected the first of these views, was ambiguous with respect to the other two. It was approved by London on May 22, 1947.[48]

Aung San, the Constituent Assembly, and Independence

Meanwhile, elections for the Constituent Assembly had been held in April, 1947. Of the 255 seats, 182 were filled by elections in Burma Proper; 24 seats were allotted to the Karen community (whose delegates were to be selected through their own organizations); 4 seats to the Anglo-Burman community; and 45 seats to the Frontier Areas.

In a vigorous election speech, reported in *The Burman* on April

6, Aung San attacked the enemies of the AFPFL, among whom he included the "Saw-Sein-Maw group," who had sought to undermine the negotiations with the British in order to pick up the political pieces in Burma; the "Thein-Than Communists," who continued to instigate labor and student strikes and the looting of rice in rural areas; and the "Red Flag" Communists whose leader, Thakin Soe, was accused by Aung San of being a "political hireling" determined on "work of destruction." Though the campaign generated considerable heat, the elections were calm. The AFPFL coalition won in 171 of the 182 election constituencies. The Communists contested in 25 constituencies that they considered to be strongholds, but they won only 7 seats. Dr. Ba Maw, Thakin Ba Sein, and U Saw, recognizing the powerful popular support for Aung San, decided to boycott the elections in order to avoid personal defeat. One Karen faction, the Karen National Union, also boycotted the elections.

Throughout the early months of 1947—from the time Aung San went to London until the decisive meeting of the Constituent Assembly in June—the question of whether the Burmese would or would not elect to remain within the British Commonwealth aroused very considerable speculation at home and abroad; speculation as to what "might have been" continued long after the event. During the January, 1947, meetings in London, Collis and Mountbatten are said to have asked Aung San whether he intended to recommend that Burma elect dominion status; both thought that he was not disinclined to do so.[49] Field Marshal Slim (who had generously compared Bogyoke Aung San with General Smuts) and, probably, Governor Rance, were among those who thought such an outcome was possible. If the wartime leaders who had had first-hand contact with the younger Burmese nationalists could have held the reins in Burma immediately after the war; if, as Mountbatten put it, Aung San had been "handled with more finesse from the start"; if the incoming Labour government had promptly set aside the White Paper of 1945—then the outcome might have been different.[50] India's subsequent decision to remain within the Commonwealth reinforces this theory. But those who have speculated about the various possibilities differ on many specific points.[51]

The clearest public argument for dominion status came from U Tin Tut, who, as a member of the Executive Council, had assisted Bogyoke Aung San in negotiating the London agreement. From December 23, 1946, until the general convention of the AFPFL officially took its stand in May, 1947, he gave his views in his journal, *The Burmese Review*. The basis of his argument was the mutual advantage of dominion status to Burma and Great Britain. As he pointed out, such a decision was not irrevocable. He also recognized some of the difficulties, criticizing the "imperial arrogance" of those Englishmen who regarded dominion status as a "privilege." Less doubtful of British sincerity than many others in Burma, he thought that the London meetings should set such suspicions at rest. On January 6, 1947, *The Burmese Review* printed a long, careful letter, signed "T. T. of Meiktila," which supported this position. On March 3, Tin Tut contributed an essay on the Irish Constitution, designed to show that even the Irish could get along within the Commonwealth. Here he played on the condescending stereotype—common in British circles and occasionally picked up by the Burmese, for whom the image had a different meaning—that pictured the Burmese as the Irish of the East. In a frontpage editorial on May 12, he recommended dominion status to the delegates responsible for making the final decision in the Constituent Assembly.

At this time the influence of Tin Tut, both in England and in Burma, was probably at its height. He had been educated at Dulwich College and Cambridge University and was the senior Burmese member of the vaunted Indian Civil Service. His three brothers also held respected positions. The oldest, then Justice Kyaw Myint, was named to head the Burmese delegation to the First Asian Relations Conference, held in New Delhi in March, 1947. Another brother, U Myint Thein (later Chief Justice of the Supreme Court), served on the Frontier Areas Committee of Enquiry of 1947. The "fourth brother" (so called by the other three), Dr. Htin Aung, was then professor at and later rector of the University of Rangoon. There can be no doubt that U Tin Tut spoke for a generation of Burmese who, not without considerable ambivalence, felt themselves closely tied to Britain. Although Tin Tut was not in the inner circle of AFPFL leadership, he was a trusted adviser to the Thakin group, and after presenting his own viewpoint for consideration, he accepted the "countervailing advantages" of the majority decision.[52]

U Ba U, who later became Chief Justice and then second President of independent Burma, was another Cambridge-educated member of the older generation who took a stand not dissimilar to that of Tin Tut. In 1945, he and his associates appear to have been willing to ask for independence, but were ready to settle for dominion status. In 1947, he clearly supported independence.[53] After independence, the attitudes of such men, coupled with AFPFL appreciation for the policies of the Labour Party once Prime Minister Attlee had made his historic decision, were important in creating and extending friendly feelings between the two countries.

But the feelings of friendship for Great Britain did not affect Aung San's drive for a free Burma. What he might have accepted when he first presented himself, as the wartime leader of a provisional government, to Field Marshal Sir William Slim and Admiral Lord Louis Mountbatten, can never be known with certainty. If in London in 1947 he again felt drawn to Mountbatten and those few others who had been willing to grant him political and personal recognition, that, too, is understandable. But these were not the sentiments that moved this remarkable young man. For almost a decade, he had set his course on independence, accepted aid from any source for independence, and shaped his anti-imperialist ideology in terms of independence. He could not change his stand now without risking the loss of popular support and further encouraging Communist and right-wing opportunist agitation. If we do not have conclusive proof of his intentions, we can at least follow his course of action once he returned from meeting with Prime Minister Attlee.

Upon Aung San's return to Rangoon after meeting with Prime Minister Attlee, a minor incident occurred in which the difficulties of translation played into the hands of those whose views differed from his own. On February 4, 1947, he broadcast in Burmese an account of the London meetings in which he called for a "free Burma," adding that he wanted Burma "to be a real and sincere friend of Britain." Enlarging on this in his conclusion, he said that "Burma should associate herself with Britain." [54] The translated word "associate" gave rise to speculation in English-language circles, but the Burmese expression used by Aung San, *tan-tu-san-gyin-de*, literally, "equal-relations desire," carries the meaning of being equal and separate—free to join in a temporary, mutually desirable relationship. Since there seemed to be some doubt about his meaning, Aung San returned to the theme at a civic reception on February 6. This time, speaking in English, he omitted any reference to association with Britain; instead, he used the phrase "complete independence," and said that "Burma when fully independent would take her due place and play her full part in all international affairs." [55]

Thakin Nu, speaking as the vice president of the AFPFL, took up the question of friendship with Britain in a broadcast a week later. He warned both British and Burmese "bureaucrats not to pull down what Sir Hubert Rance is building up with so much difficulty and so much good will" and developed the theme of a free Burma "after the demise of British Imperialism." He appealed for British friendship based on "our mutual advantage," but did not neglect to point out that because of the difficulties caused "during the last sixty years . . . it is not an easy task to foster friendship with the British." [56] In an exclusive interview with the London *Daily Mail*, April 11, 1947 (reprinted in *The Burman* on April 19), Aung San once again returned to this issue. He is quoted as having said that there is "no chance of Burma remaining in the Empire," though he personally "would like the closest relation with Britain but not as a British dominion."

The chief reason Aung San, Thakin Nu, and others made no absolute statement against dominion status was explained by Deedok Ba Choe, the leading journalist of the group and Information Minister in the Interim Government. In an interview with a correspondent of Reuters on April 23, he pointed out that although the foreign press had already referred to Aung San's intention to have Burma become an independent sovereign republic, conclusive statements by Burmese leaders were out of place. It was, he said, "for the Constituent Assembly to decide the political status desirable for Burma and to formulate a Constitution accordingly." But, speaking of the "two alternatives," he said, "I feel that a majority of the Burmese people desire Burma to be an independent sovereign state. This is not because they want to sever all connection with Britain but because they consider that it is only on the basis of complete equality of political status that Burma will be able to establish lasting friendship with the British Government and the British people." [57] Thus, in principle, until the members of the Constituent Assembly cast their ballots, the choice of dominion status or complete separation remained open.

During the House of Commons debate in early May, Under Secretary Arthur Henderson recapitulated the policy of the government, which had first been announced by Prime Minister Attlee in December, 1946, but added, "we are certain that it would be to their [Burmese] interest, as to ours, if they decided to remain within the Commonwealth and we sincerely hope they would arrive at such a decision." [58]

Whatever others had hoped, Aung San, Thakin Mya, and other AFPFL leaders had no doubts about the issue. Their independence policy was laid down in May at a stirring five-day convention in Rangoon's Jubilee Hall, the meeting place that had become the "symbol of Burma's political struggle." [59] In opening the convention on May 19, Aung San set its course by declaring that Burma must have complete independence, that monarchy in any form was out of the question, that the independent republic of Burma would be founded on the principles of socialism and administered and governed according to the principles of democracy, and that it was idle to speculate whether or not Burma would decide to accept dominion status. The AFPFL, he stated, had already decided that nothing short of complete independence would satisfy Burmese aspirations. At the end of Aung San's speech, Thakin Mya moved and Deedok Ba Choe seconded a resolution approving Aung San's views.

As the AFPFL convention began its meetings, a special committee under the chairmanship of Thakin Mya met to draft a new constitution that was to be submitted to the Constituent Assembly.[60] Its major outlines were embodied in a fourteen-point resolution[61] that began: "This convention declares its firm and solemn resolve to proclaim Burma as an independent Sovereign Republic." The second, third, and seventh points summarized the work of the Panglong Conference and the recommendations of the Frontier Areas Enquiry Report, which called for the unification of Ministerial and Frontier Burma, the latter having the right of becoming autonomous states. However, this provision applied to the Shans, Kachins, Kareni, and Chins. One point provided for a Karen Council to advise the government about Karen wishes. Other points contained recommendations for a president as head of state, an independent judiciary, and a bicameral legislature to consist of a chamber of deputies and a chamber of nationalities. The resolution affirmed Burma's commitment to democratic principles, to the rights of freedom, justice, and religious tolerance, and to the "law of civilized nations . . . international justice and morality."

The resolution was passed on the last day of the convention, May 23. Between that date and the meeting of the Constituent Assembly, Aung San convened the first of a series of rehabilitation and planning conferences at the Sorrento Villa in Rangoon. Discussing eight major economic and social problems, he advised his colleagues not to waste time and energy in attacking and blaming imperialism "for every ill in the country." In the light of the "new circumstances," he urged the Burmese to solve their own problems through "mutual cooperation," the "classic way of the people." This speech[62] and program became the bases for the Two-Year Plan later adopted by the Union Government.

The Constituent Assembly began its sessions on June 9. Since 171 out of 182 delegates belonged to the AFPFL coalition and since the 45 delegates from the Frontier Areas were either AFPFL members or supporters, the outcome of the assembly's deliberations was certain. In a thoughtful opening address, Thakin Mya, president pro tem, called for bringing the people of Burma "to the threshold of freedom" after the period "of foreign rule full of suffering and sorrow, trials and tribulations." "Political freedom," he cautioned, "is not an end in itself but an essential means for promoting the economic and social welfare of the masses." To this end he pledged, as a "guiding principle," a "democratic system of Government" in which "the social objectives and economic means for attaining them" would be paralleled by guaranteeing to every citizen his "sacred, natural and inalienable fundamental rights." [63]

The Assembly named Thakin Nu permanent president in a unanimous vote. "On Monday, June 16, 1947," *The Burmese Review* editorialized, "U Aung San, the Burmese leader, moved in the Constituent Assembly a 'directive' resolution embodying seven points [summarizing the earlier fourteen] on which the Constitution that is to be drawn up is to be based. The most important of these points is that the Constitution shall be that of an Independent Sovereign Republic to be known as the Union of Burma." [64] The resolution was approved. On June 18, the Assembly passed resolutions calling for the appointment of a continuing constitution committee and other necessary committees. The Assembly then recessed to allow the committees to do their work.[65]

The Burmese had decided on full independence, outside the Commonwealth.

The next step was to inform the British Government of the intention of the Constituent Assembly to take Burma out of the Commonwealth. In the last week of June, therefore, after the Assembly had recessed, a delegation headed by Thakin Nu (with U Tin Tut, U Kyaw Nyein, Bo Khin Maung Gale, and U Ko Ko Gyi) left Burma for England to arrange for an official meeting with the prime minister when the assembly finished its work.

During the recess, Burma suffered. On July 19, a disappointed politician, former Prime Minister U Saw, staged a mad attempt at a coup. While Bogyoke Aung San was meeting with the Executive Council, he and eight others were assassinated—Thakin Mya; Deedok Ba Choe; Mahn Ba Khaing, a Karen leader who believed in ethnic cooperation within Burma; Sawbwa Sam Htun of the Shan state of Mongpawn, who had served the same ideal as his Karen fellow Councillor; Abdul Razak; U Ba Win, an older brother of Aung San; U Ohn Maung, a member of the Civil Service; and Ko Htwe, a personal assistant to the education minister.

The nation was shocked and grief-stricken. *The Burmese Review* compared the tragic event to the assassination of President Lincoln, and could find no better expression of its feelings than to publish on the front page, in full, Walt Whitman's "O Captain! My Captain." [66]

Bogyoke Aung San had completed his main task. Without resorting to arms, he had led Burma to complete independence through a strategy of peaceful, anticolonial revolution, thus ensuring himself a place second to none in Burma's history. The performance of this young man—only thirty-two years old at his death —was extraordinary. In a chaotic situation he had won and held a deeply loyal following. For the time necessary to achieve independence, he was able to unify Burmans, Shans, Kachins, Chins, Karenni, and Karens. He recognized the internal danger of the Communists, and temporarily held them in check by removing them from the ruling coalition. He outlined the future economic direction of his government. He gained, at first grudgingly and then freely, the admiration of his immediate British adversaries. A hero in Burmese eyes, he had the qualities of great leadership that Burma sorely needed and needs.

It is a distortion of history to account for events solely in terms of the actions of a great man, and to the extent that these pages imply that, they evidence such distortion. But, given the conditions in Burma, it seemed proper to examine the record for the twelve years beginning when the Thakins first achieved political office, to the dawn of independence in January, 1948, in terms of the ambient leadership of Aung San. The words of one of his erstwhile adversaries are worth noting:

> Ever since the First World War men had been imbibing ideas of self-determination. And in 1942, with terrible suddenness, the British forfeited their right to expect loyalty by their complete inability to

protect their people from the horrors of invasion. To the Burmese Aung San was a patriot, whatever his shortcomings and his admixture of motives. His vision of independence for Burma, a rebirth of national pride for its people, and power for himself, were probably one picture, not three. He alone was able to unite his people, speak for them, and give expression to their spirit as no one else had done since the days of Alaungpaya two hundred years ago.[67]

Truly, he led the way for the generation of young nationalists who struggled for the unity and freedom of Burma.

Aung San's work, with the full cooperation of the British Government, was now quickly brought to legal fruition. Immediately after the assassination, Governor Rance appointed Thakin Nu Deputy Chairman of the Executive Council, and on July 23, the Interim Government became the Provisional Government. Thakin Nu became Prime Minister in name as well as in fact, and the members of the Executive Council became ministers of government. The first Cabinet of the Provisional Government included among its members Bo Let Ya (Deputy Prime Minister and Defence Minister), Kyaw Nyein (Home and Judicial Affairs), Tin Tut (Foreign Affairs), Henzada Mya (National Planning), Pyawbwe Mya (Transport and Communications), Saw San Po Thin (Education), Aung Zan Wai (Social Services), Thakin Tin (Agriculture and Rural Economy), Bo Po Kun (Public Works and Rehabilitation), Mahn Win Maung (Industry and Labor), Ba Gyan (Finance and Revenue), Ko Ko Gyi (Commerce and Supply), Sao Hkun Hkio (Counsellor for Frontier Areas, Shan), Vum Ko Hau (Counsellor for Frontier Areas, Chin), Sama Duwa Sinwa Nawng (Counsellor for Frontier Areas, Kachin), and Lun Baw (Chairman, Public Service Commission).

The Constituent Assembly adopted the Constitution at its third and final session, September 15-25,[68] and named Sao Shwe Thaike, a Shan *sawbwa*, provisional president. The Kareni states had formally acceded to the proposed Union on the same basis as the Shan states. A defense agreement between Britain and Burma was signed in Rangoon, and on October 17, in London, Thakin Nu signed the treaty between the Government of the United Kingdom and the Provisional Government of Burma, known as the Nu-Attlee Treaty for Independence. The treaty, containing fifteen articles, recognizes Burma as fully sovereign, succeeding to the obligations and responsibilities formerly held by the United Kingdom. British subjects could exercise the right of alienage. Various articles governed pensions, property, and contractual rights and financial obligations. International commerce and navigation, mail, aviation, and double taxation were also covered. Articles 13 and 14 referred to mutual rights with respect to the United Nations and International Court of Justice. Article 4 incorporated the defense agreement signed in Rangoon. The latter provided for the adjustment of defense charges and more especially for a United Kingdom Military Service Mission, which would train the Burma forces and arrange for the purchase of war matériel.

In December, the Attlee government proceeded to seek ratification of the treaty. A last, acrimonious debate took place in Parliament on December 10. Winston Churchill led the attack, repeating his charge against Aung San and the other Burmese "quislings" and warning Britain not to abandon its responsibilities in Burma. However, the Burma Independence Bill was approved by a vote of 228 to 114.[69]

The victorious Thakins chose January 4, 1948, as the day for formal celebration of Burma's independence. The transfer of power took place at 4:20 A.M., an auspicious hour chosen by Burmese astrologers. Kingsley Martin, editor of the *New Statesman and Nation*, attended the event and subsequently described it in a sympathetic and perceptive article, "Sunrise in Burma." He wrote:

> The ceremonies were carried out with dignity and grace and in an atmosphere of cordiality that is hard to convey on paper. . . . It is a change for us in Burma, where, with a mixture of devotion and arrogant folly, we have ruled but never been welcome. . . . One of our outstanding follies was the inclusion of Burma in our administration of India, though Burma has a proud Buddhist civilization, which, for a thousand years before the British came, had had little contact with India. A second more recent folly was our attempt after the war to ignore the revolutionary spirit of new Burma and to reimpose the old type of British rule and business interests—that way would have spelt disaster. If the attempt had been continued, Britain would now be fighting a savage war in Burma with even less chance of saving their property or prestige than the French have in Indo-China or the Dutch in Indonesia. . . . Credit for the dignified and friendly atmosphere of the British withdrawal belongs both to British and Burmans.

The approximately thousand-word Burmese Declaration of Independence—reviewing the past and calling attention "once more" to "the complete freedom that is our birthright"—and the ten-point Pledge to the Union were published on the same day. Both documents and an Independence Day broadcast by the Prime Minister paid homage to one person, Bogyoke Aung San, whose ideals and unremitting labor "brought us the coveted crown of complete freedom." Thakin Nu eloquently summed up Burmese feelings:

> We lost our independence without losing our self-respect; we clung to our culture and our traditions and these we now hold to cherish and to develop in accordance with the genius of our people. We part without rancor and in friendship from the great British nation who held us in fee. This Day of Independence dawns on a people not only free but united. . . . This is also a day for solemn thought, for in a sense, our work has just begun.[70]

PART II · THE PRESERVATION OF THE UNION

O N JANUARY 4, 1948, Burma became an independent federal republic with a bicameral legislature based on the European parliamentary system. Although some additions and changes were made in the Cabinet after independence, until October, 1958, the Anti-Fascist People's Freedom League provided the ministers that governed Burma.

The strategy of the anticolonial revolution had proved a complete success. The Thakins, led by Aung San, had been able to unite the people, and the fact that they were bound together in opposing the British was a distinct psychopolitical advantage. The ranks of their gradually yielding "enemy" were not united, but included many who supported the ideal of national self-determination for colonial peoples. In fact, both parties to the contest had been influenced by the affirmation of "the right of all peoples to choose the form of government under which they will live" that had been written into the Atlantic Charter and confirmed in the Declaration of the United Nations of January 1, 1942.

But the Thakins had, in addition, three direct sources of strength. They and their supporters had been able to build a coalition party, the AFPFL, which had won strong peasant and labor support throughout the country and had survived opposition from left and right, within and outside the party. They had early recognized the importance of national unity, and in the Panglong Agreement of February, 1947, had worked out a comprehensive though incomplete solution to the problems dividing the majority Burmans and the various ethnic minorities of the Frontier and Hill Areas. And finally, Aung San had under his control a private army, the People's Volunteer Organization (PVO). Although this trained and mobilized force never had to fight the British for independence, its mere existence was a continuing threat. Thakin Nu, as AFPFL leader first in the Provisional Government and then in independent Burma, benefited, at least for a time, from the unity that Aung San had created.

The new government acquired jurisdiction over a country that was geographically united for the first time since 1824. The immediate task of the administration was to transform itself from an anti-imperialist opposition into a functioning government, responsible for 17 million people and for an economy that had been devastated by war and was now plagued by new dislocations arising out of the transfer of power. But the newly installed leaders had not been trained in administering a state, and at all administrative levels there was a dearth of Burmese with the skills needed merely to fill the many new vacancies. Between October, 1947, and April, 1948, seventy-one of the ninety-nine Superior Civil Service members, mainly Indian or British nationals, retired or went on leave. Only four of the top twenty-five and seventeen of the top fifty remained. Equally crucial gaps appeared in the civil police forces (six were left of the top thirty-seven), in executive engineering (five, of whom two were non-Burmans, remained out of twenty-three), and in the Frontier Services (nine out of sixty-two remained).[1]

During the years when Burma had been a province of India, few Burmese had gained access to higher positions in the civil service. In fact, it was not until 1923 that any top posts were held by Burmese. Consequently, however desirable and necessary it was to fill the vacancies with Burmese nationals, it could not be done immediately, except at the cost of lowering standards of administrative efficiency. Despite repeated efforts to reorganize and improve the administration, and despite the aid provided by three United Nations public-administration advisers, difficulties due to administrative inexperience continued to plague a government already beset by greater troubles. In this respect Burma was not exceptional. Successful nationalist groups in other newly independent countries faced similar problems.

Burma, however, has been fortunate in other respects, because there is no population pressure and the land is fertile. Rural Burmese—85 per cent of the total population—are accustomed to seasonal hard work, and though the war had almost wiped out the supply of draft animals, the farmers were still able to feed, clothe, and house themselves and provide a surplus for domestic and foreign markets. Given peace, young Burmese would in time acquire the education and gain the experience necessary for good administration. In the interim the Burmese would have the satisfaction of running their own country.

But domestic peace was denied to Thakin Nu and his government, for as the need for accord diminished, the bonds that had united the Burmese in opposition to the British were strained to the breaking point. Within a few months the discord brought about by the discrepant aims and ambitions of the Communists, the People's Volunteer Organization, and the dissatisfied factions among the Karens was transformed into armed insurrection that threatened the very existence of the republic. After 1950, the situation was further complicated by the depredations of the Chinese Kuomintang troops under General Li Mi, who had retreated from Yunnan into Burma.

The Communists Begin the Insurrection

The AFPFL coalition, which had included the Socialist Party, the Communist Party, and other left-of-center groups, broke down during the postwar struggle for independence as the Socialists became acutely aware of the Communists' revolutionary intention to gain control of the government. The Communists themselves were divided. One splinter group, the Communist Party of Burma (CPB), led by Thakin Soe, had been declared illegal in July, 1946. The ban was lifted in October, 1946, when Aung San and his colleagues became the majority in Governor Rance's Executive Council, and when it was reinstated in January, 1947, the "Red Flag" Communists, as they came to be called, went underground.

The other group, the Burma Communist Party (BCP), was headed by Thakins Than Tun and Thein Pe. By October, 1946, Aung San, Thakin Nu, and Thakin Mya had succeeded in removing the members of this group first from power positions within the AFPFL and then from leadership in the labor movement. When the BCP attempted to strike against the government, Aung San took immediate action to bring about its expulsion from the AFPFL. The Supreme Council ratified the act in November. The BCP, later known as "White Flag" Communists, was not yet openly disaffected. In the summer of 1947, between the assassinations in July and the departure of Thakin Nu for London in October, it offered to cooperate with the AFPFL. The offer was accepted, and in the early fall, as the new Constitution was nearing completion, Thakin Nu invited Than Tun and the BCP to rejoin the AFPFL. Thakin Nu toured the countryside with Than Tun, a move which seemed to indicate that, except for the Soe faction, the country was united in a time of crisis and that all nationalist forces supported the new Constitution. These advances by Thakin Nu were welcomed by the Burmese press.[2]

But the *rapprochement* was a short-lived one. After the conclusion of the Nu-Attlee Treaty on October 17, the Burma Communist Party gave every evidence of a change of line. Its leaders denounced the treaty and the "rightist" elements in the AFPFL, and called for armed revolution as the way to secure freedom from "capitalists, expansionists and imperialists." Their action followed closely on the organizational meeting of the Cominform in Poland in September, 1947, and the presentation there of the new left, or militant, line by Andrei Zhdanov.

The immediate sequel to these events in Southern Asia, in general, and in Burma, in particular, was not fully appreciated at the time. It is now clear that Moscow's reorganization of the international Communist movement prepared the way for a series of revolutionary outbursts, not only in Asian lands still under imperialist control but also in ex-colonial countries that had regained, or were about to regain, their freedom. It was also at this time that the organized Communist movement in Burma sought out the support of the center of international Communism. Before this period there is no public record of direct contacts between the Burmese Communists and the Moscow leadership. It is true that in the early 1930's a state scholarship student, Thakin Thein Maung, joined the British branch of the League Against Imperialism, and in the later 1930's individual Communists, such as Thakins Soe, Thein Pe, Ba Hein, and H. N. Goshal (an Indian national born in Burma, also known as Thakin Ba Tin), had had occasional contacts with Indian Communists. These men, together with Thakin Than Tun and others, formally organized the Burma Communist Party in 1942-43. By 1947, the BCP was able to send delegates to external party conferences and to receive guidance and direction from abroad. Two members of the Party, Aung Gyi and Ba Thein Tin, were sent to the London Empire Communist Conference, and the BCP General-Secretary, Than Tun, and the "theoretician" Goshal attended the international Communist meetings in Bombay and Calcutta. At these, the Moscow-trained Indian, S. A. Dange, and other Communists from Russia, Europe, and the British Commonwealth expounded the new left line announced at the Cominform gathering in Poland.[3]

The meaning of the Zhdanov line for Burma was revealed by H. N. Goshal in an interview in December, 1947, and by Than Tun in a speech in February, 1948, both given in Calcutta.[4] They condemned the Nu-Attlee Treaty as a "fake," which imposed "national humiliation and permanent enslavement" on the Burmese. Than Tun boasted that his "tens of thousands of the finest cadres . . . and more than a lakh [100,000] of class conscious militants who have military training" could "return two blows for every blow against us" by the "Anglo-American imperialists and their running dogs, the collaborating AFPFL leadership," and he called for "links between the victorious Chinese People's Liberation Army and the onward march of the Burmese democratic movement." He expected that 1948 would be the "decisive year" during which the BCP would forge a new "united front . . . to establish real independence" and if necessary to "smash the imperialist-feudal-bourgeois [AFPFL] regime."

Toward the end of 1947, the Central Committee of the BCP had published a fuller exposition of the new line, *On the Present Political Situation in Burma and Our Tasks*, written by Goshal.[5] The committee criticized its own earlier "reformist" and "opportunist" position, and denounced its previous membership in and support of the AFPFL. It indicated that since October, 1947, the Party had begun the study of the "theory" of the "6th Congress of the Communist International," i.e., the left revolutionary strategy of the Comintern's third period, 1928-34, and since then had adopted a position calling for the "final seizure of power . . . this new line is in complete accord with the correct revolutionary understanding of the present international situation which is now available to us as a result of the deliberation and decisions of the nine Communist parties," i.e., the September, 1947, Cominform meeting. It cited Zhdanov's report on the international situation given at that conference and predicted that the attack on the "fake independence" of the Nu-Attlee Treaty and the AFPFL government would win support from the masses because of the "correctness" of Zhdanov's anti-imperialist analysis. It recommended that the British imperialists—not the actual assassin—be blamed for the murder of Aung San and the other AFPFL leaders. However, it charged that Aung San also "had reformist illusions." It castigated Thakin Nu and his government as an "imperialist tool" in the "suppression" of "freedom and democracy . . . [whose] policy leads to tightening the bonds of colonial slavery and of unleashing the civil war against the fighting people." To counteract all this it called for "a fighting united front from below" as the basis for "a *national rising.*" Only then would it be possible to have a "people's government . . . to carry through the democratic revolution."

Meanwhile, Thakin Nu made a last effort to turn the BCP from its new course. On National Day, November 8, 1947, he appealed for a revived coalition to include the Burma Communist Party, the People's Volunteer Organization, and the Socialist Party "under one common program" as a prelude to membership in "one and the same party." [6] But neither at this time nor in subsequent months, when similar appeals for unity were made, did the Communists accept his appeals. For they understood—as Thakin Nu and his colleagues did not then understand—that they were part of an organized international revolutionary movement with central direction of policy. They no longer acted merely as Burmese nationals. On November 17, 1947, the AFPFL announced "the failure of its attempt to secure unity with the Burma Communist Party," and on November 27, Thakin Nu, in a nationwide broadcast, gave a full account of the negotiations and a defense of his policy. He charged that the Burma Communist Party had "secretly instructed their followers behind our backs not to surrender their illicit arms," and that they were "as treacherous as the song of the sirens." [7]

The Communist insurrection began at the end of March, 1948.

The PVO Joins the Communists

As independence drew near, Aung San decided that private armies of all kinds, including the People's Volunteer Organization, which he had organized and used as a threat against the British, should be disbanded. He sponsored and strongly supported Section 97, Paragraph 2, of the Constitution, which forbade the formation of "any military or semimilitary organization of any kind . . . other than the forces raised and maintained by the Union with the consent of the Parliament." At the Sorrento Villa Rehabilitation Conference in June, 1947, Aung San had outlined a plan for absorbing some 10,000 members of the PVO into the regular armed forces and the police services. Others would return to farming, with assistance to be provided through land distribution, cooperatives, and credit facilities. Still others would form a temporary Rehabilitation Brigade, similar to the United States depression-born Civilian Conservation Corps.

Various estimates have been made of the size of the PVO and its following in 1947 and early 1948, ranging from 100,000 to 800,-000.[8] Taking the lower figure for an estimate would mean that with about 25 per cent of PVO members inactive and 10 per cent absorbed into the armed forces and police, some 65,000 men would still be left unplaced, a formidable number.

After the assassination of Aung San, the PVO insisted on remaining a paramilitary force and was increasingly unwilling to lose its identity. It had acquired widespread political support in many parts of the country, and though it was formally a part of the AFPFL coalition, its members regarded it as a distinct party. Sensing the dangers inherent in this development, especially in view of the path chosen by the Burma Communist Party, the Socialist Party proposed a merger with the PVO. Preliminary plans for this, announced in October, 1947, called for the disbanding of the PVO, the creation of a Rehabilitation Brigade, and the organization of the political elements of both Socialists and PVO into a new party, to be called the Marxist League.

The new League was presumably activated in the last week of November with the stipulation that the paramilitary forces "would cease to be . . . from January 4, 1948," that is, from Independence Day.[9] However, the PVO district leaders opposed the new arrangement, a pattern subsequently repeated. They were "reluctant to disband," for they were aware that their sources of power would then disappear. Thakin Nu offered a compromise, postponing the date of dissolution to April 30, 1948. But this and other suggestions, such as the proposal announced during the last week of January, 1948, to disband the paramilitary organization and to form a new party to be known as the Aung San League, separate from the Socialist Party, also failed, because the central issue, disbanding private armies, could not be resolved. In February, 1948, the PVO announced an internal division on the issue. The majority group, led by Bo Po Kun and Bo La Yaung, later known as White Band PVO, was against disbandment; Bo Hmu Aung rallied the minority group (later known as the Yellow Band PVO), which was willing to work out a compromise with Thakin Nu's government. In March, as the contest between the government and the Communists grew sharper, the majority group in the PVO proposed a new coalition of Communist, Socialist, and other AFPFL forces, within which they would provide the political and semimilitary balance of power. This time the AFPFL, aroused by the threat of the BCP, appeared to be willing to accept the PVO mediation. But the Communists, flushed with enthusiasm from the Party meetings in India, believed that rallies in up-country areas showed they had mass support, and so they rejected the advances of the PVO.[10]

The first half of 1948 was dominated by feverish negotiations and "leftist unity" policy announcements, punctuated by clashes of arms between the Communists and the government forces. Effective leadership was at an ebb. Thakin Soe, the leader of the Red Flag Communists, was arrested in mid-March, but somehow he escaped. Certain members of the press castigated the AFPFL in general and the Socialists in particular; their newspaper offices were attacked during a riot on March 12. Thakin Nu simultaneously denounced the violence of his supporters and criticized the press for its abusiveness.

The Communists opened their offensive on March 29, but then suspended hostilities on April 11 for the customary state funeral of Aung San and the other martyred dead assassinated on July 17, 1947, who had been embalmed and held for this official occasion. Thakin Nu continued to urge the BCP to give up violence, pointing out that Stalin was willing to recognize the nonviolent British approach to socialism.[11] In two speeches in May and June, Thakin Nu explained his new "Program of Leftist Unity," a fifteen-point program designed to win back both the PVO and wavering Communists by making concessions to their "leftism." [12] The Socialists, the cooperating Yellow Band PVO group, and Communist Thein Pe, who did not join his insurrectionary comrades, took joint responsibility for the program, but Thakins Nu and Thein Pe are usually considered its authors.

Briefly, the program called for political and economic relations with Soviet Russia as well as with Britain and the United States; the nationalization of "monopolizing capitalist undertakings" and foreign trade; abolishing private ownership of land and distributing it among the tillers of the soil; refusal of any foreign aid that would compromise Burma's independence; democratizing the government bureaucracy; uniting against capitalist attacks on the standard of living and privileges of the workers; reduction of house rents and house taxes and elimination of black markets; promotion of compulsory education, physical health, and culture. Point 15 was: "To form a league for the propagation of Marxist Doctrine, composed of Socialists, Communists, *Pyithu Yebaws* [PVO's] and others who lean towards Marxism and to read, discuss and propagate the writings of Marx, Engels, Lenin, Stalin, Mao Tse-tung, Tito, Dimitrov and other apostles of Marxism." In his second speech on the program, Thakin Nu explained that there was no intention to force Marxism "on the whole of the masses," and that those who favored anti-Marxist doctrines should have full freedom to propagate their views. A triumph of leftism, according to the second speech, would mean an end to private property and its evils: thefts, dacoits, prostitution, insufficient food and clothing, division of the people into classes, and wars.

The program failed to win over the majority White Band PVO, which countered with one of its own calling for a truce between the government and the Communist insurgents, treating them as equal contestants for power. The Yellow Band PVO agreed to support the program, provided Point 15 was deleted. On July 2, the AFPFL Supreme Council overwhelmingly approved the program without that point.[13]

A crisis in the Cabinet, precipitated by rumors of a scandal, led to several changes. Deputy Prime Minister Bo Let Ya and U Tin Tut resigned to join the army. Socialist chairman U Ko Ko Gyi also left the Cabinet. Thakin Nu announced his intention to resign the premiership and enter a monastery—thinking, perhaps, that someone else might succeed where he had thus far failed. He did, in fact, remove himself from public life for a few days in mid-July— thus fulfilling a religious vow made a year before—but his colleagues persuaded him to return. He reorganized his Cabinet in the August-September parliamentary session, but to no avail.

On July 29, four months after the Communist insurrection had begun, the White Band PVO, led by Po Kun and La Yaung, took up arms against the government. Like the Communists, the new insurgents had access to arms and ammunition hoarded by Aung San in earlier days and never recovered by the government. Within two weeks the rebels were joined by members and former members of the Union Military Police and of the First and Third Battalions of the Burma Rifles, stationed, respectively, at Thayetmyo on the Irrawaddy River and in the area of the Mingaladon Airport. Communist soldiers in the First Burma Rifles had defected earlier, in mid-June. Even then Thakin Nu continued his efforts at conciliation. In August, he sent Sir U Thwin, a respected Buddhist elder, to attempt mediation with the insurrectionary PVO's. This, like all previous efforts, proved futile, although the negotiations drifted on through early 1949, while the fighting continued unabated. The defection of the White Band PVO gave great impetus to the Communist insurrection.

The Karens and the Insurrection

Threats of insurrection were also made by dissident Karens, who broke with the government over the issue of the right to secede. Animosity between the Burman majority and the various Karen groups dated from pre-British days. After the First Anglo-Burmese War, many Karens abandoned their animist religion and were converted to Christianity, under the influence of the American Baptist missionaries who followed in the footsteps of their first and commanding leader, the Reverend Adoniram Judson. Although they were a minority, the Christian Karens provided educated leaders for their people. Many Karens supported the British during the succeeding Anglo-Burmese wars, the periods of pacification, and again during World War II. During the Japanese occupation, armed clashes occurred between the Burma Independence Army (BIA) and those Karens who remained loyal to Britain.[14]

Toward the end of the war Aung San and Than Tun had recognized the need for seeking a reconciliation with the Karens and for a policy that would enlist the cooperation of the Frontier and Hill peoples.[15] With the aid of the Karen National Board (KNB) and its successor organization, the Karen Central Organization (KCO, an affiliate of the AFPFL), Aung San had organized a Karen battalion of the Burma National Army—successor to the BIA—which fought effectively in the Delta region.[16]

After the war came the Panglong Conference, in February, 1947, the Frontier Areas Committee of Enquiry, and the agreement with the Frontier peoples for a federal constitution. In these years, significant Karen groups supported federal unity and Burmese independence, but other Karens persisted in keeping the old animosities alive. They feared for their future under Burma control and were determined to have an independent Karen state.

These differences among the Karens, and the untimely death in 1946 of Sir San C. Po, one of the conciliatory Karen leaders, caused a split in the KCO in late 1946 and early 1947. A minority faction led by Mahn Ba Khaing (one of those assassinated with Aung San in 1947) and Mahn Win Maung, later third President of the Union, organized the Karen Youth Organization (KYO), loyal to the AFPFL. The majority group, headed by Saw Ba U Gyi, a relative of Dr. Po, organized the Karen National Union (KNU), and withdrew from the AFPFL. Both the KYO and the KNU had branches or affiliates in the Karen districts. There were also independent loyal Karens, such as Mrs. Ba Maung Chain (Dr. Po's daughter and later the first woman member of a Burmese Cabinet) and Professor Hla Bu. They refused to join any Karen faction and played a part in the subsequent futile mediation efforts.

The Karen National Union representatives who testified before the Frontier Areas Committee in April, 1947, clearly favored "an autonomous Karen State;" they said off the record that the Karens would remain in the British Commonwealth if Burma withdrew from it.[17] The idea of a separate Karen state was not new. Proposals for such a state had been made over the years by Karens, as well as by British civil servants and Christian missionaries.[18] In 1946, the issue was not whether there should be a Karen state, but whether such a state should be created within the Union or independently of it. A separatist Karen delegation visited London in July of that year to present its arguments in favor of a Karen state that would be directly under British protection, or alternatively, would join with other Frontier Areas to become a dominion in the Commonwealth apart from Burma Proper.[19] When the British Labour government refused to support either plan, members of the KNU did not hesitate to express their bewilderment at the way in which wartime promises made by the British had become "meaningless" and "empty."[20]

The Karen National Union boycotted the Constituent Assembly, and the Karen seats went to the Karen Youth Organization. The Constitution provided (Section 180) for a future Karen state, to include the following areas: (1) the Kareni states (which had previously enjoyed a treaty relationship with Britain); (2) the Salween district, in which Karens constituted a majority; and (3) "such adjacent areas occupied by the Karens as may be determined by a special Commission to be appointed by the President." This Regional Autonomy Enquiry Commission was to ascertain the desires of the Karens in these specified areas and in nonadjacent areas, and the Karens were to advise the commission whether or not they wished to "form a constituent unit of the Union to be known as the Karen State, which shall thereupon have the same status as the Shan State." Section 181 also provided for an interim arrangement. The Salween district and the "adjacent areas occupied by the Karens" would constitute a "Special Region to be known as *Kawthulay*" (a Karen name), would be administered by a Karen Affairs Council, and would be directly represented in the Cabinet by a Karen minister. In effect, the interim arrangement paralleled that provided for the Chins; in addition, the Karens were assured that they could achieve statehood within the Union.

The constitutional provision for a Karen state, which the government had always been prepared to honor, was attacked by leaders of the Karen National Union as insufficient recognition of their territorial and political demands. Nor were they appeased when Prime Minister Thakin Nu, fulfilling an earlier promise, named a Karen, General Smith-Dun, as commander in chief of Burma's defense and police forces and appointed other Karens to leadership positions in the armed forces and the government.[21] During the summer of 1947, the KNU proceeded to organize and arm the Karen National Defense Organization (KNDO), an ex-servicemen's unit similar to the PVO, with weapons and ammunition left behind by the British forces, and in the post-monsoon season (after October) it launched a propaganda campaign among Karens in the Delta and in the Tenasserim.

The KNU refused to celebrate Independence Day and urged Karens to set aside May 5, 1948, as their own independence day. As early as February 11, 1948, these Karen separatists staged nationalist rallies in Rangoon and elsewhere in Burma. Though these rallies were not at first regarded as impressive,[22] the government made direct contact with Karens in the Pegu, Irrawaddy, and Tenasserim divisions, and in mid-March initiated discussions with a Karen delegation headed by the outstanding KNU leader, Saw Ba U Gyi, which looked toward the constitutional development of a Karen state.[23] On April 6, the government, determined to make headway under Section 181 of the Constitution, appointed the Kawthulay Boundary Commission to define the areas adjacent to the Salween district which, together with that district, would become a Karen Special Division. The work of this commission formed the background for the more broadly based Regional Autonomy Enquiry Commission set up in October with Dr. Ba U (then Chief Justice of the Supreme Court) as its chairman. Six Karens, including Saw Ba U Gyi and two members of the KNU, were appointed to the well-balanced twenty-eight-man commission. Thakin Nu directed the members on October 20 to "explore the means and ways of satisfying, without hindrance, all legitimate aspirations of Mon, Karen and Arakanese Nationals." [24] Statehood within the Union was clearly a predictable goal and was in fact recommended the following February in the Commission's preliminary report.

In the meantime, however, it had become clear that the Karen National Defense Organization, the military arm of the KNU, would settle for nothing less than a Karenistan separate from Burma. Karens speaking different languages and dialects were in a large majority in three districts of Burma: the Karenni, Salween, and Thaton. They constituted between 20 and 30 per cent in Amherst, a contiguous district in Tenasserim, and in four other districts: Toungoo (bordering the Karenni area), and Maubin, Bassein, and Myaungmya in the Delta. The KNU sought this entire area as a Karen state.

In July and August, 1948, when the PVO was mounting its insurrectionary offensive against the government, the KNDO also began to move. Desertions from the Union Military Police began in the Delta in early July, the deserters taking military and other supplies; armed attacks took place in the Karenni and in the Salween and Thaton districts.[25] The intransigence of the separatists was strengthened by their hope of covert support from abroad. According to Tinker, "British friends who had been ashamed at the abandonment of the Karens by the British Government encouraged them to believe that they would receive weapons and other aid from overseas." A plot to aid the Karens, which involved former members of the World War II British Force 136, was discovered in September.[26] Despite mounting tension and increasing disaffection among the Karens, the Regional Autonomy Enquiry Commission continued its meetings and visits to Karen areas during the fall of 1948. The government's relations with the KNU seemed to be improving; at the same time, it made some headway against the Communist and PVO insurrection.[27] In mid-September, Thakin Nu agreed to arm KNDO forces as a separate militia, provided they would help suppress the Communists and the PVO. They were given the right to guard the vital Twante Canal, the link between Rangoon and the Irrawaddy River, as well as other responsibilities, especially in "areas where the Karens were numerous." [28]

This may have been the crowning error committed by a bewildered government. Whole units of the KNDO defected. Some joined forces with the Communists, as in the Twante area; some made overtures to other Frontier peoples in an attempt to enlist them against the government; still others clashed with the PVO's and in other ways contributed to the growing lawlessness and disorder throughout Burma. The KNDO would be neither appeased nor stopped. In mid-November, its parent body, the KNU, and some dissident Mon people from the Tenasserim reiterated their demand for a Karen state that would embrace the Tenasserim and Delta districts. They were unwilling to await the recommendations of the Regional Autonomy Commission. By the end of November, the situation was deteriorating fast. On December 4, Thakin Nu admitted that "reports from all parts of the country within the past few days have given considerable ground for anxiety." [29] In the resulting confusion, those who opposed the new government seemed to be in the ascendancy. Finally, in late December, 1948, and early January, 1949, the KNDO launched an armed campaign against the government. In January and February, some of the government's Karen military and police units mutinied and joined the KNDO. The government replaced General Smith-Dun with General Ne Win, and the two Karen ministers left the Cabinet. The rebellions failed, but just barely.

Thakin Nu has declared, "Among all the insurgents, KNDO's were the most formidable, and their rebellion put the Government into unprecedented straits." [30] If the Karens had not joined the insurrection, it is quite possible that the government, supported by experienced Karen, Kachin, and Chin detachments in the army, might have routed the Communist and PVO insurgents late in 1948 or early in 1949. Instead, the rebellion grew into a full-scale civil war.

Despite the many different labels used and the factional splits that occurred, the two principal groups that took part in the rebellion may be defined as assorted Communists and ethnic Karens. The PVO's were ideologically and at times organizationally indistinguishable from the Communists. At times, smaller groups also participated in the insurrection. Among them were the Pa-os (or Taungthus), a Karen subgroup; the Mon National Defense Organization (MNDO), operating chiefly in the Mon area of the Tenasserim; and the Mujahids (Muslims of Pakistani and Burmese origin), who operated on the Arakan border of Burma and Pakistan.

Although the MNDO and the Mujahids were of little insurrectionary significance, they contributed to the civil disorder. In contrast, the Kachins, Chins, and Shans remained at the time notably free of ethnic insurrectionary activity and loyal to the ideals of federal union foreshadowed at Panglong.[31]

There are no reliable estimates of the number of insurgents involved in the fighting, and the following figures for 1948-49 represent at best a mere guess. The two groups of Communists, the BCP and the CPB, had approximately 5,000 armed members in all. They were joined by approximately 4,000 armed PVO's, 700-1,400 army mutineers, and 3,000 police and local militia (*situandans*). Thus there were approximately 13,000 armed leftists. Karens from six battalions and the police forces totaled approximately 7,000; others joined later. In February, 1949, Thakin Nu said that the government defense forces consisted of a few loyal army battalions,[32] as well as some planes and small naval vessels. At a later date, he said that the government had started with one and a half trained battalions (about 1,000 troops) and a small number of hastily recruited Union Military Police and new militia.[33] Fortunately for the government, the armed insurrectionists were never gathered together into a single striking force.

The Role of Thakin Nu: Zeal for Unity

If Bogyoke Aung San was the architect of Burmese freedom, Thakin Nu—slowly and erratically at the beginning, but with growing steadiness—became the builder of the evolving institutions designed to preserve the Union. Leadership was thrust on him, and he accepted it reluctantly, at least in the early years, always planning to resign and withdraw from political life into one of authorship and religious contemplation.[34] Twice he did resign— in 1948, for ten days, and in 1956-57, for approximately nine months. Except for these periods, however, he was Burma's Prime Minister from July 19, 1947, until October 28, 1958, and he returned to this office after the elections of February, 1960, until the military coup of General Ne Win in March, 1962.

Thakin Nu brought to the post a charisma of his own that helped sustain the fledgling state when few thought it could survive. He is, by turns, impulsive and quick-tempered, yet extremely considerate; deeply religious; quick to make little or big decisions; never fearful of taking an unpopular position if he believes it is the right one. Conviction rather than political acumen is the touchstone of his character. He is a Burman of the Delta, born at Wakema on May 25, 1907. He has told how he had been a teen-age delinquent and a heavy drinker until he worked his way through school and college. His earliest ambition was to be the George Bernard Shaw and Gorki of Burma, and he has written plays and novels, and has translated parts of the writings of Karl Marx and Dale Carnegie into Burmese. After taking his B.A. degree at the University of Rangoon in 1929, he became a schoolteacher and superintendent of education at Pantanaw, where he married Daw Mya Yee. He joined the nationalist Dohbama Asiayone in the early 1930's, and like Aung San, became a radical student leader in 1936 when he returned to the university for a law degree. From then on he was a Thakin. Arrested and jailed by the British in 1940 under the Defense of the Realm Act, he wrote one of his saddest novels, *Yet-set-par-be-kwe*, a Burmese translation of Thomas Hobbes's bitter phrase "Man is to man a wolf." [35]

On Independence Day, 1948, Thakin Nu summed up his conception of Burma, its history, and his hopes for the future:

> Thousands of years have passed since a Prince of the Sakyan race founded the first Burmese Kingdom at Tagaung in the Upper Irrawaddy, the great river which is so intermingled with our history. . . . The small beginning of Tagaung was followed by the slow but steady consolidation of the Burmese nation till, at the beginning of the nineteenth century, Burma was an empire.
>
> Then our fortunes waned. After two unsuccessful wars against the British, our empire was reduced to a small and landlocked Kingdom of Upper Burma, and after another of such wars we lost our independence to become a province of India. But even in the days when the fortunes of our country were at their lowest, the patriotic men and women of Burma were determined to be free and thousands died in the years which followed the annexation of Upper Burma in an attempt to resist alien rule. Since then many brave men and women died in the same cause down to the time of the Resistance Movement against Japan. Others suffered wounds, mutilation and imprisonment in order that Burma may be free. The last sacrifice on the altar of freedom was endured by our Leader, Bogyoke Aung San, and those who died with him.
>
> We who are alive today, as heirs of these martyrs, reap the rich reward of the sacrifices they had sown, and our hearts go out this day to the memory of those noble men and women who suffered that successive generations of Burmans may be free. Even before the sun rose today, Burma became a free and Independent Sovereign Republic, free to shape her future destiny according to the ideas of her own people. . . . In the centuries that passed, the races of Burma fought among themselves and administrative division under the British regime kept us apart. All this is now over and while the Mon, Arakanese, Burmese, the Karens, the Shans, the Kachins, and the Chins will maintain their several cultures, we are now one nation, under one flag and under one elected Head of the Burma Union. May the unity that we have achieved today, like the independence that comes with it, forever endure! [36]

The unity on which Thakin Nu depended for the future of Burma did not long survive his speech. Burma became torn by insurrection and fratricidal strife. Thakin Nu sought to hold back the civil war primarily through a path of compromise and conciliation both with the Karens and the Communists. Formulas for unity were advanced with more frequency than rationality, and each effort seemed to end in a worsened situation. His May-June, 1948, program for "leftist unity," especially Point 15, evoked outspoken criticism in the Burmese press,[37] severe condemnation by Buddhists, and violent reactions in the West. U Tin Tut, then foreign minister, tried to soften Western response by explaining Thakin Nu's program in terms of AFPFL's "party policy," not the government's. But at the time nothing seemed to work in the government's favor.

Western responses rivaled Thakin Nu's formulations in ineptness. Headlines in the London *Daily Express* and *Daily Mail* announced that "Burma is all set to go Communist." Foreign Minister Ernest Bevin demanded an explanation from the Burmese Ambassador, Sir Maung Gyee, and in response to debate in the House of Commons announced angrily that he would recommend a change in policy toward Burma if the Nu-Attlee Treaty was not faithfully carried out. Winston Churchill seized the opportunity to pay off old scores. "Burma," he said, was "descending into a state of anarchy, tempered by communism." Expression of opinion in the United States was little less censorious.[38] Yet Thakin Nu at no time repudiated his government's agreements with the United Kingdom. In a major broadcast on March 28, 1948, he had carefully defended the treaty, despite pressure from the Communists, justifying it as a "compromise involving give and take on both sides." Similarly, in his controversial second speech on "leftist unity" after the Communist rebellion had broken out, he reaffirmed at length his government's support of the treaty and its provisions. He also stated emphatically that the Burmese Communists were interested only in friendly relations with the U.S.S.R., whereas the AFPFL desired to have friendly relations with the United States and the United Kingdom, as well as with the Soviet Union.[39]

Western sympathy for the Karens also entered into the condemnation of Burma. There is evidence that the Karen organizations and the Frontier peoples were regarded as anti-Communist by some quarters in Washington, and for this reason were thought to deserve support. At a later date, a Foreign Service dispatch reported quite a different view. It noted that

> because many Karen leaders had been well known to missionaries a false impression of their objectives was taken for granted in foreign circles, and the foreign press viewed the Karen uprising as a crusade against Communism. . . . This illusion was dispelled when Karens joined the Communists in attacking and occupying Mandalay on March 13, 1949. Since then the KNDO have joined forces with the Communists, or have separated from them as momentary expediency demanded.[40]

But even after Karen actions had dispelled the illusion that they were anti-Communist, sympathy with their aspirations did not immediately die down. As late as December 24, 1949, the *Economist* proposed as a condition of British aid to Burma that "the Burmese government invite the good offices of a mediator to be appointed by the United Nations for the purpose of a settlement with the Karens." It continued, "It is intolerable that British arms and supplies should be used—as they already have been—for the suppression of a brave people to whom Britain owes an unpaid debt of gratitude." The reaction of the *Economist* was echoed in a privately printed memorandum circulated among the members of the House of Commons by a former Indian Civil Service officer with thirty-seven years' duty in Burma. The memorandum bore the same name as the published statement of the 1946 Karen delegation—"The Case for the Karens." It criticized British postwar treatment of Karens as worse than a "Munich," for the Karens, unlike the Czechs, "had fought for us . . . sheltered our fugitive and wounded soldiers, and suffered massacre." [41]

Because of sentimental or other attachments, some Western leaders found it difficult to distinguish between the Burmese Government's efforts to solve the problem of forming a Karen state by legitimate means and its attempt to prevent secession through force. Obviously, much as the Burma Government might welcome an end to the Karen rebellion, it could not, as a condition of external support, tolerate unconcealed Western sympathies for Karen rebel secessionist aspirations.[42] On the other hand, the ill-advised "leftist unity" speech, and other unsuccessful efforts of Thakin Nu to ward off insurrection at home, only added to the difficulties of the hard-pressed government, since as long as Burma was regarded as unstable and in danger of following the very course his actions were intended to avoid, there could be little hope of obtaining aid or even sympathy from abroad. Nevertheless, throughout this troubled time, the preservation—and later the restoration—of the unity of Burma constituted the essence of Thakin Nu's policy, and he did not hesitate to attempt conciliation whenever it seemed to offer some prospect of success.

The Prime Minister did not attempt to conceal the desperate state of Burma's affairs. After the KNDO joined the rebellion, he admitted that "the Union is standing on the edge of a precipice; a slight tilt would plunge it headlong into the abyss" and stated that "the whole world has opined that our days are numbered." [43] To Parliament he described the "actual state of affairs" as "an awful mess." [44] No one in a position of authority had any doubt about this, but the counsels for cleaning it up were varied and in certain instances divisive.

"An Awful Mess"

Seen from Rangoon or from abroad, the government's situation at the beginning of 1949 was exceedingly black. The Ministerial Services Union began a strike on February 4 that all but paralyzed the administration in those parts of the country that the government still controlled. The Communists, the PVO's, and the army mutineers had established themselves in the Prome area, approximately 170 miles northwest of Rangoon, while the Karens were entrenched at the Toungoo rail center. In addition, the Karens held the important area of Insein, and they raided the Mingaladon airfield arsenal. From here they attacked the capital, less than a dozen miles away, but the government forces held firm. At this stage the Second Battalion of the Karen Rifles (regular army) defected and attempted to join the KNDO at Insein. Had they reached their objective, the march on the capital might have succeeded. But on February 9, 1949, several Burma Air Force planes attacked and routed the Karen battalion, while government forces at Pegu prevented the Karens at Toungoo from coming to the aid of their stalled forces at Insein. These events led to a new round of negotiations with the two main rebel groups.

Three related efforts were made—two initiated at home, the third from abroad. When the capital was under attack, the British, Indian, and Pakistani ambassadors, with the approval of the Burma Government and the cooperation of the newly appointed "Protection Committee" (including the Chief Justice of the Supreme Court and leading nonaffiliated Karens like Mrs. Ba Maung Chain, Professor Hla Bu, and Reverend Francis Ahmya), urged negotiations, with a guarantee of safety to the KNU leader, Saw Ba U Gyi, then at Insein. During this month (February) the Regional Autonomy Commission made its Interim Report, which called for a "Karen State within the Union of Burma for the Karen people . . . irrespective of whether the Karenni State is willing to merge with the Karen State or not." [45] Thakin Nu's public endorsement of the Commission's recommendations offered a basis for negotiations. Saw Ba U Gyi came to Rangoon on April 4. An agreement was reached the next day. This was signed on behalf of the government by Thakin Nu, the chairman of the Regional Autonomy Commission, U Ba, and Minister Dr. E Maung; Saw Ba U Gyi and Mahn James Tun Aung signed for the KNU and KNDO. The Karens then returned to KNDO headquarters at Toungoo, but the KNDO leaders failed to concur in the agreement. Instead, KNDO leaders Saw Aung Sein and Saw Hunter Tha Hmwe put forward unacceptable counterproposals. Saw Ba U Gyi returned to the rebels; Mahn James Tun Aung left them to remain in Rangoon. The negotiations were terminated, and fighting flared again.[46]

In the meantime, Prime Minister Nehru, fresh from an effort at conciliation made in behalf of Indonesia in January, 1949, attempted to strengthen Burma's position in the free world and restore good relations between Rangoon and London. He persuaded the delegates at a British Commonwealth Conference in New Delhi—the United Kingdom, Australia, Ceylon, India, and Pakistan were represented—to consider the "problems raised by the revolution in Burma." Among the questions considered were a Commonwealth loan, Karen mediation, the export of Burmese rice, and the restoration of peace.[47] As a result, the Commonwealth ambassadors used their good offices in what became the last futile effort at mediation with the Karens. The conference was more successful in other matters. Relations between Rangoon and London improved. In June, a Burmese delegation to London, led by Foreign Minister Dr. E Maung and Defense Minister General Ne Win, negotiated with Prime Minister Attlee's government, and a shipment of small arms was received. Arrangements were also made for a Commonwealth loan, but the Burmese never used it.

As *The Economist* pointed out later in the spring, "the decision to help Burma had come none too soon, for there are already signs of intervention from another quarter. Bands of Chinese Communists have for some time been active in the province of Yunnan just across the frontier . . . Chinese Communist infiltration may yet become an important factor in the Burmese civil wars." [48] In fact, the more immediate danger to Burma came from the defeated Kuomintang army, but this did not become apparent until 1950-51.

The third of these interrelated efforts to bring about peace was yet another attempt by the government, late in March, 1949, to negotiate with Communist rebels, both BCP and PVO. The events in this move were widely misinterpreted in the West. On April 1, six of the Socialist and Yellow Band PVO members of Thakin Nu's Cabinet, together with their parliamentary secretaries, resigned.[49] Among them were Deputy Premier U Kyaw Nyein, Ministers Thakin Tin and Bo Sein Hman, and U Win, the Special Commissioner for Upper Burma. They issued an enigmatic statement declaring that the "resignation from office does not mean our withdrawal from the AFPFL nor does it mean the setting up of an Opposition to the Union Government. . . . Our desire is to double our efforts to restore peace, to launch free and fair elections . . . and to stabilize the Union." [50]

This move suggested that in the midst of negotiations with the Communists and the Karens, a split had developed between the Prime Minister and his major supporters in the Cabinet. Thakin Nu proceeded to construct a caretaker government, with General Ne Win as Deputy Premier and Minister of Home Affairs and Defense, Dr. E Maung as Foreign Minister, and Frontier leaders in other Cabinet posts.

Actually, what happened can be pieced together in part from Thakin Nu's own accounts.[51] On March 16, immediately after the Cabinet had approved the Interim Report of the Regional Autonomy Commission, Thakin Nu and General Ne Win had started on a tour of Upper Burma and planned the recapture of Mandalay, which then was in the hands of Communist, PVO, and Karen rebels, who had formed the Joint Political Committee.[52] A telegram from Deputy Premier Kyaw Nyein had recalled Thakin Nu to Rangoon. During his absence, General Ne Win had established political contact with Communist rebels, one of many similar moves that took place throughout the insurrection. The Communist terms of negotiation involved the premiership, Cabinet representation for their party at the expense of the Socialist Party, and new elections. So the Socialists and Yellow Band PVO withdrew from the Cabinet in order to give Thakin Nu and General Ne Win a free hand in negotiations not only with the Communists but also with the Karens. They were willing to take their chances in the "free and fair elections" which had been scheduled for April, 1949.

Thakin Nu indicated that he was willing to reconstruct his Cabinet in order "to show how sincere the Government was in its desire to conduct the general elections on really democratic lines." [53] Yet he was aware that "April 1949 was our darkest hour. . . . I felt," he writes, "as if I was wandering in a pitch-dark night with no ray of light in front. . . . I knew that the fate of the peoples of the Union rested on my decision. Shall our people lead a life of gelded oxen with no means of exercising full human rights? Or shall our people enjoy full human rights? . . . With these considerations in mind, I made my decision thus: 'this is nothing but the complete surrender of our cherished principles. I will *not* acquiesce.' " [54] Therefore he rejected the Communist demands—or perhaps made counterproposals that they found unacceptable.

After all these efforts at conciliation failed, the elections were postponed to 1951. Socialists and Yellow Band PVO's quietly rejoined an enlarged Cabinet in January, 1950. Although Thakin Nu's policy of reforging unity through negotiation was unsuccessful, it enabled him to buy time so as to rebuild the loyal forces and show his countrymen that, short of sacrificing the Union, he was for domestic peace.

The year 1949 marked the last opportunity for the insurrectionists to succeed without aid from abroad. April, 1949, was, in fact, the turning point for the Union of Burma. On April 3, government forces recaptured Mandalay, and in June they reoccupied the oil fields at Yenangyaung and Chauk. Tharrawaddy was recaptured in July, and in the same month General Ne Win set out on a diplomatic and arms mission to the United Kingdom and the United States. The government suffered occasional setbacks, as in August when the Karens took Taunggyi, capital of the Southern Shan state area, but by and large it was steadily gaining ground.[55]

In the spring of 1950, the Government of Burma clarified its stand on Communism. During a consultation in London in May, Thakin Nu assured the House of Commons that the AFPFL had no intention of letting Burma go Communist, and this time his words carried conviction. In July of that year, Burma endorsed the action taken by the United Nations Security Council in declaring

North Korea to be an aggressor and approving the sending of troops in the name of the United Nations; however, it voted against the later General Assembly resolution that named Communist China an aggressor.[56] In September, Burma signed an economic-aid agreement with the United States.[57] A new split in the AFPFL followed these actions, and in December a group of self-styled leftist Socialists withdrew from the AFPFL to form what became a crypto-Communist party, known first as the Burma Workers' and Peasants' Party (BWPP), and after 1959 as the Burma Workers' Party (BWP). The ease with which the majority in the AFPFL handled this new split gave further evidence at home and abroad of the growing strength of Thakin Nu and the AFPFL.

During 1950, the contest with the rebels continued to move in the government's favor. Government troops, regrouped, trained, and coordinated under General Ne Win, established the authority of the central government over a number of important towns in the Arakan, Delta, and Tenasserim districts and pushed steadily northward up the Irrawaddy Valley and along the Rangoon-Toungoo-Mandalay rail route. They recaptured Magwe in April, Prome in May, Thayetmyo in October. PVO rebel leader Bo La Yaung and some important sections of his troops surrendered in May, taking advantage of an offer of amnesty. The leader of the KNU-KNDO forces, Saw Ba U Gyi, was killed in August.[58]

However, a new problem emerged in 1950, that of Chinese Nationalist troops. In late 1949, Kuomintang (KMT) forces in Yunnan had given way before the Chinese Communist Fourth Army Group, and between January and March, 1950, some 2,000 KMT soldiers with their families escaped into Burma, where they regrouped in the eastern reaches of the Shan state of Kentung. Burmese troops were deeply engaged in fighting the rebels; the government, through third-country off-the-record consultations, expected that the Chinese soldiers would either quietly melt into the countryside, agree to be interned, or leave Burmese territory.

General Li Mi, commander of the KMT forces, rejected these alternatives, although about 200 men were interned at a camp near Meiktila. The KMT troops proceeded to dig in and live off the countryside, where they had access to rice and opium. During the second week of June, a unit of the Burmese army was ordered to drive them out.[59] This first brief and inconclusive encounter left the KMT still encamped in Kentung state. Li Mi's importance to the Chinese Nationalists became greater after the outbreak of the Korean War. He reinforced his position in Burma by recruiting in Yunnan, and supplies, including matériel originating in the United States, were airlifted to him from Taiwan. The Burmese, troubled by the threat of the big new Communist neighbor to the north, were fearful of the consequences of this incursion, but at that time little could be done beyond the limited military engagement of this new enemy quartered on Burmese soil. This issue became more complicated and was to involve the United States Government through 1961.

Obstacles to Victory

The back of the insurrection was broken in 1951. By and large, the government was in control, although law and order were not yet restored everywhere. The armed forces, the Union military police, and various local militia were gradually wearing down the rebels' strength, but this did not prevent the rebels from looting local treasuries, blowing up trains and water mains, and engaging in other kinds of guerrilla actions. Nevertheless, the government now felt strong enough to hold the postponed national elections. These began in June, 1951, and were concluded in January, 1952. The elections returned an overwhelming majority of AFPFL members and supporters to both chambers of the Parliament. Thakin Nu was named Prime Minister. (The elections are discussed in detail in Chapter 8.) For the first time, the Union of Burma had a democratically elected Parliament and a government that operated under the Constitution of 1947.

An example of the extent to which the nation's security had increased was the government's new policy, beginning in January, 1952, of allowing members of the U.S. economic-aid mission to fly to any of the more than two dozen airstrips serviced by the Union of Burma Airways if they gave three days' notice.

Burma's hard-won and still-being-tested unity survived the attacks of the Communists, the PVO's, and the Karens; and ultimately the Burmese, with some external aid, reduced the threat of the KMT. (It had not yet been able to resolve the issue of restive minorities.) It is pertinent to ask why it took the government so long to quell the insurrection. Despite year-by-year improvement throughout the 1950's, sporadic insurrectionary activity continued to interfere with the thorough establishment of law and order in Burma. (Burma's record on the suppression of rebel activity is not as good as India's, but it approaches that of Malaya.) [60]

The presence of the KMT forces added to the strength of the rebels, especially along the range of hills from the Kachin state south to the Tenasserim border with Thailand. They deflected the Burmese armed forces from their task of suppressing the rebels. They invited international complications: with Communist China, which might invade Burma to deal with the marauding KMT; with Thailand whose nationals engaged in smuggling operations in opium and minerals and whose territory was an occasional sanctuary for KMT guerrillas; with Taiwan, which from 1950 to 1953, utilizing a KMT-held airstrip at Mongsat, supplied General Li Mi's troops in Burma; and with the United States, whose military supplies to Taiwan were often reshipped to the KMT groups in Burma. The use in 1953-54 of the good offices of the United Nations, the United States, and Thailand in effecting the evacuation of approximately half of the KMT troops was widely regarded in Burma as an informal amende honorable. But some 1,500-2,000 KMT troops remained in a remote corner of Kentung, near the Laotian border, on a bend of the Mekong River. In 1959, the KMT were said to have built a new landing strip about one mile inside the Laos border, capable of taking a Dakota plane; they added to their forces and also engaged in counterfeiting, smuggling, and morphine manufacture. In 1960, the Burma Government again mounted a campaign against them, possibly with the aid of the Chinese Communists then working on the final demarcation lines of the Sino-Burma border.

In February, 1961, Burma again complained to the United States of KMT guerrilla action in the northeast border area, and reported the capture of American military equipment on its way to the KMT.[61] Once again an evacuation was staged. Some 4,000 KMT troops were sent by air to Taiwan, and 1,500 were sent across the border. In December, 1961, between 750 and 1,000 were said to have "settled" in this Burma border area.[62] The issue is not yet resolved.

Several factors combined to make the pacification of the country a protracted struggle. Burma's terrain permitted the insurrectionists to "fade away" in remote village and jungle areas. The monsoons made it difficult if not impossible to campaign from June through October. The government was severely handicapped by lack of trained manpower and adequate matériel, especially in the early years of the fighting. Burma's trained fighting forces were sharply divided by the insurrection, and a majority of them actually went over to the rebels. Unlike India, Burma had not inherited military forces and a military tradition from the days of British rule. In fact, until World War II the Burmans were virtually denied the opportunity of joining any armed forces. In addition, at the beginning of the rebellion, U Nu thought he could win over the rebels by persuasion and offers of amnesty. After he had belatedly discovered the futility of this tactic, he authorized the gradual building up of the armed forces and the Union military police. The rebels had access to large stores of arms, which had been sequestered throughout the countryside during the war. Despite its defense agreement with the British, the government in utter disagreement with some of the British officers assigned to this task in Burma, failed to obtain the amount and kind of equipment it thought necessary, and it suspected the West of dragging its feet in the matter of military supplies.

The government's efforts suffered from a lack of political sophistication and strong will with respect to the Communists. The leaders of the government and the leaders of the Communists had gone to school together, had lived together, and until 1947 had worked together. It was several years before the former came to believe that their fellow Thakins could be genuine Communists determined to overthrow a democratic government. At first they did not understand the implications of the founding of the Cominform and the victory of the Chinese Communists. They needed time and the bitter experience of armed struggle to learn the lessons of Communist strategy and tactics and to wear out the ties of former comradeship in the nationalist-Marxist amalgam that they had all joined so eagerly as young men.

The suppression of the rebels was complicated by the then prevalent Burmese patterns of disrespect for law and order. Crime and dacoity in Burma rose sharply after Burma became a province of India in 1862. Opposition to any central government was positively sanctioned by popular attitudes of opposition to it. The Communists were able to capitalize on this, while the KNDO was able to exploit the long-standing ill will between Karens and Burmans. Further, after the decade of prewar, wartime, and postwar agitation and disruption, it was difficult for the engaged personnel to settle down. Burma had suffered severely during the war and the Burmese had been in a state of turmoil since the elections of 1936. To revert to normal patterns of work, law, and order was not easy.

Support for the rebels was often an expression of dissatisfaction with the national government. Historically, Burma had been composed of many ethnic and linguistic groups united under strong rule, whether dynastic or colonial. The existence of real and fancied grievances made it relatively easy for the Karen rebels and other minorities to gain adherents to their cause. In addition, the divisive tendencies inherent in a plural society not yet accustomed to the workings of a national government made it possible for the rebels to recruit disaffected individuals among both Burmans and non-Burmans. Any man who did not like or could not adjust to life in the township or village tract could defect to the rebels, among whom he was assured of a welcome; he thereby joined a cause that rationalized his anarchic behavior. Any ethnic subgroup that felt that its interests were neglected in Rangoon raised the banner of separatism and potential, if not of actual, revolution. Furthermore, untrained and untried local officials and armed local militias on the government side were not always models of honest zeal and deportment. Sometimes they caused trouble and indirectly drove men to defect.

The tradition of Burmese Buddhist society made it difficult for the new government to act strongly and resolutely. Theravada Buddhism encourages tolerance and permits or accepts, if it does not approve, a wide range of behavior. For the "actor" is merely acting out his *kamma*. (For a further discussion, see Chapter 6.) His is not a predetermined role, however, for he himself determines whatever role he plays in society. Therefore, it would be argued or felt that the causes of the rebellion and the reasons for the existence of the rebels are not wholly unrelated to the rebels and to their opponents. Hence the government encountered some resistance among good Buddhists when it sought complete and one-sided acceptance of its own viewpoint. It is not easy to define this type of psychological response, which assumes that there is some good in every viewpoint and which regards with tolerance the coexistence of opposites in each man and in society. One man who illustrated this manner of thinking or feeling was Kodaw Hmaing, a vaunted nationalist and Thakin (1876-1964), who expressed his disapproval of colonialism by refusing to learn English. He consciously and publicly used the Buddhist aspect of Burmese culture in order to further his peace maneuvers in behalf of the Communist rebels. It enabled him to get a respectful hearing from U Nu's government and to gain the support of some *pongyis*. In 1954, he was rewarded by the U.S.S.R. with the Stalin Peace Prize.

In time, the government surmounted most of these difficulties and seemed to be approaching final victory over the rebels. But the cost was high, and the battle is not over yet. By the end of 1955, nearly 28,000 soldiers and civilians had been killed, and damage to private and public property had amounted to the Burmese equivalent of $950 million,[63] equal to about one full year of Burma's gross national product. More than several times this amount must have been spent up to 1965. But more important than the loss of material resources was the damage, early in the decade, to Burma's reputation abroad.

The Western attitude revealed a curious lack of sympathy for a newly independent country that was struggling against a determined Communist insurrection and other elements of political instability and inexperience. Happily, this shortsighted Western stance was not of long duration, and the wounds that it left behind have been slowly healing. Beyond the incalculable costs in human lives and reputation, the chief damage of the insurrection has been the inordinate delay it has caused in the rebuilding of Burma's economy, and the resources of leadership that have been deflected from constructive tasks into a struggle to preserve the Union of Burma. To a considerable extent, the military caretaker government that ruled from 1958 to 1960, and the military takeover in March, 1962, were the results of the protracted instability that has dogged Burma since independence—an instability arising in no small measure from the insurrection.

6 · AND WHY THE INSURRECTIONS FAILED

THE PRESERVATION OF the Union of Burma became the chief task of the government during the first decade of independence. Buddhism, nationalism frequently in cooperation with some aspects of Marxism, and the changing international political conditions brought about as a result of World War II combined to bring Burma into the comity of nations as a free and independent federal republic in January, 1948. But the wartime unity forged by Bogyoke Aung San did not long survive his assassination. The cementing struggle of the nationalist-Marxist amalgam on the road to power gave way almost immediately on the accession of power. The Burmese had suffered in prewar days from, and were not unfamiliar with, political fissionizing tendencies which interfered with the unity of the nationalist movement. Such centrifugal forces, both those that were indigenous and those brought about by the forms of British colonial rule, had made for Burmese disunity and disorganization. Nevertheless, the Burmese were almost totally unprepared for the far-reaching and debilitating effects of the Communist rebellion and its ethnic Karen counterpart.

The Communist rebellion and the Karen uprising placed an overwhelming military, economic, and social burden on the newly independent Union of Burma. Western governments were inclined to write off the country, especially between 1948 and 1950. In view of this, it is useful to ask how democratic government in Burma was in fact able to survive.[1] Its preservation was due to a variety of factors, among which the following deserve special mention here: weaknesses within the insurgent movements; the leadership of Prime Minister Nu; the Buddhist revival; the stressful unity of the three leadership groups within the government—the politicians, the armed forces, and the bureaucracy; and the four strengths of the government, symbolized in the main by the 1952 commitment to Pyidawtha, or the building of a welfare state.

Weaknesses Within the Insurgent Movements

When U Nu's government did not succumb to the first armed blows of the Communists and Karens, especially after the Karens captured Insein, less than a dozen miles from the capital, in February, 1949, some American authorities credited "the general lack of common purpose and coordination among the insurgents." [2] There was, in fact, one common purpose among all insurrectionists —the overthrow of the AFPFL government—and it brought the Communists, Karens, and Kuomintang forces together at various times. However, personal rivalry among the leaders and ideological differences among the groups repeatedly split the coalitions and alliances that were formed.

The two principal Communist leaders, Thakins Than Tun and Soe, have never been able to overcome their mutual antagonism, which dates from at least 1943, when Than Tun served as a Cabinet officer in Ba Maw's puppet government under the Japanese and, according to his opponent, was "corrupted by office and luxury." Soe was already in the jungle organizing resistance against the "Fascists." Soe also taunted Than Tun with the charge of "Browderism," an international Communist epithet signifying compromise with imperialists and opportunists. This led to their split at the Burma Communist Party's Central Committee sessions in February and March, 1946. Than Tun retained control of the BCP, and Soe withdrew to form his CPB splinter group. As far as is known, no Cominform or other representative was sent to reunite Burma's Communist parties; nor was there among contemporary Burmese Communists any leader like S. A. Dange in India, or Musso in Indonesia, who had lived in the U.S.S.R. and then returned home to take over party leadership with Moscow's backing.

Factional strife among the Burmese Communist leaders continued to have divisive effects on their followers throughout the insurrection. In addition, Than Tun and his majority group, the BCP, regularly overestimated their own strength within the AFPFL and their drawing power in the countryside. By 1945, Than Tun had become a dedicated Communist, an able organizer, and a popular figure. He was less intransigent than his brother-in-law, Bogyoke Aung San, in negotiating with the British in 1944-45, and he thought he would be able to displace the latter as leader of the AFPFL. But he failed in this contest, as he later failed to displace Thakin Nu. These political defeats at home made him the more eager to embrace the Cominform left-turn decisions in the fall of 1947. At the Communist meetings held at Calcutta early in 1948, he boasted of the size of his following in Burma. His boasts seemed to be corroborated at a Communist rally in Pyinmana, in March, where some 75,000 Burmese farmers had gathered at the end of the agricultural season. Actually, he mistook a crowd at a fair, drawn by free entertainment and sport, for serious Communist revolutionary support. Almost immediately after this rally he launched the Communist rebellion.

Than Tun[3] and his comrades were ill prepared to sustain the rebellion once its initial thrust was spent. Without the accession of defecting army units and the People's Volunteer Organization, which for the most part remained within the Communist fold, there would have been no way for the rebels to solve the problems of food supply, arms supply and repair, finances, and cooperation with other dissidents. As it was, they had to improvise. Only in the matter of ideological indoctrination were they supplied with models published in Moscow, and periodically after 1949, in Peking. When Than Tun, Soe, and the various Communist factions failed to overthrow the government by 1950, they had to regroup their forces and undertake to live in the jungle and off the villages. From this point on they engaged in guerrilla warfare; they also sent some of their cadre groups to China for training. They tried but failed to establish a Yenan-type of revolutionary base in the Kachin and Shan states, which would have given them a territorial connection with Communist China. The Kachins, Shans, and Chins—the Frontier peoples—remained loyal to the government. As the government forces pushed the rebels farther back into the jungle, they gradually became what they are today: roving bands of political dacoits, their ideology kept alive by crypto-Communists in Rangoon and Mandalay, and covertly supported from Chinese Communist sources. At one time the government placed a price on the heads of Soe and Than Tun; at other times it offered amnesty if the Communists would surrender their arms. Negotiations with them conducted by both U Nu and General Ne Win were never successful. Their declining numbers are still being hunted down by the armed forces of the government.

The weakness of the Karen rebels, despite their occasional alliances with both the Communists and the Kuomintang forces, and despite their initial military strength, proceeded from the hopelessness of their case. They were battling for secession while other Karen leaders were working for statehood within the Union of Burma. Still other Karen leaders were passive or neutral, whatever their sympathies, because they correctly believed that a Karen minority surrounded by a Burman majority could not survive by force. The units of the Karen National Defense Organization could not maintain the pace of their initial victories. As the government gradually cleared them from the Delta, they retreated to the majority Karen areas north and east of Moulmein. There, pocketed in jungle and hilly terrain, they survived, but they were forced to live off the Karen villages. On March 12, 1964, General Ne Win's Revolutionary Council government signed an agreement with the main body of the Karen rebels led by Saw Hunter Tha

Hmwe, who had headed the KNDO since 1949. At last, except for a handful of Communist Karen rebels still in the jungle, the Karen uprising was at an end (see Chapter 9).

The Leadership of U Nu

The preceding chapter referred to the personality and leadership of U Nu as charismatic. Since by definition charisma has some ineffable quality, it is obvious that the appeal of this teacher, writer, and political figure may in part elude those unpersuaded that he has the quality so named. The 30-35 per cent of the American people who did not, according to the opinion polls, respond favorably to the popularity enjoyed by General Eisenhower, were similarly "unpersuaded." Yet, like the General, the Burmese Prime Minister had no difficulty in winning three popular elections (1951-52, 1956, 1960) and retaining the overwhelming support of the people during the critical events of his decade in office. He has been described in colorful Burmese as a man "with a throne always attached to his bottom"—i.e., one destined for greatness. The Burmese people obviously believed in U Nu and seem to have been convinced of his personal morality and incorruptibility, and of his sincere devotion to Buddhism. His publicly confessed sins of omission or commission have been excused or overlooked. The popular Burmese image of U Nu is that of a man with a genuine concern for the welfare of the individual and the nation, whatever his lack of administrative ability.

U Nu moved from one crisis to another, always publicly holding aloft the ideal of a united, federal, socially advancing Burma. In return, he won the loyalty of the Shans, Kachins, Chins, Kayahs, and many Karens, most of whom remained loyal during the period of the revolts. He adopted and expounded, though he did not name, a theory of cultural pluralism capable of bridging the historical social gap that prevailed among the major ethnic groups in the Union.[4] In his search for ways to win and hold the subversive and insurrectionary left, he at times dangerously stretched the bonds among Burmese patriots. But however misguided he may have been in so doing, many Burmese have regarded his efforts as an attempt to find a way to solve the problem of insurrection. U Nu won his post as democratic leader because he convinced a majority of Burmese that he merited their confidence. He voluntarily surrendered his post of leadership in 1958 because, contrary to his preachments, he had failed to sustain the unity of his party, the AFPFL. He was finally displaced as premier by the armed forces in 1962 because he no longer seemed able to sustain his own ideal of a unified Burmese state.

The Buddhist Revival

A third major factor in the preservation of the Union has been the pervasive character of Burma's Buddhist culture. This, too, has been intimately connected with U Nu, in his roles as devout Buddhist and as Prime Minister. From the time of Michael Symes (see Chapter 1), no major commentator on Burma has failed to recognize Buddhist influence upon Burmese ways of living, thinking, and feeling. Tradition dates the arrival of Buddhism in Burma from the latter half of the third century B.C., when two monks (Thera Sona and Thera Uttara) were sent from India on an evangelizing mission. Epigraphical and other records available from the fifth century A.D. attest to the prevalence in different parts of the land of both Mahayana (Greater Vehicle) and Hinayana (Lesser Vehicle), or Theravada (Way of the Elders), Buddhism. (The Burmese prefer "Theravada" to "Hinayana," which they regard as derogatory.) The Burmans are said to have acquired Theravada Buddhism after King Anawratha conquered the Mons of southern Burma in 1057. More recent research has revealed the presence of Theravada Buddhism in Upper Burma before this event.[5] However it was received, Theravada Buddhism has been the dominant cultural fact in Burma for well over a millennium. Theravada Buddhism has great importance also for Ceylon, Thailand, Cambodia, and Laos. To understand something of this Buddhist tradition it may be useful to sketch in its main outlines.

Oral tradition associated with Prince Siddhattha (personal name) who is known as Gautama, or Gotama (the clan name in Pali), and who became a Buddha (literally, an enlightened one, a knower) some six centuries before the Christian era, was codified and canonized in Pali at least as early as 247 B.C., the year of the Third Buddhist Council. However, the first translations into Western languages do not appear until the mid-nineteenth century. Not only are the translations incomplete, they are also inexact.[6] The venerable U Thittila, a Buddhist monk who visited the United States in 1958-59 as the third U Nu lecturer, has said:

> Among the western writers on Buddhism there were some who had no intention of doing justice to Buddhism but were only concerned with showing that it was a heathen religion and inferior to the existing faith of the West. There were others again who were not only friendly but had a good intention and yet often took a distorted, and one-sided view for the simple reason that their knowledge of Pali and Buddhism was inadequate. As a result there have been some extraordinary mixtures of misconceptions and queer ideas or, in some cases of Theosophy and Hinduism that have passed for Buddhism in the West.[7]

According to Buddhist teaching, man can so conduct himself along the "Middle Way" that in his lifetime or through successive changes of living form he can arrive at the state of being a Buddha. He will have then attained *bodhi*, or wisdom. Wisdom includes intellectual and ethical fullness. Being a Buddha means that one has reached perfection, or attained *nibbana* (Pali), or nirvana (Sanskrit).

This term is perhaps the most difficult in Buddhism. It is the goal, but like the term "God" in non-Buddhist scriptures, cannot be easily comprehended. Buddha, according to both canonical writings and commentaries, refused to be drawn into metaphysical discussion as to its full meaning. But he and his Theravada followers and interpreters have used the methods of myth, parable, analogy, sermon, and dialogue to shed light upon its many characteristics. The content of these explanations furnishes inspiration for the fine and practical arts of Burma, and for the education of the young, especially in *pongyikyaungs*. *Nibbana*, whatever else it is, is *ultimate* truth, peace, deliverance, unconditioned reality. It is the end of woe, the ceasing of becoming, the ending of decay and death, the extinction of all craving, the absence of passion, cessation from the wheel of doctrine. It is not the nihilism, nothingness, or void associated with the philosophical pessimism of nineteenth-century Schopenhauerian systems. Knowledge of its attainment and its actual attainment are intrinsic to the individual, who thus knows and succeeds. There is no intercessor, no savior, no Jesus who dies for the salvation of man's soul. *Nibbana* is self-caused. It is the Buddhist ultimate solution to the problems of pain and evil.

Man determines his own fate by his *Kamma* (Pali), or *Karma* (Sanskrit), his actions. If he sins, he suffers. If he is or does good, he benefits. He will reap the harvest of his actions in this or another existence. This is the rebirth, the *Samsara*. If in this life he suffers pain, like Job, it may be, according to Buddhism, because he was evil in a previous life and is presently suffering the consequences. One's *Samsara* is at an end when one's *Kamma* has eliminated all wrong actions. Then the Buddhist may experience the realization of enlightenment. He is on the way to or has reached *nibbana*. Buddha, more than on anything else, concentrated his teachings on the "Path" or the "Way."

The Middle Way avoids the extremes of sensuality and asceticism. It moves along an "Eightfold Path," consisting of right understanding, right-mindedness, right speech, right bodily action, right livelihood, right efforts, right attentiveness, and right concentration.[8] This is known as Buddha's "First Sermon." The Eightfold Path is taken after one has initially understood the first three Noble Truths: of suffering; of the origin of suffering; of the extinction of suffering. It is in fact "the Path that leads to the extinction of suffering," or the fourth Noble Truth. While moving on the Eightfold Path, the Buddhist is enjoined to abide by the Five Precepts, or *Silas*. These are literally "steps of training," and they are similar to the commandments of the Judeo-Christian tradition. They enjoin one to abstain (1) from killing any living being, (2) from stealing, (3) from unlawful intercourse with the other sex, (4) from lying, (5) from drinking intoxicating beverages. There are a minimum of six additional commandments or rules, inclusive of an amendment to (3) above, binding on all novices and monks to abstain (6) from unchastity, (7) from eating after mid-day, (8) from dancing, singing, music, and shows, (9) from gar-lands, scent, cosmetics, and adornment, (10) from luxurious beds, (11) from accepting gold and silver.

The canonical teaching of the Buddha is known as the *Dhamma*. These scriptures, called alternatively the *Tripitakas* (Sanskrit), or the *Tipitakas* (Pali), are the "three baskets," or three great collections of the canon. The first collection includes the discourses, dialogues, verses, stories, and legends dealing with the doctrine itself and designed to elucidate the meaning of *nib-bana*, the steps of training, and the stages on the Eightfold Path. It is called the *Sutta-Pitaka*. The second collection comprises the rules or discipline of the monastic order, the *Sangha*, and is known as the *Vinaya-Pitaka*. The third collection includes the metaphysi-cal, epistemological, and psychological writings presenting the teachings of the *Sutta-Pitaka* in systematic form, the *Abhidhamma-Pitaka*.

The Buddha, his life, his attainment of enlightenment and the episodes connected with it; the Dhamma, or teachings; and the *Sangha*, or the order of monks,[9] make up the "threefold refuge" or the "three jewels" that govern Buddhism. The simple act of recit-ing: "I go for refuge to the Buddha, I go for refuge to the Dhamma, I go for refuge to the Sangha," makes it possible for one to declare himself a Buddhist. After such a declaration, the rest is up to the individual. Everything he does causally relates to his ulti-mate status in this and every other life that he will have until he attains the ultimate, *nibbana*. He requires neither church nor in-tercessor of any kind in order to arrive at this goal. His *kamma* is what he does—good and bad, to and for himself. As he gains fur-ther insight, does good, practices self-control, he can hasten his way on the Path. As he does bad, he delays himself. The various lives, human and other animal, which he may go through on the Way are his *Samsara*.

This self-responsible, moralistic conception of life has sometimes given rise to the view that Theravada Buddhism is a passive or permissive religion without love, without charity, without concern for humanity. "Let no man love anything . . . those who love nothing and hate nothing have no fetters" are among the words assigned to the Buddha. Such an interpretation violates the more profound meaning of Buddhism and disregards the experience pre-ceding the Buddha's First Sermon on the Middle Way. Prince Sid-dhattha had tried the path of austerity, of being a hermit, of, in effect, seeking his own salvation through complete withdrawal from the world, and he had found this wanting. His discourses, therefore, in the *Sutta-Pitaka* and in the *Vinaya-Pitaka*, not only emphasize one's individual actions, but also a social doctrine called **metta**. *Metta* requires active benevolence, active social participa-tion leading to the uplift of all. The individual does good, earns *kutho* (merit or worthiness), not only by observing the *Silas*, but also by aiding others to do so. The tradition of practicing *metta* toward every living thing resulted, in Theravada Buddhism, in the avoidance of those distinctions which in Hinduism led to the crystallizing of caste and class. Buddhism in its Theravada branch ignores differences of class, color, and creed.[10] In fact, at one time women were admitted to the order as bhikkhuni, or nuns. Women may be reborn in future lives as men; and only as males can they then attain Buddhahood. Over and over again Buddha preaches the rightness of charity, of cherishing kith and kin, of practicing "a boundless good will for all the world, above, below, across, in every way, good will unhampered, without ill-feelings or enmity." [11]

It has been said that "the two cardinal virtues of Buddhism are wisdom and love." [12] In discussing the latter, Pratt points out that the Buddha

. . . distinguishes clearly three attitudes of the mind which, in spite of their obvious difference, get themselves expressed in English by the word *love*. The first of these is sexual lust. The second is tender personal affection for an individual of a sort so strong and uncontrollable that it tends to occupy one's thought and make one's peace dependent on the loved one's presence, or at least on his life and welfare. The third meaning of *love* is earnest and even tender good will for all. . . . Now of these three kinds of love the Buddha sternly condemns the first, he regards the second as an unnecessary and avoidable opening to attacks of sorrow, and he approves thoroughly only the third.

Most Theravada Buddhists would endorse Pratt's analysis and judgment of the first and third kinds of love. With respect to the second kind of love, however, they would probably say that it would be rejected along with the first only insofar as it stood for uncontrollability and dependence. Insofar as it related to tenderness, consideration, and personal affection, it would be accepted and assimilated with the third. Love, in the sense of tenderness, consideration, and personal affection, is included in the individual and social doctrine of *metta*; it has been increasingly associated with the doctrine of *ahimsa*, or nonviolence; and all three—love, to use the Western word, or *metta* and *ahimsa*—are the ethical wellsprings for Buddhist attitudes on domestic polity as well as on problems of war and peace and international relations.[13]

Though the Buddha is not God—and in this sense Buddhism is agnostic or atheistic—there are gods in Buddhism. Buddhism has accommodated itself in practice to some aspects of the Hindu pantheon and to the animism or spirit worship that presumably was the original religion of those who were converted to Buddhism through the millennia. A highly committed Theravada Buddhist would probably say that animism, or, as it is known in Burma, nat worship, is an aspect of the customs of the untutored people, that it is not integral to Buddhism. However much this may be true in theory, in fact animist folk elements do exist in Theravada Buddhism and in Burma.[14] The very nature of the *Sutta-Pitaka*, with its legends, parables, and folk tales, encouraged such syncretism, a phenomenon common to all living religions. Originally a nat was a spiritual or real "feudal overlord." He was of an area and for a group of people. Like the Roman lares and penates or the local Christian saints, he could either protect or punish. He had power that could be won or lost.

Burmese Buddhism assimilated the nats or spirits of the Burmese folk religion. Frequent reference will be found in Burma to the thirty-seven nats, the chief ones, as being quite integrated in Buddhism. Actually, there are many times more than thirty-seven whose roles intimately affect the life of the Burmese.[15] There is little doubt that the overwhelming majority of Burmese Buddhists include the nats in their Buddhism. They are the local "saints" or "devils" whose holidays are observed in one or another festival throughout the land. U Nu lent his prestige to governmental participation in some of these nat festivals as well as to formal governmental observance of the festivals more commonly associated with the Buddha. Local shrines for the nats, where flowers or other offerings may be placed, are to be seen on any road in Burma. But such shrines are also regarded as *metta* offerings by Burmese Buddhists who tend to frown on nat worship. Attention to the nats is indicated in the symbolic good luck tokens placed on a house when it is being built. The Burmese use fruit or a coconut as we sometimes use a horseshoe. The nats are also involved in many Burmese folk tales.[16] They supply the local variations that one finds in most religions below the level of the highly sophisticated or austere practitioner.

J. S. Furnivall did not exaggerate in his summary of the role of Buddhism in Burma: "It is Buddhism that has moulded social Burman life and thought, and to the present day the ordinary Burman regards the terms Burman and Buddhist as practically equivalent and inseparable. The whole political and social life of Burma, from the palace to the village, centered around the Buddhist religion and monastic order." [17]

Buddhism suffered under British rule in Burma. The Sangha requested but did not receive permission to continue the royal institution of the Thathanabaing, or head of the Sangha. Responsible administration of pagoda endowments declined; holding of examinations in the Pali canon for monks lapsed; even discipline within the monasteries slackened. Burmese Buddhist scriptural and customary law—the law for the Burmese—where it was not completely disregarded was subordinated to English common law. Monastery education, which had made the Burmese one of the most literate of peoples at the beginning of the nineteenth century, was allowed to decline without the substitution of adequate secular education. Pagodas and other Buddhist shrines were officially ignored or were casually desecrated by the Western practice of wearing shoes in their sacred precincts. Little wonder then, in view of the devotion of the people to their religion, that Burmese Buddhist lay and clerical associations furnished the initial as well as a sustaining impulse for Burmese nationalism.[18]

U Nu seized on Buddhist tradition from conviction, and together with those of his Socialist and AFPFL colleagues in the Cabinet and in Parliament who appreciated its historical importance, set about revitalizing it. The political and economic ideologies, the scientific and technological education associated with the Western impact on Burma, did not inhibit this revival. Though the 1947 Constitution (Section 21) proclaimed the state's friendliness and hospitality to all religions, it accorded Buddhism a special position as the faith professed by a majority of the citizens of the Union. In September, 1961, by a constitutional amendment approved 324-28 by a joint session of Parliament, Buddhism was adopted as the state religion of Burma. This was announced by the sounding of the Maha Ganda, the 25-ton bronze merit gong in the Shwedagon Pagoda. The step fulfilled a campaign pledge made by U Nu in 1959. (When the military took over the government in 1962, it set aside the Constitution. Hence the legal status of Buddhism as the state religion is presently in question. In effect it has been disestablished.)

Early in the history of the Union, at the very height of the rebellion, Parliament enacted major legislation to improve the status of the Dhamma and the Sangha as well as to provide for Buddhist missions in Burma and elsewhere. The Ecclesiastical Courts Act of 1949 re-established the traditional authority of the Sangha to hold its own clerical courts and councils. The Pali University Act of 1950 appropriated funds for the restoration of instruction in Pali and the canon, and for the examination system designed to upgrade the Sangha and the *pongyikyaung*.* The Buddha Sasana Act of 1950 appropriated funds to support the activity of a lay society organized to promote the faith and to undertake home and other missions. In 1950, a Ministry of Religious Affairs was added to the Cabinet to represent it in all religious matters. In addition, many practices and programs of traditional Burmese Buddhist education affecting the distinctive role of the Sangha, which had been at a disadvantage in Burma ever since the final annexation of royal Burma in 1886, were publicly revived. Members of the government would probably deny that they wished to employ the assets of Buddhism as a counterfoil to Communism and other competing ideologies, for it is not proper so to employ Buddhism, but their denials would be a mere formality. Even before Parliament passed these

---

* After much public airing of the issue, the Revolutionary Council repealed these acts because of alleged abuses (*Working People's Daily*, January 19, 1965), and invited the leading Sayadaws to devise a new system (*ibid.*, May 12, 1965).

laws, it had approved and supported the Prime Minister's decision
to build the Kaba Aye, or the World Peace Pagoda, seven miles
north of the center of Rangoon, which was completed in March,
1952. A large undertaking, it carried its own meaning to those who
know Burmese history. Through the centuries, one of the first acts
of a righteous Burmese king or ruler has been to fulfill his religious
duty by building a pagoda. When U Nu, as an elected official of
the Union, decided to build the Kaba Aye Pagoda, he emphasized
the connection between central governing power and Buddhism.

Perhaps of even greater significance was the resolution of Parliament on October 1, 1951, to hold the Sixth World Buddhist
Council. This was to begin on full moon day, May, 1954, and to
last until full moon day, May, 1956. Five previous great councils
had been held during the history of Buddhism, the last one under
King Mindon in 1871.[19] Such councils are usually summoned to
clarify the meaning of the sacred writings and to serve as a source
of inspiration. The Sixth Council coincided with the celebration of
the end of the first half of the Buddhist cycle of five thousand
years. All the other Theravada Buddhist countries—Ceylon, Thailand, Laos, and Cambodia—accepted the responsibilities for the
holding of the council as a joint undertaking. Government officials
from these countries and regular Buddhist delegates were prominent in Burma throughout this period. So were the officials and
Mahayana Buddhist delegations from Japan, Communist China,
India, Indonesia, Tibet, Nepal, Sikkim, Ladakh, Vietnam, Assam,
the Andaman Islands, Pakistan, and Malaya, and even individual
Buddhists from non-Asian countries. Contacts established during
this biennium have been maintained by the Burmese. Thus far,
this has been the largest international effort that they have carried
out. Moreover, Burma, as host, appropriated some $2 million for
the construction of the necessary buildings near the Kaba Aye Pagoda, and decided that when the council had completed its labors
in 1956 a new scholarly Institute for Advanced Buddhistic Studies
should be organized there.

Prime Minister Nu attempted to enlist U.S. aid for this project,
but though he was sympathetically treated, it was decided that
support of the enterprise would violate the American principle of
separation of church and state. Paul Hoffman encouraged the active participation of the Ford Foundation in the work of the institute.

The new laws affecting Buddhism, the building of the World
Peace Pagoda, and the convening of the World Buddhist Council
were more than a demonstration of the ruling elite's attitude toward the religion of Burma. The Sixth Council showed how much
the nation as a whole was involved. The Sangha in Burma was
responsible for the clerical aspects of the council. Thousands of
monks came from all over Burma to take part in it.[20] Buddhist
laymen raised considerable sums of money, and several thousand

women and men attended to the daily cooking for the 2,500 learned monks who were the delegates to the council. Since the council continued for two years, this was no mean achievement.

Prior to independence, the political and religious leaders of the AFPFL would not brook the usual Communist antireligious and anticlerical activity.[21] In their early years of power, after 1948, they sought to reconcile their conception of Marxism with Buddhism.[22] But it was at the third AFPFL congress in 1958 that U Nu defined Marxism as Communism and rejected both because, among other reasons, they conflict with Buddhism.[23] His statement was approved by his full Cabinet.

Many other acts, both domestic and international, were associated with the Buddhist revival, including the endorsement and support of the World Fellowship of Buddhists, a type of Buddhist ecumenicity, and a more active missionary zeal among the animists in Burma. One of the most noteworthy acts took place in May, 1958, when the two rival factions in the AFPFL pledged themselves before a group of monks to abstain from violence in the conduct of their future opposition. Another was the publication in April, 1959, by Prime Minister Ne Win's caretaker government, of a national best seller, the *Dhammantaraya* (*Dhamma* [or Buddhism] *in Danger*).[24] This contained a slashing attack on the Burmese Communists for their anti-Buddhist, antireligious propaganda. It was accompanied by nationwide "exposition" meetings in which some 26,000 monks—probably 35 per cent of the total Sangha—participated. Finally, Buddhist organizations devoted to good works (*kutho* societies) and to meditation (*vipassana*, or insight, societies) have increased greatly, especially among the educated classes.

This is not to say that the Buddhist revival in Burma has been wholly consistent with the precepts of Buddhism. In practice, the abstentions called for by the Five Precepts are as much or as little observed as are religious commandments in other societies that have inherited religiously defined rules of conduct. Nevertheless, Buddhism has again become a growing and stabilizing force in Burma. As Buddhist concepts have been interpreted by contemporary Burmese, they are consistent both with the democratic and socialist aims of the government in power and they provide an ideological framework for opposition to Communism. To the extent that the government lent its resources to a renewal of the prestige of Buddhism and has fostered Buddhist behavior and ceremonial, it has won additional clerical and popular support against its opponents.

The Unity of the Three Leadership Groups

Every revolution is initiated by a group of leaders who, if successful, form the apex of a new structure of power and ideas. The nationalist-Marxist amalgam that formed the driving force of the

Burmese revolution was dominated by the Thakins who organized the Anti-Fascist People's Freedom League in 1944 and, as such, held power until 1958. The military leadership under General Aung San and Colonel Ne Win, which took shape in the war-time struggles, was itself an integral part of the Thakin movement. Both groups, political and military, maintained an uneasy relationship with a less powerful but nevertheless important group, the bureaucracy or civil service.

Largely as a result of the rebellions, each of these three leadership groups became more effectively organized at the center and because of their common danger, their members were forced to unite in order to sustain the government of the Union and to defend their own lives. Their understanding of the outside world was enhanced by the fact that the leaders in each group had had the benefits of Westernized education. With minor exceptions all of them speak English.

THE POLITICAL ELITE

On pages xxiii to xxvi of *Burma, the Tenth Anniversary,* published by the government in January, 1958, there appear thirty photographs of the ministers in U Nu's Cabinet. They include, constitutionally, the five ministers for the several states and one division (Shan, Karen, Kachin, Kayah, and Chin), and twenty-five other well-known nationalist and socialist figures. Among them are the then big four, Prime Minister Nu and his three Deputy Prime Ministers—U Ba Swe, U Kyaw Nyein, and Thakin Tin—leading Muslims, such as U Raschid and U Khin Maung Lat, and other minority leaders. Each Cabinet since independence had, by plan, been similarly representative. Altogether, in ten years, about fifty different men had held Cabinet positions.

The persistence with which these leaders held Cabinet posts over a decade might mean no more than that the top political echelon chose to play political musical chairs while sharing the rewards of office among themselves and with their followers. This is not a novel feature of political life in democratic countries. But, there is another aspect to the question. Most of these men, and their immediate associates, were among the nationalists who fought for independence during and after the war. Many of them won their spurs in the student strike of 1936 and in the prewar nationalist organizations that supported trade unions and peasant groups. Some of them were founding members of the Thakin movement in the early 1930's. Whatever their faults or mistakes, these men have always been identifiable as Burmese patriots. They share a common past, and their reaction to the Communist threat and to other rebellions not only united them for a time but also gradually clarified their policy; in time, they also came to share a general socialist ideology, never very precisely defined and usually put forward to the public as general principles and statements of objectives.

The AFPFL was their political instrument, and it dominated the political life of the country. Differences existed, and these, as we shall see, were to prove disastrous for the AFPFL in 1958. But, until the split, these socialists knew at first hand what it meant to fight together against Communist subversion, infiltration, and rebellion. They had democratically voted the Communists out of their alliance in 1946; had not hesitated to fight the insurrectionists after March, 1948; and had easily weathered the formal withdrawal of the crypto-Communists from the alliance in 1950. They, not the Communists, succeeded in reorganizing and retaining control over the economic and other organizations of workers and cultivators. They stayed up late at meetings; they organized the supporting groups and political institutions in the countryside that advanced alongside of or immediately behind the military. They traveled the country and did not flinch before the ever-present dangers. In 1951-52 and in 1956 they gave to the Burmese electorate a sense of their power—not always wisely used—and a sense of direction and unity, which the Burmese people had not enjoyed under the earlier colonial constitutions (and elections) of 1923 and 1937. For the first ten years of independence, their political leadership in and out of the Parliament provided a strong sense of unity before which the disease of Burmese political divisiveness gave way. Despite the seemingly bewildering number of party labels under which candidates ran in the elections of 1951-52 and 1956, the real political contests were quite clearly between the AFPFL leadership and two other groups—the crypto-Communist and other "left" splinters, and various right wings. The combined opposition to the AFPFL never achieved more than 25 per cent of the seats of the 250-member Parliament, though their popular vote in the 1956 elections was considerably higher. Even the split of 1958, which in the long run was to prove fatal, did not immediately displace the AFPFL, but merely divided it into two unequal parts. Two of the big four, U Nu and Thakin Tin, defeated the other two, U Ba Swe and U Kyaw Nyein, overwhelmingly in the 1960 elections, and simultaneously weakened both the parliamentary and popular support of the left and right opposition.

THE ARMED FORCES

British military tradition in colonial India and Burma had at least three main characteristics. The top echelon of the officer cadre (until 1935-37, when the Act of India was passed) had to be both white and British. The junior and noncommissioned officers were recruited from the so-called martial races, in keeping with a nineteenth-century psychobiological fantasy prevalent in British and other quarters. The general troops and military police were recruited from among the ethnic minorities in the colonies so as to insure better protection against the untrusted majority. Although the Burmese gave a good account of themselves at war with the British in the early nineteenth century and displayed great skill in jungle or guerrilla fighting until the pacification of Burma was accomplished by the mid-1890's, "the view that the Burman will never be a soldier" lasted until the eve of World War II.[25] The Burmans unsuccessfully protested against this policy, and the Thakins realized that they had to reverse it if they were to play a significant role in turning the British out of Burma.[26]

A combination of Burmese pre-British tradition, Marxist strategy, and Japanese training gave rise to the Thirty Comrades under the leadership of Aung San. This group in turn gave birth to the Burma Independence Army, the subsequent Japanese-controlled Burma Defense Army, and the Burma National Army, or Burma Patriotic Forces (BPF), which became the military component in the anti-Japanese resistance, and which helped to bring the AFPFL into existence in 1944. Of the Thirty Comrades, only General Ne Win and Major Ba La were still in the armed forces by 1960. But the officer cadre, especially the colonels, who played so prominent a role in Burma between 1958 and the elections in 1960, was composed largely of men who won their military and political spurs during and immediately after World War II: General Ne Win; Brigadier Tin Pe; Colonels Maung Maung, Aung Gyi, Kyi Maung, Chit Khine, Khin Nyo, and Kyi Win; Lieutenant Colonels Aye Maung and Win; and former Brigadier Kyaw Zaw. Immediately after the war, they were joined by such others as the late Vice-Chief of Staff (Navy) Than Pe and Vice-Chief of Staff (Air Force) T. Clift (Ret.), who had remained loyal to the Allied Forces. By agreement with Bogyoke Aung San, these officers continued in their military careers after the war and after independence was assured. They were given the responsibility of building the government's armed forces. When the insurrections broke out, they remained loyal to the Union.

Without this military leadership and a small group of loyal field officers and junior officers and men, the Union could not have survived the initial attacks of the Communist and Karen insurrectionists. Yet the army leaders were not only a military elite. Like the socialist AFPFL political leadership, they participated in the struggle for independence and were known in the countryside as Burmese patriots. They could and did attract support even after the military units of the Karens and Communists defected. Typical of these men was their leader, General Ne Win, who had been a Thakin before he became a Bo, or military leader, and who since 1932 had participated in every phase of the development of the ardent nationalist movement. During the desperate and intricate peace maneuvers between the AFPFL government and the insurrectionists in the spring of 1949, he agreed to serve in U Nu's Cabinet as Deputy Prime Minister and Minister of Home Affairs and of Defense.[27]

In the early years of the insurrection, at least half the national revenue was spent on anti-insurrectionary activity. Although the regular armed forces had equipment for only a few battalions, and had only a few planes and ships with which to fight back, they did make headway slowly and surely. As a result, General Ne Win and the colonels have not had any problem since in securing funds and recruiting personnel to build a force of approximately 125,000 officers and men. It is significant that until the Educational Reorganization Plan was inaugurated in November, 1964, of the three Burmese undergraduate colleges in Rangoon, Mandalay, and Maymyo, the one at Maymyo, founded by Ne Win in 1954 for the training of future officers, and formally opened by Prime Minister Nu on February 14, 1955, was the best in terms of its academic standards. General Ne Win left the University of Rangoon before completing his science degree, as did a number of the officers who joined with the Thakins in the late 1930's. But these men were determined that Burma's armed forces, from the enlisted men to senior officers chosen to attend the newly opened (1964) National Defense in-service educational program, should reflect Burma's traditional appreciation of education and training. For this reason, as well as for their well-established devotion to the cause of achieving and preserving the independence of the Union, they have won the respect of the Burmese population.[28]

THE (PRE-COUP) BUREAUCRACY OR CIVIL SERVICE

The visible symbol of bureaucracy in Burma is the old secretariat building in Rangoon, a sprawling, unattractive Victorian structure. This, up to 1962, was the center of the administration. The Burmese retained the main features of the Indian Civil Service (ICS) that administered Burma during colonial days. The secretariat consists of the senior career officers who serve their respective Cabinet ministers, attend Cabinet meetings when their subjects are discussed, and run the machinery of the ministries and specialized departments within the ministries. Their procedure is governed by the Secretariat Code framed in British times and largely unchanged, despite the advice given by at least three outside missions of public-administration experts. Secretaries and those with equivalent rank—in contrast to civil service specialists in various departments—are subject to rotation among the ministries and between the capital and the districts, though this is growing less frequent. Section 221 of the former Constitution required that a Parliamentary Public Service Commission serve "in matters relating to recruitment . . . and to advise in disciplinary matters."

By the beginning of World War II, approximately seventy-five

Burmese had attained a rank in the coveted Indian Civil or Police Service, Class I; they were roughly one-third the total number in that class. Members of this restricted group were required to have a university education and to have passed relatively difficult examinations. A second group of approximately 2,500 Burmese and Indian civil service officers were regarded as having a lower status because they were not admitted to the ICS. The ICS and this second, larger group were merged at independence to form the single Burma Civil Service (BCS). Their number, inevitably, has grown as the business of government has expanded. A third group consisted of junior or branch post and clerical workers; it was these employees, members of the Ministerial Services Union, who went on strike during the insurrection in February, 1949.

At the time when Burma achieved independence, considerable suspicion existed between the new political leaders and the Burmese civil servants. ICS personnel had "served" the British, and because of the civil service tradition they were nonpolitical. In that period, to be nonpolitical was to be regarded as non-nationalist. In addition, within the newly created Burma Civil Service there was much friction, based upon presumed differences of status and education, between those who had won their appointments in the ICS and those who had not. But time and experience during the insurrections have diminished the suspicion and friction. Burmese civil servants, especially those in the middle and upper ranks, have carried forward the tradition of the earlier services. Even during the most difficult days they stayed at their posts in and outside the capital; they served and were loyal to the beleaguered government because it was the government. In some cases, civil servants known to be loyal to the central government were asked by the insurrectionists to continue on duty when the insurrectionists were temporarily in control of a particular locality. This was partly because the insurrectionists had few trained civil servants among their followers, and partly because they, too, accepted the nonpolitical tradition of the civil service.

Despite occasional difficulties, the career service, especially the secretaries and near-equivalent ranks, continues to hold third place, after the political and military leadership groups, in the preservation of the Union. Significantly, when General Ne Win, as Premier, organized his "nonpolitical" Cabinet in October, 1958, he chose the Chief Secretary of Government, U Khin Maung Pyu, and several others of equivalent rank to serve as his ministers. This did not happen after the 1962 coup. However, the civil service, inhibited, no doubt, by the military in general and by frequent military counterparts attached to ministries and departments, still carries out the administrative burdens of policy.

These three elite lay groups—the politicians, the armed forces, and the civil service—were able to forge a united front with which to oppose and eventually wear down the many but uncoordinated thrusts of the assorted Communist and Karen rebels, and to handle the attacks of the Kuomintang.

The Four Strengths of the Government

The preservation of the Union was maintained through the revival of Buddhism, which won the support of the *pongyis* and lay Buddhist societies, through the charismatic leadership of U Nu, backed by the then unity of the three government leadership groups, and, finally, because the government, despite its shortcomings, acted in a manner that was generally approved by the Burmese people. There were four basic elements in the conduct of the government that gained the support of the countryside.

First, it made successful appeals to Burman and Burmese nationalism and patriotism in language noted for its free-wheeling expression, although, characteristically, the phrasing is softened when it is translated into English. The various rebels were charged, in U Nu's pungent and oft-repeated phrase, with "listening to a distant aunt" (understood as Moscow-Peking) instead of "to their mother." Their followers were "seduced by Pied Pipers," i.e., the domestic Communists. In more positive terms, a rapid process of economic and cultural Burmanization was initiated without, however, threatening the cultural autonomy of the loyal ethnic minorities. Burmese citizens got jobs formerly held by foreigners. Burmese folkways were revived or strengthened. National, nationalist, and religious holidays were celebrated in ways that enhanced the prestige of the national government. Burmese increasingly replaced English as the official language in Parliament and the courts, in the schools through the first two years of college, and in the conduct of the government's domestic affairs. A quasi-public, government-underwritten organization, the Burma Translation Society (BTS), was sponsored to translate, publish, and widely distribute works in Burmese, which were then donated to schools and public libraries and sold to the public at reasonable prices. A well-staffed Ministry of Information—whose Secretary in these early years was U Thant, now Secretary-General of the United Nations—made full use of the government-owned Burma Radio and had easy access to publishing facilities.

Second, these activities were not confined to cities and towns. As military victories made it possible for the government to advance into the surrounding countryside and to sustain its gains by night as well as by day, the government restored the normal instruments of administration and brought new public services, propaganda campaigns, and appeals to patriotism. Ministerial and other officials followed closely in the wake of the military to renew the ties between the central government and local leaders and civil servants. They likened the rebels to the dacoits who attacked villagers and townspeople whenever the central authority was weak. As the writ of the government was pushed forward, the people could feel that they were being protected from the new dacoits—the rebels.

Third, even during the worst months of the insurrection, the government fulfilled its role abroad and at home. It quickly established a diplomatic service, appointing well-known nationalist figures—among them, U Pe Kin, U Win, U Myint Thein, U Hla Maung, U Kyin—as its first ambassadors. With appropriate fanfare, it received and sent abroad accredited diplomatic missions. It promptly applied for admission and was voted into the United Nations. It participated in a variety of regional and international conferences, some of which led to Burma's cosponsorship of the Asian Socialist Conference held in Rangoon in 1953 and the Colombo Powers Meeting of 1954, which led to the April, 1955, Bandung Conference. It secured loans from members of the British Commonwealth and negotiated aid agreements with the United States, the United Nations, and the Colombo Plan powers. Despite its fear of Communist China, its representatives in the United Nations voted affirmatively for the major U.N. resolution directed against aggression in Korea; they later carried to the United Nations the government's complaint against the Kuomintang Chinese whose troops were cooperating with the rebels.

At home, the government provided for the refugees from insurrectionary-held areas and supplied them with food and shelter until they could return to their villages. It organized a center at Aung San Myo, where defectors, captives, and ex-rebels, together with their families, were housed, fed, and given training in manual and mechanical skills. Many of them were then given employment in the Rehabilitation Brigade. Although the rebels repeatedly damaged railways and water and electric-power lines, the government managed to restore service. Free schooling through the professional level was made available, though standards were lowered because of the too-rapid increase in the numbers of students admitted to make up for the wartime gap. Free or reasonably priced hospital and medical services were supplied in the larger towns, and large-scale public-health campaigns were initiated against malaria, tuberculosis, and venereal diseases. Programs and centers for maternity and child welfare were established by a partnership of government and one of the largest voluntary social-service agencies in the country, the National Council of Maternity and Child Welfare, headed by Aung San's widow, Daw Khin Kyi.

For the most part, the government backed the constitutional guarantees of freedom of the press, speech, and assembly. Parliament continued to meet regularly and acted constitutionally. The courts, especially the national High and Supreme Courts—the latter equivalent to the U. S. Supreme Court—exhibited standards of experience and conduct that won high esteem. Corruption and bribery were punished when discovered and were generally much less evident than in the last years of the British regime. The Bureau of Special Investigation was created, attached to the Premier's office, for the purpose of ferreting out official misconduct. In sum, the machinery of government continued to function in Rangoon and in the divisional and district organizations outside the capital. National leaders traveled widely and frequently throughout the country and addressed many public meetings. The insurgents could make claims, but the government in Rangoon had the inestimable advantage of being visibly, and increasingly, in power.

These three strengths of the government—its command of communications and its appeals to the nationalism and patriotism of the Burmese; its ability to serve the countryside as its military advanced; and its performance as a government at home and abroad —were reinforced and to some extent enveloped by a fourth strength, its commitment to what came to be known as "Pyidawtha," Happy Land, or, freely translated, "welfare state." (Pyidawtha is discussed in detail in Chapter 7.) The Burmese Constitution set forth the outlines of such a state in the rather unusual sections devoted to the "Directive Principles of State Policy" (Sections 32-44). In these, the government promised to work to secure for each citizen "the right to work," "the right to maintenance in old age and during sickness," the "right to rest and leisure . . . [and] education." Section 41 required planning the economy "with the aim of increasing public wealth, of improving the material conditions of the people and raising their cultural level."

Efforts to implement the constitutional provisions were begun by Aung San a month before his assassination in July, 1947. The basic principles of Pyidawtha came out of the Sorrento Villa Conference, which he convened, and which published its findings in 1948 as the Two-Year Plan of Economic Development for Burma. This fifty-five-page statement of aspirations gave the government a program on which it could set to work. Since Burma is a food-exporting country in a food-deficit area and is relatively underpopulated, the new regime started with an economic advantage. In addition, it benefited from the wartime elimination of the hated Indian caste *chettyars*, who had acquired control of considerable farmlands in prewar Burma.

Since the *chettyars* were not allowed to return to Burma after the war and since the government expropriated their properties with promises of limited compensation, there was more land available for the landless than could be adequately farmed. The first Land Nationalization Act was passed in 1948. Industrialization and a diversified economy were promised as part of the Two-Year Plan.

Thus, even in socio-economic terms, the Communist rebels had little to offer the Burmese that the existing government had not already proposed. It is true that the rebellion was effective enough to cause a sharp decline in the gross domestic product from 72 per cent in fiscal year 1947-48 (1938-39 = 100 per cent, in constant prices of 1947-48) to 61 per cent in 1949-50. It also contributed to a sharp rise in domestic prices, from 294 (1941 = 100 per cent) in 1948 to 397 in 1949. But by October, 1952, the gross domestic product had risen to 74 per cent, and prices in the same period had declined to 306. When the government convened its historic Pyidawtha conference, August 4-17, 1952, it could not only emphasize the continuity of its promises, but could also point to their partial but steady fulfillment.

In 1950, U Nu found time to write a dramatic account of Burma's fight against Communist insurrection and subversion.[29] The play, an example of the literary-political genre known as agit-prop (agitation and propaganda) in the 1930's, is called *Ludu Aungthun,* freely translated as *The People Win Through.* This, despite the tragedy and the loss incurred during more than a decade of insurrectionary activity, is what has occurred in Burma through the first dozen years of independence.

7 · PYIDAWTHA: THE BUILDING OF A WELFARE STATE

BEFORE DISCUSSING ECONOMIC planning and development in Burma, it is necessary to examine the Burmese political economy as it was before and after the British conquest and as it became after independence. Such an examination is important for greater understanding of nationalist agitation against the "colonial economy," the determination after independence to restore and to adapt traditional Burmese social patterns and values, and the contribution made by the Pyidawtha Plan to the preservation of the Union.

A Traditional Society with a Subsistence Economy

Prior to the wars with the Honorable Company, the Kingdom of Burma had evolved a rather successful subsistence economy with adequate food, fiber, and shelter produced and reasonably well distributed except in times of severe domestic strife or natural catastrophes. This economy was based on rich natural resources, a low ratio of population to land,[1] and a quasi-feudal organization of society. Between 3 and 4 million people inhabited the area roughly equivalent to Burma today. Their social organization was an intricate complex of personal allegiances regulated by customary law dating back to the thirteenth century.[2]

Burma was a society without castes or extremes of economic-class differentiation, and one in which state and church were intimately entwined. Royalty, recognized as the defender of the faith, possessing in theory absolute secular power, inhabiting the quasi-sacred precincts of the palace and its grounds, constituted the only acknowledged hereditary nobility, excepting the princes and chiefs of the Shan and vassal states.

The polygamous king and his family owned extensive royal lands

and held title to all unoccupied land. The king retained certain
highly profitable trade monopolies, received revenues from taxes,
awarded grants of land and other benefits in lieu of salary to re-
tainers and civil servants, and commanded the services of various
sections of the population. In all matters of the realm except those
affecting the Sangha, the king was aided by an appointed State
Council, or Hlutdaw, of four ministers, or Wungyis (great-burden
bearers), and by a palace secretariat, or Byedaik, supervised by four
to eight Atwinwuns (inferior-burden bearers). In practice the
Hlutdaw wielded considerable power; one member had the duty of
questioning the king's decision without fear of royal punishment.
These officers and their supporting staffs had counterparts in the
provinces, appointed by the king. The local official to whom the
Crown assigned the revenues of a provincial area was frequently
called the Myosa (eater of the province).

These officials were responsible for executive and judicial administration, and regulated the domestic economy and external trade.
The only laws were the edicts issued by the Hlutdaw in the name
of the king.[3] Members of the royal services did not constitute a
nobility. They and the military officers held their positions of
power at the pleasure of the king, and admission to their ranks was
open to any qualified male. Literacy was widespread in Burma,
since the monastery schools were open to every male child and
attendance was a religious duty. Advanced instruction in nonreligious subjects was provided in major population centers for all who
wished it, and education, however limited, was a door to advancement.

Coexistent with the secular power, but even more intimately
connected with the lives and work of the people, was the Sangha.
The Sangha and the institutions under its control—the pagodas,
shrines, libraries, monasteries, and schools—were free from secular
interference, even by the king himself. The king appointed and
could remove from office the chief monk, the *thathanabaing*. But
once appointed, this supreme ecclesiastical officer and his representative council of monks had full powers in all matters relating to
Buddhism, and these powers were further enhanced by Burmese
custom. For example, the monasteries offered sanctuary for life and
property. The *pongyi* was "the guardian of religion, the depositary
of learning, the instructor of the young, the spiritual adviser of the
elderly and aged." Nor did he hesitate to intervene in secular matters whenever he believed that some act of the administration con-
travened Buddhist and Burmese standards of right conduct.[4] The
Burmese Government supplied the heads of monasteries with
copies of all royal orders and acts. The *pongyis* were a major channel from the Crown to the people.

In return for its many services, the king, the royal officials, and
the people supported the Sangha with subsistence allowances, land,
revenues, donations, and services. Thus church and state in Burma

had evolved a sturdy interdependent relationship, each reinforcing the other, especially during the nineteenth-century struggles against British imperialism and the twentieth-century rise of nationalism.

The overwhelming majority of the people of Burma, then as now, lived in villages and rural tracts. But their governmental or administrative structure was different from what it became under the British. In the time of the kings, these villages, unlike the self-contained Indian villages, frequently were highly differentiated in social structure and occupations. It was here that the quasi-feudal character of the society appeared most prominently. For all villagers by birth or marriage belonged to an order or recognized grouping known as *athin,* or *asu.* These orders lived in villages that were either wholly charged with one function, such as being members of the king's cavalry or footsoldiers, or being weavers, potters, or rice farmers; or that housed several orders. In general, all *athin* groupings belonged to one or the other of the two major divisions of the population: *ahmudan* and *athi.* The former outranked the latter, but mobility between the two was entirely possible. The *ahmudan* consisted of those who fulfilled their duty to the state in a military or an economic service capacity. (Military service outranked economic service.) In return, they were provided with land or other perquisites for their services. The *athi* consisted primarily of cultivators who paid revenue or other taxes, usually in kind, were subject to call for miscellaneous services in their area, and could be drafted for military duty in time of war. The *ahmudan,* whether its subgroup members resided in their own or in a mixed-order village, was usually governed by its own personal leaders or officers. The *athi* was usually governed by an hereditary or chosen headman, the *thugyi.*[5] In the main, the social, rather than the territorial, relationships generated by this system determined the governance and the economy of the country. The *thugyi* and the *pongyi* gave social stability and normative leadership to the villages even in times of national disruption.

For the most part, the villagers could depend upon the self-sustaining character of the economy. Land was plentiful and relatively easily acquired, whether irrigated, as in the more populated dry-zone granary area, or watered by the monsoon rains in the less populated portions of the country. Despite the complexities of the social organization, land tenures were, as Nisbet writes, "essentially allodial. The Burmese agriculturists were peasant proprietors."[6] However, they were taxed in goods and services. Agriculture, as today, was the chief economic activity, supported by some mining, salt-boiling, fisheries, and the crafts, skills, and trades necessary to maintain household and village life. Barter prevailed for the predominantly noncoinage domestic trading patterns. The local economy was essentially complementary: rice, salt, pickled and dried fish from the delta were taken up the rivers to the central and hill areas and there exchanged for oils, sugar, saltpeter, lime, paper, lacquer ware, mineral goods, pulses, and, above all, cotton and silk goods.[7]

Prior to the wars with Britain, traders from abroad had sought Burma's exports of teak, cotton, lac, cutch, ivory, wax, earth and wood oils, lead, tin, amber, jade, seeds, indigo, and occasionally precious jewels and rice. Except for King Mindon,[8] the Burmese kings who followed Alaungpaya were suspicious of or indifferent to the traders. In a delightfully frank and admittedly exaggerated chapter, Gouger writes that "one would argue, from the state of the laws, that the Government had the definite object in view completely to exclude any commercial intercourse with other countries." [9]

The Burmese were not in principle or by law opposed to international commerce. As both Harvey and Furnivall point out, their ideas of trade "resembled, in essence, those underlying the Mercantile Theory, and there was much to be said for some of them at the time." [10] From the beginning to the end of the kingdom they continued to exchange goods with nearby trading partners. Their kings had typically expressed cautious willingness to trade with the more eager Europeans, while denying to all of them the usually sought-after monopoly.[11] But foreign trade was not highly regarded in dynastic Burma. Her people, including the conquered Mons of the seacoast, were not widely ranging seafarers. Her kings, except for the Toungoo dynasty that based itself at the former Mon seaport capital of Pegu, preferred to build their capitals in the irrigated central dry zone, at Pagan, Ava, Amarapura, Sagaing, Shwebo, and Mandalay. The first two Anglo-Burmese wars of 1824-26 and 1852, resulting in the British conquest and annexation of Arakan, Tenasserim, and Pegu (Lower Burma), made the remaining Upper Burma a landlocked kingdom and prevented any redirection of policy as contemplated by King Mindon.

Burma's Progress as a Colonial Extractive Economy

The British annexation of the provinces of Tenasserim and Arakan after 1826 did not initially bring the expected increase in domestic production, commerce, and population. At one time British officials in the area proposed that Tenasserim be restored to the Kingdom because it was not a profitable possession.[12] In time, however, the British converted Moulmein into a profitable port town, chief city of the province, given over to the milling of teak and shipbuilding. Between 1830 and 1855, 123 vessels were built in its yards. The tin mines found in the areas surrounding Tavoy and Mergui had been long worked on a modest scale, but were not to prove attractive to British interests throughout the century.[13] The British encouraged immigration of Chinese and Indians into the Tenasserim because of its sparse population. Among the Indians were the soldiers, clerks, town and mill laborers, and junior civil servants, already familiar with the British administrative system of India, as well as a caste of moneylenders—*chettyars*. The Chinese engaged in local commerce and mining. By 1852, perhaps one-third of Moulmein's 40,000 population were Indians. This was the beginning of a studied British policy, which by the beginning of World War II had resulted in a large proportion of Indians[14] and, to a lesser extent, Chinese, in the economy of Burma.

The Arakan city of Akyab, converted to a free port after 1826, began to thrive on its trade with British India, based largely on exports of rice, hides, horns, and salt, and the imports of British or Indian textiles, cutlery, and crockery.[15] Acreage under cultivation in British Burma, mostly paddy (unhusked rice), grew from 104,000 in 1830 to 530,000 in 1855, while the price of 100 baskets of paddy went from 8 rupees in 1845 to 45 rupees in 1855.[16] In the quarter-century period the population doubled.

When the British annexed the province of Pegu after the Second Anglo-Burmese War of 1852, they gained a continuous possession from the Bay of Bengal on the west to the southwestern borders of Thailand on the east. Though "the pacification of Pegu and its reduction to order occupied about ten years of constant work," [17] by the end of the century Rangoon had become "the third seaport in British India, being only surpassed by Calcutta and Bombay in the volume and extent of its trade." [18]

The increase in Burma's trade was due, first, to the productivity of the vast lands at the mouths of the Irrawaddy, Sittang, and Salween rivers, and of the alluvial land sloping westward from the Arakan Mountains. From less than 1 million acres in 1855, rice lands in Lower Burma had increased to 1.7 million acres by 1870, and between then and 1930, the area under paddy grew by an average of 1.2 million acres in each decade for a total of 9.9 million acres.[19] By the 1930's, Burma was fourth among the world's rice producers and the largest rice exporter. Rice was grown on 70 per cent of the cultivated land.

A second reason for the growth of Burma's trade was the use of steam for converting paddy into milled rice and timber into sawed wood. In 1867, there were 3 steam rice mills; by 1940, there were 673. Steam-run sawmills grew from 22 in 1878 to 116 in 1940. The use of steamships and the opening of the Suez Canal in 1869—the third factor favoring the rapid growth of trade—meant that Burma's exports could now be carried to markets even more distant than India and China without the long, slow voyages of earlier days.

Timber growing ranked second to rice, and Burma became the leading exporter of teak. Timber production increased more than seven times over between 1870 and 1940, from approximately 70,000 tons per year to 525,000 tons. Cultivation of a few other crops such as oilseeds, vegetable oils, cotton, sugar, and tobacco also increased. In the twentieth century, oil and other minerals were produced and exported on a growing scale.[20]

The accelerated growth of this predominantly agricultural economy, accompanied by the milling and processing of its products, won the approbation of the British rulers. Chief Commissioner of British Burma, Albert Fytche, writing at the end of the 1870's, remarked that "if the commerce of India bore the same proportion to population [as it did in Burma], it would be ten times greater than it is." [21] He also expressed the hope that the Government of India would attend to the further development of "this province which, in all reasonable probability, has a greater future before it than any country in Asia." British approbation was also tinged with pleased surprise. The authors of *The British Burma Gazetteer* concluded:

> To the existence of an abundance of good land, to the facility with which rights over it can be acquired, to the great demand for its produce and the still greater local demand for European goods, to the, if higher than formerly as the peasants assert, yet fixed taxation and the cessation of all irregular and uncertain collections, and to the absolute personal security enjoyed by all under the English administration are due the increase in population, the astonishing increase in the revenue, the still more astonishing increase in trade which . . . have taken place since British Burma became British territory.[22]

The annexation of Upper Burma in 1886 added to this sanguine picture. Nisbet, writing at the turn of the century, noted that "this agricultural prosperity" had not yet approached "within even distant view of the ultimate limits to which expansion of cultivation is possible. . . . So far as the possibility of future supplies for export are concerned, the rice trade of Burma may still be considered as merely in a state of normal development; and the nearly two million tons now exported will increase and be multiplied according as Burma's greatest want, population, is supplied." [23] He concluded that "the province is already one of the brightest jewels in the Imperial diadem of India; and its lustre will increase in proportion as inducements are offered for the influx of the capital and the labour necessary for more rapid development in the immediate future." [24]

The inducements were offered. Agriculture, forestry, and mining contributed the primary products that constituted the overwhelming portion of Burma's economy. Industry was largely confined to the milling and processing connected with this predominantly extractive enterprise.[25] For the decade prior to World War II, the total value of exports, mainly rice, teak and other hardwoods, oil and its by-products, silver, lead, zinc, tin, and tungsten, was more than double the value of imports. Burma enjoyed a favorable balance of trade.[26]

During these same years, revenue receipts, the largest single item of which came from the land, comfortably exceeded expenditures.[27] Burma was indeed a profitable colony. But a large share of the profits were sent abroad as overseas remittances, pensions, and dividends, or were held as undistributed profits for potential investment in Burma and elsewhere.[28] "Nation-building services," according to an official British study completed in 1943 but published later, were "sacrificed to an undue extent in favor of the more purely administrative services." [29]

Burma's Dislocation as a Colonial Extractive Economy

In the words of John L. Christian, who knew Burma well and usually wrote in sympathy with liberal British opinion, "the Burman wasn't happy. Progress and the new economic life had left him pretty much a bystander in his own country. In all this development the Burman had little share." [30] Foreign trade, both exports and imports, gravitated almost exclusively into British or other European, Indian, or Chinese hands. The other major sectors of the economy—agriculture, mining, industry, communications, power, and banking—were also owned and controlled by European (chiefly British) and Indian capital. The Chinese were a low third in this race. Not even in the capital city of Rangoon was there "a single banking, insurance, shipping, manufacturing or import firm of any size . . . owned or managed by Burmese." [31] Burmese ownership and entrepreneurship were reduced to small mills, local bazaar trade, handicraft and cottage industry. The economic success of the British in opening Burma to trade and development after the Suez Canal had become available for international commerce has accurately been called a "pioneer" effort.[32] But the success was matched by the growing distress of the Burmese, without whose basic contribution this success would not have been possible. For many reasons, some of which have already been indicated, the Burmese did not, in any substantial numbers, get into industry, trade, the professions, the white-collar private or governmental services, the army, or the police. Throughout the period of British rule, at least seven out of ten Burmese remained in some way connected with the land.[33] Since the Burmese originally came from a subsistence economy, they did not have the capital for the development of their country's major resources. They were unacquainted with Western business methods and lacked the overseas contacts on which foreign commerce thrives. The opening of the Delta to rice cultivation found them as willing in-migrants and cultivators working at what they knew. They began in traditional Burmese fashion as peasant proprietors, "holding" or "owning" the land while they "used" it. But the demand for rice transformed subsistence into commercial agriculture and required capital for the exploitation of the one cash crop. The capital, loans to tide the cultivators over the seven months' growing season and for other purposes, came mainly from the *chettyars*. The *chettyars* were spread out through some 1,400 firms with approximately 1,900 offices[34] throughout the village-tract and township areas, chiefly in Lower Burma.

This combination of Burmese peasant proprietor and Indian *chettyar* capital under a British administrative and legal system that guaranteed protection for the loans secured by mortgages resulted in disaster for the Burmese. Burmese sweat plowed, planted, reaped the "interminable [Delta] plain, 180 miles long, 150 wide" [35]—more than 90 per cent of which was devoted to rice cultivation. Burmese labor reclaimed the land from swamp and jungle. "The conversion . . . into fertile paddy land was an epic of bravery and endurance on the part of the Burmese cultivator who was then [in the earlier days] generally a settler from Upper Burma." [36] But the Burmese did not retain the land they cleared and cultivated. During the first half of the twentieth century, particularly during times of depression, they gradually lost their land to the suppliers of annual and short-term credit. In this process the Burmese peasant proprietor, more frequently than not, ended up as a dispossessed, rootless sharecropping tenant or farm laborer.[37]

After the opening of the Suez Canal, British Burma adopted a variety of land-tenure devices in order to attract settlers to the Delta. The Lower Burma Land and Revenue Act of 1876 recognized a form of squatter's rights akin to the pre-British Burma system of clearing and holding land by working it (*damaugya*), provided the cultivator paid land revenue for a period of twelve years.[38] However, the pioneer as well as the later settler "needed money for food, expenses of cultivation, for reclaiming and improving his land and for the purchase of [work] cattle and seed grains." [39] Thus arrived the trader and moneylender, some Chinese and Burmese, but mainly Indian *chettyars*. Agricultural credit was necessary and expensive. Even by Eastern standards the interest rates were frequently usurious, ranging to 45 per cent annually on fixed security (e.g., land, gold, jewels). Short-term loans against the harvests could rise to five and six times that interest rate, depending upon time factors. (The briefer loan period extracted higher rates.)[40] In good times with rising prices for rice,[41] the cultivator could pay off a considerable portion of his debts. But some debt remained, and it usually grew. In bad times, as long as land was still plentiful in the Delta, he could move on to a new holding, hoping to escape his debt and to acquire ownership by a change in economic fortunes. But as available Delta land became cleared and occupied, the peasant proprietor lost his land.

Land alienation became acute. The Burma Provincial Banking Enquiry Committee revealed in 1930 that 1.3 million acres had been transferred from peasant ownership to resident and absentee landlords. In more detailed fashion, the *Report of the Land and Agriculture Committee, 1938–1939*, showed that by 1937, 5.3 mil-

lion acres, or 48 per cent of occupied agricultural land in Lower
Burma, was owned by nonagricultural landlords. In Upper Burma,
16 per cent of 6.9 million acres was so owned. The figures for total
tenancy were even more alarming, for some of the occupied agricultural land was worked by landlords and tenants. Tenancy in
Lower Burma climbed to 58 per cent and in Upper Burma to 33
per cent. In some of the chief rice-growing districts nonagricultur-
ists owned as much as 71 per cent of the total agricultural land.
And in the thirteen principal rice-growing districts, the *chettyar*
moneylending community owned 50 per cent of the area held by
nonresident landlords, or 25 per cent of the total occupied land.[42]
Upper Burma, with a less productive and more diversified economy, suffered less than Lower Burma.

Thus the depression years after 1929, the slump in prices of rice,
the drying up of local credit facilities, and the foreclosures on Burmese cultivators, doubling the amount of acreage which went to
the absentee landlords between 1929-37, contributed in no small
way to the dislocation and malaise of Burma's indigenous majority
during the 1930's. There is no doubt that Burmese anti-Indian sentiment, which erupted into riots and physical conflict in the 1930's,
had deep-rooted foundations in Indian competition and especially
in *chettyar* expropriation of debt-ridden Burmese landholders and
tenants.[43]

No one disputes these facts. Nor did they suddenly emerge out
of an accumulation of scattered data. Every inquiry affirmed them
—and there were many between that of the generally anti-Burman
Financial Commissioner D. A. Smeaton, who in 1891 framed the
first Burma Agriculturists' Relief Bill to prevent the further deterioration of the "naturally thriftless," "free spender," "imprudent"
Burmese cultivator, and the previously mentioned *Report of the
Land and Agriculture Committee, 1938–1939*.[44] The labors of that
committee secured the passage of the Tenancy and the Land Alienation Acts of 1939. Two other committee recommendations
were adopted: the organization of three exploratory Cooperative
Land Mortgage Banks and a Government Land Purchase Scheme
for the reacquisition of *chettyar*-owned lands. But all this was done
too late. The war was soon to come to Burma, and though the
British returned, they were not destined to stay.

The committee had reported that perhaps a majority of the tenants of Lower Burma had been reduced to a "standard of living
down to a bare subsistence level [and] a state of permanent indebtedness from which there is no hope of escape." The committee concluded that it was "socially undesirable" and "politically
inexpedient" for so much of Burma's agricultural land to be in the
hands of absentee landlords, so many of whom belonged to a "professional money lending community domiciled outside of Burma."
(It was silent on British, Chinese, and Burmese landlords.) It
noted that the *chettyars* had, presumably, no desire to enter into

occupation of large areas of land but found themselves "in that position as the result of the free play of economic forces [which] may explain how the situation arose, but in no way alters the fact." [45]

These defects of the agricultural economy of Burma—the growth of indebtedness; the shift from proprietorship to tenancy; the rapid turnover of tenants working the land with depressed standards of living; the large holdings of absentee *chettyar* (and other) landlords, whose agents were routinely redistributed every few years and hence did not acquire any stable interest in the land from which they collected their exorbitant profits; the sponsored immigration of a considerable foreign population (Indian) whose standards of living were lower and whose habits of work were more exploitable than those of the indigenes; and the considerable expatriation rather than reinvestment of profits—did not undermine the European, Indian, and Chinese enterprises in Burma. For despite these defects, and the consequent economic and other dislocation of the Burmese population, especially in the Delta, the primary products of Burma continued to be extracted, processed, and marketed. (See Note 26, Tables 2 and 3.) The slump in world prices and trade during the depression of the 1930's reduced both the rate and volume of earnings on invested capital. But in every year of the decade Burma had a favorable balance of trade, as she had had since 1869. The average excess of exports over imports for 1930-40, approximately 29 crores of rupees (1 crore = 10 million rupees), was actually greater than that of the average for the high level of trade between 1920-30, approximately 26 crores. The Burmah Oil Company and Steel Brothers and Company—the two business leaders of the country—did not declare 50 per cent dividends as Steel Brothers had in the decade of the 1920's, but they managed a range from a 1932 low of 7½ per cent to a high of 20 per cent.[46]

More serious than the economic dislocation though they remained less well perceived and understood, were the political and social effects of these far-reaching agrarian changes on Burmese society, particularly in the Delta. When Burmans from the north settled in Delta villages, their ties to the king, to their *ahmudan*, even to their hereditary or elective *thugyi* were gradually attenuated or broken. Traditional Burmese society felt the corroding effects of distance from its up-country center and of the British introduction of a village-and-circle administrative system based on geographical settlement and appointive officers, including headmen. Personal loyalties and customary Burmese law were superseded by British concepts of law and order and by the presence of nontraditional and foreign officers. What the Burmese valued in their culture became inferior in status and power to what they received and did not value.

These socially debilitating changes were aggravated by the economic events of the twentieth century described above. The depression of 1907 brought the issue of tenancy to the fore, but it was then, as later, left to "the free play of economic forces." The unbridled individualism of British laissez-faire colonial economic policy in Burma had its way. Even when the conditions of the 1920's and early 1930's converted the majority of Burmese cultivators into migrant tenants, occupying land for three years or less, there was no substantial alteration in British Burma policy. At the beginning of the 1930's, J. S. Furnivall, Commissioner of Settlements and Land Records, forcibly brought the resulting conditions to light.[47] Burmese society, particularly in the Delta, gave every evidence of disorganization. Religion, art, literature, the crafts, language, education, the advantages and restraints of customary law, the loyalties to a service leader or headman—all these were experiencing the adverse effects of the economic dislocation and consequent disintegration of Burmese life. In time, the colonizing of Lower Burma and the development of its economy severely weakened, where it did not destroy, the cohesive fabric of the traditional Burmese village.[48] The breakdown in moral standards was evident in rising crime rates, particularly in the 1930's.

The disintegration of traditional Burmese society and the economic plight of the cultivators had far-reaching effects in the 1920's and 1930's, giving fuel to the rising nationalist movement. The people of the countryside, when given an opportunity, supported indigenous leaders against the British and against such easier scapegoat targets as the Indians, who were visible in considerable numbers and who accounted, in part, for their misery. They rallied to the banners of Saya San, whose rebellion in 1930-31 had political links with surviving factions of the General Council of Burmese Associations, that fount of nationalist activity of the 1920's. Saya San was a politically minded *pongyi* who, however deluded, advocated independence from the British. After much loss of life and property, the British captured, tried, and hanged him; his trial, during which he was defended by a dozen leading Burmese barristers, became the basis for his recognition as a Burmese national hero.[49]

In similar fashion, cultivators flocked in the 1936 elections to Dr. Ba Maw's Sinyetha Party, which promised an end to agrarian evils; their support resulted in his heading the coalition Cabinet that set up the above-mentioned Land and Agriculture Committee. The cultivators also engaged in frequent riots against the Indians. Perhaps most important of all, beginning with the elections of 1936, they gave their support to the most ardent nationalists, the Thakins, whose leadership promised freedom from the British Raj and relief from their economic plight.

These conditions in Burma determined the programs and policies of the Thakin movement and provided a platform for their chief parliamentary leader, Thakin Mya, who proposed tax abatement, debt relief, and giving unoccupied land to the peasants. Thakin Mya became president of the Thakin-organized All Burma Cultivators League and the leader of a workers' and peasants' political party, both of which, under new names, became major components of the Anti-Fascist People's Freedom League in August, 1944.

Independence and the Welfare State

The Thakins who ushered in the independence of Burma were committed in principle to the primary responsibility of the state for the reconstruction and development of their war-devastated, ex-colonial economy. They blamed colonialism for the plight of the peasant masses, the evils of debt and landlordism, and the disadvantageous situation of the Burmese workers and tradesmen as compared to the foreigners, whether European or Asian. The insurrections soon added to the tremendous devastation caused by the war, and they also postponed and made more costly the tasks of reconstructing and transforming Burma's monoculture into a diversified economy.

At the war's end, Bogyoke Aung San repeatedly referred to the necessity of laws to abolish landlordism and to prevent land alienation in the future.[50] This sentiment lay behind the Constitution, adopted by the Constituent Assembly in September, 1947, the Two-Year Plan, and the Land Nationalization Act of 1948.[51] Section 30 of the Constitution begins: "The State is the ultimate owner of all lands." It may "regulate, alter or abolish land tenures or resume possession of any land and distribute same for collective or cooperative farming or to agricultural tenants." The Constitution promised to end all "large land holdings" and to limit by law the "maximum size of private land." In the next section, workers are accorded protection, rights of association, and assistance "against economic exploitation." Sections 32-44 outline social and economic policies, called "directive principles of State policy." These presumably encourage the state to promote the welfare of the people.

The Land Nationalization Act of 1948 and the Two-Year Plan represented the first concrete steps to fulfill these promises. Thakin Tin said that the Land Nationalization Act was "one hundred per cent revolutionary," that it would "put an end to landlordism," something "worse than capitalism." Thakin Nu sharply called attention to "the degradation of the agriculturists," whose plight was caused by "collusion" between British authorities and landlords, by "exorbitant rates of interest and lands foreclosed for settlement of debts," and by "dishonest transactions." In defending the nationalization of land he took pains to point out the Buddhist implications. "Property," he said, "is meant not to be saved, not for gains, nor for comfort. It is to be used by men to meet their needs in respect of clothing, food, habitation in their journey towards Nirvana or Heaven." [52] In his view the yielding of property would not only end class warfare, it would confer merit on those who yielded and would help them advance toward the goal of nirvana.

Less sweeping than its supporters claimed, the new law nevertheless accomplished several immediate objectives. Peasant debts that had accumulated prior to October, 1946, had been in effect canceled by two acts passed by the provisional government in 1947. Under the new law, the government began to supply portions of the credit required by cultivators at reasonable interest rates; tenancy and revenue rates were scaled down to manageable proportions.

The land nationalization and redistribution program did not get under way until after a more careful act was drawn in 1953, amended in 1954, and then implemented.[53] *Chettyar* and certain other holdings were then nationalized or, to use another word common in Burma, "resumed." By 1959, the state had reacquired 3.35 million acres, had exempted from redistribution 1.6 million acres, and had redistributed 1.45 million acres to 190,000 cultivators.[54] In the main, cultivator families received an amount of rice land that could be worked by a yoke of cattle, about 10 acres per family. Redistributed land could not be alienated through insolvency, sold, or otherwise transferred, except under rules prescribed in the law. Those who worked the land acquired family rights in it so long as they worked it and had family units that could inherit and work it. They paid rent and revenue directly to the state or its local agencies. Thus, to a major extent, the twentieth-century problems of insecurity of tenure and of high rent and revenue have been substantially dealt with by successive Burmese governments. Once again Burma is a nation of small farmers with rights to the land accruing from its use.[55]

But other problems of land development remained. Throughout the 1950's, the government was plagued by the problem of providing an adequate flow of agricultural credit at reasonable interest rates through workable institutions, and recovering its loans to cultivators. In 1950, it had for a second time canceled cultivators' debts. Between that year and 1960, it made credit available annually in amounts ranging from kyats 33.6 to 87.6 million (1 kyat = 21 cents U.S.), but it still did not fully meet legitimate credit needs, which in some years amounted to approximately twice as much as it granted in the highest year. Collection of loans during the same period ranged from kyats 15.6 million to 63.3 million.[56] The 1948 *Two-Year Plan for Burma*, the first major statement of economic policy and planning goals for the newly independent country, represented the findings of the Sorrento Villa Conference convened by Aung San in 1947. It was assigned to produce "an economy which will ensure that a fair share of the fruits passes on to the common man." It laid down goals for a two-year period, during which a comprehensive plan of economic development was to be drafted.

This highly optimistic statement of aspirations and target dates revealed both the temper of the times and the economic inexperience of its authors. For example, it insisted—"shall be achieved" is the language used—that by October, 1952, Burmese cultivators restore and reclaim some 3.2 million acres of paddy land so as to produce some 3.1 million tons of milled rice for export, close to the highest prewar level. And although Burma had few men with industrial and management experience and even fewer economists, architects, engineers, and other trained personnel, the plan decreed that a steel rerolling factory for the utilization of war scrap metal "shall be set up" within the first six months of 1948. This was the tone of comment and commitment to goals for the eleven operative sections of the plan: agriculture, forests, industrial development, fisheries, technical education, electricity, labor, transport and communications, finance, survey of natural resources, and economic research.

What is interesting today about this document, besides its youthful optimism, is the fact that the targets so blithely set up in the flush of revolutionary fervor have persisted and have by now been partly realized. However, one can understand how and why many of the experts brought to Burma under the various bilateral and multilateral aid programs dismissed the Two-Year Plan. It was too unrefined; it lacked analytical sophistication; it was hopelessly vague on means and capabilities. Of the dozen and a half new industries that were projected, none was built on schedule; nor were the planners any more successful with other sectors of the economy.

Yet somehow the Two-Year Plan, which reflected the posthumous sanction of Bogyoke Aung San, carried its own afflatus, and especially so after the insurrections broke out. Then, perhaps even more than before, Burma's leaders became convinced that by working swiftly toward the goals expressed in the plan, they would demonstrate their concern for the people, an asset in the fight against the rebels. Certainly the Communists had nothing more to offer; they could only promise that they would do it better.

Successive Burmese governments proceeded to implement the policy, and to refine both policy and targets in the light of experience. They have not altered its direction substantially, though before the coup of 1962, they were becoming progressively less doctrinaire and widening the opportunity for domestic and foreign private investment in industry, commerce, and mining.

In April, 1951, the government convened a Conference on Current Economic Problems at which five British experts presented papers on economic development and related fiscal issues.[57] In January, 1952, a preliminary survey and plan for the national economy was presented by a team of American engineers and economists working under a two-year contract with the government, financed by the U.S. Economic Cooperation Administration. This and their final survey are known as KTA Reports, from the initials of one of the companies associated in the contract.[58] The Preliminary Report provided data for the Pyidawtha Conference of August 4–17, 1952, as did the work of U.S. and U.N. technical-assistance missions in fields such as agriculture, education, health, housing, transportation and communication, labor-management problems, and public administration. As the tide of the rebellion receded and as the complications of developing an economy became more apparent, Pyidawtha, though never unrelated to the problem of extending law and order, came to be considered as the means of transforming and improving Burma's economy and of nation-building. Comparable in many ways to the New Deal in the United States, Pyidawtha became the rallying cry for the 1950's.

Industrialization was the key word in the early years of Pyidawtha. A much lower priority was given to agriculture, despite its basic role in the economy, especially in supplying exports and foreign exchange. Burmese leaders were abetted in the drive toward industrialization by some of the foreign experts working under bilateral and multilateral aid programs.[59] The socialist philosophy of the AFPFL leaders, and their recognition of the instability of Burma's primary-product economy, also influenced them toward industrialization. They believed that it would end the stigma of Burma's role as a "colonial" economy, a raw-materials economy with its heavy reliance on a few export items sold on wildly fluctuating world markets. After independence, Burma's leaders sought to change the complexion of the economy by a rapid industrial revolution, geared to make the country free both politically and economically.

The Pyidawtha Conference of 1952 was one of the notable events in Burma's recent history. More than 1,000 delegates attended—members of Parliament and party organizations, government officials, and private citizens. It was agreed that all targets should be fulfilled by 1960, hence the name, Pyidawtha Eight-Year Plan.[60] A few projects were scheduled for completion by 1963. Where necessary, the government enacted legislation to carry out the plan; otherwise it proceeded by executive action. The mandate of the Pyidawtha Conference was ratified by Parliament in the fall of 1952, and subsequent parliamentary budget sessions had the opportunity, through the appropriations machinery, to pass on various phases of the plan.

The Eight-Year Pyidawtha Plan, 1952–60, included targets for the same sectors of the economy as the Two-Year Plan. It added more details, especially in relating capital investment and official organization to future output. Besides devoting more attention to problems of social welfare (e.g., housing, education, and health), it was concerned with the task of governmental structure and responsibility at the local level. This concern manifested itself in the Plan for the Devolution of Powers and Democratization of Local Administration for the 10,000 village tracts and 200 townships comprising the 40 districts of the Union. A new act passed in 1953 provided for the election of village, township, ward, and urban councils. Whatever system the Burmese eventually adopt—and this is not yet clear—will be designed to replace the British village administrative system with some features of traditional administration.[61] They also wish to introduce some modern ideas of local democratic responsibility and to retain some features of a federal national structure, without impairing the authority of the central government.

Under the inspiration of Pyidawtha, Burma acquired an abundance of plans, surveys, reports, and targets, and some relevant data. The data produced in the early days were based excessively on prewar findings and pre-independence policies. The desire to carry out some of the plans bred impatience with the need for painstaking inquiry that might either substantiate, modify, or reject data on hand and policies proposed for the future. The political leader and the foreign engineer held sway. The former rightly knew why he wanted something done to upgrade the economy. He did not take the time, perhaps he did not have the time, to determine what could be done best and what could be done first. The foreign engineers and associated economists, particularly in the earlier years, accepted the challenge of the political leader with a minimum expression of critical judgment and with almost no understanding of an underdeveloped Asian economy. The engineering principles for erecting a given type of bridge are constant. But the social engineering of planning and executing programs in a country such as Burma, which at independence was almost devoid of modern technological and managerial skills, requires knowledge and understanding beyond the laboratory, especially a Western-oriented one. Such knowledge and understanding were not strikingly available in the early days of Pyidawtha in Burma.

The economic and social goals of the Eight-Year Plan were clearly stated and well publicized. Since "approximately half of Burma's national capital had been destroyed" during World War II and since the insurrections "arrested the pace of reconstruction and added heavily to material loss," the Eight-Year Plan aimed at "restoring the standard of living of the people to its prewar level at the earliest possible date, and thereafter to raise it to a level where the people of the Union shall enjoy a reasonable standard of living and comfort." [62] The plan called for an approximate one-third increase in gross national product over prewar levels. Allowing for population growth, this would provide about a 9 per cent increase in per capita consumption. It would require an investment over the eight-year period of kyats 750 crores of public and private capital, or $1.575 billion, approximately two-thirds of which could, according to the KTA estimates, be raised internally. The remainder would have to come from abroad in the form of loans, grants, and later, reparations. Of the proposed governmental capital, 27 per cent, or kyats 350-400 crores, would be invested in power. Other figures were for highways, 23 per cent; ports and waterways, 16 per cent; irrigation, 13 per cent; railways and airways, 10 per cent; manufacturing and mining, 10 per cent; telecommunications, 1 per cent.[63] Essentially this was a power, transport, and communications program designed first to lay the basis for industries, and only secondarily to improve the productivity and the marketability of agricultural and mineral products.

TABLE 1

TARGETS AND FULFILLMENT, EIGHT-YEAR PYIDAWTHA PLAN, 1952–60
(*in 1950–51 prices*)

Gross kyat [a]	1938–39	1951–52 Planned	Actual	1959–60 Planned	Actual	Per Cent of Plan
Domestic product (million kyats)	5,317	3,911	3,911	7,000	5,878	84
Per capita production (kyats)	323	209	208	340	281	83
Per capita consumption	211	143	143	224	183	82

SOURCES: *Economic Survey of Burma*, 1954, p. 115; *Second Four-Year Plan*, pp. 3-4.
[a] 1 kyat = approximately 21 cents (U.S.); 1 crore = 10 million kyats.

Agriculture, the chief sector of the economy, in which a single export crop, rice, provided about 80 per cent of earned foreign exchange, was not to be completely neglected. The government set forth ambitious programs for land reclamation through irrigation and improvement of waterways and water control; for setting up new systems of land tenure and reasonable (if still insufficient) credit facilities; for providing bonus payments for higher yields per acre and for new acreage sown; and for extending health, education, and other social services to the villages. These, together with government control of prices for rice, government monopolies in the export of rice, rubber, cotton, and teak, and expansion of government agricultural research and extension services, were central features of the Agricultural and Rural Development Five-Year Plan, one part of the Pyidawtha program.[64] Nevertheless, for the first four years of the plan, agriculture was underrated, though not entirely neglected, in the operations of the central government.[65] Governmental capital expenditures for agriculture (including irrigation and forests) for 1952-56, except for an extraordinary investment (17 per cent) in 1954-55, were less[66] than for any other sector of the economy except mining—then largely in unsafe territory. The ratio of agricultural investment to other investment was not the only index of this condition. For example, graduates of the Faculty of Agriculture, University of Rangoon, entering the civil service in their specialty, received lower starting salaries than those with the same or similar qualifications who joined other branches of the government.

The decision to industrialize led to the inevitable steel mill, a rather uneconomic and costly item, but one regarded in some Burmese quarters as having prestige value. In a sense, the Pyidawtha plan for industrial development, as outlined in the KTA Preliminary and Comprehensive Reports, set forth certain indexes for Burma's future development. Though some of the projects have been carried out, the whole program could not possibly have been achieved in the eight to eleven years allotted. Of fifty proposed industrial projects (excluding transportation, telecommunications, power, and mining), eighteen had been partially or fully completed and put into operation by 1961, five of these by private capital, two by joint ventures. Four other projects are rated as "possible," and twenty-eight have been "deferred." The major new government industrial plants are in steel, jute textile and bags, pharmaceuticals, clay tiles and brick, cement, sugar refining (two plants), tea blending, silk spinning, cotton bleaching, dyeing and printing, spinning and weaving. Two of these new factories, silk and tea, have questionable futures. They were partially shut down under the Ne Win caretaker government that took office in 1958, though the former went back into production after the elections of 1960. Other industrial establishments included the nationalized brewery and bottling plants at Mandalay; the major joint ventures with foreign capital in oil, lead-silver mines, and soap; and many privately owned local and cottage industries.[67] In September, 1951, the Ministry of Housing and Labor estimated that there were some 1,350 local industrial plants (defined as employing ten or more workers) and perhaps as many as 5,000 cottage-industry units. Among the local industries there were 862 rice mills, 194 sawmills, 110 vegetable-oil extraction plants, 80 flour mills, 67 cotton ginning and spinning mills, 1 knitting mill, 1 sugar refinery, 3 match factories, 1 cement plant, and others in glass, soap, tobacco, beverages, rope, rubber products, leather goods, and printing. Among the cottage industries there were some 37 varieties of activities, from making parasols and lacquerware to highly skilled lapidary and ivory carving. By 1959-60 (excluding cottage industry), the total number of local industrial plants had grown to approximately 2,500.[68]

The excitement over and the preference for industry were somewhat diminished in 1955, when Burmese leaders became disturbed by the drop in foreign reserves consequent upon the decline in the value of rice and other exports.[69] KTA projections had been based upon a Korean war-inflated price for export rice, which had reached £80 per ton for certain grades. These projections, which were to insure Burma's ability to continue a high import level of capital goods with an initially low output ratio for industrialization, assumed that the world market price would not go below £45-50 per ton. In fact, in the post-Korean period, particularly in 1954, the price went down to £30-35 per ton, where it has remained. As a result, in 1955-56, Burma recast the character of the Eight-Year Plan. Within the framework of that plan, the then Deputy Prime Minister in charge of the industrial sectors of the economy, U Kyaw Nyein, worked out a more conservative and consolidating program of industrialization. Simultaneously, investment in agriculture was accelerated. Since there were four more years to the original 1960 date of the Eight-Year Plan, this modified program became known as the (First) Four-Year Plan.[70]

Further critical re-examination, reorganization, and some curtailment of projected and unprofitable industrial plants were instituted by the Ne Win caretaker government, which at that time (1958) also continued to encourage private capital, both indigenous and foreign. Such encouragement had started with the Industrial Policy Statement of 1949 and was climaxed by the Union of Burma Investment Act, 1959.[71] The act guaranteed against nationalization for a period of ten years, which might be extended for a second ten-year period by the president; other provisions liberalized import restrictions and repatriation of capital and earnings; allowed for the use of foreign personnel along with training programs for Burmese citizens; exempted new investors from custom duties and taxes for three years; and otherwise sought to attract private investment.

Throughout the period of the Eight-Year and Four-Year plans, 1952-60, the governments in power gave priority to investment and the development of transport, communications, and power, both for the achievement of a balanced economy and because these sectors contributed to the maintenance of security in the country. During General Ne Win's first regime much less was said or written about the Pyidawtha Eight- and Four-Year Plans, but targets derived from earlier decisions were for the most part retained.[72] The failures and successes of the plans are revealed in the economic-growth data for the period. The following tables indicate the scope and direction of governmental investment in the major sectors of the economy from 1952 to 1960.

Thus it will be seen that after the sharp decline that occurred during the worst years of the insurrections, Burma's gross product mounted steadily, except in 1957-58, when adverse weather seriously affected the rice crop. But, though the over-all national accounts for 1959-60 showed an improvement over those for the base years, Burma failed to achieve the projected one-third increase. Per capita output and consumption climbed during the period 1952-60, but never exceeded 87 per cent of the prewar level. The popula-

TABLE 2

ALLOCATION OF CAPITAL EXPENDITURES SPENT

(in millions of kyats)

Sector	1952–53	1953–54	1954–55	1955–56	1956–57	1957–58	1958–59	1959–60[a]	1952–53 to 1959–60
Agriculture and irrigation	4.6 (1.4%)	107.6 (16.9%)	6.5 (1.2%)	35.9 (7.1%)	43.8 (9.4%)	60.7 (12.1%)	40.8 (9.4%)	66.5 (12.3%)	366.4 (9.2%)
Forestry	12.2 (3.7%)	11.8 (1.8%)	2.8 (0.5%)	3.8 (0.8%)	7.1 (1.5%)	5.3 (1.1%)	5.8 (1.3%)	6.5 (1.2%)	55.3 (1.4%)
Mining	0.3 (0.1%)	2.9 (0.5%)	8.5 (1.6%)	4.0 (0.8%)	4.9 (1.1%)	3.3 (0.7%)	0.1	0.3 (0.1%)	24.3 (0.6%)
Industry	4.0 (1.2%)	47.5 (7.4%)	71.4 (13.3%)	63.7 (12.5%)	54.5 (11.7%)	34.6 (6.9%)	13.4 (3.1%)	85.4 (15.9%)	374.5 (9.4%)
Power	2.0 (0.6%)	69.4 (10.9%)	52.5 (9.8%)	78.7 (15.5%)	75.9 (16.4%)	112.4 (22.5%)	60.0 (13.7%)	54.8 (10.2%)	505.7 (12.8%)
Transportation	63.7 (19.5%)	125.1 (19.6%)	104.0 (19.3%)	78.6 (15.4%)	65.1 (14.0%)	89.8 (18.0%)	116.2 (26.6%)	127.6 (23.7%)	770.1 (19.5%)
Communication	5.0 (1.5%)	8.0 (1.3%)	16.0 (3.0%)	14.4 (2.7%)	18.6 (4.0%)	24.7 (4.9%)	25.1 (5.3%)	29.4 (5.5%)	141.2 (3.6%)
Construction	35.2 (10.8%)	67.9 (10.6%)	129.6 (24.1%)	83.7 (16.4%)	38.7 (8.3%)	17.7 (3.5%)	13.9 (3.2%)	27.2 (5.0%)	413.9 (10.5%)
Social Services	28.9 (8.8%)	32.0 (5.0%)	41.8 (7.7%)	19.8 (3.9%)	16.3 (3.5%)	18.0 (3.6%)	28.3 (6.5%)	35.5 (6.6%)	220.6 (5.6%)
Miscellaneous	106.3 (32.5%)	50.8 (8.0%)	15.4 (2.8%)	26.7 (5.3%)	32.9 (7.1%)	34.8 (7.0%)	36.4 (8.3%)	18.5 (3.4%)	321.8 (8.1%)
Law and Order	65.2 (19.9%)	115.0 (18.0%)	90.2 (16.7%)	99.7 (19.6%)	106.0 (23.0%)	98.3 (19.7%)	96.3 (22.1%)	87.0 (16.1%)	757.7 (19.2%)
Total	327.4	638.0	538.7	509.0	463.8	499.6	436.3	538.7	3,951.5

SOURCE: *Second Four-Year Plan*, p. 7.

[a] Revised estimates.

TABLE 3

GROSS DOMESTIC PRODUCT, PER CAPITA GROSS OUTPUT, AND CONSUMPTION, IN 1947–48 PRICES

(in millions of kyats)

Industry	1938–39	1947–48	1948–49	1949–50	1950–51	1951–52	1952–53	1953–54	1954–55	1955–56	1956–57	1957–58	1958–59	1959–60	1960–61
Agriculture and fisheries	1,907	1,451	1,366	1,220	1,351	1,440	1,537	1,521	1,577	1,617	1,753	1,620	1,797	1,878	1,849
Forestry	360	273	202	191	238	266	276	289	303	314	344	347	347	349	379
Mining and quarry	273	29	14	21	30	34	36	49	60	66	84	102	116	116	112
Rice processing	182	125	119	106	112	119	129	125	129	131	144	124	147	156	152
State marketing	633	286	248	236	288	248	258	278	371	460	493	434	452	572	459
State transport	117	63	19	24	43	48	56	68	79	78	76	74	82	87	84
State banking	—	1	1	1	1	1	1	2	2	9	12	14	13	18	19
Other public utilities	31	14	9	9	11	10	11	22	26	28	31	37	29	50	58
General government	153	229	218	243	79	314	376	412	435	461	487	535	570	593	613
Rental value of housing	165	151	153	153	157	162	170	177	185	194	203	210	215	220	225
Other industries and services	1,124	935	851	834	921	994	1,049	1,103	1,127	1,098	1,307	1,281	1,427	1,561	1,613
Gross domestic product:															
Millions of kyats	4,945	3,557	3,200	3,038	3,431	3,636	3,899	4,046	4,294	4,456	4,934	4,778	5,195	5,600	5,563
Index (1938–39 = 100)	100	72	65	61	69	74	79	82	87	90	100	97	105	113	112
Gross output per capita:															
Kyats	302	200						210						269	264
Index (1938–39 = 100)	100	66						70						89	87
Consumption per capita Index:															
Kyats	195	163						140						174	183
(1938–39 = 100)	100	84						72						89	94

SOURCES: *Economic Survey of Burma*, various years, and *Second Four-Year Plan*, p. 20. The *Survey* for 1964 adopted 1961–62 as the base year for constant prices. In this new series, GDP had risen from K7,443 million in 1960–61 to K8,111 million in 1962–63, but it declined in 1963–64 to K7,962 million. Per capita output fell from K234 to K224, while per capita consumption varied from K327 to K329 in the same years.

TABLE 4

Capital Formation, Planned and Actual
(in millions of kyats)

Year	Gross Government Capital Formation		Gross Private Capital Formation		Gross Total Capital Formation		Net Total Capital Formation	
	Plan	Actual	Plan	Actual	Plan	Actual	Plan	Actual
1953-54	565	435	470	398	1,035	833	655	564
1954-55	695	562	495	344	1,190	906	830	626
1955-56	745	519	570	433	1,315	952	950	662
1956-57	740	509	645	509	1,385	1,018	1,015	716
1957-58	670	533	735	602	1,405	1,135	1,030	817
1958-59	615	420	815	583	1,430	1,003	1,050	671
1959-60	590	472	865	526	1,455	998	1,070	657

TABLE 5

CAPITAL FORMATION AS PERCENTAGE OF GDP

Year	Gross		Net	
	Plan[a]	Actual[b]	Plan[a]	Actual[b]
1953-54	19.9	18.2	12.6	12.3
1954-55	21.4	18.8	14.9	13.0
1955-56	22.1	18.4	16.0	12.8
1956-57	21.9	18.7	16.1	13.1
1957-58	21.3	21.1	15.6	15.2
1958-59	21.1	18.0	15.4	12.0
1959-60	20.8	16.8	15.3	11.0

[a] In 1950-51 prices.
[b] In current prices.
SOURCE: *Second Four-Year Plan*, p. 4.

tion of Burma, estimated at just under 21 million in 1960, increased at the rate of 1.3 per cent a year.

The Outlook

Burma's gross domestic product increased from K3,200 million in 1948-49, the first year of the Two-Year Plan and of the insurrection, to K5,600 million in 1959-60, an average annual increase of almost 5 per cent. Gross public and private capital formation has moved forward during the same years from K280 million to K998 million, on an average of 18 per cent per year of gross domestic product. An examination of the foregoing tables reveals all too clearly that Burma did not reach her Pyidawtha goals. Faulty planning and management, the insurrections, and the sharp dislocations in world prices for primary products were at the core of the failure. The decline in the export unit value of rice, especially in relation to the cost of Burma's imports, highlights the imbalance between the economies of primary producers and others. However, statistics show that Burma's economy is not stagnant, even though it was set back by its relative neglect of agriculture in the first four Pyidawtha years and its heavy investment in indirect productive capital, that is, the infrastructure necessary for economic development. If the cultivators are given the necessary incentives, they will achieve a breakthrough in paddy to match the growing production in jute, groundnuts, and one or two other crops now being cultivated to supplement the six or seven months of rice growing. The incentives will probably be given. In the interim, the considerable capital investment in transport, power, communications, construction—all with low output ratios—will more readily sustain both the extractive industries of agriculture, forestry, and mining, and the modest industrial plant based on the resources that Burma has so painfully acquired during the past decade. If these rates of growth, redirected capital investment, and capital formation can be sustained, if law and order continue to be extended throughout the

TABLE 6

Some Economic Indicators, Prewar and Today

	Prewar[a]	1959–60 Actuals	1959–60 (as a Percentage of Prewar)
1. Paddy-sown acreage (thousand acres)	12,832	10,667	83
2. Paddy production (thousand tons)	7,426	6,916	93
3. Rice export (thousand tons)	3,303	2,080	64
4. Total agricultural sown acreage (thousand acres)	19,166	17,720	91
5. Index of agricultural production	100	102	102
6. Agricultural exports other than rice (thousand tons)	249	311	125
7. Teak production (cubic tons of round logs)	453,481	250,474	55
8. Teak export (cubic tons of round logs)	215,000	90,591	42
9. Non-teak production (cubic tons of round logs)	501,866	660,843	132
10. Non-teak export (cubic tons of round logs)	40,600	10,070	25
11. Petroleum production (thousand gallons)	275,673	143,342	52
12. Mineral production (tons)[b]	188,992	70,061	37
13. Mineral exports (tons)[c]	139,402	44,457	32
14. Electric power—installed capacity (kw)	33,800	190,668	564
15. Electric power—installed capacity units generated (mil. kw)	48	246	513
16. Railway passenger traffic (passenger-miles in million)	433	950	219
17. Railway freight traffic (ton-miles in million)	3.1	2.6	84
18. IWTB passenger traffic (passenger-miles in million)	8.0	5.0	62
19. UBA passenger traffic (passenger-miles in million)	. . .	20.2	. . .

SOURCE: Second Four-Year Plan, p. 17.
[a] Prewar period for which data available: 1. 1936-37 to 1940-41, average; 2. the same; 3. 1938-39; 4. 1936-37 to 1940-41, average; 5. the same; 6. 1938-39; 7. 1936-37 to 1940-41, average; 8. 1938-39; 9. 1936-37 to 1940-41, average; 10. 1938-39; 11. 1939; 12. 1939; 13. the same; 14. 1938-39; 15. the same; 16. 1939-40; 17. 1937-38 to 1940-41, average; 18. 1937-38 to 1940-41, average.
[b] Tin ores and concentrates, tungsten ores and concentrates, mixed tin and tungsten, lead ores and concentrates, zinc concentrates, iron, manganese, copper, and nickel.
[c] Tin, tungsten, mixed tin and tungsten, lead and lead unwrought, zinc, manganese, nickel, copper, and other base metals.

country, and if there is no catastrophe or war, Burma should be able to attain her modest Pyidawtha goals in the decade of the 1960's. This conclusion was reached by the U.S. Special Technical and Economic Mission to Burma after it rejected the excessive optimism and projections of the KTA Preliminary Report. It still seems sound today.

The investment in planning will probably produce more dividends in the future than it has to date. In addition to the two KTA Reports, there are at least 1,500 technical and data papers on many aspects of the economy.[73] These, together with an impressive volume from the Robert R. Nathan Associates,[74] provide descriptive and analytical material capable of serving Burma's interests for the next ten years. The expenditure of so much energy devoted to planning must have appeared bewildering, if not frustrating, to the handful of political leaders and civil servants who were responsible for Burma's economy. But it bought time, if not wisdom, for the Burmese, and time was important. Those already in power had to transform themselves from preindependence agitators without governmental or economic experience into officials capable of directing an expanding economy; in this process they gained, however painfully, some necessary economic experience and insight. The Burmese will inevitably reject, as they should, many of the recommendations of the planners of the 1950's, but they will be able to do so on some basis of fact and further exploration.

In the long run, the significance of Pyidawtha lay not in the facts of hasty and faulty planning, of inexpert execution, of waste and some corruption (this last vastly exaggerated by the Burmese themselves), of political interference and maladministration, of questionable advice from parties-at-interest, domestic and foreign. Informed Burmese and other commentators would recognize some truth in these criticisms, which were offered in Burma at the time and certainly afterward. Rather, it is the fact that the thin layer of Burmese leadership, political and bureaucratic, launched and partially carried out a huge socio-economic program of reform and development while its military counterpart was slowly and painfully grinding down the Communist and ethnic rebellions that threatened the survival of the new state.

General Ne Win's government, in office from October, 1958, to February, 1960, helped greatly in appraising the results of Pyidawtha. The General then had no stake in defending or excoriating the AFPFL leaders who had been so deeply and often divisively involved in the plans and their execution. Burma thereby gained a breathing time to look at the outcome of Pyidawtha without prejudice. Ne Win was able to cut out or cut down questionable industrial projects, dear to the heart of one or another of the AFPFL rivals, and to reorganize others so that their output would prove more valuable. He then continued to encourage private enterprise, and took steps to reduce the cost of living.

When U Nu again took over the leadership of the government in April, 1960, he was apparently in no way dismayed by the changes produced during the Ne Win regime. During 1960-61, he concentrated primarily on economic re-examination of the past, including his own devotion to the plans. Out of that came the Second Four-Year Plan—embodying a more judicious and cautious approach to the future. But before it could begin to execute the plan, his government was displaced in March, 1962, by the second Ne Win regime—this time a complete military takeover. (This is discussed in the next two chapters.)

The slogan of Pyidawtha was seldom used after 1958, but by 1960, the Pyidawtha program had made a contribution to Burma greater than is revealed by statistics. It had reached the people and their leaders in the cities. It had reached the rural masses through land nationalization and distribution, credit and cooperative facilities, schools and health programs, and in other ways. It had initiated the process whereby the traditional and later "colonial" economy was placed on the road to modernization. In Burma as elsewhere, economic development has been a factor in decreasing political apathy and isolation. The Burmese rural masses had not been apathetic during the struggle for independence or in the battle against the insurrections. But tangible and intangible Pyidawtha programs made them aware that their government, regarded in former times as one of the "five evils"—"fire, water, storms, robbers and rulers, these are the five great evils"—could be a force for progress in welfare. The welfare goals were not all achieved, but some progress was made. Pyidawtha thereby helped the government sustain the Union. The goals were not achieved on time, but Burmese Buddhists are generally a patient people.

WHEN A NATION ACHIEVES its independence, there is no blueprint that can be followed automatically. Citizens of long-established nations with well-developed economies tend to forget how many decades and even generations were needed to reach present levels, and they tend to assume that the solutions that worked for them are readily transferable to other countries. Leaders of newly independent nations, impatient for tangible improvements in their well-being, tend to ignore its necessary preconditions. No matter how highly they regard their own culture, they too often accept external models instead of patiently developing their own. They tend to ignore the fact that nation-building tasks and skills are far different from those of nation-begetting ones. Though certain of these tasks and their solutions can be generalized, for example the establishment of a level of general education, health, and other forms of social well-being, improvements in the extractive processes of primary-products economies, and introduction of modern technology for whatever degree of industrialization an economy can sustain, there are no uniform blueprints that can be automatically assigned to and adopted by each new nation-building "construction team." Burma has been no exception, for example, in the acceptance of foreign and domestic economic planning that was largely unrelated to its own cultural and economic conditions.

Burma weathered the insurrections and the economy has moved forward, even if the Pyidawtha goals have not yet been fully won. But what of the art of politics during this period from 1948 until the coup of March, 1962, which established a military regime and abrogated the Constitution?

How has this newly independent country maintained its political life in the particular democratic climate that its founding fathers had originally chosen? Can it elect or choose governments capable of governing with consent and satisfaction, or will it fall prey to right or left or military dictatorship? And, if the latter, for how long? Can it devise and execute policies and programs that contribute to well-being and security for its population, to material and normative progress, to rational and friendly international discourse? Can it, in the final analysis, create a unified nation out of a colonial past that deliberately accentuated a plural, communal organization of society?

The Political and Institutional Setting

Mention has been made of the "founding fathers." This has become a comfortable phrase for Americans about other Americans because we can identify the individuals, know something of their biographies, their labors, and their period. There is a similar group for the Union of Burma, and all but a few of them are alive today (though a number have been jailed since the coup). They gave inordinate vitality and single purpose to the nationalist movement that ultimately secured independence from England. They called themselves Thakins, in mockery of the foreign ruler who had to be so addressed. But apart from names and name calling, it is significant that political leadership in Burma from 1948 to 1962 revolved about this group of Thakins who "made the revolution." They were the activists, the Burmese patriots of the 1930's, whose nationalist movement succeeded. They were and still are called "extremists," and less polite names by outsiders and by others who do not agree with them; but they are the founding fathers of the Union of Burma. They were jailed for political activity; they joined Japan against England the better to conduct their struggle; and when they became convinced that this was an error they advanced their cause by joining England and the Allies against Japan. Their status in Burma today, depending on political and other circumstances, may be high or low, bright or tarnished. But there is scarcely a prominent leader who did not have a genuine connection with the Thakin movement in the critical decade before, during, and immediately after World War II. This is a fact that must be taken into account when analyzing the political life of newly independent Burma.

These pages have attempted to convey a sense of Burma's political background, through the prisms of the struggle for and the achievement of independence, the survival beyond the dark days of the Communist and Karen insurrectionary flood tide, and the launching of the Pyidawtha program. It is now necessary to examine Burma's political institutions and to assess the importance of the breakup and replacement of its major political party, the AFPFL, the coalition that carried Burma through its first decade of independence.

After the 1951 elections, the AFPFL leadership was able to run the country with a diminishing sense of the danger that had plagued its course from the beginning. Though the leadership could not yet afford to relax its vigilance, and though the country as a whole needed time and dedicated and enlightened energy for rehabilitation and development, it was clear by the beginning of 1952 that the political institutions of the state and government could begin to function with some degree of normalcy. This is not to imply that these institutions had been suspended during the height of the insurrectionary crisis. On the contrary, even during the trying years after 1948, the government leaders carried on within the framework of the democratic Constitution, and avoided the form and substance of dictatorship. (One of the few exceptions was the Public Order [Preservation] Act.)[1] But after the first national elections, Prime Minister U Nu and his colleagues had to demonstrate in a period of reconstruction the viability of the political institutions that they had so enthusiastically adopted and zealously defended.

It is relatively easy to describe these institutions and it is also relatively easy for Westerners to understand them, since they draw heavily on Western sources for their inspiration. But Westerners have a tendency complacently, or perhaps unimaginatively, to accept the flattery of such imitation while ignoring or undervaluing its significance. For the Burmese nationalist march toward independence can be characterized as a revolt against alien white man's political, economic, racial, and cultural domination. This fourfold revolt[2] is the basis of the anticolonialism and anticapitalism so vigorously championed by Burmese and other nationalists in South and Southeast Asia since World War I. Hence, when Burma's nationalists designed their state, they might have been expected to reject the social and political institutions of the West.

Within their own and certainly their fathers' memory they had been familiar with and had respected the traditions of dynastic Burma. The kings of Burma had been in theory absolute and hereditary monarchs. But the theoretical despotism, as in imperial China, was limited by the risk if not the right of rebellion, by the difficulties of communication, the role of the local *wuns* (literally, burden-bearers), or governors, the customary law and practical democracy of the villages, the presence at the capital of the *thathanabaing*, who administered ecclesiastical law and order, and especially by the institution of the Hlutdaw. Mingyi-thet-taw-she, the Council Minister who was under any circumstances exempted from the penalty of death, was, in fact, the chief officer of the Hlutdaw.[3]

But Burmese nationalism exhibited little if any desire to restore the crown. The Ko Min Ko Chin Party (One's Own King, One's Own Kind), which in 1936 elected three representatives to the legislature, has sometimes been regarded as having desired a royalist future for independent Burma, the more so because its leader, U Ba U (not to be confused with the second president of Burma), came from Mandalay, the "kingly" capital. However, it is most probable that this group selected its name to show cultural, not dynastic, continuity with the past. Further, the Burmese phrase *ko min*, "one's own king," may be related to the Chinese term for revolution, *ko ming*, which Bodde translates literally as "transferring the Mandate." Even if U Ba U's group had been genuinely royalist, it would have been the only such group.[4] In this connection, two additional points are worth noting. First, despite the opportunistic flirtation with Japanese militarism and fascism that led to the "one blood, one voice, one command" nationalist merger under Adipati Ba Maw[5] in August, 1943, the nationalist movement quickly rid itself of any fascist intellectual sympathies, if it had any.[6] This is indicated not only by the name chosen for the major war and postwar coalition, Anti-Fascist People's Freedom League, but by the very nature of the institutions that the Burmese attempted to root in the body politic. The second point is perhaps more significant. Despite the attraction that the Russian Revolution and Communist doctrine had for some of the younger nationalists between 1936 and the founding of the Communist Party in 1942-43, the sociopolitical institutions that the Burmese adopted at independence by and large rejected such influences. In principle and in practice, these nationalists accepted a variety of Marxist ideas, but they discarded the totalitarian potential in Marxism. They chose Western parliamentary, multiparty democracy in preference to a one-party monolithic state. In doing so they were influenced by the impact of Western education and their experience under British rule to select the forms and instruments of constitutional government.

"Due process," a government of laws not of men, the rights of citizens guaranteed by law, contractual relations subject to determination of fact not compromise, the social responsibility of the state extending beyond that of the family—these are among the major concepts that the Burmese nationalists, in part spiritual descendants of American and French revolutionaries, incorporated in the Constitution of 1947. This is the Preamble of their Constitution:

WE, THE PEOPLE OF BURMA including the Frontier Areas and the Karenni States, Determined to establish in strength and unity a SOVEREIGN INDEPENDENT STATE, to maintain social order on the basis of the eternal principles of JUSTICE, LIBERTY AND EQUALITY and to guarantee and secure to all citizens JUSTICE, social, economic and political; LIBERTY of thought, expression, belief, faith, worship, vocation, association and action; EQUALITY of status, of opportunity, and before the law, IN OUR CONSTITUENT ASSEMBLY this Tenth day of Thadingyut waxing, 1309 B.E. [September 24, 1947], DO HEREBY ADOPT, ENACT AND GIVE TO OURSELVES THIS CONSTITUTION.

The Constituent Assembly of 1947 resolved that Burma was to be "a Sovereign Independent Republic to be known as the Union of Burma." It created a federal union with strong central features and with limited rights of secession reserved to several of the constituent states; a bicameral Parliament consisting of a Chamber of Nationalities and a Chamber of Deputies; a cabinet system of government headed by a prime minister; a president as titular and ceremonial head of state elected by Parliament; and a strong and independent judiciary. The Constitution also set forth in some detail a number of political, economic, and social policies that the Union undertook to pursue for the benefit of its citizens, amounting to a veritable Bill of Rights. The Constituent Assembly deliberately sought Western ideas and contributions. In addition, Burma's own corps of well-trained lawyers felt completely at home in British and continental European law, and they enlisted the aid of the distinguished Indian judge Sir B. N. Rau. Experts were sent to India, the United Kingdom, and the United States to learn techniques of constitution-drafting and to obtain treatises and model constitutions. The German Weimar and Irish constitutions influenced the section on the Directive Principles of State Policy, including the right to work, social security, education, protection from all forms of exploitation, and economic planning for better living conditions.

From the constitutions of Yugoslavia, Canada, South Africa, and the United States the Burmese drew provisions dealing with the representation of the states in the Chamber of Nationalities and their relations with the central government. British common law and judicial concepts and organization, together with principles of the Indian constitution, made a pervasive contribution in such matters as the nature, operation, and responsibilities of Parliament, the role of the Union executive, and provisions relating to ministers and the courts. The Constitution made the right of secession exercisable after ten years (Sections 201-6), except for the Kachin state, which included numerous Burman and Shan residents (Section 178). This unusual provision for secession may have come from the Soviet constitution of 1936, but it was probably devised to accommodate the Shan sawbwas who were reluctant to yield their feudal rights completely.[7]

The Burmese shared with their eighteenth-century Jacobin prototypes biases against property and privilege. They would pursue life, liberty, and happiness, but not—as in Locke's formulation—property. Their views were derived from their cultural background with its emphasis on family and communal social responsibility, a general absence of caste or class structure below the royal family, and a commitment to the view that in principle the land and its resources ultimately belong to the king or the state. They had also acquired an ill-defined amalgam of Marxist ideas.

The result is to be found in various sections of the Constitution.

Section 23 guaranteed "the right of private property and of private initiative in the economic sphere," but stated that "no person shall be permitted to use the right of private property to the detriment of the general public." Monopolist organizations, i.e., cartels and trusts, were forbidden. If public interest required, the state might nationalize or expropriate property, "but only in accordance with law which shall prescribe in which cases and to what extent the owners shall be compensated." Chapter III, in two sections, covered "relations of the State to Peasants and Workers." It began with the declaration—traditional for Burma—"The State is the ultimate owner of all lands." Section 42 calls on the state to encourage cooperative undertakings. It may assist workers to associate and organize themselves for protection against economic exploitation. The Constitution also upheld the right to work, to education, to rest and leisure, and to maintenance during sickness and old age.

In the judgment of J. S. Furnivall,

> . . . the Constitution as finally adopted agreed very closely with the original conception of a national government uniting all the peoples of Burma for their common welfare. . . .
>
> Both the original conception and the final product embody two conflicting principles: the principle of individual freedom under the rule of the law, characteristic of British rule; and the principle of social obligation as a reaction against the social disintegration and economic disabilities resulting under British rule through free enterprise under the rule of law. The Constitution voices socialist propensities; yet through the whole document the emphasis is on individual rights; obligations are imposed upon the State, but not one clause imposes any duty on the people or suggests that individual rights are in any way conditional on the performance of social duties. Perhaps it may best be summarized as a liberal Constitution with socialist aspirations. How these will blend in practice is as yet uncertain.[8]

The uncertainty of which Furnivall writes is a long-range one. Until 1962, the Burmese did not tinker very much with their Constitution. Four amendments had been passed under provisions stipulated by Chapter XI, three of which affected the names and the incorporation of the Kayah, Karen, and Shan states in the Union. The fourth, discussed below, was an amendment limited in scope and time.[9] The Constitution proved flexible enough to withstand the trials of the past. The Supreme Court, as the highest judicial authority with the duty of constitutional interpretation, enjoyed great respect in the country. It had not been unwilling to bend the language of the Constitution so as to permit by interpretation certain types of joint ventures in which the government became a minority stockholder. At the same time it had not hesitated to "thwart" the government when, in its opinion, the latter violated the rights of citizens or otherwise "offended" the Constitution.[10]

Electoral Successes and Party Fissures, 1948–58

The first national elections, which had been postponed four times because of the insurrections and other internal problems,[11] began in June, 1951.

There appeared to be a multiplicity of parties in the 1951 campaign, as there would be again in 1956, but there were in fact three well-defined groups: the majority AFPFL and its supporters in the various states and election districts, who did not always use the AFPFL label; a crypto-Communist group centering around the Burma Workers and Peasants Party (BWPP) and its allies; and a non-Communist opposition. The last-named was led by remnants of the older generation of nationalist leaders—Dr. Ba Maw, Thakin Ba Sein, U Ba Pe, and Sir Paw Tun. A right-wing faction led by U Kyaw Min also won a number of seats in the Arakan division.

Elections were held in all but two dozen of the 250 constituencies, and were spread over a seven-month period to ensure protection for the voters. The elections were conducted fairly.[12] The AFPFL easily captured both houses of Parliament. Thakin Nu, as Prime Minister, announced that since the Burmese were now masters in their own home through democratic and constitutional means, he would no longer use the prefix "*Thakin*," but would prefer to be called by the ordinary honorific prefix "*U*"—"uncle," or "mister."

Throughout these first years of the Union, the AFPFL easily sustained the government in power. Its huge parliamentary majority insured the passage of any legislation desired by U Nu and his Cabinet. Burma in effect had one-party rule within a democratic framework. But the AFPFL and the government suffered in popular esteem from the defects of the power so wielded. On the local scene there was dissatisfaction because of the misconduct and bad reputation of some district leaders. One-party rule led to increasing bureaucratization and inefficient public administration. The government was accused by some of rewarding its friends and thus alienating others who failed to profit from the measures it adopted. Though the country as a whole applauded acts of expropriation, nationalization, and especially agrarian reform, the government frequently lacked Burmese management and skills to replace the foreigners and to execute its reforms. Its welfare and Pyidawtha resolutions were not and could not be speedily translated into popular benefits. The economic recession in 1954-55, following the drastic fall of export rice prices after the Korean War boom, added to disaffection. Some of the *sawbwas* resisted, as did some other minority-group leaders, the gradual imposition of central-government control. The government was charged with "Burmanization" at the expense of the minorities. Finally, differences between the top leaders of the AFPFL also emerged. For these and related reasons, the AFPFL was less successful, though still victorious, in the second national elections of 1956.[13]

In the 1956 elections, a coalition National Unity Front (NUF) was formed by the BWPP, other crypto-Communists, and a new centrist group, the Justice Party, led by Dr. E Maung, formerly a Supreme Court justice. The NUF captured 48 seats and more than 30 per cent of the popular vote, surpassing by far the total opposition (37 seats) in 1951. Of these 48, the assorted crypto-Communists held 32 seats (as against 12 in 1951), while the Justice Party won 16. Right-wing Arakanese (5) and other minorities and independents (15) raised the potential opposition to 68. This still left the AFPFL and its allies with 182 seats, but the size of the opposition vote, registering the dissatisfaction in the country, prompted U Nu in June, 1956, voluntarily to step down from the premiership for "one year" in order to "clean up the party." U Ba Swe became prime minister and U Kyaw Nyein his deputy. Their policies were endorsed by U Nu when he resumed office ahead of schedule in March, 1957.[14]

The history of the AFPFL parallels in certain respects that of the Congress Party of India. Before independence, both parties constituted the main organizational and political force of the nationalist movements of their respective countries. They were composed of individuals, all types of groups, and various affiliates, including trade unions and the Communist and Socialist parties. In both countries, the Communists were eventually excluded from the coalition by the leadership of the broad organization. With independence these movements had to transform themselves into political parties, complete with programs and electoral purpose, capable of winning in an election the endorsement of a majority of the voters.

The internal life of these parties is not without some analogy to political party life in the United States and elsewhere in the West. The principle of democracy is served in theory; in practice, the party leaders and bosses command a majority of the votes of the faithful within the party, act in their names, and otherwise maintain their positions by pursuing public policies that bring rewards and favors to the faithful. If we profess to see something of an Asian emphasis on leadership and "followership" in the careers of Pandit Nehru, U Nu, and Dr. Sukarno, it might be worth reminding ourselves that this leadership is not unlike that of President Roosevelt, Prime Minister Churchill, or General de Gaulle.

From its organization in 1944, to January, 1958, the majority group in the AFPFL had succeeded in maintaining a balance of centripetal political forces, though it had been shaken somewhat by the results of the 1956 elections. Modest reform measures and exhortations from within, rather than attacks by outside parties, have been the standard Burmese devices for reducing graft and corruption. Party leaders gave increasing attention to party programs, structures, and grass-roots organizations. Because the AFPFL was composed of both individual members and group affiliates (Trade Union Congress of Burma, All-Burma Peasants Organization, Federation of Trade Organizations, women's and youth groups, minorities), its leaders devoted considerable attention between elections and after 1956 to demonstrating their accountability to the electorate. Cabinet members and other party leaders devoted an extraordinary amount of time to public appearances and to making pronouncements at party or affiliate meetings throughout the country. Their speeches were widely and critically reported in the press. The specific actions flowing from the party program of democratic socialism and neutralist foreign policy were placed before a wide variety of audiences. As a result, the AFPFL built itself up not only as the historical patriotic force that brought independence to Burma but also as the action agency, admitting some mistakes, but seeking and in the main winning approval for its efforts to establish Burma as a welfare state.[15]

At the beginning of the tenth year of independence, 1958, it appeared that the AFPFL had learned its lessons and was geared for a continuing period of governmental leadership and electoral success. Certainly, during its first decade as a republic, Burma exhibited an interesting if somewhat unexpected political phenomenon: it was predominantly, though neither by law nor by power-decision, a one-party state, but it was essentially as democratic as any of its Western prototypes. To all outward appearances there was a high degree of political unity, and the AFPFL could apparently look forward with confidence to the next regular election of 1960. U Nu had been the prime minister for almost all these years.

In February, 1958, the AFPFL concluded its Third All-Burma National Congress by approving, in an apparent burst of unity, a resounding four-hour speech by Prime Minister U Nu in which he dedicated the party to democratic socialism and Buddhism and opposed Communism and Marxism, identified as synonymous.[16] The tenth year of Burma's independence, however, proved to be a troubled one, disturbing both to citizens and to friends abroad.

In April, 1958, the AFPFL split irretrievably into two bitterly hostile factions.[17] Each side was led by two of the country's four most prominent political figures, who had been in constant association since the early days of the struggle for independence and who had previously formed an inner group in the Cabinet. Prime Minister U Nu and Deputy Prime Minister Thakin Tin headed the faction known as the "Clean" AFPFL. Deputy Prime Ministers Ba Swe and Kyaw Nyein commanded the other group, which they called the "Stable" AFPFL.

This political crisis severely tested constitutional and democratic continuity. Each side sought to win a majority of the members of the Chamber of Deputies in order to control the government. In a special session of Parliament in June, the Nu-Tin faction won by a slim majority of eight votes, 127 to 119. This was done by making concessions to the five-member Arakanese National Unity Organization (ANUO) led by U Kyaw Min (major stockholder in the English-language daily, *The Nation*, in opposition to the AFPFL), who became Finance Minister in the reconstructed Cabinet, and to the NUF coalition, which included 32 crypto-Communists. Dr. E Maung, leader of the non-Communist Justice Party in the NUF, became Minister of Justice. The crypto-Communists of the BWPP were not given any Cabinet posts, but they wrung from U Nu concessions that dangerously liberalized the amnesty offered to the underground Communist rebels (see below). Prime Minister U Nu next faced the regular budget parliamentary session of September, 1958, where a switch of four or five votes could overthrow his government. He had in the meantime announced that national elections would be held in November.

Political Marriage and Divorce

The immediate cause of the split within the AFPFL was not doctrinal or ideological, as subsequently reported or charged in factional diatribes. Rather, it was precipitated by a conflict over an appointment to the AFPFL secretaryship, a most essential control point for patronage, election maneuvers, and power in Parliament and in the Cabinet.

U Nu supported Thakin Kyaw Tun,[18] a prominent peasant leader and one-time Cabinet minister of low moral repute, whom he regarded as completely loyal to him and who had publicly resolved henceforth to be morally good in Buddhist fashion. U Kyaw Nyein rejected Kyaw Tun as excessively partisan and incompetent. But long before this contest there had been a variety of conflicts within the Cabinet. These men and their wives—some of whom were politically and socially active in a variety of causes—had lived and worked together for almost two decades. Irritation, suspicion, and arguments frequently marked their relations. They had been together too long. They had carried too many burdens for their numbers. They did not know how to broaden their ranks and lighten their loads. They may have been reluctant to do this or they did not have the time for it. Frequently they merged their roles as Cabinet officers and policy-makers with the daily tasks of operating the regular departments of government including public sectors of the economy. They completely overlooked the fact that, though they were still comparatively young (U Nu was born in 1907; his ally, Thakin Tin, in 1903; most of the others around 1915), they had been engaged in the wearying business of active daily leadership of the nationalist struggle, the war, and independence, without interruption, for twenty years.

As in the case of a marriage that is breaking up, the fights over an alleged ouster move against U Nu in 1957 and over the secretaryship in 1958 were merely the final incidents in a long train of personal and organizational strains. What became the issue, though it was never clearly articulated, was the very nature and character of a one-party democracy in which provision for change was institutionally available but was not freely used. "Throw the rascals out"—a slogan known in the United States—had its Burmese equivalent in the 1956 elections. The AFPFL was still safely in power, but the strains and stresses were dangerously evident. Unless the inner Cabinet group—U Nu, Thakin Tin, Ba Swe, and Kyaw Nyein—found ways to dilute the intensity of their constant association, to broaden the bases of actual power, to divest decision and policy making from administration and execution, it was obvious that they would break apart, as they did in the spring of 1958.

In both India and Burma there has been some evidence that government can operate democratically under a one-party system when the party represents a coalition of functional and geographical units. But when control is confined to the top few the strain becomes intolerable, the base becomes flabby, and the few at the top wear out or collapse. They can stand each other no longer and seek separation. This is the conclusion U Nu reached between February and April, 1958. He would no longer compromise with other Cabinet leaders, even over an appointment to a party post. The time had come for a divorce.

In view of the socialist character of the AFPFL, is the foregoing explanation adequate? After all, socialists are concerned with ideology, and in Japan, India, and elsewhere their organizations have split over it. Why should Burma be an exception? Some Western reports suggested—and the acrimonious name-calling, mudslinging campaign adopted by both sides supported the suggestion—that one faction was pro-Communist, the other pro-West. Such charges were entirely erroneous. To understand this it is necessary to take a closer look at the AFPFL leadership.

In the 1930's, the principals in the AFPFL read and absorbed somewhat indiscriminately an anticolonial ideology that justified their struggle against British power. They found their inspiration in the Marxist literature published by the Nagani Book Club of Rangoon. When they organized the AFPFL in 1944, they did not distinguish too finely among socialists, Communists, and other Marxists. At that time it seemed logical to combine all forces into an organization like that of the People's Front in the period from 1935 to 1939.

But such political innocence did not last long once Burma was confronted with the realities of independence. This was evidenced as early as 1946, when the AFPFL leaders ejected the Burma Communist Party from the coalition. After independence the AFPFL was severely tried by the Communist insurrection beginning in 1948; by the crypto-Communists who split off in December, 1950, to form the BWPP; by the overt and covert support tendered to the BCP by the Sino-Soviet axis before Stalin's death in 1953;[19] and since then in more subtle ways. For example, Burmese Communists are known to have been in Moscow and Peking at least through the summer of 1965. Communist China never ceased being a training ground for Burmese Communist cadres. The Chinese embassy in Rangoon was accused of aiding the crypto-Communists in the elections of 1956. The continuing dangers arising from the China-Burma border issue (*infra*) and from illegal Chinese immigration[20] into Burma also broadened the political experience of the AFPFL socialist leadership.

Gradually, the AFPFL leaders came to realize that no matter how Marxist they remained, they were socialists and not Communists. They set about the task of clarifying their socialist outlook while retaining the anticolonial basis of their original ideological orientation. The top four and other leaders undertook extensive travel in Europe and elsewhere in Asia to confer with other socialists.

These developments help to explain Burma's leading part in founding and directing the Asian Socialist Conference (ASC), which first met in 1953 and was housed in and directed from Rangoon while it actively survived. Members of the Nu-Tin and Swe-Nyein factions participated vigorously in all the meetings of the ASC. Their emerging ideological agreement at home made possible their effective and united stance at ASC gatherings on international questions and on problems of socialist development. Gradually they espoused a philosophy of democratic socialism in concert with the humanist approach of such socialists as Sjahrir of Indonesia, Asoke Mehta of India, Sharett of Israel, and Djilas of Yugoslavia—all of whom attended the founding conference at Rangoon.

There were minor differences among the AFPFL leaders—differences in Marxist vocabulary and definition—that were evident even at the AFPFL Third All-Burma Conference in January-February, 1958. But these differences in no way accounted for the split. U Nu's strongest political ally, Thakin Tin, regards himself as a Marxist of socialist persuasion. He did not like U Nu's equation of Communism and Marxism and his antagonism to both. Similarly, U Ba Swe did not like U Nu's insistence on the irreconcilability of Marxism and Buddhism, for he had expounded a view that combined and reconciled the two. But U Kyaw Nyein, U Nu's sharpest opponent in the conflict, vigorously supported U Nu's defense of democratic socialism without Marxism. The split was not caused by an ideological conflict over the various shades of socialist thought. Anti-Communist U Nu accepted the expediency of crypto-Communist parliamentary support in June, 1958, in order to defeat his rivals, but the charge that he was "pro-Communist" had no more basis in fact than the Nu-Tin cry that Swe and Nyein were "tools of American imperialism."

After the split, months of shameful, demoralizing campaigning by both factions, in anticipation of elections that were to have been held in November and December, 1958, revealed no ideological conflict. Charges and countercharges of corruption and maladministration, the whole panoply of alleged scandal, character assassination, and unfaithfulness filled the newspapers with the bitterness of a divorce between political partners who had so long been together. The principals found some psychological release in the exposure of respective weaknesses and foibles now grossly exaggerated. Friends and distinguished elders intervened unsuccessfully to stop the disgraceful public fight. In disgust and sadness the English-language *Guardian* (October 20, 1958), in the hope of putting an end to "blind vindictiveness," called editorially for "a halt to the reciprocal recrimination . . . in the interest of the nation."

The Advent of the Caretaker Government

During the summer and early fall of 1958, many citizens feared that the verbal violence of the conflicting groups would deteriorate into physical violence. Some of the Communist rebels, especially those associated with the former People's Volunteer Organization, took advantage of the government's new amnesty offers and "came out into the light" on August 15. The amnesty terms completely exonerated all surrendering rebels, including criminals. Almost immediately, 2,000 former PVO members formed a legal party known as the People's Comrades Party (PCP), and proposed to contest the November election with an openly pro-Communist international and domestic program. Those who remained underground and still fighting, led by Communist Than Tun, stepped up their campaign for a negotiated peace with the government, a campaign abetted by a Communist-front peace group led by the late Thakin Kodaw Hmaing.[21] The armed forces fighting the rebels had not approved the current amnesty actions and had proposed a counterpolicy of wiping out the rebels.

Public and private industry and commerce slowed down because of the uncertainty, as did work in government offices. In addition, drought and flood diminished the 1957 harvest and the 1958 export of rice, while lower world prices for other primary products, chiefly minerals, further impaired the economy. A general feeling of uneasiness prevailed in the economy and in the community, especially in Rangoon and Mandalay.

Several times during 1958, the armed forces, speaking through Commander in Chief Ne Win and his close associates, made it clear that they would continue to assist any government to keep law and order, would impartially carry out their duties as policemen for peaceful elections, and would refrain from playing politics. General Ne Win warned both AFPFL factions against the use of violence, cautioned Prime Minister Nu against accepting parliamentary support from the Communists, and rejected all attempts at inducting any of the surrendering rebels into the armed forces.

Further, it was an open secret in Rangoon that the army was disturbed by the latitude of the amnesty order of August 1, 1958.

The mounting crisis caused Prime Minister U Nu to broadcast to the nation on September 26 that he had decided to resign and turn the government over to General Ne Win, and that the elections scheduled for November had been postponed to April, 1959. The armed forces deployed troops to all major locations. In a public exchange of letters, U Nu urged the General to suppress "wrongs and acts of violence," to strive for the "prize of internal peace," to ensure "a free and fair election," and to maintain "the policy of strict and straightforward neutrality in foreign relations." Ne Win agreed to do this.

On the surface, it appeared as if the army had forced the so-called invitation and had staged a coup in order to thwart any danger from the aboveground or underground Communists. Such an interpretation, though reflecting the anti-Communist stand of the armed forces and the state of apprehension that pervaded Burma, fails to account for Burmese political realities. It should be noted that both factions in the AFPFL had agreed in advance to General Ne Win's takeover.

During the summer and early fall of 1958, it became increasingly evident to the factional campaign leaders that neither side was assured of victory if elections were held on the November-December schedule. Though it was probable that all the principals would be easily re-elected, it was by no means certain that either the inspirational leadership of U Nu or the organizational abilities of Swe and Nyein would be sufficient to carry either group to parliamentary power. The AFPFL and its constituent functional and geographical units had become so faction-ridden and disoriented, so uncertain of support in the countryside, that neither the Nu-Tin nor the Swe-Nyein group could be sure of winning a majority in the new Parliament. A determined minority, crypto-Communist or ethnic in composition, might easily acquire the balance of power in Parliament. However much U Nu might desire to keep the Prime Ministership—he already had had to pay dearly for his eight-vote majority in the June session of Parliament—he did not look forward to being once more a minority Prime Minister. But if the elections could be honorably postponed, he might succeed in building a new party potentially capable of winning a majority in a later election. The Swe-Nyein group had already determined to build a more coherent and stable political organization, and therefore they, too, welcomed a postponement of the elections.

Finally, it was clear in August and September that the National Unity Front was splitting on national and international issues. The Justice Party, which held sixteen of the NUF parliamentary constituencies, formally dissociated itself from the NUF on October 27. The former rebels who had formed the People's Comrades Party also gave evidence of fragmentation. Both the Nu-Tin and

Swe-Nyein factions hoped to bolster their respective organizations by absorbing some of these elements. Each faction believed it would benefit from a delay in the elections, provided it had a fair opportunity to build its own organization. The armed forces, however much disgruntled over the amnesty policy, knew, perhaps better than most, that there was in fact no chance for a Communist takeover unless foreign forces came to their aid. There is therefore little reason to doubt U Nu's assertion that he invited General Ne Win, in his personal capacity, to assume the premiership in order to insure the peace and to provide for free and fair elections at a later date.

When Parliament was called into special session on October 28, U Nu referred to General Ne Win's earlier Cabinet service (April, 1949, to September, 1950) as a precedent, and explained that this time he was to be elected Prime Minister for a six-month period, with a group of nonpartisan, respected civilians (e.g., the former Chief Justice of the Supreme Court, the Chief Justice of the High Court, the Chief Secretary of Government) as members of what was called a caretaker government. The General was elected Prime Minister by an uncontested vote.[22]

It should be borne in mind that the armed forces in Burma had achieved a most respected position. They had never evidenced dictatorial ambitions, and there had never been any serious contest between services or groups within a service. Along with other patriotic Burmese they accepted the constitutional means that were used to establish a caretaker government, headed by a General who promptly appointed an all-civilian Cabinet, committed to guarding the conditions for democracy.

The advent of General Ne Win's government closed the dismal tenth year of Burma's independence with a promise of stability and renewed hope for its democratic future. This solution saved face for all parties involved in the factional conflict. Popular response was strong and affirmative.[23] The Nu-Tin group gained politically from having stepped down, even though it yielded the advantage of contesting the next election from the superior position of being the government. The Swe-Nyein group avoided the necessity of repudiating in Parliament international loan and aid agreements, particularly with the United States, to which they had given assent while members of U Nu's Cabinet. In an opening statement to Parliament, Prime Minister Ne Win pledged his government to hunt down the remaining Communist insurgents relentlessly and to treat them as criminals. Thus, the Burma Defense Services could feel that their sacrifices in suppressing the insurgents would not be vitiated by a dangerously generous amnesty policy. After months of fearful speculation and postponement, a regular session of Parliament was held in late October and November, 1958, which passed the annual budget and otherwise provided for the continuing operations of government.

The new Prime Minister, formally elected to that office on October 28, 1958, reduced the number of Cabinet members from thirty to fourteen. He eliminated all the politically appointed parliamentary secretaries, of whom there had been thirty-eight in the Nu-Tin Cabinet. He thoroughly reshuffled eighteen of the top-level civil servants who as secretaries and commissioners administered various ministries and departments of government. At the completion of his reorganization, General Ne Win announced that his Cabinet, pledged to uphold the Constitution and democracy, would address itself primarily to four major tasks: the restoration of law and order; preparation for free and fair elections within six months, if law and order were restored and the political parties cooperated; lowering the cost of living; and seeking remedies for the economic chaos in the country.

The General's Government and the Elections of 1960

Thakin Shu Maung, known however, since his command position among the "Thirty Heroes" by his alias, Bogyoke Ne Win, Chief of Staff of the Burma Defense Services (army, navy, and air force), was born on May 24, 1911, near Prome. He was more than a military officer assuming power; he was also an ardent nationalist who had quit the University of Rangoon in the early 1930's and had joined the newly organized Dohbama Asiayone, fount of the Thakin movement. He was one of the Thirty Heroes who had received military training under the Japanese, returning to Burma with Bogyoke Aung San in 1942 as second in command of the Burma Independence Army. He remained in military life, entering the postwar (British) Burma Army in 1945 as a lieutenant colonel, becoming colonel in 1947, major general in 1948, and replacing the Karen, Smith-Dun, as lieutenant general and supreme commander in February, 1949. He became a full general on January 1, 1956. During the worst days of the insurrections he had served as Deputy Prime Minister and Minister for Defense and for Home Affairs in U Nu's Cabinet. Confidence in General Ne Win was based on more than his campaigns against the insurgents. He had carefully built up the armed forces, selecting and training good men, initiating and supporting educational institutions—the Defense Services Academy at Maymyo and the National Defense College (later discontinued as a college and reorganized as "in-service" training programs) for senior officers in Rangoon—and he sponsored the anti-Communist Psychological Warfare Division.

This thumbnail sketch is relevant to an understanding of what happened in Burma from October, 1958, until after the national elections of February, 1960, when General Ne Win turned over the government of Burma to the democratically elected U Nu. For General Ne Win and his commanding officers, many of whom assisted him during these months, regarded themselves as committed to a national ideology compounded of "Freedom, Democracy, and

Socialism," in that order. Their point of view was formulated at the Meiktila Defense Services Conference on October 21, 1958, just prior to General Ne Win's takeover. Then, as a "second phase," the Defense Services defined their role in support of the ideology. It was "to restore peace and the rule of law, to implant democracy, to establish a socialist economy." [24]

The preparation of an ideology and the definition of the accompanying role of the military are unusual departures, but they are understandable in the light of the nationalist backgrounds of the chief participants in the endeavor. The sources of the ideology are set forth as the Constitution and the founding documents of Burma's first Parliament in 1948. The nationalist spirit behind the ideology is revealed in the following quotation:

> The Defense Services are not an upstart organization newly formed after Independence. Neither is their leadership. These Defense Services fought in the vanguard of the pre-independence struggle, and following Independence they gave an estimable account of themselves against the forces of evil [insurrectionists]. Under loyal and heroic leadership they have always been staunch defenders of freedom and democracy in the Union. As long as this strength remains, the Constitution shall remain inviolate.[25]

General Ne Win's civilian caretaker Cabinet[26] was supported by a considerable number of military officers assigned to various executive and administrative posts in the civil departments of the ministries. Approximately 150 such appointments were made, with several officers holding more than one post. Approximately one-third of these officers had been decorated with the "Order of the Star of the Revolution for Independence," instituted by presidential decree on November 3, 1953, for service with the armed forces during World War II.[27] Twenty of these officers had started their nationalist careers with the Burma Independence Army, under the leadership of Bogyoke Aung San.

The addition of these officers to the Ne Win administration gave it a military complexion. Government policies were executed with unaccustomed dispatch. Burma experienced a variation of that historical stereotype, a "Puritan" or "Cromwellian" regime. Every phase of national life felt its impact as the government set austerely about redeeming the promises that General Ne Win had made in October, 1958.

The chief target was the suppression of insurgency. At the beginning of the regime it was estimated that there were still about 4,000 Communists, a like number of Karen and other ethnic rebels, and about 1,300–1,400 former Kuomintang guerrillas in the eastern Shan hills, living off the opium trade. In addition, some 6,000–7,000 individuals still aided and abetted these insurgents. The government undertook vigorous military offensives; it established a system of rewards and protection for "People's Reporters" who informed the government of insurgent activity. About 2,000 rebels were killed and a like number wounded; some 1,200 were captured and 3,600 surrendered. Considerable quantities of rebel arms, totaling about 160,000 pieces, were recovered. At the beginning of 1960, the remaining strength of all rebels and their supporters was estimated at just over 5,000. Those who surrendered were registered and repatriated to their own towns, or given agricultural training at army-administered schools and then resettled.[28]

Progress in national security and in the related campaign against crime[29] was constantly reported in the press and by radio, usually in six-month totals. Symbolic of the improving conditions, instanced in terms of "the restoration of vital communications" of the railways, roads, and waterways, was the following excerpt from an editorial in *The Guardian* for January 3, 1960:

> On December 30, thirty rafts of logs manned by two hundred men arrived at Rangoon from the Chindwin river area, and their arrival was fittingly hailed as an achievement because it was the first time, since the outbreak and spread of the insurrection, that such a journey could be accomplished without armed escort and molestation from the lawless elements. The simple feat of logs and raftsmen floating safely down the two arteries of Burma, the Chindwin and the Irrawaddy rivers, signifies that after many long years of life-giving struggle, the armed forces of the country have prevailed over the forces of destruction to the extent that the common and humble people can now follow their lawful avocations with freedom from fear and physical loss in an important stretch of the country. Rendering the chief rivers of Burma safe for travel is a job which may not be as dazzling as a speech on democracy, but it is a harder task which in the long run will promote democracy more effectively than an election campaign.

The cost of living, especially in Rangoon, was lowered by controls on prices and profit margins, revamping the Ministry of Cooperatives and Commodity Distribution, opening some two-score military and civilian fair-price shops, and creating a number of commercial enterprises under the direct control of the Defense Services Institute. The composite index (1952 = 100) was brought down from the 1957 high, 116.5, to 99.7 in 1959. The decline in the cost of food and clothing was even more marked.[30] In order to strengthen the economy, the government sought to curtail or eliminate unprofitable industrial enterprises, while placing greater stress on agriculture and encouraging initiative in the private sector. It was helped considerably by the good planting and harvesting season of 1958, and spectacularly by the early arrival of earth-moving and other equipment procured under a U.S. dollar-loan agreement of $5.4 million, signed in December, 1957, and delivered in April, 1958. The equipment was used to accelerate land-reclamation and water-control projects in the Delta.

A central feature of General Ne Win's economic policy is illustrated by the State Timber Board (Amendment) Act No. 1 of 1959. It provided for special audits of the board's funds and expenditures by the auditor-general and for submission of this audit to the Chamber of Deputies. This set a pattern for the careful examination and parliamentary scrutiny of the fiscal operations of all government-sponsored boards and corporations operating in the public sector of the economy. This drive for fiscal and operating efficiency, sorely needed as it was, could nevertheless have slowed down the never very fast pace of Burmese economic decision-making and performance. But because senior military officers had been assigned to the ministries, and because they had the full confidence of the Prime Minister, the total effort made for considerable progress.[31]

In a fair appraisal on January 12, 1960, *The New York Times* pointed out: "Burma's financial and economic situation took a turn for the better last year. The military government of General Ne Win made good progress in eliminating corruption, inefficiency, and bureaucracy, and a record rice harvest paved the way for a favorable trade balance." Furthermore the government's policies were in line with those of the Four-Year Plan of 1956, and it carried them out more effectively. What Ne Win's government demonstrated was its ability not only to execute policies but also to find ways of enlisting the economic initiative and energies of the people while eliminating some of the bureaucratic obstacles within the government itself. This was true in agriculture, industry, and commerce. The carrot was accompanied by a stick, but except in the area of security the stick was not used.

One aspect of the economic drive was the decision to do something about the filth and deterioration of Rangoon. On November 29, 1958, President U Win Maung officially discharged the elected Councillors of the Corporation (city government) of Rangoon as incompetent. On December 1, a new administration, headed by Colonel Tun Sein, the brother of Burma's former Ambassador to the United States, took office and accomplished a minor miracle. Rangoon was partially restored to its prewar high level of cleanliness and sightliness. The slogan "Let us wash the city with our sweat" enlisted thousands of citizens in weekly cleanup campaigns, while the government made provision for moving to new satellite towns on the outskirts of Rangoon some 160,000 people from 24,000 slum dwellings and bamboo huts.[32] The maintenance of Rangoon will be a minor but not unimportant test for future governments.

A new nonpolitical, nationwide organization was formed in the spring of 1959, officially unconnected with the Ne Win government but prodded into being and officered by its military and civilian leaders. The Kyant-Khaing-Ye Ahphwe, or National Solidarity Association (NSA), was pledged to foster patriotic loyalty and good citizenship. It promised to uphold the Constitution and the laws, to combat enemies, traitors, and economic insurgents, to provide rural leadership and advance community development, to help maintain public morality. Though the NSA was organized on a national basis, its local associations were authorized to govern themselves, provided they abided by national rules. Every *thugyi* (ward leader) was empowered to form a local association. In November, 1959, the NSA held a mass rally in Rangoon attended by members and delegates from thirty-four districts.[33] Its sponsorship as a lay organization related to the military leadership made it capable of being transformed into a political party supporting the military.

General Ne Win had been charged with the responsibility of holding free and fair elections within six months of taking office, i.e., in the spring of 1959, provided law and order were restored and the political parties cooperated. In the absence of these conditions, Ne Win resigned in February, 1959. Not being an elected member of Parliament, he could not legally serve as a minister longer than six months. Section 116 of the Constitution was temporarily amended on February 26 to permit him to serve without being elected to Parliament, until the elections were held in 1960. The Constitutional Amendment Act, 1959, was passed in a joint session of the two houses, 304 to 29, with only the crypto-Communists opposed. On February 27, 1959, General Ne Win was again elected prime minister, and his second government was sworn in that evening.

One of its urgent tasks was to insure that the postponed elections would be held. Work had already been started on a house-to-house check to provide new and untarnished electoral rolls. This was completed by the end of the summer of 1959. Any fears that Ne Win's regime might have then become a continuing military dictatorship gave way as his government steadily prepared to redeem its pledge of free and fair elections. Gradually, it appeared that the new target date would conform to the constitutional requirement for a general parliamentary election "in no case later than April 1960." [34] The President dissolved Parliament as of December 19. This, in turn, dictated the constitutional timetable ("within 60 days") for the filing of candidates and the holding of the general election, which was fixed for February 6, 1960.[35]

Throughout the period, from the AFPFL split in April, 1958, to the election in February, 1960, the "Clean" and "Stable" factions continued their political warfare and organizational efforts in preparation for the electoral showdown. The Burmese press was filled with the charges and countercharges of this protracted campaign. No blow was too low for delivery. No promise to the electorate was too extreme. During the summer of 1959, when it became clear that the general elections would be held in early 1960, each faction set about redefining its political philosophy and electoral program. In late September, the Nu-Tin Clean AFPFL held a four-day Supreme Council meeting at which it decided to build a socialist state, support "active neutrality" in foreign affairs, reject negotiations with the insurgents, and make Buddhism the state religion.[36] The Swe-Nyein Stable AFPFL prepared its program in a fifteen-day seminar. It stood for a socialist state, "active neutrality" in foreign affairs, and an eleven-point program for the propagation of Buddhism, without any commitment on the issue of the state religion. It also rejected negotiation with the insurgents.[37] Obviously, the choice of the electorate would be determined less by the appeals of the competing programs than by its estimate of the competing leaders.[38]

Both factions agreed in late October to convert all presplit AFPFL funds and properties into a memorial for their founder, Bogyoke Aung San. But they also decided to retain the AFPFL label while campaigning.

During the campaign, whispering charges were made that the army favored the Swe-Nyein group, and that President U Win Maung inclined toward the Nu-Tin side. As a result, General Ne Win issued a stern warning to officers and civil servants that they remain absolutely impartial in the coming election.[39] U Win Maung, in an unusual departure, sent a public letter to the Prime Minister, commending him for his impartial role and urging that it be emphasized throughout the country until the campaign was over.[40]

These events were taking place while the Clean AFPFL was scoring an overwhelming series of victories in the municipal elections, which began in October and were generally completed by the end of 1959. To the surprise of most, the Nu-Tin group won a total of 367 out of 526 municipal seats, taking control of 33 out of 42 towns. This victory foreshadowed the outcome of the national elections the following February.

All this was by way of preparation for the general elections of February 6, 1960. A total of 934 candidates filed for the 250 seats in the Chamber of Deputies. The Clean faction put up 204; the Stable, 202; the NUF (from which the Justice Party had split off to join the Clean AFPFL), 135. Independent candidates and those of smaller parties and sectional groups totaled 393. Out of 250 constituencies in the Chamber of Deputies, free elections were simultaneously held in 229. Elections were initially postponed in 15 due to insurgent activities. The death of a candidate postponed 1, and 5 constituency elections were contested in the courts.[41]

U Nu—whose picture on traditional Buddhist yellow background adorned the Clean AFPFL ballot boxes by way of identifying his party—and his colleagues and allies in the various states won an extraordinary victory. They captured at least two-thirds of the popular vote in a total of about 6 million. When Parliament convened on April 1, 1960, the following distribution was on record:

Clean AFPFL (renamed the Pyidaungsu, or Union League, Party)	159
Stable AFPFL (retaining the AFPFL designation)	41
Arakanese National Unity Organization (ANUO)	6
Mon National Front	3
Chin National Organization	3
Kayah State	2
Shan State, independents, and others	23
	237

U Nu's new government could easily count on Mon, Chin, Kayah, and some Shan votes; he also had the occasional support of the ANUO, especially as he proceeded to honor his campaign promise of Arakan statehood. The opposition AFPFL attracted some support from among the Shan, Karen, and Kachin independents, but it was barely able to muster the fifty votes required to put a parliamentary motion of no confidence. The crypto-Communists of the NUF failed to capture a single seat. (In the West, the Mon group was sometimes confused with the NUF because one of its three winners had formerly been an NUF associate.) The NUF received about 300,000 votes, i.e., 5 per cent of the total, as against about 1.3 million, or approximately 38 per cent in 1956, when the NUF had included the Justice Party. U Nu had acquired for his new party a majority as impressive as that achieved in the AFPFL landslide of 1951.

Even more impressive were the results in Rangoon, where the Clean AFPFL won all nine seats. Dr. E Maung, by no means a popular figure, defeated by more than a two-to-one majority former Prime Minister U Ba Swe, who had always been ranked next to U Nu in the united AFPFL. Similarly, Thakin Tin defeated U Kyaw Nyein by a better than two-to-one vote; U Raschid, outstanding Muslim leader, swamped his fellow Muslim, U Khin Maung Lat, three to one. In the elections for the 125-member Chamber of Nationalities, begun on February 29, 1960, U Nu's party scored similar victories. His supporters carried fifty-three seats against twenty-nine for the Stable AFPFL; the remaining forty-three seats were assigned to the designees of the several states.[42]

Tillman Durdin, one of the best U.S. correspondents for Asia, reported in *The New York Times* (February 9, 1960): "The polling was carried out in an exemplary fashion. The results are evidence that the voters successfully exercised independence of judgment since the losing . . . faction had seemingly important advantages . . . of more money, more party workers, better organization, and more transportation with which to carry voters to the polls."

The election was primarily an endorsement of U Nu. His devotion to Buddhism, and his promise to make it the state religion, undoubtedly won him support throughout the country from the influential Sangha. As recently as 1959, he had spent forty-five days in a Buddhist retreat, emerging from it with a new series of five lectures on the virtues and compatibility of non-Marxist socialism and Buddhism.[43] He had added the advantage of the vigorous support of the widow of General Aung San, Daw Khin Kyi, who subsequently became Burma's first woman ambassador (to India). U Nu constantly warned the country against fascism, meaning by implication the danger of continued military rule with its abrupt discipline, foreign to Burmese custom. This rule was associated with the Stable AFPFL, which allegedly was favored by the armed forces.[44]

Further, the Swe-Nyein campaigners, confident in the summer of 1959, appear to have lost heart after their defeats in the municipal elections. They had expected to have a strong appeal among the urban population. They also had better resources for reaching the educated, the youth, and the trade unions; the last had been regarded as a stronghold of U Ba Swe's. On the other hand, Thakin Tin and Thakin Kyaw Tun had for years worked with and led the All-Burma Peasants' Organization. The Swe-Nyein forces were unable to balance their losses in the cities by gains among the rural masses.

The campaign was fought as if there were two major parties in conflict, a healthy departure in Burmese politics. However, the outcome left the defeated faction with so small a parliamentary fraction that it would experience difficulty in acting out its part as the official parliamentary opposition. Short of an unpredictable catastrophe or a split in his newly named party, U Nu's government could expect to have the constitutional four years in office.

General Ne Win turned over the reins of government to U Nu at the opening of the parliamentary session in April, 1960. Between the election and the new session, U Nu and his colleagues gave up their Clean AFPFL party label. In mid-March they reorganized as the Pyidaungsu, or Union League, Party and adopted a new constitution and four resolutions governing their policy with respect to internal peace (no negotiations with rebels); electoral justice (a permanent department for future registration and supervision); foreign policy (active neutrality); and national economy (balanced between agriculture and industry).[45] In naming his Cabinet, U Nu followed Ne Win's practice of having one minister hold several portfolios, thus reducing the total number of ministers to thirteen[46] and the parliamentary secretaries to thirteen. His opening speech to the Chamber of Deputies on April 5, entitled "Crusade for Democracy," began with the comment that "Burma has just passed through a period in her history which is unique not only in our own experience but that of other countries in the world." He reviewed the promises he had made during the campaign and indicated that he would make every effort to fulfill them.[47]

U Nu's estimate of the recent period in Burma was both accurate and perceptive. For contrary to expectations in many quarters, and to actual experience in quite a few countries, a military group that was invited into power scrupulously honored the terms of the invitation. General Ne Win's civilian caretaker government and its military-infused administration strengthened the stability of the country at a time of sharp and devastating political conflict. They protected Burma against Communist subversion, and, in seventeen months of rule, drastically reduced the possibility of Communist success in Burma, barring outside intervention. When it was time to withdraw from governing, they did so. There may have been some military grumbling at turning back unfinished work to less efficient civilians. There may have been some vocal or suppressed criticism at the possibility that their handiwork would be disregarded or altered by U Nu's new government. But the changeover after the elections went smoothly and speedily, according to the wishes of the retiring and incoming premiers.

Bogyoke Ne Win and his civilian and military officers did more than re-establish stability in a newly independent country; they provided a demonstration lesson in nonbureaucratic efficiency and puritanical incorruptibility; they also provided a sufficiently different, if not unique, example of military and civilian support for nationalist ideals and a commitment to democratic processes and goals. Ne Win took office on a democratic timetable. Typically Burmese in their optimistic scheduling, Ne Win and his colleagues thought that they could deliver what they had promised within six months. Ne Win promptly acknowledged the error, secured more time, and fulfilled his commitments in a longer but still relatively short period. He might have held power a few more months without jeopardizing his reputation. But he and his officers preferred to hold to their revised timetable to restore Burma to a constitutionally elected civilian government.

Their role in Burma, at a time when the military were taking control in several other Asian countries, inevitably gave rise to the question: Are Western-style representative institutions unworkable for countries newly emerged from colonialism? And it also raised doubts as to whether or not it is desirable to encourage the growth of these armies, independent of whatever representative institutions the respective countries may have established or hope to establish.[48] These questions will be answered in Chapter 9. The example of General Ne Win's voluntary acceptance of the return of democratic government to Burma ended *for the time being* what had seemed to be Burma's movement toward a typical military dictatorship. The Union was preserved, as were its democratic institutions.

The Crusade for Democracy Falters

WHEN PRIME MINISTER U NU delivered his policy speech to the Chamber of Deputies on April 5, 1960, he took pains to reiterate the more significant promises he had made in the election campaign.[2] He said that there was "no alternative to democracy," and to that end he pledged "action," until "it becomes native to our soil." He announced that his Pyidaungsu Party, despite its huge majority in the Parliament, would operate in "strict compliance with the true principles of democracy." It would respect and welcome "constructive" opposition in and out of the Parliament. Above all, he pledged that the "politicians" would not interfere with "the administration." He reviewed the many "undemocratic" mistakes that he and his party had made during the previous years of rule, mistakes which he would seek to avoid making again. This meant, among other things, that in the economic sphere his party and government would act with restraint, and that there would be limits to the intrusion of the state in further developing a new four-year plan for a balanced economy.

U Nu indicated that if the desire for statehood was "real," he would implement his promise to this effect for the Arakanese and the Mons; and in this connection he would seek to promote the unity, stability, and prosperity of the Union, while at the same time recognizing that such unity "does not" require the sacrifice of the "specific characteristics" of cultural, national, or religious groups. However, he also indicated that he expected to carry out the promise "to make Buddhism the State Religion of Burma," while protecting "the rights and privileges of the other religions in the state."

This was another notable U Nu speech on a moving occasion before the newly elected Parliament. The speech was an indication that U Nu would seek to carry out as policies the aspirations to which he had previously given voice, and that, at the same time, he would try to heal the wounds caused by the bitterness of the political split and the hard-fought election campaign. Curiously, he was silent on one of the central issues faced by all earlier governments: what policy he would follow with respect to the insurrectionists, Communist and ethnic—an issue which, as we have seen, had brought him into conflict with the armed forces in 1958.

There were no items among his promises, save that of statehood to the Mons, which could not be reasonably defended, and which, if carefully carried out, would not command sizable majorities in the Parliament and in the public at large. Statehood for the Mons was at best a sentimental gesture to eighteenth-century Burmese history, for except for a few tens of thousands of Mons who lived in noncontiguous Tenasserim villages and who still retained their language (but who were otherwise culturally indistinguishable from the Buddhist Burmans), there was no geographic, economic, or cultural basis for a Mon state.

U Nu had certain advantages as he proceeded on his path. Gross domestic product (1947-48 prices) stood at the then all-time high of 113 per cent for 1959-60, and the estimates for 1960-61 (not in fact reached) were slightly higher. Rice exports reached an all-time postwar high of almost 2.1 million tons for 1959-60; and though the volume for the succeeding year was estimated somewhat lower, the value of these exports was expected to be increased by the 7 per cent rise in world prices. In addition, at the beginning of 1961 the government negotiated with Peking an interest-free, ten-year line of credit for $84 million, and a second World Bank loan for the further development of the Burma Railways. Except for the rise in the cost of living that followed the ending of the price controls instituted by the Ne Win regime, Burma seemed well set for the launching of the Second Four-Year Plan in 1961. As if to signify the hands-off policy of the armed forces, General Ne Win at the end of May, 1960, went off to the United Kingdom and the United States for medical treatment. *The Times* of London (February 3, 1961) commented favorably on the "improvements" in Burma during 1960, brought about, it said, by General Ne Win and U Nu, who learned to "trim" their "overbold attempts at national planning."

Politically, however, all was not well. A number of overlapping factors combined to cause uneasiness, and in the end, they brought to a close U Nu's crusade for democracy. These factors were dissension and division in U Nu's Union Party; the promulgation of Buddhism as the state religion; the rise of insurrectionary activity, particularly among the KNDO's and other minorities, complicated by the remnants of the Kuomintang troops still active in the Shan states; new demands for "federalism," particularly among the Shans —demands that were interpreted as an indirect attack on the unity of the Union; and U Nu's inability or unwillingness to use his great popular appeal to restore order where it was lacking or where it was under attack. At almost any time during this period he could have dissolved the Parliament, dismissed his factional government, and asked the people for a new mandate, which most probably he would have received. Instead, he exhorted and temporized while disunity spread.

These issues facing the regime reached a crescendo that suddenly, and without explanation, brought on an "army reshuffle." On February 7, 1961, it was announced that the recently promoted Brigadiers Aung Shwe and Maung Maung would be named as ambassadors, five senior colonels would be assigned abroad as military attachés, and five more "will resign to go into politics and business." [3] Though no official explanation has ever been forthcoming, the following may serve as an interpretation of this event.

Dissension within the Union Party had broken out shortly after victory in February, 1960. From then on there was conflict over the issue of membership on the party's executive committee. (A party ruling had barred officers of the constituent organizations, such as the All-Burma Peasants Organization, the Federation of Trade Organizations, the Union Labor Organization, from holding posts on the executive committee.) Tension grew between two groups of party leaders, subsequently identified as the Thakins (i.e., those who led the above-named organizations) and the U-Bos (i.e., those who presumably supported U Nu's insistence on an individual-membership party). In December, 1960, U Nu announced that he would soon resign his party leadership, though he would presumably remain as Prime Minister. It appeared as if the new Union Party would, like the old AFPFL, split apart.

In the same month the Chins, who unlike the Mons had at least some geographic and cultural unity, put forward their claims to statehood to parallel those of the Arakanese and the Mons, while the former President of Burma, Sao Shwe Thaike, one of the leading Shan *sawbwas*, submitted a bill of particulars designed to loosen the federal-state structure of the Constitution. He obviously spoke for a group of his peers who sought either a better financial settlement from the central government for relinquishing their princely rule, or an actual "separation" or "secession" from Rangoon. Some of his associates had been suspected of encouraging Shan rebels, who had given Ne Win difficulty during his regime. The Constitution allowed for such secession during a period of ten years, i.e., to 1958. But at that time the central government and the armed forces, partially located in the Shan states, had no intention of allowing any secessionary move. Sao Shwe Thaike included criticism of the armed forces because it "could station units in [Shan] State territory and recruit personnel without reference to the State concerned." [4] On a narrower issue, also raised in December, U Nu appeared to take a negative stand against continuing the National Defense College established by the Ne Win regime, and against the creation of a Central Intelligence Organization, both of which Brigadier Maung Maung, one of the two leading officers in the army after Ne Win, had specifically encouraged. Earlier in the year, U Nu had removed the police from army jurisdiction and given it responsibility for its own training, thus weakening the strength of the armed forces in their campaigns against insurgency. He also announced that the new Burma Economic Development Corporation would gradually relieve the armed forces of their hold on various economic activities previously carried on under the management of the Defense Services Institute. (The latter had originally started as a kind of post exchange operation. During the caretaker regime it created or absorbed some thirty commercial and manufacturing enterprises.)

It was no secret in Rangoon that some military men were of the opinion that the country was going downhill and that a new military takeover was desirable. U Nu is said to have confronted General Ne Win with this situation. In February, 1961, Ne Win sided with U Nu and against the politically minded officers, presumably expecting that the Prime Minister would straighten things out. The above-mentioned officers were assigned to posts out of the country or were allowed to resign. Later that month, on February 26, the Prime Minister spoke at Myitkyina, and said that "if not for his tension-easing campaign the country would have by now suffered a similar fate to that of the Congo or Laos." [5] He also agreed to retain the leadership of the party for "a year more" and proceeded to revamp the membership of its executive committee in order to harmonize the differences between the two factions. He bemoaned the "16,000" problems—a Buddhist reference to troubles—that he and his colleagues faced. [6]

Thus ended the first internal crisis of U Nu's most recent regime.

In a two-hour address at the opening of the March, 1961, meeting of Parliament, the Prime Minister gave a full account of his stewardship during the past eleven months, and especially of his efforts "to redeem the election pledge to build democracy." [7] He also presented the outlines of the Second Four-Year Plan and renewed his promises on such issues as statehood and the state religion. He expected to have his proposals on the latter ready for the August, 1961, meeting of Parliament, and he announced the formation of state preparatory commissions for the Arakanese and Mons.

The state-religion issue had already aroused considerable minority opposition. In October, 1960, the Burmese Baptist Convention, representing 250,000 Baptists in Burma, issued a statement to the effect that they feared Christians would lose their "fundamental rights" if Burma officially adopted Buddhism as the religion of the state.[8] Early in 1961, representatives of the Baptists, Burmese Muslims, animists, and even some Buddhists, particularly from the Shan and Kachin states led by Sao Shwe Thaike, organized the National Religious Minorities' Alliance (NRMA) to oppose U Nu's determined drive to secure enactment of the necessary legislation. The former president indicated that such legislation would violate "the Panglong spirit," [9] referring to the Panglong Conference of February, 1947, which insured the unity of the majority Burmans and the minorities of Burma.

There was virtually no opposition to statehood for the Arakanese, since the area they inhabit in Burma is located west of the Arakan Yoma and south of the Pakistan border. Their language is a somewhat differently accented Burmese; they are a Buddhist majority with some Burmese Muslims. Few, however, took the proposals for a Mon state seriously. In the final analysis, it was expected that the Arakanese, and eventually the Chins, would join the Kachins, the Shans, the Karens, and the Kayahs as peoples in Burma entitled to some form of statehood, provided all remained in a united Burma.

Criticism of a state religion was sincere, and it was treated seriously by U Nu so as to reassure the religious minorities. But on any test of public sentiment in Burma, and in the light of experience outside of Burma, where there were successful and peaceful examples of state religions with toleration for religious minorities, it was clear that this issue, by itself, would not damage the fabric of Burmese unity.

Of greater significance, and not unrelated to the statehood issue, particularly in the Shan state area, was the gradual decline of security from the peak that had been achieved under the Ne Win caretaker regime. It is quite probable that Burma had no national counterinsurgency plan prior to the advent of that regime in 1958. Earlier, strategy was developed as the Burmese armed forces proceeded to recruit, train, and arm regular units (usually at the platoon level), constabulary and paramilitary police, and one form or another of local anti-insurgent defense groups. Maximum tactical authority was given to commanders in the field in conjunction with what is now called "civic action" local leadership. Since 1958, the armed forces had prepared anti-insurgent manuals and had stepped up their psychological-warfare campaigns. They had come to believe that the latter, in conjunction with their use of the offensive, their morale, their military training and civil-military action, had ground down and pushed back the rebels to the point of defeat.[10] The task had been long and costly.

At the beginning of U Nu's 1960 government, it appeared as if the assorted Communist rebels were close to exhaustion and certainly to ineffectiveness. The complete defeat of the NUF in the 1960 elections had accentuated this condition. Though there was still a hard core of Communist rebels, they were on the run. Leaders in the ranks were captured, including Party Central Committee member Bo Tin Thein, who had been "in charge" of the Communists in the Delta.[11] Well-known Communist wives were coming "out of the jungle" and were apprehended; for example, Daw Khin Gyi, wife of BCP Politbureau leader Thakin Than Myaing, in May, 1960, and Daw Hla May, wife of the second most important BCP leader, H. Goshal, in November. In this same month, military intelligence cracked a Communist rebel headquarters concealed in the Rangoon area;[12] and in January, 1961, an important group of seventeen Red Flag Communists who had been operating in the Insein and Maubin districts surrendered with a considerable quantity of arms. When Communist leader Than Tun renewed, by letter to U Nu, his readiness to "negotiate" peace with the government, its arrival caused neither surprise nor much interest.[13] The Communist rebels could occasionally make trouble in outlying areas, but they were not a major threat to the security of the country.

Despite this improvement in one sector of the long-fought battle against insurgency, difficulties increased in the ethnic insurrectionary areas. Early in Ne Win's caretaker regime, after the Shan *sawbwas* by constitutional arrangements had turned over their remaining powers to the federal Shan state and the central government in return for compensation for their loss of hereditary and other rights, a small group of rebels took up arms against the central government.[14] Their ire was directed against the army, which had positioned detachments in the Shan state to combat remnants of the KMT's and roving bands of the KNDO's, and also to anticipate any trouble that might be caused with the ending of the power of the hereditary sawbwas in 1958. With the beginning of U Nu's new government in 1960, Shan insurgent activity increased.[15] Concurrently, the KNDO's were able to step up their campaign against the government in apparent concert with the Shan rebels.[16] By the end of the year Rangoon was worried at the deterioration of security in these rebel areas.[17]

Further complications arose in November, 1960, when the Army, which was engaged in the task of demarcating the Sino-Burmese boundary in cooperation with official detachments of the Chinese Communist army, encountered newly trained and equipped (with some American material) KMT forces at Keng Lap and other border areas in the Shan state of Kentung on the Laos-Thailand border. In ensuing battles at the beginning of 1961, Shan and later KNDO rebels joined forces with the KMT's. This new conflict between Rangoon and Taipeh created a furor in Burma, especially when, after a Chinese-manned American plane had been shot down, it was reported that the English-language *China News* (Taipeh) admitted its participation as "another case of overflight" for a "noble cause"; and that "if we are caught we are caught." Students rioted in February before the American embassy in Rangoon in protest against "American complicity." The opposition AFPFL party, ordinarily not unfriendly to the United States, called upon the U Nu government to make representations to both the U.S. and the U.N.—which it did.[18] A small remaining KMT group, estimated at about 750, merged with the Shan and Karen rebels, and together they continued to carry out insurrectionary actions.

The country seemed to be alarmed by these events. U Nu stated that "though some people were inclined to panic, the situation was not out of hand." He blamed "luck for the worsening security . . . and admitted that the security conditions in the country were bad but comparatively not so bad as things were in 1949-50." [19] The press in Burma did not take kindly to U Nu's attempt to blame "luck." They called upon him to increase the size of the armed forces, especially of rear protective elements that could hold territory cleared in an offensive.

It is probable that if U Nu could have proceeded constructively from this point forward (early 1961) he would have maintained control of the situation. For the country then rallied in the face of an external aggressor, the KMT's, and soured on the claims of Shan and Karen separatists and rebels who made common cause with the hated Kuomintang Chinese. But once again party friction and factionalism broke out, and in the end they triggered the quick temper of General Ne Win.

U Nu decided to adhere to his one-year-more schedule, after which he would resign leadership of the party—though keeping the post of prime minister. This meant that in 1962, at the All-Burma Conference of his Union Party he would relinquish control of the party. Concurrently he had at first privately, then publicly, indicated that he would retire from politics at or after the next regular elections in 1964. Thus at stake within the Union Party were two posts, one imminent and the other potential: party leadership in 1962 and the premiership in 1964 (which, if the Union Party won the election, usually fell to the party leader).

Signs that U Nu's attempt to revamp the Union Party were not succeeding appeared in the press in May, 1961. His six-man reorganization committee, designed to harmonize the two factions, the Thakins and the U-Bos, was ignored by the organizational leader of the former, Thakin Kyaw Tun, who, it will be remembered, had precipitated the split in the AFPFL in 1958, when he had been appointed to the party secretaryship by U Nu.

During late May and June of 1961, while U Nu withdrew for another long forty-five-day Buddhist retreat, party factional activity remained in the background. Early in July, the Shans, led by Sao

Shwe Thaike and then apparently joined by the foreign minister and head of the Shan state, Sao Hkun Hkio, staged a minority people's conference in Taunggyi. There they sought alliances to press their demands for a looser, more federalized type of constitution. The tone of the conference was reported as so bitterly anti-Burman and anti-army that leading Kachin, Chin, and Karen representatives disassociated themselves from it. However, U Nu indicated that since the Shan proposals were democratically proposed, they should be treated "with love." No one, least of all his Constitution Revision Committee concerned with the proposed amendments for the state religion and for the new states, knew how to interpret Nu's reference to the Buddhist doctrine of Metta.

The Buddhist State Religion Amendment was passed by the August session of Parliament, which later passed a second amendment protecting the rights of religious minorities. Each amendment created a vocal opposition. And troubles multiplied. The monsoon brought devastating floods, described as the worst in twenty-five years. Some 200,000 people were made homeless and 300,000 acres of paddy land lost the crop for the current year. The cost-of-living index was rising, and taxes were increased.

At the end of the monsoon in October, the Union Party factions began to prepare for the 1962 conference, now scheduled for January 27, 1962. There followed a vicious countrywide primary fight for control of the party, if anything more severe than that of the two factions of the AFPFL after the split in 1958. No one seemed to know where U Nu stood—except that, apparently aloof from the struggle, he was going to step down. Charges and counter-charges by each faction filled the press in the late fall and early winter of 1961-62. When the January conference was over, it appeared that U Nu had given the nod to the Thakin faction which was joined by Minister Dr. E Maung (holding several new portfolios in addition to those to which he had been appointed in April, 1960) and his political secretary, U Ohn. Led by E Maung, the Thakins emerged as the party leadership in February, 1962; and the Union Party was for all practical purposes split. Almost as a last irrational gesture U Nu withdrew the remaining 15 per cent of the import business from the private sector, in apparent violation of his promise to involve the state less rather than more in the economy of the country. The affected sector of the business community staged a three-day protest strike, shutting down their premises.

Why did U Nu, who had done so much for the country, allow this deterioration in public life? Former political allies who are not personally unfriendly to him accuse him of political weakness. They cite various events since 1947 to prove that U Nu "follows" and "fronts" for strength, that he is really unable to lead. Others in the same camp accuse him of being a shrewd politician who is patient enough to wait for his opponents and subordinates to knock each other out by the virulence of their conflict, thereby affording him the opportunity to pick up the pieces and appear as savior. Some of his former political allies exonerate U Nu because he followed the bad advice of such men as E Maung or U Ohn. Others charge him with an increasing involvement in Buddhist life which, however praiseworthy, unfitted him for the political realities of the day. Certainly, there is some truth in all of these statements: he has been a temporizer when decision-making was necessary; he has been wily; he has listened to bad advice and has stood loyally by these advisers because of past or present connections; and he has increasingly become persuaded that the Buddhist way is what he prefers to tread. No one has ever called him a *religious* hypocrite.

These are all partial explanations. I have called him a charismatic leader. By its very nature charisma is in part indefinable. Certainly he demonstrated that he could win the population of Burma when he *wanted* their support. But after his election in 1960, he appears to have become somewhat disorganized, never fully using his popular appeal, unwilling or unable to maintain the unity of his party and of the country's essential institutions—without such unity Burma has in the past disintegrated—always preaching to leader groups and hoping, perhaps, to convert them in one evangelical Buddhist effort. In this he certainly failed. I believe, though it cannot be demonstrated, that U Nu's final failure was largely psychological, that he could no longer reconcile the requirements of political leadership with his desire to achieve Buddhist religious integration and carry out its consequences in public life.[20]

The Coup and the Revolutionary Council

Early in the morning of March 2, 1962, the armed forces led by General Ne Win staged a *coup d'état*. Ministers, including U Nu; the President; the Chief Justice of the Supreme Court (who had certain constitutional powers that could legally thwart the army); and certain Shan leaders in Rangoon (who were charged with advocating policies and possibly instigating action that would help to break up the Union of Burma) were all arrested and placed in an army-camp jail just outside of Rangoon. The political leadership of the parties—Union (both factions), AFPFL, and NUF—was initially not molested. What was then called the Union Revolutionary Council, and later the Revolutionary Government, took power and set about restoring order to the country. The coup was generally greeted by a feeling of relief: now, at least, the slide downward would be stopped.[21]

General Ne Win's announcement of the coup, on March 2, 1962, was brief. He advised the people of the Union that the armed forces had "taken over the responsibility and the task of keeping the country's safety owing to the greatly deteriorating conditions of the Union." [22] He appealed to the people to carry on with their daily tasks, to the government servants to attend to their duties without interruption, and he specifically asked that the education authorities continue with the then-current examination period. This time there was no reference to the Constitution, the Parliament, and other democratic institutions. Nor was there any promise of a caretaker government, which looked forward early to free and fair elections. It was announced that the Revolutionary Council—at no time has it been called a cabinet—consisted of its chief or chairman (General Ne Win), and sixteen other high-ranking officers who were to take over the various ministries. Later, it was also announced that the General retained the powers of the former president as well as "supreme legislative, executive and judicial authority." A separate Communiqué No. 3, also dated March 2, called for friendly relations with all nations, based on international justice and morality; "whole-hearted" support for the principles of the United Nations as embodied in its charter; and the determination of the government to continue its policy of "positive neutrality." [23]

The Revolutionary Council proceeded swiftly to announce its domestic policies. It set aside the Constitution, dissolved both Chambers of Parliament and the existing State Councils, replacing the latter by new State Supreme Councils with a central military figure as one member. It deferred for at least two years the change in the import policy, instituted by U Nu just before the coup; that is, it restored the private import sector to its business. It banned horse racing, public gambling, and beauty contests. It reinstituted its practice of controlling the prices of essential household commodities but otherwise proceeded slowly on economic measures. It reduced the former ministerial and councillor salaries to those drawn by top officers. It abolished the existing Supreme and High Courts, replacing them by a Court of Final Appeal (later called Chief Court). It reinstituted its former practice of raising animals for meat and abolished the sabbath day of leave (an extra holiday if it occurred on a workday) recently allowed by U Nu. However, with respect to the state religion it pursued a cautious policy, announcing its respect for freedom of religion that "did not emphasize one religion at the expense of the other." Above all, it promised to take immediate action "to stamp out" insurgency, and on April 23 and May 1, respectively, it announced the capture of the headquarters of the KNDO at Maingmaw and of a combined Shan-KMT group at Naungpalan. To heighten its security offensives it took steps to reabsorb the constabulary police force into the regular armed services, and it set about recreating central, regional, and local security councils for more effective prosecution of its civic-action and psychological-warfare campaigns to wipe out insurgency "in one year." [24]

The Revolutionary Council indicated its desire to maintain a "no Press-censorship policy," in which the press was free to criticize the Revolutionary Government "so long as they did not support the insurgents." Initially, it had indicated its acceptance of the existing political parties. Later, however, it announced that it would organize a new, All-Burma Party, which the existing parties would be asked to accept.

More startling was its first major domestic-policy declaration, "The Burmese Way to Socialism," which appeared on April 30, 1962. In it the Revolutionary Council stated as its leaders had in the earlier document of 1958, "The National Ideology and the Role of the Defense Services" [25] its commitment to a socialist domestic policy in keeping with the outlook of Burmese nationalist leaders at least since the Two-Year Plan of Economic Development for Burma was adopted at Aung San's 1947 Sorrento Conference. A number of passages in this declaration repeat or parallel the third part of the 1958 document, "To Build a Socialist Economy." There is, in effect, little novelty in its classic exposition of and support for a planned socialist economy, which nonetheless rejects "neglecting the owners of national private enterprise" and expects to "enable them to occupy a worthy place in the course of further national development." However, those who committed themselves to the policy statement this time were disciplined military accustomed to a command-and-control system that expected performance and, as the government, would discipline negligence.

What is new in "The Burmese Way to Socialism" is its break with parliamentary democracy. It acknowledges the superiority of the latter system as "the best in comparison with all . . . preceding systems," but it goes on to point out that it has failed in Burma "due to its very defects, weaknesses and loopholes, its abuses and the absence of a mature public opinion . . . until at last indications of its heading imperceptibly toward just the reverse have become apparent." Elsewhere the Revolutionary Council had made clear that the coup had been made necessary by the breakdown in the political-party process, by the decline in the economy, by the demands for a loosely organized federal structure and for the state religion, and by the continuing phenomenon of insurgency.

Hence, the declaration went on, the Revolutionary Council "must develop, in conformity with existing conditions and environment and ever-changing circumstances, only such a form of democracy as will promote and safeguard the socialist development." This development is possible "only when the solidarity of all the indigenous groups has been established," only when, in the words of Aung San quoted in the declaration, the "people acquired a sense of oneness . . . and a will to live in unity through weal and woe that binds a people together and makes them a nation and their spirit a patriotism."

How to acquire this sense of oneness, the will to live in unity, to build the nation with a spirit of patriotism, has been the continuing objective of Burmese governments since independence. The Revolutionary Council proceeded to carry out this objective in a series of moves which were compounded of military severity, vigorous nationalism (frequently applied in terms of far-reaching Burmanization,[26] especially in economic matters), and socialism. Efforts have been made to reduce all foreign influence—cultural and economic—while stressing the goal of completing the "revolution for workers and peasants." The General's new regime is unlike his caretaker regime; this time he has determined to build a new political order to serve the objectives that he and all other Burmese nationalists have, in their fashion, sought.

"The Burmese Way to Socialism" was followed by an effort, announced on May 18, to form a single party uniting the military interests with those of the three major existing parties—the Union Party, the AFPFL, and the NUF. Only the NUF, renamed the United Workers Party, accepted General Ne Win's terms, which called for an end of parliamentary democracy. Thus rebuffed, the Revolutionary Council on July 4 announced its decision to build its own national cadre party—"other parties can also exist by themselves"—with recruitment open to all citizens eighteen years of age and over. Known as the Burma Socialist Programme Party (BSPP), it became in fact the only legal political organization in Burma. All other political parties were subsequently banned, while the expenses for the BSPP were paid by the government, since it presumably represented the workers and peasants, that is, the majority of the population.[27]

The first test of the Revolutionary Council followed within two days of the decision to organize a new party, though it probably had been planned before the July 4 announcement. The Rangoon University Students' Union had long been under the control of a Communist-sympathizing student group. On July 6, the RUSU Executive Committee called for a demonstration to protest "oppressive new hostel regulations" and other measures that the newly appointed senates and committees of Rangoon and Mandalay universities had adopted earlier that month. The demonstration was held on July 7; it turned into a violent riot. Unable to quell it, the police called for aid from the armed forces. The latter arrived, failed to disperse what had become a fighting mob of students, warned them, and then fired on them. Scores of casualties—dead and wounded—resulted. The next day the security forces deliberately demolished the RUSU building. The authorities also closed all universities and colleges.[28] The country was shocked. Long accustomed to the irresponsibility and political machinations of the RUSU, the people had not expected such draconian measures from the government. It was a costly and harsh lesson, but for a time it stopped the political agitation carried on by a determined minority group within the universities that used its position to perpetuate the rebellion. The institutions, closed until August, 1962, were reopened under an uneasy truce, which lasted for a little over one year.[29]

The Burma Socialist Programme Party, having adopted a formal constitution in July, 1962, became the chief political vehicle for the Revolutionary Council. In January, 1963, it published a "philosophy," or ideology, called "The System of Correlation of Man and Environment," [30] based partly on the Buddhist *Abhidhamma-Pitaka* (the "third basket" of the Buddhist canon), partly on humanism, and a nondogmatic Marxism. This credo must be accepted by all members and candidate-members of the BSPP. When in July, 1963, the Revolutionary Council established the Central School of Political Science for training party cadre leaders, "The Burmese Way to Socialism," the party's constitution, and the "Philosophy" were made part of the curriculum "to guide the Party along the line of non-deviation towards right or left and . . . remove all the impediments in its path." Fourteen months later, the BSPP issued a tabulated document outlining its "specific characteristics" and distinguishing features that presumably marked it off from Social Democratic and Communist parties in other countries.[31]

An inspection of the BSPP's specific characteristics confirms its continuing omission of a return to parliamentary democracy. It is also clear that it has dropped U Nu's commitment to Buddhism as the state religion, and instead sponsors full freedom of conscience and religion to believers and nonbelievers as well.[32] It remains the single political party in a state dedicated to a socialist society. However, because many of its members accept the Buddhist doctrine of ceaseless change, it affirms its adherence to progress in human society, and because of that belief, remains open-minded as to the means of achieving its goals. No economic, political, or social treatise is regarded as an infallible guide to serve the interests of all citizens and to serve the unity of the Union of Burma. All citizens (not "classes"), save "those who live by exploitation of their fellowmen" are eligible for membership in the party.

The rapid development of the BSPP was paced in 1963 by popular measures nationalizing banking, big industry, and commerce. These in turn were supported by new laws, authorized in March and April, 1963, improving land tenure and tenancy and increasing the amounts and availability of loans to the cultivators.

This combination of events contributed to the growing confidence of the Revolutionary Council and led it once again to seek an end to the insurrection by offering amnesty to the rebels. On April 1, 1963, it announced its terms, allowing until July 1 for acceptance. (This was later extended to January 31, 1964.) The provisions for amnesty were as generous as those offered by U Nu in August, 1959, which at that time so alarmed the military. All rebels would be pardoned, and even those charged with rape and murder would receive "lenient treatment." On June 11, this offer was enlarged. The Revolutionary Council proposed unconditional negotiations—called parleys—with guarantees for safe passage to and from the underground, and "three days immunity from arrest or hostile action" for those who returned to the underground.[33] The offer was astounding. It was what the Communists had demanded for years, a demand previously rejected by all governments.

A number of prominent Communist rebels—Ye Htut, Sein Tin, Ye Maung, Tha Doe, Aung Din, among others—accepted the April 1 offer, and have since been given either important civilian posts, or membership in the BSPP, or both.[34] However, these surrenders were overshadowed by the rush of underground delegations that arrived in Rangoon for negotiations. The first group appeared on June 26, representing the Red Flag Communists. On August 10, Thakin Soe, their leader, arrived. He attacked the revisionism of Khrushchev, the opportunism of the Chinese Communists, and called for free national elections and freely chosen organizations. Eleven days later, the Revolutionary Council announced that its peace talks with the Red Flags had been "broken off." [35] The Red Flag contingents were followed by the White Flag Communists (BCP), including a group of Burmese Communists who had been living and training in Communist China. These latter were led by General Ne Win's erstwhile friend from the Thirty Heroes' days, Bo Zeya. The Burmese press (other than the irrepressible Thein Pe Myint in the *Botataung,* which supports Moscow against Peking in their current debate) diplomatically (or perhaps on orders) refrained from mentioning Communist China. It used the euphemism "foreign country." The BCP members were followed by delegations from various ethnic groups of rebels, the Shan State National Front and Independence Army, the Kachin Independence Army (KIA), the Karen National Defense Organization, and others. The ethnic rebels excepting the "formidable" KNDO rebels (U Nu's word for them in 1949) led by Saw Hunter Tha Hmwe, demanded the irrevocable right of secession as the minimum price of peace. The BCP requested democracy, legalization, and freedom of action for revolutionary parties, rights for national minorities, and other political sundries.[36]

The extravagance of the demands was initially ignored in the general satisfaction at the fact of the parleys. During the summer and early fall of 1963, the Burmese press could not have extended itself further than it did in meeting, photographing, and quoting the insurgents. Peace was in the air, and the press and the people apparently thought they smelled it. The government joined in these efforts, offering fetes along with the negotiations. All these measures—except the talks with the KNDO—failed. By November, the Revolutionary Council publicly acknowledged its failure.[37] It was forced to swallow the proverbial bitter pill, but it benefited in popular esteem by having demonstrated its willingness to try the path of negotiations, so dear to the conceptions of Burmese Buddhists. Few—other than those who covertly supported the rebels—blamed the government for its decision to end this episode.

The proof of the government's good will and good intentions

was supplied by the agreement with the KNDO—ending the Karen rebellion of all except the Karen Communists. This was a solid achievement of the peace parleys. The able rebel leader of the Karens since 1949, Saw Hunter Tha Hmwe, arrived in Rangoon on October 22. Negotiations continued until March 12, 1964. On the latter date, the peace agreement with the KNDO insurrectionists was signed.[38] One month later, the Karen state was given its traditional Karen name as a symbol of the agreement with this second largest minority ethnic group. Henceforth, it would be known in Burma as Kawthoolei (or Kawthoolay) state.

At the end of 1964, though the Communists could blow up a bus and otherwise engage in isolated attacks, it seemed clear that the Revolutionary Government did not doubt its ability to ferret out and crush the assorted rebel Communists, and it was proceeding to do this. The two remaining groups of ethnic rebels, the Shans and the Kachins, represented another kind of problem at the end of 1964, for they could call on local ethnic loyalties in support of their efforts against the majority Burman group—a residue of the issue not fully solved by the Panglong Agreement of 1947. The Kachin Independence Army was regarded as the more serious threat. For the Kachin state presented a variety of difficulties: high mountains, heavily forested; sparse population with many and disparate tribal groups whose languages or dialects the central government was ill-equipped to handle; proximity to Communist China, to which the rebels could (and did) easily repair. Of all Burmese territories it was the least known to the government; was the most inaccessible; and had few main settlements or urban centers from which to operate.[39]

Nonetheless, the Revolutionary Council was determined to preserve the unity and Union of Burma. In January, 1964, it announced its decision to have one set of laws for all Burmese states within the Union, thereby replacing some of the autonomous legal privileges that had remained in the several states under the old Constitution. On Union Day, February 12, General Ne Win indicated that his government would continue to respect, even enhance, the individuality of the several ethnic groups (called "nationalities," or "races," in Burma), but would confine this to "their own languages, literatures, cultures, religious beliefs and customs." [40]

From its inception, the Revolutionary Council moved to fulfill its commitment to a nationalized and socialist economy. This it understood in terms of state or national corporate ownership of the means of production, distribution, and external trade. This, however, did not include the collectivization of agriculture—though in time the government sponsored a number of experimental cooperative villages in the Israeli kibbutz manner.[41] Nor would the government have much to do to complete the process of state trading in rice and timber, and state ownership of the few large industrial enterprises (steel, cement, jute, textiles, pharmaceuticals, hydro-electric power, some new rice and sugar mills, and a few others), which had been started earlier under civilian plans. Transportation, communications, and power had long been national enterprises. But there remained a sizable, if minor, sector of industry, trade, and banking in private hands, both domestic and foreign. This private sector, as to be expected, became the government's initial target.

One of the first major acts of the government, effective January 1, 1963, was to nationalize the Burma Oil Company (BOC). This joint venture of the 1950's had been a 51-49 per cent partnership between government and British private interests. The Revolutionary Council bought out the private shares for K62.5 million, payable in sterling within two years. In similar fashion it got rid of Steel Brothers and Anglo-Burma Tin—companies whose pasts go deep in colonial records.[42] The next major step, on February 23, resulted in nationalizing the twenty-four banks in Burma. Ten of these were Burmese-owned. The remaining fourteen were divided among the Dutch (one), Pakistani (one), Communist Chinese (three), British (four), and Indian (five).

The Revolutionary Council did not, as previous civilian governments had, proceed from any over-all two-, four-, or eight-year plan. Rather, it moved along on an operational basis in the manner of the caretaker regime. Within each major operation there might be a long-range plan, for example the four-year plan for reclaiming 1.5 million acres in the delta. The government acted slowly at first, and then, toward the end of 1963 and in the first half of 1964 it moved with almost bewildering speed. Expiring private contracts and import licenses were not renewed. Foreign trade became a government monopoly. Exchange control was extended to all remittances. Privately owned businesses in the hands of foreigners began to dry up as imported merchandise and exchange became difficult for them to acquire. Liquidation also proved difficult. Burmanization, a long-sponsored nationalist policy, was being accelerated.

In the fall of 1963, a series of laws and orders were promulgated that were designed to hasten the process. These included the People's or Civil Stores Corporation Law; Burma Income-Tax Amending Law; People's Film Production Board of Management Law; Enterprises Nationalization Law; and Imported Commodities Regulation Order. Earlier in 1962, a Printing and Publishing Act with rules and registration requirements had been issued.

These and related laws, orders, and regulations facilitated the nationalization of private enterprise, among which were included all saw mills, a number of the larger rice mills, five oil-producing companies, six cigarette companies, the joint Burma-Japan venture for cultured pearls and fisheries, and the almost fifty firms under the jurisdiction of the now-defunct Burma Economic Development Corporation and the Burma Defense Services Institute.

The most far-reaching effort of this kind was made in March and April, 1964. It began in Rangoon, where all big stores, co-ops, wholesale businesses, brokerage firms dealing in essential consumer commodities, and general-merchandise wholesale and retail establishments were nationalized. This process was extended to the whole country, under the administration of the Socialist Economic System Establishment Committee, headed by the Minister for Industry and Labor, Colonel Than Sein.[43] By the end of May, some 3,000 firms had been nationalized (with compensation promised), and approximately 1,000 of these had been declared superfluous. Former owners and employees were requested to continue in their respective tasks as salaried personnel until the government made a final determination as to the future of these enterprises.

The month of May saw the capstone fitted onto this design. On May 17, the Revolutionary Council promulgated the Demonetizing Law, 1964, effective from that day. It declared that K100 and K50 notes "ceased to be legal tender." Those who held such notes in whatever quantity were given one week (later extended for a limited period) to turn them in to the nearest township Security Affairs Office. The latter was authorized to give each such depositor a receipt for his money and up to K500 in smaller notes if the deposit reached or exceeded this amount. Penalties for noncompliance were severe. The Minister of Information explained the action in terms of eliminating a "black market," stopping the outflow of such currency by those who had converted goods and other movables into cash since the banks had been nationalized, and by the fact that, of the money in circulation, some K223 crores, more than half was in these high notes and was being used in ways that were damaging to the economy.[44]

The cumulative effect of nationalization and demonetization in 1964 was a disruptive one in the lives of most Burmese families, and the Revolutionary Council knew it.[45] Domestic-commodity distribution of good rice and cooking oil—essentials of daily living —faltered. Shortages arising from governmental mismanagement and from disgruntled people caught up in these changes were widespread during the summer of 1964. The demonetization procedure affected 1.36 million individuals, more than 1 million of whom were Burmese citizens who surrendered K500 or less.[46] Whatever purpose was served by the demonetization law could have been achieved by other measures. Apparently the Revolutionary Council had not understood that citizens of Burma—as in many other Asian countries—accumulate their savings without benefit of banks. The equivalent of the traditional New England cookie jar, hidden desk drawer, removable floorboard, or old sock is traditional in Burma also.

As the government became aware of its mistakes, it took several steps to cope with its difficulties. It assigned the task of commodity distribution to a high-level team headed by Brigadier Tin Pe, and lowered and fixed the prices for rice throughout the country.[47] It began to denationalize the smaller shops and bazaar stalls that had been caught up in the March-April measures,[48] thereby assisting ordinary distribution channels. It announced in mid-August that all deposits of notes up to the sum of K4200 would be refunded in full. Those who had deposited larger sums would also receive refunds, minus income tax, but not less than K4200. The refunding process, it was stated, would be carried out in three stages during September-November, 1964. It "ceased" in January, 1965.[49]

During 1964 members of the Revolutionary Council, led by General Ne Win, addressed the people frequently, explaining, exhorting, and always citing evidence as to where improvements had been made, where mistakes had been corrected, and how the government hoped to advance the fortunes of the workers and peasants. Holidays and other occasions were used for bringing together the Council and the citizens. Ne Win inaugurated the year with a Peasants Seminar on January 2, 1964, attended by 1,200 "delegates" and many others, and continued to use the seminar technique in various parts of the country.[50] Similar attention was paid to the urban workers, for whom a Workers' Basic Rights and Responsibilities Law was presented in draft form to the usual big May 1 rally by General Ne Win[51] and U Ba Nyein, ex-BCP member and financial adviser to the government. The draft became law later in May, retroactive to May 1. The seminar technique and mass rally have since been repeated annually.

The transition to the first full economic year (October 1, 1963, to September 30, 1964), under the impact of "The Burmese Way to Socialism," was not without its to-be-expected liabilities. The net effect of the plunge into nationalization of the private sector, demonetization, faulty distribution, and related measures became evident when the Revolutionary Council published the provisional summaries of its annual economic survey. Gross domestic product in constant prices declined "by 1.8 per cent" as compared with the previous year. The consumer price index for low- and middle-income families in Rangoon rose about 2-3 per cent. Sector declines in private industrial production and in the volume and value of exports were registered. However, curtailment of imports brought about an increase of K39 million in foreign-exchange reserves. Adverse weather and crop conditions (floods and pests) combined to reduce over-all agricultural production "from 112 per cent of prewar in 1962-63 to 109 per cent in 1963-64." But the concern of the government for the individual farmer—a concern made manifest by successful land reclamation, new crop loans, and government-guaranteed purchases of paddy—increased the sown acreage and production of rice, the bellwether of Burma's economy. The harvest was expected to yield 7.72 million tons as against 7.54 million in the preceding year.[52]

In presenting its third, 1964-65 budget, the Revolutionary Council said that it had incorporated "rectifications" for its "shortcomings"; but insisted that it had scored several victories, among which it listed the nationalization program, standardization of rice prices, and demonetization; and that it planned further to consolidate its victories in socialist construction to "provide more employment . . . produce more goods—enhance the value of money . . . raise the standard of living of workers and farmers." [53] This new budget is constructed somewhat differently from past ones. It is presented in two parts; one devoted to the national budget, showing over-all estimated receipts and expenditures; the other covering the government's fiscal proposals for its own investment in the state-managed boards, corporations, banks, and allied organizations of the national economy. Thus it is designed to reveal more clearly the public sector of the economy, which for 1964-65 is expected to equal approximately half of the total.

The New York Times, in its annual economic survey of Asia, summed up the situation quite fairly. It said:

> Burma rushed toward its Socialist goals during 1964 as the army-run Government refused to be deterred from its program of rapid nationalization by any disruption to the economy. . . . Spokesmen for the Government of General Ne Win conceded that production had been set back because Government managers of state enterprises were mostly army officers who lacked experience. . . . However, this was accepted by the Government as a price worth paying for taking the nation of 24 million people down the "Burmese road to Socialism." [54]

The Union Survives

As the government celebrated the eighteenth anniversary of independence on January 4, 1966, it could say that it had created a single party, the BSPP, in an almost unitary state; had reorganized the judiciary; had extended military and police security in much of Burma; had full control over the machinery of the civil service and the organizations of workers and peasants; had Burmanized as well as nationalized most of the economic life of the country; and had utilized efficiently the strong appeals of Burmese nationalism while extending social-welfare benefits among the people in widening circles. It has rejected parliamentary democracy for the present, but has substituted for it involvement of the people in a great variety of ways designed to further what it calls the "Burmese Way to Socialism." Decision-making remains in the hands of the military.

The Revolutionary Council, however, has achieved one of its chief reasons for being. By and since its *coup d'état* of March 2, 1962, it has been able to preserve the Union of Burma. The armed forces have demonstrated throughout the period since independence their loyalty to this ideal, essential if there is to be any Burma at all. It will never be known whether the Union of Burma would have survived under its previous civilian regime, but it is clear that it was in very grave danger. At the time, the armed forces appeared to be the only institution in Burma capable of preserving some unity in the country. How Burma will develop in the future we must leave to the future. How the Burmese have fared under the military social-ist regime these pages have suggested. Burma has survived to cele-brate her seventeenth anniversary—no mean achievement in the light of the past.

It is now possible to return to questions raised at the end of the preceding chapter: Are Western-style representative institutions unworkable for countries newly emerged from colonialism? Is it desirable to further the careers of their armies, independent of whatever representative institutions these countries may have es-tablished or hope to establish?

Such questions merit sober and intensive examination without prejudice to one's own institutional loyalties. Certainly the second question is in a sense the more difficult to answer. For apart from the questionable short-run-policy implications of promoting Cae-sarism, we have little data about these new armies, and they differ too much to be compared. The scope and purpose of these armies, their size and capability, are directly related—or ought to be so related—to problems of their respective countries. Cambodia, for example, has thus far been spared the plight of Burma or Malaya. Its armed forces, therefore, have a very different history and com-plexion in comparison with those of its Southeast Asian neighbors. Obviously, each new country needs a law-and-order force to insure that the writ of its governmental mandate is respected throughout the land. Whether such a force is police, constabulary, militia, or regular army is of little moment. What counts is the size of its task and its ability to carry it out.

Normally—whatever that word may mean—a law-and-order force is proportionately small. New York City, with 8 million in-habitants, has about 27,000 police. Burma, with a population al-most three times as large, only recently acquired armed forces in-cluding a police force that is four times the size of New York's. And Burma has had an extraordinary problem of insurgency since 1948. British estimates in Malaya called for a more than 15 to 1 ratio of armed forces to insurgents. At the start of the rebellions in Burma the proportion was 10 to 1 in favor of the rebels!

It seems that we do not know enough, nor do we have data enough, to guide us toward sound judgment on the second ques-tion. There are too many variables and too many as yet untried propositions in the complicated question of newly independent and unified nation-*cum*-problem of law and order-*cum*-size, com-mand and control, and deployment of armed force.

The first question, the workability and applicability of Western-style representative institutions to countries newly emerged from colonialism, is much easier to answer. For such institutions are relatively recent in the West and not all have had so continuous a history as we sometimes think when we call medieval England or Iceland the "Mother of Parliaments." Western-style democracy found short shrift in too many countries in Europe and Latin America for us to feel that its institutional base and structure can be readily transplanted to differing societies. Where such institutions have worked, they have been attractive and have lured others to imitation. However flattering such imitation is, it hardly suffices to sustain the transplant. Each new country will have to search out those unifying, as well as diversifying, elements in its culture pattern that permit the transplant to survive. Without these elements there will certainly be no nation, and most probably no state. Our task is to help others discover and utilize their own culture patterns, permit and help them to borrow from us what is relevant to them, but carefully avoid the futility of superimposition. Useful as this device is in geometry, it has no place in free politics.

One of the themes basic to this study is that Burma at this stage in her history, as U Nu said on reassuming office in 1960, exhibits certain unique features, which require fundamental exploration and understanding before conclusions can be reached. The military and civilian leaders who now govern and defend Burma still have much to learn about their own country. Only recently have they reacquired the opportunity to study their own history other than through old chronicles and folklore. Only recently have they acquired the right and the duty of seeing and experiencing their own country and its people. We may have an opportunity to share in that enterprise, provided we approach it sympathetically and have the patience to work at it in depth.

The military regime set up by General Ne Win is, in 1966, a dictatorship. It "promulgates" (its word) the law. It has instituted a far-reaching socialist nationalized economy. It relies heavily on central planning and "common ownership" to promote "sufficiency and contentment of all." Its trade-union policy has been adapted from the U.S.S.R. It has outlawed opposition parties and has limited the action of all nonreligious organizations by various means including registration. It has not suppressed the nongovernmental press and other expressions of opinion but it is easily provoked into punitive action by sharply expressed criticism. It has used the device of protective custody or political jails for former political leaders.

But such tendencies to totalitarianism have been paralleled by contradictory ones. The regime's philosophy, party constitution, and program exhibit deeply imbedded Buddhist and other Burmese traditional values that it seeks to preserve and enrich. These values are both individual and social. They readily support a grass-roots democratic social structure. The regime clearly recognized the "spiritual" in life based on its Buddhist analysis of the interacting "material," "animal," and "phenomenal" worlds (respectively, *okasaloka, sattaloka, sankharaloka*). Because of its adherence to the doctrine of ceaseless change (*paticcasamuppada*), which it likens to "the law of [Marxist] dialectics," the government asserts that its ideology and programs are not "final," are not "beyond the need of amendment and alterations."

The affirmation of traditional Burmese beliefs and values may be seen in the regime's special emphasis on and support for peasant proprietorship and cooperative undertakings (which it calls "collective" undertakings). Insistence on compliance with its laws and orders is paced by its search and desire for consensus and by its genuine dedication to public welfare.

The effort to reconcile modern socialism (including Marxist totalitarianism) with traditional Burmese values and beliefs is once again on trial in Burma. In one form or another, this has been the case under every government in Burma since independence. What the outcome will be is uncertain. But, in my view, no Burmese regime—military, socialist, or other—could long survive in Burma if it deeply offended or violated the meaning of Buddhism for its Burmese adherents. I believe the military leaders of Burma are aware of this; hence their efforts at reconciliation.*

It may now be said that the Burmese, in their not quite so newly independent country, have discovered that a major degree of law and order can be established, but it must be sustained; that a genuine nationality- and nation-building effort must be restarted; that their state is politically viable if it is unified; and that unity requires both freedom and responsibility. Burma's difficulties between 1948 and 1966 have been real, but political continuity has been sustained through a variety of Burmese solutions. We can watch, wait, and see, or we can help the Burmese to have what they say they now want—unity, order, socialism, and democracy—in that order.

* The BSPP held its first national "Seminar," or gathering in December, 1965, three and a half years after its inception. General Ne Win opened and closed the Seminar with a sharp call: "It is no use," he said, "building up a party if it is not for the interests of the people. It will be simply a source of danger." One danger he clearly recognized—and labeled—was the current inadequacy of his economic program. Parts of it were a "mess"—a word U Nu used to characterize the state of security in 1949.

PART III · BURMA'S FOREIGN RELATIONS

FROM THE SEARCH FOR POWERFUL
ALLIES TO NEUTRALISM

BURMA'S FIRST STEPS toward the re-establishment of international relations were taken in 1947 before the independent government assumed full power. This was possible because under the Aung San–Attlee Agreement signed in London at the end of January, Burma's Interim Government was given the right "to raise, consider, discuss and decide on any matters arising in the field of policy and administration" affecting "matters concerning defense and external affairs." On February 28, U Kyin, Finance and Revenue Secretary of Burma, concluded negotiations in London for a Lend-Lease settlement with A. W. Boyd of the United States. The agreement made available to Burma military and other supplies that had remained in the country at the end of the war. Their value at $7.5 million was reduced to $5 million. Payment was to be made over twenty years at 2⅜ per cent interest. Of this, 80 per cent was to be spent on educational projects that were to be mutually agreed upon by the United States and Burma, and the balance was to be used by the United States to cover its representational costs within Burma. The agreement was received with "the thanks of the people of Burma . . . for this generous and sympathetic attitude." It was, according to *The Burmese Review*, "the first occasion on which since the annexation of Upper Burma in 1885 a Burmese government has successfully negotiated without British intervention an agreement with a Foreign Power." [1]

An interesting echo of the Kellogg-Briand Peace Pact was incorporated in Burma's Constitution: "The Union of Burma renounces war as an instrument of national policy, and accepts the generally recognized principles of international law as its rule of conduct in its relation with foreign States" (Section 211). In the next section, "The Union of Burma affirms its devotion to the ideal of peace and friendly co-operation amongst nations founded on international justice and morality." In pursuit of this ideal, decision-making power has resided generally in a small group of leaders whose major foreign-policy spokesman has been the Prime Minister or, since 1962, the Chairman of the Revolutionary Council. To a large extent U Nu, like Nehru, was his own foreign minister. General Ne Win has made more use of his Foreign Affairs Minister, U Thi Han. These leaders have enlisted strong public support behind their basic international policies. Almost the only opposition has come from insurrectionists and from crypto-Communists who follow the shifting policies of the Sino–Soviet bloc.

With no further preliminary steps than these, independent Burma entered into formal relations with other nations.

"We Cannot Live Alone"

On April 19, 1948, Burma entered the United Nations, sponsored by the Nationalist Government of China. During that year two Foreign Ministers, U Tin Tut and U Kyaw Nyein, concluded exchanges of recognition with China, France, India, the Netherlands, Pakistan, Thailand, the United Kingdom, and the United States. An agreement with the U.S.S.R for the establishment of diplomatic and consular relations was announced in August, 1950, but was not implemented until February-April, 1951.[2] However, in 1948, neither U Nu nor the successive Foreign Ministers made many specific public statements about Burma's new role in international affairs. At this time the dominant concern of the government was unity within Burma, and the main expressions of foreign policy, viewed in the context of incipient civil war, may be construed as attempts to preserve that unity.

Yet these statements caused considerable alarm in the West, especially when, two months after the actual outbreak of the Communist insurrection, U Nu made known his "Fifteen Point Program for Leftist Unity." Responding to Western expressions of alarm, U Tin Tut immediately held a press conference on June 17, 1948, in the hope of dispelling the "misapprehensions abroad in regard to Thakin Nu's plans." This program, which U Nu discussed on May 25 and again on June 13, included in its first and fifth planks the following statements:

> To secure political and economic relations with Soviet Russia and the democratic countries of Eastern Europe in the same way as we are now having these relations with Britain and the United States.

> The refusal of any foreign aid of a kind which will compromise the political, economic and strategic independence of Burma.[3]

In his June 13 speech on "The Nature of Leftist Unity," U Nu vigorously defended the conduct of his government against the in-

surrectionary Communists and took that occasion to outline what
became a cornerstone of his foreign policy: "the wish that Burma
should be in friendly relations with all the three" great Western
powers, the United Kingdom, the United States, and the U.S.S.R.
The formulation of this policy, he attempted to make clear, was
dictated by Burma's strategic weakness, economic needs, and the
wish to avoid the devastating consequences of a new war. "Our
country," he said, "suffered the most by the war and seeks peace
for the whole world. We do not wish to see dissension between the
Big Powers, and we shall support any measure for securing unity
between Britain, the United States, Russia and other Powers." He
rejected the Communists' push for "friendly relations" only with
the U.S.S.R.[4]

Burma's foreign policy in this and the past decade has been expressed in its version of neutralism. Prime Minister Nu, in his policy speech to the Chamber of Deputies on April 5, 1960, reiterated
many earlier pronouncements that Burma is "pledged to the policy, *followed since independence*, of positive neutrality, nonalignment with any block, doing our utmost to promote peace in
the world, giving our full support to the aims and objectives of the
United Nations and our full and active cooperation to its working
and taking all measures in our power to promote the closest relations of friendship and amity with neighboring countries [italics
added]."[5]

Despite these references to the policy followed "since independence," nonalignment or neutralism was *not* the initial position of
the Burmese Government. Nor was it at that time, as Hugh Tinker
suggests, a policy in any way based upon what he calls Burma's
traditional, pre-British "isolationist" policy.[6] Burma's foreign policy was originally anchored to the Bo Letya–Freeman Defense
Agreement, signed in Rangoon on August 29, 1947, and included
as an annex to the October 17, 1947, Nu-Attlee Agreement, the
Independence Treaty between the United Kingdom and the Provisional Government of Burma. The annex called for the evacuation
of British troops from Burma, certain financial concessions with
respect to defense matters, the provision of a United Kingdom
navy, army, and air-force training mission, facilities for training
Burmese nationals in the United Kingdom, and the purchase of
war matériel. The agreement was to run for at least three years
after the transfer of power, and was subject thereafter to twelve
months' notice before termination. The agreement specifically referred to the possibility of a future military alliance with the
United Kingdom, while the treaty reserved to each country the
ordinary rights of sovereign powers to enter other international
agreements in conformity with the Charter of the United Nations.
Obviously, Burma at the time contemplated entering into alliances
and agreements with other powers.

Burmese Communists attacked the defense agreement even before independence on the grounds that it favored the "imperialists." Again and again the Prime Minister publicly defended his government's course of action. He used arguments of self-interest and security; he cited the many similar agreements into which the U.S.S.R. and other countries had entered; he examined, however loosely, the words of Lenin, Trotsky, and Stalin to support the presumed theory behind such practices in his endeavor to justify his policy of seeking and having alliances. Above all, he declared that because it was difficult to maintain freedom "we need good allies" —good allies who were also "powerful." Any alliances had to be based on what Buddhists called "*Attahita-Prahita*, that is, mutual benefit." A careful reading of the Prime Minister's statements and speeches from November, 1947, to September, 1949, amply demonstrates that in its first stage, Burma's foreign policy was directed toward achieving security through a system of beneficial alliances and through whatever additional protection the U.N. might offer its members.[7]

In seeking good allies U Nu was clearly following in the path chartered by Bogyoke Aung San, who had declared that "a free and independent Burma is quite ready to enter into any arrangement with other nations for common welfare and security. . . . Our nation as indeed all other nations, cannot live without allies. We must have our allies and friends, and if we can't win the friendship of one we must try the others. We cannot live alone." [8]

It has been suggested in some quarters that the lack of experience of Burmese leaders in foreign affairs and their intense preoccupation with the insurrections of 1948 conspired to obscure the intent of their search for alliances. But by mid-1949, no one should have failed to understand Burma's foreign policy. For U Nu's speech of June 14, 1949, "Democracy versus the Gun," clearly favored treaties on economic and defense problems. He reaffirmed his nation's earnest desire to "cooperate as closely as possible with countries of common interest, in economic, political and defence matters, with a view to the achievement of common ends." He lamented the fact that "although our independence is over a year old, we have up till now no economic or defence treaty on which we can fall back in time of need." And he added, "it is obvious that we cannot go on in this fashion indefinitely. It is now time that we should enter into mutually beneficial treaties or arrangements, defence and economic, with countries of common interest. The Union Government is at present considering this question in all its aspects." [9]

The West Does Not Respond

When General Ne Win, then Deputy Prime Minister, and Dr. E Maung, Minister of Foreign Affairs, visited the United Kingdom and the United States during the summer of 1949, the Foreign Minister expressed Burma's willingness to consider a Pacific area security pact.[10] General Ne Win was seeking arms. But at this time the United States was cool toward collective defense arrangements in the area, and cited in support the views of Prime Minister Nehru in opposition to such arrangements.[11]

On September 28, 1949, after his emissaries had returned virtually empty-handed, U Nu began to recast his policy. In a speech to Parliament, he rejected "anti-Left or anti-Right pacts," but supported "anti-aggression" pacts. Using long excerpts from Lenin and Stalin, he justified Burma's economic need for "help of foreign countries both for men and material." [12]

However, in this speech[13] and a later one of December 11—just seven days before Burma recognized the Communist government of the People's Republic of China—he examined the possible consequences of Burma's inability to acquire good and powerful allies and sounded the theme for "an unwavering Union [of Burma] attitude," which would avoid "any false step in our foreign relations." His prescription was to "follow an independent course and not ally ourselves with any power bloc . . . any other course can only lead the Union to ruin." The significance of his phrasing in the December 11 speech, especially in contrast with that of June 14, is unmistakable:

> In drawing up a political programme, it will just not do to lay down, for example, a pro–Anglo-American programme simply in the belief that the Anglo-American powers will crush Soviet Russia in the event of war. Similarly also we must not lay down a Communist programme merely because Chinese Communists are over-running China and therefore we must adopt a pattern acceptable to them. Such political programmes adopted without conviction are the work of opportunists. The only political programme which we should pursue is the one which we genuinely believe to be the most suitable for our Union whatever course the British, the Americans, the Russians and the Chinese Communists might follow. Our salvation lies in our own hands, and no matter what help foreign capitalists or foreign Communists may give us it will be of no avail if we are divided and lack the ability to steer our own ship of state. They will not merely form a low opinion of us but they will take full advantage of our weakness and meddle in our affairs until our sovereignty vanishes. Just look at the world today, and be they Capitalist or Communist they behave in exactly the same way.
>
> Therefore in our attitude towards foreign powers we should do away with any inclination to "long for the aunt" at the expense of the mother and all opportunistic tendencies.
>
> Be friendly with all foreign countries. Our tiny nation cannot have the effrontery to quarrel with any power. If any country comes with an offer of a mutually beneficial enterprise, welcome it by all means and work closely and honestly. But do not forget to strengthen yourself and to be fully equipped for your dealings with foreign countries. In laying down political programmes do not forget to ensure that it is fully suited to the requirements of the Union.[14]

From these statements it is clear that by December, 1949, U Nu had definitely rejected the earlier policy of defense treaties and pacts and had formulated those ideas that have become central to Burmese foreign policy from that time to the present. Such an independent course was the only alternative left to the Burmese unless they were to move into the Sino-Soviet orbit. It is also significant to note that this was the first occasion on which the Prime Minister publicly, in a major address, referred to the Chinese Communists as "over-running China." But from this time forward, irrespective of the language of diplomacy, Burmese policy took cognizance of Communist China as a clear and present danger. The Burmese were aware of the hostility expressed toward them by Liu Shao-chi at the Peking-sponsored Conference of Trade Unions of Asia and Oceana. Liu had openly called for support of the Burma Communist Party's "war of national liberation" against U Nu's government and for the adoption by the BCP of the "path taken by the Chinese." [15]

There were other factors besides the emergence of Communist China that led to the change in policy at the end of 1949 and the beginning of 1950. During the period when U Nu was making a last futile effort to choke off the Communist insurrection, the Burmese were officially informed of Western disapproval of his proposed terms of internal political unity. The Burmese were also aware of outspoken criticism by leading newspapers in the West. Their requests in September, 1948, and again in 1949, for increased military assistance to combat the insurrectionists, were answered parsimoniously or turned down. The United States felt constrained by the Anglo-Burmese Defense Agreement to defer to the United Kingdom in a recently emancipated colonial Asian area. Britain was to have been the supplier of defensive arms, but Britain and Burma never agreed upon the quantity and types of arms to be supplied—a major issue that led later to the abrogation of this pact. When Burma attempted to purchase military supplies through U.S. commercial channels, which had been suggested to her officials in 1949, she found difficulties in the way of securing the necessary export licenses. Quite possibly, Burma requested types of military hardware that were in short supply in the United States and which, even if available, would have been difficult to integrate with the predominantly British matériel then being used in Burma. Whatever the reason, Burma received virtually no help from the United States during the 1948-49 upsurge of Communist rebellion.

In 1948 and early 1949, the Burmese Government also suffered because the United Kingdom and the United States tended to regard the Karens as strongly anti-Communist, and hence viewed with dismay the growing tension and rebellion between the central government and this disaffected ethnic minority. (It has already been pointed out that the rebelling and separatist Karens made common cause with the Communists whenever it suited their purpose, though this fact was largely ignored in the West until more sober political reporting eventually reached and affected the policy of the Department of State.) The Burmese were told that the United States hoped there would be no civil war with these groups.

During the first crucial eighteen months of independence, the Burmese tended to regard the United States as a "cardboard" figure. They felt that they could not get in touch with the U.S. in a meaningful way. Prior to the fall of China to the Communists, U.S. policy had not been geared to relate to Burma in particular or to South and Southeast Asia in general. The influential State Department Policy Planning Staff, initiated in 1947 and headed by George F. Kennan, was then largely, if not exclusively, Europe-centered. This was accentuated by the understandable concentration on Western Europe, including those countries with extensive interests in Asia.[16]

Three theories have been advanced to explain this early period in Burma's foreign relations. One is that the countries of common interest with which U Nu desired defense arrangements were mainly Burma's neighbors. This interpretation is not persuasive, for the Burmese leaders clearly expressed their desire for "powerful allies." Although there were warm relations with some Indians in and around Nehru's government and although the Burmese eagerly participated in the first and second Asian Relations conferences at New Delhi in March and April 1947, and in January, 1949,[17] they did not then, nor do they now, regard India as a powerful ally. Nor were they then particularly knowledgeable about their other neighbors. Their sympathy with the anticolonial struggles of the Vietnamese and Indonesians was based on a general antipathy toward imperialism rather than on an understanding of specific issues.[18] Treaties of friendship were signed with Indonesia (March 31, 1951); India (July 7, 1951); Pakistan (June 6, 1952); and Thailand (October 15, 1956). The long-sought treaty with China was not secured until 1960 (see Chapter 11). Nevertheless, in Burmese eyes these treaties and the more important trade agreements, particularly with the food-deficit countries of Asia, did not meet the need for strong allies.

A second theory is that in the first years of independence Burma's leaders lacked a clear conception of how to carry out any foreign policy. Undoubtedly there is some truth in this. The Burmese leaders, political and civil service, had had practically no diplomatic training or experience. Prior to the war, the University of Rangoon had not offered courses in political science or international relations, though minor elements of these subjects were included in the history (mainly British and European) and the law curricula. Neither Asian nor Burmese history was taught. Of the twenty-four different members of the 1948 and 1949 Cabinets, only a few had traveled widely abroad, and only two had received a university education in England. It is entirely possible, therefore, that Burmese leaders were at first insufficiently prepared to execute the foreign policy that they had formulated; the West, however, failed to make allowance for this.

A third theory has been concisely expressed by Hugh Tinker:

> U Nu did not . . . suggest whither Burma should look for allies, probably because the AFPFL and the country were acutely divided upon the issue. The Socialists would wish to go to Soviet Russia, but this would have alarmed all the conservative elements in the country. The Karens, and to a lesser extent the Shans and the Kachins, would have preferred to conclude an alliance with Britain: but this would have been repugnant to the Socialists as a "sell-out" to the "Imperialists." And so nothing more was heard of the desirability of allies.[19]

This view, despite sturdy support in London and Washington, is, in the author's opinion, based on an incorrect interpretation of the actual situation. It served to misdirect Western policy at a crucial time, and it inhibited the Western response to the foreign policy that Burma's leaders had formulated and were attempting, somewhat unsuccessfully, to implement. It is worth examining, nevertheless, in order both to establish an accurate record and to obviate similar errors in the future.

There were three major flaws in this interpretation. In the first place, it assumed the existence in Burma of a pro-Western group that included members of the non-Burman minorities—Karen, Shan, Kachin, Chin, Mon, and others—but overlooked their varied motivations. These minorities were regarded in the West as anti-Communist; among their numbers were a considerable body of Christians who had long had relations with Anglo-American churches; and many of their leaders were known to World War II Allied forces in the China–Burma–India Theater as loyal anti-Japanese friends. Sentiment and the desire to reward such friends played legitimate if confused roles in this estimate.

It has already been pointed out that when the Karen National Defense Organization joined the insurrection it did not hesitate to make common cause with both the Communists and the Kuomintang troops. Its goal was secession from the Union of Burma. Together with its ethnic ally, the Mon National Defense Organization, the KNDO sought support for this goal in Western capitals. Their pro-Western policy was based less on ideological anti-Communism than on a hopeless, romantic nationalism. The Kachins and Chins who did not join the rebellion were both pro-Western and pro-AFPFL. That is, they continued in their wartime sympathy for the West, which they found quite compatible with their support for the socialist-oriented AFPFL. There were then few more ardent "socialists" or "state planners" in the economic sphere than the leading Kachin chief and Cabinet member, Sama Duwa Sinwa Nawng (later Ambassador to Communist China).

The Shans, led by Burma's first President, Sao Shwe Thaike, and by the Foreign Affairs Minister, Sao Hkun Hkio, were then preoccupied with the problem of retaining some of their feudal states rights. They wanted to postpone or avoid altogether the role allotted to their Indian counterparts, or to settle the issue of their state powers on the most favorable terms. For obvious reasons, then, the Shan *sawbwas* felt and feel more strongly drawn to the West than to the U.S.S.R. But their days as rulers—not as individual leaders —had become limited by the growing demands, even among the Shan people, for democratic state and local government. Correlatively, the AFPFL had a growing membership and following in the Shan states, which, if anything, had been held back because the central government expected to work out, on a reasonable basis, its relation with the *sawbwas*. General Aung San, U Nu, and the AFPFL had agreed to this at the Panglong Hill Peoples' and Frontier Conference of 1947.

The *sawbwas* may properly be regarded as "conservative elements," to use Tinker's phrase, which presumably stands for "capitalist" elements. Within the Arakanese National Unity Organization as well as among some non-Burman businessmen's circles, there were similar conservative elements. But "capitalism," or "conservatism," as the Burmese understood and used the term, was hardly a popular concept in the early days of Burmese independence. It always carried the connotation of "exploitation" and "colonial economy" against which all nationalists of whatever color or stripe had united. Not until U Nu's speech of June 8, 1957, "On the Four Year Plan," was the phrase "profit motive" used by a Burmese leader with some approval.

In the second place, during the early days of independence there was strong pro-Western sentiment not only among the non-Burman minorities and the conservative elements, but also within the Socialist-dominated AFPFL, the civil service, and the armed forces. The overwhelming majority within these three groups were extremely gratified at the way in which Prime Minister Attlee's government had negotiated the various agreements that led to independence. The British Labor Party, then in power, both collectively and through many of its public and press leaders, was favorably regarded in Burma. One small but influential contingent among the Burmese, led by U Tin Tut, and not without influence in the AFPFL, had, as we have seen, openly argued for the choice of dominion status within the Commonwealth, at least until the Constituent Assembly in 1947 decided against it. Admiral Mountbatten, Governor Rance, Prime Minister Attlee, Commissioner Malcolm MacDonald, Lord Ogmore, and a host of others in or near the Labor Party had won for Britain a considerable amount of good will, only partially dissipated by Foreign Secretary Bevin and the British Military Mission in Burma. U Nu could accurately state for himself, for his government, and for the AFPFL, that Britain was "the closest to us" of the big powers. No figure in the West, even Tito of Yugoslavia, received the warm welcome and political respect accorded to Attlee when he visited Burma in connection with the First Asian Socialist Conference in January, 1953, a conference that was organized by the socialists of the AFPFL.

If the United Kingdom was closest to the Burmese, the United States, although it had had much less contact with Burma, was not far behind. President Franklin D. Roosevelt and Secretary of State Cordell Hull had helped to build up in Asia an anticolonial image of America. The United States' withdrawal from the Caribbean (Inter-American conferences at Montevideo, Buenos Aires, and Lima, 1933-38); its setting of July 4, 1946, as the date for Philippine independence; and its role in launching the Atlantic Charter and the United Nations gave substance to this image. The assignment of Ambassador Edwin F. Stanton of Thailand as the official United States representative at the birth of the Union on January 4, 1948, was an appreciated gesture. The Marshall Plan and the Point IV Program initiated by President Truman also contributed favorably to the Asian view of the United States.

This postwar image became somewhat tarnished by what George V. Allen once described as the American dilemma (international version): the basic sympathy of the United States for the independence and nationhood of emerging states, limited by its relations with friendly powers who have stakes in their status.[20] Similarly, when the U.S. aid program became mixed up with a military program in 1951-52, it lost some of its appeal. But these are latter-day events, postdating the early Burmese search for allies.

During these first years of Burmese independence, the United Kingdom and the United States had a tremendous advantage over the U.S.S.R. It is true that the Russian Revolution had been an inspiring event to Asians and that Marxist theory, chiefly in the Leninist version of imperialism, had influenced Burmese nationalists, Socialists, and Communists. But the Communists, following the 1947 Cominform "left strategy," soon set out to rule or ruin both the AFPFL and the Burmese Government. Furthermore, AFPFL leaders, including the Socialists, were generally aware of the antagonistic attitude toward their party that prevailed in the U.S.S.R., at least until the period immediately prior to the visit of Bulganin and Khrushchev in December, 1955. In *Premier Reports to the People*, U Nu recalled that "when we became independent, the Soviet Union apparently decided to treat us as 'on probation' . . . as the Communist rebellion gathered momentum, her attitude underwent a change [for the worse], and indications were that she came to look upon us as reactionaries standing in the way of the people's liberation." Earlier in the same speech he remarked, "can we ever forget that it was the so-called Southeast Asia Youth Conference [sponsored by the international Communist movement] held in Calcutta in February 1948 which was the signal for the start of the Communist rebellion." [21]

Before the Bulganin-Khrushchev visit, *Pravda* (January 19, 1953) and *For a Lasting Peace, For a People's Democracy* (January 30, 1953) used their choicest billingsgate to characterize the "medley of Right-Wing Socialist Betrayers in Rangoon," and singled out Burma's "Socialist Traitors" for a special attack because they were "dealing harshly with detachments of the people's opposition." Material on Burma, the AFPFL, the Socialists, and U Nu that appeared in the second edition of the *Large Soviet Encyclopedia* is almost wholly derogatory.[22]

In the early days of independence, non-Communist Burmese, including the Socialists, respected and feared the Soviet Union and would have accepted an agreement, but in 1948 the Kremlin would not even exchange diplomatic missions. The Burmese hoped for an agreement with the U.S.S.R. as one means of cutting off the local insurrectionary Communists from their outside sources of support. U Nu was as much a spokesman for this position as he was for similar agreements with the United States and United Kingdom. But to suggest, as Tinker does, that the Socialists would "wish to go to Soviet Russia" as a viable political or diplomatic alternative to having Western allies, is to misread completely their intentions and conceptions. For they, more than any other group in Burma, were aware of the personal and political catastrophes awaiting them if Burma turned to the Soviet Union as its "powerful ally."

A third element in this Western misinterpretation of Burmese foreign policy arises from the relation between U Nu and "the Socialists." [23] One view is that U Nu was not a Socialist, but an "independent" who held the balance of power between the Socialists and the non-Socialists in the Cabinet and in the AFPFL. A differing view holds that U Nu was the captive of the Socialists, who, acting privately outside the Cabinet, determined policy and transmitted it to him. Still a third opinion is that U Nu and the independents constituted a faction in conflict with the Socialists and that both factions survived in the Cabinet by means of shifting majorities, but that U Nu continued as Prime Minister because neither faction had any strong candidate of its own.[24]

If Tinker, Cady, and others use the word "Socialist" to mean those within the AFPFL in the 1948-50 period who had belonged to the Communist Party, but who did not go underground and join the insurrection in March, 1948, and who later came to be called "Left Socialists," then there is no doubt that this group supported a pro-Soviet Russia policy within the AFPFL and was outspokenly against the "Anglo-American bloc." But this was a group of consistent crypto-Communists, not in the Cabinet, which became the Burma Workers and Peasants Party when it finally split from the AFPFL and the Socialist Party in December, 1950. However, this is not what is usually meant by reference to the "social-ists" in Burma; nor is there any indication that Tinker or Cady have this crypto-Communist group in mind.

The Socialist Party of Burma was at one time formally a member of the coalition party, the AFPFL. However, regulations adopted before independence by the AFPFL, instigated by the Socialists and primarily directed at breaking up the Communist-Party caucus within the AFPFL, decreed that only organizations of an eco-nomic nature would be accepted as member organizations of the AFPFL. All other membership would be on an individual basis. Thus the Socialist Party became technically an organization out-side the coalition AFPFL. However, its members remained in AFPFL leadership as officers in trade unions, and peasant, coopera-tive, and other organizations.

When U Nu became *de facto* Prime Minister in 1947, he with-drew from membership in all organizations affiliated with the AFPFL, including the Socialist Party, which he had helped to or-ganize. The only office he retained was that of president of the AFPFL, which in principle represented all its constituent organiza-tions and members. This step, which the Burmese regarded as proper conduct for the president of a coalition, may have given rise in the West to the mistaken notion that U Nu was not a Socialist; that he was an "independent"; and that he held views politically distinct from the predominant socialist cast of his various cabinets.

None of these propositions is true. Until 1958, there was no break in his long and intimate political association with members of the Socialist Party, particularly such leaders as U Ba Swe, U Kyaw Nyein, Thakin Tin, Bo Khin Maung Gale, U Tun Win, Thakin Tha Kin, U Raschid, U Win, and others. These leaders had belonged to the Thakin group together with Aung San, Thakin Mya, and the other men who were assassinated in 1947, and in 1944 they had laid the groundwork for the AFPFL. Under the leadership of Aung San, Thakin Mya, U Nu, and U Kyaw Nyein, the same group organized the Socialist Party in 1945 in order to promulgate a Marxist, non-Communist policy, and later, as a group, they expelled the dissident Communist Party from the AFPFL coalition.[25]

There had, of course, been disputes among the Socialists and within the Cabinet prior to the 1958 and 1962 splits. Party conflicts are as common in Burma as elsewhere. U Nu had always been closer in personal ties and program to some of his colleagues than to others. But, as we have seen, the topmost Burmese political leadership held one general, socialist ideological viewpoint until 1958, despite occasional deviations and inevitable disputes on cur-rent issues.

Perhaps the best demonstration of this ideological consensus was the unanimous approval given by the Third All-Burma AFPFL

Congress in 1958, when U Nu, with the support of the Socialist Party leadership, rejected Marxism, which he equated with Communism, and defined the goal of the AFPFL as democratic socialism.[26] Throughout the party split in 1958, U Nu again and again expounded the theme of democratic socialism, and he returned to power in part by incorporating this ideology in the platforms of the Clean AFPFL and the reorganized Pyidaungsu Party after the elections.

It appears clear that U Nu, as Prime Minister and AFPFL president, was not speaking for himself alone in formulating foreign policy. When he sought strong allies between 1948 and 1950, he had the active cooperation of his ministers, including the Socialists, several of whom went abroad on missions in search of arms and other aid to help quell the insurrections. In answer to its requests, the government received sympathy, but little assistance, from the West. The search for allies proved abortive. Perhaps the conduct of the search was inexperienced, even inept. But the fact remains that the Burmese were unable to get the support in the West that they needed for their security. Their disappointment, as well as subsequent events beginning with the Communist takeover in China and the gradual emergence of a third force, or neutralist Asian approach to problems of the day, led the Burmese to reassess their foreign policy. By the beginning of 1950, the Burmese Government had adopted the outlines of that neutralist foreign policy to which it has clung ever since.[27]

"Neutrality Free from Any Entanglements"

Burma's foreign policy since 1950 has been a stable compound of policy and practice, but the terms used by the Burmese to describe it have changed somewhat over the period. What U Nu called an "independent course" in December, 1949, he renamed "our policy of non-partisanship" in an important speech on Korea, on September 5, 1950.[28] Later, in a famous speech at the Pyidawtha Conference on August 4, 1952, he called it "our policy of strict neutrality." [29]

When General Ne Win first addressed the Parliament on October 31, 1958, as premier for the caretaker government, he announced that he intended "to continue in the practice of strict neutrality free from any entanglements." [30] He used the phrase, "positive neutrality," when he established his Revolutionary Council as the government in March, 1962.[31]

Neutralism or neutrality, qualified by strict, or positive, or active; independent, nonpartisan, or nonaligned—these are the shorthand references for this second and continuing stage in Burma's foreign policy. There is no point in seeking a definition of these imprecise terms which would apply to all countries that employ them. The term "neutralism" has in fact been used in such a variety of ways by spokesmen of different countries that it seems less desirable to try to stretch any one definition to cover every case than to understand its meaning in the context of actual policy in each case.

The Burmese use neutralism—or a near variant of the term—to sum up what they have done in international affairs since 1950. They have supported the United Nations, though not without some skepticism as to its effectiveness. They are understandably proud to have contributed one of their distinguished civil servants, U Thant, to the post of Secretary-General; and they are also pleased to have served twice as a regular member of the Trusteeship Council. They have avoided all big-power bloc or pact alliances, even though they are aware that in recent years United States power and interests in Asia have counterpoised Sino-Soviet power and interests. The avoidance of such alliances has not inhibited their participation in any presumed tension-reducing conference, such as the one held in Geneva, 1961-62, in the matter of Laos, in which both blocs were represented. Necessity and interest have combined to make them promote a wide variety of "mutually beneficial" trade and aid agreements.[32]

The Burmese ministers of every Cabinet have sought friendship with all nations, especially those which have recently claimed their independence. To this end Burma became one of the five "Colombo Powers" that convened the first Afro-Asian Bandung Conference in 1955. Since then, with some caution, Burma's delegations at the U.N., and at various locations such as Belgrade and Cairo, have participated in meetings of the Afro-Asian groupings.

Above all, within the self-imposed limits of small-power ability, Burmese neutralists have acted on their conceptions of independence and international morality by speaking out on such critical issues as Korea, Hungary, the Suez, and others.[33] Despite the opposition of its big Communist neighbor to the north, Burma signed the Washington-and-Moscow-sponsored limited Nuclear Test Ban Treaty of 1963. Burma may be a neutralist country, but her policy has not been neuter.

In the main, Burmese leaders prefer to present their neutralist interpretation of foreign policy as if it had been consistently held and expounded from the beginning of independence. Since they disentangled themselves from the Anglo-Burma Defense Agreement in 1954 by invoking the appropriate clause that led to its termination; and similarly disengaged themselves from the first U.S.–Burma Aid Agreement signed in September, 1950, this reading of the past has been facilitated. But it is an inaccurate reading, one which obscures both the understanding and the implications of Burma's earlier attitude and policy.

Burma did not begin as a neutralist nation, she became one. Enough has been indicated to demonstrate that one cannot lump all neutralist countries under one concept of "neutralism"; just as one cannot lump the policies of Western nations under one "democratic" policy. Burma's neutralism is based, as one would expect, on her own requirements and considerations. The Burmese, like most other people, have a strong aversion to war, strengthened by the fact that their country was devastated in World War II. They see their future security in a world at peace. They see a direct connection between military nonalignment and peace. Thailand, however, with relatively the same area and population, the same religion, the same economic resources, and almost the same problem of relations with China, seeks security through membership in the Southeast Asia Treaty Organization. The difference between the two countries can be explained in terms of their past experiences. Burma has only recently escaped from alien domination, whereas Thailand had managed to stay free by steering a careful course among the various imperialist powers. Despite their similarities, Burma and Thailand have adopted contrasting solutions for the problem of security. The contrast between Burma and Thailand suggests the need to understand each country in some depth before attaching to it some convenient label that fails to cover the instant case.

Burma today is a neutralist country; that is, she will not join power blocs or pacts promoted by one side or the other in the Cold War. She has sought to be friendly with all nations, especially with ex-colonial ones. Burma concerts her policies with like-minded countries to advance the cause of peace, deciding each issue that arises on its own merits, not on the basis of prior commitments. Burma does this within and outside the United Nations. Membership in the United Nations is not considered prejudicial to neutrality, since both the Soviet and Western blocs are also members.

Burmese neutralism, however unpopular it may have been in Washington in the first half of the 1950's, cannot be charged with being neutralist in favor of the Moscow-Peking axis. A previously mentioned example is that in 1950, the Burmese voted to send United Nations troops to defend South Korea, although, along with India, Burma opposed a later resolution condemning China as the aggressor. On all colonial and trusteeship issues, Burma's vote is predictably against colonialism or imperialism and for hastening the end of trusteeships. Burma has voted with the Afro-Asian bloc on all such issues, including resolutions on Suez and Algeria. But Burma joined the West in a vote against the U.S.S.R. on the revolt in Hungary, for she considered that intervention in Hungary and aggression in Egypt were basically the same.[34] At the Asian Socialist Conference in 1953, at meetings of the Colombo powers, and at the Bandung Conference in 1955, the Burmese condemned all imperialism including, by name, the Soviet variety.

The Burmese have been somewhat less consistent in their approach to economic-aid matters. At one time they expressed a desire to accept all kinds of public and private aid—grants, loans, lines of credit—provided it came "without strings." Their experience with bilateral and multilateral aid programs caused them to modify their position. At other times they would not accept any grant aid; at still other times they emphasized trade, not aid. Their present policy (since March, 1962) is to accept only government–to–government and multilateral (U.N., Colombo Plan) aid. Perhaps their basic desire is to do without any aid. But such a goal, however desirable and understandable, is not yet practicable.

Burma has established strong ties with Yugoslavia and Israel, two countries that are held in varying degrees of political disesteem by the Sino-Soviet bloc. Burma's membership in the Afro-Asian bloc, which has excluded Israel in deference to Arab feelings, has not prevented cordial diplomatic and technical-assistance relations from developing between Burma and Israel. Indeed, Burma urged, though unsuccessfully, that Israel be invited to the Bandung Conference. During his trip to the Middle East after that conference, U Nu planned to visit both Egypt and Israel. When Egypt asked him not to visit Israel, he refused, carried out his visit to Israel, and canceled the one to Egypt. During the caretaker regime, Prime Minister Ne Win visited both countries. Similarily, even at the peak of Stalin's (and later, Mao's) cold war against Yugoslavia, Burma maintained her cordial relations with President Tito's government.

Even those who are strongly antineutralist should find it difficult to charge Burma with favoring the Sino-Soviet bloc. Yet such charges have been made, especially when Burma spoke out in favor of banning the A-bomb and H-bomb, and also when she opposed the formation of SEATO. We sometimes forget that prior to the Geneva Conference of 1954, the United States had expressed little support for such a regional security pact in Asia. In brief, Burma has been neither a docile satellite nor a small neutralist power afraid to take an independent stand.

Burmese security can be supported by respecting Burma's conceptions of security, and by aiding where possible the measures Burma has taken to preserve her security and independence. In the geopolitical context of Asia, Burma's most severe test has been her relationship with China, especially in connection with the many hundreds of miles of the formerly undemarcated border. It is to that relationship that we now turn.

N O INTERNATIONAL CONCERN has been as important to Burma
as her relations with China. Kuomintang China had encouraged
the Burmese nationalists and had sponsored Burma's entry into the
U.N., but had also exhibited (in various published maps and in
other ways) traditional Chinese expansionist tendencies toward
Burma and mainland Southeast Asia. Most of all, after 1950, Kuomintang China endangered Burma's relations with Communist
China by her active, irresponsible support for her troops who had
escaped via Yunnan into northeast Burma. However much the
Burmese may have initially and quietly tolerated the presence of
these KMT "escapees,"—a view which has been unofficially hinted
in some Burmese and American quarters—expecting that they
would either merge into the Burma population or quickly repatriate to Taiwan, at the end of the first year of experience with these
troops the Burmese became justifiably alarmed, repeatedly sought
but did not receive assistance from the United States for this repatriation, and eventually, in 1953, officially took the issue to the
United Nations.[1] (It was this issue that brought U.S. prestige and
relations with Burma to a postwar low.)

The relations between Burma and the People's Republic of
China, with their approximately 1,500 miles of unprotectable border, are certainly correct and, on the surface, friendly. However, a
more revealing estimate of the Burmese attitude will be found in
an interview given by U Kyaw Nyein on March 30, 1951.[2] Kyaw
Nyein said:

> Small nations always mistrust bigger ones, especially those close by.
> For years past, every Burman has mistrusted China, whether un-
> der Mao or Chiang. They also mistrust India; for that matter they

* This chapter originally appeared in *The Journal of Southeast Asian History*,
V, No. 1 (March, 1964). Some editorial changes have been made in the present version.

also mistrust Soviet Russia and even America. We don't consider China a menace, but we accept a possibility of China one day invading us. We are not alone in this concern. Our neighbors will also be perturbed as our fate may likely be theirs. We are entering into closer relations with India, Pakistan, Indonesia, and are trying to find a formula for peaceful coexistence in this part of our world. We don't want to do anything that will provoke China, but if she does invade, I am confident that the national spirit of our people will stand firm against her. We don't want Communist Russia or Communist China, but being a small nation, we must find ways and means of avoiding embroilment in power blocs.

Burma was the first non-Communist country to recognize the People's Republic of China (December 18, 1949)[3] and to agree on an exchange of embassies. The first Chinese cultural delegation arrived in Burma approximately two years later, on December 9, and departed on December 28, 1951. The compliment was returned by the Burmese, April 19-June 6, 1952. From then on various missions were exchanged (Thakin Tin, August, 1952; Bo Hmu Aung, May-June, 1953), leading up to the exchange of good-will visits on the prime-ministerial level. Chou En-lai came to Burma on June 28, 1954, at which time he and U Nu issued their joint communiqué endorsing the Sino-Indian "Five Principles of Peaceful Coexistence" (a three-year trade agreement, the first, had been signed on April 22, 1954), and U Nu returned the visit on November 11 of the same year. Since then there have been more meetings and exchanges. Barter and regular trade between the two countries have improved. In 1961, the Chinese agreed to make available to Burma an interest-free ten-year loan of $84 million to be used for Chinese supplies and technical assistance.[4] The two governments apparently agreed to "seal off the borders against anyone entering or departing without proper authority," [5] thus curtailing not only the traditional free movement across the borders but also the large-scale illegal emigration of Chinese nationals into Burma. The Burmese were aware that Communist China had repulsed several re-entry attempts made by the KMT troops located in Burma. They were also aware, though it was not published, that Chinese Communist troops had settled in several northeast border areas as a "defensive" measure against KMT disruption. However, throughout the 1950's the basic issue between the two countries was the border question, in dispute at least since the British annexed Upper Burma in 1886.

A brief backward glance at Sino-Burman relations is necessary to understand this issue.

The Burmese are Sinic peoples whose high cultures after the third-century fall of the Han dynasty are derived mainly from Indian sources. When the neolithic ancestors (Ch'iang tribes?) of the present Burmese descending from "Kansu, between the Gobi Desert and northeast Tibet," first came to Burma is not known. Chinese records of the second century B.C. note a kingdom in what is now Upper Burma and refer to a trade route through the mountain passes of southwest China linking it to Burma, India, Central Asia, and the Indian Ocean. The majority group, the Burmans, refer to themselves as Tibeto-Burman. This latter term, of linguistic and geographical derivation, is broad enough to include such major Frontier or Hill peoples as the Chins and Kachins of northern Burma. The Shans, like their cousins the Thai and Lao and probably the Karen, were originally from southwestern China, closely related to the Yunnanese.

The borders of this northern and northeastern area where Burma meets China, Laos, and Thailand are largely cartographical, not ethnic, for members of various subgroups inhabit both sides of the respective frontiers. There are, in addition, many tribal groups living on both sides of the northeast border area whose identification is less clear. Among these, one of the most numerous and isolated groups, estimated at about 100,000, is the Wa—animist, occasionally until well into the twentieth century, given to head-hunting, and probably of Mon-Khmer origin. Their territory, like that of the Kachins and the Shans, will figure in subsequent Anglo–Burma–China border issues. Their language is probably a Mon-Khmer variant. The latter are the chief bearers of Theravada Buddhist culture to all of Burma. The word "foreigner" in Burmese, when referring to the Chinese, is *paukpaw*, or "cousin"; when referring to other foreigners it is *kala* (or *kula*—caste people—Indians), sometimes used in a pejorative sense. The Burmese vocabulary has about 1,000 words of exclusively Tibetan origin; about 750 of exclusively Chinese origin, and many thousands common to both. But racial, linguistic, and some cultural affinities between the Burmese and the Chinese, however much stressed since 1954, have not been the bases of their political relations during the centuries.[6]

During the period of the Tang Dynasty (618-907 A.D.) some small states in Burma were probably in some kind of tributary relation to China. Up to the eleventh century, when Burma was unified for the first time under the Pagan Dynasty, founded by Anawratha in 1044, such tribute, if indeed it was that, probably went to the T'ai Kingdom of Nanchao and possibly through it to the Sung Dynasty in China. Nanchao was the landlocked area of Yunnan, Laos, northern Thailand, and the eastern area of the (Burma) Shan Plateau. The Mongols under Kublai Khan finally defeated and absorbed Nanchao in their victorious march to the south, thereby removing a buffer state between Burma and China. Between 1271 and 1273, Kublai Khan twice demanded that the Burmese kings at Pagan acknowledge their token submission to his throne by tributary payments. The Burmese refused; and were defeated in 1277 in the battle described but not seen by Marco Polo.[7] The Chinese (Mongols) then withdrew, but six years later were again forced to subdue the Burmese, who had apparently failed to remain properly submissive. This time their king fled—earning the

nickname Tarok Pye Min (now a Burmese term for cowardice)—
"the king who ran away from the Chinese." Subsequently he returned, attempted to pay tribute, and was murdered by one of his
sons in 1287. Within a few years the Pagan dynasty expired under
the last of the Mongol attacks and the rising power of the Shans,
who maintained a series of feudal kingdoms in Burma from then
on.

This was, in a sense, the beginning of Sino-Burma relations. The
Shan states produced one leader known as Tarok Kan Mingyi, "the
king who defeated the Chinese," in the early fourteenth century.
Mongol power gave way to the Ming dynasty (1368-1644), which
reasserted with some success its suzerainty over the states of Upper
and eastern (Shan) Burma. It is on the bases of Mongol and Ming
history that modern Chinese assert claims on Burma. Burmese historians corroborate these Chinese successes up to the end of the
fifteenth century. But then a new Burmese dynasty became powerful, particularly under the leadership of Bayinnaung, 1551-81. His
conquests not only unified Burma for a second time but also vastly
extended the area owing suzerainty to Burma during his long reign.
These include the Chittagong area of what is now East Pakistan
and Manipur on the west; roughly the same northern boundaries as
today; the "Chinese" Shan states of Santa, Hotha, Latha, Mowun,
Kaingma, Kenghung (Kiang Hung), considerably to the east of
the present borders, including the watershed of the Taiping River
and roughly bounded by the Mekong River on the northeast. G. E.
Harvey says that states "as far east as Annam and Cambodia probably sent proprietary homage to Bayinnaung." [8] Certainly Bayinnaung reversed the direction of tribute. It came to him by virtue of
conquest—including states that had formerly acknowledged Ming
authority. Actually, as the Ming withdrew before the advancing
Manchus, some of their remnants (the last Ming pretender, Chu
Yu-ang, or Prince Kuei, and his family) sought and received asy-
lum in Burma, at Bhamo, in 1656. But Burmese power also slid
downhill in the seventeenth century. Burma surrendered the Ming
to the Manchus in 1662.

Sino-Burman relations for the next hundred years do not appear
to be in conflict over their boundaries or over the mobile, border-
crossing populations. Nor are there any Burmese records of tribute
missions to China. But on a pretext—mistreatment of Chinese
merchants by the Burmese (how frequently this occurs in imperialist histories), Ch'ien-lung (1736-95), the powerful Ch'ing emperor,
attempted to reimpose vassalage or at least some form of the tributary system on Burma. He made his first move in 1765. [9] The power
and reputation of the Ch'ien-lung era has vastly overshadowed its
Burmese counterpart. However, a fairly obscure local chief in Upper Burma was on the way to becoming the founder of Burma's
third unifying dynasty. He first took the name of "The Victorious"
and then "Embryo Buddha," or Alaungpaya of Shwebo. Between

1752 and his death in 1760, he succeeded in again reuniting Burma and in establishing outposts in Manipur and Siam. The Chinese viceroy of Yunnan recognized his kingship. One of his sons, King Hsinbyushin (1763-76), finally subdued Siam, capturing and destroying its capital at Ayuthia in 1766. This event, perhaps more than the treatment of the Chinese traders, stirred the Chinese Emperor. He thereupon intensified his campaign against the Burmese, sending a considerable armed invading force to compel compliance with the traditional Chinese practice of tribute.

The Burmese call this the period of the "Four Invasions." [10] In the first, three Chinese armies led by the Viceroy of Yunnan attacked successively at Kentung, Mogaung, and Bhamo. Each of them was defeated. The leading Burmese General was Maha Sithu. "Large military stores were seized from the Chinese after their defeat and a large number of Chinese were also taken captive to Ava and these formed a useful settlement in Burma." A second avenging invasion followed close upon the first. This time a great Burmese General, Maha Thiha Thura, took the field against the Chinese who had entered Burma near the Hsenwi border. The Chinese were again defeated. The Burmese, as in the time of Bayinnaung, reoccupied the nine Shan states (the *ko shan pye* referred to in n. 8), thereby indicating that these states had reverted to the Manchus during the decline of the Burmese Toungoo dynasty.

The third and fourth invasions, 1767-69, again brought forward General Maha Thiha Thura, who had already won fame during the second invasion, and who now succeeded in defeating the Emperor's son-in-law, Ming-jui. (The latter had previously achieved distinction in the Manchu wars in Turkestan.) General Ming-jui had initially won a series of battles, almost reaching the Burmese capital at Ava—and certainly had gotten as far as the Gokteik Gorge, considerably to the west of Lashio. Harvey places his furthest advance as "three marches from Ava." [11] Another source has him near what is now Maymyo, approximately 50 miles east and north of the then capital. Ming-jui, in traditional pattern, committed suicide after his defeat. His successor, General Fu-heng, a relative of the Chinese Empress, fared no better in the fourth invasion. The Burmese won the wars of 1765-69. The Chinese generals sued for peace which, as later events disclose, was contrary to the wishes of the Burmese King. The Burmese General and thirteen of his officers met with thirteen Chinese officers to draw up a "written contract of settlement." [12] The Chinese departed in peace. Trade was restored, and to prevent further misunderstanding, it was agreed to exchange decennial missions "of some sort"—the phrase is Parker's—between the two sovereigns. Neither monarch apparently ratified the treaty. The Chinese were not happy at their costly defeat at the hands of a smaller power. The Burmese royal household never quite forgave General Maha Thiha Thura for his leniency in not completely wiping out the Chinese armies. Manchu historical accounts, as Hinton points out, refer to this Chinese failure at arms as one of the ten great victories of his (Emperor Ch'ien-lung's) reign by virtue of its permitting Burma to enter the ranks of the vassal states! [13]

This brief account of Sino-Burman relations is a necessary background for understanding the future role of the exchange of so-called tribute missions and the long-continuing border question. The Burmese and Chinese in fact exchanged missions beginning in the 1770's, but after the wars of 1765-69, the Burmese never acknowledged any obligation to pay tribute. The Chinese never acknowledged their defeat. The relations between the two countries revolved primarily about trade. The Chinese, from time to time, acted out their role as if the Burmese were paying tribute. The Burmese stopped sending missions after 1795 for approximately two decades during the reign of King Bodawpaya when they felt affronted by Chinese treatment.[14] As Christian concludes, "certainly there is little evidence of a seigneural position between the two countries after the Burmese defeat of the great Chinese invasions of 1765-1769." [15]

The advent of the British in nineteenth-century Burma, especially as a consequence of the three Anglo-Burmese wars and the gradual disintegration of nineteenth-century China, likewise unsuccessful in rebuffing or restraining the corroding forces of Western imperialism, changed the situation between Burma and China.

The Burmese, in the nineteenth century, were increasingly preoccupied with growing English power. Both the English and the French eyed competitively the potential trade with southwest China. The presumed key to this lay in control of the Irrawaddy River and the overland route from Bhamo and Lashio to Yunnanfu (Kunming)—the road to Mandalay and the Burma Road. English interest in a trade route into southwestern China is marked by a notable series of reports, surveys, and missions, following closely upon each other from just after the First Anglo-Burmese War, 1824-26, until after the third in 1885.[16]

King Mindon, in what proved to be a vain attempt to bolster the fortunes of his kingdom, sought to establish some kind of diplomatic relations with various powers other than Britain. He sent missions to the United States (1857), Italy and France (1872), and China (1874). It was the last mission from royal Burma sent, not in tribute, but as a diplomatic device to redress the balance against advancing English encroachment.

After the British annexed Upper Burma and incorporated it into their Indian provinces, they largely ignored or were indifferent to Burma's border-area history, and immediately sought to work out commercial and other arrangements with the Chinese, especially since they feared the rapidly growing French competition. France had already gained access to China's southern provinces via the Indochinese Red River Valley and was building up its commercial

and political influence in Thailand.[17] British authorities, preoccupied with the pacification of Upper Burma, were also concerned
lest the Chinese operating out of Yunnan would use the initial
confusion of the annexation period to carve out a piece of Burma
for themselves before British power could be established over the
north and northeast border areas. Immediately after occupying
Mandalay,[18] the British sent a steamer to Bhamo to forestall possible seizure of that river port. Some six months later, on July 24,
1886, England signed the O'Connor Convention with China "Relative to Burma and Thibet." In return for doing "whatever she
deems fit and proper" in Burma (Article II), stipulating that there
shall be established a "Delimitation Commission" on boundaries,
and securing agreement on a Frontier Trade Commission "to protect and encourage trade between China and Burmah" (Article
III), England agreed, in an apparently meaningless gesture to as-
suage Chinese sensibilities, "as it has been the practice of Burmah to send a decennial mission to China," to continue this arrangement, provided that its members would be Burmese, not British!

Thus England yielded on the "tribute mission" (Article I). She
regarded it as an empty gesture because she was interested in the
Southwest China trade, and simultaneously she had determined to
deny the Chinese "a large hunk of Burmese territory in the
North," [19] which the Chinese demanded as the price for trade concessions. Boundary surveys begun in 1893 led to the signing, in
London, in March, 1894, of a convention "giving effect to Article
III of the convention of July 24, 1886." Seven articles were devoted
to boundary questions (and providing for further rectification)
and twelve to trade development. Later that year, in September, a
second convention, "regarding the junction of the Chinese and
Burma telegraph lines," was signed in Tientsin.

As part of the 1894 convention the British yielded to China
some of the territory of the old *ko shan pye* area, "formerly possessed by the Kings of Ava concurrently with the Emperors of
China," with the stipulation that China "shall not cede" such territory to any other nation. Nevertheless, in those turbulent days of
Anglo-French rivalry in mainland Southeast Asia, the Chinese were
forced in the following year to yield Kenhung (Kiang Hung) to
France.[20] As punishment, while recognizing the questionable Chinese sovereignty over the area, the British obtained, in a new and
important convention of 1897, "a perpetual lease" at a fixed rent
(later determined at rupees 1,000 per year) of the so-called Namwan Tract on Burma's border, near Bhamo, and ended the tribute
missions. Variously estimated as between 60 and 100 square miles,
the area of the tract, defined in Article II, continues to figure in all
subsequent negotiations between Burma and China. Modifications
of the boundaries were also negotiated in this and later agreements.[21]

Thus, the first decade of Anglo-Chinese negotiations on the Sino-Burma boundary and trade carelessly or confusedly set the stage for a protracted debate, which persisted throughout the first half of the twentieth century and endangered the security of Burma once the Chinese Communists came to power. The Chinese were given the ammunition of British recognition for their assertion of traditional rights in Burma. Parenthetically, it may be remarked that some derogatory qualification, as here used, is clearly supported by the evidence. Britain's imperialist depredations against China rightfully arouses sympathy for the latter. But this in turn has obscured the traditional Chinese imperialist role vis-à-vis the *Nanyang* in general and Burma in particular.

The demarcation of the border proceeded episodically but not always peacefully after the creation of a new Boundary Commission following the adoption of the 1897 convention. Armed clashes between the British and the Chinese occurred in the Kachin, Shan, and Wa states areas at least three times between 1900 and 1911 and again in 1934-35.[22] After the clash in 1935, the two governments agreed to the appointment of a League of Nations Boundary Commission, consisting of two representatives from each government and presided over by a neutral chairman, Colonel Frederic Iselin of Switzerland. The commission worked on defining the Wa state border, including the possible participation of Chinese interests in certain silver mines "of the Lufang ridge." Its labors were completed in April, 1937, just prior to the July Marco Polo Bridge episode which heightened the Sino-Japanese conflict. As a result of this new convulsion, ratification did not take place until June 18, 1941; however, the agreement presumably settled only one of the border-area disputes, that of the Wa state line.[23]

In the closing years of the Manchu dynasty, China continued to base her claims on Burmese territory on her version of the ancient tribute-and-vassalage system. As the dynasty "gave way to foreign pressure and penetration from the coast," it "tended to look for new compensatory activities . . . [and] fields of expansion elsewhere." [24] After the fall of the Manchus, the rising tide of Chinese nationalism intensified China's imperialist claims to Burmese territory. In his fourth lecture on the *Three Principles of the People*, Sun Yat-sen blandly, and with almost childlike arrogance, referred to the many states which "wanted to bring tribute and adopt Chinese culture . . . [and] considered it a great favor for China to annex them." He claimed that Siam was a country which "would gladly renew . . . allegiance to China and become a province of China"—a Siamese, he adds, told him so. He regarded Burma, Nepal, Tibet, and Bhutan as "having belonged" to China.[25] Other Chinese frequently referred to Britain's "actions of aggression" along the Yunnan-Burmese border as typical imperialist impositions on China. Apparently they never questioned the validity of China's own claims.[26]

In sum, the Chinese position was based on vague sentimental or medieval historical claims of Chinese suzerainty in mainland Southeast Asia deriving from the traditional tributary system. The Western Powers, so the Chinese legend goes, usurped the lands that belonged to them. In chauvinist accounts of Mongol, Ming, Manchu, and Republican history, the claim for *all* of Burma is made and, when power to establish such a claim vanished, grandly waived. A more dangerous claim took its place after the British annexed Upper Burma. The Chinese sought all Burmese territory north of Myitkyina to the Himalaya Mountains, west to the India border and east to Yunnan. This trans-Himalayan claim, voiced by Sun Yat-sen among many others, was incorporated in the oft-referred-to maps published by the Kuomintang National and Chinese Communist governments.

The Kuomintang Government, in fact, was even unwilling to abide by the joint delimitation of the Wa state border, achieved under the impartial auspices of the League of Nations, which it had ratified on June 18, 1941. Its attempt to reopen negotiations in August, 1941, was shelved only by the outbreak of the war in the Pacific. "After the war," as Hinton points out, "various Chinese officials proposed that the [boundary] question be resolutely taken up again." The National Government put forward a strong claim to the area north of Myitkyina, buttressed by the fact that Chinese troops fought there against the Japanese. In 1946, General Chiang Kai-shek sent a force into Burma "on the pretext of hunting for deserters." The threat of an air attack was necessary to make the troops leave.[27]

The Chinese Communists, as we shall see, continued and extended this aggressive policy, beginning with their action against Tibet in 1950.

Independent Burma inherited this problem. *The New York Times* of December 2, 1947, carried a story, with a map, to the effect that the "Chinese [were] preparing to lay claim to territory in Northern Burma" about equal in size to the state of Oklahoma. The advent of the Communists to power in China did not alter the situation—the same or related Chinese maps were published at least once, with the explanation that the Communists did not have time to alter "older" maps, which were merely reprinted.[28] Burmese leaders, acutely aware of the provocation provided by KMT troops on their soil, voiced their anxiety over possible Chinese encroachment "into our territory." [29]

There are some variations in these Chinese maps, but whether Kuomintang or Communist, they most frequently refer to three areas: The first includes all territory north of latitude 25° 35′ along a line from above Myitkyina. On the west it reaches the Assam border; on the north it extends through Putao to the northern watershed of the upper Irrawaddy River at the Tibetan-Sikiang border, the so-called McMahon line,[30] drawn in 1914 under the Sino-

British conventions of 1886 and 1897; on the east it is defined by the area beyond the N'mai Kha River to the watershed shared with the Salween River, with the High Conical Peak as the southern anchor and the Izurazi Pass as the northern one. In this northern area, in major part referred to as the "Triangle" (approximately 60 square miles), there are three Kachin villages—Hpimaw, Gawlum, and Kangfang—destined to become famous in the ensuing events. The second territorial claim, located in the Shan states, is the Namwan Tract, a tract of land wedged in south and east of Bhamo to the Shweli River. It was assigned to Burma on "perpetual lease" as part of the 1897 revision of the 1894 convention between China and England. The third disputed area is a portion of the Wa state, east of Lashio, and east of the Salween River, which at this point runs well inside the Burmese border. Its boundary of some 200 miles had been surveyed and fixed by the 1941 Iselin agreement between England and China; both the Chinese Communists and the Kuomintang Chinese sought to repudiate this agreement.

Despite their republication of these maps, the Chinese Communists made no territorial moves in the direction of Burma until the summer of 1953. The Burmese attempted to clarify these questions with China after they formally recognized the People's Republic in December, 1949. At that time, according to U Nu, the Chinese Communists "had their hands so full . . . with more urgent problems" that the Burmese were asked "to shelve the boundary question for the time being." [31] However, without any further discussion or warning, "five units of the Red China People's Army, a little over 200 men" entered Burmese territory and established camps about 25 miles inside the northern Wa state.[32] These detachments were stationed there presumably to hold off any further attacks against Yunnan staged by the KMT troops located in Burma. The Burmese Government did not publicly acknowledge their presence until it released on June 3, 1957, for limited distribution, a 1953 report on the border with Yunnan prepared by Colonel Saw Myint. However, there is ample evidence that the Cabinet was not only aware of the problem but soon took steps to handle it.

After the Burmese gained the cooperation of the U.N., the United States, and Thailand for the evacuation of about half of the KMT troops in 1953-54, they sought to secure the withdrawal of the Chinese Communist "defensive" forces stationed in Burma and to open discussions on the border issue. Negotiations on these issues between Communist China and Burma followed their adoption, June 20, 1954, of the so-called "Five Principles of Peaceful Coexistence": mutual respect for territorial integrity and sovereignty; nonaggression; noninterference in internal affairs; equality and mutual benefit; peaceful coexistence. Conversations were begun in a preliminary manner during Prime Minister U Nu's first visit to China at the end of 1954. A trade and diplomatic communiqué was released on December 12, 1954, in which reference was made to the need "to settle this question [incomplete delimitation of the boundary line] in a friendly spirit at an appropriate time through normal diplomatic channels." [33] At the Bandung Conference of April, 1955, Chou En-lai also referred to a possible settlement of the border question. Apart from such statements little else was done. The Burmese had interpreted the presence of the P.R.C.'s troops as counteraction to the Kuomintang troops which on several occasions had made sorties back to Yunnan. They expected, or at least hoped, that in 1954-55 the partial evacuation of the KMT and the pervasive Bandung spirit would cause the Chinese Communists to withdraw to their side of the border. On this issue U Nu returned home empty-handed from his 1954 visit. He did get some kind of commitment for negotiations.

But the path of negotiation was neither swift nor always peaceful. Chou En-lai, reporting to the First National People's Congress in July, 1957, said:

> In November, 1955, just as the Chinese and the Burmese sides were respectively making active preparations for the settlement of the boundary question, an armed clash unfortunately occurred owing to misunderstanding between the outpost units of the two countries in the border region. This incident was properly dealt with through the joint efforts of both sides, but at the same time it made the governments of both countries realize the need for an early settlement of the boundary question between the two countries.[34]

Actually the armed clash of November 20, 1955, in which the Burmese "lost one dead and three wounded, the Chinese lost one man killed and seven wounded," [35] was not publicly revealed until a series of news reports began to appear in the Burmese press in late July and August, 1956. Then, in crescendo fashion, a flood of information was made available to enterprising Burmese reporters. The story was first reported by *The Nation*. It carried an account, July 23, of a small detachment of Chinese soldiers discovered in the far northern area, about 80 miles above Putao. (It is to be noted that this is in the far north area, a considerable distance from the Chinese troops who clashed with the Burmese in the Wa state.) A second story on July 25 described the arrest of Chinese "Red Army men of Political Branch" near Sima in the Burma Kachin Hills, 63 miles west of Tengchung, Yunnan. They were involved with a Kachin (Zaw Naw) who had been arrested earlier while recruiting for a "liberation army." Then came the main story on August 1, which revealed that Chinese troops had entrenched themselves in the Wa state, had clashed with Burmese troops in November, 1955, and again in April, 1956. Headlines proclaimed that the Chinese "hold 1,000 square miles of Burmese territory" in the Wa state and that their garrison was approximately 1,500 strong. The Chinese first denied the story, then became silent. Burmese leaders first refrained from talking about it, but then the Prime Minister held a press conference, as mentioned, and U Nu, not then in office, sent a personal letter via the Burmese Ambassador, U Aung Soe, to Prime Minister Nehru, seeking his aid. Public opinion was stirred in and out of Burma, to the embarrassment of the Chinese and Burmese Communists. The "Five Principles of Coexistence" and the "Bandung spirit" were watchfully invoked as all Burma became aware of a three-pronged Chinese armed probe in the three regions historically claimed by China.[36]

It is interesting to note that the details that appeared in the Burmese press could not have appeared without the cooperation of the armed forces and the government; and that the story of the clash was published shortly after the elections of April, 1956, at a time when the Anti-Fascist People's Freedom League felt that it had to regain some of the nationalist fervor and popular support that it had in part lost to the National Unity Front, the Communist-infiltrated coalition. Perhaps, too, as the following timetable suggests, the AFPFL leaders hoped that by arousing domestic and foreign public opinion they would be able to press negotiations with Peking on the border issue in general and secure the withdrawal of the Communist troops.

The main features of this story had appeared between July 23 and August 1, 1956. Radio Peking denied the story on August 5. As if to answer Peking, additional details, especially about location points and numbers of Chinese troops at each post, were published in *The Nation* of August 6. At his press conference on August 7, Prime Minister Ba Swe implied that he had taken steps [by an exchange of letters] to ask Chou En-lai to withdraw the Chinese Communist troops. (Though this correspondence has not been published, a summary of it appears in U Nu's "Speech of April 28, 1960.") A careful round-up story appeared on August 11. U Nu sent a personal letter of appeal to Nehru on August 15, which was reported in the press, although the text was not released. On August 17, there appeared the first public references to Chinese-sponsored "Free Wa," "Free Kachin," and "Free Thai" movements. The encroachments on Burmese territory indicated in the Chinese Communist maps were published on August 20 under a *Nation* headline, "Red Chinese Imperialism." Further details concerning the presence of Chinese troops in the Myitkyina district were given by the same paper on August 23 and 25. The press campaign was kept up intensively until it was announced on September 22 that U Nu had for the second time been invited to China in October "to talk about the boundary question." The same announcement carried with it the dates for U Nu's first visit to the anti-Communist regime in Saigon, Vietnam, November 11-15, 1956.

There is no evidence on this point, but it is not unreasonable to suppose that Peking was unhappy over the worldwide unfavorable attention it had attracted by its border depredations and machinations in Burma—a Bandung state, already neutralist in policy, and committed to a campaign for China's admission to the United Nations. It was also a time when Chinese Communist policy was directed at wooing the Bandung states. In terms of Communist strategy and tactics, this latter motive was probably more important to the Chinese than any reaction from the non-Communist world. This was the background to the renewal of border negotiations between Rangoon and Peking in late 1956.

The Chinese Communists, like their predecessors, based their claims on the fluctuating course of traditional Sino-Burmese history, interpreted, however, solely from the Chinese chauvinist viewpoint. They did not refer, as such, to the ancient and no longer relevant meanings of tribute. They emphasized the more congenial ideological charge that the settlements with the British between 1886-1941 had been forced on a "weak" China by imperialist power, while ignoring the obvious character of past and present Chinese imperialism among the non-Han, Mongoloid peoples of Tibet, the trans-Himalayan areas, and mainland Southeast Asia. The extent of their recognizable territorial aspirations, without respect to continuing international Communist efforts at infiltration and subversion, was initially coterminous with the high points of Imperial and Republican China's actual and fancied expansion. That such Chinese territorial aims may erupt in future aggression against the independent countries of Asia, as they already have in Tibet, Korea, mainland Southeast Asia, and India, is a clear probability.

Ethnic and linguistic analysis offered no resolution of the difficulties over the Sino-Burma border issue. Related peoples of the disputed areas are minorities in both Burma and China, and straddle both sides of the border. Transborder traders, permanent and seasonal migrants, and practitioners of religio-cultural observances have moved freely across the mountain passes and river valleys without observing the niceties of border locations. Flag marches, the placing and replacing of the border stone-markings or pillars (in General Joseph W. Stilwell's colorful phrase, "the Chinese carried the border stones in their knapsacks"), the findings of field surveys over the course of years have varied as a consequence of domestic and international factors. Beginning in 1956, the Burmese sought a settlement that would cost them "least loss," but which at the same time would give them a stabilized border with their feared neighbor. They banked on their demonstrated friendliness to all powers, their neutralism in the Cold War, and their championship, together with India and Indonesia, of the P.R.C.'s entry into the U.N.

The policy of least loss was essentially the one retained by successive Burmese Cabinets at and subsequent to the time when U Nu renewed negotiations with the Chinese at Chou En-lai's invitation to Peking in October, 1956. On his return to Burma he broadcast a report, "On the Sino-Burmese Boundary Question." [37]

From this and other reports it became clear that the Burmese position, more carefully prepared than it had been in 1954, was presented and defended on the basis of the Sino-British and League of Nations boundary documents of 1886-1941. Throughout these negotiations the Burmese requested the removal of Chinese troops from their territory. They wished to retain the McMahon Line on the north, the N'mai Kha-Salween watershed on the northeast, and the Iselin Line as the eastern border of the Wa states. They were prepared for the possibility of having to surrender the leased Namwan Tract, since the British documents that they used implied that this area had belonged to the Chinese. U Nu, as the chief negotiator in November, 1956, was sanguine about persuading the Chinese to permit the Burmese either to retain permanently this tract that provides ready access between Bhamo and the Shan states, or at least to maintain the existing "perpetual lease."

The Chinese, as a matter of policy, rejected the British documents and while they did not out of hand reject the Iselin Boundary Commission findings, they threw doubt upon their validity. However they won some initial advantage by agreeing to the withdrawal of their troops from the Wa state (and did so "within one month");[38] and by their silence with respect to former Chinese claims to the Triangle, west of the N'mai Kha River. Their counteroffer came to be called the "Package Deal," for Burma would have to accept all or none of it. It included what appeared to be acceptance of the northern McMahon line, which was henceforth called the traditional line, retention on the northeast of the N'mai Kha-Salween watershed from High Conical Peak to the Izurazi Pass, provided that Burma cede as allegedly Chinese-owned the Kachin area of the three villages, Hpimaw Kangfang and Gawlum, to the west of that watershed. This area affords the Chinese a favorable route through mountain passes northward to Tibet. Finally, it provided for approval of the Iselin line as the boundary of the Wa state and for the abrogation of the lease on the Namwan Tract, the method and consequences of which would be subject to further negotiation.

The Burmese delegation, returning from Peking in mid-November, 1956, characterized the Chinese offer as "fair and reasonable," despite the Chinese demand for territory in the Kachin State. The proposed cession of the three villages occasioned an anguished outcry among the Kachins and, generally, throughout the country, contributing to a much "cooler" reception for Chou En-lai when he returned U Nu's visit the following month.[39] Premier Chou En-lai wooed Burmese opinion by a speech in which he declared that a border settlement would be made not on the basis of problems "left behind by [imperialist] history," but on the basis of the "Five Principles of Peaceful Coexistence." [40] According to

U Nu and U Ba Swe, he agreed to yield the Namwan Tract to Burma in return for the Kachin village area. Prime Minister Ba Swe and his cabinet thereupon decided to accept the "Package Deal" [41] in order to bring the thorny border question to a speedy end on the basis of "least loss." On February 4, 1957, the Burmese Government sent an official letter (with accompanying maps) to the People's Republic of China. Signed by Premier Ba Swe, the letter sought confirmation of the Burmese understanding with Chou En-lai. It included reference to the traditional line, demarcated by the Upper Irrawaddy watershed, the Iselin line, and the agreement to yield some 56 square miles of the Kachin villages for the approximately 60 square miles of the Namwan Tract.[42]

At the end of the month U Nu reassumed the premiership, and shortly after proceeded, somewhat optimistically, to conclude the agreement by visiting with Premier Chou En-lai in Kunming. He was doomed to disappointment. For by now the Chinese had revised their demands upward, on the strength of U Nu's 1956 admission that their claims on the Kachin villages and on the Iselin line had some justification because of British "imposition." At U Nu's suggestion to Chou En-lai, the new Chinese demands were presented to the Burma Government by way of a letter-map reply, dated July 26, 1957, in response to U Ba Swe's letter and map communication of February 4. Chou now insisted that the three Kachin villages unconditionally belonged to China and that the territory amounted to 186 square miles[43] instead of the Burmese 56 square miles; that if the Burmese were to receive the Namwan Tract, defined as 86 square miles, they had to yield some equivalent territory along the Iselin line in the area inhabited by the Panhung and Panglao tribes; and that the traditional northern line required modification of the Upper Irrawaddy watershed, which he proposed could be turned over to a new Joint Boundary Survey Commission to be set up by the two governments.

The Burmese were dismayed. On every major point, with the exception of the withdrawal of Chinese troops, they would now have to yield more than they had expected to on the basis of the tentative agreements of 1956. The political implications of protracted negotiations were not lost upon them. The new Chinese demands for Burmese territory would make for greater unrest and unpopularity at home. Yet, if their objective was to close out the border question as quickly as possible, they had little bargaining power.

During the remainder of 1957, the Burmese Government sent two missions to Peking, one headed by Supreme Court Justice Myint Thein, the former Ambassador to China, and the other by Deputy Prime Ministers Ba Swe and Kyaw Nyein. In February-March, 1958, the Burmese Ambassador to Peking, U Hla Maung, who had been called home the previous month for consultations on this issue during the Third All-Burma Congress of the AFPFL, was returned to his post instructed to make yet another attempt at a solution. In each instance, the Burmese were prepared to yield to the new demands by exchanging the Panhung and Panglao territory for the Namwan Tract and by accepting a modification in the traditional line to the north where it crossed the Taron River valley, provided the rest of that line could be settled on the watershed principle. They continued to agree to the cession of the three villages, but tried to whittle down the size of the area demanded by China. All the negotiators had the backing of a Cabinet decision of October 14, 1957. They were prepared to go to almost any lengths, within the new set of Communist Chinese terms in order to settle the matter. All the missions failed. In a letter of July 30, 1958, Chou En-lai summed up the cat-and-mouse game he had been playing during the eighteen months following his December, 1956, visit to Rangoon. Typically, where he appeared to accept in principle the Burmese restatement of terms he added some new reservations with respect to boundary line or to the size of territory to be exchanged, or some other new feature that would require the Burmese either to make further revisions or to become alarmed lest the new reservation endangered the future.

The 1958 split in the AFPFL interdicted any further efforts in this matter by Prime Minister Nu. However, General Ne Win, his successor, after consulting with the leaders of both the Clean and Stable AFPFL in mid-1959, determined to make another try. On June 4, 1959, he proposed a settlement to the Chinese along the lines that had been approved by the presplit Cabinet in October, 1957. The Chinese again temporized, suggesting in a reply dated September 24, 1959, that the problem be turned over to negotiating delegations. The Burmese had steadfastly declined such an arrangement, convinced that it would lead to further delay. General Ne Win reiterated this view in his reply (November 4), and offered to go to Peking if the Chinese government would agree to close the gap of their respective disagreements on the basis of his "fair and equitable compromise" proposals of June 4, 1959.

This new Sino-Burmese correspondence roughly coincided with the more overt "beginnings" of the Sino-Indian border conflict in Ladakh and in India's northeast territory, the boundaries of which had been presumably settled by the Durand and McMahon lines; and with the Sino-Indonesian conflict about the "overseas Chinese" being removed from the rural areas in Indonesia.[44] Perhaps as a consequence of these events and the unfavorable Asian as well as world reaction, the Chinese suddenly decided to show themselves in at least one friendly stance in Asia. Premier Chou En-lai responded to General Ne Win's November letter with an invitation to the latter to visit Peking in January, 1960. The Burmese accepted. General Ne Win; the Foreign Minister, U Chan Tun Aung; the Vice-Chief of Staff (Army), Brigadier Tin Pe; and others visited the People's Republic between January 24-29. The outcome was a "Ten Year Treaty of Friendship and Mutual Non-Aggression between the Union of Burma and the People's Republic of China" and an "Agreement . . . on the question of the Boundary between the two countries." [45]

The Boundary Agreement would "cease to be in force when the Burmese-Chinese Boundary Treaty . . . comes into force" (Article IV). In the interim, a "Joint Committee," meeting regularly in the two capitals, was charged with the responsibility "to discuss and work out solutions on the concrete [border] questions . . . enumerated in the major article of the Agreement" (Article II) and to prepare the Boundary Treaty designed to "cover not only all the sections of the boundary as mentioned in Article II of the Agreement, but also the sections of the boundary which were already delimited in the past and need no adjustment" (Article III). In this latter article, later reaffirmed in the Boundary Treaty (Article IV) the Chinese renounced their right to participate in the mining enterprises at the Lufang Ridge, which they had been awarded by the Iselin Commission in the Sino-British League of Nations Notes of June 18, 1941. (There is some professional opinion to the effect that the known deposits of these mines are nearly exhausted.) The joint committee was also given jurisdiction over "joint survey teams," which were to "conduct on-the-spot surveys, determine the location of boundary markers and, otherwise, help the Joint Committee to arrive at conclusions with respect to the amount of any area transferred from one sovereignty to another."

Basically, this agreement (Article II) incorporated the increased demands put forward by Chou En-lai in his letter of July 26, 1957, instead of those which the Burmese had accepted in the U Nu–U Ba Swe agreement summarized in the latter's official letter and maps of February 4, 1957. Nonetheless, the Burmese readily accepted the Chinese proposals and hailed General Ne Win for bringing back an agreement. Shortly after the re-election of U Nu as Prime Minister in February, 1960, it fell to his government to pilot this agreement through Parliament. Approval was voted on April 28; instruments of ratification were exchanged on May 14; the Supreme Court on June 17 ruled that the action accorded with the Constitution, though it required a minor amendment. On June 27, the Chinese-Burmese Joint Boundary Committee held its first meeting in Rangoon. Two subsequent meetings were held in China while survey teams worked at the border regions throughout the difficult monsoon months.[46] On August 22, Prime Minister Nu reported to Parliament on the progress already achieved and announced that the Boundary Treaty would be ready for signature on October 1. It was. To celebrate this historic event Burmese Government gifts consisting of 2,000 tons of rice and 1,000 tons of salt were distributed to approximately 1 million inhabitants of Yunnan, living in close proximity to the Burmese-Chinese boundary; and the Chinese reciprocated by distributing 2.4 million meters of printed textiles and 600,000 pieces of porcelain plates to 1,200,000 Burmese citizens.[47] Parliament approved the new Chinese-Burmese Boundary Treaty on December 5, and instruments of ratification were exchanged in Rangoon on Independence Day, January 4, 1961.[48] Chou En-lai headed the Chinese delegation.

The new boundary treaty evidenced the completion of the task of delimiting the Sino-Burma border, leaving for future determination only the "western extremity" at the junction of China, India, and Burma (Article V). This is an area south of the Indian-Tibet McMahon line which the P.R.C. has invaded and claimed. There also remained very minor adjustments of the boundary line where it bisects several small villages in the Wa state. It was proposed that certain of these villages be wholly included in China, others in Burma (Article III). Conventional international practice governs the location of lines where the latter follow rivers (Article VIII). Provision is made for prompt location of boundary markers and preparation of appropriate maps (Article X), and for settling any future disputes "through friendly consultations" (Article XI).

Otherwise the ratified treaty of twelve articles provided that:

(1) Burma agrees to return to China the Kachin area of Hpimaw, Gawlum, and Kangfang, about 59 square miles, which "belongs to China" (Article I).

(2) China agrees to turn over to Burma the Namwan Assigned Tract, about 85 square miles, though it, too, has "belonged" to China. In exchange, Burma agrees to turn over to China 73 square miles of territory under the jurisdiction of the Panhung and Panglao tribes (Article II).

(3) Except for certain villages that might be bisected as indicated above, the June 19, 1941 Iselin line in the Wa state area is accepted by both parties (Article III).

(4) Except for the Kachin villages (as in (1) above), the traditional line, including the demarcation established by the 1914 McMahon determination, is retained from the High Conical Peak in the northeast, north to the Upper Irrawaddy watershed, and west to the western extremity, which latter will ultimately be fixed as the junction of Burma, India, and China (Articles V-VII).

The treaty calls attention in a preamble to the fact that since 1954 the two countries had supported the "Five Principles of Peaceful Coexistence" that served them in their negotiations. The accompanying Exchange of Notes[49] signed by the two Premiers stipulated that the former practice whereby peoples on either side of the border migrated seasonally in cultivation of community-held land should cease within three years, i.e., January, 1964, of the coming into force of the treaty. Intermediate steps were to be taken in the intervening period to bring about this sealing off of the borders.

The signing and ratification of the treaty between October 1, 1960, and January 4, 1961—each an auspicious day in the respective calendars of China and Burma—gave the Burmese, for the first time since pre-British days, an agreed, delimited border with China. *The Guardian* cautiously summed up the prevailing Burmese attitude: "The ratification [of the treaty] has evoked general satisfaction in all quarters which have made a study of Communist China's relations with its neighbors." [50]

The Kachins, in the interest of Burma as a whole, have quietly accepted the treaty, despite the loss of part of their state. With characteristic Burmese humor, they referred to the lost area as one that grows certain trees desired by the Chinese for the making of coffins—which they would not wish to deny to their neighbors. They have already taken steps to repatriate their kinsmen from the three ceded villages. Provision of new land inside the Burmese border has been made available to some 2,000-3,000 Kachins who wished to leave their former village areas. How many more will be thus accommodated is not yet known. What the Panhung and Panglao tribesmen, who are Burmese citizens, have done about the transfer of the 73 square miles remains unreported.

These arrangements for the pursuit of boundary and friendship treaties did not include any overt reference to the problems created by the illegal entry of Chinese into Burma, or to the position of the "overseas Chinese" in Burma who have not opted for Burmese citizenship. Expectedly, they were also silent on clandestine relationships between Burmese and Chinese Communist cadres.

The problem of illegal Chinese entry, aggravated during the period of protracted negotiations, has reflected conditions in Communist China. There are no accurate estimates as to the size of this influx. It is commonly stated that in the immediate postwar period the overseas Chinese population in Burma amounted to 300,000; and that it has more than doubled since then. Not until February, 1958, did the Chinese embassy in Rangoon propose that the two countries consider a Dual Nationality Agreement along the lines of a similar (but unsatisfactory) one adopted by China and Indonesia.[51] Burma has not responded favorably to the suggestion, for thus far she has refused to recognize the concept of dual nationality. Instead, Chinese and Indian nationals "long resident in Burma had been encouraged to opt for citizenship" under sections 11 and 26 of the (now suspended) Constitution, supported by a series of citizenship and immigration acts and amendments, 1948-56. Such naturalized citizens have been freely mobile in Burmese society. Intermarriage between Burmese and Chinese is common, as neither religion nor caste is an inhibiting factor. (Intermarriage between Burmese Buddhists and Hindus, and between Burmese Buddhists and Burmese Muslims, is much less frequent because of differences in concepts of caste as well as religion.) Burmese citizens of Chinese extraction and Sino-Burmans (descendants of mixed marriages) have readily attained high economic and political status, including membership in several Cabinets.[52]

In the absence of reliable data, one can gather only piecemeal information from newspaper stories that illustrate the problem of illegal entry. For example, *The Nation* (October 15, 1958) referred to "9,000 non-Han Chinese" and "1,000 racial Chinese" who have entered Burma in this fashion. It was at this time, as indicated above, that Burma and China agreed to seal off the border. This decision, confirmed in the exchange of notes in October, 1960, was probably precipitated by a Burmese Kachin raid in late August, 1958, against a Chinese border outpost, in which twenty Chinese soldiers were killed. Peking officially protested the "affront." [53] Chinese- and Kachin-language leaflets, printed in Communist China, have been found on the Burmese side of the border area; they promised that Peking would take no punitive action against any refugees who returned and that their property—or its value—would be restored to them. There has been no information about the return of any such refugees. It is not improbable that on another and later occasion Burma will have to face the unpleasant prospect of treating a Chinese Communist demand for the repatriation of the illegal immigrants. Conceivably the latter might be absorbed into the total population, but that prospect is a difficult one for those noncitizen "overseas Chinese" in Burma who looked with genuine or practical approval on protection and support from Peking, either directly, or indirectly through the Chinese Communist-controlled banks and other economic instrumentalities that freely and legally operated in Burma until the nationalization-of-banks measures adopted in the spring of 1963. The future of this question, and the related one of the closed borders in and after January, 1964, is still unclear.

Undoubtedly the boundary treaty represented a forward step for Burma's security. But even if the almost 1,500 miles of the border are at long last peacefully demarcated and agreed upon, the danger to Burma from the north is not yet removed. A swing in Peking's policy, a pretext based on the illegal immigration, or on Burma's treatment of the noncitizen "overseas Chinese," or on some presumed violation of the friendship treaty, certainly an inhibiting factor in the free exercise of Burma's foreign policy decision-making, might activate the danger. Some of these refugees, when rounded up, have proved to be Communist agents.[54] And the illegal traffic does not move only in one direction. Occasionally, stories appear about Burmese Communist cadres, who, from 1950 onward, have been sent to China for training; they have to make the illegal crossing when leaving and re-entering Burma.[55]

Whatever the actual numbers, the overseas Chinese form only a small proportion of the total population of Burma (approximately 3 per cent),[56] and in terms of domestic politics are not important. Their potentiality as a future fifth column is entirely a speculative matter. Little is known about their present attitudes toward Com-

munist China, whose propaganda and economic assistance have
certainly reached them. Any sympathy among them for Nationalist
China would have to be concealed, not only because of the justifia-
ble antagonism of the Burma Government and population over the
KMT issue, but also because of the era of good feeling which cur-
rently finds expression in Rangoon and Peking.

At the beginning of the Revolutionary Council's regime, there
were five Chinese-language newspapers published in Rangoon.
Since then a politically neutral one, the *Southeast Daily* (*Tung
Nan Jih Pas*), has ceased publication. The anti-Communist *Freedom Daily* and three pro-Peking Communist papers survive; and a
new one has been added. The latter, all dailies, are the *Zin Min,
New China, China Commercial Times,* and *New Rangoon Evening Post.* Prior to the nationalization of the banks they were probably financed through a variety of sources emanating from the
Communist Bank of China of Rangoon.

The friendship and border treaties, the $84-million, interest-free,
ten-year line of credit, the direct air-transport connection between
the two capitals, the frequent cultural exchanges and state visits,
have brought about a rapprochement between Burma and China
in the 1960's. Perhaps the high-water mark in this *paukpaw* relationship came in the seven-day good-will visit to Burma of Chairman Liu Shao-chi of the P.R.C., April 20-26, 1963. The dour Communist was wined and dined throughout the land. In response to
the many speeches and toasts he spoke as follows in his farewell message: "May the *paukpaw* friendship between China and
Burma remain ever green." A careful reading of the joint communiqué issued before his departure reveals little beyond the reaffirmation of policies approved in and before 1960. The inevitable
"Five Principles of Peaceful Coexistence" and the "Bandung Conference spirit" were explicitly mentioned. The Burmese reiterated
their desire to see the P.R.C. in the United Nations; and expressed
the hope that the Indians and Chinese would find a solution to
their problems on the basis of the proposals put forward by the
Colombo Powers. Both nations expressed their satisfaction with
the solution for Laos brought forward by the Geneva Conference
of 1962 in which they participated.[57]

There are those who have charged the Burmese with subservience to the Chinese. But to do so is either to be ignorant of Burmese history or to misunderstand Burmese attitudes toward their
neighbor to the north. No modern Burmese regime, and certainly
not the present one, would risk repeating the experience of King
Narathihapate, mentioned earlier as the king whose nickname,
Tarok Pye Min, has given the Burmese a term for cowardice—"he
who ran away from the Chinese." Similarly, every Burmese school
boy now learns of successful Burmese resistance to the eighteenth-
century "four invasions" of Emperor Ch'ien Lung. The Burmese, I

believe, understand that they are not to "provoke" China; but they also, as Kyaw Nyein pointed out, "will stand firm against her" if necessary.

The principal risks to Burma derive from the possibility that Communist China needs and may seek the *lebensraum* and the actual and potential food surplus of mainland Southeast Asia. How the People's Republic of China solves this twin problem in the generation ahead will determine peace or war in Asia. At least one major question is worth considering in summing up these protracted negotiations and their present amicable settlement. Why has Peking behaved in this fashion toward Burma? To put it another way, why have the Burmese received so favorable a conclusion to their long search for a recognized and equitable boundary with China?

It has been pointed out above that both Nationalist and Communist China have exhibited the same claims on Burma. Should, therefore, Peking's behavior toward Burma before and after 1949 be regarded as a species of traditional Chinese expansionism toward the *Nanyang*, the South Seas Area? In part this question may be answered affirmatively. Irrespective of the government in power, the Chinese, in times of strength, exert pressure on ill-defined border regions. In times of weakness they emphasize the idea of Chinese pre-eminence in the contiguous areas by recalling past glory and former tributary relationships.[58]

In the case of the Chinese Communists, however, this explanation of traditional policy is insufficient, for their policy contains additional elements which, though less susceptible to documentation than the traditional Chinese policy, add up to a circumstantial case of political, and, as in the instances of Korea, North Vietnam, Tibet, and northern India, military aggressiveness. From 1947, when Mao Tse-tung gave public support to the revival of the "Left Strategy" of the Cominform, through the November-December 1949 Peking Asian-Australian Trade Union Conference, to the Asian-Pacific Region Peace Conference in Peking, October, 1952, the Chinese Communists had waged an incessant political campaign against both colonial regimes and the leaders and governments of the newly independent Asian nations. Burma was included in this attack. During those years Burma acutely feared Peking's intervention, particularly because the provocation of the KMT on her soil invited countermeasures from the Communists. Fortunately, Burma was not then the prime target of Peking's attack, probably because the Chinese Communists had more immediate issues to resolve: namely, the consolidation of power at home; the adventure in Korea; the support of the Viet Minh in French Indochina; the imposition of suzerainty in Tibet (1950); and their continuing conflict with Taiwan.

Though Burma was not a prime target during this period, 1947-53, she was not ignored. For, in conformity with typical "Left

Strategy" policies, the Chinese Communists created on Burma's perimeter a number of "free" or "autonomous" movements (Kachins, Was, Lao, and Thai) that served the purposes of political agitation and military harassment across the borders, and set up training centers for Burmese and other Southeast Asian Communist cadres at Kunming. Discussing this period at a later time, Prime Minister Nu said about China: "But our relations with the new Chinese regime [even after mutual recognition and exchange of ambassadors] remained uncertain for a number of years. The Communist rebellion was still going strong, and the new Chinese Government seemed inclined to give our Communists their moral support, apparently regarding us as stooges of the West. Broadcasts from Radio Peking at the time did not attempt to disguise this attitude." [59]

A few months before the death of Stalin in March, 1953, the international Communist line changed again. From then on, with some consistency, the Sino-Soviet over-all strategy was to intensify the neutralism of Southern Asian countries. The Russians and the Chinese have endeavored to accomplish this by means of unremitting attacks on Western diplomacy, by trade, barter, and aid with the neutrals so as to tie their economies wherever possible with those of the Communist bloc, and by exchanging cultural missions and exhibits at an incredible rate. It was in this context that the "Five Principles of Peaceful Coexistence" and the "Bandung spirit" represented the face of Chinese and U.S.S.R. policy.[60] Burma's adoption of a neutralist foreign policy in late 1949 or early 1950; her participation as one of the Colombo Powers which convened the Bandung Conference; her genuine conflict with Taiwan and consequent abrogation of the first U.S. Aid Agreement in March, 1953; her vigorous sponsorship of the Chinese entry into the U.N. fitted into this international Communist gambit. On the surface, therefore, the Chinese should have been willing to settle the border issue after the subject was reopened in 1954.

However, to a certain extent, the Burmese may have compounded their own difficulties, and in at least two ways may have contributed to the delaying tactics so expertly pursued by the Chinese Communists. They acted with great independence on a number of important foreign-policy matters,[61] and they made initial diplomatic errors in accepting Chinese interpretations of the Sino-British border agreements of 1886-1941, basing the negotiations on them before they had carefully considered possible alternative bases for negotiations.

When U Nu opened negotiations with China in 1954, he was less than well prepared to meet the historical claims of the Chinese, and he had not sufficiently restudied Burmese history from Burmese sources. The Burmese had earlier assigned to Dr. Htin Aung, Rector of the University of Rangoon, and Professor Kyaw Thet the task of research on Sino-Burmese border records. Their labors, undertaken in the United Kingdom and the United States, were never completed. Hence the Burmese were in effect compelled to accept the Sino-British records and agreements as the basis for negotiations, and the Burmese Government in 1956 made some damaging concessions about these. The Chinese took the position that these agreements had been forced on a weak China by an imperialist power—an argument that the Burmese, by the very nature of their own colonial experience, could not very well refute. The Chinese also invoked but later "graciously" set aside the traditional Chinese claims in Southern Asia, while making every attempt to push back the frontiers reached as a result of the Sino-British conventions.

Alternatively, the Burmese could have claimed that Burma, too, had suffered under imperialism, and that the British, by annexing Upper Burma in 1886, had reopened border questions that had been settled at least since the eighteenth century. All the disputed border areas had been in the possession of royal Burma throughout the Konbaung dynasty and had also been Burmese in earlier periods. The British border concessions, the Burmese might have argued, were designed to facilitate other British interests in China, in competition with French interests. If such an argument had been advanced, the Chinese could not then have claimed territory "lost" through British action.[62] The Burmese might have proposed that both countries return to their "pre-imperialist" borders. But the Burmese made no such arguments. Once they relied on the Sino-British conventions, agreements, and disagreements between 1886-1941 they had to take the consequences. Yet an initially more profound and detailed understanding even of these might have spared U Nu from coming home in 1956 with the statement about Chinese "fairness."

Correlatively, it served Peking's interest to keep alive the cat-and-mouse game on the border issue. It was a Damoclean sword poised to sustain China's neighbors' consciousness of Communist China's strength and punitive power. It kept Burma busy on the border, detracting from other constructive enterprises. It weakened the central Burmese Government's position vis-à-vis the minorities of the border area, particularly among the Kachins, and to a lesser extent the Shans, whose territory would be yielded, while furthering Peking's threat and probable ambitions in the Salween-Mekong watershed. It gave comfort and training to Burma's insurgent Communists. It helped to keep alive within China the idea that the Communists were concerned with looking after Chinese traditional interests; and in any event helped to distract the Chinese from some of the woes imposed by Communist domestic policy. By deliberately keeping its intentions on the border issue ambiguous for a decade, Peking was able to place unacknowledgeable restraints on Burma's cooperative relationships with Western democracies.

When Peking decided to move toward a final border, trade, and loan agreement, it did so by exacting minor territorial concessions from Burma, thus gaining the public advantage of appearing to abide by the "Five Principles of Peaceful Coexistence" and the "Bandung spirit," and demonstrating that the People's Republic of China could live together in amity with a neutralist neighbor. Such a demonstration was useful at a time when China's aggression in Tibet, her border conflict with India, and her "overseas Chinese" conflict with Indonesia were detracting from the favorable image she wished to create among the newly independent nations of Afro-Asia. Even so, the Boundary Agreement and the ten-year Treaty of Friendship appear to impose on Burma the continuing need of extreme caution in its relations with the West. Finally, the conclusion of the boundary and friendship agreements with Burma (like the later ones with Nepal and Pakistan) probably prevented any immediate revival of a Colombo Power or Southern Asian group spearheaded by the then mutual troubles of India, Indonesia, and Burma with the People's Republic of China.* Burma was the temporary beneficiary of this Communist strategy at the very time when India, stirred out of a decade of relative complacency over Sino-Indian relations, might have taken some initiative in building a non-Communist regional grouping aroused by Communist China's aggression and territorial ambitions in free Asia.

For her part, Burma felt great relief at the conclusion of the Boundary Treaty. Burmese leaders not insensitive to India and Tibet, and aware of the plight of their Laotian neighbor, privately acknowledged the opportunistic nature of their present position, but justified it on the grounds of the uncertain future posed by the power of their rampant northern neighbor. For the same reason Burma has campaigned vigorously for Peking's entry into the U.N. She expects to find in this, if and when necessary, some modicum of protection and public support for her legitimate position. The Burmese may have doubts, which they have expressed, that the U.N. will in fact be able to protect the smaller powers in the same way as it does the big powers, but they still believe that the small nations require whatever safety it can provide. That Burma has carefully nurtured friendly relations with Communist China is but another form of security insurance. In a very real sense Burma has settled for the peaceful policy of "least loss." She ardently wishes to avoid the fate of North Korea, North Vietnam, Tibet, and Laos. This she has achieved for the time being—but for how long?

* It will be recalled that the Colombo Powers—Burma, Ceylon, India, Indonesia, and Pakistan—the convenors of the Bandung Conference, came into being in the spring of 1954 in part to offset Secretary of State Dulles' call for a Southeast Asia organization designed to take "united action" against the Viet Minh, and in part to alert Peking that its further 1954 thrust in Tibet was not particularly liked by the trans-Himalayan states.

S INCE INDEPENDENCE, in addition to devoting attention to China, Burma has steadily, if not vigorously, cultivated relationships with her other Asian neighbors. At first Burma was most friendly with those South Asian countries—India, Pakistan, and Ceylon—which had elected to remain within the British Commonwealth. They had all shared in varying ways in the pre-independence British colonial system, despite differences in race, religion, and cultural backgrounds. Their histories within the British Empire, their egress from imperial power, their partial retention of English, both as an official language and a lingua franca, their initial, modified adoption of British civil and legal institutions, helped to cement friendly relations.

Indonesia was the first to be admitted into this grouping, primarily because the four nations had ardently championed her struggle for independence after 1945. Subsequently, Burma established relations with all the other nations of Southeast and East Asia, except Taiwan, though it has withheld formal recognition from divided Korea and Vietnam.

Burma, India, and the Other Colombo Powers

In the spring of 1954, representatives of Burma, India, Pakistan, Ceylon, and Indonesia met at Colombo, Ceylon, and again in December at Bogor, Indonesia. As a result of their first meeting in Ceylon's capital, they came to be known as the Colombo Powers (not to be confused with the cooperative economic association of Western, Pacific, and Asian nations known as the Colombo Plan). Out of these meetings came the decision to hold the Bandung Conference of twenty-nine African and Asian states, or territories on the way to independence, which convened in April, 1955. Its purpose was to consider the political and economic problems of the newly independent nations, and to aid them both to assert their independence in international affairs and to promote world peace and cooperation by serving as a possible bridge between the Cold War antagonists. The People's Republic of China, though not the Soviet Union, was invited to attend Bandung as an Asian power. India had joined with Burma in holding that Communist China's participation might lead it to alleviate its pressure on mainland Southeast Asia and to relax its covert support for indigenous Communist movements.

At Colombo, Burma had joined Ceylon and Pakistan and opposed India in attempting to secure condemnation of Soviet as well as Western imperialism. At Bandung, the debate on this issue sharply divided the nations between those who opposed Soviet colonialism as much as Western imperialism and those who, like Prime Minister Nehru, favored omitting any mention of the Soviet variety. The Bandung compromise, which declared, "Colonialism in all its manifestations is an evil which should be speedily brought to an end," helped to bring the conference to an amicable conclusion.[1] But it left the issue unresolved. Despite efforts made by President Sukarno of Indonesia, there has been no further meeting of the Bandung or Colombo Powers as a distinct grouping. (It is alleged that the Algiers conference originally scheduled for March, 1965 [later postponed to June, and again to November] is to serve as the second "Bandung Conference.") Burma was not one of the nations supporting the conference.

Burma has usually been regarded as a close follower of India's foreign policy because of the intimate personal relations between Prime Ministers Nehru and Nu and the fact that both countries are neutralist or uncommitted. But this view misreads Burma's policy and the attitudes of many Burmese leaders. Frequently, the two countries have been in agreement on foreign-policy issues in and out of the United Nations. But on such key issues as Korea and Hungary, and on the degree to which they condemn all varieties of imperialism, the cleavage between India and Burma is as strong as is their agreement on other questions. The varieties of neutralist policy are as numerous as those of Western democratic policy.

The differences between Burma and India over the issue of imperialism were paralleled by similar divergences that arose at the meeting of the Anti-Colonial Bureau of the Asian Socialist Conference held in May, 1954, at Kalaw, in Burma. There, speaking for the Burmese, Kyaw Nyein denounced Soviet imperialism as "even more degrading and even more dangerous [than traditional Western colonialism] because it is more ruthless, more systematic and more blatantly justified in the name of world Communist revolution." [2] The Burmese position, endorsed by a majority of the delegates, was opposed by some Indian Socialists.

These differences between India and Burma are not merely variations in ideology. They found concrete application when the Soviet Union invaded Hungary. India's response was delayed and, when it came, anemic. Burma's response—"There, but for the grace of God, go we" [3]—summed up her stand in the United Nations, and it resounded throughout the world.

U Nu constantly and sincerely advocated friendship with India, especially with Nehru.[4] He frequently reminded Burmese audiences of the times Nehru came to the aid of Burma, including the latter's promotion of a Commonwealth loan in early 1949, and his other more direct assistance during the height of the insurrection. A treaty of friendship between India and Burma was signed in Rangoon, July 7, 1951. India, a relatively good customer but a hard bargainer for Burma's rice, extended a loan of approximately $40 million to Burma in 1956-57, and privately supported Burma throughout the early stages of the boundary negotiations with China. Under General Ne Win's caretaker regime these same general conditions prevailed.

Burma joined Cambodia, Ceylon, Ghana, Indonesia, and the United Arab Republic at a conference held in Colombo, December 10-12, 1962, to seek "an atmosphere conducive to the opening of negotiations between China and India" following the further outbreak of their border conflict in September. General Ne Win led the Burmese delegation, which included his government's Foreign Minister, U Thi Han, the ambassadors to Peking and New Delhi, and other leading officials. Ceylon was deputized by this conference to serve, if possible, as the "friendly and impartial" mediator between the contestants.[5]

Since this intervention failed, General Ne Win apparently decided or was persuaded to essay direct negotiations. In anticipation of a mid-February, 1964, five-day "friendship visit" from Prime Minister Chou En-lai and Foreign Minister Marshal Chen Yi, he made what was called a flying visit to see Prime Minister Nehru to "enquire after the latter's state of health." Senior Burmese officials who accompanied the General were "to have talks with their counterparts in the Indian External Affairs Ministry." [6] Paragraph 14 of the Sino-Burmese joint communiqué issued on the departure of the Chinese called attention to the December, 1962, Colombo proposals, and to "the hope" that China and India would enter into direct negotiations to achieve a friendly settlement of their boundary question. In printing the communiqué, the Burmese press headlined this "hope" for an "amicable settlement." [7]

The generally good relations between the governments of Burma and India are based on a common colonial past and a hope to share a future as socialist or "socialistic" (Nehru's word) countries.[8] Burma's tradition of drawing upon the Indian and especially the Buddhist heritage provides less intercultural sustenance than might be expected. Relations between Indians and Burmese as individuals are not as good as they are between the two governments.

Some of India's leaders show an attitude of intellectual condescension toward Burma. For their part, the Burmese people resent Indians because of their role in colonial days. The Indian moneylenders and landowners are mostly gone from Burma; the Indian laborers and businessmen remain in considerable though steadily declining numbers. Neither group is popular in Burma. The Indians (Hindus and Muslims), who numbered well over a million in prewar days, are now estimated at about half that number. Many Indians—both capitalists and laborers—quit Burma in the aftermath of the 1963-64 nationalization program. The Burmese were generally glad to see them go.[9] With perhaps unintentional irony, *Forward*, August 1, 1964, editorialized to the effect that Burmese officials "spared no pains to facilitate the departure" of the Indians.

Burma's relations with other Colombo Powers have grown more friendly over the years. In early February, 1950, Pakistan granted a loan of £500,000 to Burma, and in March of that year participated with India, Ceylon, Australia, and the United Kingdom in arranging a second but unused loan of £6 million. Pakistan and Burma signed a treaty of peace and friendship in Rangoon on June 25, 1952. Over the years they have had a continuing trade relationship in which Burma has, as in her trade relations with other Asian nations, been the supplier of rice; and, in the case of Pakistan, has been a buyer of jute for rice-bagging. However, the two countries have a border problem where the Arakan province touches on East Pakistan. Historically, since the days before the First Anglo-Burmese War, this area, based on the fluctuating boundary lines of the Naaf River estuary, has been the locus of a law-and-order problem. Illegal immigrants, escapees from justice, and organized bandits known as *mujahids*—Muslims from both sides of the border—have disturbed the peace of the zone.[10]

Periodically the two governments have reviewed this problem and have made joint efforts to resolve it. In October, 1959, General Ne Win and Ayub Khan agreed to set up a Joint Burma-Pakistan Border Commission. After a meeting in Rangoon, May 5-9, 1960, the commission submitted a report (unpublished).[11] In 1964, efforts were renewed. Again meeting in Rangoon, the two Foreign Ministers, Zulfiqar Ali Butto and Thi Han, signed a joint communiqué, which provided for a hydrographic survey of the Naaf to determine the international boundary and agreed to joint rights of navigation on its waterways. These efforts led to a "rousing reception" for General Ne Win when he visited Pakistan in February, 1965. At that time, he and Marshal Ayub Khan took official notice of the satisfactory way in which their two governments were proceeding on the boundary and all other bilateral issues.[12]

Ceylon and Burma agreed to exchange legations on June 6, 1949; they were later raised to embassies. The two countries have been drawn together increasingly as a consequence of their shared heritage of Theravada Buddhism. This bond was especially noticeable during and since the Sixth World Buddhist Council held in Rangoon between May, 1954 and May, 1956. The membership of the two countries in the Colombo Powers, and in the six-nation conference to mediate the Sino-Indian conflict, has helped to maintain such friendly but not overactive relations. Burma sells rice to and buys tea from Ceylon.

Burma has actively supported Indonesia since its independence, especially in all matters affecting Indonesian-Dutch relations. The two countries signed a treaty of peace and friendship in Rangoon, July 7, 1951. In some ways, relations between the Burmese and Indonesians are friendlier than those between the Burmese and the peoples of India and Pakistan. There appear to be fewer psychological problems between them. Both the government and the press in Burma unfailingly backed Indonesia in its claim to West Irian (or Dutch New Guinea). U Thant (acting in his capacity as United Nations Secretary-General), was influential, together with former U. S. Ambassador Ellsworth Bunker, in bringing the disputants to the end of their conflict on this issue. The final settlement was reached in July, 1962.

More recently, however, the Burmese press has been outspokenly and unprecedentedly critical of Indonesia's policy of force with respect to the "confrontation" with Malaysia and the withdrawal from the United Nations. The anti-Western papers, neutralist in-favor-of-the-Communist-bloc, such as the Burmese-language *Rangoon Daily*, characterized Indonesia's action as a "thoughtless line" which "will not only damage UN but also Indonesia herself." [13] Neutralist Burmese-language papers such as the *Hanthawaddy* and *The New Light of Burma* likened Indonesia's quitting the U.N. to "Hitler's leaving the League of Nations," and suggested that though the United Nations is "not able to solve all problems," it still is the "only world body that can prevent an outbreak of fresh fire in the world." The former counseled that Indonesia would do better by "fighting from within" the United Nations for what she believes, while the latter thought it doubtful that other countries would "approve the course Indonesia has taken." [14] Indonesia is Burma's largest customer for rice.

Burma and the Other Countries of Mainland Southeast Asia

The southward spurs of the Himalayas divide Southeast Asia by a series of high north-to-south ridges and rivers. These natural barriers have impeded contacts but have not averted conflicts. The Shans of Burma, the Thai, and the Lao are related ethnically and linguistically; together with their cousins in Yunnan, they made up the Kingdom of Nanchao, until it fell before Mongol power in the thirteenth century. Their borders are blurred by a common Shan-Thai-Lao language and a common Buddhist culture. The Burmans, who belong to a different branch of the Sinic peoples, had re-established their unity under their Toungoo kings of the sixteenth century, and had extended their control over much of this area. Chiengmai, in what is now northern Thailand, became a Burmese city.

In spite of cultural, religious, and ethnic affinities, Burmese-Thai relations were traditionally unhappy and marked by numerous wars. After the great Burmese victory and sack of the Thai capital at Ayuthia, in 1767, the experience of the two countries differed vastly. Thailand preserved her independence in the nineteenth century by becoming a buffer state between the French and the British colonies. The different conditions of the two nations not only separated Thai ruling families and cliques from the royal and later the nationalist leadership of Burma, but also affected the writing and teaching of history in each country. Every Burmese schoolchild learns of the glories of Burmese arms and especially of Ayuthia; every Thai child learns of Burmese cruelties there. One learns of the loss of independence, the other of its retention. A residue of historical bitterness still prompts occasional suspicion of the Burmese by the Thai and some mild degree of mutual disdain. Both countries were under Japanese military control during World War II, and initially this experience drew them together. Certainly Thailand helped General Aung San by providing a staging and a recruiting area for the Burma Independence Army, which entered Burma from Thailand in 1942. Relations were later exacerbated, however, by Thailand's toleration of the Kuomintang troops who entered Burma in 1949 and 1950. These troops had easy access to the Thai border areas, bought supplies there, and received some supplies and services from Taiwan by way of Thailand. Eventually the Thai Government joined the United States in the Good Offices Committee that helped to evacuate most of these troops in 1953-54, and again in 1960-61.

There is very little trade between Burma and Thailand, as both nations export the same major products. To some extent Thailand's rice exports have captured a portion of Burma's prewar trade. But both countries have the common problem of finding markets. Since the United States has become the third largest exporter of rice and has engaged in large-scale disposal of surplus food and fiber, both the Burmese and Thai have found their normal trade in part dislocated by what they consider dumping. Both U Nu and Pibul Songgram expressed their concern about this problem when they visited the United States in 1955.

Ever since the preparations for the Sixth World Buddhist Council and the Bandung Conference, the Burmese have made an effort to draw closer to the Thai. The result has been a complete turnabout in their historic, antagonistic or indifferent relationship. They face the same danger on the north. In January, 1953, Communist China announced the creation of a "Thai Autonomous People's Government," which geographically would tend to re-establish the old Nanchao territory out of Burma's Shan state, northern Thailand, Laos, and Yunnan. In a forthright statement to the Bandung Conference, and in the presence of Chou En-lai, the then Thai Foreign Minister, Prince Wan Waithayakon, called attention to this danger.[15] The new era of cordial relations between Burma and Thailand began officially in 1955 with an exchange of good-will missions—the first since they had established diplomatic relations in August, 1948—the waiving by Burma of World War II claims against Thailand, and an apology from Burma for the sacking of Ayuthia almost 200 years before.[16] On October 15, 1956, the two countries signed a treaty of peace and friendship. Since then there have been inconclusive and cautious discussions of joint rice-marketing arrangements. In early 1960, while the caretaker regime still held the reins of government, the King and Queen of Thailand received a most cordial reception in Burma. The Burmese press was unanimous in praising this popular royal couple and expressing good will toward their people.

The fact that Thailand has sought its security through the Southeast Asia Treaty Organization and bilateral agreements with the United States has obviously not interfered with the growing relationship between Thailand and neutralist Burma. Shortly after the Revolutionary Council took power, General Ne Win paid a state visit to Thailand, where on December 14, 1962, he was received in an unusual ceremony at the Dom Muang Airport (Bangkok) by the King himself.[17] The social ceremony was followed by the preparation in March, 1963, of a Burma-Thai Agreement on Border Arrangements and Cooperation, ratified on May 15.[18]

The agreement provided continuing diplomatic and military high-level and operational units to supervise the Thai-Burma border, which had been freely crossed by insurrectionist ethnic groups and Kuomintang troops hiding out in its recesses. Though security was the prime goal sought by the agreement, it also made provision for economic and cultural cooperation. Since then the responsible ministers and officers have met frequently and taken action on matters relevant to all the terms of the agreement.[19]

Burmese leaders have been keenly interested in the long struggle in French Indochina, despite their attitude of public reserve. They believed that the Vietnamese nationalists, among whom they included the Viet-Minh in 1946-48, were fighting a battle for national liberation against the French. They did not regard the restoration[20] of Bao Dai as a real solution, and they looked upon the French in Indochina as incorrigible imperialists, perhaps even worse than the Dutch. But they also became aware that Ho Chi Minh and the Viet-Minh were Communist in character and were supported by the People's Republic of China. Hence Burmese leaders were silent on the Indochinese issue at the First Asian Socialist Conference in 1953, though they named and condemned all other vestiges of colonialism. They welcomed the Geneva settlement in July, 1954, and in August, 1954, Burma recognized and exchanged legations with Cambodia and Laos.

Norodom Sihanouk, then King of Cambodia, was invited to Burma in November, 1954. Burma gave some evidence of hoping that the ridges that divide Laos and Cambodia from Vietnam, both North and South, would be held as a safe boundary against further Communist (or other) encroachment. On the occasion of the King's visit Dr. Ba U, President of Burma, called attention to Cambodia as "one of the stabilizing factors in South East Asia" and pointed out that the Cambodian people were linked to Burma by common ethnic origin, culture, and religion (through the Mons and Buddhism). He promised that Burma "shall watch and follow the progress of Cambodia with sympathy, interest and best wishes." [21] It has been indicated in some quarters that U Nu urged Nehru to take a similar position—a thus-far-and-no-further line—to safeguard the independence of Laos and Cambodia. If Indian policy seems to have been less clear than Burma's on this point, it may have been due to India's responsibilities, as a member of several International Commissions for Supervision and Control set up by the Geneva Conference.[22]

The Burmese are particularly interested in Laos because of their common border and proximity to China. During the crisis in Laos following the August, 1960, coup of Kong Le, which returned Souvanna Phouma to power, Burma took the stand that Laos should be neutralized. Unlike India, Britain, France, and the U.S.S.R., she did not then immediately extend support to the government formed by Souvanna Phouma. Her leaders apparently regarded the coup that brought him back with as much as doubt and distress as they had General Phoumi Nosavan's overthrow of the government of his erstwhile ally, Phoui Sananikone, in December, 1959. (Burmese intelligence on Laos appears to have been better than on the other former French-Indochinese states, though the Burmese press has become more vociferous and tendentious on the subject of Vietnam). They welcomed the initiative of Sihanouk of Cambodia in January, 1961, when he proposed a fourteen-nation conference on the subject of Laos. For, as far as they were concerned, both blocs would be represented if the conference were to be held, and Burma would also attend under the formula for conference representation proposed by Cambodia (i.e., as a state bordering on Laos). The conference was opened by Prince Sihanouk on May 16, 1961. Burma was represented by her Foreign Minister, Sao Hkun Hkio, and by her then permanent Secretary of the Foreign Office, James Barrington.

In the published records of the International Conference on the Settlement of the Laotian Question, Burma's delegates do not appear to have intervened frequently, though they, like all other par-

ticipants, voted for the final settlements. However, early in the
sessions, Foreign Minister Sao Hkun Hkio made a definitive statement on Burmese policy for Laos and for mainland Southeast
Asia,[23] which has remained in effect under General Ne Win's government. In conformity with Burma's past position on divided
countries such as Korea and Vietnam, he opposed partition for
Laos. "It has proved no solution" whenever applied. He reminded
his audience of the connection between Burma and Laos. They
shared a common border and "close ties of religion and culture."
He asserted that any solution for Laos "must be accepted by the
Laotian people, exercising, through a fully representative government, their full sovereignty." He strongly supported the reapplica-
tion of the relevant 1954 Geneva Agreement, especially the provision creating the machinery for supervision and control (the
International Control Commission) but with "conditions . . .
under which it can operate efficiently and effectively." He hoped
that "an independent and neutral Laos" would emerge "as a result
of our endeavors," and while he explicitly rejected Sihanouk's call
for the creation and guarantee of a "neutral zone" including Cambodia, Laos, and Burma, on grounds of variations in the conditions
and policies of the several countries, he reaffirmed Burma's policy
of nonalignment, and "hoped" that "there will come into being a
continuous stretch of non-aligned States from India in the West to
Laos and Cambodia in the East, a *de facto* neutral zone."

In a carefully phrased letter dated September 11, 1962, General
Ne Win, responding to another attempt on the part of Sihanouk
to convene yet another conference to guarantee Cambodia's neutrality and territorial integrity, reaffirmed Burma's position as outlined above and suggested that Cambodia seek the resolution of
her difficulties through direct discussions and negotiations. However, he did not close the door on a conference if "all the parties
concerned" wished to see one convened.[24] Similarly, at the conclusion of a spring, 1963, state visit from King Savang Vatthana of
Laos, a joint communiqué was issued seconding the conclusions of
the International Conference on the Settlement of the Laotian
question, and expressing the "desirability [of] close cooperation
among the countries in Southeast Asia . . . in matters of common
interest affecting the region as a whole." [25]

Essentially Ne Win supports the view that the "small countries"
want to, and should, be "left alone." He seems to regard their troubles in no small measure as the consequence of big-power rivalry.
This is certainly the attitude of Burma toward the two Vietnams.
Since she has not formally recognized these divided countries, her
relations with them have been conducted on a cautious basis of
exchanges of visits. The first visit was made to Saigon in 1956, followed by one to Hanoi in 1958. When in the latter year Ho Chi
Minh visited Burma, *The Nation* (February 15) and *The Guardian* (February 18) mixed their welcome with warnings about Ho's

"brand of Communism." Since then, the general position of the government and the non-Communist press has been summed up by the two leading Burmese-language newspapers: "All in all the situation in Laos, Cambodia and South Vietnam is in a dangerous state and there are signs of a conflagration taking place in the whole of Indochina which was once dominated by France." [26] Since Burma fears such a conflagration more than anything else because she believes that it will engulf her, and since her leaders at least until early 1965 believed that the Communist Viet Cong were winning in South Vietnam, it would appear that she then favored what *The New Light of Burma* suggested: "We think the only way to solve the issue is for South and North Viet Nam to merge together and elect a government truly representative of the people. We would urge therefore all concerned to implement the terms of the 1954 Geneva Agreement." [27] Or, it may be added as a reflection of Burmese views, convene a new conference embracing *all* the interested parties to effect some compromise that will in fact create a zone of neutrality from the Bay of Bengal to the China Sea. For the Burmese seem to feel at this time that however skeptical they may be, they must act as if the words about peaceful coexistence and the "Five Principles of Peaceful Coexistence" introduced by Chou En-lai in 1954 are still valid.

Burma's relations with the countries of mainland Southeast Asia, including Malaysia,[28] have steadily grown more cordial. Regional activities and organizations such as the Sixth World Buddhist Council, the United Nations Economic Commission for Asia and the Far East (ECAFE), the Colombo Plan, and the Bandung Conference have supported bilateral relations but have not supplanted them. The countries of the mainland are divided politically between those like Burma, which seeks its international security in neutralist policies, and those like Thailand, which belongs to the Southeast Asia Treaty Organization. On August 18, 1954, the Burmese Ambassador to the United States, James Barrington, advised Washington that, though his government would not join the proposed organization, it would maintain a "benevolent neutrality" toward it. Unlike India's hostile attitude toward SEATO, the Burmese position has occasionally made possible cooperation between Rangoon and SEATO on minor projects. This cooperation, as such, has not altered her relations with the Asian SEATO members—Pakistan, Thailand, and the Philippines. Differences between Asian countries over the issue of SEATO have had little effect on their intergovernmental relations.

Burma and Japan and Other Asian Relations

Burma's relations with Japan are not close, though Burma was the first Asian country to conclude a peace-and-reparation agreement with Japan (November 5, 1954). Wartime memories are still alive in Burma. These include Burma's acceptance between 1940 and 1942 of Japanese aid in the struggle for independence, as well as Burma's rejection of and military resistance to Japan's imposition of a puppet government.[29]

The Treaty of Peace and the Agreement for Reparations and Economic Cooperation between Japan and Burma entered into force on April 16, 1955.[30] Japan was to pay $200 million for reparations and $50 million for investments in joint ventures in Burma over a ten-year period. In December, 1956, the terms of the agreement with respect to the rate of reparations payments and the nature of investments, but not the total sum, were revised in Burma's favor. During a visit to Burma by Prime Minister Nobusuke Kishi in 1957, Prime Minister Nu remarked that the new and improved relations between the two countries had come about because Burma's leaders had "decided to turn our backs upon the unhappy past." [31]

Prior to the treaty and agreement, the United States had quietly encouraged the improvement of relations between the two countries. Within the terms set by Congress, efforts were made, with some success, to encourage Burma and other Asian countries to purchase Japanese goods with U.S.–aid dollars and to encourage Japan to help other Asian nations by training their technicians. Though these efforts did not bulk large, they helped to diminish anti-Japanese feeling left over from World War II.

Under the terms of the Reparations Agreement, Burma retained the right to reopen the issue in the event that Japan concluded a more favorable agreement with Indonesia and the Philippines. When this latter occurred, Burma exercised her right. Negotiations were begun in late December, 1959. They continued with some interruptions, partly because of the changeover in Burmese governments, partly because Japan was a tough bargainer. Finally, in January, 1963, Brigadier Aung Gyi, leader of the Burmese delegation, and Japanese Foreign Minister Masayoshi Ohira agreed on new terms. Burma was to receive an additional $140 million in goods and services, and commercial loans totaling $30 million.[32]

With the gradual elimination of what the Burmese call hitches in the reparation programs and in deliveries of Japanese goods and services, both countries have come to recognize the complementary character of their economies. Japan needs Burma's rice, and markets in Burma for its industrial exports. Burma needs the Japanese market and can benefit from Japanese technology. Both appear to be getting what they seek.

Burma exchanged ministers with the Philippines in 1956, and more purposeful relations began to develop during Ramon Magsaysay's presidency. The Philippines have only recently begun to look westward to Asia. (Nor had the South and Southeast Asian nations previously embraced the Philippines in their outlook.) In a speech made in September, 1957, U Nu reminded his people that the Philippines had regained their independence in 1946 "in fulfillment of a ten year old promise given by the United States." He continued, "This great act of statesmanship on the part of the United States undoubtedly started the chain reaction which has now resulted in the independence of all the countries of South and Southeast Asia." The following year in May, 1958, the Philippines signed two agreements with Burma for the purchase of 50,000 tons of rice. Since then the pattern of trade contacts and exchange of high-level visits have continued on a modest basis.[33] The impetus for these comes from Manila, which has actively sought to develop its Asian relations in a variety of ways—through regional organizations, university and research enterprises, and even through some technical assistance.

A few other aspects of Burma's relations with its Asian neighbors may be noted. Burma offered to help solve what U Nu called "an element of insecurity in our region," the quarrel over Kashmir. The offer was not accepted. Burma and Afghanistan signed a treaty of friendship in November, 1956, and agreed to exchange diplomatic missions. Burma also agreed the following year to exchange diplomatic missions with the Mongolian People's Republic. For a long time Nepal has had a consulate in Rangoon to look after the sizable Gurkha population in Burma, a number of whom are members of Burma's armed forces. Burma applies the same policy to Korea as she does to Vietnam; that is, she does not recognize *de jure* either the 38th or the 17th parallel demarcation lines. Therefore Burma's contacts with the two Korean states are formally limited to economic and cultural matters. The volume of trade between Burma and South Korea far exceeds that between Burma and North Korea.

When Burma recognized Communist China, she declared that Formosa belonged to China. In U Nu's 1957 review of foreign relations for the Parliament,[34] he referred to all Asian nations, but omitted reference to Formosa. This omission does not mean any diminution of the strong anti-Chiang sentiments in Burma. The KMT issue is still very much alive. But it may mean that Burma may wish to revise her position on Formosa and the Formosans when Chiang inevitably joins his ancestors. If the Formosans were successful in launching a campaign for self-determination on the island—there is a non-Communist Formosan independence movement with headquarters in Tokyo—Burma would have to consider anew her policy on the question.

Burma and Regional Organizations

Ever since Burma participated in the Asian Relations Conference held at New Delhi in 1947, she has sent many official and private missions to a wide variety of meetings and conferences held in Southern Asia. As we have seen, Burma and the other Colombo Powers convened the Bandung Conference. Burma joined ECAFE at once and takes an active part in its work. (A Burmese, U Nyun, now heads the organization.) Burma has also been an active member of the Colombo Plan since she joined it in 1952. Burmese membership in the various specialized agencies of the United Nations carries with it participation in their Asian and world-wide meetings. The two Burmese universities have joined the Association of Southeast Asian Universities. Burma has also served as host for the Asian Socialist Conference (1953), the Sixth World Buddhist Council (1954-56), the Conference on Cultural Freedom in Asia (February 17-20, 1955), and for many other meetings. Burma formerly—until the second Ne Win regime took the opposite position—encouraged nongovernmental gatherings, such as those of the International Junior Chamber of Commerce, the Rotary International, the Inter-Parliamentary Union, and those of groups devoted to Buddhism, social service, law, international relations, science, travel, and sports.[35]

Such a view of Burmese and other Asian activity suggests an optimism in respect to the development of regional integration that more careful analysis does not yet sustain. Prior to World War II, Southeast Asia had been primarily a cartographical region. In time, common external problems such as fear of Communist China, and the common internal problem of transforming backward, raw material-producing economies, may bring the nations of the region closer together. They may even develop a regional organization more or less analogous to the Pan-American Union. But that is at best a future possibility, and any institution like the European Economic Community is even more remote. Regionalism depends on a mutuality of interest and on a commitment to multilateral institutions that promote such interests. Asian nations have not yet found a sufficient range of common interests on which to base new regional institutions. The only continuing, though not profoundly creative, exception has been Asian participation in the regional efforts of ECAFE, and Asian membership in the Afro-Asian grouping within and outside the United Nations. Even the Colombo Plan represents, essentially, an organized form of bilateral cooperation.

It may be possible further to cultivate regional economic proposals. The Mekong River Valley development project, affecting the four riparian countries of mainland Southeast Asia, is the first such major proposal to have won regional support. In order to succeed, such projects need international support, including skilled manpower not available locally and external capital.

The first attempt to establish a basis for Asian regional economic development proved abortive. In May, 1955, a conference met at Simla to consider a U.S. proposal to create an Asian Regional Development Fund of $200 million for financing regional projects. The proposal was unsuccessful. Burma had declined to attend the conference. In general, the smaller nations in the area were reluctant to participate in such a fund because they expected India and

Japan to receive the largest share. If there is a lesson to be drawn from this failure, as well as from the similarly abortive Asian Nuclear Reactor Center, which was to have been located in the Philippines, it is that factors of gain, pride, and prestige play as much a part in the lives of the Southern Asian nations as they do elsewhere in the world.

Burma's role in the Afro-Asian bloc (her leaders are affronted by the word "bloc"; they tend, as did their Foreign Minister, to use the phrase "the emerging nations of Asia and Africa" [36]) has been persistent ever since the 1955 Bandung Conference. But since then she no longer acts as a convening nation of such conferences. Prime Minister U Nu attended the Afro-Asian meeting at Belgrade in September, 1961, and Foreign Minister U Thi Han attended the related meeting at Cairo in October, 1964. In both instances, the Burmese took moderate and independent positions. At Belgrade, U Nu expressed the hope that the "unaligned countries," collectively or individually, might contribute to a "cooling-off process" between the big powers, and to "the restoration of a calm atmosphere free from frenzy or hysteria" as the "first pre-requisite for a sane and sober conduct of negotiations." Both U Nu and U Thi Han restated Burma's conception of nonalignment, which among other things, as the latter pointed out, supports "the right of every nation to think and act on any issue according to its own convictions and according to its best judgment." [37] Hence, for example, at Cairo, the Burmese explicitly expressed and maintained their differences with the Arab nations on what was called there the "Palestine Question." Burma continues her friendly relations with Israel and with the Arab states.

Burma also continues her interest in the Afro-Asian group at the United Nations. Her permanent representatives to the U.N.— particularly James Barrington (two tours), U Pe Kin, and U Thant—have exercised considerable influence in its deliberations during their tours of duty. Certainly the election of U Thant to the office of Secretary-General was facilitated by his effective role in the Afro-Asian nonaligned bloc.

However, neither fear of Communist China, the obvious desirability of regional economic marketing and other cooperative developmental measures, nor participation in Afro-Asian or Asian conferences has, as yet, produced a sustained collective regional response. Various proposals for a regional security pact have been broached, for example at the May, 1950, Baguio Conference convened at the suggestion of President Elpidio Quirino of the Philippines. The nations attending—Indonesia, Thailand, Ceylon, Pakistan, India, and the Philippines, but not Burma—failed to agree on anything remotely resembling a security pact. The Manila Pact for the creation of SEATO was signed in September, 1954, but this pact split the Asian countries between those who welcomed it and those who rejected more or less vehemently the interjection of

Western power into the security problems of Southeast Asia. Burma was one of the less vehement objectors.[38] Subsequent efforts have had as little success in attracting support or surviving. In 1959, the Malayan Prime Minister, Tengku Abdul Rahman, sponsored the suggestion for a non-Communist Southeast Asian Friendship and Economic Treaty Organization (SEAFET). Other than from Philippine President Carlos P. García there was no favorable response.[39] The Association of Southeast Asian States (ASA) proposed by Thailand in 1961 led to one meeting in Bangkok attended only by the host country, the Philippines, and Malaya. In 1963, Philippine President Diosdado Macapagal made his bid with a "Malay Race" regional organization, Maphilindo, to embrace his country, Indonesia, and Malaya. It foundered on the rock of the Malaysian-Indonesian "confrontation" issue. Burma refrained from participation in any of these ventures.

Nevertheless, regional collective or cooperative arrangements—political, social, economic, and cultural—are inescapable in the future. Because the United States has only recently emerged from isolationism, Americans tend to be somewhat impatient in urging others to follow the alternative policy of collective action. But such a policy must grow from within nations. The merit of regional cooperation and organization will in time be recognized and sustained by Burma and her neighbors in South and Southeast Asia. But both time and motivation from within the area are necessary. These must overcome the warring dynasties of the past, the isolating effects of colonialism, and the relative instability and uncertainty of the post-independence period. Positive factors must have a chance to work themselves into the fabric of Southeast Asian lives. Theravada Buddhism, shared by Ceylon, Burma, Thailand, Laos, and Cambodia, may contribute, but, as seen in the conflict between Thailand and Cambodia, it is not enough. Economic competition for markets is keen, but it may yield to ideas already bruited in Burma and elsewhere in Southeast Asia for economic community. Security in Southeast Asia has been sought in a variety of ways, none of which has thus far been wholly successful. The search will go on, and cooperative or collective effort may result.

Historically, Burma enjoyed its relatively isolated position on the Southeast Asian mainland, set apart from the main sea-lanes in the Indian Ocean. However, at least three times in their past the Burmese pursued an aggressive Southeast Asian policy—in the Middle Ages and in the sixteenth and the eighteenth centuries. Their experience under the British Raj, their cultural and national tendency to live at home (few Burmese have ever emigrated), and their contemporary estimate of power relations in the world have combined to reinforce during the current Ne Win regime the tendency toward a mild form of isolationism under the general slogan of nonalignment. The Burmese would prefer to be left alone in the competition among the powers. But they also realize that they no longer can enjoy or afford the luxury of such a policy. Hence they make careful sallies toward their neighbors in Asia and their fellow members in the United Nations, in order to yoke responsible, if minor, participation in regional and world affairs to the preservation of security at home.

Burma's security—a goal that foreign policy always seeks to maintain—can be supported by respecting Burma's conceptions of security and by aiding where possible measures adopted by its leaders to preserve Burma's independence and security. It is fitting, in closing this section on Burma's foreign relations, to quote from an official expression of policy:[40]

> Burma's historical understanding of the meaning of non-alignment may be stated in this manner. The non-aligned nations have been brought together not by any treaty obligations but by their common understanding towards various international problems and their common approach towards their solution. The non-aligned nations do not and should not constitute any bloc. Nor is non-alignment merely the striking of an attitude between the different power blocs. Non-alignment preserves independence of thought and action. It is characterized by the qualities of detachment, good sense and goodwill. That is why non-alignment does not believe it is its duty to condemn this or that nation in any conflict or controversy. Its entire effort is dedicated to the search for peaceful solutions acceptable to all parties to a conflict. It is prepared to search till all peaceful means have been exhausted. . . . Burma's conduct in international relations is based upon honesty of purpose, sincerity of feeling and generosity of act. It may be stated without righteousness that Burma does what she says she will do and that she says only what she can do. Burma observes scruples in her international conduct; she holds no double standards. And Burma can so conduct herself because she jealously guards the position that she is not answerable to anybody in her foreign policy. She is answerable only to her convictions and her conscience.

PART IV · BURMA AND THE UNITED STATES

Intercourse between the United States and Burma began
with sailing ships searching for trade and profits in the Indies; the
first American ship apparently reached the port of Pegu in 1789.
The captain and crew must have displeased the authorities for they
were imprisoned, but little more is known about them.[1]

American shipping to the Orient[2] began with the "*Empress of
China*, on a speculative voyage to Canton" in 1784, and with "the
visit of the brig *Hope* of Salem to Batavia in 1786." Between 1784
and 1786, the *Grand Turk* reached the Ile de France (Mauritius) "with a cargo of provisions." After the federal government
was organized in 1789, and especially after the wars in Europe that
began in 1793, American shipping forged rapidly ahead in the
scramble for the risky but highly profitable Asian trade. To further
this development, and to compensate for the fact that the United
States, unlike the European powers, had no colonies or factories in
Asia, a consular service was established in 1790. Our first consul to
the "Indies," Benjamin Joy of Newburyport, arrived in Calcutta in
November, 1794. A John B. Davy of Pennsylvania "was named
consul at Rangoon in the Burman Empire" in January, 1811. But
whether he functioned there is not known, "the records have long
since vanished." [3] Restrictive trade policies established by the colonial powers and the War of 1812 severely interrupted American
commerce and consular activity in the Indies. The Calcutta consulate was not reopened until 1843, forty years after the departure
of the last-known consul. After the First Anglo-Burmese War, the
authorities of the port of Calcutta (and hence the American consulate as well) regarded Rangoon as within their jurisdiction. The
American consular practice conformed to British custom in this

respect. American shipping and trade with Burma reached their nineteenth-century peak just before the Civil War.[4]

The Pre–World War II Connection with Burma and Southeast Asia: Continuity Without Depth

The true beginning of the presence of Americans in Burma dates from the arrival in Rangoon of the converted Baptist missionary Adoniram Judson, and his wife, Ann, on July 13, 1813. The impulse that brought them to Asia was part of the great evangelical and missionary movement that succeeded the Age of Reason in Europe and the United States. Judson, a former Congregationalist, had already voyaged to England seeking support for the missionary enterprise which he and a group of young Americans had adopted as their true vocation. When he decided to go to India, it was to join the English Indian Mission at Serampore near Calcutta. At that time, the end of the first decade of the nineteenth century, India already had at least thirty-five English missionaries "who preached the gospel, three in Hindoosthan, sixteen in Bengal, two in the Telinga country, one at Bombay, eight in the Southern part of the peninsula, three in Ceylon and two in the Burman empire." [5]

The first American missionaries went to Burma because the British East India Company would not allow them to remain in India. They then set out for Java, but their vessel carried them to Rangoon—and there they remained. Later the Honorable Company was to find full use for their services in Burma. As Parker Thomas Moon pointed out in 1926: "Going out to preach the kingdom not of this world, missionaries found themselves very often builders of very earthy empires. Sometimes they promoted imperialism quite unintentionally. . . . Protestant missionaries representing national churches have doubtless been particularly disposed to regard themselves as representative pioneers of their own nation." Throughout the nineteenth century, American missionaries in Asia served as officials of the U. S. Government or as aides to those who were so appointed. More restricted in their movements than merchants or traders, they were the more eager to seek treaty protection and other advantages through the intercession of their own government.[6]

Just before the First Anglo-Burmese War, 1824-26, there were seven American Baptist missionaries in Burma: the Judsons and Dr. Jonathan Price (a man who knew something of surgery), who were then visiting the Burmese capital at Ava; and the Wades and Houghs in Rangoon. They were aware that trouble was brewing between the British and the Burmese, but thought that war might be averted, and that if it came, Americans would fare better than Englishmen because, as Judson wrote in a letter dated February 19, 1824, "the distinction between Americans and Englishmen is pretty well understood in this place." Price, in a letter dated December 24, 1822, had written: "Our manners, as missionaries, are so different from those of the captains and merchants here who speak our language that they [the Burmese] are all desirous of a further acquaintance with Americans, supposing all our nation are entirely destitute of the hauteur they have observed in our European neighbors. American ships would be received with peculiar favour until some imprudent fellow should set them [the Burmese] on their guard." [7]

When the war came to Burma, the authorities did not distinguish between Americans and Englishmen. Nor is it clear that the missionaries were neutral. Judson and Price were imprisoned in Ava. The missionaries in Rangoon were imprisoned briefly but were quickly freed as a result of British arms.[8] And American ships did not then find their way to Burmese shores.

The American Baptist missionary contact with Burma dominated the personal and official contact between the United States and Burma for most of the nineteenth century. Many Americans had their first contact with people from Burma in 1833, when the missionary Jonathan Wade and his wife brought two "native Christians" to the United States: "Moung Shway Moung, a Burman, and Ko Chet-thing, a Karen." The missionaries brought them "to render their visit still more entertaining, and as a means to increase interest in the heathen." [9]

Burma's first diplomatic contact with the United States arose out of King Mindon's search for allies to help deter further encroachments by Britain after Burma's defeat in 1852. In September, 1855, King Mindon invited the missionary, the Reverend Eugenio Kincaid, to visit him at Amarapura. The latter arrived on April 11, 1856, and had a long audience with the king, during which Mindon "requested us to write to the newspapers in America, and to inform our fellow-citizens, that he would do everything to promote trade. He hoped merchants would come and settle in his kingdom . . . he would afford them every opportunity to obtain riches." The following January, the Reverend Kincaid again was invited to visit the king who requested him to carry a message to President Pierce "engaging to pay all expenses of the overland passage and back to Burmah." Kincaid delivered the "Royal letter," according to his biographer, "into the hands of the President." [10] It follows:

His Majesty, whose glory is like the rising sun, ruling over the kingdoms of Tho-na-pa-yon-te, Ton-pa-de-pa,[11] and all the eastern principalities, whose chiefs walk under golden umbrellas—Lord of Saddan, the King of Elephants, and Lord of many white Elephants—whose descent is from the royal race of Alompra,—also the great Lords and officers of State, ever bowing before his Majesty, as water lilies around the throne, to direct and superintend the affairs of the Empire—

Send salutations to the president and great officers of State residing in the city of Washington, and ruling over many great countries in the continent of America.

His Majesty, whose shadow, like that of his royal race, falls over the entire kingdom, desires to govern so as to promote wise and useful regulations, such as the greatest of rulers has ever made it his study to accomplish. His Majesty is aware that it has always been the custom of great rulers to be on terms of friendship with other nations, and to pursue measures tending to perpetual amity.

As the American Teacher, Rev. E. Kincaid, has come to the royal city, without hindrance, and he has permission to go in and out of the Palace when he pleases, and has permission to look on the royal countenance, he will be able to address the President of the United States, and the great officers, on all subjects pertaining to the government and kingdom of Burmah. Should this royal kingdom and the great country of America form a friendly intercourse, there is on our part the desire that the two great countries through all coming generations may cultivate friendly relations—and that the merchants and common people and all classes may be greatly benefitted. For this purpose this royal letter is committed to Mr. Kincaid. Should he be charged with a letter from the President and great officers of State, to bring to the royal city of Ava, for his Majesty and the court, and should the President and great officers say, let the two countries be on terms of friendship, and that our children and grand-children, and all merchants and the common people, may through all generations reap great advantage—should such a message come, it will be heard with great pleasure.

Kincaid carried back to King Mindon a reply from President Buchanan, who succeeded President Pierce in March, 1857. It follows:

James Buchanan,
President of the United States of America

To His Majesty the King of Ava, whose glory is like the rising sun, ruling over the Kingdoms of Tho-na-pa-yon-te—Ton-pa-de-pa—and all the Eastern Principalities, whose chiefs walk under golden umbrellas; Lord of Saddan the King of Elephants; and Lord of many white Elephants, whose descent is from the Royal race of Alompra;— Greeting. I have received from the Reverend Eugenio Kincaid the letter which he informs me your Majesty delivered to him in April 1856 of the Christian Era. It has been a gratification to me to learn from that communication that so worthy a citizen of the United States as Mr. Kincaid has had free access to Your Majesty. It would be a further gratification if others of my countrymen who might resort to Your Majesty's dominions as merchants or as travellers might also be hospitably received. Your Majesty may be assured that the subjects of Burmah who may visit this country shall be received in the same manner.

We heartily reciprocate your Majesty's wish for the cultivation of friendly relations between the two countries, and as we have no interest, the promotion of which so far as can be foreseen, would render it necessary to desire that your Majesty's sovereignty should be diminished or in any way put in jeopardy, we trust that peace and good will may be perpetual between us. This letter will be delivered to Your Majesty by Mr. Kincaid whom I have authorized to make known to Your Majesty orally also the amicable sentiments of the government and people of the United States towards Your Majesty and Your Majesty's subjects.

And so I pray the Almighty to have Your Majesty in His safe and holy keeping.

Written at Washington this 19th. day of May Anno Domini, 1857.
By the President   James Buchanan

    Lewis Cass,
    Secretary of State[12]

Nothing came of this exchange, or of the other efforts made by King Mindon to save his kingdom. On November 17, 1882, the U. S. Minister to Siam, John Halderman, in a dispatch to Secretary of State Frederick T. Freylingheusen,[13] accurately predicted the coming end of royal Burma. Three years later, after the fourteen days of the Third Anglo-Burmese War, in November, 1885, Britain annexed King Thibaw's "dominions, treasures and monopolies, and incorporated them one and all in Her Britannic Majesty's Indian Empire." In time, the United States appointed "commercial agents" in British Burma—at Akyab, Moulmein, and Rangoon. In 1908, a consulate was established in Rangoon.

At the beginning of the twentieth century there was a flurry of American business activity in Burma, but this was not followed by greater official interest. In 1899, the Pennsylvania Steel Company beat its English competitors to a contract for the great single-track viaduct over the Gokteik Gorge between Mandalay and Lashio.[14] In 1903, Herbert Hoover helped to reopen the Bawdwin Mine for the British-owned Burma Corporation at Namtu. Between 1904 and World War I, American oil drillers were indispensable to the Burmah Oil Company. In 1910, one estimate placed their number at 400. (One of these old-time American oil drillers, married to a Burmese lady, was killed by insurrectionists while working on a U.S.-Burma aid project during my tour of duty, 1951-53.)

The generally low level of official U. S. interest in Burma and the surrounding region in the nineteenth century did not apply to East Asia and the Pacific region. The word "China," according to one authority, appears in a public presidential message or paper for the first time in 1831. The word "Japan" appears in 1852.[15] From May 8, 1843, when President Tyler appointed Caleb Cushing of Newburyport, member of the House Committee on Foreign Affairs, as resident commissioner in China, and authorized him to negotiate a treaty for American trade and extraterritorial rights, the United States became intimately involved in East Asian affairs, and has been ever since. But neither President McKinley's determination to retain the Philippines after the war with Spain (the treaty was ratified February 6, 1899), nor the earlier decision to complete the annexation of Hawaii[16] led the United States to extend her interests (other than with Siam) to the Southern Asian colonial empires of England, France, or Holland.

One of the earliest uses of the term "Southeast Asia"—to describe the region from Burma to the Pacific Ocean—appears in a report published in 1839. The American Baptist Missionary Society had sent Howard Malcom "to examine into, and with the missionaries adjust, many points not easily settled by correspondence . . . and to gather details on every point where the Board lacked information." On his return, he published an account of his *Travels in South-Eastern Asia embracing Hindustan, Malaya, Siam, and China . . . and . . . The Burman Empire*. For the next century, "Southeast Asia" was rarely used. The names "Further India," "Indochina," "East Indies," "Island India," or variants thereof, as well as references to the names of the countries in the context of colonial empires, dominate the nomenclature. As late as 1941, despite the title of his work,[17] J. S. Furnivall refers to the "Tropical Far East" as the designation for the region. The concept of "Southeast Asia" reappears in the perceptive historical writings of J. C. van Leur, particularly in *De wereld van Zuid-Oost Azië*, which he prepared for a volume on Dutch Colonial history.[18] With World War II, "Southeast Asia" (or "South-East Asia") as an imprecise regional concept and name, came into its own. The creation of the South-East Asia Command, decided upon at a May, 1943, U.K.– U.S. Washington conference, contributed largely to the continued usage of the name.[19]

Up to World War II, Southeast Asia in general and Burma in particular held little place in the international concerns of various American administrations. Even the consulate in Rangoon declined in importance. Nor, excepting in missionary circles in the United States, was there much interest evinced in the area in nongovernmental quarters. For example, the Council on Foreign Relations launched its annual series, *The United States in World Affairs*, in 1931, though it had begun earlier (1928) to issue an annual *Survey of American Foreign Relations*. East Asian Pacific topics appear in relative bulk up to the war in both the *Survey* and the subsequent series; however, there is no indication throughout these volumes of any significant U.S. interest in Burma and the rest of Southeast Asia. Burma is mentioned but once (as a place of Chinese emigration) in the four *Survey* volumes, 1928-31.[20] The subsequent series, starting with 1932, does much better. Burma appears in connection with the Burma Road in 1939 and 1940. The Council's influential quarterly, *Foreign Affairs*, founded in 1922, from its second issue onward frequently treated the problems and relations of Great Britain (but not the United States) with respect to India, of which Burma was a province until 1937. However, reference to Burma as an independent subject does not appear until

1932, followed by an article on the Burma Road in 1939. Southeast Asia as a name for the region was used in *Foreign Affairs* only late in the war. Until then, in the long series of articles on U.S. foreign policy, it had not been used.

When the war in the Pacific began, it would not be an exaggeration to say that except for the Philippines, the United States Government and the American people entered the fateful period of wartime concern for Southeast Asia with an almost incredible lack of policy, of knowledge, and of scholarly preparation. The United States had had a century of sustained diplomacy and knowledgeable contact with East Asia and the Pacific, but did not have trained manpower resources (other than missionaries) and American scholarship on which to rely for Southeast Asia (save in the Philippines).[21]

The Impact of World War II: Anticolonialism and Compromise

Just before Pearl Harbor, the United States was heavily involved in the problem of the Burma Road as a supply route for China. The U.S. had sent a transportation expert, Daniel Arnstein, to Rangoon to expedite the flow of American war matériel and other supplies. Arnstein was probably the first emissary from Washington to have direct contact with a governor-general of Burma. But this activity was China-oriented and was not related to the nationalist or defense problems of Burma.

Pearl Harbor and the war in the Pacific altered with perhaps irreversible direction the indifferentist course of American interest in South and Southeast Asia. The Roosevelt-Churchill meeting in August, 1941, which led to the adoption of the Atlantic Charter, represents perhaps the first U.S. expression of future involvement in the area. In Article III, the signatories declared that they "respect the right of all peoples to choose the form of government under which they live." Though Churchill regarded the charter as a reference " 'primarily [to] the restoration of the sovereignty, self-government and national life of the States and nations of Europe now under the Nazi yoke, and the principles governing any alterations in their territorial boundaries which may have to be made,' it was not long before the people of India, Burma, Malaya, Indonesia were beginning to ask if the Atlantic Charter extended also to the Pacific and Asia in general." [22]

Traditional U.S. anticolonial feeling, in both official and unofficial quarters, was heightened by the idealism of the war, which saw the coming peace settlement as a great opportunity to make fresh beginnings and eliminate some of the evils of the past. But nations owning colonies approached the problem from a different point of view. They found it hard to understand why they should lose their overseas possessions because they were fighting a war of survival against the Axis.

A special U.S. Committee on International Organization, set up in July, 1942, under the chairmanship of Under Secretary Sumner Welles, proposed a system of trusteeships limited to territories mandated to League of Nations members after World War I, and dependent territories to be detached from Italy and Japan. The committee's draft of a United Nations Declaration on National Independence of March 9, 1943, stated in its preamble that "opportunity to achieve independence . . . shall be preserved, respected and made more effective." In the body of the document, colonial powers were urged to cooperate fully with the peoples in their dependencies and to aid their progress toward self-government and independence. It recommended setting up a timetable for this. No action was taken on this or on a British draft declaration.[23]

Only in the unfolding drama of the war, and more particularly during and after the March, 1943, Roosevelt-Eden meetings, did the obvious application of the Atlantic Charter to Asian colonies held by the Allies come to be openly discussed among the Allies. On March 27, at which time Roosevelt, Eden, Hull, Halifax, and William Strang met at the White House, the President continued the general discussion of the organization of the United Nations foreshadowed at the Atlantic Charter meeting, and by the Declaration on National Independence. The President again supported the still vague notion of trusteeships for various former colonies. In this connection, Portuguese Timor and French Indochina seemed to be among the chosen examples of colonies that would not necessarily be restored "to the countries which owned or controlled them prior to the war." Apparently, Roosevelt had also "once or twice urged the British to give up Hong Kong as a gesture of 'good will.' " [24] Whether India, Burma, Malaya, and Indonesia were discussed at these 1943 meetings has not thus far appeared in the published record, though India and Malaya were referred to as possible agenda topics.[25]

The year 1944 saw considerable friction between the United States on the one hand and the British and the Free French on the other over the colonial question.[26] On March 21, Secretary of State Cordell Hull sternly called attention to the duty of nations to prepare dependent peoples "for the duties and responsibilities of self-government and to attain liberty." The same year, the Division of Territorial Studies of the Department of State for the first time added Burma to the list of countries for study, looking toward the postwar period.[27] Whether there was any connection between this and the Secretary's reaffirmation of the traditional American anti-colonial policy is not known. There is nothing in the published record of the war period to suggest that the United States had developed either a short- or long-range policy relating to the Burmese. After the United States had burned its fingers on the Indian question, as John C. Campbell has pointed out, and after General

Joseph W. Stilwell's comment on Burma (see *supra*, p. 62), the U.S. refrained from gratuitous criticism of the British, and, in the absence of an international agreement on the future of colonies, "the United States pursued a cautious policy calculated not to give offense to its allies, the European colonial powers." Campbell continued: "With the division of command in the Far East, assigning the Philippines and Japan to MacArthur's theater, Lower Burma, Malaya, and the Dutch East Indies to that of Lord Louis Mountbatten, the United States accepted in practice the legal argument that the colonial territories should be restored to their prewar status, at least as a starting point for any changes." [28]

The war that was taking place in Burma was seldom related to discussions of the future of Burma. While Chinese maps showed northern Burma as within China's borders, Chiang Kai-shek looked upon the Burma campaign as logistical support for his armies in fighting first against the Japanese and then against the Chinese Communists. The Churchill government in Britain never doubted that Burma, punished and perhaps contrite for her wartime collaboration with the Japanese, would be restored to her prewar colonial status. Throughout the war, the British Burma government-in-exile at Simla was making detailed plans for its return to a British-ruled Burma. At the Cairo Conference of November, 1943, the three powers—United States, Britain, China—discussed only the military aspects of the campaign to retake Burma, which in fact was postponed until after the great channel invasion of Nazi-held France. During the war in Burma, English officers developed afresh their connection with one minority, the Karens, while the Americans were befriended by the Kachins, whose behind-the-lines efforts for the Allies were made the subject of promises never fulfilled.

When the great powers met at Dumbarton Oaks in 1944[29] to draft the Charter of the United Nations, the U.S proposals on trusteeships followed those of the State Department's Special Committee on International Organization. Promotion of self-government in colonial territories was stated as the basic objective. No strong effort was made at the San Francisco Conference to bring colonial peoples under the proposed trusteeship system. The new system was to be applied to League of Nations mandates, former enemy territories, and any colonial areas that might be placed voluntarily under the system. However, Chapter XI of the Charter went beyond the Covenant of the League in requiring U.N. members that administered non-self-governing territories to promote the well-being of the inhabitants, which included the development of self-government, and to report to the Secretary-General on economic, social, and educational conditions in the territories. Independence as the goal for the peoples of all colonial areas no longer appeared as such in these documents.

If U.S. foreign policy toward Burma throughout the Stilwell

command was notably absent and if policy toward other sections of Southeast Asia was at best a vague expression of education for self-government or for trusteeships under the still unclarified approach of a United Nations organization, what of presumably informed, nonofficial expression on these subjects? Two wartime examples are considered here as illustrative.

In August, 1942, the editors of *Time, Life,* and *Fortune* issued a thirty-two-page supplement on the general theme of "the United States in a New World," called *Pacific Relations.* The following quotations are from this supplement to *Fortune.* The editors expected that we would win the war; that the victory would offer an opportunity "to think greatly and act nobly" so that "Asia's revolution into modernity" would lead into "patterns of fruitful, dramatic and harmonious intercourse between West and East." In keeping with this aim, the editors proposed "that the Western powers surrender all their exclusive rights or preferential position in Asia after this war." This would be, in their words, "the end of imperialism." Specifically, Britain was called upon to complete the "devolution of British imperial rule." This apparently meant that India should be free (though the report discusses India very little) and that India and a reborn China, together with the West and some kind of "international authority," or United Nations, should strive "to build orderly free societies in Asia, capable of producing higher levels of living for their depressed classes and poverty-ridden peasant masses."

In traditional American fashion, China was the focus of *Pacific Relations* and of its policy derivatives. China was to become one of the senior members in the United Nations, the dominant power in a new *Pax Asiaticus Sinica* depending upon a partnership with the United States for building an economic base necessary and sufficient to sustain its political position vis-à-vis Japan and even free India. The latter was Britain's responsibility, though the United States had a share "to an important degree" in helping to sustain its integrity and independence.

But if the editors of *Time, Life,* and *Fortune* were characteristically at ease and relatively well supplied with information in making policy recommendations for East Asia and for India, when they turned to "Southeastern Asia" they betrayed a combination of arrogance and ignorance which would be difficult to exceed. For example:

1. China and Japan are described as "peoples integrated nationally with proud traditions and long histories." But Burma, Thailand, Indochina, Malaya, the Netherlands Indies (along with Borneo and Timor), are described as "for the most part illiterate, heterogeneous, completely lacking in common traditions or political training." Ignored is the fact that Burma then had the highest percentage of literacy in Asia; and that Burma and the countries of Indochina and Indonesia also had "long histories" and "proud tra-

ditions," disrupted in no small measure by the advent of colonialism.

2. Thailand's long history of independence is described as "formal" rather than "real." It is ruled by "a small, pro-Fascist clique of palace despots" who have "persecuted a minority of 2,500,000 Chinese with the systematic cruelty of Germans towards Jews." Any uninformed Western reader would be forced to conclude from such an irresponsible statement that the Thais, like the Nazis, engaged in mass racial and ethnic murders, or otherwise physically mistreated the Chinese. No reader would learn from these editors anything about the true and advantageous role of the "overseas Chinese" in the economy and intermarried society of Thailand. Nor would he be clear as to whether the "palace despots" referred to the limited constitutional monarch and royalty or to the military who ended the absolute powers of the monarchy by the 1932 coup and who then ruled Thailand with some modest regard for the introduction of limited constitutional reforms.

3. Burma is described as having "a high degree of [political] autonomy before the outbreak of the Pacific War," but as being a "disappointment to the friends of Burmese freedom." Her politicians could agree only on "their dislike of the British, their hatred for the Indians, and their distrust of the Chinese. . . . The Buddhist church of Burma . . . has regularly tended to promote anarchy, and social and political unrest." It will therefore have to be redirected as a "prerequisite for the eventual establishment of full Burmese autonomy and independence." No one, unless informed, would gather from these editors that Burma "enjoyed"—their word—such autonomy only since 1937; that the British had long encouraged the emigration into Burma of both Indians and Chinese, who, in that order, rated after the British in the control of the Burmese economy; that second to the British, the Indians had historically been given the preferred positions in the civil service; and that Buddhism in Burma, as did Islam in Indonesia, as did Protestantism in the American colonies, nurtured the early nationalist, anti-colonialist aspirations of the indigenes. Nowhere in this screed would the reader learn why Southeast Asians welcomed the Japanese in preference to their former colonial masters.

The policy recommendations of the editors are in keeping with their descriptions of the area. They are:

1. Thailand, British Malaya, Netherlands Indonesia, and Portuguese Timor should be combined into one state, whose capital would be located in Batavia (Djakarta). A supreme council made up of representatives of the United Nations having a "direct interest in the area, such as Australia, Britain, China, the Netherlands, India, Portugal and the U.S. will administer the state . . . with an obligation to combine intelligently the best features of various colonial policies" until such time as "a government responsible to a literate and politically informed electorate" will be produced from

"an adequate educational program." Such a policy is advocated because the area has in the main been characterized by "abortive nationalistic drives . . . aimless reactions against Western colonial policy rather than the stirrings of real nationhood." The "colonial genius" of the Dutch will be employed because they know how to achieve a "kind of practical penetration" of the area by one people, the Javanese, and how best to make "the Moslem faith of the inhabitants a factor for unity rather than division. Thus in the new Indonesian state the task and responsibility of the Dutch colonial administrators will be greater, not smaller, than in their sovereign past."

2. Indochina will be assigned to a "strongly represented" French-Chinese U.N. Commission, which "would guarantee to prepare the territory for self-government."

3. Burma will be similarly assigned to an "International Commission on which Great Britain, India, China and the U.S. will be strongly represented."

4. Self-government will be restricted in any of these states or territories "where it is used for the suppression of minorities."

5. Population pressures in India and China will be relieved by "an intra-Pacific migration agreement" through which "each country will be forced frankly to consider its neighbors' problems as well as its own."

6. Security will be achieved by a chain of "fortified islands," a trans-Pacific U.N. defense belt anchored at Formosa as a United Nations-controlled base.

There is nothing reprehensible in proposing in 1942 a series of trusteeships, with or without a timetable for self-government and independence, under a United Nations organization for erstwhile colonial possessions. What gives these specific proposals their bizarre cast is the series of fantastic value judgments, false statements, and incredible misreading or ignorance of history that undergird them. That Thailand, an historically independent Buddhist country with a viable economy, should be sliced out of mainland Southeast Asia in order to form a state with Muslim Indonesia and Malaya makes no sense at all. In the final analysis, what the editors propose is a superficial dilution rather than "the end of imperialism." Exclusive English, French, and Dutch colonial hegemony in Southeast Asia is to be merged into a Western, Indian, and Chinese condominium, which will serve to relieve the "population pressures" of the latter two by migration into that area only.

The editors exhibited little appreciation for or understanding of indigenous nationalist movements and national backgrounds. They sought to guard against any future revival of Japanese militarism while they failed to accord any significance to the effect of Japanese "liberation" upon the Southeast Asian nationalists who, at least since the end of World War I, had been organizing to secure true liberation. Burma and the rest of Southeast Asia were still a piece of faceless geography, ready to be carved up and served to a partnership of Western and Asian powers.

The second example of nonofficial expression on postwar settlement is taken from the Eighth Conference of the Institute of Pacific Relations, held at Mont Tremblant, Quebec, December 4-14, 1942. The published *Preliminary Report*[30] makes clear that the conference made no recommendations and passed no resolutions. But areas of agreement and consensus are indicated where relevant. Seemingly the conference ardently supported all eight points of the Atlantic Charter, while carefully rejecting or otherwise interpreting Churchill's narrow application of it to those nations overrun by the Axis powers in Europe. Similar support was voiced for the United Nations and for any derivative security system that would in effect create a Pacific or regional council to which the Pacific powers, large and small, already or newly independent, would be admitted. In these two general respects, there was no difference between the editors of *Time, Life,* and *Fortune* and the IPR conferees. They were in similar agreement on the postwar independence of India and its consequent role; though the IPR conference, in contrast to the *Pacific Relations* editors, paid considerably more attention to India and her problems than to China. The latter was expected to assume importance in East Asia and in the councils of the U.N. The Anglo-American declaration that called for an end to all special privileges, concessions, and extraterritorial rights in China was uniformly approved. Repeatedly the British members declared, to the satisfaction of most, if not all, present, that in their opinion India, after the war, would be able to take any decision with respect to determining its own future. (There was no Indian National Congress member present.) The extensive discussion on India revolved about the relations between Hindu and Muslim, the failure of the Cripps mission, and ways of ending the deadlock between the Congress Party and the Churchill government.

Southeast Asia, "the central arena of old imperial rivalries," was taken more seriously at the IPR conference than by the editors of *Pacific Relations*. The *Preliminary Report* made no effort to create new states and did not reveal an attitudinal pattern comparable to that of the editors; nevertheless, it did not represent significant political progress beyond the logic of the *Time, Life,* and *Fortune* editors. There is in it no bold, democratic, anti-imperialist vision, no understanding or treatment of the motives that led so many Asians to accept the Japanese at the beginning of the war in Asia. It is, above all, a cautious document seeking to inch forward under the protective panoply of a new international organization, the bona fides of presumably reformed erstwhile colonial powers. The aims of the Atlantic Charter, when applied to the area, would "require an unusual amount of specialized adaptation to diverse needs." The Philippines and Thailand would regain independence, but there was "still much to do before 'self-determination' could for the masses of the people have the desired reality, in social and economic as well as in political life." Trusteeships or some form of "international supervision" would be applied to the former French and Portuguese colonies. The Netherlands Indies were agreeably left to the vague postwar reconstruction plans announced by Queen Wilhelmina[31] and to the even more vague idea of a "complete partnership."

For Burma, "the case was less clear but no obstacle was seen to a relatively early assumption by that country of a status of self-government within the British Commonwealth."

In all such matters, the conference was prepared to accept some kind of "International Authority," provided the participating members of the authority were prepared to accept "their proportionate share of responsibility for the security and economic development of the peoples concerned."

Thus some representative and influential sections of American and Western opinion, while bravely supporting the aims of the Atlantic Charter and the organization of the United Nations, and viewing with varying degrees of satisfaction the prospective independence of China and India, did not at this time (1942) envisage at the war's end the free determination of their respective futures by the colonies of Southeast Asia. At best, these colonies would be allowed to exercise some forms of self-government or home rule. It was not clear whether these forms would be the same or in advance of what they had in prewar days. Independence, the "end of imperialism," to use the editors' phrase, the clear recognition of the nationalist aspirations of the former Southeast Asian colonies, was not yet an acceptable policy. Some American opinion at the IPR conference, particularly Tyler Dennett's exposition of his views in "Security in the Pacific and the Far East," insisted that the American war purpose and fundamental, traditional American policy could be realized only if the third article of the Atlantic Charter were accepted and applied to colonial areas. This he regarded as a "minimum demand." His was very much a minority voice.

The Asian Price for Containment in Europe: A U.S. Policy of Ambivalence

The slow evolution of U.S.–Burma relations can be understood only in the context of the development of U.S. foreign policy for Asia. At the war's end the United States Government, and for the most part the American people, were committed to the necessity for an international, in contrast to an isolationist, foreign policy. This time there was to be no return to the presumed security of the two oceans or to the Western hemisphere. Residual impulses toward withdrawal, toward some kind of American isolation, remain in the diversified political stream of American life, but these have become recessive strains in the body politic. What William James once called the "rivalry of the patterns" polarized the world between the United States and the U.S.S.R. America no longer holds the illusion of "One World." But America knows—and knows it from the days of World War II—that she is inexorably entwined in the world.

Within the first few postwar years, the United States witnessed the crumbling of old empires and the making of new ones more dangerous and more ruthless than many of their predecessors. New states, but old nations, were to emerge from the former empires in Africa and Asia, whereas the Marxist-Leninist world of Russia, and later China, gradually engulfed hapless nations and peoples. That a polarized world of competing systems and sovereignties should develop out of wars is ineluctably inherent, according to its believers, in the nature of Marxian dialectical and historical materialism. So long, therefore, as the Sino-Soviet Marxist world professes its belief in the necessary struggle of the "Two Camps," the artifice of coexistence is merely an interim stage until the conditions necessary for a final transformation in its favor arrive. Long before the war, some Americans had acquired a clear understanding of Soviet ideology and the uses to which it had been put by the Stalinist hierarchy. But generally, throughout the war, the government and the people of the United States hoped and acted as if the wartime alliance might be continued into the postwar world.

The organization of the United Nations, and the expression in its charter of moral and quasi-legal concepts of world order, became a cornerstone of United States foreign policy, acceptable to the majority of American people because it gave expression to their hope of continuing the wartime alliance in the making of peace and because it seemingly reflected the broad, general, benign self-image Americans entertain of themselves and of their country. No better example of this self-image need be cited than that reflected in President Truman's speech at a Navy Day celebration in New York on October 27, 1945. In this speech he restated the twelve "fundamental principles of righteousness and justice" on which "United States foreign policy is based":

1. We seek no territorial expansion or selfish advantage. We have no plans for aggression against any other state, large or small. We have no objective which need clash with the peaceful aims of any other nation.

2. We believe in the eventual return of sovereign rights and self-government to all peoples who have been deprived of them by force.

3. We shall approve no territorial changes in any friendly part of the world unless they accord with the freely expressed wishes of the people concerned.

4. We believe that all peoples who are prepared for self-government should be permitted to choose their own form of gov-

ernment by their own freely expressed choice, without interference from any foreign source. That is true in Europe, in Asia, in Africa, as well as in the western hemisphere.

5. By the combined and cooperative action of our war Allies, we shall help the defeated enemy states establish peaceful, democratic governments of their own free choice. And we shall try to attain a world in which Nazism, Fascism, and military aggression cannot exist.

6. We shall refuse to recognize any government imposed upon any nation by the force of any foreign power. In some cases it may be impossible to prevent forceful imposition of such a government. But the United States will not recognize any such government.

7. We believe that all nations should have the freedom of the seas and equal rights to the navigation of boundary rivers and waterways and of rivers and waterways which pass through more than one country.

8. We believe that all states which are accepted in the society of nations should have access on equal terms to the trade and the raw materials of the world.

9. We believe that the sovereign states of the western hemisphere, without interference from outside the western hemisphere, must work together as good neighbors in the solution of their common problems.

10. We believe that full economic collaboration between all nations, great and small, is essential to the improvement of living conditions all over the world, and to the establishment of freedom from fear and freedom from want.

11. We shall continue to strive to promote freedom of expression and freedom of religion throughout the peace-loving areas of the world.

12. We are convinced that the preservation of peace between nations requires a United Nations Organization composed of all the peace-loving nations of the world who are willing jointly to use force if necessary to insure peace.[32]

There is nothing notable or new in these twelve points. Together they express the traditional American desire for peace, security, well-being, and freedom, and opposition to armed force, coercion, and territorial aggrandizement as instruments of policy. They lean heavily on the general outline provided by President Franklin D. Roosevelt and Secretary Hull. Not only was the U.N. required "to insure peace," but President Truman underlined, as a supporting theme, the special responsibilities and hope for the maintenance of the wartime alliance. Communism was not listed along with Nazism and Fascism, as it came to be later; and Russian collaboration with "other peace-loving people" was a required and invited element for the future. The difficulty, of course, is not in formulating such principles or objectives—most, if not all, states indulge in the exercise—but in applying them. Events somehow get in the way. The expression of such principles is not infrequently referred to as "idealism" or "moralism" in foreign policy; whereas their application and modification in terms of "interests" are referred to as "realism." Such a disjunction is philosophical nonsense, though it causes endless argument between respective proponents, and, as frequently, leads to political ambivalence even within any one group. The "idealists" or "moralists" temper their principles with the anticipated difficulties of policy execution; the "realists" color their expressions of policy with objectives derived from past or future valued goals. Actually, all such assertions or propositions about the principles and direction of foreign policy, whether couched in the terms used by President Truman or by others, are made in whatever reality this world has. Their application in concrete situations depends solely upon the administering will of the authorities in any state. Their success or failure in application, that is, the risks of principle, depends solely upon the capacity of a state, alone or in concert with others, to carry out its will.

There is no need here to do more than to mention the broad changes which, shortly after President Truman spoke, shattered his hopes for a world of organized peace. Russia under Stalin had no intention of remaining a friendly peacetime ally. In early 1946, Stalin began to make the moves on the Soviet chessboard that led to the 1947 revival of the Comintern, now called the Cominform. Gone was the practice of the "soft" or "right" strategy, which had been revived after the Nazi invasion of Russia on June 22, 1941. Stalin, as a good Leninist, was determined to use war-weariness and war depletions as the springboards for a Communist political offensive. Non-Soviet Europe was the main target, or so it appeared. I have suggested elsewhere[33] that during this crucial period, 1946-49, Stalin, having pushed westward into Europe as far as he could go without further war, was primarily concerned with China; that Communist actions in Europe and South and Southeast Asia were calculated risks designed largely to distract the anti-Communist world and thus afford Stalin and Mao their long-awaited victory in China. Stalin's defeat at the hand of the Kuomintang in 1926-27 was soon to be wiped out. He could not help but know how badly Chiang was faring in 1946 and 1947—specifically so after General Marshall returned from his "failure of a mission" and after the United States publicly withdrew on January 29, 1947, from any mediatorial role between the Chinese Communists and Chiang Kai-shek.

Whether or not this interpretation of Stalin's Chinese orientation in 1946-49 is correct, there is no question that Europe was in a parlous state after the war, and could ill withstand any determined onslaught on her weakened economies and political structures. Hence Truman's decision to counter the Stalin offensive in Europe was a momentous one. The aid to Greece and Turkey, the announcement of the Marshall Plan, the specific and generalized policy of "containment," went far to give non-Soviet Europe the economic and political stimulation necessary to put its house in better order.

Containment of the Soviet world came to represent the central conception of our foreign policy. The crisis and challenge in Greece and Turkey that the Truman Doctrine, announced on March 12, 1947, sought to meet, the implementation of the Marshall Plan through the European Recovery Plan, following the Secretary's speech of June 5 at Harvard University, were but the opening rounds in the execution of this policy. The Communist coup in Czechoslovakia, in February, 1948, followed by the Soviet bar to Western land traffic to Berlin in June, accentuated United States determination to block the Soviet European offensive. Peacetime conscription, proposed by Truman in March, 1948, was passed by the Congress in June along with a considerable peacetime military budget for those days ($14 billion), which laid the basis for military preparedness, utilizing the Strategic Air Command (and the atom bomb) as the striking weapon of a proposed seventy-group air force. The North Atlantic Treaty Organization, April, 1949, capped these actions. War with the Soviet Union was a possibility publicly discussed.[34]

But what of Asia? And more particularly of Southeast Asia and Burma? The United States Government had attempted to base its immediate postwar Asian policy on a hoped-for strong and free China, on a demilitarized Japan, and on a series of to-be-fortified islands (the *Pacific Relations* editors' proposals) that the U.S. acquired as U.N. trustee, but which our armed forces had in any event insisted upon controlling. This, in a sense, was traditional American Asian policy.

These policies, interpreted in the setting of postwar alliances and United Nations sentiment, were largely incorporated in a speech given by John Carter Vincent, then Director of Far Eastern Affairs, Department of State. The Vincent speech upheld the necessity for "understanding, friendship and collaboration between and among the four principal powers in the Pacific"—China, the Soviet Union, the United States, and the United Kingdom—as the basis for this traditional Asian policy.[35] Where the United States had to make a relatively new decision was in the application of its anticolonial posture to the Asian colonial areas of its wartime allies. In this respect, Vincent repeated what had been generally stated in the various wartime declarations on United Nations policy with respect to dependent and colonial peoples. While affirming the principle of colonial freedom, he vaguely circumscribed it by apparently advocating the goal of "self-government." [36] The right to self-government, in the vocabulary of colonial policy, is not equal to the right of independence.

This ambivalence and uncertainty with respect to colonialism is a persistent feature of U.S. foreign policy. No matter how high-sounding the declaration for freedom for dependent or colonial peoples, somehow or other "circumstances" or "interests" interfere to water down the application of the principle in the adopted course of United States action. Much of what Wendell Willkie called the Asian "reservoir of good will toward the United States" has been wasted, not because of an absence of an Asian policy, but rather because of the disparity between United States profession and practice on colonial issues. For example, Vincent said in this same speech: "In Southeast Asia a situation has developed to the liking of none of us, least of all to the British, the French, the Dutch, and I gather to the Annamese and Indonesians. [He was silent on Burma.] With regard to the situation in French Indo-China, this government does not question French sovereignty in that area. Our attitude toward the situation in the Dutch East Indies is similar to that in regard to French Indo-China." Such a statement directly contradicts or ignores presidential and departmental expressions, indicated above, of the United States wartime position with respect to a proposed trusteeship for Indochina outside the French empire. At no time did the U.S. publicly promise to restore Dutch sovereignty as such. If secret commitments were made they, too, violated the frequent promises for self-determination and self-government made during the war. Certainly, Vincent's exposition of colonial policy and its application in Southeast Asia is at variance with President Truman's virtually simultaneous presentation of the "fundamental principles of righteousness and justice" on which "United States foreign policy is based."

Throughout this period, 1945-49, the United States, with the honorable exception of its policy toward the Philippines, was not conspicuous at any stage in living up to its anticolonial professions of principle. Out of deference to its European allies, it refrained from offering moral or material support to the nationalists of South and Southeast Asia. But if the United States had been largely unaware of the significance of prewar Asian nationalism, it could no longer take refuge in such ignorance in the immediate postwar period, when the strengths and the aims of nationalist movements were clear. As John C. Campbell sums it up:

> . . . the native nationalist movements in Burma, Indo-China and Indonesia, *already strong before the war*, made tremendous gains. Their leaders, on the defeat of Japan, were ready to strike out for independence. . . . The colonial peoples were little interested in the world ideological conflict between democracy and fascism except as it affected their own goal of national independence. . . .
>
> In the early part of the war certain influential officials in the United States Government hoped for the adoption after the war of a "new deal" for colonial peoples which would grant independence to those which were ready for it and establish international trusteeships for those which were not. In the absence of international agreement on such a program, the United States pursued a *cautious* policy cal-

culated not to give offense to its allies, the European colonial powers. [Italics added.][37]

What Campbell calls a "cautious policy" is in fact a policy of ambivalence. That is, United States policy could be said to be cautious with respect to the Philippines, slowly building up the institutions of self-government, providing for a legislative timetable under the terms of which the Philippines would at a certain time become completely independent and sovereign. But the many United States wartime statements, and the postwar actions flowing from such statements, reveal the United States not as "cautious," but as simultaneously verbalizing pronouncements that appear to be in favor of the self-determination of colonial peoples and yet temporizing, or withholding, or backing off from the steps necessary to effectuate the announced policy. Political ambivalence, like psychological or personal ambivalence, consists of developing an approving image of or attraction to an object, replete with pleasant feelings and emotions, and simultaneously being repelled or inhibited by unpleasant, nonapproving feelings and emotions toward the same image or object.

The United States acquiesced in the British armed intervention that reimposed Dutch and French sovereignty respectively on Indonesia and Indochina, but it warned its allies "not to use against the native peoples, lend-lease equipment bearing labels of its American origin." [38] It took no stand on the policies involved in the return of the British to the Indian subcontinent, Burma, and Malaya. The United States did, however, use its influence and aid to get Chiang Kai-shek's armed forces out of Burma and Indochina.[39] It was not until after the first Dutch "police action" against Indonesia, in July, 1947, that the United States offer of "good offices" was tendered and accepted by both sides. This led to the Renville Agreement of January 17, 1948, negotiated by Dr. Frank Graham. Only when this agreement was violated by the second Dutch police action, December 18, 1948, did the United States take a strong stand against the Dutch, bilaterally by suspending ECA aid to Holland and multilaterally through a most forthright denunciation of Dutch policy, made by United States delegate Philip C. Jessup in the U.N. Security Council.[40] Yet the United States continued to balance its decision in favor of Indonesian independence with its concern for Dutch interests in the area, especially after the initial public disapproval of Dutch police actions had waned.

The changeover in Britain from the Churchill to the Attlee government in July, 1945, made this ambivalent United States policy toward South Asia and Burma seem more tolerable. For the Attlee government on December 4, 1945, announced its intention of abiding by Labor's promises for Indian independence. No similar declaration concerning Burma was forthcoming from Britain for another twelve months, during which time the Burmese nationalist

movement led by General Aung San pursued its eventually successful campaign. Nonetheless, British Labour policy toward the Indian
subcontinent and Burma made it possible for the United States in
the early postwar years to maintain its ambivalent stance in this
area without suffering from excessive foreign criticism or twinges of
violated conscience at home. Britain's transfer of power to Pakistan, India, Ceylon, and Burma was peacefully completed by January 4, 1948, but it was certain of completion by January, 1947.
Through the wisdom of British Labour in accepting gracefully what
I believe was inevitable anyway, the Free World scored one of its
great victories. If the reservoir of Asian good will toward the
United States did not thereby directly benefit, at least considerable
English waters were added to its storage.

These events coincided with growing tension between the West
and the Soviet Union. U.S. policies in Europe, in contrast to those
in Asia, were clear and vigorously executed. The collapse of the
wartime alliance during late 1946 and early 1947 was precipitated
by the Stalinist political offensive in Europe and Asia, to which the
United States responded with the policy of containment.[41]

There is no doubt that containment in Europe and the Middle
East was pursued vigorously and effectively by the United States,
culminating in the North Atlantic Treaty Organization, signed
April 4, 1949. But if containment was a sound policy in Europe
and the Middle East, why was it not a sound policy for Asia? Large-
scale but not absolute U.S. withdrawal from China resigned that
country to the growing military success of the Chinese Communists, who had established contiguous borders and supply lines with
Soviet Asia. The Wedemeyer report,[42] dated September 19, 1947,
had if anything strengthened the opinion that the grave situation
in China threatened strategic and political interests. Everyone
agreed that a victory for the Chinese Communists would be a defeat for the United States. Yet the great debate on China, which
took place in the United States after 1947, posed the issue as a
disjunction: for or against the Communists; for or against Chiang
Kai-shek and the Kuomintang. Though I do not propose to enter
the "China tangle," it seemed to me then and now that disjunc-
tions may be logical but not necessarily political constructs. The
terms of the debate and the debaters obscured the real issues and
blocked a proper search for alternatives to the Chinese Communists. The difficulty was compounded by the apparent failure to
assess correctly the potential danger of an aggressive Chinese Communist regime in control of mainland China. It was predictable
that such a regime, protected on the north and west by Soviet
power, would be concerned with its eastern flank where it faced
U.S. power in occupied Japan and Okinawa, and with South and
Southeast Asia. Here were important sources of minerals, rubber,
and rice for China's growing population and production. And here,
as the self-proclaimed inheritors and dispensers of Chinese tradi-

tion, the Chinese Communists would especially seek to establish a sphere of influence. The *Nanyang*—Burma, Thailand, and the then Indochina area—had long been regarded not only as a "spill-way" for Chinese population and civilization, but also as an area where ancient, and, as in the case of Burma, frequently dubious claims of suzerainty might be reasserted. Only the immediate choice of tactics to be pursued by the Chinese Communists was open to speculation. But that they would vary or combine standard and well-known international Communist strategy and tactics was also predictable. Meanwhile, the Communists succeeded in advancing their power throughout 1947 and 1948. They were not contained, either by the Kuomintang or by diminishing American involvement in Asia.

Obviously, containment as a policy was not applied to mainland China. British—not U.S.—policy made it possible for four newly independent nations in Southern Asia to join in the concert of free nations. This left in Southeast Asia, apart from British Malaya, which had been offered a choice but had put aside its decision, the problems of the French in Indochina and the Dutch in Indonesia. Apparently, as indicated above, the effrontery of the second Dutch police action and the effective criticism voiced by the Soviet bloc in the U.N. finally decided United States policy-makers to move in the direction of recognizing and supporting Indonesian independence. This belated action in late 1948 and early 1949 came after the Indonesian nationalists in power suppressed an attempt at an armed Communist rebellion (Madiun) in September 1948.

Throughout the long devastating years from the postwar 1945-46 return of the French in Indochina to Dien Bien Phu in 1954, the United States with incredible consistency supported the imperialist aims of France in Indochina. If corruption, mismanagement, failure to win popular support, rejection of necessary reform, indifference to the plight of the overwhelmingly rural masses, dictatorship under the façade of parliamentarianism were among the potent reasons for turning away from Chiang Kai-shek, then U.S. support for French imperialist policy in Indochina was all the more unwise, for all these factors, plus the additional one of white foreigners imposing alien rule, were present in the French debacle in Indochina. If the advent of a Chinese Communist regime was believed by the administration to be a tragic but perhaps inescapable consequence of Kuomintang inner rot (a view the author rejects), then steps could have been taken at the end of World War II, and certainly before 1954, to bring about a genuine transfer of power in the states of Indochina that would have had a chance of saving more from the Communists than the area south of the 17th parallel. No amount of rationalization about the need for France in NATO, or in the unborn European Defense Community, or in the stillborn Western European Union serves to explain why the United States continued to support France's last-ditch

Asian colonial venture long after America had become the beneficiary of the British decisions in South and Southeast Asia, and after the United States had belatedly decided that the Dutch should be relieved of most of their self-imposed white man's burden in Indonesia. Support of the French in Indochina can be made to fit into the policy of containment of Asian Communists only by the dubious assumption that the French in Indochina were the sole alternative to a Communist take-over. If such an assumption was made, circumstances before and since 1954 have demonstrated its falsity. For there were and are genuine anti-Communist nationalists in Indochina who gave their lives to fight against French and Communist imperialism.

An Interim Policy for Asia and Its Emptiness for Burma

Perhaps we should examine United States relations to Asia and Asian events apart from the policy of Communist containment in Europe, a policy developed there more intensively after the withdrawal of the United States from underwriting a Chiang victory in China. This does not mean that the United States was less concerned with the dangerous east-and-west thrust of Soviet imperialism and with Communist infiltration, subversion, and revolution. It means rather that the United States could no longer anchor its Asian policy to the wartime goal of building up a strong, democratic China. What were the alternatives to this? Until further disclosure of classified material it would appear that pending the final outcome in China, the fearfully awaited victory of Mao Tsetung over Chiang Kai-shek, a sixfold interim policy for Asia was in the making even before Secretary of State Acheson delivered his National Press Club speech on the "Crisis in Asia—An Examination of United States Policy." [43] First, Japan would replace China as the basic American Asian ally.[44] Second, American strategic security would be anchored to a line of island defenses running from the Aleutians through Japan and Okinawa to the Philippines.[45] Third, the United Kingdom would have primary defensive responsibility for the Asian Commonwealths, remaining British-Asian colonies, and Burma.[46] Fourth, there would be acceptance and recognition of Indonesian independence, while *faute de mieux* France was accepted as having paramountcy in Indochina. Fifth, the U.S. would pursue a policy of noninvolvement in such Asian regional efforts as the Nehru-sponsored Asian Relations Conference at Delhi (1947); the abortive Southeast Asian League (1947-48, Bangkok), which grew out of the Delhi Conference and had received some impetus from the Burmese; the second, primarily Indonesian-concerned, Asian Conference at New Delhi (1949); and related occurrences. The exception to this was U.S. interest in the U.N. agencies concerned with Asia. Finally, collective security pacts were considered premature and were therefore to be avoided.[47]

The emptiness of U.S. policy toward Burma can be traced in the pages of the Department of State *Bulletin*. Burma's struggle for independence is met with virtual silence there. Twice during 1945-46 there are references. The first is when the U.S. consulate general at Rangoon was reopened.[48] A few months later, the United States and the United Kingdom discuss the possibility of prohibiting the production in and export of opium from Burma except for medicinal purposes. This theme recurs in 1947. Once the 1947 negotiations between Burma and the United Kingdom set in motion the machinery leading to Burma's independence, then the United States responds with alacrity. We wish to be friendly. Secretary of State Marshall sends a warm greeting on June 10, 1947, to Thakin Mya, Chairman of the Constituent Assembly then in session in Rangoon. The message follows:

> On this historic occasion I extend to you as chairman of the Constituent Assembly and through you to the Burmese people the sincere good wishes of the United States government and the people of the United States of America for a successful conclusion of the important task you are about to undertake. Burma's peaceful and steady progress in rehabilitation is being watched with sympathetic interest. Freedom loving people throughout the world hope that you will lay the foundation for a stable and peaceful Nation.[49]

Thakin Mya replies to Secretary Marshall's greetings with a letter dated June 13, 1947:

> On behalf of myself and the Constituent Assembly of Burma, I desire to thank you most warmly for your very kind message of good will and good wishes which has been most deeply appreciated by the Constituent Assembly and country. Such cordial greetings and sincere good wishes from the government and people of the United States of America at the outset of our deliberations would be a source of inspiration and encouragement to us in the task of framing a Constitution for free and United Burma. I can assure you that free Burma will regard it as its special duty and privilege to maintain most cordial and friendly relations with your country and to make all possible contributions to the peace and happiness of the world.[50]

While Burma was still a provisional government within the British Commonwealth, the United States determined to raise the rank of the consulate general to an ambassadorship. Consul General E. L. Packer was promoted to Chargé d'Affaires while the United States and Burma agreed to an exchange of ambassadors.[51] Burma's first Independence Day, January 4, 1948, occasioned the sending of greetings from the United States.[52]

> *Message from President Truman to Sao Shwe Thaike, Saopha of Tawnghwe, President of the Union of Burma, on the occasion of the establishment of the Union on January 4, 1948:*

> It is fitting that on this day, the day of the birth of a new nation, a sovereign independent republic, the Union of Burma, I should ex-

tend to you, to the Prime Minister and to the people of the Union, on behalf of the people of the United States of America, my sincere best wishes. We welcome you into the brotherhood of free and democratic nations and assure you of our firm friendship and goodwill, anticipating that the Union of Burma will take its rightful place among the nations of the world and by constructive participation will assist in the advancement of the welfare of all mankind. We in this country have confidence in the people of Burma and in their leaders. I am sure that our friendship will continue in the future and will be expressed in the same close and cordial relations as have existed in the past.

Robert A. Lovett, Acting Secretary of State, addressed the following message to the Ambassador of Burma on the occasion of the flag-hoisting ceremony at the Embassy of Burma in Washington on January 4, 1948:

This is a memorable occasion for the world as well as for Burma itself, for on this day the Union of Burma, a sovereign independent republic, has joined the family of nations. I extend to Your Excellency and to the people of Burma the welcome of the people of the United States. May the flag first flown today be dedicated to democratic principles of freedom, to the cause of peace, and to the advancement of all peoples. It is of singular pleasure to us here in the United States that you have seen fit to use the colors red, white, and blue, and to represent your various peoples by white stars on a blue field. Needless to say red, white and blue, and white stars on a blue field are especially dear to all Americans. We are confident that this new flag will symbolize the cordial meeting of the East and the West for the betterment of the entire world.

Shortly before this, in November, 1947, the first official Burmese delegation, a youth mission from the Department of National Planning, arrived in the United States for a visit. On December 8, 1947, the United States Senate confirmed the late J. Klahr Huddle as Ambassador to Burma;[53] two days later the Burmese Ambassador, U Soe Nyun, presented his credentials. A procedure for filing war claims in Burma was also announced that month.

Just before the Burmese gained independence, the United States and Burma signed an agreement (December 22, 1947) putting into operation the program of international exchanges authorized by the Fulbright Act (PL 584, 79th Congress). The agreement, signed by U Tin Tut, Minister of Foreign Affairs, and R. Austin Acly, United States Chargé d'Affaires, was incorrectly heralded by the Department of State *Bulletin* as "Burma's first agreement with any foreign country to be signed in Burma." (The first such signed in Rangoon was the United Kingdom–Burma Defense Agreement, August 29, 1947—the so-called Bo Let Ya–Freeman Annex to the London-signed Nu-Attlee Independence Treaty of October 17, 1947.) It established the United States Educational Foundation in

Burma with a joint Burma-American Board with funds (local currency) derived from the sale of surplus property in Burma.[54]

Between this agreement and the fall of Nationalist China in September, 1949, the United States and Burma negotiated several minor agreements; one, for example, for the exchange of official publications and for the regulation of air communications.[55] During the summer of 1949, Burma's Foreign Minister, Dr. E Maung, met in Washington with Secretary Acheson for a "full and frank exchange of views." [56]

Thus, after a period of indifference on the part of the United States, official relations with Burma began with good will and the expectation of friendly relations on both sides. The United Kingdom maintained its primary responsibility for military assistance to Burma and for the training of Burmese defense forces. Since London and Rangoon had parted in a most amicable fashion, Washington did not have complications such as it had faced with Paris and the Hague. In addition, the United States welcomed Burma's entry into the United Nations on April 19, 1948. And in November, 1949, Burma joined the Far Eastern Commission that watched over the U.S. occupation of Japan until the peace treaty of 1951.

At this time, early 1948, despite the socialist cast of her ideological leadership and administration, Burma fitted rather snugly into the context of American-Asian policy: She was friendly with (but worried about) China; her independence, like that of the Philippines, was evidence of the declining significance of Western imperialism; she elected to remain within the economic sterling bloc despite having left the Commonwealth; and to some extent her defense was tied in with the United Kingdom. Since the United States had no great political, economic, or security interests in Burma, we could, without having made any prior postwar exertions, afford to regard the Land of Golden Pagodas, along with Pakistan, India, Ceylon, Thailand, the Philippines, and even Malaya, in conformity either with the "fundamental principles of righteousness and justice" itemized by President Truman as far back at 1945 or with the newer sixfold interim policy then aborning.

The first significant event to mar this comfortable outlook was the outcome in Burma of the series of Soviet-directed meetings held at Bombay in November-December, 1947, and at Calcutta, February-March, 1948. The Cominform had determined to strengthen its revolutionary efforts in South and Southeast Asia. India, Burma, Malaya, and Indonesia, in that order, were to experience the consequences of this insurrectionary thrust beginning in late March, 1948; action had already been initiated in Indochina and the Philippines. As indicated earlier (see Chapter 5), the Burmese Communists and their allies initiated their armed rebellion upon their return from the meetings in India, barely three months after the beginnings of independence.

U.S. intelligence in and out of the State Department was aware of this Soviet thrust. Whether or not it regarded the Communist rebellions as a feint to draw Western attention away from Europe and China is not especially relevant here. What is clear is that during late 1947, and all of 1948, the United States was keenly aware of the Communist advance in China but had elected to play what has been called a wait-and-see role in that quarter. There was no sign that it foresaw a possible link between a Communist China and the Communist rebellions in Burma and elsewhere in the region. Nor that, if it foresaw any such possible linkage, it would take steps to thwart it. Curiously, the burst of Communist rebellions in the region did not bring forth any prompt or urgent reaction in the United States. The U.S. did transfer eight to ten patrol boats and some lend-lease ammunition to Rangoon shortly after the rebellion started, but otherwise avoided any significant measures to aid the beleaguered Burmese Government. On the other hand, when the Burmese Government sought to block the Communist rebellion by vain attempts at leftist unity, it was criticized for this in England and in the United States. The U.S. Government hoped that the United Kingdom, with its long experience in the area, would somehow be able to help Burma put down the insurrection. In fact, the United States, in September, 1948, turned down a Burmese request for military assistance, suggesting that Burma turn to the British and to U.S. commercial channels. That the latter were subject to federal export controls which the government would not readily ease was not lost on the Burmese. In 1949, after the Karen National Defense Organization joined in the rebellion, U.S. policy toward Burma, because of mistaken regard for the Christian-led Karen rebels, seems to have forgone even the element of sympathy. George McT. Kahin, writing about Indonesia, remarks that "with the spring of 1949 came the nadir in America's position in Indonesia." [57] I would add, in Burma, too.

How does one read and evaluate American foreign policy in Asia in 1948-49—during the last months before China fell to Mao? The antipathy to Communism, the bold and successful moves to halt Stalin in Europe, need no further elaboration. The gradual Kuomintang withdrawal from the China mainland to the fortified islands and bases offshore is clear, however debatable its wisdom. But did this also mean a U.S. withdrawal from mainland Asia wherever the Communists happened to be vigorous and successful? Such a view makes no sense whatsoever even if U.S. economic-assistance programs and military lines in 1948-49 were overextended. Perhaps the U.S. was husbanding its military strength to face a Soviet invasion of Western Europe. The then Chief of Staff, General Omar Bradley, is quoted in *The New York Times* of April 26, 1948, as saying: "We are not sure that there is no war right away." A House Report of the Armed Services Committee for May 7, 1948, presented as its opinion the "new and ominous possibility that the Soviet Union may now be willing to risk a showdown." [58]

But such speculation still leaves unexplained why the United States made such an inadequate response to Communist maneuvers in Southeast Asia and in Burma in 1948 and 1949. The usually well-informed authors of the Council on Foreign Relations series, *The United States in World Affairs*, shed no light on this glaring fact, although they recognize it. For example, Richard P. Stebbins remarks that "though the United States refused to go to the rescue of the Chinese Nationalists or to be hastened into collective measures for the defense of other threatened areas, it still clung to certain elements of a strategic policy for the Far East. That policy, *so far as could be discerned*, was as yet [mid-1949] neither very comprehensive nor particularly vigorous [italics added]." [59] He later adds that "American policy for Southeast Asia had to await an adjustment by public and official opinion to the new events in China" [60]—a sort of anticipatory "agonizing reappraisal," to use the Dulles phrase of another period.

It might be argued that U.S. concern for Europe, evidenced in the dramatic and far-reaching policies initiated and executed by the first and second Truman Administrations, was so great and constituted, as implied above, such a drain on our economic resources and demobilized military that we could not afford any further drain in Asia. If such an argument is made, the burden of proof must accompany it, for there is no evidence that the American public and economy were asked to meet the threat in Europe and Asia.

The argument of hindsight, that "things did not go too far wrong," that no great tragedy befell Southern Asia because of weakness or ambivalence in U.S. policy, provides little truth and no comfort. The loss in mainland Southeast Asia, not yet at an end, is real and tragic. This argument, if made, glides over the Communist victory north of the Vietnamese 17th parallel and the Communist gains and continued threat in Laos and elsewhere in Southeast Asia. It also overlooks several additional items: the dire cost, in lives, treasure, and internal stability, of the Communist rebellion borne by Burma and other affected countries; the thwarted desire of the Burmese, especially in 1948 and early 1949, for some kind of Western strong-power alliance, which, when it was offered, came too late; and the pervasive feeling, difficult to document, but known to observers of Southern Asia, that somehow the West, because of race, culture, and past colonial traditions, was less concerned with Asian difficulties once it was removed from the seats of colonial power in Asia.

There is still another kind of loss. The newly independent countries of Southern Asia, Burma included, had little reason to acquire confidence in Western expressions of democratic and humanitarian concern. They were, at least until 1950, left to fend for themselves. This is, of course, what they said they wanted as they came out of the colonial era. But a helping hand, generously proffered when it was most needed, might have made a considerable difference. To speculate now on what might have been the outcome during those years if policies similar to those adopted toward Europe had been applied in Asia is not a fruitful theme. However, I believe that a strong program in Asia, comparable in time and related to the program in Europe, would have profoundly altered the course of history in that area. I believe it still can, if tried.

The end of 1949, which witnessed the Communist take-over in China, also marked the end of the wait-and-see policy. Secretary of State Acheson's "defensive perimeter" speech was a sign of this transition. The Acheson speech was a masterful lawyer's statement, but it was also an evasive one. Acheson answered his own question, "Has the State Department got an Asian policy?" by charging the questioners with "a depth of ignorance." However, he avoided a direct answer on the recent past by hiding behind the "incredibly diverse" patterns of Asia as the factor inhibiting the formulation of "a uniform policy." As if uniformity of policy were a necessary criterion for policy! One commonly expects that the broad outlines of any over-all policy, if such exists, must be suited to the instant case and perhaps thereby modified. Secretary Acheson removed U.S. military, political, and economic policy from the shores of mainland East Asia, and left Communist-embattled South and Southeast Asia as they had been during the previous years—under the primary leadership of America's Western allies. India and Pakistan were to be helped, but the major "responsibility is not ours." The short-lived Federal Indonesian–Dutch solution, following the action of the U.N. and the Round Table Conference at the Hague, was hailed as "a great success," as a result of which the improbable prediction was made that "relations of this government [Indonesia] with the Dutch will be very good." "The British have and are discharging their responsibility with the people of Malaya and are making progress." France was applauded for its alleged progress in Indochina, and the United States "would not want . . . to add to the burdens" carried by its Foreign Minister. Burma was dismissed with the curt and tendentious statement that "the situation . . . is highly confused . . . where five different factions have utterly disrupted the immediate government of the country."

There is no doubt that in early 1950, the U Nu government could not yet enforce its writ throughout the country—nor would it be able to do so for some time. But for the Secretary of State to describe that country in such journalistic and unreliable terms seems hardly fitting. Nor was it honest reporting at the time. Essentially Burma faced, in 1949 and early 1950, the combined difficulty of a Communist and ethnic rebellion. There were factions in each grouping; the rebellious forces were located in different parts of the country; their attacks were made under different flags and slogans, but basically, behind the newspaper headlines, it was evident that the Communists sought to overcome the government and the Karens sought an autonomous state outside the Union. The United Kingdom was either unwilling or unable to supply the legitimate government with the arms necessary to combat the Communist and other rebellious groups. By 1949, Burma had almost been "written off." [61] The West regarded it as a poor risk for military investment. No attempt had been made or proposed by Secretary Acheson to find any solution to the impasse. And a detachment of Kuomintang troops, defeated in their own country, were allowed or encouraged to stay in Burma, which further threatened her security.

Despite the Secretary's words about the countries of South and Southeast Asia, a new approach was in the making. Ambassador-at-Large Philip C. Jessup, a member of the group designated as Asian consultants to the State Department, was assigned to a tour of Asia. He left in December, 1949, and returned the next spring. In February, 1950, the Griffin Economic Cooperation Administration mission was similarly assigned to a rapid tour of Asia. From these and related developments, a new and more vigorous approach to South and Southeast Asia was cautiously broached. The outbreak of the Korean War in June, 1950, removed the basis for caution. Burma among others became a beneficiary. In September, the United States and Burma signed an agreement for economic aid to Burma.

Beginning in late 1949, U.S. policy toward Southeast Asia was in the process of being overhauled and strengthened. The stimulus to this reappraisal came from many directions. Among them were the complete Communist victory in China, domestic attacks on the administration's policies toward China, the inability of Britain and France to defend non-Communist Asia, and the resulting pressures on the United States to take over more and more responsibilities in the area. The Korean War gave additional urgency to policy formulation and helped to clarify U.S. objectives. Signs of the changed policy were not slow in coming.

Annus Mirabilis: A Year of Policy Formulation

On December 15, 1949, Philip C. Jessup was designated Ambassador-at-Large to review the situation in Asia and make recommendations. This new effort had been carried on since the preceding August by the committee consisting of Jessup, Raymond B. Fosdick, Everett Case, and John Leighton Stuart. In February, 1950, Ambassador Jessup presided over a regional conference of U.S. envoys at Bangkok, which considered "the affirmative steps which could be taken by the United States to carry out its announced policies of extending friendly support to the states in Asia which may desire such assistance." The conference recommended that the United States provide military and economic support for states resisting Communist aggression.[1]

It was also announced in February that a mission headed by R. Allen Griffin would visit Rangoon, Bangkok, Saigon, Singapore, and Djakarta "to prepare the way for the most expeditious and efficient use of whatever technical assistance funds may become available for that area."[2] In his inaugural address in January, 1949, President Truman had proposed as a supplement to the Economic

Cooperation Act (the Marshall Plan) the Point IV program of technical assistance, and as a result of the new direction of policy this program was to play an important role in Asia beginning in 1952 and 1953. In May, upon his return to Washington, Griffin recommended a $60 million economic- and technical-assistance program to be drawn from unexpended funds of the China-aid appropriation. Later he was appointed Southeast Asia Director for the Economic Cooperation Administration. Meanwhile, on March 21, 1950, the first formal trade agreement between Burma and Japan had been announced, providing for the two-way exchange of $49 million in goods during 1950.[3]

Other new and important policy statements were giving a fresh direction to U.S. policy. In a preface to the State Department's report on *United States Relations with China with Special Reference to the Period 1944-1949*, Secretary Acheson had in effect closed the book on a long tradition of support for Nationalist China. On January 12, 1950, in his "Crisis in Asia" speech, Acheson announced that the United States accepted the "necessity of assuming the military defense of Japan," and that the defensive perimeter of the Pacific, defined as "the Aleutians to Japan and then . . . to the Ryukyus," must and would be held. Later, on March 15, in an address before the Commonwealth Club in San Francisco, he suggested without further clarification that the United States would support free peoples resisting subversion by armed minorities or outside pressure.[4]

On January 31, in an address on "United States Economic Relations with South Asia," Assistant Secretary of State George C. McGhee demonstrated the growing importance of U.S. trade with Asia.[5]

In March, Ambassador Loy W. Henderson delivered an important address on "Objectives of U.S. Policies Toward Asia" before the Indian Council of World Affairs. This offered an impressive list of difficulties and handicaps, many of which are still relevant today:

> . . . deficiency of knowledge and understanding . . . of the points of view and the particular problems of various peoples of Asia . . . insufficiency of human and natural resources in the United States in the face of the world-wide demand . . . a high degree of sensitivity at any action on the part of foreigners which might even remotely be construed as an effort to influence the conduct of their internal affairs or of their relations with other countries.

Henderson went on to refer to fears in Asia of "some kind of economic imperialism" and power politics, the fear that cooperation with the United States might arouse the hostility of powerful forces, and the existence of national, religious, class, and other animosities.

Henderson then mentioned each of the countries of non-Communist Asia in turn, stressing U.S. willingness to assist their progress toward "economic stability, political independence, or self-government, and territorial integrity." Unlike the cavalier and superficial remarks on Burma made by Secretary Acheson and Assistant Secretary McGhee, Ambassador Henderson's references to Burma—the first such since the exchanges on Burma's first Independence Day—were thoughtful and sympathetic:

Of all the new states of Asia, with the possible exception of Korea, Burma has suffered the greatest vicissitudes. Severely damaged by war, it became independent before these damages were repaired and before its economy had recovered from the effects of military occupation. Then a series of terroristic acts deprived it of some of its most able leaders; and internal strife has added to the misery already existing as a result of world war. Nevertheless, the Burmese leaders and people had displayed both courage and tenacity in their efforts to maintain the integrity of their country. . . . I am not aware of the specific needs of Burma from the United States or of the extent to which the United States might be able to assist Burma just now. There can be no doubt, however, of the desire of the United States to do what it can in the circumstances to assist the Government and people of Burma in keeping their ship of state on a level keel.[6]

On the day of Henderson's address, March 27, Deputy Under-Secretary Dean Rusk, who was known to have a strong interest in Asian affairs, was appointed Assistant Secretary in charge of Far Eastern Affairs. Shortly afterward, the retirement of George F. Kennan from the State Department gave an added impetus to Asian interests, for Kennan's influence, it was widely and correctly assumed, had reinforced the traditional Department emphasis on European problems.

Thus, by 1950, the United States, by choice and necessity, was beginning to assume a more active role in Asian areas formerly left to British responsibility and a more active role toward the Republic of Indonesia; it had also made the decision to support French policy in Indochina by extending recognition (February 7, 1950) to Vietnam, Cambodia, and Laos as so-called independent states within the French Union. Apparently the new turn was concerted with the major Western allies. For example, in January, 1950, a Conference of Commonwealth Ministers, convened by the United Kingdom at Colombo, resulted in the launching of the Colombo Plan for Asia, which in turn was strongly backed by the United States through its economic-aid programs.[7]

This major shift in emphasis took place to the accompaniment of domestic disputes over U.S. foreign policy. Senator Joseph R. McCarthy's irresponsible attacks on the State Department were at their height in the first half of 1950. Within the Republican Party, the bipartisan foreign-policy approach, until then associated with the names of Senator Arthur S. Vandenberg and consultant John Foster Dulles, had come under continuous attack.[8] Seldom in the twentieth century had a Secretary of State been so bitterly attacked by the opposition as was Secretary Acheson during this period. His concept of a defensive perimeter supported by situations of strength was fiercely debated. It won little confidence in national and international circles.

Then Communist aggression created a new situation favorable to the administration's Asian policy. The invasion of South Korea at 4 A.M. on June 25, 1950 (an event which, according to one important spokesman of the State Department, had not been anticipated), accentuated American interest in Asia. There is no question that the administration had determined several years before the final event that it could not stop the Communists in China; there is also no question that within hours of the invasion of Korea the administration determined that it would contest by arms this evidence of Communist aggression in Korea. The final debacle in mainland China, and the response to it by sincere as well as malevolent forces at home, precipitated this need for an accentuated Asian policy. The Korean War gave additional urgency and character to its formulation and execution. As John Foster Dulles, then a consultant to Secretary of State Acheson, said: "The Korean attack opened a new chapter in history. No one knows how that chapter will end." [9] The Korean attack opened the way for the administration to press forward with the new Asian policy that had been in the making since late 1949.

This policy, which was to remain basically unchanged until the French disaster at Dien Bien Phu in May, 1954, was clearly set forth by Assistant Secretary Rusk in a speech given on September 9, 1950, on "Fundamentals of Far Eastern Policy." [10] It opened by stressing both hopes and obstacles. The United States entertained "hopes for Asia and the world," hopes of "freedom, equal partnership, security, peaceful progress, material well-being, cultural exchange and good neighbors." Among obstacles he listed ignorance and indifference: "We have much to learn and unlearn . . . we are inclined to forget that we have relations with other people, not control over them." He said that Americans sometimes proposed solutions for the problems of other peoples that often had "nothing to do with their situation in fact, nor with their cultural traditions, their moral codes, their capabilities, or their needs." Referring to domestic discrimination against Asians and other nonwhites in American communities, Rusk reminded his listeners: "The peoples of Asia are sitting as a great jury and are passing judgment upon our way of life; there is no place for us to hide from our own performance."

Assistant Secretary Rusk went on to outline a program for action. The United States could help Asian peoples and governments, but "we cannot take over." The United States had no desire for privilege. It would support the aspirations of the peoples of Asia to be free, to determine their own institutions. It would act vigorously and loyally as a member of the United Nations to deal with aggression, to carry out U.N. resolutions in favor of a free and united Korea. It would seek a peaceful settlement of the Formosa problem by international action while sustaining the historic ties of friendship between the American and Chinese peoples. It would strongly support the full and equal participation of the nations of Asia in the family of nations, and would back applications of Ceylon, Indonesia, Nepal, and Korea for membership in the United Nations. It proposed to move toward a peace settlement with Japan. It viewed with sympathy Asian regional efforts for security[11] and welfare and would work with its friends in Asia to strengthen their own institutions. It would provide military assistance to Indochina and the Philippines, and to other nations in Southeast Asia whose security was being threatened. It would offer economic and technical assistance, and would support the Point IV and U.N. aid programs for Asia. It proposed to expand its information and exchange programs in this part of the world.

The statements of Henderson, Rusk, and others constituted forward-looking Asian policy. One could point out that they retained the now-typical ambivalence: the oft-repeated statement of support for the freedom of the peoples of Asia and the simultaneous support for the French in Indochina.[12] They also suffered from certain illusions illustrated in Secretary Acheson's view: "We still believe that the Chinese are going to be Chinese before they are going to be Communists. We believe that the people of Indo-China will see this menace which is coming towards them." [13] But no one could deny that here was a reasoned and reasonably full U.S. Asian policy adopted in this *annus mirabilis*. Its test would be its application to Asia in general and to specific countries. Then, as now, the presence and threat of Communist China helped to stimulate the formulation and execution of Asian policy in the United States.

The new policy toward Asia had immediate results for Burma. Both the Jessup and Griffin missions included visits to Burma. The Griffin mission arrived in Rangoon on March 23, one day after Prime Minister Nu had issued a new invitation to foreign capital to invest in Burma as an "instrument for upholding democracy." [14] One result of the mission was the signing of an agreement on economic cooperation, on September 13, 1950. On the occasion of the signing, Ambassador David McK. Key explained its purposes:

The purpose of agreement . . . is to assist Burma to achieve those sound economic conditions and stable international economic relationships so necessary for the maintenance of individual liberty, free institutions, and independence. Under the agreement the United

States is prepared to furnish economic and technical assistance toward these ends.

The detailed working out of the economic cooperation program will be decided by mutual agreement between the Government of Burma and the Government of the United States. The nature of the projects to be carried out will be determined on the basis of the proposals put forth by the Government of Burma. In playing her part, the United States can provide physical equipment and technical experience to be applied to recovery, rehabilitation, and economic development in a wide variety of fields, including agriculture, mining, transportation, communications, medical, and general health projects. The program can also include the provision of consumer goods of importance to general welfare.

The United States Government will look forward to receiving from the Government of Burma her detailed proposals and is fully confident that, aided by our joint efforts, Burma will move steadily along the road to recovery and economic strength.[15]

The text of the agreement spelled out the purposes and procedures in some detail and defined the status of the U.S. Special Technical and Economic Mission (generally known as STEM), leaving specific decisions to be worked out within the general framework of its provisions.

Two months later the United States made available to Burma ten river patrol craft—the Burmese home minister insisted that only eight arrived—under the U.S. Mutual Defense Assistance Program adopted in October, 1949. Patrol craft were of special value because of "the unique importance of the navigable river systems of Burma to commerce and the over-all well being of that country." Training for Burmese naval personnel and spare parts for the completely rehabilitated vessels were also provided.[16]

The new U.S. policy was off to a good start in Burma. Useful economic and minor military programs were steadily added to modestly expanded cultural- and educational-exchange programs. In the immediate turmoil of the Communist takeover in China, and especially in the stress of the war in Korea, Congress was willing to provide substantial funds for these and similar purposes.

The new U.S. missions to Burma, and, above all, the aid agreement, gave a tremendous boost to Burmese morale. Their effect was all the greater because 1949 had been a perilous year, in which the survival of the republic had been at stake. Within Burma, satisfaction over the shift in U.S. policy, and especially with the aid agreement, was heightened by the contrasting delays in negotiating a Commonwealth loan. Using Nehru as an intermediary, Burma had asked for aid from the United Kingdom in 1949; about thirteen months later, at the end of June, 1950, it received a Commonwealth loan of £6 million. To the Burmese, the delay was a mark of no confidence. The negotiations had been accompanied by statements of Commonwealth leaders in favor of the rebellious

Karens and by a dispute over Burma's preindependence debts to India and Britain. In the end the loan was never used. The only attacks on the U.S. aid as "American imperialist intervention" came from the crypto-Communists who still held membership in the Anti-Fascist People's Freedom League. It was soon after their failure to block its ratification in the Chamber of Deputies on October 5, 1950, that this group split off from the AFPFL to form the Burma Workers and Peasants Party.

The Application of U.S. Policy: The Dominant Partner

The major focus of U.S. policy toward Burma during 1950 and the next several years was on economic and technical assistance. The aid program was designed to build strength through technical and material aid to essential services and through economic rehabilitation and development, as in other countries of Southeast Asia that were "not secure against internal subversion, political infiltration, or military aggression." [17] It was based on the expectation that the national government would gain political strength and stability through the aid program, which would also demonstrate "the genuine interest of the United States in the welfare of the people of Southeast Asia." Productivity, political stability, and a concrete demonstration of U.S. friendship were the prime goals, as a contribution to thwarting any further expansion by international Communism in general, and by Communist China in particular.

Although the Griffin mission and the STEM staff consulted Burma's leaders about the content of the proposed program, Washington rapidly became the senior partner in determining its specific objectives. These objectives were to be achieved quickly in order to justify the initial decision to undertake a crash program. In the first years only a few, unheard voices were raised to say that the task was essentially a long-range one.[18] At that time, of course, the United States had relatively little knowledge and even less experience in Southern Asia. Nor could it rely on the experience of its Western allies, since they were then the recent, not especially loved, ex-colonial rulers. The senior partner-and-donor relationship was initially less onerous for the Burmese to bear because there was general agreement within Burma and between Burma and the United States with respect to the problems that had to be solved.

Burma needed to establish internal security, law, and order. After repairing the physical damage caused to the economy by war and insurrection, the Burmese would have to restore and expand existing transportation, communications, and public utilities, and develop agriculture, forestry, mining, processing, and export trade. In the meantime, the nation required substantial imports of certain urgently needed commodities. Burma would have to develop numerous technical and administrative skills, as well as technical assistance and equipment for its development plans. It would have to train a skilled labor force for industry, mining, agriculture, and government, as well as managers, executives, scientists, teachers, and students.

Burma lacked, and would now need, new institutions for capital formation and investment; creation and expansion of facilities for private, public, and foreign investments and savings; systems of commercial banking available to rural and smaller urban areas. It would have to provide effective incentives to the city worker and rural cultivator to encourage them to acquire the skills needed to increase productivity in all enterprises. Public administration and local self-government would have to be improved, and the forms and practices of self-proclaimed democratic ideals would have to be introduced into state and district governments. Finally, there was the problem of providing better health, education, housing, and other services. Obviously, problems of this magnitude required long-term and patient efforts; they could not be solved by a crash program.

Burma had, it is true, made encouraging progress in the postwar years 1945-48. Its national product in fixed 1947-48 prices had moved up from 61 per cent of the prewar level (1938-39 = 100) to 72 per cent at independence. The catastrophic series of insurrections reversed this trend sharply, reducing it by 1950 to the postwar low. Villagers were streaming into the cities in search of security, creating squalid and unhealthy shantytowns. Per capita production was about four-sevenths, and per capita consumption about two-thirds, of prewar levels. Rice exports had declined to one-fourth, while Burma's entire foreign trade was but a fraction of its prewar volume. Revenues had been declining in a time when expenditures were rising, in good part to combat the insurrections.

To help Burma cope with its multifaceted emergency, the Griffin mission had outlined a broad program of projects in many fields: agriculture; public health; education; industry, transport, and communications; public administration; engineering and economic planning; exchange of governmental leaders, and the provision of sorely needed commodities. It estimated that the program would cost about $12.2 million between March, 1950, and the end of U.S. fiscal year 1951.[19]

Apart from UNICEF aid, which provided dried milk from U.S. contributions, the STEM program was the first major foreign-aid effort in Burma. Begun in the fall of 1950, it was continued formally until June 30, 1953. For the first two years the program in the United States was under the independent jurisdiction of the Economic Cooperation Administration and its successor, the Mutual Security Administration. In July, 1952, control over it was transferred to the Technical Cooperation Administration (Point IV) of the Department of State.

The STEM programed total appropriations of $31 million for the fiscal years 1951, 1952, and 1953, as follows:

TABLE 1

FUNDS OBLIGATED TO BURMA PROGRAM [20]
(*in millions of dollars*)

	Agri-culture	In-dustry	Transpor-tation	Health	Public Adminis-tration	Edu-cation	Commu-nity De-velop-ment	Miscel-laneous	Total
Fiscal year 1951	1.25	.02	3.62	1.79	.04	.65	.80	2.63	10.80
Fiscal year 1952	3.75	1.53	3.40	2.10	1.12	.48	—	1.29	13.67
Fiscal year 1953	2.27	.21	.33	2.72	—	1.28	—	.12	6.93
Total	7.27	1.76	7.35	6.61	1.16	2.41	.80	4.04	31.40

After STEM was terminated, on June 30, 1953, certain projects already budgeted and under way were continued and concluded with U.S. funds and staff as late as 1955; others were stopped and the funds were released. In all, of the $31 million appropriated, approximately $21.2 million was expended, as follows:

TABLE 2

FUNDS EXPENDED FOR BURMA
(*in millions of dollars*)

Transportation, public works, and communications	5
Commodity imports to relieve shortages	4
Agriculture	3
Health and sanitation	3
Industry and natural resources	1.5
Education	1.5
Engineering, mining, and economic contract services	2
Other	1.2
Total	21.2

These expenditures were substantially increased by Burma Government funds for a variety of purposes in connection with the program; and by what came to be called the counterpart fund. This fund—in domestic currency—was generated by the sale in the local market of $4 million of U.S.-supplied commodities and by deposits equivalent to the "commensurate value" of landed dollar materials required for approved projects. No final accounting was made of these funds. STEM calculated that Burma had committed herself to an expenditure of kyats 100 million (approximately $21 million) in order to complete the projects originally projected for fiscal year 1951-53; this total was later reduced when the Burmese Government canceled the aid agreement and abandoned many of the projects.

The Burmese Government appointed a Burma Economic Aid Committee (BEAC), composed of the leading secretaries of the ministries primarily involved in the program, to serve as its formal agency in dealing with STEM. The first chairman was U Hla Maung, a former member of the Indian Civil Service and subsequently Ambassador to Yugoslavia. The second chairman, U Tin Pe, lost his life in a plane accident while on an official mission. Formally, BEAC reported to the National Planning Minister, U Win, who later became Ambassador to the United States. In practice, the Prime Minister and other Cabinet members were frequently involved in decisions. At the height of the program STEM had approximately seventy-five Americans, including professional and office personnel, on its immediate staff. At least another fifty-five Americans were recruited for various U.S. contractual services that were supplied to Burma but paid for by STEM appropriations. There were also about 200 local employees, ranging from guards to professionals. Expenditures under the program were designed to cover more than ninety individually negotiated project agreements, under the system instituted and controlled by Washington—a system that placed a premium on multiple projects "across the board" of production and social capital investment.

The task of fitting the American staff physically and psychologically into overcrowded, battle-scarred, and insanitary Rangoon presented constant problems, and these were further complicated by the difficulties and delays of recruitment and security clearances for those who were willing to accept posts there.[21] Salaries for the noncontractual personnel, modest at best in comparison with their salaries at home, did not make the posts especially attractive. People needed for senior posts frequently accepted the same salaries as they would have received at home and occasionally suffered a financial loss. Contract personnel were able to negotiate considerably better financial arrangements, as they were employed by "private industry"; in addition, by remaining in Burma for more than eighteen months, they enjoyed substantial reductions in their federal income taxes. Both these groups were better paid than the career foreign-service officers and staff, who did not consider that their own permanent tenure justified the disparity in salaries. These problems, not peculiar to Burma, have arisen wherever U.S. aid and related programs operate in underdeveloped countries.

The difficulties that beset American personnel were compounded by the conditions that prevailed in Burma. The small number of capable senior civil servants and ministers had far too much to do. They could neither create suitable conditions nor find the qualified technical and administrative personnel to work with the Americans on the large number of projects that were approved. Burmese planning ambitions had clearly run ahead of Burmese hands; and these ambitions were furthered by some American engineers and economists who failed to understand the significant noneconomic factors that are required for successful economic development. Conflict between chairman Hla Maung of BEAC and his lifelong friend, Edward Law Yone, editor of *The Nation*, over the allocation of funds for a Burma Journalist Association building erupted into a bitter public fight and a lawsuit for libel and defamation of character instituted by Hla Maung. As one consequence of this private folly, STEM became the target of a sustained attack from *The Nation*.[22] These difficulties, however, did not affect the political relations between the governmental agencies of Burma and the United States.

The first major political difficulty arose after the U.S. Congress passed the Mutual Security Act of 1951. Prior legislative authority for the aid program in Burma stemmed from the terms of the China Area Aid Act of 1950, incorporated as Title II of the Foreign Economic Assistance Act of 1950, and not from the Point IV title of the same act. This legislative decision made Burma eligible to receive aid through the Economic Cooperation Administration as an independent Washington agency. Such aid in goods and services, unlike that of Point IV administered by the Department of State, was not limited to programs based primarily on technical assistance. The 1951 act, on the other hand, brought all previous aid legislation and administration together under the Mutual Security Administration, with the general aim "to assist other peoples in their efforts to achieve self-government or independence under circumstances which will enable them to assume an equal station among the free nations of the world and to fulfill their responsibilities for self-government or independence." [23]

In Section 2 of the Act of 1951, Congress amplified its purposes. These were:

> to maintain the security and to promote the foreign policy of the United States by authorizing military, economic, and technical assistance to friendly countries to strengthen the mutual security and individual and collective defenses of the free world, to develop their resources in the interest of their security and independence and the national interest of the United States and to facilitate the effective participation of those countries in the United Nations system for collective security.

It then defined "eligibility for assistance" in Section 511, under which the recipient country must agree to the following conditions:

> (a) No military, economic, or technical assistance pursuant to this Act (other than assistance provided under section 408(e) of the Mutual Defense Assistance Act of 1949, as amended) shall be supplied to any nation in order to further military effort unless the President finds that the supplying of such assistance will strengthen the security of the United States and unless the recipient country has agreed to—

(1) join in promoting international understanding and good will, and maintaining world peace;

(2) take such action as may be mutually agreed upon to eliminate causes of international tension;

(3) fulfill the military obligations which it has assumed under multilateral or bilateral agreements or treaties to which the United States is a party;

(4) make consistent with its political and economic stability, the full contribution permitted by its manpower, resources, facilities, and general economic condition to the development and maintenance of its own defensive strength and the defensive strength of the free world;

(5) take all reasonable measures which may be needed to develop its defense capacities; and

(6) take appropriate steps to insure the effective utilization of the economic and military assistance provided by the United States. (b) No economic or technical assistance shall be supplied to any other nation unless the President finds that the supplying of such assistance will strengthen the security of the United States and promote world peace, and unless the recipient country has agreed to join in promoting international understanding and good will, and in maintaining world peace, and to take such action as may be mutually agreed upon to eliminate causes of international tension.

The temper of Congress was fairly clear. The House Foreign Affairs Committee indicated that the United States "can help effectively only those of our friends who help themselves, help each other and help us." Some commentators have held that Congress was merely elaborating the declared purposes of the act.[24] In any case, it was clear that Congress sought to secure an overt or more direct commitment to U.S. concepts of collective security on the part of the recipients of aid, especially from those who had adopted a neutralist foreign policy.

Section 511 met with immediate disfavor abroad. Those countries that had security pacts with the United States saw no reason for making new pledges under section 511(a). At the least it would mean writing amendments to existing bilateral aid agreements and treaties, and it might even make it necessary to renegotiate them. It was felt abroad that section 511(b) appended meaningless but offensive conditions to offers of nonmilitary aid. Asian suspicions and anxieties were accentuated when an Indonesian government (the Sukiman Cabinet) fell, apparently because it had been willing to accept section 511(a), contrary to parliamentary and popular opinion. "Aid with strings" became a favorite complaint leveled at the United States.

In Burma the immediate reaction to the new legislation was quite heated. The press construed the new act to mean that Burma would have to accept military aid as a condition for receiving economic assistance, and this, it was widely felt, would endanger Burma's neutralist foreign policy. On January 10, 1952, the government temporarily suspended the aid program pending clarification of the issue, while Parliament plunged into debate over it. On February 6, the government agreed to an exchange of notes and to the resumption of the program.[25] Burma rejected section 511(a). Finally, after protracted negotiations in which State Department officials tried to appease Asian sensibilities without departing from Congressional requirements, a watered-down interpretation of section 511(b) was agreed upon, under which Burma pledged her support for the principles of peace as expressed in the United Nations Charter.[26] The episode served as a political irritant. It ran counter to other U.S. interests in Burma and elsewhere, and it exacerbated the widespread suspicions in Asia about which Henderson and Rusk had spoken so clearly. It gave strong support to anti-American propaganda, which criticized the United States for exacting a political price for its assistance. "Aid without strings" became a counter-demand even among those Asians friendly to the United States.

The aid program in Burma rode out the flurry caused by the "strings" of section 511. For the fiscal year ending June, 1952, STEM and BEAC were working on a $14 million program appropriation. Operational difficulties gradually gave way to better knowledge and understanding on both sides. STEM began to plan for fiscal 1953—beginning on July 1—in more genuine bilateral terms than had been possible in the earlier days of the crash program. In the spring of 1952, Prime Minister U Nu indicated that ECA aid had "contributed substantially to economic reconstruction and development," but that "the aid has been too restricted in amount to make a substantial impression in all the spheres that it has covered, with the result that even after two years of aid, the ostensible results are not many." He continued, "This is inevitable, having regard to the emphasis on quality rather than quantity, but it has also been responsible for many of the criticisms that have been made of ECA." He thought that ECA's many projects had helped initiate work that would enable the Burmese to continue on their own. He therefore suggested that "the time has come to consider whether the aid received under ECA should not be applied to certain concentrated spheres, so that not only would the contribution it makes be effective but the results would be seen and appreciated by the people of the Union of Burma." In particular, he proposed, beginning with fiscal year 1953, "to apply the bulk of ECA aid received in future to two main spheres, namely Public Health and Education." He did not wish to exclude entirely all other departments, but if they retained limited access to ECA dollar procurement the Union budget would expedite their execution. Among tentative suggestions for large-scale projects, he proposed a hospital and public-sanitation program, a dairy farm, an agricultural college, a second medical college, a veterinary institute, and a technical institute.[27]

These proposals for social capital aid, which would be large, significant, and visible to the Burmese, originally met with objections on the part of several Burmese Cabinet ministers and secretaries whose departments would thereby lose the benefit of dollar aid. But they were approved by the Cabinet and transmitted to Washington as the basic program for the new fiscal year beginning in July, 1953. They had acquired strong political and public backing in Burma and were based on the expectation of receiving from the United States for fiscal year 1953 an aid allocation approximating the $14 million received in fiscal year 1952. These proposals and request for funds were sent as usual to the independently administered ECA sector of Washington's Mutual Security Administration. However, without prior consultation with the Burma Government or STEM officials in Rangoon, the Burma aid program was suddenly transferred (with others) from ECA to the Technical Cooperation Administration. The latter, lacking previous contact with the program in Burma, now had the duty of quickly passing on its content and allocating funds for it for fiscal year 1953. TCA, again without consultation in Rangoon, cut the proposed budget to 50 per cent of the previous year. Since this cut was proportionately much greater than those imposed on the programs of other countries, the Burmese concluded that this had been done in retaliation for their stand on section 511. The only rational ground for Washington's decision was the rapid growth of Burma's foreign-exchange earnings because of the increase in prices of rice and other primary export products during the Korean War. If this was a factor in Washington's decision, it was not communicated to the Burmese. Nor was the impending decline of rice prices, which began in mid-1953, taken into account.

Despite the reduction from $14 to $7 million, Prime Minister Nu was determined to ask the Point IV administration to approve the concentrated type of program he had earlier suggested. In principle, such programs of social capital investment had been acceptable to Washington under previous aid policies, though greater stress had usually been placed on the use of aid dollars to stimulate production. Burma, which was enjoying the temporary benefits of the Korean War boom, was willing to spend its ample foreign-exchange reserves, primarily sterling, for capital goods required to stimulate production, and therefore preferred to use dollars to build social capital in ways that would benefit Burma and reflect well on the United States. Though the Burmese decision was based on political and humanitarian considerations, it can be argued that their proposed U.S.–Burma investment in infrastructure would enhance other investment in production. However, TCA's response to these proposals was far from encouraging; it was now inclined to stress production projects. U Nu therefore decided to send a Cabinet-level mission, headed by an able business executive and cabinet member, M. A. Raschid, to discuss the program with the Washington officials. At the request of Prime Minister Nu, the author, as director of STEM, also went to Washington, so that if the decisions were made promptly, their execution could be expedited.

The Burmese mission received a somewhat reluctant invitation to Washington. There it found that the type of program proposed by U Nu was not congenial to TCA conceptions. (The mission encountered another kind of lack of congeniality: While sightseeing on his own, its leader, a Burmese Muslim born of Indian parents, was refused service in a Washington restaurant on grounds of color.) Finally, after considerable Washington "persuasion," a much-compromised program of more than twenty projects was accepted by the Burmese.[28] It did not have the characteristic that U Nu had so wisely sought: a small number of substantial and visible projects that would benefit Burma and reflect well on the United States.

These experiences strengthened the view among Burmese that American aid brought with it a number of undesirable strings. Whether or not STEM might have brought about some improvements in the situation during the following year will never be known, for at this very time the problem of the Kuomintang troops who had escaped into Burma entered an acute stage. These forces, it was estimated, had grown tenfold between 1951 and 1953, from 1,200 to 12,000.

Disruption and Dissolution

In February, 1953, a combined KMT-Karen force attacked the airfield at Loikaw, capital of the Kayah state. Burmese troops repelled the attack, but only after the home of an American aid official had been hit by random bullets, happily without personal damage to its occupants. With the cooperation of the embassy's plane and crew, I flew to Loikaw and evacuated the family. In March, the press gave wide currency also to a second story that "three white men," presumed to be Americans, had been killed in battle while aiding the KMT.[29] The three men were "white"; their nationality could not be discovered. One cannot interrogate dead men.

After having attempted unsuccessfully to enlist the good offices of the United States in the matter, the Burmese Government decided to take its complaint against the KMT to the United Nations and simultaneously to terminate the bilateral aid agreement. These decisions were influenced by a variety of factors.

The boldness of the KMT attacks in February-March, 1953, was perhaps the factor that triggered Burma's move. But, in addition, Burmese leaders were dismayed at their inability—and the inability of U.S. ambassadors in Burma—to get any help from Washington, which they regarded, rightfully, as having considerable influence with Taipeh, the source of the trouble. They were also unhappy with the outcome of the Raschid Mission, with the sharp curtailment in the magnitude and content of the aid program, and with the earlier disturbance over section 511. These experiences did not conform to their conception of "aid without strings." Some among their more ideologically minded socialist leaders, for example Kyaw Nyein and Ba Swe, anticipated new difficulties from the change of administrations in Washington. To them, the Republicans resembled British Tories, for whom they had little regard. They expected that the Republican victory in 1952 would strengthen Chiang Kai-shek's position; this in turn might strengthen the KMT forces on Burma's soil, thereby opening the way for Peking to put severe pressure on Burma. Her vulnerability to this pressure was enhanced because, despite her willingness to accept aid from any quarter, Burma had thus far received aid only from the West, and chiefly from the United States. Burmese leaders thought this was a danger worth accepting if the aid—of all kinds—was worth accepting and if political relations between Burma and the United States and other Western countries were warm and effectively friendly. Doubts about these matters made the political hazard of one-source aid less attractive.

The attitude of Burma's leaders was also influenced by their misreading of the country's economic prospects. In early 1953, Burma's economy was booming because of the Korean War, and despite signs to the contrary, Burmese leaders and U.S. contract advisers were excessively optimistic about the future. During 1951-52, rice exports had climbed from one-fourth to one-third of their prewar high, and were rising both in quantity and price. By 1952-53, gross national product (in constant 1947-48 prices) had also climbed from the 1949-50 low of 61 per cent to 79 per cent. American aid was a relatively small item in this rosy financial situation, whether measured against gross national product or against the government budget.

Finally, Burmese leaders were highly encouraged by the international response to their leadership in the First Asian Socialist Conference, which they had called together at Rangoon in January, 1953. Political currents in favor of a "third force," free from the international entanglements of capitalism and Communism and critical of both, were running strong.

Thus, it was a combination of reasons that led Burma to abrogate the U.S. aid agreement on March 17, 1953—the first such instance in U.S. experience. In a letter to Ambassador William Sebald, Foreign Minister Sao Hkun Hkio wrote as follows:

I am to request you under Article V of the Economic Cooperation Agreement between our two governments that the Government of the United States of America will accept notice that we do not desire the aid program to continue beyond June 30, 1953. The Government of the Union of Burma, however, wish to put on record their appreciation and gratitude for the materials and services received under the Economic Cooperation Agreement which are of great help to them in implementing their rehabilitation programs.

The original language of the above note had referred to the provocation of the KMT forces in Burma, but this passage was deleted by informal agreement between the Embassy and the Foreign Minister. Only in 1960 did Prime Minister Nu publicly relate the "cessation of American assistance in 1953" to the "aggression [of] the Chinese Kuomintang group which owes its very existence to American support." [30]

With this step, Burma's relations with the United States suffered a very serious setback, though not a mortal blow. Reporting for the *New York Herald Tribune*, March 29-31, 1953, Homer Bigart, then in Rangoon, described it as a "painful defeat" for American policy in Southeast Asia and India. In the meantime, just a few days previously U Nu had met with Prime Minister Nehru in the Naga Hills on the Indo-Burmese border to enlist India's backing for Burma's complaint to the United Nations. Indeed, it was in large part because of India's firm support that the Seventh General Assembly adopted a Mexico-Lebanon-Argentine-Chile resolution (fifty-nine votes in favor, none against, China abstaining), condemning "the presence of these forces in Burma and their hostile acts against that country" and endorsing the "good offices of certain member States" designed to remove the KMT forces from Burma.[31]

Almost simultaneously with the announcement of the end of the aid agreement and before Burma's complaint was successfully upheld by the Seventh General Assembly, Washington belatedly offered its good offices to help solve the KMT problem. Burma accepted. A four-nation committee representing the United States and Thailand, meeting separately with Burma and China (Taiwan) began to arrange for the voluntary repatriation of KMT troops.[32]

The termination of the aid agreement took effect on June 30, 1953. Phased close-out procedures were adopted satisfactory to both governments. Burma assumed sole responsibility for approximately $4.65 million of incompleted projects, including retention of a number of American engineering and economic contractual services that had previously been paid out of U.S. funds. This continuing support was in a sense an endorsement of some aspects of the U.S. aid program.

Ironically, the termination of the aid program and the belated setting up of the good-offices committee that the Burmese had earlier requested in vain served to bring Burma more sharply into focus in U.S. policy-thinking. In November, 1953, Vice-President and Mrs. Nixon visited Burma. They were lodged in the Presidential House and otherwise feted, and the press gave them a warm welcome, publicizing their appearance in Burmese national dress at a presidential reception. The following month Burma was also visited by a congressional mission to Southeast Asia and the Pacific, headed by Walter H. Judd. In its report, it recommended "careful consideration to the problems and effects resulting from the termination of the Burma program with a view to ascertaining the lesson that may be applicable to other programs."[33] Unfortunately, the lessons were not drawn in time to affect the sequence of events surrounding the "Burmese Rice Case," which led to the large-scale barter, trade, and aid program of the Sino-Soviet bloc with Burma and elsewhere in Asia. (See Chapter 15.)

As Burma felt the pinch of a recession in late 1953 and especially in 1954, her leaders made new overtures to the United States. They were prepared for a resumption of American aid, but not on a grant basis.[34] In February, 1955, Secretary of State Dulles, after attending a three-day SEATO conference at Bangkok, made a brief stopover at Rangoon where he conferred for ninety minutes with Prime Minister Nu. He went there, he said, neither "to woo or to be wooed," but to explain U.S. SEATO and other policies.[35]

In return, Prime Minister Nu was invited to Washington to meet with President Eisenhower. His visit, from June 24 to July 16, 1955, was not only one of courtesy. In the two years since the end of the aid program, Burma's economic fortunes had taken a turn for the worse. The price of rice had fallen sharply after the Korean War. Though Burma's exports had steadily mounted in volume, their value had declined substantially. The price of rice, for example, had fallen from the Korean War boom average of K849 per long ton to K513 in the first quarter of 1955.[36] This decline, together with the rising demand for capital and consumer goods, was causing considerable strain on Burma's foreign reserves.[37] As a result, Burma's leaders were preparing to cut back their planned targets, which they did at the end of 1955 by adopting the more modest First Four-Year Plan. During his visit, U Nu asked the United States to assist Burma in selling its rice stocks for cash or credit.[38] He did not succeed in this, but his visit contributed to a new interest in Burma's problems and later to a renewal of U.S. economic aid on a new basis.

The Application of U.S. Policy: The New Phase

U Nu's visit brought its first fruits seven months later. On February 8, 1956, the U.S. agreed (*TIAS* 3498) to deliver to Burma $22.7 million in surplus agricultural products, with payment in local currency, as authorized by the Agricultural Trade and Development Assistance Act (P.L. 480) of 1954. Of the total, raw cotton, to be used for processing in third countries into textiles for sale in Burma, accounted for $17.5 million. The purpose of these textile imports, processed in Japan, India, the United Kingdom, and West Germany, was to lower the cost of living in Burma. The balance of the agricultural deliveries consisted of $2 million in dairy products, $2.1 million in tobacco leaf, and $200,000 in fruits; $900,000 was allocated to transportation costs.[39] Burma was to pay for these commodities either in kyats or dollars over forty years at 4 or 3 per cent interest, respectively. Thus the "sales" under P.L. 480 were in effect a loan. However, about 80 per cent of the funds, equivalent to more than $17 million, was to remain in Burma for the purpose of promoting economic development, and the balance was to be used for U.S. local expenditures in Burma.

This innovating device of P.L. 480 "sales" for local currency of U.S. surplus commodities to Burma (and other countries) renewed the government-to-government aid relationship and provided beneficial results to both parties. The United States was able to diminish its agricultural surpluses and storage costs; Burma was able to conserve foreign exchange in the implementation of her development programs. The sales of the needed commodities to domestic consumers helped to restrain rises in the cost of living, and provided a fund which was then used in Burma as "loans" and "grants" for projects jointly approved by the two governments. Since the recipient country, in this case Burma, enjoys the option of paying for these commodities in local currency—usually nonconvertible—it is questionable whether those portions of the "sales" designated as loans will ever be repaid. Sooner or later the United States will find it expedient to write off remaining loans. In the interim, these P.L. 480 sales to Burma, and additional direct dollar-grant aid, have constituted the substance of U.S. aid to Burma since 1956.

In March, 1956, the International Cooperation Administration announced that it had purchased 10,000 tons of Burma's rice for shipment to Pakistan (*TIAS* 3619, signed June 30, 1956). Payment of approximately $1.1 million was to be made by making certain training facilities in the United States available for Burma's needs and by sending American technicians to Burma. This barter arrangement and the P.L. 480 sale or loan were extremely well received in Burma.

One year later, on March 21, 1957, the United States and Burma signed a new Economic Cooperation Agreement (*TIAS* 3931, entered into force on October 9), which extended to Burma a line of credit not exceeding $25 million. This could be repaid on the same kyat or dollar basis as the earlier surplus-products agreement. This agreement was amended twice, in September, 1959, and June, 1960 (*TIAS* 4326 and 4601).

In 1958-59, four additional agreements were concluded. The first was a second P.L. 480 sale (May 27, 1958; *TIAS* 4036, amended, on March 11, 1959, October 10, 1960, and June 1, 1961), amounting to approximately $18 million, with a related assignment for development projects of kyats equivalent to approximately $15 million. The second was a U.S.-financed Indian Textile Agreement (August 25, 1958, *TIAS* 4104) equivalent to $5 million in Indian rupees

acquired by the United States from commodity sales to India, for
the sale of Indian textiles in the Burmese market. The third was a
$10 million police-equipment loan (June 24, 1958, TIAS 4081)
also repayable over forty years in kyats or dollars at 3.5 per cent
interest, "to help further develop [Burma's] continuing program
of building internal security as one basis for its economic development." The fourth agreement was a somewhat more complicated
one. It involved both a dollar grant and an assignment of earlier
P.L. 480-generated funds to several projects. Through notes exchanged on June 24, 1959 (TIAS 4325) for "Special Economic
Assistance," provision was made for an immediate grant of $1 mil-
lion for a feasibility study and other studies of two major projects:
a modern highway from Rangoon to Mandalay, and new facilities
for intermediate college students (first two years) at the University
of Rangoon. In addition, $6 million in kyats were made immedi-
ately available from earlier sales of surplus products under P.L. 480.
At the same time the U.S. Ambassador notified Prime Minister Ne
Win that the administration would request a $30 million appropri-
ation from Congress over a four-year period as a further contribution to these projects.[40]

There was no difficulty in implementing the university project,
subsequently renamed the Liberal Arts College project, once the
surveys and designs were on hand. Started in 1960, it and other
related university projects have been completed. To these, approximately $2.25 million have been allocated out of the $30 million
grant. The road project, however, which occasioned much comment in and out of Burma,[41] ran into difficulties. The U.S. technicians assigned to it did not agree with the Burmese. Compromises
were temporarily effected in December, 1960.[42] The wrangle over
the design and the path of the road was presumably solved by an
agreement to build two 100-mile extensions to the existing Rangoon-Mandalay road rather than (as the Burmese preferred) a new
highway between the two major cities of Burma. Finally, the Burmese Government under the Revolutionary Council decided to revert to its earlier plans for the highway, and on May 22, 1964,
notified the United States to cancel its participation in the project.[43] Thus Burma forfeited some $27 million remaining in the
$31 million road and university project initiated under the grant
agreement of June 24, 1959. But the Burmese have started to
build the Rangoon-Mandalay highway according to their own
plans; and in early summer, 1965, they earmarked initial funds for
the reconstruction of the Rangoon-Mergui highway.

In 1961-62, two further agreements were negotiated: a $750,000
grant for the Namsang area-development program in the southern
Shan state—a resettlement project for former military personnel;
and the third P.L. 480 agreement (TIAS 5198, November 9, 1962)
for $10.7 million, mostly in cotton.[44]

Since the renewal of aid to Burma a number of significant projects have been completed, among which are those devoted to improving agriculture by reclaiming and restoring land (about 1.85 million acres, including the Kabo Dam); by providing mechanized equipment for extracting, milling, and processing timber and rice; and by other projects related to crop diversification (1 million acres) and water resources. Agriculture (including forestry and irrigation) has thus received the bulk of allocated funds, with transport and communications a very close second. Public health, education, and applied research are the next major fields. Together these five categories account for virtually all U.S. aid funds in Burma.

The $10 million police-equipment loan approved in June, 1958, deserves special mention. Though the suppression of insurrectionary activity and the extension of law and order throughout Burma had been a most pressing problem since 1948, this was the first time since the United States provided Burma with patrol boats in 1950 that a project of this type had been jointly approved. The United States made the $10 million available as a line of credit to be used for procuring security matériel and for providing training facilities in the United States and third countries. It was a "soft" loan, spread over three fiscal years, 1958-60, to which the Government of Burma was to add in kyats the equivalent of approximately $5 million. This program, to the quiet satisfaction of American and Burmese security personnel, was supplemented by a military-sales agreement also signed in June, 1958, permitting Burma to buy military equipment from the United States with local Burmese currency.

No further agreements have been negotiated since 1962. As of July, 1965, there remained between $3 and $4 million of allocable grant money from earlier agreements and various balances from the proceeds of P.L. 480 sales. A considerable portion of the remaining grant dollars has been assigned to the construction and development of a teak mill.

Total U.S. aid to Burma, 1950-65, amounts to approximately $145 million. However, this sum may be reduced to approximately $118 million, depending on the final decision with respect to grant funds earmarked for the Rangoon-Mandalay highway. Also, the amount of local currency generated by P.L. 480 sales and used for U.S. expenses in Burma should be deducted from the total. This figure is unavailable. However, whether the total is $145 or $118 million, it does not include the cost of defense matériel (patrol boats and later military equipment); nor does it include a relief fund of $1.8 million and $5 million made available to Burma before 1950 for the Fulbright and related educational programs.[45]

Table 3, below, summarizes aid to Burma, 1950-65.

To supervise the carrying out of the 1956-65 agreements for sales, loans, and grants, a small economic staff, not an operating mission, was added to the U.S. embassy in Rangoon. However, since the loans and grants were not entirely free ones, the two governments

TABLE 3

U.S. AID TO BURMA, 1950-65
(*in millions of dollars*)

Grant aid
    ECA (MSA-TCA-FOA), phased out by 1955[a]   21.2
    ICA-AID (college and road programs)[b]   31.0
    Namsang area development   .75
        Total   52.95

Dollar loans
    March 21, 1957, Economic-Cooperation Loan   25.0
    June 24, 1958, Police-Equipment Loan   10.0
        Total   35.

Special projects
    June 30, 1956, Rice for Technicians   1.1
    August 25, 1958, Indian Textiles   5.0
        Total   6.1

P.L. 480 "sales"
    February 8, 1956   22.7
    May 27, 1958   18.0
    November 9, 1962   10.7
        Total   51.4

        Grand total   145.45[c]

[a] See Table 2.
[b] The preliminary surveys and designs for the road cost $1.6 million; the college program, $2.25 million. This leaves approximately $27 million in this grant, which may be canceled.
[c] The final total will reflect (a) the decision on the college and road grant; and (b) the amounts of the "sales" allocated to grants, loans, and use by the U.S. of local currency in Burma. In all such summaries of aid accounts there are discrepancies because of variations in categories and time factors related to commitments, obligations, and expenditures. The figures presented by AID, *Proposed Mutual . . . Programs, Fiscal Year 1966, Summary to the Congress March, 1965* (Washington, D.C.: Government Printing Office, 1965), p. 227, are useless.

had to work out agreements on the general developmental purposes for which the dollars and kyats were to be spent, and also on the specific projects. With the exception of the canceled Rangoon-Mandalay highway project, the U.S. aid program benefited from past experience. There was less second-guessing and less rigid control by Washington; there was also less need for a crash program. The earlier American insistence on across-the-board programs, with its proliferation of projects—and consequent Burmese criticism of "aid with strings"—quietly gave way to mutually agreeable plans. For several years the successful and respected operations of the International Bank for Reconstruction and Development[46] have made clear even to new and sensitive sovereign nations that soundness of concept and ability of the recipient to achieve the purposes of a loan are legitimate conditions for lending money. And though Congress has not withdrawn "Buy American" provisions in the Mutual Security and Foreign Assistance acts or similar provisions in the Mutual Defense Assistance Control (Battle) Act, these and related political conditions imposed on U.S. aid administrations have been interpreted flexibly in most, if not all, instances where neutralist countries, as in the case of Burma, are in fact neutralist.

In addition, the Government of Burma has demonstrated its willingness to accept assistance from any quarter, including the Sino-Soviet bloc (see Chapter 15). Between 1950 and 1965, it received from the U.N. Specialized Agencies and Expanded Technical Assistance Program a total of approximately $10.75 million.[47] The Colombo Plan countries have supplied materials to Burma, as a member, averaging annually since 1952 about $500,000, along with technical assistance and over 1,000 training fellowships for her nationals. A highly appreciated Israeli aid program was begun shortly after the exchange of ambassadors in 1953. More than 500 Burmese have received training in Israel, and about 100 Israeli technical assistants have served in Burma. Yugoslavia, on a lesser scale than Israel, has also been of assistance, while India, in March, 1957, and West Germany, in July, 1962, have advanced loans for development programs amounting to $42 million and $44 million, respectively.[48]

This influx of capital, goods, and services from the United States and other sources has given a considerable boost to Burma's economy, helping it to recover faster from the post-Korean War recession. Short of a catastrophic depression, and with continuing modest external assistance, Burma has the resources and the earning power to finance a reasonable capital-development program without undue inflationary strain.

An Assessment

Since Burma started on her path of neutralism or nonalignment, there has been no turning back to her earlier search for "powerful allies." Hence Burma carefully avoided joining the Southeast Asia Treaty Organization, which the United States launched in fulfillment of policies initiated in the last years of the Truman Administration. Burma's political relations with the United States have taken place largely in the context of multilateral situations such as the United Nations and the 1961-62 Geneva Conference on Laos. This in effect has meant that the U.S.–Burma aid program has been the primary focus of their bilateral relationship.

The path of U.S. aid in Burma since the first agreement in 1950 has not been any easy one. Though in the main it has been possible to reconcile the respective general interests of the two countries, the specific programs on foreign aid suffered from conflicting policies originating in each capital. Originally, the United States desired a crash program to prevent any further losses to the Communists. If poverty, disease, illiteracy, political instability, are characteristic of underdeveloped new nations, then a slashing attack in order to promote development is the presumed cure. For entirely different reasons, Burmese leadership elected to accept the American concept of a slashing attack. For the Burmese, economic development meant large-scale planning and industrialization, designed to wipe out the stigma of being a "colonial," primary-product economy. Washington was not prepared to carry out its attack on any long-range basis; it did not then appreciate the size and complexity of the task. Rangoon could not create among its people any sustained sense of urgency for development, any willingness to make the continuing self-sacrifices required for economic development. The frustrations thus caused were compounded by political conflict. Washington for a brief time wished to exact a political price for its support. This in the early days of the aid relationship included acquiescence in the role of the KMT on Burmese soil. However willing Rangoon may have been to pay some price, it could not keep its self-respect if it paid the price then required by Washington.

In this first encounter many Americans and many Burmese in fact cooperated so as to build up a partnership to relieve what General Ne Win has called the economic backwardness of Burma. Though the first formal economic agreement was abrogated in 1953, it is significant that many of its salient efforts remained alive in Burma and in the United States. In time these were successful in healing the breach.

The second phase (which began when U Nu visited the United States in 1955, though at the time he went home empty-handed) had a more reasoned, more modest, and more accommodating basis for continuity. This time the Burmese were consulted about their needs as they saw them; and this time the Burmese had a better understanding of their needs and capabilities. The First Four-Year Program adopted in 1956, which replaced the overly optimistic, overly ambitious Eight-Year Plan of 1952, recognized the relationship between economic progress and productivity in proven Burmese sectors of the economy. At this point the U.S. aid program could be more effective—and so it was.

Unhappily, these correctives in Burmese plans and adaptations in U.S. aid programs could not be fully exploited. Burmese disunity, and the consequent increase in insecurity, conspired against optimum performance. The Four-Year Plan was underfulfilled. The crisis in security called forth the first Ne Win regime and resulted in a period of consolidation with increased expenditures for law and order, fewer for economic development. In this, too, virtually for the first time, the U.S. found ways to assist Burma without compromising Burmese sensitivity on her neutrality policy. It is perhaps unprofitable to speculate about what might have been if joint action like this had been taken in the early years of the insurrection, when U Nu's government had indicated, however inexpertly, its desire for such assistance. At that time the United States, however politely, refused to make police loans or sell for local currency military supplies necessary to counter Communist insurgency. I do not believe that the United States did not then want to help the Burmese. I believe that America did not think through the consequences of a negative response or try hard enough to find a positive one.

U Nu's return to power in 1960 did not signalize any change in U.S.–Burma economic-aid policy. Nor did the U.S. exert any effective influence on the declining powers of leadership exercised by the Prime Minister. The Burmese spent some fifteen months working out their disagreements in the formulation of the Second Four-Year Plan, 1961-65. This was a somewhat more ambitious plan than the First Four-Year Plan of 1956. It contained greater emphasis on the private sector and allocated a larger share of government investment to agriculture (including irrigation and forestry), mining, transport and communications, industry, and the social services. It expected that law and order would require a lower investment.[49]

But U Nu was not to have a third chance at fulfilling an economic plan. As we have seen, in March, 1962, General Ne Win took over the government, established his military regime, and proceeded on the "Burmese Way to Socialism." The U.S. aid relationship had just enough joint momentum to continue despite Ne Win's personal disenchantment with Washington following his unofficial visit to the United States in the spring of 1960; and despite Washington's inability to find ways of accommodating to the doctrinaire expression of the Burmese Way to Socialism. That momentum was jolted if not fully braked by the final controversy over the Rangoon-Mandalay highway project, a project that the Ne Win regime had specially cultivated for security, as well as for economic, reasons.

U.S. fiscal year 1966 may well be a watershed year for Burma and for the U.S. on the question of economic aid. The administration and the U.S. Congress are rapidly approaching an overdue final accounting of the extraordinary effort begun on that fateful day in June, 1947, when Secretary of State Marshall told the graduating class at Harvard that "any government willing to assist in the task of recovery will find full cooperation on the part of the United States." And Burma now has a sounder basis for estimating what her still unchanged and unfulfilled goals of development require if they are to be realized. In such respective enlightenment there should be grounds for a new bilateral relationship based not on "aid," with its concomitant irritant, the donor-receiver syndrome, but on mutuality of interests and cooperation. But this belongs to future decisions in Washington and in Rangoon.

IF THERE WERE NO COLD WAR, if the Sino-Soviet world did not threaten the security of the United States and the rights and liberties of free peoples everywhere, there would be little need to discuss the question of the changing trends and directions of Burma's foreign trade. In a relatively free world, no serious political problem arises when some countries replace others as trading partners. If some countries cannot develop their economies as rapidly as they wish by marketing their surplus goods an economic problem may arise, but sooner or later trade finds its own levels and channels.

If countries and peoples need Burma's rice, teak, and minerals, they will pay for them with goods, services, or money. In a food-deficit area, Burma's capacity to export rice is the key enabling her to import goods for development and consumption. Prior to 1954, Burma neither traded with nor received aid from the Sino-Soviet bloc. Nor were the United States and Burma major trading partners. For the five years 1958-62, the United States exported to Burma goods valued annually at about $9 million; it imported from Burma goods valued at $1.26 million. U.S. exports included industrial machinery, automobile parts and accessories, medicinal and pharmaceutical products, chemical specialties, lubricating oils, nonfat dry milk solids, and tobacco. Tungsten ore, crude rubber, and animal products made up the bulk of U.S. imports from Burma, together with unmanufactured shells, teak, bamboo, and precious and semiprecious stones.[1] In those same years, Burma's total annual exports to all countries averaged around $217 million, and its total annual imports stood at around $226.5 million.

Since the death of Stalin in 1953, the United States has become acutely aware of the impact of the Sino-Soviet "trade and aid" economic offensive, which has been directed especially toward less developed nations. The Burmese "rice case" showed how vulnerable the free world is to this Soviet trade offensive.[2]

Under British colonial administration Burma, in the years preceding World War II, had become the world's leading exporter of rice, with its annual exports averaging 3.3 million tons. Rice plays an even more strategic role in the exports of independent Burma. In pre-war Burma, rice accounted for approximately 47 per cent of export earnings, with oil, metals, and teak following it in importance. Today, rice accounts for approximately 70 per cent of Burma's earnings, though the volume of its rice exports has not exceeded two-thirds of the pre-war level. The remaining exports consist of a variety of products, no one of which amounts to 5 per cent of the total. The export of other products can be expected to rise faster, but for many years to come rice will remain the key to Burma's export earnings. The growing of rice is carried on by private enterprise, but since independence the government has controlled the prices paid to the farmer through the State Agricultural Marketing Board (SAMB) and successor agencies. It has also had a near monopoly on the export trade. Under the Revolutionary Council this monopoly is complete, and the previously private milling of rice has been nationalized. The spread between the fairly steady SAMB domestic buying price and the export sales price provides substantial revenue for the government and is the chief source of foreign-exchange earnings which, in turn, finance other imports.

Throughout the Korean War period Burma's rice trade boomed in a buoyant seller's market. The resulting wave of optimism was encouraged by the questionable predictions of the private American firm of economic consultants, Robert R. Nathan Associates, Inc., participating in the general contract of the Knappen, Tippetts, and Abbett Engineering Company. Their report foretold a decline in prices, but not as big a one as actually occurred.[3] There were several reasons for this. Pre–World War II buyers of Burmese rice, especially India and Ceylon, were gradually replacing imports of Burmese rice with homegrown bumper-year crops and with imports of lower-priced rice and other cereals.[4] Between 1952 and 1953, sales of Burmese rice to India and Ceylon combined dropped by about 346,000 long tons. Together with other losses, this resulted in a net export decline of approximately 300,000 tons and a decrease in value of approximately K145 million ($30,450,000). As a result, Burma's foreign-currency reserves declined sharply. In late 1953 and early 1954, unsold carry-over rice stocks and lower world prices were danger signals that aroused the Burmese government. Apart from the expected fall in prices following the end of the Korean War boom, a buyer's market continued to dominate trade in rice. No one expected that the Korean War high of £70 per ton for government-to-government sales, and £85 for private sales, would continue. But the fall to £60 in late 1953, to less than £50 in 1954, to £40 in 1955, and to less than £34 in 1956, gave substance to Burmese alarm. Carry-over rice stocks, for which there were no adequate storage and pest control, and a new exportable surplus in 1954 of approximately 1.5 million tons, added up to 2.5 million tons available for export. Delivery contracts for 1954 with India, Japan, Ceylon, Malaya, the Ryukyus, Mauritius, Indonesia, and other customary trading partners accounted for less than 1.6 million tons. Foreign-exchange reserves declined from the all-time peak of approximately $265 million in June, 1953, to the all-time low of about $108 million in 1955.[5]

The difficulties of 1954 were duplicated in 1955. Carry-over stocks and the new crop again added up to a total of exportable rice at least as large as that of 1954. Burma's development program was in some danger, and this blow to the economy came at a time, in late 1953, in 1954, and early 1955, when Burma's relations with the United States were cool and distant. The earlier aid program had been closed down at Burma's request. The presence in Burma of Kuomintang forces endangered relations with Communist China. The United States, which was laying the groundwork for the Manila Pact, was not particularly pleased with the negative reaction of the Asian neutralists, including Burma.[6]

Meanwhile, a new factor had entered into the already complicated rice picture. After 1948, the United States became a rice exporter, though its total production, for example in 1959-60, was about half of Burma's estimated output of almost 7 million long tons. From 1952 through 1956, the United States exported an annual average of 640,000 tons, a substantial increase over earlier postwar years; most of its exports went to Asian markets—to Korea, Japan, Indonesia, the Ryukyus, Ceylon, India, and Pakistan. These countries, except for Korea, had customarily been purchasers of Burmese rice. In addition, U.S. rice exports enjoyed special advantages, for they were sold not only through normal channels but increasingly through the Mutual Security Act programs, especially after Public Law 480, the Agricultural Trade and Development Act, was enacted in July, 1954.[7]

P.L. 480 and associated laws and programs were devices for disposing of U.S. farm surpluses. Officially, their aim was "to promote the economic stability of American agriculture" by expanding trade and increasing "the consumption of United States agricultural commodities in foreign countries," and "to make efficient use of surplus commodities in furtherance of the foreign policy of the United States." [8] This included accepting payments in foreign currencies.

This program, it may be noted, has been criticized on general grounds in an independent study prepared for the Committee on Foreign Relations of the U.S. Senate. The report stated: "In recent years, the U.S. surplus disposal program has tended to depress world prices and to undercut, through sales for local currency, the normal markets of allied and friendly nations. While the legislation states that the program should not 'unduly' affect the normal trade, the repercussions indicate that it has." The study urged a careful examination of the program from the point of view of U.S. foreign policy, and pointed out that if our competitors followed a similar program they would earn the wrath of Congress, farmers, and the public at large." [9]

Prior to the end of 1953, when Burma began to find difficulty in disposing of its rice stocks, its leaders apparently were relatively indifferent to the U.S. commodity-disposal programs. Under the 1950-53 ECA aid program Burma had received over $4 million in U.S. commodities, mostly cotton, and similar results were expected from P.L. 480 sales when the aid program was renewed in 1956. However, the falling market of 1953-54 caused the Burmese to become aware that considerable amounts of U.S. rice, in comparison to their own exports, were entering their normal markets. U.S. domestic agricultural price-support policies and P.L. 480 agreements for disposing of surpluses for local currencies were now seen as a real threat to Burma's share of the Asian rice market. No matter how the export figures for the United States and Burma are analyzed, it is obvious that the increase in American rice exports to Asia—the United States now ranked third after Burma and Thailand—was having a serious impact on Burma. U.S. wheat and other cereal exports to Asia during the same period must also be taken into account, for they involved a comparative price advantage of wheat over rice (approximately £3 to £4 per ton) and consequently a partial substitution of wheat for rice. If these additional factors are brought into the picture, the Burmese reaction is readily understandable.[10]

It may be argued that there was no necessary equivalence between increased sales of U.S. cereals and diminished sales of Burmese rice. Yet it is quite probable that there was some economic relation between the two. In any case, there was a strong reaction in Burma, which could hardly further U.S.–Burma relations. In October, 1954, the Burmese charged that the U.S. surplus-disposal plan was a "kiss of death" to Rangoon and that "dumping of American rice in Asia will force us to go to China on our knees. . . . We will have to depend upon China for our rice market and this will naturally tie our economy to Red China." [11] In hearings before the House Committee on Foreign Affairs, Chester Bowles, Ambassador to India, remarked, "A lot of our present problems in Burma are because we dumped American rice all over Asia. We knocked Burma out of her markets." [12]

Beginning in late 1953, Prime Minister Nu sought a resumption of U.S. aid, proposing that the United States purchase Burmese rice for re-export to Asian rice-importing countries, while Burma would use the dollars thus earned "to hire U.S. technicians and buy machinery for a stepped-up national development program."

In this connection U Nu declared, "Burma is willing to accept U.S. economic aid but we do not want it free. We prefer to pay for it, as this forms a more solid basis of friendship than accepting gifts." Though he was prepared to send a negotiating mission to the United States, he found that there was "no enthusiasm" in official U.S. circles for such a proposal.[13]

The problem of rice exports led the Burmese cabinet to adopt several drastic steps. It organized a new Ministry of Trade Development and placed in charge one of its ablest members, U Raschid, a businessman and a comrade-in-arms of U Nu since the student strike in 1936. The State Agricultural Marketing Board, which handled over four-fifths of all government-to-government rice contracts, underwent a reorganization. Between 200,000 and 300,000 tons of low-grade, broken, and spoiled rice were written off from carry-over stock. A vigorous international campaign was undertaken to dispose of approximately 2 million tons of rice in 1954-55 and again in 1955-56. At the same time the government imposed import restrictions and slowed down the rate of capital investment in some of its development plans.

To dispose of its surplus rice, Burma found itself obliged to redirect its patterns of trade. The Sino-Soviet bloc, which had had no prior trade or aid relations with Burma, moved vigorously into the picture. Between November, 1954, and February, 1956, Burma negotiated a series of agreements with China, Czechoslovakia, Hungary, East Germany, the U.S.S.R., Poland, Rumania, and Bulgaria. The new trade partners were willing to take Burma's surplus stocks, provided they could do so under clearing accounts, in other words, in barter rather than for cash sales. Burma disposed of its rice, but in return it had to take large quantities of Sino-Soviet bloc goods and technicians.

In April, 1954, Burma and Communist China signed their first three-year trade agreement covering a small part of Burma's surplus rice. After the failure of its overtures to the United States, the Burmese Government announced in November that a new agreement with China had been arranged; together with three contracts signed on March 28, 1955, this agreement would dispose of 150,000 tons of rice per year. Eighty per cent of payment was to be made in Sino-Soviet bloc goods, the balance in sterling. Burma's trade with China since 1957 has been on a cash basis, with China having a favorable balance until 1961, when China imported 355,000 tons of Burma's rice to relieve her pressing shortages. In 1957, China also agreed to advance to Burma a credit of about $4.2 million at 2.5 per cent interest to enlarge a 20,000-spindle textile factory.

On July 1, 1955, Burma signed the first barter agreement with the U.S.S.R., involving 150,000 to 200,000 tons of rice per year for the next three years. On a visit to Burma at the end of March, 1956, Anastas Mikoyan negotiated a supplementary trade agreement and a protocol extending the period to 1960. Under the extension Burma agreed to deliver 400,000 tons of rice annually in exchange for Soviet machinery and other goods and services.[14] Apparently no cash payment was involved. Similar agreements were signed with Czechoslovakia and East Germany on February 14 and 27, 1955; with Hungary on February 21, 1955; with Poland on November 1, 1955; with Rumania on February 7, 1956; and with Bulgaria on May 16, 1956.

These agreements tied a significant portion of Burma's export rice trade, possibly as much as 40 per cent by volume, to Sino-Soviet bloc goods and technicians. However, since Burma retained the right to renegotiate the quantity of annual exports, actual deliveries at their peak never exceeded 25 per cent of the exportable rice crop. The barter arrangements brought with them other economic and political consequences. Though Burma has expressed some dissatisfaction with the prices and quality of Soviet goods and has not been able to balance her rice-trade account with the U.S.S.R., a number of new agreements followed the Bulganin-Khrushchev visit to Burma, December 1-7, 1955. These included some technical and material assistance for agricultural development and irrigation and an "exchange of gifts." [15] The gifts were listed in an agreement signed on January 17, 1957. Soviet promises covered the building of an institute of technology and a hotel in Rangoon, and a 200-bed hospital in Taunggyi, as well as a theater, a sports stadium, a swimming pool, a conference hall, and a permanent exhibition hall. In return the Burmese were to pay the local costs and to return the value of the Soviet gifts by delivering rice over a twenty-year period. Public opinion in Burma did not take kindly to the cost of these supposedly free gifts. The first three have been completed, and the other five were postponed and later canceled by the Ne Win caretaker government. The first three will have cost the Burmese K30 million in local currency and K55 million to be paid in rice to the Soviet Union. If all had been completed, the cost to Burma would have been over K210 million.[16]

In January, 1958, the U.S.S.R. agreed to lend Burma between $4 and $7 million (in rubles) at 2.5 per cent interest for twelve years to build two long-deferred irrigation dams, and to supply teams of experts for this and related agricultural purposes. The Burmese cancelled another project credit amounting to approximately $3 million for the construction of an agricultural-implements factory. Apparently, the U.S.S.R. also agreed to share with other bloc governments some of Burma's surplus clearing balance. This concession enabled Burma to purchase goods from Czechoslovakia, East Germany, and Poland, which appeared to be of more satisfactory quality than merchandise from the Soviet Union.[17]

The amount of rice exported by Burma under these barter arrangements never reached the proportions originally envisaged. In the peak year 1955-56, approximately 480,000 tons were delivered, approximately 25 per cent of Burma's foreign trade by volume and value. In 1956-57, the volume declined to 300,000 tons, including 33,000 tons in barter deliveries to Yugoslavia and Israel. In 1957-58, it declined to 128,000 tons, of which 29,000 tons went to Yugoslavia. Barter agreements lapsed in that year, except those with the U.S.S.R., Czechoslovakia, and Yugoslavia. In 1958-59, barter accounted for 85,000 tons, a little more than 5 per cent of Burma's foreign trade by volume and a little less than 6 per cent by value.[18] The total value of trade between the Sino-Soviet bloc and Burma during 1955-59 may have been somewhere between $225 and $250 million, while Burma's total trade for the same period was approximately $2,000 million.[19] Sino-Soviet bloc credit and "gift" aid through 1964 amounted to more than $105 million, as follows:

	In Millions of U.S. dollars (Approximate)
U.S.S.R., "gift" credits	11.5
U.S.S.R., dam- and irrigation-project credits	3.9
U.S.S.R., tractors, parts and related project credits (possibly in pounds sterling)	1.1
Czechoslovakia, the same	.5
People's Republic of China, textile credits	4.2
People's Republic of China, interest-free ten-year credits	84.0
Total	105.2

It is certain that the Burmese were aware of some of the risks involved in the barter deals with the Sino-Soviet bloc. In the annual ministerial address to the Burma Chamber of Commerce on February 8, 1956, U Raschid, Minister of Trade Development, remarked: "Many of our friends [in the West] keep on reminding us of the difficulties of such arrangements. Some of them even tell us that there are 'hidden dangers.' We are not unaware of the difficulties and implications involved. Our position is that we have rice to sell and we must sell it if we are to survive." Somewhat plaintively he went on to say, "We are willing to sell all our rice for cash [so that Burma could buy imports at competitive prices, but] it may yet take some time before we can dispose of all our rice for cash." (Certainly during the crucial years of 1954-56 the Burmese could find no Western customers, though Burmese rice went to Western customers in France and West Germany and elsewhere through resale by the barter countries.) He concluded, "It is not for us to go into the motives of our customers." [20]

But motives[21] of customers are certainly a factor in foreign policy. The Sino-Soviet bloc came to the aid of Burma in the rice case because it suited its interests to cultivate the neutralist nations of Asia. Neither the United States nor the other Western powers were willing to act. The *Economist* (London), January 7, 1956, in an unsigned article on "Rice and Rouble Diplomacy," gave a clear analysis of the bloc strategy, but was completely unsympathetic to the plight of the Burmese. "Naturally," the article concluded, "no one would expect the Burmese simply to refuse the Soviet offer if it represented for them the only alternative to being saddled with an unmarketable surplus. But this problem would not have arisen if they had been prepared in the first place to adopt a more flexible policy in selling their rice to established customers." The article was wholly silent on Western policies other than those relating to the virtues of the free market. It even placed the sole blame for Ceylon's 1952 rubber-for-rice agreement with Communist China on Burma's rice-pricing policies.

The issue, it should be obvious, is bigger than the free market-place and fluctuations in world prices of primary products. Ceylon, contrary to the *Economist's* view, was similarly forced into a rubber agreement with Communist China in 1952, because it could not sell rubber profitably to the West.[22] Ceylon has to sell rubber at good prices in order to buy from Burma and other countries at least 500,000 tons of food grains per year. Similarly Burma, in order to dispose of its major cash crop, had to seek new outlets and accept unorthodox terms of trade since alternative markets were not available in the West. Through the barter agreements Burma gained a respite from her temporary economic difficulties and an opportunity to work out a long-range basis for her foreign and domestic economic policy. But Burma paid a price for the experience.

These agreements with the bloc were less than satisfactory for a variety of reasons: the prices of goods that Burma imported were not competitive; their quality was below specifications; shipments arrived improperly or failed to arrive; Burmese purchasing missions sent to the bloc countries were relatively unequipped for their tasks. In 1957, Burma also became aware that the market for cash sales was decreasing the need to rely on barter agreements, and the latter have continued to decline in practical importance, though they will probably be remembered for both their pluses and mi-nuses. Certainly they served one purpose of the Sino-Soviet bloc in that they showed it was willing to be of service to a newly inde-pendent, ex-colonial Asian nation.

Beginning in late 1955, and continuing in 1956, Burma's leaders proceeded to revise downward the Eight-Year Pyidawtha Plan. They decided to improve and diversify the country's agriculture, to give up the fetish of industrialization, and to build instead a mod-est industrial base for a more balanced economy. The barter agree-ments added a formidable burden to those already carried by the decision-makers of a newly independent country that was still suffering from the blight of war and armed Communist and other insurrections. Their attachment to democratic values might have been blunted by the exigencies of bloc barter trade, by the blan-dishments of "gifts," by the extraordinary volume of cultural exchanges and propaganda that followed in the wake of these agreements, and by accommodation to several scores of Communist experts who accompanied the various bloc projects. The disposal of some 800,000 tons of rice to the Sino-Soviet bloc during the critical years, 1954-57, was potentially a heavy weight to bear on the scales of Burma's foreign and domestic policy.

How, in the light of later developments, should the effects of the Sino-Soviet economic intervention in Burma be assessed? Before, during, and since the barter agreements, Burma's neutralist foreign policy has been maintained. Her political independence has weathered a variety of crises. Most of the barter agreements have expired, but they have promoted new trade relationships between Burma and several of the bloc countries.[23] The political conditions that led to the rupture in aid relations between the United States and Burma have been removed. What then, other than as an episode in history, remains of the Burmese rice case?

Insofar as normal U.S. rice exports and P.L. 480 wheat and rice shipped to Asia between 1952 and 1956 exceeded exports of earlier years, the Burmese charge of dumping, though perhaps somewhat exaggerated, had merit. More to the point is the continuing problem of U.S. surplus commodity "sales" in the same markets. After more than a decade of experience since P.L. 480 was legislated, the United States has not yet answered effectively the key question: Since accelerating rates of production will continue to create surpluses, can these be marketed in deficit areas without disrupting the normal direction of trade of the primary producers who look to these same markets for their foreign-exchange earnings? In November, 1959, when the United States proposed shipments of rice to India, Indonesia, Pakistan, and Ceylon amounting to 250,000 tons, the Burmese press immediately expressed concern.[24] The U.S. embassy in Rangoon took the usual step of issuing a press release indicating that the American Government had "regularly consulted with friendly rice exporting countries before making any sales of American P.L. 480 rice in their markets" and that in the future such sales would be made only after recipient countries have "undertaken to continue to buy normal amounts" from their usual sources.[25] This yardstick is a good one, but no device for applying it has yet been written into a P.L. 480 agreement.

The policy of consultations before making P.L. 480 sales was initiated only after the Burmese rice case had come to play a prominent role in the context of the Cold War. The new policy is an improvement on the past. Is it enough of an improvement? Is the concept of what has been called the "additional principle" as applied to P.L. 480 sales sufficiently flexible both for the United States and for recipient countries, and does it protect third-country interests sufficiently? Such questions are particularly pertinent when the small role of rice in U.S. trade is considered. The cost of *not* exporting American rice to Asia while our rice-exporting friends, Burma and Thailand, still have stocks on hand, may be less than the cost of repairing the damages arising from the charge of dumping. Certainly, U.S. charges that the "dumping practices" of Communist China constitute a "special threat" to "free-world trade in the Far East" carry little credibility in Asia under the circumstances.[26]

In this connection it is of interest that the United States and Canada have taken the issue of food and fiber surpluses to the United Nations General Assembly, which approved a Freedom from Hunger Campaign designed as a concerted attack on the problem of providing adequate food for food-deficient peoples." [27] It also emphasized that any action taken should proceed "with adequate safeguards and appropriate measures against the dumping of agricultural surpluses . . . and against adverse effects" on the economies of food-exporting countries.

It is to be remembered that Congress designed these disposal programs both to promote the economic stability of American agriculture and to further the foreign policy of the United States. U.S. surplus-food-and-fiber-disposal programs have helped American agriculture *and* have raised consumption levels in less privileged friendly societies. But the Burmese rice case revealed that these programs may also have a boomerang effect on U.S. foreign-policy objectives, as they did when they gave the Sino-Soviet bloc the opportunity to appear as a friend in response to Burma's distress signals. Although the United States has recently displayed caution in handling these programs, the anxiety of friendly exporting countries has not yet been relieved. The argument that the Soviet bloc's intervention in the Burmese rice case was neither lasting nor disastrous to the Burmese or to the United States overlooks the residual importance of an incident like this in the Cold War. It also overlooks the continuing economic opportunities in Burma and elsewhere for similar actions by the Sino-Soviet bloc.

There remains to be considered another line of thought about the Burmese rice case, which would put the blame primarily on Burma. This view holds that the inexperience of Burma's leaders in dealing with the world rice market, the inefficiency of Burmese milling and storage, which lowered the quality of rice exports, the stubborn insistence on boom prices after the decline had already set in, contributed substantially to the difficulties. Further, it is claimed that Burma's experience with the barter-trade agreements was a valuable if costly lesson, which she had to undergo in order to avoid future illusions. It is also argued that Burma can ill afford to complain about P.L. 480 sales and loans to others when she, too, has been a beneficiary of these same surplus disposal programs. In addition, while the United States has demonstrated willingness to help solve some of the problems of underdeveloped countries, she cannot solve all of them. In any event, the United States has to solve her own problems, including that of surplus crops, in order to be able to help other countries with their difficulties. Furthermore, as it happened, Burma's problem of disposing of her rice between 1953 and 1955 arose at a time when her normal trading partners in Asia had had the benefit of two or three good crop years and were therefore importing less rice than usual. Finally, it stands to reason that seasonal and price fluctuations are inevitably bound to plague primary product exporting economies. Actually, Burma was fortunate in making a rapid recovery from this crisis without suffering any lasting adverse effects. Hence, it has been argued, the Burmese rice case has been something of the proverbial tempest in the teapot.[28]

Yet these arguments—even were they all true—do not dispose of the case or diminish its importance. As long as friendly underdeveloped countries, newly independent or otherwise, in Asia, Africa, or Latin America, continue to depend on one or a few primary products for their basic livelihood, the United States has many reasons —political, economic, and humanitarian—to consider their problems as well as her own. What is at issue is not whether one sovereign nation has a moral obligation toward another, as individuals have a responsibility toward other individuals. However, as long as the United States continues to make decisions that affect other nations—for the purpose of advancing her interests, safeguarding or enhancing her security, containing or rolling back hostile forces, providing for national well-being, or upholding the values of a free society—then, in terms of both logic and practical advantage, her leaders must take a close and friendly interest in the impact of their decisions on any countries that are not hostile to us.

As it happened, the Burmese rice case found its own solution without entailing any dire consequences for Burma or the democratic cause. Does this mean that we can count on similar good fortune in the future? Can we stake the future on a trust in the long-range efficacy of *laissez faire* on an international scale, i.e., on the automatic balancing of wildly fluctuating international commodity markets? The answers to these questions are negative; the solutions are difficult to find, but they must be sought in concert with other friendly powers.

The major focus of U.S. policy toward Burma in the 1950's was on economic and technical assistance. As mentioned earlier, the United States contributed to Burma's development, through grants, sales, and loans, the equivalent of $145 million, including $51 million in P.L. 480 "sales." If Burma had been able to sell her rice between 1953 and 1957 through normal channels at the post– Korean War price of $90 to $100 per ton, instead of bartering it with the Sino-Soviet bloc, and had spent those proceeds in purchases from her traditional non-Communist trading partners, she would have earned from $80 to $100 million more than she in fact earned. Obviously, however disruptive U.S. shipments of rice and wheat to Asia may have been to Burmese markets, the total U.S.

impact on the rice trade has been quite small. Just as obviously, on the other hand, if the United States had stopped exporting rice to Asia, if it had bought up Burmese rice to sell or give to needy countries, as U Nu had proposed in 1954, or had bilaterally sought out some other hopeful solution, the cost of U.S. aid to Burma might have been substantially lower, or the aid granted might have been put to better use, and the political costs from charges of U.S. dumping would not have been incurred.

The Burmese rice case illustrates a persisting difficulty that plagues U.S. foreign policy. Except in the war years of 1939-45 and 1950-52, domestic policy toward farm surpluses has been inconsistent with some major aspects of foreign policy and badly needs overhauling. A variety of international approaches have been proposed and discussed, including single- and multiple-commodity agreements, stabilization agreements for marketing and stockpiling, food and fiber banks, and buffer stocks. What is clear is that there are legitimate alternatives to the periodic chaos that afflicts international commodity markets today; that it is imperative for the United States, in concert with both producing and consuming nations, to define and adopt such alternatives; that this is as important to U.S. foreign and domestic policy and security as are NATO and the other security pacts.

In one sense this otherwise difficult task may prove simpler because the raw-materials economy of Burma and of the other primary-product-exporting countries of mainland Southeast Asia complement the economy of Japan and, potentially, that of India. This appears to be sound projection even after consideration has been given to Japan's increasing ability to raise its volume of rice production. Burma, despite her adherence to the multilateral trading principles of the General Agreement on Tariffs and Trade (GATT), is desirous of balancing her trade, especially where it is possible to do so with major rice buyers; and Japan and India will for the next foreseeable period remain net food importers. Though rice exports from Burma and Thailand, the major Asian exporters, total only about 2 per cent of Asian production, even minor fluctuations in the production and export of rice have major repercussions in the economies of mainland Southeast Asia. Now that the United States has become the third ranking exporter of rice, it cannot avoid, except at the cost of a political disaster in Southeast Asia, treating the problems of Burmese and Thai rice sympathetically and effectively.

Since rice accounts so overwhelmingly for Burma's economic viability, U.S. and Western failure to act may prove tantamount to handing a bloodless victory to the Sino-Soviet bloc.[29] Although Sino-Soviet credits to Burma had been relatively insignificant in the 1950's, China's 1961 $84-million interest-free line of credit coupled with continuing credits (1963-64) from the U.S.S.R. and East European bloc countries, has altered this situation.[30] Bloc trade with

Burma has been growing. In the five-year period, 1958-62, Japan and the United Kingdom rank first and second as the major suppliers to Burma (though the Commonwealth and sterling area as a whole rank first), while Communist China has inched ahead of India to third place with approximately 9 per cent of Burma's total imports.[31] Nevertheless, there still remains a major opportunity to strengthen Burma's economic trade ties with the Free World, based as they are on trading habits and desires built up over decades on a preference for trademarked goods imported largely from the sterling area. In addition, there are new opportunities to strengthen the developing pattern of trade with Japan and to restore trade with India, which are much less dangerous partners for Burma than the Sino-Soviet bloc.

The Burmese rice case—like the Ceylon rubber case, the Latin-American coffee case, the African cocoa case, the Canadian wheat case, and others—can serve merely as an early illustration of the Sino-Soviet use of trade as a strategic weapon in the conduct of their foreign policy. It can be argued, of course, that when the Sino-Soviet powers develop their trade with extra-bloc nations for political purposes they impose additional strains on their own economies, and that the greater these strains are the better for the rest of the world. This reasoning overlooks the ultimate purpose of the Sino-Soviet bloc, which is to win the ideological allegiances of its weaker trading partners. Through its long-range projects it seeks to train nationals of the recipient countries and to give its own nationals new opportunities to work and propagandize abroad.

It has also been argued that Sino-Soviet trade with non-Communist countries may serve to divert the Communists from the goal of world revolution and thus promote the peaceful coexistence of differing political systems. A major test of this view was made in effect after the U.S. recognition of the U.S.S.R. and especially after the seventh meeting of the Comintern in 1935. The Nazi-Soviet Pact disproved this view; and the postwar reorganization and conduct of the Cominform in and after 1947, along with the successive failures of the agreements reached at Geneva in 1954 and 1962 concerning Laos and Vietnam, should have dispelled any lingering illusions on this score. That such illusions remain, are even revived because of post-Stalin Soviet policies and because of real but exaggerated tensions between Moscow and Peking, is regrettable. This argument overlooks the fact that protracted conflict between the Communists and the free world is inherent in the nature and goals of the Communist system.

If Sino-Soviet trade outside the bloc grows it will be safer for such trade to be conducted with technologically advanced and internally stable countries, for they are better equipped to withstand this formidable challenge. It would be unwise and unnecessary for newly independent countries to reject all Communist trading overtures, but they should not be left to drift into the orbit of Sino-

Soviet trade strategy either by default or as a consequence of erroneous U.S. policies. The ultimate lesson of the Burmese rice case is that Burma's leaders made determined and successful efforts to avoid such an outcome and thereby gave the free world a second chance to avoid a catastrophe in the strategic rice bowl of mainland Southeast Asia—a target area of Communist China. The outcome is by no means certain.

U.S. POLICY TOWARD ASIA in general and Burma in particular was reshaped in the heat of crisis following the Communist victory in China in 1949 and the outbreak of the Korean War in 1950. During subsequent crises, those guidelines for policy have been restated and reinforced, but have not been changed substantially. In classic diplomatic style a system of bilateral and multilateral security and defense treaties, initiated in 1951 with Japan (renewed in revised form, January, 1960), the Philippines, Australia, and New Zealand, was subsequently enlarged to include Korea (1953) and the Republic of China (1954). Finally, the Southeast Asia Collective Defense Treaty, which established SEATO, was signed at Manila on September 8, 1954. SEATO included among the Asian signatories the Philippines, Pakistan, and Thailand, and the three Protocol-covered states, Cambodia, Laos, and the Republic of Vietnam.[1]

These agreements, together with U.S. military forces and bases under the U.S. Pacific Command, provide the framework of U.S. security policy in Asia. Burma, though not a party to any of these alliances, is strongly affected by them. Since 1950, the United States has negotiated economic-aid and cultural agreements of various kinds with each country of free Asia, and some kind of military-assistance program with all the countries of free Asia except Nepal and Afghanistan.

It will be recalled that up to the last quarter of 1949, Burma had expressed an interest in some kind of Pacific Area Security Pact. At that time the United States was cool toward collective defense arrangements in Asia and even cited Prime Minister Nehru in support of its position. After 1950, the United States changed its position, but so had Burma. Burma and other Asian nations elected to emphasize their support of neutralism. In the 1950's, Washington did not find this attitude a congenial one. It had forgotten or did not regard as relevant America's long attachment to neutrality. It preferred to ignore the anti-Western memories and suspicions on which Asian neutralism feeds. It insisted that these Asian countries should share its analysis of the evils and dangers of Sino-Soviet imperialism and support for local revolutions. Perhaps the high-water mark of Washington's irritation with the neutralist position was Secretary Dulles' speech at Iowa State College on June 9, 1956. "Neutrality," he said, "has increasingly become an absolute conception and, except under very exceptional circumstances, it is an immoral and shortsighted conception." A month later, under protests from India and other countries, he modified this assertion by saying that there were "very few" immoral neutrals. Since then the United States has more carefully sought an accommodation with bona fide Asian neutralism.

Among the neutralists Burma has been less given than others to overt criticism of SEATO and other U.S.–Asian defense agreements. Her leaders, in every regime since the 1954 abrogation of the defense treaty with the United Kingdom, have been determined to avoid commitments that involve choosing between "East" and "West." They have rejected all military alliances and have explicitly accepted Article III of the 1960 Treaty of Friendship with the People's Republic of China, which excludes "any military alliance directed against the Contracting Party." As a participant in the Geneva Conference on Laos, Burma endorsed its neutralization, and despite the continuing failure of that solution supports those who call for another Geneva-type conference for the resolution of conflict in South Vietnam. Were the Burmese to have a choice between the hazards of continuing or extending the war in mainland Southeast Asia and its neutralization guaranteed by what they call the "Power blocs," they would prefer the risks of the latter. They would add that they are not unaware of these risks, for they have been fighting to suppress a Communist rebellion since 1948.

It is sometimes argued that as a neutralist nation Burma gains advantages from both worlds, and that she benefits indirectly from the Asian policy of the United States without joining in any defense treaties. This argument rests on the twin assumptions that in the event of a big war the United States would regard the defense of Burma as one of its objectives, and that in the event of Burma's subjection to a limited war or other forms of encroachment, the United States would be drawn into the struggle as it has been in Laos and Vietnam. Neither assumption offers Burma historical grounds for optimism. The British wartime defense of Burma failed, although the defeat of Japan in other areas finally resulted in Burma's liberation. Nevertheless, the physical and psychological scars of the battle still remain. Outside support to Burma against the Kuomintang encroachments of 1950-54 and 1960-61 came only after Burma had taken her complaint to the United Nations. And once Burma had been forced to depend largely on her own resources in combating the initial thrust of the Communist and ethnic rebellions, she decided that self-reliance in these matters was a wise if not complete insurance policy for the future.

In terms of power politics, little Burma fears big China—as well she might—despite the Treaty of Friendship and the settlement of the border conflict. China looks to Burma's space, food, and access to the Indian Ocean for its landlocked western areas. If a large-scale war should break out on the Asian mainland, Burma would probably be involved; and even though in the long run she might regain her freedom, she would necessarily succumb to China even if, as Burmese spokesmen have repeatedly claimed, she should fight to preserve her independence. Burma has fought before.

But if a big or limited war or other armed encroachments should occur, would the United States come to the defense of Burma? Existing defense treaties and expressions of official policy offer U.S. allies no such firm commitments outside of NATO Europe. The U.S. record, and therefore credibility in its policy, is an ambiguous one if we cite the differing cases of Korea and Laos. The record is better with respect to the offshore islands of Taiwan and Vietnam. But it is clear that U.S. policy and public opinion do not respond with alacrity to local or brush-fire wars, or to Communist insurrectionary activity 12,000 miles away. The inconclusive outcome of the struggle in Korea, despite its high cost in American casualties; the remoteness of Laos and the consequent turnabout to seek a neutral Laos through the doubtful pursuit of an understanding with the U.S.S.R. in June, 1961; the incredible confusion within Vietnam after the successful November, 1963, coup against Ngo Dinh Diem and the uncertainty of U.S. policy in that arena until President Johnson's decision of February 7, 1965, actively to combat the North Vietnamese source of the conflict within South Vietnam: all help to make this American attitude understandable, if not reliable.[2]

Aware of such difficulties, Burmese conceptions of security, however ineffectual they may prove against a ruthless Communist enemy, are drawn from their own brand of socialist-nationalist ideology framed largely in a Buddhist cultural pattern. They have, of course, been willing to enter into friendly relations with all powers and to support the principles and aspirations of the United Nations Charter.

During the 1950's, Burmese leaders believed that U.S. commitments elsewhere in Asia did not embrace Burma. They appreciated the somewhat tardy expressions of sympathy such as those the United States offered during the height of the Communist insurrection in Burma; also the aid and later military and police supplies. But they could not expect the United States to risk a big war for their sake. Hpimaw, Gawlum, and Kanfang, the lost Kachin

village areas of the border treaty with China, were even more remote than the provinces of Laos. Hence, those who say that Burma's neutralism affords her the advantages of both worlds ignore
the power realities of a small, faraway nation. At Washington, in
July, 1955, Prime Minister Nu said:

> In the present circumstances of Burma her membership in any alli-
> ance with a great power military bloc is incompatible with her con-
> tinued existence as an independent state. . . . Burma has no choice
> but to pursue her policy of neutrality if she wishes to preserve her
> independence, and that to us is more important than anything else.
> It is part of her defense, and an important part against subversion
> . . . she cannot abandon her neutrality without increasing the risk
> of losing her independence through subversion.[3]

No succeeding Burmese chief of government has altered this basic
position. There is little, if any, likelihood of a change, short of a
Communist takeover. When General Ne Win took office in October, 1958, he stated: "My Government does not entertain any notion to introduce any changes whatsoever in the foreign policy being pursued [it] intends to continue in the practice of strict neutrality free from any entanglements." When he reassumed chief
office after the coup of 1962, he reaffirmed this policy.[4]

Nor, despite Burma's sincere adherence to the principles of the
U.N. Charter, has there been any discernible trend in Burma to
regard the United Nations in its present constitution as a bulwark
of defense. Burma's role in the United Nations as an uncommitted, anticolonial, and underdeveloped nation has been and still is,
in part, predictable. As a member both of the Afro-Asian bloc and,
for two terms, of the U.N. Trusteeship Council, Burma's delegations consistently supported the right of all peoples to self-
determination and, where possible, independence. They have
voted for resolutions in support of U.N. multilateral aid programs;
and they have ranged themselves on the side of those who would
lessen "tensions" and mediate Cold-War disputes. In this latter
connection they have always favored the admission of Communist
China, on the basis of a proposed "universal membership" clause,
and they have supported hopes for arms control and disarmament
while voting for the limited nuclear-test-ban treaty (contrary to Peking).

However, as mentioned earlier, Burmese delegations, unlike
other neutralist members of the Afro-Asian bloc, voted for U.S.–
U.N. intervention to stop aggression in Korea and for condemnation of the U.S.S.R's invasion of Hungary (as well as of Western
aggression in the Suez incident). The Arab nations' policy toward
Israel has not kept Burma, unlike India, from having a friendly and
cooperative relationship with Israel.

Burmese satisfaction in the election of their U.N. ambassador to
the post of U.N. Secretary-General is evident in the attention that

the country's press gives to U Thant.[5] But a more careful appraisal of Burma's attitude toward the U.N. has been made by the then U.N. Ambassador, James Barrington, who also served in that capacity between 1950 and 1955. In a speech at Colby College, Maine, he referred to the quickening of the Burmese imagination by the U.N. Charter, calling for a world "in which peace would be maintained by collective security and collective action," in which the "traditional underdog, the masses of Asia and Africa and Latin America would at long last begin to enjoy a fairer store of the good things in the world . . . with dignity." He analyzed the serious undermining of the collective-security system by the "emergence . . . of two antagonistic blocs," and the consequent difficulties for any small nation that wanted to remain uncommitted. He described Burmese "disappointment" in the treatment it received over the Kuomintang issue. He concluded with an expression of "faith in the future" of the U.N. "despite its shortcomings. . . . If it has not been the great success we prayed for, it is because of the human element. . . . It can absorb new ideas, abandon outmoded ones. This can be brought about by discussion and persuasion. We continue to feel that the United Nations is a valuable forum for these purposes."

There has been no change in the Burmese attitude toward the U.N. since Barrington delivered this speech, "The United Nations Through Burmese Eyes," March 18, 1954. It was repeated by General Ne Win, at the nineteenth annual celebration of U.N. Day, October 24, 1964, at which time he still regarded the U.N. as expressive of Burmese "aspirations" for world order and peace, serving as the necessary "forum" for "harmonizing the varied interests of nations" and as the institution which should "ensure universality of membership" for these purposes.[6] The Burmese are grateful for the technical assistance they have received from the U.N. They are active, serious participants in the work of the General Assembly and its committees and in those organs of the U.N. that they have joined. But the Burmese know the limits of the U.N.'s ability to help defend their country in the event that they are involuntarily drawn into a conflict between the "two antagonistic blocs."

Why, then, it may be asked, do Burmese political leaders so strongly advocate that the United States reach an agreement with Communist China, or at least withdraw obstacles to the seating of the People's Republic of China in the United Nations?[7] The answer seems to me to be relatively simple. The Burmese are as much concerned with Communist China as are the American people, perhaps more so. They regard the United Nations as a source of moral and, in a very limited sense, material defense in the event of overt trouble betwen the P.R.C. and Burma. They feel that the P.R.C. in the United Nations will be less dangerous to them—and others—than if it remains outside. Burma's security would be enhanced, they believe, if there should be some kind of political settlement between the Sino-Soviet bloc and the West. Hence, Burma's strong advocacy of seating Communist China is more for reasons of national security than out of Asian pride or any doctrinal sympathy for Communist China. Burma, in effect, argues that if the United States recognizes the U.S.S.R., then why not the P.R.C.? If the U.S.S.R. is in the United Nations, then why not Communist China? Her leaders understand American anti-Communist feelings on this matter but do not appreciate what they call American inconsistency. They believe that with Communist China in the United Nations, they (and all other Southeast Asians) would gain additional support if the border settlement should become unsettled, or if China were to seek other ways to encroach in the rice bowl of Asia.

Obviously the Burmese know that the United States is not going to remake its China policy to satisfy the interests of Burma or any other country. They also know that the United States can veto the entry of Communist China in the U.N. Security Council. But, they argue, the growing membership of the U.N. alters the balance of voting strength in the General Assembly, and therefore it is possible that the United States may be defeated on the issue of seating a delegation from Peking in forthcoming sessions of the General Assembly. Such an event, the Burmese fear, could cause major reconsideration by the United States of its participation in the United Nations. They view the "seating" issue, as they do the dispute over Article 19 (concerning overdue payments from the U.S.S.R., France, and others), and the withdrawal of Indonesia over the Malaysian issue, as endangering the future existence of the U.N. itself. And they wish to "Preserve U.N." [8]

It is in the light of these factors that the Burmese—as have some Latin American friends—put forward the proposal for a universal-membership clause, which would require an amendment to the Charter. The Burmese see in such a clause—they optimistically do not recognize the difficulties of amending the Charter—several advantages. If the amendment were accepted before a final showdown vote on the seating of Communist China in the General Assembly, it would, they believe, avoid the ultimately expected defeat for the United States on this issue. It conceivably would pave the way for the recognition and admission of the two Koreas, the two Vietnams, the two Germanies. It would provide India with another forum for discussing the Chinese Communist incursions into its territory. If the Communist Chinese then continued this adventure or other similar ones in mainland Southeast Asia, and if the United States chose to come to the aid of aggrieved friendly states under a U.N. umbrella, it would, so the argument runs, more readily be supported by other nations, including some neutrals.

The foregoing Burmese argument is not without logical merit. However, it tends to view a strengthened United Nations more in legal than in political terms. The U.N. becomes a supreme court, or what has been called a supranational body with some executive powers. In such a context the anxieties of the rimlands of the Himalayas, including Burma, always under the threat of a rampant China, would become somewhat lessened. But it is an argument running counter to the deep political rift in the world, a rift that shattered similar hopes expressed by President Truman on that far-off day in October, 1945, when he restated the twelve "fundamental principles of righteousness and justice" on which "United States foreign policy is based."

It is because the Burmese leaders are not unaware of the seeming futility of what has been called here their legal argument for a strengthened U.N. that they hold the more tightly to their policy of "strict neutrality" and "nonalignment." They believe that the United States has at long last accepted the responsibility for the defense of its allies in Southeast Asia—that is, for the Philippines, Thailand, Vietnam, and possibly Laos. They hope that the course of this defense can be successfully concluded before a war with China engulfs them, as it would were it to occur. They also support without great enthusiasm another Geneva-type conference[9] to avoid such a war, provided all parties to the dispute were to participate. That is as far as their nonalignment takes them.

Burmese neutralism no longer requires a stubborn defense in or out of Burma; nor does it at present offer an obstacle to the intensive and extensive cultivation of bilateral relations between the United States and Burma on a government-to-government basis. Burma is a good illustration of a newly independent country committed to some form of "socialist democracy" (Ne Win's phrase; before him it had been "social democracy" or "democratic socialism") and to suppressing Communist rebellion and subversion, and which is willing to acquire from the free world the means of defense to carry out these purposes. From the earliest days of independence, when foreign policy was fluid because the policy-makers were young and inexperienced, in addition to being as doctrinaire as they are today, nothing has prevented Burma from seeking and accepting such aid when it was freely offered. The Bo Letya–Freeman Defense Agreement of August, 1947, was abrogated in 1954, mainly because of inept British actions in Burma at that time. Some of the training practices begun under it, however, have continued without an agreement. The military shopping list that Burma submitted to U.S. officials in 1948 may have been considered an example of Burmese inexperience and political naïveté, to be turned down in a cavalier manner; it may also have been rejected because American policy-makers believed that the equipment would be wasted since Burma would not survive the rebellions. Ten years later, the United States handled such a list more sympathetically through local currency purchases and loans. It should not be necessary to wait ten more years to draw the obvious inferences. Making the cost of counteracting Communist subversion as inexpensive as possible is in Burma's interest because it contributes to stability and eventually, I believe, to the return of democracy without any qualifying adjective. It is also in the interest of the United States and furthers our policy everywhere in free Asia, and especially in mainland Southeast Asia.

Since Burma is predominantly a Buddhist country, and since Buddhism exhibits pacifist tendencies, the question of its relationship, if any, to foreign policy arises. Buddhism as a way of life rests on a philosophy of constant change, on the interplay of individual intent and behavior in the context of external reality, on the pursuit of tolerance and the "Middle Way" between all extremes. During this past millennium, the majority of Burmese have adopted as their own one of the two major strains of Buddhism, Theravadism. Their commitment to this, as their history amply demonstrates, has enriched their lives and shaped their culture. But Buddhism has not inhibited Burmese aggression under the kingdoms or kept them from militant self-defense whenever such action seemed to be required.[10]

There is nothing in the culture of Burma, particularly her Theravada Buddhism, that inclines her people to peace at any price, to surrender to a competing, militant ideology. Buddhism within Burma may seek the path of compromise and peaceful resolution of conflict, but never at the expense of its own survival. Nor has it ever counseled submission to an external force, whatever its source. Buddhism in Burma is pacific when it is allowed to grow freely. It has frequently demonstrated its power to take a different course when obstructed or thwarted. Buddhism is not an ally of any political power in any direct sense; to so regard it would be in Buddhist eyes to demean it by overtly mixing worldly power and faith. By the same token, Theravada Buddhism cannot be made to serve Asian racial or Marxist class interests. There is little or no likelihood of a concordat between Burma's Buddhism and a Communist anti-religious or nonreligious society. For example, during Ne Win's caretaker regime over 1 million copies of a pamphlet prepared by the armed forces, exposing anti-Buddhist documents and teachings of the Burma Communist Party, were distributed as part of a psychological-warfare campaign against the Communists and Communism in Burma.[11]

Thus present Burmese policies, summed up under the general headings of neutralism, nonalignment, and socialism, are designed for self-defense; for combating Communist insurrection; for living in peace with Burma's neighbors; for participating modestly in those post–World War II multilateral institutions that already have, or, in the Burmese view, should have, representation from all the big powers; and for preserving Burma's unity while developing her resources according to plan. That the Burmese have become even more nationalistic during Ne Win's second regime than they were before (some critics have called this xenophobic or isolationist) is to a considerable extent understandable. Burma wishes to preserve her independence at all costs. Her leaders believe that Burma's independence is threatened in two ways: by the on-going big-power struggle in Southeast Asia and by the fact that Burma is geopolitically situated between her two most populous and now contending neighbors, Communist China and India. Since the threats are real, Burmese desires to avoid their dangerous consequences are rational. That Burmese leaders, in a much divided and contending world, elect to carry out the defense of Burma's independence by means that do not always coincide with those adopted by some of their neighbors or with some of those utilized by the United States, is also understandable. This does not as such make them anti-foreign, or anti-West, or anti–Sino-Soviet; it merely makes them, if anything, more pro-Burma.

On the other hand, the United States has repeatedly stated its foreign-policy objectives in terms of a world order under the "rule of law," symbolized in part by the United Nations and other multilateral agencies, and more specifically in terms of assisting Southeast Asian countries to maintain their freedom and independence, and in halting Communist expansion in Asia. Since these objectives are similar to those advanced by the Burmese, there should be no insurmountable barrier between the United States and Burma in reaching an understanding regarding their respective policies and in cooperating wherever possible in means to carry them out.

Strengthening and deepening direct relations between the United States and Burma means supporting identifiable and shared interests and setting aside those on which agreement cannot be reached at present. There is more to these shared interests than either Burma or the United States has as yet explored, while the disagreements have been unduly highlighted on both sides. To strengthen and deepen bilateral relations between Burma and the United States is not to argue for an "American showcase" among Asian neutralists or to support the view that Burma is a Southeast Asian "domino" whose fate, like that of Vietnam, will necessarily affect the other nations in that embattled arena. Rather, it is to support the mutuality of interests and reciprocal advantages between a democratic, noncolonial big power and an anticolonial small power seeking to become eventually a stable democracy of its own delineation, and presently trying to preserve its unity and independence.

The primary focus of this study emerged from the materials of Burmese history. The record reveals a dedication to independence not always supported by a constituency wise and effective enough to maintain it. The secondary focus arose from concern for Burma's independence and the relation to it of domestic and foreign policy—her own and that of the United States and other countries.

The emphasis of Parts I and II was on the insistence of the Burmese on maintaining, or fighting to regain and retain, their sovereignty. However nationalism may be defined, the Burmans in royal Burma and the multiethnic Burmese of the Union of Burma have always had a strong sense of identity with their land. To preserve it against the outsider and against internal rebellion and subversion has been a dominant concern. To build a national identity on the foundations of a modest welfare state, to improve the conditions of life, has been the overriding ambition of Burma's leaders since World War II. Therefore, to assist Burma to sustain and build a nation, to help her solve the major problems attendant upon these tasks while she develops relations abroad (Part III), become foundations for U.S. policy toward Burma (Part IV) as well as toward other newly independent nations in Asia and elsewhere. There has been no absence of policy on the part of the United States— though this has been a frequently met charge. Some policies of questionable wisdom and effectiveness, such as SEATO, have been hastily adopted. Others, such as the tacit toleration of early Kuomintang operations within Burma, have been pure folly. Mostly as a consequence of U.S. policies, Burma–U.S. relations have ranged up and down the political thermometer. What has been frequently lacking has been the will to apply existing benevolent policy vigorously, consistently, and continuously.

Three propositions that underlie this study are directly related to the overriding issues of security, stability, and improvement in the conditions of living for the Burmese. The first is that Burma's freedom and independence, in whatever terms the examination of them takes place—historical, political, economic, cultural—are worth preserving. Second, as a continuing objective of policy the United States wants friendly relations with Burma, one of the newly independent countries, and is seeking, not without interruption, to establish a free and open society capable of providing some modest modern benefits to her people. Third, the U.S. wants to prevent further Communist encroachments into the Asian rice bowl. We want to do this, not because we cannot live with Russians and Chinese, but because we are convinced that their system wishes to extinguish completely the idea and the practice of freedom, without which we and the Burmese and all other Southeast Asians cannot live and thrive.

As we approach the close of the second decade in our relations with Burma, we can see more clearly that U.S. foreign economic policy, intimately related to domestic policy, especially farm policy, and to world-wide food shortages, is an essential and major item in the conduct of over-all U.S. foreign policy. It is also clear that we shall have to invent or refine new bilateral and multilateral economic arrangements so that we and our friends can prosper. Certain types of aid may be offered "with strings," as the International Bank for Reconstruction and Development has demonstrated;

other types are better offered "without strings." There is no universally applicable principle here, just as there is no panacea in any one of the aid devices such as grants, soft or hard currency loans, credits, or use of surplus commodities. Nor is there any virtue in applying these devices exclusively to productive or social capital investment. There is the essential need for the adoption of long-range policies, plans, and appropriations, subject to U.S. executive and congressional review but without the annual uncertainties and public wrangling over the year-to-year authorizations and appropriations. At whatever point aid—any kind of aid, economic, military, political—is applied it can liberate the resources of the recipient for other purposes. What is required is first a commitment to be of genuine assistance, and then joint discovery of how best to carry out the commitment in terms of the requirements, priorities, and resources of the developing society and our own. There is need to apply some old words that are still relevant: imagination, flexibility, partnership.

I can offer no blueprint for the future, for the essence of my recommendation for U.S.–Burma bilateral relations, in economic as in all other matters, is that we must prepare the blueprint after we have made the commitment, and on the basis of mutual discovery and capability. The task of mutual discovery is not an easy one. The two countries' knowledge of each other is still in short supply. Both countries tend to be doctrinaire in the expression of their economic philosophy. The Burmese sloganize about the "Burmese Way to Socialism"; the Americans about their "free enterprise system." Burma, as one of the newly independent nations, tends to be sensitive to the kind of treatment she receives abroad; whereas the United States, having taken on global responsibilities, is upon occasion insensitive in its treatment of other member countries on the globe.

After a number of starts, and despite a number of errors, the U.S.–Burma relationship has survived. But neither its strength nor its quality is impressive. This condition provides a frame of reference within which relations can be improved. (At this stage there is in my view no reason to consider the opposite proposition, namely, that U.S.–Burma relations will cease.) Burma still needs imaginative and continuing assistance *of all kinds* in order to achieve the domestic goals with which she started at independence. Her security, however, against external Communist or other large-scale aggression depends largely on arrangements outside her control, whether these be bilateral agreement or through multilateral arrangements.

But this is not all that must be considered within the frame of reference to improve U.S.–Burma relations. The relations between the United States and other Western countries are set against a common cultural background that facilitates, though it does not guarantee, common understanding. The nations of Judeo-Christian and Greco-Roman traditions share many intellectual, ethico-religious, and esthetic values. The continuity of these traditions, the patterns they have formed, do not make it easy to establish an international discourse between nations as different as the United States and Asian countries such as Burma.

In Southern Asia, Burma has taken the leadership in revivifying Theravada Buddhism. Important segments of her leadership have adopted and vigorously expounded a domestic version of a cultur-ally pluralistic philosophy. Burma has taken major steps toward providing her people with compulsory free public education through the level of the professions. English, at least until the end of the 1960's, will remain in considerable part either the language of instruction in higher education or the required second language begun rather early in the lower schools. Burma sends several hun-dred students abroad each year. She is making a valiant effort through governmental channels to reinvigorate the traditional arts and crafts. It is a commonplace to say, though it is a saying that is not always honored, that an understanding of the culture of an-other country and its people is essential to building close relations with them.

For the time being, actual and potential bicultural contact has been inhibited by the decision of the Ne Win regime to accept only government-to-government programs. He has requested pri-vate American foundations (and related Russian ventures in this field) to withdraw from Burma. But even this retaliatory step may have had its origin in American insensitivity to Burmese concepts of cultural and personal respect. Intercultural understanding on a governmental as well as on a private level is not only intrinsically meritorious, but, in addition, as it is achieved it supports and en-hances the more common and more prominent political and eco-nomic aspects of international diplomacy.

U.S. policy in Asia should not be hinged to any one country in the area, be it big India, or advanced Japan, or Buddhist Burma. As we approach the 1970's, the United States has an opportunity to redirect her outlook, retain what has been good in the past, and forge ahead as she did at the beginning of the 1950's. The United States must begin with, though not necessarily stop at, building strong and direct relations with each of the countries of non-Communist Asia. In this context, Burma is a key country in South-ern Asia. The United States can and should do more to discover how to assist Burma in her progress toward economic growth, do-mestic security, and political stability. Where relevant we should encourage Burmese initiative in Asian affairs, especially among neighbors with a similar Buddhist culture. Americans engaged in official and private affairs should strengthen friendly relations with all levels of Burmese leadership. All too frequently Americans abroad tend to move diplomatically at the summit, forgetting that there are other levels of leadership in being or developing. We do not need to endorse all Burmese policies nor expect endorsement of all our policies. We do need to have understanding where differences may exist.

During the 1950's and 1960's, the United States rebuilt its military strength in response to the Communist challenge. Partly because of the Korean War, and more recently because of the war in Viet Nam, U.S. policy has understandably been heavily weighted in the direction of military security factors. Decisions, attitudes, and arguments flowing from security conceptions have affected and colored political, economic, and cultural foreign policies and actions, not always to their advantage. This in turn has affected our relations with Burma and other nations in free Asia. But to the extent that such U.S. military security policies succeed in their objective—to help the newly independent countries maintain their freedom—they will gain basic acceptance, if not expressed approval. In this sense, the U.S. role in Vietnam since February, 1965, is being carefully watched by Burma and all other free Asian countries. And in this sense, also, since I believe the Republic of Vietnam will survive as a free state, we need and can afford to take a longer view.

What should be the purpose and hopes of U.S. policy toward Burma? We covet no territory. We are not in dire need of Burmese or other Southeast Asian resources. Our primary interest is in regional peace and stability, so that Burma and all other still free Asian countries can enjoy the fruit of their own independent efforts. Our hopes must spring from a clear analysis of the forces and meanings inherent in Burmese life, as well as in our own. Without an understanding, or with an insufficient understanding, of Burmese aspirations for peace and security, political and economic stability, and cultural renascence, we cannot proceed. But with such understanding—one that must be cultivated on both sides—there can result a surer foundation for friendly relations between the two countries—and that is our purpose.

Such relations do not require either identity of outlook on the means to common ends or the subservience of one country to the other. Friendship between Burma as an Asian and Buddhist country and the United States will open two doors: mutual cultural enrichment and mutual cooperation for peace, freedom, and development in an important part of the world. Burmese quiet awareness of the dangers posed by Communist imperialism, of the bitter, costly experience with Communist insurrections, of the fact that Western imperialism has virtually disappeared from her part of the world, strengthens Burma's commitment to some variant of socialist democracy without aligning foreign policy to either big-power bloc. U.S. policy toward Burma is a test, albeit a partial one, of America's ability to work closely with a small, unaligned country in furtherance of shared hopes and purposes. This offers a challenge to Americans to replenish their fund of moral capital through wise, tolerant, and generous treatment of a distant and different people. Moral capital, it is true, brings only respect and perhaps admiration. But it is something without which free peoples and free nations, big or small, cannot meet the challenge of our turbulent age.

NOTES

Chapter 1: Burma Meets the West

1. The quotation is from Ralph Fitch's account, reprinted in J. Horton Ryley, *Ralph Fitch: England's Pioneer to India and Burma* (London: T. Fisher Unwin, 1889), pp. 156–57. See also Arthur P. Phayre, *History of Burma, Including Burma Proper, Pegu, Taungu, Tenasserim and Arakan From the Earliest Time to the End of the First War With British India* (London: Trübner, 1883), pp. 261–74. This is the first full history of Burma written by a Western scholar who was, as well, a British administrator. Its concluding chapter, "Early European Intercourse With Burma," is the first connected account of this subject, though Phayre and subsequent authors such as Hugh Clifford and D. G. E. Hall undoubtedly made use of "Notes on the Intercourse of the Burmese Countries With Western Nations," in Captain Henry Yule, *A Narrative of the Mission Sent by the Governor-General of India to the Court of Ava in 1855 With Notices of the Country, Government and People* (London: Smith, Elder and Co., 1858), pp. 204–19.

2. G. E. Harvey, *History of Burma, From the Earliest Times to 10 March 1824. The Beginning of the English Conquest* (London: Longmans Green, 1925), pp. 174–76. Harvey, seldom favorably inclined toward the Burmese, relies here on the account by Caesar Fredericke. See also his note, "Pegu Merchants Abroad," pp. 341–42.

3. D. G. E. Hall, *Europe and Burma, A Study of European Relations With Burma to the Annexation of Thibaw's Kingdom, 1886* (London: Oxford University Press, 1945), p. 14. See also U Myo Min (ed.), *Old Burma as Described by Early Foreign Travellers* (Rangoon: Hanthawaddy Publications, 1947). This book, edited by Professor Myo Min of the University of Rangoon, was compiled to enable Burmese students to learn something of the Western portrayal of their land: "Even where they intended to be honest recorders of what they saw, they were at a disadvantage through ignorance of language, customs, and background, and through misunderstanding and pre-conceived notions."

4. Albert Fytche, *Burma Past and Present With Personal Reminiscences of the Country* (2 vols.; London: Kegan Paul, 1878), I, 4–13. The East India Company also sent a mission to Ayuthia, the capital of Siam, in 1611, which arrived the following year. Some members from this group proceeded north to Chiengmai, then part of the Lao States. Fitch had also visited and reported on this area. See D. G. E. Hall, *Early English Intercourse With Burma (1587–1743)* (London: Longmans Green, 1928), pp. 19, 31–33.

5. Marguerite Eyer Wilbur, *The East India Company and the British Em-*

pire in the Far East (Stanford, Calif.: Stanford University Press, 1945), pp. 13, 17–22. Fitch is not listed among the original 101 subscribers to the Company's capital (pp. 455–58), but he appears as an adviser or informant in at least two documents related to the Company. See Ryley, *op. cit.*, pp. 198–99. D. G. E. Hall, A *History of South-East Asia* (New York: St Martin's Press, 1955), remarks on p. 227, without further documentation, that the story of a "Dutch corner in pepper . . . often quoted [is] entirely legendary." Though that may be, the fabulous profits to be made from the pepper and spice trade, especially in the first half of the seventeenth century, provided a real incentive to compete with the Dutch traders who charged high prices for these commodities. See Kristof Glamann, *Dutch Asiatic Trade 1620–1740* (Copenhagen: Danish Science Press, 1958), chaps. iv, "Pepper," and v, "Spices," pp. 73–111.

6. For brief reviews of Anglo-Dutch and Anglo-French rivalry, with special reference to Burma in the seventeenth and eighteenth centuries, see Hall, *Europe and Burma* . . . , pp. 29–51, 60–73.

7. *The Imperial Gazetteer of India, the Indian Empire, Historical* (Oxford: Clarendon Press, 1909), II, 454–59.

8. *Ibid.*, pp. 459–60.

9. Virginia McLean Thompson, *Dupleix and His Letters, 1742–1754* (New York: Ballou, 1933), "The French East India Company," pp. 65–86.

10. L'Abbé de Choisy, *Journal du Voyage de Siam, 1687*, quoted in Maurice Collis, *Siamese White* (London: Faber and Faber, 1951), pp. 46–47. Writing some fifty years earlier, Jeremias van Vliet, the Dutch agent in Ayuthia in 1629–34, described the city as a "great conglomeration of streets, alleys, canals and ditches . . . the houses are of poor construction, but the town is adorned with about 400 fine temples and monasteries, which are all cleverly and sumptuously built . . . the palace of the king is great and magnificent." "Description of the Kingdom of Siam," trans. L. F. van Ravenswaay, in *Journal of the Siam Society* (Bangkok, 1910), VII, Part I, p. 13.

11. The 1,200 miles from Madras to Mergui could be covered in three weeks. River and land portage from Mergui to Ayuthia took some ten to twelve days. The alternate route from Madras to Ayuthia by way of the Straits of Malacca and the Gulf of Siam, a distance of 3,000 miles, "might take six months if winds were unfavorable." Collis, *op. cit.*, p. 31.

12. Phaulkon, White, and the port of Mergui are fascinating subjects. Collis' *Siamese White* is all the interested reader needs to know of Mergui; and the piratical White, whose petition against the Company was presented to the House of Commons on April 18, 1689, decidedly helped to reinforce the triumph of the Whigs. A contemporary account of Phaulkon by the Jesuit Père d'Orléans, *Historie de M. Constance* (Tours, 1690), appears in translation of Sir John Bowring, *The Kingdom and People of Siam; With a Narrative of the Mission to That Country in 1855* (2 vols.; London: John W. Parker, 1857), II, 385–407. A curious historical sidelight is that Elihu Yale, founder of the university that bears his name, a president of the British East India Company's factory at Madras and sworn enemy of Samuel White, was implicated in a private deal in rubies with King Narai which, according to Collis, did not reflect well on him. Phaulkon had been decorated by Louis XIV for his diligent labors in converting the Siamese to Roman Catholicism: see his letter to the Jesuit priest Père la Chaise (November 20, 1686) in *Mémoire du Père de Beze sur la Vie de Constance Phaulkon, Premier Ministre du Roi de Siam, Phra Narai, et sa Triste Fin, Suivi de Lettres et de Documents d'Archives de Constance Phaulkon*, ed., with notes, by Jean Drans and Henri Bernard (Tokyo: Presses Salésiennes, 1947), pp. 170–95. The *Mémoire* by Father de Beze was written *circa* 1691, and is published here for the first time, with the letters.

13. W. A. R. Wood, A *History of Siam From the Earliest Times to the Year A.D. 1781, With a Supplement Dealing With More Recent Events* (rev. ed.; Bangkok: Siam Barnakich Press, 1933), pp. 194–211.

14. *The Imperial Gazetteer of India* . . . , II, p. 460.

15. Collis, *op. cit.*, "Behind the Scenes in London and Madras," pp. 183–202. The quotation is on p. 189.

16. *Records of the Relations Between Siam and Foreign Countries in the 17th Century Copied From Papers Preserved at the India Office* (5 vols.; Bangkok, 1915–21), IV (1686–87), 35. (Printed by order of the Council of the Vajiranana National Library.) In the Company's view, Phaulkon was the villain. He "fears the revenge deserved by him from us, and it may be from the Dutch likewise, which has forced him in his Master's name to the craving of succour from the King of France" (p. 114). These records (Vol. IV, as well as Vol. III [1680–85]) are invaluable for the study of the period.

17. Wood, *op. cit.*, pp. 212–17.

18. *Records of the Relations Between Siam and Foreign Countries*, V (1688–1700), *op. cit.* 106. "We take it for granted that Phaulkon is killed, and the French being gone our war is at an end with those people, rather because the last advice we had from Siam was that the new king was sending an ambassadour to the Fort [St. George] to compose all differences, which we hope took effect accordingly; if not fully concluded we would have you take the first honourable occasion for concluding a firm peace with that king, not that we have any esteem for the trade of that place." (Extract from a letter from the Court of Committees to the Council at Bombay, January 31, 1690.)

19. See, for example, the criticism of Alexander Hamilton, "A New Account of the East Indies," in John Pinkerton, *A General Collection of . . . Voyages and Travels* (London: Longmans . . . , 1811), VIII 429–30. Hamilton accused the Company of harassing the "English free merchants [who] were settled at Merjee [Mergui]," of threatening the King of Siam with a sea war though his government was "mild" and "indulgent," and of provoking and killing "some Siamers, without just cause." Such conduct led to the Siamese reprisals and loss of "innocent" English lives at Mergui. Captain Hamilton had been "trading and travelling" from 1688 to 1723. His *A New Account of the East Indies* was first published in 1727.

20. *Records of the Relations Between Siam and Foreign Countries*, IV, 230. Hall, in *A History of South-East Asia* (p. 322), points out that Weltden's claim of Negrais for the Company in 1687 had been preceded by an "abortive attempt to seize the island" in 1686. However, Syriam—opposite modern Rangoon—not Negrais, became the important naval station.

21. Sir Edward Blunt, *The ICS: The Indian Civil Service* (London: Faber, 1937), pp. 9–10.

22. *Ibid.*, pp. 26–34.

23. See Hall, *A History of South-East Asia*, p. 318; and the author's review of this important work in *Far Eastern Quarterly*, XV, No. 3 (May, 1956) 433–38.

24. *The British Burma Gazetteer, Compiled by Authority* [H. R. Spearman] (2 vols.; Rangoon: Government Press, 1880), I, 294–95, notes: "The Burman sovereigns and their officials, and indeed the whole of the inhabitants of Chin-India, had the most supreme contempt for non-Boodhistic foreigners, and our ignorance of their laws and traditions and the resulting mistakes we made, especially as individuals, by no means tended to produce greater friendliness [and] subsequent events only proved how right they were."

25. Hall, *Europe and Burma . . .* , pp. 24–28. The quotation is from a document of 1626.

26. See "Embassy of Mr. Edward Fleetwood to Ava in 1695," in *Reprint From Dalrymple's Oriental Repertory, 1791–97 of Portions Relating to Burma* (Rangoon: Government Printing, 1926), p. 216. Hereafter cited as Dalrymple, *op. cit.*

27. Hall, *Europe and Burma . . .* , pp. 32–34. In *Early English Intercourse With Burma* (p. 105), Hall rejects the reference in Dalrymple (*op. cit.*, p. 2) to the Chinese as a "wild assertion," but offers no contrary evidence and, in fact, acknowledges a seventeenth-century report that tends to confirm Dalrymple.

28. Dalrymple, *op. cit.*, pp. 6–7; see also *The British Burma Gazetteer*, p. 295.

29. The documents pertaining to Fleetwood and Bowyear appear in Dalrymple, *op. cit.*, pp. 187–254. Higginson was working for the Company, and in his own interests, as a private trader. The Fleetwood documents consisting of Higginson's instructions, the transcript of the letter to the King, Fleetwood's "Diary of Transactions," (October 14, 1695, to March 17, 1696), and the King's letter of committal to Fleetwood, are gems of seventeenth-century international discourse.

30. *The British Burma Gazetteer*, I, 295–96. Hamilton, *op. cit.*, p. 423, reported, *circa* 1709, that Alison had served "twice [as] ambassador from the Governor of Fort St. George, or his agents at Syriam, to the court of Ava."

31. It is not wholly clear whether these agents were officials of the Company or private traders who also handled some of the Company's affairs. The unknown author of a letter dated June 23, 1759 (Dalrymple, *op. cit.*, pp. 9–10), regards the residents as "mere Supervisors of the Private Trade and not immediately in the Service of the Company." Hall holds that these agents were proper "residents," appointed upon payment of a security fee to the Company, "to take charge of [its] shipbuilding," *Europe and Burma . . . ,* pp. 57–58, and *Early English Intercourse With Burma*, pp. 189–242. The Burmese believed they were dealing with officials.

32. Thompson, *op. cit.*, pp. 86, 89, 92; see also pp. 720–21. Harvey (*op. cit.*, p. 353) remarks that Dupleix "liked Syrian because it was out of the way of the English; he regarded it as his chief shipbuilding center, because labor and material were cheap." Harvey also points out that "in the eighteenth century their [the French] shipwrights were probably the best in Europe, and it is from them the Delta [Burma] received its first lessons in shipbuilding." The Burmese were and are good woodworkers.

33. Michael Symes, *An Account of an Embassy to the Kingdom of Ava Sent by the Governor-General of India in the Year 1795* (London: W. Bulmer, 1800), pp. 10, 19–23. "The French favored the Peguers whilst the English leaned to the Burmans. . . . Their partialities were manifested by petty assistance lent in secret, and supplies clandestinely conveyed, probably more with a view to private emolument, than from any enlarged political consideration." Symes, of course, was writing an official account of his mission of 1795. (Hereafter cited as Symes, *An Account*.) Sonnerat, *Voyage aux Indes Orientales et à la Chine, 1774–1781* (Paris, 1782), II, 40, charges that the French broke a neutrality agreement, which caused the Burmans to kill some officers who fell into their hands and make prisoners out of the soldiers and sailors. One of these later served against the British. There is some confusion about these engagements. There is a record of a single "engagement [that] lasted seven days" which found *both* the French and the English on the side of the Mons in an assault, in 1755, on the Burman-held city of Dagon (later renamed Rangoon, or "End of Strife"). This episode contributed to the subsequent massacre at and destruction of the British factory at Negrais in 1759. See Dalrymple, *op. cit.*, pp. 61–63; and *ibid.*, for Captain George Baker's *Journal of a Joint Embassy to the King of the Buraghmahns* [Burmans]; and *English at Dagon* (pp. 81–104). Between 1743 and 1759, the English made several attempts, in which they eventually succeeded, to regularize their position at Negrais. In addition to Baker's *Journal* and *Observations at Persaim* [*Bassein*], see Dalrymple, *op. cit.*, for the various accounts by Governor Saunders (*circa* 1750), Ensign Robert Lester (1757), and Captain Walter Alves (1759 and 1760), and *ibid.*, pp. 182–83 for the King's letter in October, 1760, to the Governor of Madras after the Negrais massacre. See also Symes's account of how the British and French combined against the Burmans in 1755, *op. cit.*, pp. 23–25. He called the episode "a strain on the national honor which the lapse of more than forty years has not been able to expunge."

34. Dalrymple, *op. cit.*, "Lester's Embassy, 1757," pp. 104–30. Unless

otherwise indicated, all quotations in the following paragraphs are taken from Lester's account.

35. Both the letter "Plate of Gold, with Rubies set around it" and the letter to the Company were sent by the King through Ensign Dyer in 1756. Hall gives a translation of the former in *Europe and Burma . . .* , pp. 65–67. He refers to the fact that King Alaungpaya sent his letter "to the King of England in person [and] would not demean" himself by an agreement with a mere local official of the Company. There is no record of a suitable reply.

36. Hall, *Europe and Burma . . .* , from the translation of the letter.

37. It is reprinted in Dalrymple, *op. cit.*, pp. 127–30.

38. *Ibid.*, "The Loss of Negrais," pp. 131–38. All quotations are from Captain Walter Alves, who gives what amounts to an eyewitness account, supported by his further inquiries both in 1759 and when he returned, at the Company's orders, in 1760. See *ibid.*, "Alves' Embassy, 1760," pp. 139–81. Phayre, *op. cit.*, p. 168, was inclined to accept the reliability of the report that Negrais officials sold arms and ammunition to the Mons rebels.

39. Symes, *Embassy to Ava*, p. 56; see also pp. 44, 56–62.

40. Sonnerat, *op. cit.*, pp. 42–45. Sonnerat adds that the French East India Company did not "profit from these advantages." The letter is dated Burmese Era 1132, i.e., 1770. However, what Yule, (*op. cit.*, p. 218) refers to as the "apprehension of French intrigue in Burma" continued to occupy the British.

41. See Symes, *Embassy to Ava*, pp. 51–53, for an estimate of this King who, "whether viewed in the light of a politician, or soldier, is undoubtedly entitled to respect. The wisdom of his councils secured what his valour had acquired: he was not more eager for conquest, than attentive to the improvement of his territories, and the prosperity of his people [and] his heroic actions give him an indisputable claim to no mean rank among the distinguished personages in the pages of history."

42. *The Imperial Gazetteer of India*, II, 488.

43. William Francklin, *Tracts, Political, Geographical and Commercial on the Dominions of Ava and the Northwestern Parts of Hindostaun* (London: Cadell and Davies, 1811), p. 2. "As no adequate idea of the power and authority of the British Government in Asia, has hitherto been entertained by the Burma court, it appears from the treatment experienced both by Captains Symes [1795] and Cox [1797], that their characters as Ambassadors was not sufficiently understood, or if it was, the Court of Ava pretended ignorance of the circumstance, by considering, and treating, those gentlemen in the inferior light of commercial agents only; in consequence of which, they did not experience that personal respect which was undoubtedly due to the representatives of the Governor-General of India." Francklin, a major in the East India Company, prepared these papers in 1801 "by command of the Most Noble Marquis Wellesley, then Governor-General." He called attention to "our inveterate enemy," the French (p. 11), and urged that the Company's ambassadors "be empowered to require the total expulsion of the French from the dominions of Ava" (p. 13).

Chapter 2: Empire and Kingdom: The Irrepressible Conflict Between England and the Kingdom of Burma

1. Father Vincentius Sangermano, *Description of the Burmese Empire*, with an Introduction and Notes by John Jardine (Westminster, England: Archibald Constable, 1893), pp. 70–71. Father Sangermano, a Barnabite missionary, arrived in Burma in 1782. He returned to Italy in 1808 with a pension from the British Government as a reward for his map-making and intelligence work. He prepared this account on his retirement to Italy where he died in 1819. It was translated into English by William Tandy and was first published in 1833, although Father Sangermano had shared his notes

and his knowledge with English missions to Burma beginning, in 1795, with that of Captain Symes. His work was extensively used by most nineteenth-century Western writers on Burma, who rarely questioned the missionary bias. Jardine's edition is the most valuable one; it retains the text of the translation as it appeared in 1833.

2. *Ibid.*, p. 74.

3. Phayre, *op. cit.*, pp. 230–31.

4. D. G. E. Hall (ed.), *Michael Symes' Journal of His Second Embassy to the Court of Ava in 1802* (London: George Allen & Unwin, 1955), p. lxv. (Hereafter cited as *Symes' Second Embassy*.) A reading of Hall's valuable eighty-page introduction is required to correct the distortions of Symes's work that appear in most earlier English writings about him. Here, Hall not only corrects his own earlier views, but also gives the best account of the events surrounding the renewal of British East India Company relations with Burma, *circa* 1795.

5. Harvey, *op. cit.*, p. 271.

6. For a substantial account of Rangoon as a socio-economic and political center in the second half of the eighteenth and the first half of the nineteenth centuries, see the fine folio volume, B. R. Pearn, *A History of Rangoon* (Rangoon: American Baptist Mission Press, 1939), chaps. iv, v, pp. 49–109. Pearn, at the time, was a British civil servant. These chapters give an account of the private and demiofficial trade relations between the Burmese and the English from the time of Alves.

7. Yule, *op. cit.*, pp. 218–19.

8. Phayre, *op. cit.*, p. vii. See Harvey, *op. cit.*, p. xvi: "It has long been the fashion to deny the existence of historical [vernacular] material in Burma. But it is a question of standard and the native material though modest in quantity and quality, is better than in the rest of Indo-China."

9. John F. Cady, *A History of Modern Burma* (Ithaca, N.Y.: Cornell University Press, 1958), pp. vi–vii. What Cady says of English-language sources would apply to works in other Western languages, and also applies to the period before 1800.

10. Pearn, *op. cit.*, pp. 69–70.

11. There is some evidence that King Bodawpaya and his grandson and successor, King Bagyidaw (1819–37), sounded out the Indian princes who were in opposition to the Company, about the possibility of an alliance that might regain for Burma the Chittagong-Dacca area, formerly a dependency of the Arakan overlords. See Phayre, *op. cit.*, pp. 224–24; and quotations from Lady Amherst's diary in A. T. Ritchie and Richardson Evans, *Lord Amherst and the British Advance Eastwards to Burma* (Oxford: Clarendon Press, 1894), pp. 64–65, 121–22.

12. Quoted from the summary by Pearn, *op. cit.*, p. 93. Most, if not all, authorities would agree with Pearn's conclusions, however differently they might weigh the separate factors. For Pearn essentially reproduces the contemporary materials and the instructions given to Michael Symes. See Symes, *Embassy to Ava*, pp. 456–64.

13. Symes, *Embassy to Ava*, pp. 487–93.

14. *Ibid.*, p. 483.

15. *Asiatick Researches or Transactions of the Society Instituted in Bengal* (London, 1801), VI, 163–308. Some of this material, translated by Dr. Buchanan from the notes of Father Sangermano, and used by the latter in his later *Description of the Burmese Empire*, had been extended by the surgeon through his own inquiries. Dr. Buchanan was obviously well acquainted with the researches initiated by Sir William Jones, pioneer of English Orientalist studies in India and founder-president of the (Royal) Asiatic Society of Bengal in 1784. Both Buchanan (p. 307) and Sangermano (*op. cit.*, pp. 180–81) call attention to the high degree of literacy in Burma brought about by the *pongyis*, "monks."

16. Symes, *Embassy to Ava*, pp. 456–64.

17. From a letter dated March 9, 1796, quoted in Vincent A. Smith, *The Oxford History of India From the Earliest Times to the End of 1911* (Oxford: Clarendon Press, 1920), p. 574. Smith, wholly admiring the strong governors-general who advanced the cause of England in India, calls Shore "the worst of the few really incompetent Governors-General."

18. This is the subject of Hall's fine introduction to *Symes' Second Embassy*, for which he drew on the largely unpublished contemporary sources, the Bengal Secret and Political Consultations and the Bengal Political Consultations. Cox severely criticized Symes and the Burmese in dispatches to Bengal. His son Henry posthumously published his *Journal of a Residence in the Burmhan Empire and More Particularly at the Court of Amarapoorah* (London: Warren and Whittaker, 1821). The *Journal*, which is militantly anti-Burmese, does not contain the anti-Symes material. This, as Hall points out, appears in a long unpublished dispatch to Bengal, dated November 27, 1797.

19. From Captain Cox's general letter of instructions quoted in William Francklin, *op. cit.*, pp. 3–10. The *Tracts*, gathered from Cox's papers, were prepared by Francklin in 1801 at the request of Marquis Wellesley, Shore's successor.

20. *Symes' Second Embassy*, p. 241. This story was told to Lieutenant Canning by a Catholic missionary. See also Pearn, *op. cit.*, p. 95.

21. "I was either somebody or nobody," Cox wrote in his *Journal*, p. 207.

22. *Ibid.*, pp. vi–vii. He arranged to resettle refugees from Arakan at the place still known as "Cox's Bazar."

23. *Symes' Second Embassy*, p. 256.

24. *Ibid.*, pp. lii–lxi. See also B. R. Pearn, "King-Bering," *Journal of the Burma Research Society*, XXIII, Part II (1933), 55–85. "King-Bering" is the Arakanese Chin Byan who, operating from English territory, raided this border area from 1811 until his death in 1815; this confirmed the Burmese suspicions of British "treachery." See also Phayre, *op. cit.*, pp. 222–26.

25. *Symes' Second Embassy*, pp. lix–lx.

26. *Ibid.*, pp. 97–100.

27. George Macaulay Trevelyan, *A Shortened History of England* (London and New York: Longmans Green, 1944), p. 422. See also Smith, *op. cit.*, pp. 578–608, for a wholly sympathetic account of Wellesley's regime. Governor-General Lord Minto (1807–13) and Thomas Stamford Raffles pursued Wellesley's policies with regard to the French possessions of Mauritius and nearby islands in the western reaches of the Indian Ocean and the (French) Dutch Indonesian islands. Louis Napoleon then occupied the throne of Holland. Despite Raffles, Java was returned to the Dutch in 1816, as a consequence of English policy at the Congress of Vienna and because of doubts in the London offices of the Company about the profitability of this colony.

28. All quotations, unless otherwise indicated, in this and the following pages are taken from the documents in *Symes' Second Embassy*, pp. 93–266, which include instructions, letters, his journal (September 25, 1802, to February 3, 1803); and appendixes to the journal which include the new exchanges of agreements between Symes and the Court of Burma, and instructions to Canning.

29. See Collis, *Siamese White*, pp. 226–38.

30. Symes subsequently visited with the Prince of Toungoo, the potential contestant for the throne in the event of an abdication. He found him to be "a man of ability, courage and enterprise," but no longer able to bid for power. He had already tried and failed. In the second set of instructions, the report to Symes, concerning the abdication, was apparently in error. See *Symes' Second Embassy*, the journal entry for December 25, pp. 216–17, for a possible explanation of how the story of the abdication may have gained currency. Bodawpaya outlived his son and heir, who died in 1808, but he had no difficulty in naming his grandson to be his successor.

31. *Op. cit.*, "Observations, etc., on the Instructions of the Envoy to the Court of Ava, Delivered to Mr. Edmonstone, July 1, 1801," pp. 1–25. N. B. Edmonstone was Secretary to Government. He prepared the various "observations" of the Governor-General, and instructions given to Symes in 1802.

32. Smith, *op. cit.*, p. 606.

33. Symes officially disavowed any British intention to extend her territorial acquisitions, because he felt that this was what the Burmese feared. See *Symes' Second Embassy*, the journal entry for December 20 (p. 169) and the second of the four articles of the proposed agreement (p. 245).

34. *Ibid.* See, for example, pp. 146–47, 175–77, 181 (a story of how the king had formed a French diplomatic mission, including an American, Mr. Bevan, in order to embarrass Symes), pp. 185 ff.

35. The treaty, consisting of an introduction, eleven articles, and an "additional article" governing the payments of the indemnity, was reprinted several times. Contemporary military writers, such as Captain Thomas A. Trant and Major J. J. Snodgrass, included it in their published accounts of the war, as did John Crawfurd, who was sent to Burma, first in 1826, as a civilian commissioner, then as an envoy to Ava from September, 1826, to February, 1827, to negotiate the above-mentioned commercial agreement and to arrange for the exchange of ministers. See his *Journal of an Embassy From the Governor-General of India to the Court of Ava* (2d ed.; 2 vols.; London: Henry Colburn, 1834), II, Appendix, 35–43. (The first edition appeared in 1829.) Crawfurd summarized the commercial agreement (Appendix, pp. 11–34). It added nothing to previously negotiated similar agreements. But he did arrange for the appointment of a resident minister at Ava—Major Henry Burney, who remained there from 1830 to 1837. Crawfurd's *Journal* is important in at least two respects. It contains (Appendix, pp. 86–115) Adoniram Judson's "Deposition" as a prisoner, an understandably partisan document, in view of Judson's twenty-one months in prison, "seventeen in irons," which placed the blame for the war on the Burmese; and it is another detailed description of Burma and the Burmese, the prototype of which was Symes' *An Account*. For a more convenient copy of the Treaty of Yandabo, see Maung Maung, *Burma in the Family of Nations* (Amsterdam and New York: Djambatan and Institute of Pacific Relations, 1956), pp. 155–57. Burney is another in the line of distinguished soldier-scholars who added to the rich legacy of English writings on Burma. See also *infra*, n. 37.

36. There is, as yet, no single, modern, full-length study of the three (1824–26, 1852, 1885) Anglo-Burmese wars. Readable secondary accounts of the wars will be found in Phayre, *op. cit.*, pp. 232–60 (first war); and in Pearn, *A History of Rangoon*, pp. 111–30, 163–73, and (to a lesser extent) in *The British Burma Gazetteer*, pp. 325–46, 354–75 (first and second wars). John Leroy Christian, *Modern Burma, A Survey of Political and Economic Development* (Berkeley, Calif.: University of California Press, 1942), pp. 27–36; and Cady, *op. cit.*, chap. iii, glide quickly over all three wars but their works, like the Pearn volume, are useful for bibliographical references to original sources. Important English-language contemporary and published original sources not mentioned in these three books are: Captain W. White, A *Political History of the Extraordinary Events Which Led to the Burmese War* (London: C. Hamilton, 1827); G. W. de Rhé-Philipe, *A Narrative of the First Burmese War, 1824–1826 With the Various Official Reports and Dispatches Describing the Operations of the Naval and Military Forces Employed, and Other Documents Bearing Upon the Origin, Progress, and Conclusion of the Contest* (including two Appendixes of biographical notices of officers mentioned in these records and an alphabetical roll of British officers killed, wounded, and captured) (Calcutta: Government Printing, 1905); D. G. E. Hall (ed.), *The Dalhousie-Phayre Correspondence, 1852–1856*, with introduction and notes (London: Oxford University Press, 1932); and "Frontier and Overseas Expeditions From India Compiled in the Intelli-

gence Branch . . . Army Headquarters, India," *Burma* (Simla: Government Monotype Press, 1907), Vol. V.

37. Reference has already been made to the chief published records of Symes, Crawfurd, Phayre, and Yule. Burney's writings are largely unpublished, though a number of articles appeared during his lifetime in the *Journal of the Asiatic Society of Bengal*; including his important "Some Account of the Wars Between Burma and China," VI (January to December, 1837). He is supposed to have revised Dr. G. T. Bayfield's "Historical Review of the Political Relations Between the British Government in India and the Empire of Ava," in R. B. Pemberton, *Report on the Eastern Frontier of British India* (Calcutta: Government Printing, 1835), but it difficult to say what part he played in the preparation of this tendentious and important account by a member of his staff during the time of the Residency of Ava, 1830–40. See W. S. Desai, *History of the British Residency in Burma, 1826–1840* (Rangoon: University of Rangoon, 1939), and D. G. E. Hall, "Henry Burney, Diplomat and Orientalist," *Journal of the Burma Research Society*, XLI (December, 1958), Parts I and II, 100–110.

38. Hall, *A History of South-East Asia*, p. 519.

39. Crawfurd, *op. cit.*, I, 304.

40. Pearn, *A History of Rangoon*, chap. vii, "Tharawaddy's Rangoon," 130–60.

41. *Ibid.* See also Desai, *op. cit.*, pp. 56–61, 130–41.

42. Maung Maung, *op. cit.*, p. 42.

43. *The Political Writings of Richard Cobden* (2 vols.; London: William Ridgeway, 1867), II, 25–106. General Lewis Cass, U.S. Senator from Michigan, spoke in Congress in strong agreement with Cobden. Excerpts from his speech are quoted on the penultimate page of Cobden's text. See also Dalhousie's own views, quoted in Hall (ed.), *The Dalhousie-Phayre Correspondence*, pp. xx-xxix and *ibid.*, "The Proclamation of the Annexation of Pegu," December 20, 1852 (pp. 4–5).

44. During his reign, there was one war scare with regard to the Burmese and the British. It followed the difficulties between the English and the Chinese (the Margary murder affair of February, 1875), in which the Burmese were also suspected. British India decided to send a special mission, headed by Sir Douglas Forsythe, to King Mindon's court because "it was thought that a third Burmese war would be the result." See an interesting account of this episode in C. H. E. Adamson, *Narrative of an Official Visit to the King of Burmah in March, 1875 From Notes Made at the Time* (Newcastle-on-Tyne: J. Bell, 1878).

45. Hall, *The Dalhousie-Phayre Correspondence*, p. 392. See also the exchange of letters covering the 1855 mission and its preparatory stages, pp. 341–93. Phayre (*op. cit.*, p. 380) records how the King asked for the "health of the English ruler"—"the old ambiguity as to the English ruler, and English country was retained." Phayre "expressly, however, named *Bengal* [italics in original]" in his answer; that is, he referred to the Company as the ruler.

46. Fytche, *Burma Past and Present*, I, 205. See, in contrast to such frank opinions, the conversations between the King and Fytche as the latter reports these in *ibid.*, II, Appendix C, 252–85.

47. There is an annalistic account of his reign, translated from the Burmese, in J. George Scott and J. P. Hardiman, *Gazetteer of Upper Burma and the Shan States* (5 vols.; Rangoon: Government Printing, 1900), I, Part I, 29–81. See pp. 81–96 for a similar account of King Thibaw; see also pp. 97–115. Hereafter cited as *Gazetteer of Upper Burma*.

48. There can be no defense for such actions. However, subsequent British commentators almost invariably call attention to Burmese brutality and pointedly ignore, for example, the equally brutal mass executions carried out by the British Provost Marshal in Burma immediately after the fourteen days' war in 1885. This ignominious story remained buried in the files of *The*

Times (London), January, 1886. It has been exhumed recently, by D. P. Singhal, *The Annexation of Upper Burma* (Singapore: Eastern Universities Press, 1960), p. 83.

49. *Gazetteer of Upper Burma*, pp. 107 ff. The documents that outline the difficulties occasioned by the Bombay Burmah Trading Corporation, the Burmese negotiations with the British and French, the ultimatum and its reply from the Burmese, the orders to march on Burma, and even the projected possibility for the annexation will be found in *Burmah* (1886), *Correspondence Relating to Burmah Since the Accession of King Theebaw in October, 1878, Presented to Both Houses of Parliament by Command of Her Majesty*, Cmd. 4164 (London: Eyre and Spottiswoode, 1886). Hereafter cited as *Burmah* (1886) *Correspondence*. See especially pp. 221, 230–31, 240–46, 247–66.

50. *Gazetteer of Upper Burma*, pp. 108–15.

51. Cady, *op. cit.*, pp. 130–32.

52. Li Chien-nung, *The Political History of China, 1840–1928*, ed. and trans. by Ssu-yu Teng and Jeremy Ingalls (Princeton, N.J.: Van Nostrand, 1956), pp. 12–46.

53. II, 194–95.

54. Christian, *op. cit.*, "Trans-Burma Trade Routes to China Before 1900," pp. 212–25. The fullest treatment of this subject will be found in Ma Thaung, "British Interest in Trans-Burma Trade Routes to China, 1826–1876" (Ph.D. dissertation, University of London, 1954).

55. J. S. Furnivall, *Colonial Policy and Practice, A Comparative Study of Burma and Netherlands India* (Cambridge: Cambridge University Press, 1948), pp. 69–70. See also John P. Cady, *The Roots of French Imperialism in Eastern Asia* (Ithaca, N. Y.: Cornell University Press, 1954). Cady amply documents the Anglo-French rivalry, though he is inclined, without giving adequate evidence, to place major responsibility on "aggressive policies pursued by successive French ministries."

56. Quoted in Christian, *op. cit.*, pp. 34–35.

57. Hall, *A History of South-East Asia*, pp. 546–47. The unwillingness to adapt to local customs was by no means limited to government officials or Englishmen, e.g., John Crawfurd, *op. cit.*, I, 63, refers to Burmese disapproval of Adoniram Judson, the American missionary who wore shoes while visiting the Shwesandaw Pagoda at Prome.

Chapter 3: Nationalism

1. *Burma's Fight for Freedom, Independence Commemoration*, issued by the Department of Information and Broadcasting, Government of the Union of Burma (Rangoon: Superintendent of Government Printing and Stationery [1948]), p. 27. (Government publications of independent Burma will hereafter be cited as GUB, place, and date.) This 119-page book reprints a number of official documents relating to the reoccupation and later transfer of sovereignty; among them are the British White Paper of May, 1945; the August, 1944, Manifesto of the Anti-Fascist People's Freedom League, and the "Immediate Programme" of May 25, 1945; the Aung San–Attlee Agreement of January 27, 1947; The (Fourteen Points) Resolution of the AFPFL Convention of May 23, 1947; some of the pertinent statements of the Constituent Assembly of 1947; the treaty between the Government of the United Kingdom and the Provisional Government of Burma (the Nu-Attlee Agreement of October 17, 1947); the Bo Let Ya–Freeman Defence Agreement (August 29, 1947) appended as an annex; and the Independence Bill enacted by the Attlee government.

2. Cady, *A History of Modern Burma*, pp. 125–54, 185–424; see also Frank N. Trager *et al.*, *Burma* (3 vols.; New Haven, Conn.: Human Relations Area Files, 1956), III, 959–1042.

3. John Nisbet, *Burma Under British Rule—and Before* (2 vols.; Westminster, England: Archibald Constable, 1901), I, 46. For extended accounts of the last years of the monarchy and the period of pacification, primarily based on English sources, see *ibid.*, pp. 26–101; A. C. Bannerjee, *Annexation of Burma* (Calcutta: A. Mukherjee and Co., 1944), pp. 141–318; and Charles H. T. Crossthwaite, *The Pacification of Burma* (London: Edward Arnold, 1912) (Sir Charles was the chief civilian officer during 1885–90).

4. Maung Maung said that "the resistance of the Chins was finally broken in 1894" (*op. cit.*, p. 69).

5. See *The Burman* (Rangoon), November 15 and 17, 1946; *The Review* (Rangoon), November 10, 1947.

6. There were, of course, some British civil servants who, aware of the pervasive significance of Buddhism in Burma, urged that more favorable consideration be given to Burmese Buddhism. Dr. Maung Maung (*op. cit.*, p. 76) refers to the *Reports on Criminal and Civil Justice in British Burma, 1870–1874*, in which the British sought "authoritative treatises" or "living authority in Buddhist Law"; they offered at one time a prize of 1,000 rupees to "the composer of the best essay on the sources and history of Buddhist Law as it prevails in the province." In this connection, see the Introduction by John Jardine (a judicial commissioner of British Burma) to his edition of Father Sangermano, *op. cit.*, pp. xv–xix, and n. 1, pp. 221–23. See also G. E. Harvey, *British Rule in Burma, 1824–1942* (London: Faber, 1946), pp. 25–29, where the views of Sir Edward Sladen in 1884, "If only we did not interfere with religion so seriously as we have done since we took possession of [Lower] Burma," are cited with approbation.

7. U May Oung, "The Modern Burman," *Rangoon Gazette*, August 10, 1908, reprinted, with a brief introduction by J. S. Furnivall, in *Journal of the Burma Research Society*, XXXIII (Rangoon, 1950), Part I, 1–7. See also Maurice Collis, *In Hidden Burma, An Autobiography* (London: Faber, 1953), pp. 147–48, for a brief description of this "most eminent man of his generation," who died in 1926. His son, U Tun Hla Oung, and daughter, Daw Mya Sein, have continued the family tradition.

8. U May Oung, *op. cit.*, p. 1.

9. Harvey, *British Rule in Burma, 1824–1942*, pp. 45–47. Of the 400 who thus acquired degrees, a considerable number were Indians and Anglo-Indians domiciled in Burma. Until 1923, the Indian Civil Service, the bureaucracy that administered Burma, was almost exclusively English; in 1942, out of a total of 145 of these officers, who almost invariably had English university training, 81 were English, 10 Eurasian, and the remainder Burmese. This is not the place to discuss, at length, the character and extent of the colonial government's role in Burmese education. Hugh Tinker has written that from about 1870 to 1900, "primary education throughout India and Burma stagnated," in *The Foundations of Local Self-Government in India, Pakistan and Burma* (London: University of London, 1954), p. 249. Furnivall, summing up the situation, wrote: "It might be claimed sixty years ago [1870–80] that Burma was the best educated country in the tropical Far East, with the possible exception of the Philippines. It would be difficult to repel the charge that at the time of its separation from India (1937) it was the worst educated." *Colonial Policy and Practice*, p. 211.

10. Harvey, *British Rule in Burma, 1824–1942*, p. 28. The word "placid" had originally been used by the Governor, Sir Reginald Craddock, in *The Dilemma in India* (London: Constable Co., 1929), p. 109. For a thoughtful account of this "white-man's-burden" Governor and his relation to dyarchy, see Tin Tut, "The Early Days of Dyarchy," *The Burmese Review* (Rangoon), III, No. 4 (October 6, 1947). U Tin Tut, C. B. E., received an Honours B.A. (mathematics and economics) from Queens College, Cambridge. He received a second B.A. from Dublin; M. A. (*Cantab.*), and became a barrister-at-law (Middle Temple). In 1921, he won appointment to the ICS, the

first given to a Burman. His weekly journal, cited here, which was first printed on May 20, 1946, is an indispensable source. A profile about him appeared in *The Burman,* January 20, 1946, and again on October 3, 1946, after General Aung San invited him to join the Governor's Executive Council. He was killed in 1948; his three remaining brothers are U Kyaw Myint, a leading barrister; U Myint Thein, a former Chief Justice of the Supreme Court; and Dr. Htin Aung, former Rector of the University of Rangoon.

11. F. S. V. Donnison, *Public Administration in Burma: A Study of Development During the British Connexion* (London: Royal Institute of International Affairs, 1953), pp. 50, 52.

12. Hall, *A History of South-East Asia,* p. 626. See also Hugh Tinker, *The Union of Burma: A Study of the First Years of Independence* (London: Oxford University Press, 1957), p. 2. Tinker believes that the treatment accorded Burma "did more than anything else to arouse national pride and to direct this pride towards a demand for political freedom," but he, too, regards the various protest actions as "sudden" and "unexpected."

13. *Joint Report on Indian Constitutional Reforms,* Cmd. 9109 (1918), para. 198.

14. Furnivall, *Colonial Policy and Practice,* pp. 143, 160–62.

15. Maurice Collis, *The Journey Outward* (London: Faber, 1952), p. 260; see also pp. 222, 248. Collis was an officer with this regiment when it served in India and Palestine.

16. "Burmese Politics—1917–1931," *The Burmese Review,* I, No. 17 (September 9, 1946), 1, 7. In 1959, U Maung Gyee came out of retirement to organize a Buddhist Democratic Party to contest the 1960 elections as a way of expressing his disapproval of the factionalism that split the dominant party in 1958.

17. Prior to 1897, when Burma was incorporated into India as a province, it had been governed by a chief commissioner. Between 1897 and 1923, the effective date of the dyarchical constitution, its chief officer was the lieutenant governor. The latter was advised by a predominantly nominated or appointed legislative council with a modestly expanding membership: there were seventeen members after the 1909 Morley-Minto reforms in India; thirty in 1915. Since 1909, the European business community in Burma had been entitled to elect two legislative members. See Ma Mya Sein, *Administration of Burma: Sir Charles Crossthwaite and the Consolidation of Burma* (Rangoon: Zabu Meitswe Pitaka Press, 1938).

18. Collis, a civil servant in Burma at the time, points out, for example, that the distinguished appointed member, U May Oung, "had to go warily" because the ICS could reach the governor directly. "Moreover, he was not treated as a social equal by the Europeans in Rangoon. The British officials and businessmen did not invite him to dine in their houses, nor, had he stood for the British clubs, would he have been elected." (*In Hidden Burma,* pp. 147–48.)

19. Cady, *A History of Modern Burma,* p. 228; and Tinker, *The Union of Burma,* p. 3. For a full and illuminating account of the state of Burmese opinion at that time, see Burma Reforms Committee, *Report and Appendices* and *Record of Evidence* (4 vols.; Rangoon: Government Printing, 1921–22).

20. Christian, *op. cit.,* p. 241.

21. *Joint Committee on Indian Constitutional Reform, Session 1933–34, Report* (London: HMSO, 1934) I, Part I, 248–49. The Joint Committee reaffirmed the view of the Simon Commission: "We hold that the first step towards the attainment of full responsible government in Burma is the separation of Burma from the rest of British India." Though the Simon Commission did not define, in constitutional outline, what such full responsible government would mean, it left no doubt that it favored what the Burmese opposed, viz., a dyarchical and communal type of government. See *Indian Statutory Commission,* Cmd. 3572 (London: HMSO, 1930), III, 510–12.

22. Maung Maung Pye, *Burma in the Crucible* (Rangoon: Khittaya Publishing House, 1951), p. 32.

23. Christian, *op. cit.*, p. 103. This section of his work is based on his "A New Constitution for Burma Under the Government of India Act, 1935" (Master's thesis, Stanford University, 1936).

24. Furnivall, *Colonial Policy and Practice*, pp. 168–70.

25. Maung Maung, *op. cit.*, p. 86.

26. Based on Christian, *op. cit.*, p. 83. F. Burton Leach, *The Future of Burma* (Rangoon: British Burma Press, 1936), pp. 57–60, presents a different breakdown: Burmese (95), Karen (12), Indian (13), Chinese (1), Anglo-Burman (2), and European (9). The Burmese held 72 per cent of the seats, but comprised 82 per cent of the population.

27. Leach, *op. cit.*, p. 63.

28. Christian, *op. cit.*, pp. 76–81. See also Government of India Act, 1935, Part XIV, section 326.

29. Maung Maung, *op. cit.*, p. 87.

30. Quoted in Maung Maung Pye, *op. cit.*, pp. 36–37.

31. Speech at Meiktila, August 11, 1926, *Collected Speeches* (Rangoon: Government Press, 1927), p. 155.

32. "The Thakins," *The Burmese Review*, I, No. 26 (November 11, 1946), pp. 8–9.

33. One of the most interesting and revealing accounts of the 1936 student strike and its Thakin leaders was written by one of the participants, Dr. Tha Hla, a one-time rector and professor of geology at the University of Rangoon—"As I Remember: The 1936 Rangoon University Strike," *New Burma Weekly* (Rangoon), June 21–August 2, 1958. Written at a time of political fission, this retrospective account makes the point that Burmese nationalism thrived when Burmese nationalist leaders were unified.

34. I am indebted for details in this paragraph to the lively account by Dr. Maung Maung, *Burma's Constitution* (The Hague: Nijhoff, 1959), pp. 35–44.

35. Frank N. Trager (ed.), *Marxism in Southeast Asia: A Study of Four Countries* (Stanford, Calif.: Stanford University Press, 1959), see especially the chapter by John S. Thomson. See also Frank N. Trager, "Nationalism and Communism," in J. J. Kirkpatrick (ed.), *The Strategy of Deception* (New York: Farrar, Straus, 1963), pp. 135–64.

36. Cady, *A History of Modern Burma*, pp. 415–16. The Burma Revolutionary Party (BRP) included both socialists and Communists. The present Burmese Communist Party now claims it for its own and in 1959 celebrated the BRP's twentieth anniversary. This is a spurious claim. The formal Communist Party was organized in 1942–43. The identifiable Communists in the BRP at the time numbered, at best, four or five individuals, viz., Thakins Soe, Ba Hein, Thein Pe, H. N. Goshal, and Than Tun. Furnivall, in his introduction to Thakin Nu, *Burma Under the Japanese, Pictures and Portraits* (London: Macmillan, 1954), p. xxiv, writes that "before the war" there were "only two or three [who] went so far as to call themselves Communists." He may be right, for Thein Pe probably had not, as yet, made up his mind, and Goshal and Than Tun may not have been fully committed at that time. See Frank N. Trager, "Marxism and Nationalism in Southern Asia," *Far Eastern Survey*, XXIX, No. 5 (May, 1960), 75–77.

37. Sketches of ten of the Thirty Comrades appear (in Burmese) in Mya Daung Nyo (Aung Thein), *Yebaw Thongyeik* (2d ed., Rangoon, 1954); the text, except for a new introduction by U Thant, is unchanged from the first edition of August, 1943. Dr. Maung Maung, *Burma's Constitution*, pp. 49–52, gives a brief account of this episode, with a full list of the Thirty. One died on Formosa; two, according to General Aung San, were not formally in the group. Aung San prepared an autobiographical sketch and a collection of speeches, *Burma's Challenge* (Rangoon: The New Light of Burma Press, 1946), which contains much useful data. See especially "The

Resistance Movement," Speech, August 29, 1945, pp. 7–45. Excerpts from it also appear in Maung Maung, *Aung San of Burma* (The Hague: Nijhoff, 1962), pp. 31–40.

38. Not all details on these Thakin and Japanese moves are available. The British Government of Burma published several relevant items: *Burma Handbook* (Simla: Government of India Press, 1943); *Burma During the Japanese Occupation*, Vol. I (Simla: [Burma Intelligence Bureau], October, 1943) and Vol. II (Simla: Government of India Press, 1944). *Burma Handbook* (pp. 112–13) and *Burma During the Japanese Occupation*, I (pp. 18–19), tend to confirm the main outlines of the account which appears in Burmese and Japanese sources. See Dr. Maung Maung, *Burma's Constitution*, pp. 49–53, and Aung San, *Burma's Challenge*, pp. 3–5, 21–27. Colonel Suzuki had served for a few months in Rangoon, in 1939, as the ostensible secretary of the Japan-Burma Association. It would appear that this Japanese officer had been charged with the responsibility of organizing subversive forces in general and, in particular, of forming some kind of Japanese OSS or Wingate-type long-range penetration group. See also W. H. Elsbree, *Japan's Role in Southeast Asian Nationalist Movements, 1940–1945* (Cambridge, Mass.: Harvard University Press, 1953), "The Japanese Blueprint," pp. 15–41. When, in the course of an official assignment to Burma, this author took time to reintroduce the first postwar Japanese Consul General to various Burmese friends and associates, he found that both sides were reluctant to review the pre-1941 episodes because of the unpleasant events that occurred in 1942–44.

39. Thakin Nu, *op. cit.*, pp. 1–2. Before the U.S.S.R. entered the war, only the Fabian socialist, Deedok Ba Choe, and one Communist, Thakin Soe, appear to have argued against the pro-Japanese policy of the majority of the Thakins.

40. U Saw, "Journey Perilous, the Adventures of a Prime Minister," *The Burmese Review* I, No. 1 (May 20, 1946). See also Nos. 2, 14, 16, 17, 19, and 20. For confirmation of the essential points of U Saw's account, see "Burma . . . ," a paper submitted by a group of members of the Royal Institute of International Affairs to the Eighth Conference of the Institute of Pacific Relations (Quebec, December, 1942 [mimeographed]) pp. 19–20, 22–24.

41. Dr. Maung Maung, *Burma in the Family of Nations*, p. 93.

42. F. S. V. Donnison, *British Military Administration in the Far East, 1943–1946* (London: HMSO, 1956), p. 345. Donnison estimates that "perhaps 5,000 had fought on the side of the Japanese against the British" (p. 71).

43. B. Prasad (ed.), *The Retreat From Burma 1941–1942, Official History of the Indian Armed Forces in the Second World War 1939–1945* (Calcutta: India and Pakistan—Combined Inter-Services Historical Section, 1952), p. 250.

44. Thakin Nu, *op. cit.*, p. 7; the full account is given on pp. 2–13. This insightful book was written between August and November, 1945. It was intended to be one of several such accounts by leading participants (which, for the most part, have not appeared). Tetpongyi Thein Pe, a founding member of the Burma Communist Party, now a prominent journalist-spokesman for a Moscow-oriented "Burmese Socialism," expanded his wartime *What Happened in Burma* (Allahabad: Itabistan, 1943; also available in mimeographed form, Institute of Pacific Relations, 1944) into *Sit Atwin Hkayithe* (*Wartime Traveler*) (Rangoon: Shumwa Press, 1953). A former Minister of Information, Tun Pe published his wartime memoirs as *Sun Over Burma* (Rangoon: Rasika Ranjani Press, 1949). Very few other Burmese who remained in Burma during the war have written about their experiences. See for example U Khin (Recorder) *U Hla Pe's Narrative of the Japanese Occupation of Burma*, Cornell University Data Paper 41 (Ithaca, N. Y., 1961).

45. U Tin Tut, on his return to Burma in 1945, as reconstruction adviser to Governor Dorman-Smith, broadcast an account of their Simla work; the speech is quoted in Maung Maung Pye, *op. cit.*, pp. 72–80. In a generally descriptive pamphlet, Daw Mya Sein in *Burma* (London: Oxford University Press, 1943) refers to the "substance of political power" inherent in the 1935–37 Constitution (p. 32). She implies that it was reapplied in Burma after the war, but also calls attention to the need and desire for an improved "economic life." Maurice Collis, *Last and First in Burma, 1941–1948* (London: Faber & Faber, 1956), *passim*, gives the most favorable account of Burma's penultimate governor. Some Burmese, who did not go to Simla, are nonetheless inclined to accept that estimate of Dorman-Smith which depicted him to be much more kindly disposed to Burma than was allowed him by his Conservative government.

46. Vice-Admiral Mountbatten of Burma, *Report to the Combined Chiefs of Staff by the Supreme Commander, Southeast Asia, 1943–1945* (New York: Philosophical Library, 1951), pp. 142–45. In *Burma During the Japanese Occupation*, II, 154, reference is made to the "traitor Burmans" of the BIA.

47. Thakin Nu, *op. cit.*, pp. 21, 38ff. This is the principal account written by an insider. Dr. Ba Maw has not yet published his autobiography; some parts have been serialized in *The Guardian* (Rangoon). The first installment appears in VI, No. 10 (October, 1959), 17. (Unless otherwise indicated, all subsequent references to *The Guardian* are to the magazine published in Rangoon.)

48. Thakin Nu, *op. cit.*, p. 27.

49. *Ibid.*, p. 42.

50. *Ibid.*, p. 67. Ba Maw's independent attitude toward the Japanese is confirmed by an English source. See F. C. Jones, *Japan's New Order in East Asia* (London: Royal Institute of International Affairs, 1954), p. 356.

51. Thakin Nu, *op. cit.*, p. 42. In August, 1942, Ba Maw was chief executive or *ahnashin*; in August, 1943, he became head of state or *adipati* of Burma's "independent" government. The lists of his fellow officers in 1942 and 1943 are given in *Burma During the Japanese Occupation*, I, 6, 10–12. The Constitution of "independent" Burma is in *ibid.*, II, 247–52. It is also reprinted in Dr. Maung Maung, *Burma's Constitution*, pp. 223–28. Dr. Ba Maw and the Thakins severed relations with each other after the war.

52. Ian Morrison, *Grandfather Longlegs: The Life and Gallant Death of Major H. P. Seagrim* (London: Faber & Faber, 1947), pp. 112–14, 194ff.

53. Donnison, *British Military Administration*, pp. 345–48. It is interesting to note that Communist Thein Pe's *What Happened in Burma* was published with the cooperation of the British Burma Government at Simla. See Collis, *Last and First in Burma*, pp. 194–97.

54. Sir William Slim, *Defeat Into Victory* (London: Cassell, 1956), p. 484.

55. Maung Maung Pye, *op. cit.*, pp. 82–85, 177–83. See also Maung Maung, *Burma's Constitution*, pp. 62–67. Aung San refers to meetings in August, 1943, when the Communists "discussed and approved my proposal" for the Resistance and for the general organization of "the Anti-Fascist Peoples Freedom League and the first manifesto draft" (*Burma's Challenge*, p. 36).

56. Donnison, *British Military Administration*, p. 348. For similar critical expressions, see Morrison, *op. cit.*, p. 133; or Mountbatten, *op. cit.*, pp. 201 C, 68; C 69–100.

57. Cady, *A History of Modern Burma*, p. 497.

58. Theodore H. White (ed.), *The Stilwell Papers* (New York: William Sloane, 1948), p. 106. The causes of the defeat, and the giving back and retaking of Burma require a separate study.

59. *Burma Statement of Policy by His Majesty's Government*, 1945, Cmd. 6635 (London: HMSO, 1945). All quotations in this paragraph are from Part II, paras. 3 and 7.

60. Slim, *op. cit.*, p. 518. See also the instructions sent by the British Cabinet to Admiral Mountbatten on March 30, 1945, insisting that he treat the Resistance leaders as "ex-collaborators [who] have a lot of leeway to make up" and that he should proceed "with caution" lest they claim "political concessions which HM Government would not consider." Quoted in Donnison, *British Military Administration*, pp. 353–54.

61. The phrases occur in a House of Commons speech by Churchill in 1947. Quoted in Donnison, *British Military Administration*, pp. 369–70.

62. Slim, *op. cit.*, pp. 519–20.

63. *Burma Under the Japanese*, p. 99.

64. The Manifesto, issued by the AFPFL in August, 1944, called for "a constitution for independent Burma" and for a "People's Government." It is reprinted in *Burma's Fight for Freedom*. See also Slim, *op. cit.*, p. 517.

65. Collis, *Last and First in Burma*, pp. 229–30.

66. *Report to the Combined Chiefs of Staff*, p. 202 C72.

67. Quoted in Collis, *Last and First in Burma*, pp. 209–12.

68. *Ibid.*, p. 241. Collis' opinion is confirmed by Donnison, *British Military Administration*, p. 338.

69. Donnison, *British Military Administration*, pp. 334, 353.

70. Cmd. 6635.

71. Collis, *Last and First in Burma*, p. 189. The period before full self-government was to allow for reconstruction and the orderly transfer of government after national elections and constitution-drafting.

72. Tin Tut, "The Burma and the India White Papers, a Comparative Study," *The Burmese Review*, I, No. 4 (June 10, 1946).

73. Collis, *Last and First in Burma*, p. 243.

74. A mixed attitude toward Bogyoke Aung San still is expressed by various British authorities. Tinker wrote in 1957: "It is not easy for an Englishman to see the attainment of this young man free from all prejudice." (*The Union of Burma*, p. 27.) And in the superb biography of *Orde Wingate* (Cleveland, Ohio: World Publishing Co., 1959), p. 403, Christopher Sykes unhesitatingly refuses to accord to Aung San even the ordinary respect given to a war enemy, referring to him as "a jackalish youth in Japanese employ."

75. See Frank N. Trager, "Aung San of Burma," *Asia*, III (June, 1965), and Trager, "Aung San: Father of the Union of Burma, an Appreciation of the Fiftieth Anniversary of His Birth," *The Guardian*, March, 1965, pp. 37–40.

76. Quoted in Collis, *Last and First in Burma*, p. 251.

Chapter 4: Independence

1. *Conclusions Reached in the Conversations Between His Majesty's Government and the Delegation From the Executive Council of the Governor of Burma*, Cmd. 7028 (London: HMSO, 1947): "Conclusions as to the methods by which the people of Burma [including the Frontier peoples] may achieve their independence, either within or without the Commonwealth as soon as possible."

2. Collis, *Last and First in Burma*, chap. xxx, "The Contest With Aung San," pp. 253–82; a most interesting account written primarily from the viewpoint of Sir Reginald Dorman-Smith, who left Burma because of "illness," in mid-June, 1946. He was replaced by Major General Sir Hubert Rance on July 31, 1946. Under him, events moved rapidly forward to the meeting with Attlee. Rance had been Mountbatten's nominee, first to replace Pearce as Chief Civil Affairs Officer (May, 1945), then to replace Dorman-Smith as governor. The Burmese have consistently recognized the Admiral and the General as sincere friends and, since independence, have extended official honors on both of them.

3. For the "Manifesto" and related documents, see chapter 3, n. 1.

4. Donnison, *British Military Administration*, p. 356. Donnison gives a concise account of the various conferences and negotiations between the Allied

and Burmese officers (pp. 356–65). See also Collis, *Last and First in Burma*, chaps. xxvii–xxviii, pp. 232–52; and Slim, *op. cit.*, pp. 515–20.

5. Donnison, *British Military Administration*, p. 365. Approximately 5,000 men were individually reincorporated into the new Burma Army. General Aung San politely rejected a British officer to serve as a brigadier in the Burma Army, but, apparently by prearrangement, Colonel Ne Win, second in military command of the Burmese officers in the BNA, accepted a command post. Donnison estimated that General Aung San's troops amounted to approximately 13,500 men. Cady, *A History of Modern Burma*, estimated that "they numbered 25,000 men with actual fighting experience" (p. 519). Dr. Maung Maung, a member of the BNA, is the source for an earlier reference to 50,000 men. Subsequent events support a larger figure than that suggested by Donnison. However, the differences in these estimates may possibly be explained in terms of variations between organized troop units and guerrilla forces under Thakin leadership. If both are included, a more accurate estimate would probably fall somewhere between the figures suggested by Cady and Maung Maung. It is also certain that large stocks of arms remained in the possession of AFPFL forces.

6. Maung Maung Pye, *op. cit.*, pp. 85–86. The original nine were: General Aung San (President), Bo Ne Win, Bo Let Ya, Saw Kya Doe, Thakins Kyaw Nyein, Ba Swe, Chit, and two avowed Communists, Thakins Soe and Than Tun; the last-named was secretary. As the Council was enlarged, it included Thakins Mya, Nu, Thein Pe, and Ba Hein. It worked closely with officers (Bos) Aung Gyi, Maung Maung, Yan Aung, Ye Htut, Zeya, Tin Pe, Chit Khine, Aye Maung, Khin Maung Gale, Win, and Mahn Win Maung.

7. For a series of documents covering the period from August 1, 1944, to November 18, 1945, see *The New Burma in the New World: From Fascist Bondage to New Democracy* (Rangoon: Nay Win Kyi Press, 1945–46). The ten-page political introduction is followed by approximately 100 pages of speeches, resolutions, and reports covering nineteen separate themes (partial and complete texts). Among the reports is Thakin Than Tun's account of the events that took place from the Naythuyein Hall meeting in August to the November 18 Shwedagon affair.

8. *Ibid.*, p. 76.

9. Quoted in Collis, *Last and First in Burma*, pp. 189–207.

10. J. S. Furnivall, "Twilight in Burma: Reconquest and After," *Pacific Affairs*, XXII, No. 1 (March, 1949), 14.

11. *Ibid.* The "newly returned British Government took away the land and forged new chains of debt."

12. Cady, *A History of Modern Burma*, pp. 518, 521. For a measured defense of his administration, see the Governor's *Address to the Legislative Council*, February 28, 1946 (Rangoon: Superintendent, Government Printing and Stationery Burma, 1946).

13. This incident is well described by Collis in *Last and First in Burma*, pp. 267, 272–77.

14. Maung Maung, *Burma's Constitution*, pp. 75–76.

15. *New Times of Burma* (Rangoon), May 5, 7, 1946. This British-owned newspaper had, at an earlier date, incorporated the Rangoon *Liberator*.

16. "General Aung San Replies to Government Communiqué," *The Burman*, May 11, 1946. *The Burman* was Burmese-owned. See also *New Times of Burma*, May 10, 12, 1946.

17. *The Burman*, May 28, 1946, p. 2. The Dorman-Smith papers are quoted in Collis, *Last and First in Burma*, pp. 268–69.

18. *The Burman*, May 18–19, 21–24, 1946. Reprinted as *Presidential Address Delivered by Major General Aung San at the Second Session of the Supreme Council of the A.F.P.F.L.*, May 16, 1946 (Rangoon: The New Light of Burma Press, n.d.). Also reprinted as "Critique on British Imperialism" in Aung San, *Burma's Challenge*, pp. 97–159.

19. *Presidential Address*, p. 32. See also *The Burman*, May 25, 1946. A

previous reference to dominion status appears in a speech given on August 29, 1945, by Aung San, quoted in his *Burma's Challenge*, p. 44. But see below, n. 55.

20. *The Burman*, May 28, 1946.

21. Quoted by Collis, *Last and First in Burma*, p. 278. As Collis points out, this solution was adopted by the Labour government after Sir Reginald's departure from office.

22. On June 9, 1946, *New Times of Burma* and *The Burman* carried this account of the debate.

23. *The Burman*, June 7, 1946.

24. Quoted in Collis, *Last and First in Burma*, p. 280.

25. *New Times of Burma*, August 25, 26, 1946. For a partial but extensive text of the speech, see *The Burman*, August 27–30, 1946; and Aung San, *Burma's Challenge*, pp. 167–80.

26. The Executive Council, consisting, in fact, of the Governor and nine others, was appointed the next day. In addition to Bogyoke Aung San, the AFPFL members were Thakin Mya, Home Affairs; U Ba Pe, Commerce and Supplies; Thakin Thein Pe, Agriculture and Rural Economy; Mahn Ba Khaing, Industry and Labor; U Aung Zan Wai, Social Services. This group represented the Socialists, Communists, Arakanese, Karens, and the older generation of ardent GCBA nationalists. The other members were U Tin Tut, first Burmese member of the Indian Civil Service, Finance and Revenue; Thakin Ba Sein, Transport and Communications; and Sir Maung Gyee, also a former GCBA leader. U Saw was later appointed by the Governor as the eleventh member. There is no doubt that this was a distinctly nationalist council.

27. *New Times of Burma*, September 27, 28, 1946. The full text of Sir Hubert Rance's broadcast and of the AFPFL's acceptance also appeared in *The Burman*, September 27, 1946.

28. Kyaw Nyein, "The AFPFL Directive," reprinted in *The Burman*, September 20, 1946.

29. *The Burman*, October 1, 1946.

30. *The Burman*, October 13, 22, 30. The November 3, 1946, issue also carried the story. See also Trager, *et al.*, *Burma*, III, 1022–26, 1077–96; and John S. Thomson, "Marxism in Burma," in Trager (ed.), *Marxism in Southeast Asia*, p. 34.

31. *New Times of Burma*, October 30, 1946.

32. *New Times of Burma*, November 13, 1946.

33. *The Burman*, November 13, 1946.

34. *New Times of Burma*, December 5, 1946.

35. Cmd. 7029 (London: HMSO, 1947). Herbert L. Matthews, in a London dispatch to *The New York Times* on January 29, 1947, cabled: "The chances of Burma's being free in a year are very slim, it is conceded here. The British, however, are convinced that Thakin Ba Sein, U Saw, and the Communists will not be able to cause much trouble." His information was wrong on both counts. See U Tin Tut, *The Burmese Review*, I, No. 39 (February 10, 1947), for a Burmese view of the *Conclusions*.

36. There is no richer treasure trove for information about Upper Burma than J. George Scott and J. P. Hardiman, *op. cit.* See I, Part I, 117–86; and II, 515–60, for the period of postannexation pacification and administration.

37. For a comprehensive account of predyarchical British administration based almost exclusively on official sources, see Alleyne Ireland, *The Province of Burma; A Report Prepared on Behalf of the University of Chicago* (2 vols.; Boston and New York: Houghton Mifflin Co., 1907). For a brief account, see F. S. V. Donnison, *Public Administration in Burma*, pp. 16–50; and A *Study of Development During the British Connexion* (London: Royal Institute of International Affairs, 1953).

38. Donnison, *Public Administration in Burma*, p. 33.

39. J. S. Furnivall, *The Governance of Modern Burma* (2d ed.; New York: Institute of Pacific Relations, 1960), p. 22. For another view that is friendly

in its way to the Excluded peoples, but which sees them as being separate from the Burmans, see Harvey, *British Rule in Burma, 1824–1942*, pp. 84–86.

40. *Burma During the Japanese Occupation* I, 14; II, 169. The four brief articles of the treaty were signed in Rangoon on September 25, 1943.

41. Thakin Nu, *op. cit.*, pp. 98–101.

42. *New Times of Burma*, November 27, 1946; and December 5, 6, 1946.

43. There is no full study of the Excluded Areas and the events leading up to the major Panglong Conference and committee hearings. (I have interviewed a number of Burmese who were participants in these events and they have contributed to my knowledge, though they are in no way responsible for my views. Among these are U Vum Ko Hau, Sama Duwa Sinwa Nawng, Sao Shwe Thaike, Sao Hkun Hkio, Mahn Win Maung, U Pe Kin, U Myint Thein, and U Nu.) The basic document which deals with this material is the *Report*, Frontier Areas Committee of Enquiry (Rangoon: Government of Burma, 1947). (Hereafter cited as *Frontier Areas Report*.) Part I contains a concise summary of the problem, the work and composition of the committee, and its recommendations and observations. It reprints the Panglong Agreement signed on February 12. Part II is composed of four appendixes of the verbatim record and contains some of the early 1946 agreements between Aung San and the Frontier peoples, resolutions, notes on the areas, and maps. A variety of relevant autobiographical data are included in Vum Ko Hau, *Profile of a Burma Frontier Man*, printed privately by the author while serving as his country's ambassador to Indonesia (Bandung, 1963).

44. From the text of the agreement, *Frontier Areas Report*, pp. 16–17. See also the analysis of the agreement by U Tin Tut, *Burmese Review* I, No. 40 (February 17, 1947), 7, 10. The newly appointed (August 1, 1946) American Consul General in Rangoon, Earle L. Packer (prior to this, the United States was represented in Burma only by a consul), attended the conference.

45. Rees-Williams, later Lord Ogmore, was officially honored by the Burma Government on June 18, 1956. The other members were: U Tin Tut; Thakin Nu; Bo Khin Maung Gale; U Myint Thein for Burma Proper and Councillor Sawbwa Sam Htun; and Deputy Councillors Sama Duwa Sinwa Nawng and U Vum Ko Hau, representing the Frontier Area Shans, Kachins, and Chins, respectively. The last three mentioned had received their appointments to the Executive Council immediately following the Panglong Conference. Saw Sankey, who represented the Karen National Union, was also one of the four Karen observers at the Panglong Conference. See *Frontier Areas Report*, pp. 18–19.

46. *Frontier Areas Report*, Part I, pp. 22–31.

47. *Ibid.*, Part II, pp. 119–69. According to the census estimate of 1941, there were, in all, about 1.5 million Karens in a total population of 17 million. Some 50,000 lived in the Salween District. See *Burma Handbook*, pp. 4, 7. The 1941 estimates were based on an estimated 12 per cent increase in population over the 1931 census.

48. Cmd. 7138 (London: HMSO, June, 1947).

49. Collis, *Last and First in Burma*, p. 286.

50. See, for example, U Tin Tut's analysis, "The Burma and the India White Papers, a Comparative Study," *Burmese Review*, I, No. 4 (Rangoon, June 10, 1946).

51. George Orwell, who had served in Burma, stated in *The Tribune* (London), February 7, 1947, that if a specific date for dominion status had been offered to the Burmese in 1944 they would have "gladly accepted" it. Hall wrote: "Moreover there is reason to believe that Aung San had determined to work out a settlement which would enable Burma to remain within the Commonwealth." (*A History of South-East Asia*, p. 710.) But he furnished no evidence. Nor did Tinker, *The Union of Burma* (p. 26), who shared this view. In contrast, Cady, *A History of Modern Burma*, described the Burmese decision to leave the Commonwealth as "ultra nationalist," but considered that "only wishful thinking could have imagined a different outcome" (p. 556).

52. *The Burmese Review*, June 23, 1947.
53. U Ba U, *My Burma: The Autobiography of a President* (New York: Taplinger, 1959), pp. 180–81, 192–93.
54. *The Burman*, February 6, 1947.
55. *Ibid.*, February 7, 1947. Aung San had referred earlier, on at least two important occasions, to Burma's entering the Commonwealth; see *supra*, n.18, 19, and accompanying text. In his *Burma's Challenge*, he explained the first reference in a footnote indicating that he was not referring to his or to the AFPFL's policy, but to "declared British" policy. There is no further explanation for his statement in May, 1946, which I have called his one unexplained reference to dominion status. (See *supra*, p. 73.)
56. *The Burman*, February 16, 1947.
57. *Ibid.*, April 23, 1947.
58. *Ibid.*, May 4, 1947.
59. *Burma's Fight for Freedom*, pp. 48–49, 58.
60. For text, see Maung Maung, *Burma's Constitution*, pp. 231–50.
61. The text is reprinted in *Burma's Fight for Freedom*, pp. 49, 58; also in Maung Maung Pye, *op. cit.*, pp. 113–18.
62. The text is partially but extensively reprinted in Maung Maung Pye, *op. cit.*, pp. 121–41.
63. *Burma's Fight for Freedom*, pp. 91–92. See pp. 86–91 for a list of the delegates by election district and Frontier Area; also for the members of the constitution committee and others.
64. "The Political Front," June 23, 1947, p. 8.
65. The June recess was followed by a second session, July 29–August 16, to consider the draft of the constitution and to adopt various interim reports on the national song, state seal, and flag. See *Burma's Fight for Freedom*, pp. 63, 92–93, for the text of Aung San's "Seven Points."
66. July 21, 1947.
67. Donnison, *British Military Administration*, pp. 368–69.
68. The text of the Constitution has been printed separately by the government in Rangoon. It also appears in Maung Maung, *Burma's Constitution*, pp. 258–308. Originally written in English, it has since been translated into Burmese by the librarian-scholar U Thein Han.
69. The documents are: *Treaty Between the Government of the United Kingdom and the Provisional Government of Burma, With Annex and Exchange of Notes*, Cmd. 7240 (London: HMSO, 1947); the Annex consists of the "Defence Agreement" that was signed August 29 by Bo Let Ya and John Freeman, and the Burma Independence Act, 1947 (11 Geo 6, chap. iii). These three documents, with minor excisions, are reprinted in *Burma's Fight for Freedom*, pp. 101–14. For a brief summary of the debate in Parliament, see Cady, *A History of Modern Burma*, pp. 569–72.
70. Maung Maung Pye, *op. cit.*, pp. 170–75, and Appendixes III, IV, V, pp. 204–12.

Chapter 5: The Insurrections

1. Furnivall, *The Governance of Modern Burma* (2d ed.; New York: Institute of Pacific Relations, 1960), p. 26.
2. Editorial, *The Burmese Review*, October 14, 1947.
3. For a detailed examination of the implications for Asia from these meetings (held in India), see Frank N. Trager (ed.), *Marxism in Southeast Asia*, pp. 263–73; John S. Thomson, "Marxism in Burma," *ibid.*, pp. 14–57; and *The Burman*, February 21, 28, March 4–6, 14–20, 1947.
4. Interview on "Goshal's Thesis" (mimeographed; Calcutta, December 21, 1947) and Than Tun's "Speech of Greeting to the Second Congress of the Communist Party of India" (mimeographed; Calcutta, February 28, 1948) (in author's possession). See also Frank N. Trager, "Nationalism and Communism in Burma," in Kirkpatrick (ed.), *op. cit.*, pp. 135–64.

5. A copy of this confidential document is in the author's possession. It is also referred to as "The Revolutionary Possibilities for 1948," or as "Goshal's Thesis." (It has been described as a "26-page typescript in English" and as "twenty-seven pages of closely typed document.") See also Thakin Nu, *Towards Peace and Democracy* (Rangoon: GUB, 1949), p. 50; and *Burma and the Insurrections* (Rangoon: GUB, 1949) pp. 4–5. Actually, the paper by Goshal is an elaboration of the material presented in his interview (*supra*, n. 4) and runs to forty-one typed pages. The opening section is called "A Decisive Period of Revolutionary Possibilities." A new section, "Noted on Programme," begins on p. 27. The quotations in this paragraph are from the Goshal document.

6. *Towards Peace and Democracy*, "The Road to Unity," pp. 10–19.

7. *Ibid.*, "Communist Allegations," pp. 20–29. It is interesting to note that later, in a speech given by U Nu on September 27, 1957, he remarks that "as the Communist rebellion gathered momentum . . . indications were that [the U.S.S.R.] came to look upon us as reactionaries standing in the way of the people's liberation" while the Communists in Burma were "following to the letter the dictation given to them by their 'Big Brothers' abroad" (Rangoon: GUB, 1958).

8. There are no accurate records and claims were typically inflated. J. S. Furnivall, in "Twilight in Burma," rejected the higher figure and guessed at a figure of 300,000. Tin Tut is responsible for the lowest figure that is used here. Recruitment for the PVO among ex-servicemen, and others who had not shared in guerrilla and resistance fighting, had been spurred by Bo Po Kun, who had attained the rank of major during the war, and Bo La Yaung, one of the Thirty Heroes; on the strength of his success, Bo Po Kun had no difficulty in securing a Cabinet post in Thakin Nu's provisional and first independent governments.

9. *The Burmese Review*, October 13 and December 1, 1947. After the latter date, the Rangoon newspapers carried various stories about the new Marxist League.

10. *Burma and the Insurrections*, p. 17.

11. Broadcast, "I Choose Democracy," April 3, 1948, *Towards Peace and Democracy*, pp. 55–64; see also broadcast, "Lawlessness Will Be Suppressed," March 28, pp. 50–54, for an account of the earlier negotiations.

12. "The Programme," May 25, 1948, and speech, "The Nature of the Leftist Unity," June 13, 1948, in *Towards Peace and Democracy*, pp. 92–97, 106–38, respectively. The Fifteen Points appear on pp. 92–94. Because the fifteenth point (see below) evoked sharp criticism at home and abroad, it was subsequently dropped. The text of the points as given in the later *Burma and the Insurrections*, pp. 41–45, lists only fourteen points.

13. *Burma and the Insurrections*, pp. 19–22, 45–56.

14. See John F. Cady, "The Karens," in Frank N. Trager (ed.), *Burma*, II, 883–88.

15. Thakin Nu, *Burma Under the Japanese*, pp. 98–99.

16. *Frontier Areas Report*, Part II, p. 169. The KNB consisted of twelve leading Karens, both Christian and Buddhist, including Dr. Sir San C. Po, Saw Hla Pe, a minister in Ba Maw's Cabinet, Saw Ba U Gyi, and Sidney Loo Nee. The KCO was listed as an AFPFL member organization by Aung San at a press interview on May 14, 1945, but it was not formally organized until June 30–July 5, 1945. At that time, the KCO did not win the support of the older Buddhist Karen National Association. See Trager (ed.), *Burma*, III, 1121–28.

17. *Frontier Areas Report*, Part II, pp. 162–63. The KNU spokesman was Thra Tha Htoo.

18. See, for example, San C. Po, *Burma and the Karens* (London: Elliot Stock, 1928). Dr. (later Sir) San C. Po argued that the Karens were "a nation second in importance of the indigenous races . . . [and] desire to have a country of their own." He proposed a federation, modeled on Switzerland or

the United Kingdom (he likened the Karens to the Welsh), in which the Burmans, the Shans, the Arakanese, and the Karens would have separate states. The Reverend Harry I. Marshall, *The Karen People of Burma: A Study in Anthropology and Ethnology* (Columbus, Ohio: Ohio State University, 1922), pp. 310–14, calls attention to the rise of "national spirit" among the Karens at the time of the Third Anglo-Burmese War. The Karen levies serving "for the most part under their missionaries as officers," did "much to establish peace throughout the province of Burma." But Marshall, unlike other missionaries, advocated an accommodation of the Burmans and the Karens within a single political entity. See also J. S. Furnivall, "The Karens" (Rangoon, 1958), pp. 28–32 (unpublished manuscript in the author's possession). Karen Christians (chiefly Baptists) from the delta districts led the hill Karens and the KNU. This fact gave rise to the view that the differences between the Burmans and the Karens were in major part caused by traditional differences between indigenous Buddhism and imported Christianity. This view, applicable to the period before World War I, had unfortunate repercussions in Burma and in the Christian West after World War II. However, there were Christian Karens whose independent political outlook was entirely compatible with loyalty to the existing government and Union.

19. Cady, A *History of Modern Burma*, p. 553. The Karen delegation published its plea as *The Case for the Karens* (London, 1946). Cady's interpretation of Karen-Burman relations generally favors the Karens.

20. *Frontier Areas Report*, Part II, p. 176.

21. Edward Law Yone and David G. Mandelbaum, "Pacification in Burma," *Far Eastern Survey*, XIX, No. 17 (October 11, 1950), 183.

22. See *The Burmese Review*, February 16, 1948.

23. See *ibid.*, March 15, 1948. This action may have been precipitated by a KNU–KNDO conference, March 3–5, which rejected the constitutional provisions of secs. 180–81.

24. "Address to Members," *Towards Peace and Democracy*, p. 156. See also *KNDO Insurrection* (Rangoon: GUB, 1959), pp. 13–15.

25. A detailed chronology of desertions and attacks from July 2, 1948, to June 26, 1949, appears in *KNDO Insurrection*, Appendix A, pp. 31–45.

26. Tinker, *The Union of Burma*, p. 37. The men involved were Lieutenant Colonel J. C. Tulloch, then in Calcutta; Alexander Campbell, then a Rangoon correspondent for the London *Daily Mail*; and a British missionary, the Reverend J. W. Baldwin. Earlier, insurgent Karens in Insein had freed Captain David Vivian from Jail. Vivian, a British officer, had been found guilty of supplying U Saw with weapons in the plot to assassinate Aung San.

27. See A *Brief Review of Disturbances in Burma* (Rangoon: GUB, June 30, 1949), p. 3; and *Burma and the Insurrections*, "Chronology," p. 62.

28. *KNDO Insurrection*, pp. 14, 19–20; and p. 34, items 61 and 62. See also Furnivall, "Twilight in Burma," pp. 167–68; Yone and Mandelbaum, *op. cit.*, p. 183; and *The Karen Rising* (Rangoon: GUB, 1949), p. 7.

29. A *Brief Review of Disturbances in Burma*, p. 4.

30. Speech, "Democracy versus the Gun," in *Towards Peace and Democracy*, p. 201.

31. Naw Seng, a Kachin, acquired some prominence as a leader of the Karen rebels. He was last reported to be in Communist China. A Communist group, led by Marang La Dee, tried to establish a foothold in the Kachin state; the first and probably only attack by this group was reported in November, 1956. In more recent years, General Ne Win's government has experienced difficulties in the Shan and Kachin states, but these are not directly linked to the insurrections that began in 1948.

32. "Review of the General Situation," *Towards Peace and Democracy*, p. 168.

33. U Nu, *An Asian Speaks*, Speech, Washington, D.C., July 1, 1955 (Washington, D.C.: Embassy of the Union of Burma, 1955), p. 15.

34. For a characteristic statement of his intentions, see Thakin Nu, *Burma Under the Japanese*, pp. 29, 70–71.

35. The novel, in English translation, was serialized in *The Guardian*, beginning with Vol. I, No. 8 (June, 1954).

36. Quoted in Maung Maung Pye, *op. cit.*, pp. 210–12.

37. See, for example, *The New Light of Burma* and the *Bamakhit* (Rangoon), June 16 and 17, 1948.

38. See *The New York Times*, June 16, 1948; *New York Herald Tribune*, June 18, 1948.

39. *Towards Peace and Democracy*, pp. 55–58, 110–17. In an editorial, the *New York Herald Tribune*, on June 19, 1948, "quoted" a statement that was not contained in the speech, and distorted the expression of friendship for the U.S.S.R. by omitting any reference to a similar desire for friendship with the United States and the United Kingdom. The editorial concluded with a statement that the present chaos in Burma "was foreseen" and that Burma's future was "unpredictable." As late as February 17, 1950, this newspaper reported that "British experts predict Burma will fall to the Reds."

40. Department of State, *Review of First Four Years of Burma's Independence* (Washington, D.C., June 20, 1950). The BCP and the Karens formed the "Joint Political Committee" and adopted a program of work in late March or early April, 1949. See *Burma and the Insurrections*, pp. 55–59, for reprint of Manifesto and Program. My mimeographed copy of their document varies from the government-printed text in unimportant ways. The name used is the "Affiliated Political Committee" of the "United Resistance Parties."

41. C. F. Grant, "The Case for the Karens," January 4, 1950.

42. The persistence of such sympathy may be gauged from a reference to these events in a September, 1955, background bulletin of the Department of State, "The Union of Burma." It reads: "Presently elements of the Karens, resenting refusal of their request for a separate state, rebelled." There was *never* any refusal for a separate Karen state within the Union. But there was rejection of such a state out of the Union of Burma. Continuing, the bulletin minimizes the extent of the Karen rebel agreements and cooperative ventures with the Communists and omits entirely the pre-1954 contact between the KNDO and the Kuomintang troops, which it calls "Chinese irregulars." There was nothing "irregular" about Chinese General Li Mi and his staff, nor his original troop force. For the "Chinese irregulars," see below.

43. Speech, February 27, 1949, "The Political Scene," in *Towards Peace and Democracy*, pp. 180–81.

44. Speech, "Democracy versus the Gun," June 14, 1949, in *Towards Peace and Democracy*, p. 201.

45. See *Burma and the Insurrections*, pp. 28–30, 52–53, for the Interim Report by the Regional Autonomy Commission, February 19, 1949, which was reprinted with the March 14 official acceptance and the terms of an interim cease-fire announcement. The Karen state was excluded here because of armed strife between Roman Catholic and Baptist Karens, which broke out when a KNDO Baptist group tried to enlist the Catholic Karens. See *KNDO Insurrection*, pp. 16–17.

46. For the documents, see *Burma's Freedom, The Second Anniversary* (Rangoon: GUB, 1950), pp. 27–29. See also Yone and Mandelbaum, *op. cit.*, p. 185.

47. *The New York Times*, February 26, 27, March 1, 12, 1949. It is questionable whether these efforts made by India's chief neutralist were properly evaluated in the free world, nor are they always remembered with the appreciation they deserve.

48. May 28, 1949, p. 976.

49. See, for example, the *New York Herald Tribune*, April 4, 1949, which reported that the resignations took place as a consequence of the "rejection of

Communist proposals for an all-Leftist government," presumably advanced by the Socialists and turned down by Thakin Nu. Tinker, writing in 1956 (*The Union of Burma*, p. 43), relying on a 1954 story in the Rangoon *Nation*, takes the same view. The resignations gave rise to a belief held by some members of the State Department for several years, viz., that U Nu and the "independents" in the Cabinet were at loggerheads with the Socialist Party leadership. There had been differences between Cabinet members, but not over this issue. The fallacy of this view was finally exposed when the group led by U Nu, Thakin Tin, and Kyaw Htun split with Ba Swe, Kyaw Nyein, and others in 1958. Avowed socialists and Socialist Party members were on each side.

50. *Burma's Freedom, The Second Anniversary*, pp. 18, 27.

51. Broadcast, April 1, 1949, in *Towards Peace and Democracy*, pp. 192–95; Thakin Nu, *From Peace to Stability* (Rangoon: GUB, 1951), pp. 202–5. In the final analysis, however, my interpretation is based on personal interviews with many of the chief participants in the affair.

52. See *supra*, n. 40. The Red Flag and White Flag Communists were temporarily united at this time but split again on April 1, just before government forces retook Mandalay on April 3 (information from manuscript, "Four Weeks with the Burma White Flag and Red Flag Communists," April 8, 1949, by Mon Hallsberg, chief Swedish representative of the Swedish-owned Burma Match Company [in author's possession]). On March 11, Hallsberg had gone to Mandalay to protect the company's property; he returned to Rangoon on April 6.

53. *Burma's Freedom, The Second Anniversary*, p. 27.

54. *From Peace to Stability*, pp. 202–3.

55. See "Maps for 1949" in *Burma and the Insurrections*, pp. 63ff. The "Chronology of Events" included in each anniversary issue of *Burma*, a quarterly published by the government, is also useful. (This chronology is found in issues between 1949 and 1954; after 1954, it was omitted.)

56. The government statement of July 8, 1950, is quoted by Thakin Nu in *From Peace to Stability*, p. 95. See also Frank N. Trager, Patricia Wohlgemuth, and Lu-yu Kiang, *Burma's Role in the United Nations 1948–55* (New York: Institute of Pacific Relations, 1956), p. 7.

57. The change in United States–Burma relations is illustrated by the following: Assistant Secretary of State George McGhee had passed through Rangoon in December, 1949. He regarded Burma as "unstable." Ambassador Philip Jessup, who attended the February, 1950, Bangkok Conference of U.S. Ambassadors to Asian countries, is quoted in the *Daily Telegraph* (London), March 25, 1950 (repeated in Tinker, *The Union of Burma*, p. 367), as saying that the situation in Burma "is well nigh hopeless." In a conversation with him, Mr. Jessup denied the quotation. The U.S. Economic Aid Mission, headed by R. Allen Griffin, arrived in Burma on March 23 for a nine-day survey. Its recommendations formed the basis of the September 13 United States–Burma ECA Agreement.

58. "Drive Towards Peace," in *Burma, the Third Anniversary*, I, No. 2 (January, 1951), 73–78. See also John Dennis Sitterson, Jr., "Communism and Conflict in Burma" (Master's thesis, Georgetown University), pp. 120–30, for a careful account of General Ne Win's 1950 offensive. Colonel Sitterson was in Rangoon in 1949–50.

59. Maung Maung, *Grim War Against KMT* (Rangoon: Nu Yin Press, 1953), p. 8. See also a more precise account with documents, *Kuomintang Aggression Against Burma* (Rangoon: GUB, 1953), p. 9.

60. There are, of course, too many differences between the two countries to permit any true comparison to be made. But it is instructive to note that the insurrections in both countries began shortly after the Calcutta Communist conferences in 1948. The Malays had extensive leadership and support from England and the Commonwealth. Hence, the following story from *The New York Times*, January 17–18, 1958, approximately ten years after the insurrec-

tions began in each country, suggests the inherent problems in Communist (and other) insurrections. *The New York Times* account states:

A brigade of British Commonwealth troops, two battalions of Malay troops and hundreds of policemen, special constables and home guards have been deployed in the largest concentrated effort in nine years of fighting here to break a Communist organization in one area. The rebel force is estimated at 275 or more men.

Central Perak has proved an unbreakable stronghold for the Communists so far, and the Government said it did not expect any spectacular results "for some months" from the new operations, which are based on the principle of denying food to the terrorists. More than 10,000 troops and police, operating in a 1,200-square-mile area, were engaged in this one drive on 275 Communists.

61. *The New York Times*, February 18, 1961.

62. "Chinese Nationalists at Large in Burma," *The Guardian*, December 16, 1961.

63. U Nu, *Premier Reports to the People*, p. 51.

Chapter 6: And Why the Insurrections Failed

1. Trager *et al.*, "Why the Insurrections Failed: The Road to Unity," in *Burma*, III, 1172–1201.

2. S. B. Thomas, "Burma," in L. K. Rosinger, *et al.*, *The State of Asia* (New York: Alfred A. Knopf, 1950), p. 320; see also Virginia Thompson and Richard Adloff, *The Left Wing in South-East Asia* (New York: William Sloane, 1950), pp. 106, 109; and Lennox A. Mills, *The New World of South-east Asia* (Minneapolis, Minn.: University of Minnesota Press, 1949), pp. 170–72.

3. See Maung Maung, "Thakin Than Tun," *The Guardian*, III (October, 1956), 33–36, for a profile of this leading Communist.

4. See, for example, his three-hour speech, *Towards a Welfare State* (Rangoon: GUB, 1953), delivered at the opening of the August, 1952, Pyidawtha Conference, through which his appeal to all groups, "Burman, Shan, Kachin, Karen, Kayah, Mon, and Arakanese," suns like a diapason. The speech was also reprinted in U Nu, *Burma Looks Ahead* (Rangoon: GUB, 1953), pp. 56–123.

5. Burmese historical chronicles report that King Anawratha (1044–77) conquered the Mons *because* they refused to share their Buddhist scriptures with the Burmans. See *The Glass Palace Chronicle of the Kings of Burma*, trans. Pe Maung Tin and G. H. Luce (London: Oxford University Press, 1923), pp. 70–80. However, more recent research, especially by the young Burmese scholar Dr. Than Tun, disproves this account. See his "A History of Burma Down to the End of the Thirteenth Century," *New Burma Weekly*, August 23, 1958–February 28, 1959, *passim*. A revised version of this paper appears in *Bulletin of the Burma Historical Commission*, I, Part I (Rangoon, June, 1960), 39–57. See also Than Tun, "Religion in Burma, A.D. 1000–1300," *Journal of the Burma Research Society*, XLII, Part II (Rangoon, December, 1959), 47–69.

6. R. L. Slater, *Paradox and Nirvana—A Study of Religious Ultimates with Special Reference to Burmese Buddhism* (Chicago: University of Chicago Press, 1951), pp. 4–5; and N. Ray, *An Introduction to the Study of Theravada Buddhism in Burma* (Calcutta: University of Calcutta, 1946), are useful studies in connection with the localization of Buddhism in Burma.

7. *Rangoon University Pali Association Magazine*, Vol. I (1954–55).

8. These terms are defined in Nyanatiloka, *Buddhist Dictionary; Manual of Buddhist Terms and Doctrines* (Colombo: Frewin & Co., 1950), pp. 81–83, 147, 148. The author, a German Buddhist (born Anton Gueth), has written

extensively on Buddhism. See also his *The Word of the Buddha: An Outline of the Teaching of the Buddha in the Words of the Pali Canon* (Colombo: The Word of the Buddha Publishing Committee, 1952). Each step on the Path is fully developed in the Pali canon and commentaries.

9. The word "monk" has been used throughout this chapter for the Buddhist canonical word "bhikkhu" or the Burmese word "*pongyi*." Here is a simple example of the difficulties of translating the word "bhikkhu." It has been translated as "beggar," "priest," and "monk." However, since the bhikkhu does not beg, he is not a beggar; since he performs no mediational or sacramental service, he is not a priest; and he has made no lifelong vows that bind him to the order. He may elect to enter or leave it at any time. Only while in the order does he accept its discipline. The Burmese have several words for bhikkhu indicating the stage of his training in the order, i.e., from novice to chief "monk." The latter is known as the *thathanabaing*, or moderator. He becomes such by holding the post of presiding judge of the chief Ecclesiastical Court, re-established by the Act of 1949 (repealed in January, 1965). The head of a monastery is usually called a Sayadaw *pongyi*; monks are called *pongyis* and *rahans*.

10. U Thittila, "The Meaning of Buddhism," *Atlantic Monthly*, CCI, No. 2 (February, 1958), 145.

11. From the Khuddaka-Patha-Nikaya, one of the five main divisions of the *Sutta-Pitaka*. See F. L. Woodward (trans.), *Some Sayings of the Buddha According to the Pali Canon* (World's Classics [London: Oxford University Press, 1949]), pp. 53–67. See also the rules for the monks in the *Vinaya-Pitaka* governing "the sick," *ibid.*, pp. 126ff.

12. J. B. Pratt, *The Pilgrimage of Buddhism and a Buddhist Pilgrimage* (New York: Macmillan Co., 1928), pp. 36, 51.

13. See Frank N. Trager, "Reflections on Buddhism and the Social Order in Southern Asia," in Burma Research Society, *Fiftieth Anniversary Publications, No. 1* (Rangoon, 1961), pp. 529–43.

14. Dr. Htin Aung is the foremost scholar on those folk elements associated with Burmese Buddhism. See his articles in the *Journal of Burma Research Society*: "Burmese Initiation Ceremonies" (August, 1953); "Burmese Alchemy Beliefs" (December, 1953); "The Nine Gods" (December, 1954); "The Lord of the Great Mountain" (June, 1955); and "The Thirty-Seven Lords" (June, 1956). These articles, with additional material by the author, also appear in *Folk Elements in Burmese Buddhism* (London: Oxford University Press, 1962).

15. A casual reading of the opening pages of *My Burma*, the autobiography by U Ba U, Burma's second president, will confirm this point.

16. See Htin Aung, *Burmese Folk Tales* (London: Oxford University Press, 1948), pp. xv–xvii, xx, and *passim*.

17. Furnivall, *Colonial Policy and Practice*, pp. 12–13.

18. See, for example, two such otherwise differing authorities as Harvey, *British Rule in Burma, 1824–1942*, pp. 25–29; and Furnivall, *Colonial Policy and Practice*, pp. 199–201, 211.

19. The Third Council of 247 B.C. was held during the reign of King Asoka, the great Buddhist monarch of India. Of the two previous councils, the first is believed, traditionally, to have been held shortly after Buddha's death, *circa* 483 B.C.; the second, *circa* 376 B.C. These three councils were held in India. The fourth council was held in Ceylon, *circa* 29 B.C. Not until King Mindon's time was the fifth council held. He had the sacred texts incised on the marble slabs that composed the platform of the Kuthodaw Pagoda at Mandalay, where they still can be seen.

20. There has been no exact census of monks in Burma. One estimate quoted from a Parliamentary account, in *The Nation*, March 5, 1954, placed the figure as high as 800,000. This surely must have referred to all males, including the novices and students, who were at some time in the *pongyikyaungs*. An official report, made in 1953, which probably differentiated between

the monks and the novices (who may attend for a week or less) gave the more probable figure of 100,000. More recent figures (in 1959) have reduced this number to approximately 60,000 regular *pongyis*. But the total number would depend on what definitions were used. Monks and the *pongyikyaungs* are to be found in all cities and towns and in most of the 18,000 villages of Burma. Each monastery houses relatively few permanent monks. Five would be a high average for the larger village and town monasteries. In a town, there may be more than one monastery; in a city, there is always more than one.

21. In 1945, they forced the then Communist leader, Thein Pe (now known as Thein Pe Myint), to apologize publicly for his anticlerical book, *Tet Pongyi* (*Up-to-Date Monk*), published in 1935.

22. See, for example, *The Burmese Revolution* (Rangoon: GUB, 1952), a pamphlet published by U Ba Swe, a former prime minister.

23. Speech of January 29, 1958, reprinted in *The Nation*, January 30, and *Burma Weekly Bulletin*, February 6, 1958; subsequently reprinted as *Towards a Socialist State* (Rangoon: GUB, 1958). General Ne Win's policy on this issue as expressed in the "philosophy" and "program" of the Burma Socialist Program Party, "gives full freedom of conscience and religion to those who believe and worship, and to nonbelievers and free thinkers alike." See, for example, the "Specific Characteristics of the BSP Party" (a comparison with Social Democratic and Communist parties), *Forward*, III, No. 3 (September 13, 1964), 4–6.

24. There are various editions of this pamphlet, the first of its kind in Burma; originally issued by the Ministry of Information and the Ministry of Defense. As of September, 1959, more than 1 million copies had been distributed. See Fred von der Mehden, "Burma's Religious Campaign Against Communism," *Pacific Affairs*, XXXIII, No. 3 (September, 1960), 290–99.

25. Harvey, *British Rule in Burma, 1824–1942*, pp. 40–42. See also E. C. V. Foucar, *I Lived in Burma* (London: Dobson, 1956), p. 105. Foucar, a British barrister who became an officer in Burma, calls this policy "a grave political error." A brief account of the British military and police forces in Burma just prior to the separation from India in 1937 appears in Leach, *op. cit.*, pp. 107–17. There were, at that time, approximately ten battalions of soldiers and military police, one mountain battery of artillery, and one company of sappers and miners, in addition to the police of the districts.

26. Collis, *Last and First in Burma*, p. 27. In 1938, the British Parliament was told that there were approximately 6,200 men with 278 officers in the armed forces in Burma. The distribution was: 159 Burmans; 3,040 other indigenous "races"; 1,423 Indians; 1,587 British. Among officers there were 4 Burmans; 75 other indigenous "races"; 36 Indians; and 163 British. Quoted in Maung Maung, *Burma's Constitution*, p. 42.

27. See Maung Maung, "General Ne Win," a profile, *The Guardian*, I, No. 12 (October, 1954), 55–60. See also *The Guardian*, VI, No. 1 (January, 1959), 37. There is no history of the Burma armed forces in the World War II or postwar period. Colonel Ba Than, now retired, as Chief of the Psychological Warfare (anti-Communist) Branch, had been responsible for building the Burma Defense Forces Historical Research Unit, which was charged with the task of producing such a record. Since retiring, he has published a long article, "The Revolution, A Brief History of the Defence Services of the Union of Burma and the Ideals for which They Stand," *The Guardian*, March 27, 1962, special supplement; see also *Working People's Daily*, March 27, 1965, for a supplement, "The Armed Forces and the Working People."

28. There is a brief description with photographs of the Defense Services Academy (undergraduate) in *Burma, the Eleventh Anniversary*, IX, No. 2 (January, 1959), 149–75. (The role of the military in Burma since 1958, especially after the coup in 1962, is treated in Chapter 9.)

29. U Nu, *The People Win Through* (Rangoon: Society for the Extension of Democratic Ideals, 1952). There is an American edition (New York: Tap-

linger, 1957). The play was presented in the United States by the Pasadena Players and has been made into a film. The latter was shown widely throughout Burma under the auspices of the Psychological Warfare Branch of the armed forces. For a political biography of this leader, see Richard Butwell, *U Nu of Burma* (Stanford, Calif.: Stanford University Press, 1963). For a sensitive review of this book, see James J. Dalton, *The Asian Student*, March 13, 1965.

Chapter 7: Pyidawtha: The Building of a Welfare State

1. The population figures for preconquest Burma have been the subject of frequent speculation. The early figures of Symes and Cox were grossly overestimated; Symes suggested a figure of 17 million. Crawfurd, *Journal of an Embassy . . . To the Court of Ava* (pp. 234–48), using a variety of data based upon the household tax, the consumption of certain essential goods, and other sources, arrived at a figure of 4 million. He also offered some interesting comparative figures on urban wage rates and food costs and the condition of the peasantry, figures which support a benign view of the economy. Harvey, *History of Burma* (pp. 333–35), confirms Crawfurd's estimate.

2. Htin Aung, "Customary Law in Burma," in Philip Thayer (ed.), *Southeast Asia in the Coming World* (Baltimore: Johns Hopkins Press, 1953), pp. 203–16. See also D. Richardson, *The Dammathat or the Laws of Menoo*, in Burmese, with English translation (2d ed.; Rangoon: Mission Press, 1874); S. C. Lahiri, *Principles of Modern Burmese Buddhist Law* (5th ed.; Calcutta: Eastern Law House, 1951), chap. i, "Sources of Burmese Buddhist Law," pp. 1–5; and Maung Maung, *Burma in the Family of Nations*, "Law and Administration Under the Kings," pp. 14–20. At times, this body of law has been referred to as the "code" of the mythical Hindu law-giver, Manu; at other times, as Burmese Buddhist law. It is neither Hindu nor Buddhist as such, though the influence of both can be found in its corpus. See the Preface to Htin Aung, *Burmese Law Tales, The Legal Element in Burmese Folk-lore* (London: Oxford University Press, 1962), p. vii, and Maung Maung, *Law and Custom in Burma and the Burmese Family* (The Hague: Nijhoff, 1963), chap. i, pp. 1–19.

3. Cady, *A History of Modern Burma*, pp. 3–38; there is a useful summary of older sources in chap. i, "Government in Old Burma." I do not agree with Cady that the kings (at least from Pagan days) were "divine" in the Indian manner, despite the persistence of Brahman priests and practices at the Court until 1885, or that the royal administration was "the Indian type." The Indian elements were more prominent in other Theravada countries, for example, Cambodia. The Burman dynasties ruled directly in Burma Proper; they ruled indirectly through feudalistic arrangements when they conquered the Shan princedoms, and Kachin and Chin tribal and clan territories.

4. Scott and Hardiman, *op. cit.*, II, Part I, 1–5. Most Western commentators on the Burmese scene have noted such intervention. Some hold that it is inconsistent with Buddhist doctrine. What such commentators see as inconsistency arises from their incomplete exploration of the social content of Buddhism.

5. He could be the headman of a village tract or township area, hence a *myothugyi*; of a circle or somewhat larger area, especially in British times, hence a *taikthugyi*. See chaps. ii (J. S. Furnivall) and iv (John Brohm, Charles Brant, and M. Lois Jackim), in Trager, *et al.*, *Burma*, I, 38–43, 105–10.

6. Nisbet, *op. cit.*, I, 268–69. See also Richardson, *op. cit.*, "The Law regarding the perfect or imperfect proprietary right in land," pp. 227–30.

7. Crawfurd, *Journal of an Embassy . . . to the Court of Ava*, p. 191. See also Walter Hamilton, *The East-India Gazetteer* (2d ed.; 2 vols.; London: William H. Allen, 1828), pp. 85–86. Coinage had been known in the old kingdom of Arakan, but it did not take root in dynastic Burma until its introduction by King Mindon. Burma had monetary units based on the

weight of silver or gold bullion (a tical or kyat equal to one-hundredth part of a viss of approximately 3½ pounds). In the sixteenth and seventeenth centuries, a lead-copper amalgam called ganza had also been monetized. See description by G. H. Luce, "Economic Life of the Early Burman [the Pagan period]," *Journal of the Burma Research Society*, XXX, 283–335. Reprinted in Burma Research Society, *Fiftieth Anniversary Publications, No. 2* (Rangoon, 1960), pp. 343–75.

8. In November, 1862, and October, 1867, the respective British Chief Commissioners of Lower Burma, A. P. Phayre and Albert Fytche, concluded treaties "for the Protection of Trade" with King Mindon. These treaties, like their predecessors, did little to arrest the struggle between Burma and Britain. The texts of these treaties will be found in that extraordinary compendium of documentary material on British Burma after 1886, Alleyne Ireland, *The Province of Burma*, I, 349–53.

9. Henry Gouger, *Personal Narrative of Two Years' Imprisonment in Burmah* (2d ed.; London: John Murray, 1862), p. 61. Gouger arrived in Burma in 1822 (chapter cited deals with that time). He was a daring businessman who was responsible for the story repeated by others of how he bought £3,000 of goods in Calcutta and sold them for £8,000 in Ava. However, restrictions on the removal of precious metals, jewels, and other commercial valuables from the country seemingly made it impossible for him to take his profits out of Ava. He decided to "extricate himself by bribery" (p. 65) and return later to Burma to begin trading in "rice" (p. 66), because he would guarantee the Burmese cultivators a market which would be of "incalculable value." Gouger did not do this, but his prediction about the rice trade was later fulfilled.

10. The quotation is from Harvey, *History of Burma*, p. 350; see also J. S. Furnivall, *An Introduction to the Political Economy of Burma* (Rangoon: People's Literature Committee and House, 1957), p. 153, see also pp. 30–41. This third edition of a work first published in 1931 contains a new preface of forty-five pages. Furnivall had made a special study (still partially unpublished) of the preconquest records, some of which are still preserved in Rangoon and embodied in the *sittans*, or "depositions," of those in local authority, which formed the basis for the Royal Inquests (tax, census, and revenue records) of 1783 and 1802. King Thalun is supposed to have made the first of these Inquests in 1638 (since lost). I have had access to Furnivall's social and economic study (mimeographed) based on the *Annual Reports on the Administration of Burma* and other *Annual Reports* since 1862. I am indebted to him as always. (Copies of both unpublished studies are in the author's possession.)

11. For another picture of preconquest trade and commerce, see Francklin, *op. cit.*, "On the Commerce of Ava" (largely based on Hiram Cox's papers), pp. 26–122; "Topography and Population of Ava," pp. 127–34. See also Crawfurd, *Journal of an Embassy . . . to the Court of Ava*, II, 187–99. The remainder of Crawfurd's chapter (199–225) describes the "natural products" of Burma.

12. The most illuminating account of the arrival of the British administration in the provinces will be found in *Selected Correspondence of Letters Issued from and Received in the Office of the Commissioner Tenasserim Division for the Years 1825–26 to 1842–43* (new ed.; Rangoon: Government Printing, 1928); and its index volume, *Correspondence* (new ed.; Rangoon: Government Printing, 1929), both edited by J. S. Furnivall. See in particular pp. 61–64, 69–72, 95–98, 99–111; and "The Statistical Statements Relating to the Tenasserim Provinces" for the Receipts, Expenditures, Imports, and Exports for 1833, 1836, 1839, *Correspondence*, pp. 98–99. There is an interesting account of Arakan written from a missionary point of view by the Reverend G. S. Comstock, "Notes on Arakan," *American Oriental Society Journal*, I, No. 3 (1844), 219–59. Comstock had spent the preceding ten years in Arakan for the American Baptist Missionary Society.

13. Nisbet, *op. cit.*, pp. 395, 418–19.
14. Furnivall, *Colonial Policy and Practice*, pp. 42–47, 59–61, 116–23. See also Furnivall, *The Political Economy of Burma*, pp. 244–55, for the population figures gathered by B. N. Kaul for the Arakan, Tenasserim, and Pegu provinces, 1830–1921. The census data for 1941 were almost completely lost during the war. However, some portions were preserved and are available along with fuller summaries of the 1931 data in *Burma Handbook*, pp. 4–12. The first regular census was taken in 1872, followed by decennial counts after 1881. Previous estimates were based on revenue and other related data. The actual figures for 1931 (total population, 14.6 million) and projections for 1941, before the exodus caused by the war, yield an Indian population of approximately 7 per cent out of the total Burmese population of 16.8 million. For Lower Burma, it would be at least 11 per cent. Rangoon had an Indian majority after the turn of the century. See *Census of India, 1931*, Appendix B, with Burma Racial Map (Rangoon: Government Printing, May, 1933); James Baxter, *Report on Indian Immigration* (Rangoon: Government Printing, 1941), pp. 6–14, 116–17; and B. R. Pearn, *The Indian in Burma*, Racial Relations Studies in Conflict and Cooperation, No. 4 (Ledbury, England: LePlay Press, 1946). Three special studies should also be noted: E. J. L. Andrew, *Indian Labour in Rangoon* (London: Oxford University Press, 1933), pp. xxxiii, 300; C. Kondapi, *Indians Overseas 1838–1949* (London: Oxford University Press, 1951), p. 558; and Usha Mahajani, *The Role of Indian Minorities in Burma and Malaya* (Bombay: Vora, 1960), pp. xxx, 344.
15. Nisbet, *op. cit.*, pp. 417–18.
16. These figures for the Arakan and Tenasserim divisions are taken from J. W. Grant, *The Rice Crop in Burma, Its History, Cultivation, Marketing, and Improvement*, Agricultural Survey No. 17 of 1932 (Rangoon: Government Printing, 1933), pp. 3, 44.
17. Nisbet, *op. cit.*, p. 24.
18. *Ibid.*, pp. 419–20.
19. Grant, *op. cit.*, pp. 44–45.

TABLE 1

PADDY ACREAGE SOWN AND PRICES PER 100 BASKETS
(*1 basket = 46 lbs.*)

Year	Area in Lower Burma (in Thousands of Acres)	Area in Upper Burma (in Thousands of Acres)	Total	Prices in Rupees
1855	993	a	...	...
1860	1,333	a	...	45
1870	1,734	a	...	45
1880	3,102	a	...	100
1890	4,398	1,357	5,755	95
1900	6,578	1,972	8,550	95
1910	7,808	2,142	9,950	110
1920	8,588	1,751	10,339	180
1930	9,911	2,459	12,370	130

a No records until Annexation in 1886.

Grant reports that 1920 was an abnormal year in Upper Burma. He arrived at the 1920 figure by averaging the 1919–21 results. By 1940–41, total average sown equaled 18.8 million acres, with rice grown on 12.5 million acres. See *Season and Crop Report of Burma, 1945–46* (Rangoon: Government

Printing, 1946), pp. 34–39. This is a useful series for annual crop data. See also *The British Burma Gazetteer*, I, 423, for a table of crops grown in the years 1869–78. Chapters xiii and xiv, "Arts, Manufactures, Agriculture and Prices" and "Population, Revenue and Trade," pp. 410–76, are invaluable sources for the period.

20. *Burma Handbook*, pp. 25–29. See also Furnivall, *Colonial Policy and Practice*, pp. 187, 191; and Appendixes I and II for data on seaborne trade, 1869–1940.

21. *Burma Past and Present with Personal Reminiscences of the Country*, I, 320–21.

22. *The British Burma Gazetteer*, I, 441.

23. Nisbet, *op. cit.*, I, 433–34.

24. *Ibid.*, p. 453.

25. In 1940, there were 1,027 factories (defined as using power and having twenty or more workers). Among these were 673 rice mills, 116 saw mills, 54 cotton gins, 29 vegetable-oil mills, 19 printing presses, 10 oil and related-products refineries, and assorted other plants. These industries engaged about 90,000 workers of a total labor force of approximately 7 million. These figures are compiled from the 1931 *Census of India*, and the *Annual Reports on the Working of the Factories Act XXV of 1934 in Burma*. See also O. H. K. Spate, "Beginnings of Industrialization in Burma," *Economic Geography*, XVII (1941), 75–92. He refers to the "big mills"; the rice mills numbered only 5 per cent of the total but employed more than 40 per cent of the workers. These mills were "practically all European-owned . . . and had practical monopoly of the Western markets."

26. This is indicated in the following tables:

TABLE 2

BALANCE OF TRADE IN SELECTED YEARS
(IN MILLIONS OF RUPEES)

Year	1868–69	1872–73	1903–4	1913–14	1926–27	1936–37	1939–40
Total exports	32.6	45.9	206.7	389.1	659.5	499.1	547.5
Total imports	27.6	32.2	145.3	254.1	386.9	217.8	251.6
Balance	5.0	13.7	61.4	135.0	272.6	281.3	295.9

TABLE 3

VALUE OF SELECTED EXPORTS
(IN MILLIONS OF RUPEES)

Year	1868–69	1872–73	1903–4	1913–14	1926–27	1936–37	1939–40
Rice products	20.5	29.4	148.9	264.7	391.5	218.4	250.4
Teak and other timbers	6.9	7.0	16.8	22.3	49.9	39.7	35.5
Oil-well products	...	...	21.6	54.3	110.0	129.9[a]	143.5[a]
Metals and ores	...	...	.33	5.3	41.4	51.3	62.2

SOURCE: J. S. Furnivall, *Colonial Policy*, p. 187, and *Burma Handbook*, n. 20.
[a] Excludes duty on oil products, about Rs.65 million.

During the prewar decade, the rupee ranged in value from 24 to 37 U.S. cents. In October, 1940, it was equal to 29.85 cents. James Baxter furnishes a yearly table of values for total imports and exports from 1900–1901 to 1938–39. (*Op. cit.*, p. 126.) There are minor discrepancies in the tables, depending on the exclusion or inclusion of re-exports, excise duty on mineral oils, and transfers of gold and specie.

27. J. Russell Andrus, *Burmese Economic Life* (Stanford, Calif.: Stanford University Press, 1947), pp. 317–22. See also Furnivall, *Political Economy of Burma*, pp. 198–225, for a discussion of the revenue system in Burma.

28. Christian, *op. cit.*, p. 125. H. G. Callis, *Foreign Capital in Southeast Asia* (New York: Institute of Pacific Relations, 1942), p. 93, estimates dividends at a 20 per cent yearly average. Andrus quotes some yearly dividend statistics of four leading British companies ranging up to 50 per cent. (*Op. cit.*, p. 186.)

29. B. O. Binns, *Agricultural Economy in Burma* (Rangoon: GUB 1948), p. 105.

30. *Burma* (London: Collins, 1945), p. 44.

31. Christian, *Modern Burma*, p. 128. See also pp. 124–42. Callis (*op. cit.*, pp. 88–96) estimates European investments (held by fewer than fifty major banks and companies) at £47.2 million. The Burma Provincial Banking Enquiry Committee in its *Report* (Rangoon: Government Printing, 1930), and the Chettyar Association of Burma, estimated Indian investment, chiefly of the money-lending caste of *chettyars*, at between 600 and 750 million rupees (approximately £40–£50 million). Chinese investment, according to Andrus, is given as a low £2.8 million (*op. cit.*, p. 184). The population of the three groups before World War II was European, 10,000; Indian, more than 1 million; and Chinese, less than 195,000.

32. E. H. Jacoby, *Agrarian Unrest in Southeast Asia* (New York: Columbia University Press, 1949), p. 79.

33. See tables on page 391.

34. Tun Wai, *Burma's Currency and Credit* (Bombay: Orient Longmans, 1953), p. 44. Other estimates suggest a much larger number of local offices; the highest estimate I have seen is 5,000.

35. Harvey, *British Rule in Burma, 1824–1942*, p. 50.

36. *Report of the Land and Agriculture Committee, 1938–1939* (reprint; Rangoon: GUB, 1949), Part II, p. 37. The report (hereafter cited as RLAC) was published in four parts: I, *Tenancy*, pp. 1–33; II, *Land Alienation*, pp. 35–70; III, *Agricultural Finance; Colonization; Land Purchase*, pp. 73–175; IV, *Regulation of Moneylending*, pp. 177–98. RLAC and Binns' study, *Agricultural Economy in Burma*, are the major documents on pre-independence agriculture in Burma.

37. RLAC, Part I, pp. 13–14, for figures on short-term tenancies (one to three years), in selected districts, from a low of 34 to a high of 78 per cent.

38. Furnivall, *Political Economy of Burma*, pp. 48–60.

39. RLAC, Part II, pp. 39–40. See also pp. 39–55 for a review of various legislative attempts, beginning in 1891, to deal with the problem.

40. See Tun Wai, *op. cit.*, chaps. iv and viii; the revised edition published in 1962 does not change this material, although the pagination varies.

41. See Table 1 above. Paddy prices are difficult to report because of seasonal, locational, and quality variations, and because of the fluctuating supply and demand of the market. V. D. Wickizer and M. K. Bennett, *The Rice Economy of Monsoon Asia* (Stanford, Calif.: Stanford University Press, 1941), pp. 330–31, report prices for one quality of 100 baskets of milled rice (75 lbs.) for 1920–39. Their five-year averages for Rangoon "Big Mills Special" are: Rs.470, 434, 217, and 220. Tun Wai (*op. cit.*, p. 39) quotes several sources for the same period on prices for 100 baskets of paddy (46 lbs.) which indicate approximately the same relative decline in the twenty years, i.e., an average of Rs.187 for 1919–29 to Rs.98 from 1930–39.

42. These figures are taken from RLAC, Part I, pp. 7–8; Part II, pp. 37–39; and from Binns, *op. cit.*, pp. 9–12, 17. The Burma Tenancy Bill of 1908 was discussed for six years without action being taken. It was opposed by European businessmen and the *chettyars* and other landlords. Other relief bills had a similar fate.

TABLE 4 ª

OCCUPATIONAL DISTRIBUTION OF INDIAN AND INDIGENOUS
WORKERS IN BURMA, 1931

Occupation	All Races	Indigenous Races	Indians	Percentage of Indians
Exploitation of animals and vegetables	4,321,356	4,094,240	176,208	4.0
Exploitation of minerals	39,505	20,037	14,752	37.3
Industry (including crafts)	664,376	536,995	104,767	15.8
Transport	222,055	108,390	101,536	45.7
Trade	557,248	408,445	96,211	17.3
Public force	30,816	14,543	13,995	45.4
Public administration	44,867	28,434	13,762	30.8
Professions	198,890	182,912	10,418	5.2
Domestic service	44,689	17,575	24,326	54.4

SOURCE: *Census of 1931.*
ª There is some distortion due to seasonal labor factors. However, if the data for cottage industry and crafts and for local trade were separated out of these categories, the proportion of alien to indigenous workers would be higher.

TABLE 5

OCCUPATIONAL DISTRIBUTION OF INDIAN AND INDIGENOUS WORKERS
IN BURMA'S IRRAWADDY DELTA, 1931

Occupation	All Races	Indigenous Races	Indians	Percentage of Indians
Exploitation of animals and vegetables	1,605,556	1,502,430	95,692	5.3
Exploitation of minerals	407	237	129	31.4
Industry (including crafts)	203,706	117,943	73,887	36.3
Transport	100,650	30,304	66,258	36.3
Trade	275,856	178,422	65,746	65.8
Public force	10,696	5,301	4,291	40.0
Public administration	20,566	8,476	10,730	52.1
Professions	63,354	53,186	7,028	11.1
Domestic service	25,306	6,872	17,287	67.9

SOURCE: *Census of 1931.*

TABLE 6

OCCUPATIONAL DISTRIBUTION OF THE TOTAL WORKING POPULATION,
1931 AND 1953–54
(*In Per Cent*)

	1931 (6.23 million)	1953–54 (8.5 million)
Agriculture	69.6	62.7
Industry and crafts	10.7	10.6
Transport	3.6	1.8
Professions and managerial	3.2	3.1
Trade and sales	9.0	9.8
Services (domestic and public)	1.9	11.1
Mining	.6	0.5
Miscellaneous	1.4	0.4
Total	100.0	100.0

43. See *Interim and Final Reports of the Riot Inquiry Committee* (Rangoon: Government Printing, 1938 and 1939).

44. In addition to the formal inquiries and official notices about these conditions, and the cited works of RLAC, Furnivall, and Binns (both of whom had served as ICS Commissioners of Settlements and Land Records), there are considerable data in the long, occasional, official series of *Reports on Settlement Operations*, and *Revisions* of these reports, gathered in the districts of Burma and published by the government. These *Reports* and *Revisions* were primarily designed to aid the government in imposing revenue rates on the land and other related taxation. See, for example, *Report on the Revision Settlement Operations in the Maubin, Myaungmya and Pyapon Districts, Season 1905–06* (Rangoon: British Burma Press, 1907), pp. 2–3, 14–15 (on the rise in tenancy). See also Maung Maung Gyi, *Report on the Revision Settlement of the Bassein District, Season 1935–39* (Rangoon: Government Printing, 1941), pp. 3–4, pp. 41–45. Tenancies, in this district, had soared from 37 to 74 per cent, while 67 per cent of all tenancies were for three years or less.

45. RLAC, Part I, p. 10; Part III, p. 147. For a provocative but unconvincing defense of the *chettyar* caste, see Chester L. Cooper, "Moneylenders and the Economic Development of Lower Burma—an Exploratory Historical Study of the Role of the Indian Chettyars" (Ph.D dissertation, American University, 1959). Cooper also accepts the historical necessity of British *laissez faire* policy between 1880–1930, because to do otherwise "was not the way to build and preserve an empire" (p. 113). Obviously, the empire was not so preserved.

46. Andrus, *op. cit.*, p. 186.

47. *Political Economy of Burma*, pp. 65–67, 189–94; see also Binns, *op. cit.*, pp. 2–3. It may become fashionable to discount the data and insights of ex-colonial civil servants such as Furnivall, the late B. W. Swithinbank, H. F. Searle, B. O. Binns, and others, who attempted to reform from within. This is what C. L. Cooper (see *supra*, n. 45) tries to do (*op. cit.*, pp. 107–8, 113). But to do so is to ignore the facts on which the insight was based. The late U Maung Maung Gyi, Settlement Officer for the Bassein District Revision in 1935–39 (see *supra*, n. 44), was my neighbor in Burma from 1951 to 1953. We spent many hours poring over his report and the detailed data, not all of which got into the published record. He regarded this as his most important piece of work. Though he knew Furnivall, Swithinbank, Searle, Baxter, Binns, and other ICS'ers rather well and was interested in their outlook, he, and the few other Burmese admitted to the upper ranks of the ICS, arrived at similar conclusions independently; he could support his conclusions with immense knowledge.

48. Jacoby, *op. cit.*, pp. 86–87.

49. The late February–early March, 1965 "Peasants Seminar" commemorated, especially, the Saya San rebellion. See General Ne Win's speech in the March 4, 1965, issue of the *Working People's Daily* (Rangoon). (All subsequent references to *Working People's Daily* are to the Rangoon newspaper.) Some 400,000 farmers and others attended rallies and meetings during the week. See also Christian, *Modern Burma*, pp. 158–59, and Furnivall, *Colonial Policy and Practice*, pp. 131–41. Both authors suggest a relationship between crime and agrarian unrest. This subject requires further study.

50. See Aung San, "Presidential Address. Second Session of the Supreme Council of the AFPFL, May 16, 1946," *Burma's Challenge*, pp. 107–13.

51. *The Constitution of the Union of Burma* (reprint; Rangoon: GUB, 1954); *Two-Year Plan of Economic Development for Burma* (Rangoon: GUB, 1948); *The Land Nationalization Act, 1948*, together with speeches by Thakin Tin, Minister for Agriculture and Forests, and Prime Minister Thakin Nu (reprint; Rangoon: GUB, 1950).

52. *The Land Nationalization Act, 1948*, pp. 1, 2, 16, 19, 28–31. This act in part replaced and supplemented the *Tenancy Standard Rent Act, No.*

XXIV, the *Agricultural Debts Moratorium Act, No. LXXII*, the *Agricultural Debt Relief Act, No. LXXVIII*, passed in 1947, and the *Disposal of Tenancies Act, No. IV*, passed in 1948. Thakin Tin referred to these as examples of "piecemeal" legislation. Unless otherwise indicated, statistics for the post-independence period in this chapter are taken from the annual series *Economic Survey of Burma* (Rangoon: GUB). The data in this series, the most reliable for Burma, were gathered and consolidated, chiefly by the Central Statistical and Economics Department, from the various reports prepared by the ministries, departments, directorates, boards, and banks of government. This series may be supplemented by the *Bulletin*, Union Bank of Burma, published as a quarterly (with some interruptions) since 1952; data compiled for the suspended *Second Four-Year Plan for the Union of Burma (1961–62 to 1964–65)* (Rangoon: GUB, 1961); and the related publications of the two Ne Win governments. Since the Revolutionary Council became the government, the above series have been supplemented by two compendiums of statistical material. The first, *Burma National Economy* (Rangoon: GUB, 1964), covers the period from March 2, 1962, to March 1, 1963. (A second volume is promised for the same period.) The second item is extremely helpful, especially when used with the annual *Survey* series. It is the first issue of the *Statistical Year Book 1961*, prepared by the CSED as a summary of data since 1950 (Rangoon: GUB, 1964).

53. *The Land Nationalization Act, 1953, as Amended by Act No. 22 of 1954* (Rangoon: GUB, 1955).

54. *Economic Survey of Burma, 1959* (Rangoon: GUB, 1959), pp. 77–79.

55. Exempt (or exempted) land refers (1) to rice land up to 50 acres, held and worked by a cultivator, whether former tenant or landlord; (2) to specified amounts of acreage in crops other than paddy; and (3) to acreage in the possession of religious institutions. See *The Land Nationalization Act, 1953*, Schedule 1, pp. 21–23. The government has steadfastly refused to recognize a *legal* right to compensation for the ex-landlords. However, on moral grounds, it has agreed to some compensation. In 1956, the Compensation Department was created, and charged with the responsibility for processing landlords' claims. A total of 21,389 claims were instituted by December 31, 1959. The number of new claims and settlements were noted in the annual *Economic Surveys* through 1962.

56. *Statistical Year Book 1961*, p. 129; and U Sein Win, "The Peasant Problem, Agrarian Development in Postwar Burma," *Far Eastern Economic Review, Burma Supplement*, March 17, 1960, pp. 598–600. Credit and collection facilities steadily improved, especially after 1958, when the Ne Win caretaker government was installed. See *Is Trust Vindicated?* (Rangoon: GUB, 1960), pp. 160–71.

57. *Conference Papers on Current Economic Problems of Burma, 1951* (Rangoon: GUB, 1951).

58. The contract, dated August 8, 1951, was held by the Knappen, Tippetts, and Abbett Engineering Company, in association with Pierce [Mining] Management, Inc., and Robert R. Nathan [Economic] Associates, Inc. See *Preliminary Report on Economic and Engineering Survey of Burma* (Rangoon; GUB, 1952); and *Comprehensive Report, Economic and Engineering Development of Burma* (2 vols.; London, August, 1953), I, 1–491; II, 495–841. (These reports are hereafter cited as KTA, *Preliminary Report;* and KTA, *Comprehensive Report*.) After 1953, the KTA and Robert R. Nathan Associates were retained in Burma under separate contracts, financed by the government, until the Ne Win regime terminated their services in February, 1959.

59. For a discussion of the earlier, partial neglect of agriculture, when the emphasis on industry was being excessively promoted by some experts, see Frank N. Trager, *Building a Welfare State in Burma 1948–1956* (2d. ed.; New York: Institute of Pacific Relations, 1958), pp. 35–51, 92–106, and Postscript, pp. 111–15.

60. *The Pyidawtha Conference August 4–17, 1952, Resolutions and Speeches* (Rangoon: GUB, 1952). Hereafter cited as *The Pyidawtha Conference*.

61. *The Times* (London), September 11, 1959, called attention to various administrative changes within Burma and to the revival of the traditional headman's influence (*awza*) in the reorganization of village life.

62. *The Pyidawtha Conference*, p. 35.

63. KTA, *Comprehensive Report*, II, 836–41; Table XXV–1. See also Plate 2 for list of projects within each group.

64. *The Pyidawtha Conference*, pp. 23–34, 44–56; and *Pyidawtha, The New Burma* (Printed for the Government of Burma, in England, 1954), pp. 31–52.

65. See Trager, *Building a Welfare State in Burma*, "Agriculture," pp. 35–55; and pp. 89–109 for the KTA–GUB planning for the early years.

66. *Second Four-Year Plan*, p. 7.

67. See KTA *Contract Completion Report*, February 28, 1959, Chap. ix, "Burmese Industries," pp. 1–25; *Appendices for Contract Completion Report* [n.d. to November, 1958], "Industry," pp. 13–18. These are unpublished reports submitted to the GUB (in the author's possession). See *Second Four-Year Plan*, pp. 122–24, for summary of major industrial development.

68. See *Statistical Year Book 1961*, Tables 83, 85, and 86, pp. 161–65; and Louis J. Walinsky, *Economic Development in Burma 1951–60* (New York: The Twentieth Century Fund, 1962), "Implementation of the Program for State Manufacturing Industry," pp. 299–317.

69. Foreign-exchange reserves dropped from the all-time high of K1,186 million in September, 1953, to K516.3 million in September, 1955.

70. Trager, *Building a Welfare State in Burma*, pp. 111–18. See also a series of papers prepared by Robert R. Nathan Associates: R. B. Bangs, "Evaluation of the Domestic Fiscal Impact of the Three [later four] Year Development Programme" (mimeographed, January 25, 1956); S. Takahashi, "The Rice Export Situation and Outlook" (mimeographed, June 18, 1956). (Both are in the author's possession.) See also Walinsky, *op. cit.*, which is an indispensable reference for these years. This is a massive and impressive if somewhat defensive study, written by the outstanding director of the Robert R. Nathan Associates in 1953–59. See also Thet Tun, "A Critique of Louis J. Walinsky's 'Economic Development in Burma 1951–1960,'" *Journal of the Burma Research Society*, XLVII, Part I (June, 1964), 173–81.

71. For the text of the act and favorable Western reaction see Bank of Burma *Bulletin*, third quarter (Rangoon, 1959), pp. 103–5; and *The Times* (London), August 24, 1959.

72. *Economic Survey of Burma, 1960* (Rangoon: GUB, 1960), p. 107, refers to the completion in September, 1960, of the "First Four-Year Plan," and to a new one in preparation, subsequently published by the government as the *Second Four-Year Plan*. However, after the March, 1962, military coup, all previous plans were again subjected to review. They were later shelved.

73. Reference to these will be found in KTA, *Appendices for Contract Completion Report* (1958). (In author's possession.)

74. Robert R. Nathan Associates submitted "Thirteen Final Papers" (mimeographed; Rangoon, 1959), which in turn refer to many others, e.g., "Capital Programme Evaluation 1952–53 to 1957–58" (mimeographed; Rangoon, 1958). (In author's possession.)

Chapter 8: Political Viability: Fissures and Continuities

1. Known popularly as POPA. Adopted in 1948 and amended in 1949, it gave the government authority to arrest individuals suspected of committing or planning to commit "political" crimes, and to hold them pending long-delayed trials. The act was modeled on earlier British legislation. In June, 1963, the military regime extended the application of POPA to all

states in the Union. (Until then, it had been confined to Burma Proper.)

2. See Frank N. Trager, "The Impact of Marxism: Historical Overview and Judgment," in Trager (ed.), *Marxism in Southeast Asia*, pp. 240–99.

3. The last person who held such a position, U Gaung, known as the "Kinwun Mingyi," or "Chief Minister of the King," died in 1908. He had served Kings Mindon and Thibaw with some distinction and, after the end of the monarchy, had briefly served the British. One of the few Burmans who had an appreciation of Western military power in the second half of the nineteenth century, he advised Thibaw to avoid a military contest with the British. "From humble birth he rose through sheer merit to the highest post to which a Burman without royal blood could rise. His career will remain an inspiration to all young Burmans seeking to be of service to their country." From Maung Tun Tin, "The Kinwun Mingyi," *Burmese Review*, I, No. 10 (July 22, 1946), 7–10.

4. Derk Bodde, "Authority and Law in Ancient China," *Journal of the American Oriental Society*, Supplement No. 17 (1954); *Authority and Law in the Ancient Orient*, p. 49. See also John L. Christian, *Burma and the Japanese Invader* (Bombay: Thacker, 1945). Christian reported "some lingering royalist sentiment in Upper Burma" (p. 353). Prime Minister U Say restored King Alaungpaya's tomb in Shwebo; Dr. Ba Maw removed some of the earth from this place to Rangoon, while two princes volunteered to join his services in 1943. In general, Ba Maw has been charged with investing his leadership, under the Japanese, with a kingly "aura of splendour." See, for example, U Ba U, *op. cit.*, p. 170.

5. *Adipati* or *Adipadi* has been mistranslated by some to mean *Führer*, with all its unpleasant connotations. It is a Pali word meaning "chief," and is still in use to mean Chancellor of the University. Ba Maw, according to Christian (*op. cit.*, p. 353), may have had "a Herman Goering fondness for bright clothes and multiplicity of uniforms," but the fascist tones of the "independence" conferred upon Burma by Japan in 1943 were, even then, the butt of Burmese jokes. There is no doubt that the Constitution that the Japanese permitted legally created a dictatorship. For the text see Maung Maung, *Burma in the Family of Nations*, Appendix VI.

6. Maung Maung, commenting on the Thakins, writes that "they were Marxists, they were Fabian Socialists, they admired Hitler and Mussolini, they consumed with great hunger the stories of the Irish struggle for freedom" (*Burma in the Family of Nations*, p. 88). He is writing here of the group in the late 1930's, at a time when the average age was less than twenty-five.

7. The feudal hereditary rights of the Shan *sawbwas*, or *saophalongs*, ended officially on April 24, 1960, when their states were incorporated into the popular Shan State Government. The hereditary rulers were to receive an already determined compensation. See *Burma Weekly Bulletin*, May 21, 1960. Earlier, in December, 1959, the Central Government, by agreement, took over the responsibility for development of the more remote areas of the Shan and Kachin states. See *The Guardian*, December 17 and 29, 1959.

8. *The Governance of Modern Burma*, p. 31.

9. *Burma Weekly Bulletin*, May 21, 1959; and *GUB 1958 Nov.–1959 Feb.* (Rangoon: GUB, 1959), pp. 15–17. See also Maung Maung, *Burma's Constitution*, pp. 195–96.

10. Maung Maung, *Burma's Constitution*, pp. 148–57.

11. One such internal problem arose during 1949–50, from a financial scandal involving a leading AFPFL Cabinet minister (Ko Ko Gyi, Commerce and Supplies). This led to the 1951 law, already mentioned, that set up the Bureau of Special Investigation. This Bureau, which was to report directly to the prime minister, was empowered to make summary arrests of those suspected of corruption involving government funds and property.

12. The elections were supervised by a highly respected Commission, which included Supreme Court Justice Dr. E Maung and other prominent jurists,

such as U Kyaw Myint and U Thein Maung. See *The Nation*, June 13, 1951; Tinker, *The Union of Burma*, pp. 71–75; and Dorothy Woodman, "Rangoon Polls," *New Statesman and Nation*, XLII (July 7, 1951), p. 8. These sources all agree on this issue.

13. The electoral rolls for 1951 (there was universal suffrage for those eighteen years and over) were estimated at 8 million; for 1956, 8.57 million. In 1951 and 1956, there were, respectively, approximately 1.5 million and 4.1 million votes cast. See *The Nation*, May 15, 1956; and Josef Silverstein, "Politics, Parties and National Elections in Burma," *Far Eastern Survey*, XXV, No. 12 (December 1956), for accounts of the 1956 elections. (Hereafter, all subsequent references to *The Nation* are to the Rangoon publication.)

14. *Premier U Nu on The Four-Year Plan*, Speech, June 8, 1957 (Rangoon: GUB, 1957). See also U Nu, *Premier Reports to the People*.

15. In an interview during the summer of 1956, one of the deputy prime ministers said to me: "Either we are capable of serving and achieving or we deserve to be thrown out at the next election" (i.e., in 1960).

16. *Towards a Socialist State* (Rangoon: GUB, 1958).

17. The following pages are based on the author's "The Political Split in Burma," *Far Eastern Survey*, XXVII, No. 10 (October, 1958), 145–55; and on his "Political Divorce in Burma," *Foreign Affairs*, January, 1959, pp. 317–27; also on many interviews with civilian and military leaders in Burma during the critical summer of 1958.

18. Sein Win, in *The Split Story* (Rangoon: *The Guardian*, 1959), p. 15, refers to the individual, Kyaw Tun, as belonging to the "uneducated" group within the leadership (friction existed between those who had had university education and the others who had barely finished elementary school). Kyaw Tun, although "cleared," had also been allegedly involved in a notorious kidnapping-ransom scandal. (The truth about this has never been fully disclosed.)

19. U Nu refers to this in *Premier Reports to the People*, pp. 36, 41–42. See also the revelations of A. Kaznacheev, former information officer, Soviet Embassy, Rangoon, in *The Nation*, March 21, 1960, "Soviet and Chinese Economic Warfare in Burma"; since amplified and republished in his book *Inside a Soviet Embassy, Experiences of a Russian Diplomat in Burma* (Philadelphia: J. B. Lippincott, 1962).

20. *The Nation*, November 6, 7, and 9, 1959, reports on the illegal immigration and on an interview with an ex-Kachin Communist trained in China; and also summarizes some of the data relating to Burmese Communists trained in China from 1949 onward. These stories appeared simultaneously in the Burmese- and English-language press. Similar stories had appeared in earlier years. They could not have been published unless the government in power had assisted reporters in getting (or releasing) data. Reporters in Burma do not travel much outside the two main publishing centers of Rangoon and Mandalay. Travel is costly, and in the up-country and border areas it requires military or police acquiescence.

21. See *The Times* (London), August 5 and 22, 1958, "Burma Tries to Coax Rebels into Surrender" and "Concession to Communists in New Burmese Amnesty." Various generous amnesty offers had previously been made, some of which were successful in persuading rebels to surrender. However, the Indemnity Order of August 1, 1958, broadened excessively the then prevailing amnesty regulations. Between July 26 and October 11, 1958, some 4,373 rebels took advantage of the current leniency. They "came out into the light"—the Burmese expression for surrender—were lavishly greeted by government officials, but frequently left their weapons behind them. The Indemnity Order of August 1 was withdrawn when U Nu demitted office in October. General Ne Win then publicly commented on this. See *The Times* (London), November 1, 1958.

22. The timetable for these events (from U Nu's broadcast on September

26 and the exchange of letters with General Ne Win to the session of Parliament on October 28) was fixed by the Constitution, which required a thirty-day notice before Parliament could be convened. All the documents relevant to this transfer of power are conveniently gathered in *GUB 1958 Nov.–1959 Feb.*, pp. 2–24.

23. *The Times* (London), September 30, 1958, carried a summary headlined, "Burmese Press Praises U Nu," which referred to the transfer of power. The issue of October 7, 1958, suggested that U Nu "thrust greatness" upon a "great patriot, General Ne Win."

24. The texts appear in *Is Trust Vindicated?*, pp. 534–41. This 567-page work contains "A chronicle of the various accomplishments of the Government headed by General Ne Win during the period of tenure from November, 1958, to February 6, 1960"; it is the indispensable official record and public accounting. See also John S. Thomson, "Supplement on the Ne Win Administration, A Second Chance for Burma," in Furnivall, *The Governance of Modern Burma*, pp. 133–54.

25. *Is Trust Vindicated?*, p. 536.

26. Its members, in addition to the Prime Minister, were: Former Chief Justice of the Supreme Court, U Thein Maung; Chief Justice of the High Court, U Chan Tun Aung; Chief Secretary of Government, U Khin Maung Pyu; civil servants U Kyaw Nyein, U Chit Thoung, and U Ka; respected elders U Ba Kyar and U San Nyunt—and the five designees of the states and division, Sao Hom Hpa (Shan), Dr. Saw Hla Tun (Karen), Duwa Zau Lawn (Kachin), Sao Wunna (Kayah), and U Htang Lian, later replaced by U Ral Hmung (Chin). After February, 1959, the Prime Minister reshuffled his Cabinet, relieving two of the older members, U Thein Maung and U Ba Kyar. Their replacements were U Thi Han, U Lun Baw, and U Tun Tin. One military officer, Brigadier Tin Pe, was also added.

27. There are three "degree" awards depending upon the period of service: First Degree for those whose careers began with the Burma Independence Army, January 6–July 26, 1942; Second Degree for any two periods, the second beginning with that of the Burma Defense Army (under the Japanese), July 27, 1942–March 26, 1945; Third Degree for any one period, the third beginning with that of the Burma Patriotic Forces, the Resistance against the Japanese, March 27–August 15, 1945.

28. *Is Trust Vindicated?*, pp. 19–58.

29. *Ibid.*, pp. 2–18. During Ne Win's regime "important" crimes such as murder, robbery, and kidnaping declined from 9,635 cases to 6,201. See also *The Nation*, May 15, 1959, "Crime Rate Continues to Fall; No Negotiations with Rebels."

30. *Is Trust Vindicated?*, pp. 489–500; and *The Nine Months After the Ten Years* (Rangoon: GUB, 1959), pp. 26–31. In January, 1960, the Central Statistical and Economics Department introduced a new Index with 1958 as the base year, using six subgroups of approximately eighty commodities and services. Thus, the use of cost-of-living statistics after January, 1960, when compared with pre-1958 indexes, requires great care.

31. Two major sections of *Is Trust Vindicated?* contain the detailed record of this progress: "National Economy," pp. 113–340; and "Social Service," pp. 343–500. The list of senior officers and their assignments follows:

Selected Senior Officers	*Assignments in Economy*
Brig. Aung Gyi	Chairman, Budget Allocation Supervision Committee
Col. Kyi Win	Agricultural Resources Development Corporation; Income Tax Department
Col. Kyi Maung	State Timber Board
Col. Hla Aung	Survey Department
Col. Mya Win	Union Purchase Board

Selected Senior Officers	Assignments in Economy
Brig. Tin Pe	Ministry of Mines; Ministry of Public Works, National Housing and Rehabilitation
Col. Khin Nyo	Trade Development Corporation; Burma Railways
Lt. Col. Mya Thaung	State Agricultural Marketing Board
Capt. B. O. Barber (Navy)	Burma Pharmaceutical Industry
W/Comdr. P. Aye Cho	Industrial Development Corporation
Lt. Col. Ba Kyin	Electricity Supply Board
Sqn./Ldr. Khin Maung Gyi	Chief Executive Officer, Steel Mill
Comdr. T. Clift	Union of Burma Airways
Col. Kyaw Soe	Inland Waterways Transport Board
Lt. Col. Ba Ni	Directorate of Telecommunications
Lt. Col. Saw Mya Thein	Port Commissioners
Comdr. Baroni (Navy)	Union of Burma Shipping Board
Lt. Col. Chit Khaing	Directorate of Labor
Lt. Col. Bo Thaung	Union Stevedoring Board
Col. Sein Win	National Housing Board

At least four other officers should also be cited: Col. Maung Maung, Member of the Central Security Council; Col. Min Thein, Union Constabulary (Police); Col. Tun Sein, Corporation of Rangoon; and Col. Ba Than, Ministry of Information and Psychological Warfare Officer. They had considerable responsibility for a variety of interdependent political and economic decisions.

32. *The Nine Months After the Ten Years*, pp. 64–73.

33. *Burma Weekly Bulletin*, June 4, 1959, published the rules for the organization. The issue of November 17, 1959, is devoted entirely to the November meeting. It includes the names of about forty nationally prominent military figures and civilians who had participated. Many of them became officers and members of the NSA's Central Executive Council.

34. *The Nation*, June 9, 1959. At a press conference, Colonel Maung Maung, speaking for the Central Security Council, said that the "general election was seven months away" (i.e., February or March, 1960), and he added emphatically that "no army officer" would stand for election to Parliament. See *The Nation*, August 25, 1959. The well-informed Deputy-Attorney General Dr. Maung Maung suggested a slightly accelerated schedule, i.e., January or February, 1960, in an article in the London *Forum-Service*, reprinted as "The Interlude" in *The Guardian*, October 3, 1959. Colonel Maung Maung later confirmed this possibility; see *The Nation*, November 11, 1959.

35. *The New York Times*, December 16, 1959. A detailed timetable was published in *The Nation*, December 20, 1959.

36. *The Nation*, September 27–October 2, 1959. Muslims in the Clean AFPFL, led by U Raschid, disagreed with U Nu on the issue of Buddhism as the state religion. They were permitted to express their disagreement and to oppose this majority policy before and after the elections without suffering any disciplinary measures. U Nu expanded on this program at various times. See, for example, *The Nation*, November 17, 1959; and *The Guardian*, November 17 and 24, 1959, and January 23, 1960. In a press interview on May 24, 1960, Prime Minister Nu confirmed the independence of Cabinet minister Raschid on the state religion issue. See *Burma Weekly Bulletin*, June 2, 1960.

37. The seminar began on October 19, 1959. Its views on these issues were published intermittently. See *The Guardian*, October 20, and December 14 and 23, 1959; and January 20 and 23, 1960. See *The Nation*, November 12, and December 15 and 23, 1959. The December 23 issues of both papers carried the Stable AFPFL "Election Manifesto." The third political grouping, the NUF, also issued an election manifesto, calling for "unity and parliamentary

democracy." See *The Guardian*, October 22, 1959. An interesting curiosity of the elections was the Buddhist Democratic Party, otherwise known as the Buddhist People's Party. It was founded in 1959 by Sir M. A. Maung Gyee, one of the original members of the pre-World War I Young Men's Buddhist Association, forerunner of Burmese nationalist organizations.

38. Albert Carthy, Secretary of the Socialist International, while visiting Burma (see *The Nation*, November 22, 1959), inexcusably acted and spoke as if the Stable AFPFL were the only socialist grouping in Burma. In doing this he ignored, or was ignorant of, the legitimate socialist claims of the Nu-Tin Clean faction, perpetuating thereby the kind of error previously made in the Socialist International. For, however real and bitter the split, it was based not on ideology, policy, or program, but on warring personalities.

39. *The Nation*, December 22, 1959.

40. *The Guardian*, January 19, 1960.

41. *Is Trust Vindicated?*, p. 67. There may be some small discrepancy in this count. *The Nation*, March 1, 1960, indicated that 226 seats were filled. A later report from the "Official Returns for Lower House," *The Guardian*, March 29, 1960, decreased the number of postponed elections due to insurgent activities from 15 to 12. See also the *New Times of Burma*, March 20, 1960. There was no single official source for all elections, except insofar as a successful candidate claimed his seat in Parliament.

42. In addition to those cited above, useful sources for the results of the elections include: *The Nation*, March 1, 1960, for the voting records in the constituencies; *The Guardian*, April 8, 1960, for the Chamber of Nationalities; Lee S. Bigelow, "The 1960 Elections in Burma," *Far Eastern Survey*, XXIX (May, 1960), 70–74; Richard Butwell and Fred von der Mehden, "The 1960 Election in Burma," *Pacific Affairs*, XXXII (June, 1960), 144–57; and Maung Maung, "New Parliament in Burma," *India Quarterly*, XVI (April–June, 1960), 139–44. Almost 10 million Burmese were eligible to vote; more than 60 per cent exercised their right to do so.

43. *New Times of Burma* and *The Nation*, November 17, 1959.

44. Several reporters called attention to the coupling of the army and the Stable AFPFL, and to the fact that army discipline violated certain Burmese customs, e.g., killing of pariah dogs, legalizing the slaughter of beef (promptly repealed after U Nu came back to power). See, for example, Tillman Durdin, *The New York Times*, February 9, 11, 1960; Richard Butwell, "The New Political Outlook in Burma," *Far Eastern Survey*, XXIX (February, 1960), 27; and Kingsley Martin, "Nu's Victory," *New Statesman*, March 12, 1960, *passim*. The three men were in Burma during the elections.

45. *New Times of Burma*, March 19 and 20, 1960.

46. The Cabinet members were U Nu, Prime Minister and Defense, Home Affairs, Democratization and Administration of Local Bodies, Information, Relief and Resettlement; Sao Hkun Hkio, Foreign Affairs and the Shan State; Thakin Tin, Finance and Revenue, National Planning; Bo Hmu Aung, Transport, Posts and Telegraphs, Marine and Civil Aviation, Public Works, Housing and Rehabilitation; Dr. E Maung, Judicial Affairs, Education; U Raschid, Industries, Mines and Labor; U Ba Saw, Social Welfare and Religious Affairs, Union Culture, Health, Immigration and National Registration; Thakin Tin Maung, Agriculture and Forests, Land Nationalization, Cooperatives and Commodity Distribution; U Thwin, Trade Development, Civil Supplies and Supplies; Dr. Saw Hla Tun, Karen State; Sima Duwa Sinwa Nawng, Kachin State; Sao Wunna, Kayah State; and U Za Hre Lian, Chin Affairs.

47. *Burma Weekly Bulletin*, April 7, 1960. On April 25, it was announced that a five-member advisory committee to the Union Government had been appointed to consider such questions as statehood for the Arakan and Mons areas, and other campaign promises. It was headed by the second President of the Union, Dr. Ba U. See the May 12, 1960 issue. Similarly, lay and clerical commissions were appointed to advise the government on the state-religion issue.

48. See, for example, Guy J. Pauker, "Southeast Asia as a Problem Area in the Next Decade," *World Politics*, XI (April, 1959), 325–45.

Chapter 9: The Failure of U Nu and the Return of General Ne Win

1. The material in this chapter is based on the author's article with a similar title in *The Review of Politics*, XXV (July, 1963), 309–28; and on another visit to Burma in 1964.

2. The quotations in this and the following paragraphs are from his speech "Crusade for Democracy," printed in the *Burma Weekly Bulletin*, April 7, 1960. The themes were substantially repeated at the August meeting of Parliament (*ibid.*, September 1, 1960).

3. *The Guardian*, February 7, 1961. Some less senior officers also "decided . . . to retire . . . and take up business." See also *The New York Times*, February 19, 1961.

4. *The Guardian*, December 23, 1960.

5. *Ibid.*, March 3, 1961.

6. *Ibid.*, March 17, 1961.

7. U Nu, Speech, Chamber of Deputies, March 13, *Burma Weekly Bulletin*, March 23 and 30, and April 6, 1961. In this speech, U Nu lauded the army for its role against the KMT "aggressors," upbraiding the latter for joining forces with the Shan and Karen rebels, and insisting that the United States put a stop to the KMT activity in Burma.

8. *The Guardian*, October 20, 1960.

9. *Ibid.*, February 13, 1961.

10. Studies of the Burmese military strategy and tactics are not available. Certain insights may be gained from two articles by Major Thoung Htaik, which were published in the U.S. Army Command and General Staff College *Military Review* (June and August, 1961); "Encirclement Methods in Anti-guerrilla Warfare," pp. 90–95; and "What It Takes: Essentials of Special Operations," pp. 12–16. For a more general view, see Colonel Trevor N. Dupuy, "Burma and Its Army: A Contrast in Motivations and Characteristics," *Antioch Review*, XX (Winter, 1960–61), 428–40. Colonel Dupuy was Visiting Professor of Military History at the University of Rangoon, 1959–60. The chapter by Lucian Pye in John J. Johnson (ed.), *The Role of the Military in Underdeveloped Countries* (Princeton, N.J.: Princeton University Press, 1962), is so general in scope and treatment as to be of little use.

11. *The Nation*, August 28, 1960.

12. *The New York Times*, November 9, 1960.

13. *The Guardian*, January 22, 1961.

14. See editorial, "Shan Rebellion," *The Nation*, August 27, 1959.

15. *The New York Times*, February 12, 1960; *The Nation*, March 7, 1960; and *The Guardian*, April 19, 1960.

16. *The Nation*, August 27, 1960.

17. See editorial, "Elusive Peace," *The Guardian*, December 28, 1960.

18. *The Burma Weekly Bulletin*, March 2, 1961. During March–April, the U.S. and Thailand again helped to evacuate considerable numbers of KMT's. The first group numbered about 1,200 (*The New York Times*, March 15, 1961). They were to be followed by about 4,000 to 5,000 more (*The Guardian*, March 17, 1961); the precise number has not been published.

19. *The Guardian*, April 1, 1961. The worst year of the insurrection had been 1949.

20. In an article ostensibly devoted to "The Military Take-over in Burma" (*The Guardian*, March 9, 1962), Dr. Ba Maw analyzed the failure of U Nu which he assigned to "four causes": U Nu lacked political interest; he had no firm political faith; he confused democracy in government with license; and he exhibited an inability to impart the necessary drive in the people for sustained progress. Though Dr. Ba Maw, wartime *adipati* for the Japanese, has frequently been a special pleader, his analysis here is a shrewd one.

21. John S. Everton, then U.S. Ambassador to Burma, subsequently described the situation as "generally one of relief and expectation; expectation based in part on memories of the efficiency of the caretaker government two years earlier and the assumption that this would somehow be similar." "The Ne Win Regime in Burma," *Asia*, No. 2 (Autumn, 1964), p. 6.

22. *The Burma Weekly Bulletin*, March 8, 1962.

23. *The Guardian*, March 3, 1962, published the broadcast message of General Ne Win after the coup; the list of forty-two prominent officials and other individuals who were arrested; and the names of the seventeen members of the Revolutionary (or ruling) Council were listed as follows: General Ne Win, Commander-in-Chief; Brigadier Aung Gyi, Vice Chief of Staff (Army); Commodore Than Pe, Vice Chief of Staff (Navy); Brigadier T. Clift, Vice Chief of Staff (Air); Brigadiers Tin Pe, San Yu, Sein Win; Colonels Thaung Kyi, Kyi Maung, Maung Shwe, Than Sein, Kyaw Soe, Saw Myint, Chit Myaing, Khin Nyo, Hla Han, Tan Yu Saing. Various ministries were assigned to several of these officers. U Thi Han, a student strike leader in 1936 and a long-time civilian friend of General Ne Win, was added as Foreign Minister. Since that time, there have been changes in the Council due to death, resignation, retirement, and reassignment. The Revolutionary Council (RC) in turn created the Revolutionary Government (i.e., a cabinet). It is sometimes called the Council of Ministers. On September 17, 1964, an enlarged Council was designated by the RC. Its members—not all of whom were in the Revolutionary Council—and their portfolios included: General Ne Win (Commander in Chief), Chairman of the Council of Ministers and Minister of Defense; Brigadier Tin Pe, Minister of Supply and Cooperatives and Minister of Trade Development; Brigadier San Yu (Vice Chief, Army), Minister of Finance and Revenue; Commodore Thaung Tim (Vice Chief, Navy), Minister of Mines; Brigadier Thaung Dan (Vice Chief, Air), Minister of Information and Minister of Culture; Brigadier Sein Win, Minister of Public Works and Housing; Colonel Thaung Kyi, Minister of Agriculture and Forests and Minister of Land Nationalization; Colonel Maung Shwe, Minister of Industry; Colonel Than Sein, Minister of Labor; Colonel Kyaw Soe, Minister of Home Affairs, Minister of Judicial Affairs, Minister of Democratization of Local Administration and Local Bodies, Minister of Religious Affairs, and Minister of Immigration, National Registration and Census; Colonel Hla Han, Minister of Education and Minister of Health; Colonel Ba Ni, Minister of Transport and Communications; Colonel Maung Lwin, Minister of Relief, Resettlement, and National Solidarity, and Minister of Social Welfare; and U Thi Han, Minister of Foreign Affairs and Minister of National Planning. (This list is taken from *Working People's Daily*, September 18, 1964.)

24. From March 2, 1962, the Burmese daily press is the indispensable source for accounts of the rapid changes that occurred. For a short time after the coup, the official *Burma Weekly Bulletin* was continued. During the summer of 1962, it was suspended; in August it was replaced with a new, official biweekly, *Forward*. Still later, at the end of 1963 and beginning of 1964, the government established its own daily newspaper, the *Working People's Daily* (also published in Burmese). *Forward* and the *Working People's Daily* chronicle the actions of the government. *Forward's* fortnightly column, "Diary of Events," is particularly useful.

25. This will be found in *Is Trust Vindicated?*, pp. 534–41. All other references to the policies, decisions, and acts of the Revolutionary Council noted above are taken from the *Burma Weekly Bulletin*, March 8 to May 31, 1962. See issue of May 3, 1962, for the text of *The Burmese Way to Socialism*.

26. This has particularly affected the Indian minority in Burma. See, for example, S. B. Mookherji, "The Exodus of the Overseas Indians," *Eastern World*, XVII (November, 1964), 13–14. By the end of 1965, the *Working People's Daily* reported that more than 100,000 "foreigners (chiefly Indians and Pakistanis) left Burma."

27. The process by which the BSPP at first coexisted and then replaced all

the legal parties was gradual. In the summer of 1963, when leaders of the parliamentary parties, the AFPFL and the Union Party, warned against such a development (see, e.g., the mild speech by U Ba Swe at the Martyrs' Mausoleum, July 19, widely reprinted and commented upon in the Burmese press of the period), they were jailed. Later in November, when the aboveground Communists blamed the government for the failure of the peace parleys they, too, were jailed. For an account of the BSPP's subsidization, see *The Guardian,* October 8, 1963. The ban on political parties was achieved by Law No. 41 of March 28, 1964, the National Solidarity (Protection) Law.

ANALYSIS OF PRISONERS HELD BY RGUB UNDER EMERGENCY
OR SPECIAL LEGISLATION, AS OF MAY 5, 1965

	Arrested	*Released*	*Jailed*
Top leadership			
March 2, 1962	53	10	43
Other dates	36	3	33
AFPFL and Union Party politicians			
August 9, 1963	12	1	11
Other dates	306	175	131
NUF politicians and supporters			
November 15, 1963	904	912 [a]	1,726
Other dates	1,734		
Students			
December 2, 1963	91	291 [b]	81
Other dates	281		
"Economic criminals"	871	505 [c]	366
Pongyis, politicians, and others (April 27, 1965)			
Pongyis	142	3	139
politicians, and others	205	—	205
Total	4,635	1,900	2,735

SOURCE: Figures are taken from newspaper reports and are not official.
[a] Includes 351 political prisoners released on May 1, 1964, and 216 political prisoners released on January 3, 1965.
[b] Includes 141 student prisoners released on May 1, 1964, and 2 student prisoners released on January 3, 1965.
[c] Includes 496 economic criminals released on August 4, 1964, 9 economic criminals released on January 3, 1965.

28. *The Guardian,* July 7–11, 1962.

29. The problem of higher education in Burma has been a troublesome one. Rangoon University was a seedbed for the pre–World War II nationalist movement. After independence, it offered higher education to all who could pass matriculation examinations at fairly low levels. It never recovered its prewar standards. Its indiscipline was in part encouraged by the formation of student groups loyal to the existing political parties—above and under ground. Since independence, it has had five rectors. There has been a tendency in Burma to blame "colonial education" for the university's difficulties. This is a convenient form of scapegoating hardly commensurate with the facts. More at issue, in addition to the above, has been the willingness in Burma to abide by the "lecture-cram-exam" system of education and indecision with respect to the language of instruction. The advocates for Burmese faced an enormous

gap in study and research materials, while those who supported English were faced with a deteriorating capability in that language among students. Other factors—large classes, excessive teaching loads, insufficiently trained staffs— also contributed their share to the educational malaise. In November, 1963, the political students, utilizing an examination issue but timing their renewed demonstrations to the failure of negotiations with the Communist rebels, again challenged the government. The Revolutionary Council swiftly closed all institutions, arrested the agitators, and sent the other students home. The technical schools and faculties were reopened shortly thereafter. The arts and science faculties remained closed for one year. In April, 1964, Colonel Hla Han, Minister for Education (a physician by training), conducted a national four-day seminar on education. Out of this have come a number of reforms. All faculty members became civil servants, and all higher-education institutions were placed under the jurisdiction of the Ministry. A new Higher Education Law was passed, and a Reorganizing Committee was authorized with the Minister as Chairman. Burmese was to become the language of instruction, with English as a second language. Provision was made for more translations and the preparation of college texts in Burmese. The focus of education was shifted from general arts and science to technical, vocational subjects and other specializations, e.g., economics. The structure of the universities was reconstituted into constituent colleges and institutes with smaller student populations, larger faculties, and separate rectors for each college or institute. The system was inaugurated with the opening of the November 2, 1964, term. See *Working People's Daily*, April 17, May 29–30, and October 13, 1964; see also *The Guardian*, May 29–30, for accounts of the seminar and the law; the *Working People's Daily*, September 28, November 2, 1964 (four-page supplement) for the list of colleges, institutes, and rectors; and *Forward*, November 15, 1964, for details on the opening of the new term.

30. This is a document of "thirty-six typewritten foolscap" pages, published in full in *The Guardian* and *The Nation*, January 18, 1963. It has since been published as a small book (Rangoon: Beikman Press, 1964).

31. *Forward* frequently chronicles the progress of the BSPP. The above quotation will be found in the issue of March 7, 1963, p. 2; the tabulated specific characteristics in the September 15, 1964 issue, pp. 4–6. At the opening of the first training course (six–seven weeks) for the BSPP, General Ne Win made a three-hour inaugural speech in Burmese, expounding the views of the Revolutionary Council as contained in these documents, and the history and prospects of his government. I do not believe there is a full text of this speech. In June, 1964, the Ministry of Home Affairs opened a similar school, the Central Service Training School, for training civil servants "to transform the present bureaucratic machinery into one based on socialist democracy."

32. On April 1, 1964, the government ordered the registration of all organizations in Burma. At first, this included the religious organization of the monks, the Sanghas. (See *The Guardian*, April 2, 1964.) On April 18, 1964, it issued a statement to mollify the Sanghas, whose members opposed the registration order, and again called attention to its support for freedom of worship, pointedly adding the provision that it "would never misuse the Sanghas." The agitation continued. The government, finding itself in trouble, backtracked with regard to its policy toward the Sanghas. (See the *Working People's Daily*, May 4, 1964.)

33. See *Forward*, April 7, 1963, for the amnesty; see the June 22, 1963 issue for the parleys. This episode did not end the regime's troubles with the Sanghas. The repeal of the 1949–50 Ecclesiastical Court and Pali University Acts (*Working People's Daily*, January 19, 1965) initiated a variety of protest meetings by "dissident Sanghas" which erupted into violence (*ibid.*, March 26, 1965) and led to the arrest of some *pongyis*. A new draft of a law was presented to the all-sect Sanghas convention on March 19 and 20. The dissident Sanghas charged the government with interference in religious matters and with fostering Communism. The government initiated another round of

pacification by assigning the 107th Burma Regiment in Mandalay to "washing and cleaning the important Maha Myatmum Pagoda in Mandalay" and then enlisted the aid of the "24 senior-most *sayadaws* of Mandalay" to assist in redrafting the Ecclesiastical Court law (*ibid.*, May 10, 12, 1965). At this time, the regime seems to have found, once again, a workable relationship with the Sanghas.

34. See *The Guardian*, August 5, 1963, for Ye Htut's appeal for cooperation with the RC's peace parley. (Ye Htut was a former Central Committee member of the BCP.)

35. *Ibid.*, August 14 and 21, 1963. See also editorials in the August 14 and 22, and September 8, 1963 issues. Soe, as pointed out in this study, is a "character." He has no foreign attachments; I have looked upon him as the De Leon of Burma—an isolated radical incapable of agreement with anyone who purports to be his equal. His group has frequently, and mistakenly, been called Trotskyist. *Forward*, August 22, 1963, carries the official statement breaking off negotiations.

36. *The Guardian*, August 16, and September 2, 3, and 10, 1963. The demands of the KIA were published in a long article in the Mandalay press, September 10, 1963. The *Ludu* (Mandalay) (a pro-Peking Communist paper in Burmese), ably edited and apparently financially secure, although it does not have much advertising, featured the KIA statement, which began by acknowledging its insurrectionary activity for "an autonomous state. Frankly speaking we do not think of a union."

37. *Forward*, December 7, 1963, pp. 2–4. See also *The Nation*, November 16, 24, 1963; *The Guardian*, November 16–17, 19, and 23, 1963; and the *Working People's Daily* for that period. The English- and Burmese-language press—other than the pro-BCP paper, the *Ludu* (Mandalay)—in general, shared the views of the sober Burmese-language daily, the *Hanthawaddy*, whose columnist Ye Din, on November 17, 1963, summed up the situation by saying that the failure of the negotiations is not a matter for "rejoicing": that no government could have or ought to have acceded to the demands of the rebels, "no matter how ardent the people are for peace. They [the people] will not be in favor of the mockery of domestic peace" proposed by the underground.

38. *Forward*, March 22, 1964, pp. 3–6.

39. See *The New York Times*, December 4, 1964, and January 11, 1965. On February 2, 1965, the *Working People's Daily* carried a story to the effect that the "KIA depradations in Kachin State have laid waste about K17 lakhs worth of property [$1.7 million]." However, during the spring of 1965, various Kachin and Shan rebel "surrender" stories were printed. On June 7, *The Guardian* published a six-month summary: "3,164 rebels surrendered bringing in 1,241 pieces of fire-arms and 26,536 assorted ammunition."

40. Speech at Mandalay, *The Guardian*, February 14, 1964. In this important policy speech, General Ne Win indicated that "a fully representative national convention might be held at an appropriate time to formulate just and permanent relations between all the races in the country, uniting them all in a United Burma." This was the first major pronouncement concerning such a future constitutional convention. See also "The Meaning of the Union Day," *Forward*, February 7, 1964, pp. 7–10. In June, the RC authorized the Shan State Affairs Council—the equivalent of a state government with limited powers—"to form an eleven-member committee for the purpose of promoting the Shan language, literature, customs, and the Shan national way of life." See editorial, *The Guardian*, June 24, 1964. In December, a similar twenty-two-member committee was appointed for the Kachin State (*The Asian Student*, December 26, 1964).

41. "Cooperative Villages for Landless Farmers," *Forward*, May 22, 1963, pp. 6–13.

42. The details for these and subsequent acts are to be found in the Burmese press. For actions taken before March, 1963, see *Burma National Econ-*

omy (Rangoon: GUB, 1964). A second volume in this series is promised. The move with respect to Steel Brothers occurred at the time when the BOC was nationalized; Anglo-Tin was bought out the following spring. The *Economic Survey of Burma, 1963* contains the standard series of Burma's statistics for the revolutionary government's first year in office. Gross domestic product (1947–48 prices) jumped from 112 in 1961–62 to 121 (estimated) in 1962–63 (1938–39 [base year] = 100).

43. It was reported that the action was taken in order to forestall "capitalists' sabotage" and to reduce "the cost of living for all the peoples of the Union." For the Rangoon event, see *The Guardian*, news and editorial pages (and any other Burmese daily) for March 20, 1964. For the countrywide event, see *ibid.*, April 10, 1964.

44. See news and editorial, "The Elimination of Black Money," *Working People's Daily*, May 18, 1964. See also supporting editorials in *The Nation*, May 18, 1964, and *The Guardian*, May 19, 1964.

45. Apparently, a briefing session for some 600 officers was at least one place where the RC revealed its awareness of the difficulties. See "Brigadier Sein Win Meets Commanders," *The Guardian*, June 20, 1964; and the editorial in the same issue.

46. See table, *Working People's Daily*, August 12, 1964.

47. *Working People's Daily*, June 20, 1964; *The Guardian*, July 12, 1964.

48. This was done, at first, outside of Rangoon—in Mandalay, Bassein, and other cities. See *The Guardian*, June 14, 1964. As of that date, 142 shops were restored to former owners in Mandalay.

49. *Working People's Daily*, August 12, 25, 1964. The first stage of the refund was almost completed by September 15. For an account of subsequent stages, see *ibid.*, September 15, 1964, and January 28, 1965.

50. It was called a seminar because instruction, based on current government data, was given. Questions and answers were permitted. General Ne Win's speeches (translated texts in the author's possession) on these occasions, particularly the ones at Popa on January 2, and Kabaung on March 2, were important in revealing its program and implementation. Other members of the Council and government also participated. See for example *The Guardian*, during the Kabaung Seminar, March 2, 3, 4, and 5, 1964. See also S. C. Banerji, "Burma's Peasant Seminars," *Far Eastern Economic Review*, July 30, 1964, pp. 204–5.

51. Ne Win spoke at Chauk, the historic oil fields where nationalist labor first made headway in the 1930's. See *The Guardian*, April 29, 30, and May 1, 3, 1964; and *Working People's Daily*, May 20, 21, 1964. The comparable seminars and mass rallies for both peasants and workers, held in February–March and May, 1965, respectively, were massive affairs. In addition to the meetings at the national level in Rangoon, regional gatherings were also held throughout the country. At all these meetings, there were important announcements embodied in the major addresses given by General Ne Win, e.g., that farmers would be freed from the obligation to pay tenancy fees to landlords; exhortations to workers to avoid "wastage" during work hours and in the handling of machinery. They were repeated, in substance, by members of the government. See *Working People's Daily*, March 2, 4, and 23, 1965, and especially the supplement, "The Farmer and Socialist Revolution," March 2.

52. "The Economy in 1963–64, A Summary," *Working People's Daily*, October 30, 1964. This document also appeared in *Forward*, III, No. 7 (November 15, 1964).

53. *Working People's Daily*, September 13, 1964.

54. "Despite Shock, Burma Rushes to Socialism," January 18, 1965.

Chapter 10: The Two Stages of Policy: From the Search for Powerful Allies to Neutralism

1. The editorial, "The Lend-Lease Agreement," March 24, 1947. The same editorial referred to a trade agreement with India, in 1940, and to the uncompleted negotiations with China and India on immigration problems, but Burma's foreign relations during the period of Japanese occupation were ignored. During March, the interim government also sent a delegation of seventeen members, headed by Judge Kyaw Myint, to the First Asian Relations Conference which was convened by Nehru in New Delhi. A short while later, Aung San invited representatives from nationalist movements in French Indochina and Indonesia to Rangoon to consider the formation of a regional organization.

2. The Communist Information Bureau (Cominform) launched its journal, *For a Lasting Peace, For a People's Democracy,* in November, 1947. For the next ten years, it denounced the independent government of Burma as a "puppet," controlled by the "big imperialist monopolies." See, for example, R. Palme Dutt, "Right Wing Social Democracy in the Service of Imperialism," No. 21 (24) (November 1, 1948), pp. 6–7.

3. See *supra,* chap. V, p. 101; and Thakin Nu, *Towards Peace and Democracy,* pp. 92–93. This, and subsequent collections of the Prime Minister's speeches, are the major source for policy statements.

4. Thakin Nu, *Towards Peace and Democracy,* pp. 117, 130–34.

5. *Burma Weekly Bulletin,* April 7, 1960. Earlier typical U Nu statements are to be found in his Martyrs' Day Address, July 19, 1954, *For World Peace and Progress* (Rangoon: GUB, 1954), in which he calls Burma a "neutral nation" and describes the Burmese as "neutralists in power politics"; in *Resurgence, A Collection of Three Speeches* (Rangoon: GUB, 1955), made at the April, 1955, Bandung Conference, in which he refers to and defines the role of the "uncommitted" nations; in the speech given before the Washington National Press Club, July 1, 1955, *An Asian Speaks About Neutrality* (Washington, D.C.: Embassy of the Union of Burma, 1955); in his speech, March 4, 1956, at the AFPFL mass conference (*Burma Weekly Bulletin,* March 8, 1956), where he refers to Burma's "line of action receiving the approbation of even those persons and those countries which had in the past criticized our neutral policy and suspected our motives"; in his long review of foreign relations in *Premier Reports to the People,* where he refers to Burma's "independent foreign policy"; in the exchange of letters between U Nu and General Ne Win, September 26, 1958, reprinted in *Is Trust Vindicated?,* pp. 543–44, where promises were made (and kept) to pursue "a policy of strict and straightforward neutrality"—and in many other documents. After General Ne Win's coup on March 2, 1962, the Revolutionary Council issued a four-paragraph text of foreign policy. Paragraph 3 states that the Council "reaffirm their conviction that the policy of positive neutrality pursued by the Union of Burma *ever since independence* [italics added] is the policy best suited to her in the context of prevailing world conditions, and that its faithful pursuance best serves the larger interests both of Burma and the World." *The Guardian,* March 3, 1962.

6. *The Union of Burma,* pp. 337–38. It is true that in pre-British times, Burma had little interest in Europe. But it frequently was involved with its neighbors, i.e., India, China, Siam, and other parts of the Indochinese peninsula. During the reigns of Kings Mindon and Thibaw, Burma made determined efforts to enlist the interest of the United States and France as potential allies in her struggle for survival with Great Britain. This was one cause of the Third Anglo-Burmese War. An effort was also made to enlist Germany's interest. (A convention between the two countries was recently discovered in the German archives. The Burmese copy has been lost. See *Working People's Daily,* April 4, 1965, for reprint of the text [in German].) Tinker's reading of

the past is a typical example of a European-centered reading of Asian history. See my review of D. G. E. Hall's *A History of South-East Asia*, in *Far Eastern Quarterly*, XVI (May, 1956), 433–38.

7. For U Nu's defense of the Anglo-Burmese treaty, see his statements about strong allies and his examples of similar Soviet agreements, etc., *Towards Peace and Democracy*, especially "The Road to Unity" (November 8, 1947), pp. 15–16; "Communist Allegations," (November 27, 1947), pp. 20–29; "Towards a Lasting Peace" (December 20, 1947), pp. 32–34; "I Choose Democracy" (April 3, 1948), pp. 55–61; "Warning to Leftists" (May 1, 1948), pp. 79–80; "The [Leftist Unity] Programme" (May 25, 1948), pp. 92–93; "The Nature of Leftist Unity" (June 13, 1948), pp. 110–19, 130–34; "Insurgents Can Never Wrest Power" (August 23, 1948), pp. 140–44; "Democracy versus the Gun" (June 14, 1949), *passim*, but especially p. 209; "Peace Within One Year" (July 19, 1949), pp. 223–25. For the role of the United Nations, see Thakin Nu, "Martyrs' Day Speech" (July 19, 1950), *From Peace to Stability*, p. 89.

8. "An Address to the Anglo-Burman Council," Rangoon, December 8, 1946.

9. *Towards Peace and Democracy*, p. 209. *The Christian Science Monitor*, July 30, 1949, quotes U Nu in a reiteration of the above.

10. *The New York Times*, August 14 and 16, 1949. See also Cady, *A History of Modern Burma*, pp. 597–98.

11. Department of State *Bulletin*, XX (May 29, 1949), 696.

12. "Bullets versus Ballots," *From Peace to Stability*, pp. 22–26.

13. *Ibid.*, p. 21.

14. "Insurrection, An Analysis and a Remedy," *ibid.*, pp. 44, 51, 52–53.

15. The speech was reported in the New China News Agency, November 23, 1949. It was printed with some variations as "Speech of Liu Shao-chi at the Conference of Trade Unions of Asia and Oceania," *For a Lasting Peace, For a People's Democracy*, No. 33 (60) (December 30, 1949), p. 2. The following month, both the "Manifesto" of the conference and additional, though similar, remarks of Liu were added to the record. See *For a Lasting Peace, For a People's Democracy*, No. 1 (61) (January 6, 1950), p. 1; and No. 4 (61) (January 27, 1950), p. 1. The Burma Communist representative at the conference, Aung Win, is quoted as calling for "the complete destruction of the Thakin Nu government," New China News Agency, November 29, 1949. The conference took place between November 16 and December 3, 1949. For an early, accurate analysis and appraisal of this conference, see Milton Sacks, "The Strategy of Communism in Southeast Asia," *Pacific Affairs*, XXIII (September, 1950), 227–47.

16. This policy has been referred to as "American non-involvement [which], of course, sometimes favored one party, sometimes the other and brought criticism from both. If the official American attitude seemed to lean more to the side of the colonial powers, that was because they were so important to us in Europe." John C. Campbell, *The United States in World Affairs, 1947–1948*, with an Introduction by Dean Acheson (New York: Harper & Bros., 1948), p. 184.

17. The second conference was primarily concerned with aiding the Indonesian cause. Both Prime Minister Nu (in April, 1949) and Foreign Minister E Maung (in December, 1949) visited India in connection with various proposals that would bring Commonwealth aid to Burma. Dr. E Maung was also concerned with the issue of recognizing Communist China (see below, Chapter 11). A Commonwealth loan of £6 million was ultimately approved, March 24–May 9, 1950, but never used by the Burmese. See "Commonwealth Loan to Burma," *Commonwealth Survey* (London), March 31 and May 26, 1950.

18. The Burmese attitude was succinctly summarized by Aung San: "I hate Imperialism whether British or Japanese or Burmese. I believe in the inherent right of a people to revolt against any tyranny that people may have over them." *Burma's Challenge*, p. 185.

19. Tinker, *The Union of Burma*, p. 342. There is no change of this in later editions (last edition published in 1961). Cady offers a variant of Tinker's view. He suggests that U Nu and Dr. E Maung were opposed by "the Socialist-controlled parliament," and, though he cites no evidence, that the Socialists had tended to praise the successes of the Communist revolution in China.

20. Department of State *Bulletin*, XXXIV (April 30, 1956), 718. My paraphrase is less polished than the original but I have not changed the meaning. Allen was then an Assistant Secretary of State.

21. Speech, September 27, 1957, pp. 41 and 29.

22. See G. A. von Stackelberg, "U Nu and Burma, a Study in Soviet Inconsistency," *Bulletin*, Institute for the Study of the U.S.S.R.: III, No. 4 (April, 1956), 30–35. An excerpt follows:

> The *Encyclopedia* describes the army as the tool of the Burmese puppet government, used by U Nu in the struggle with the Burmese people's national liberation movement. . . . that by August 1949 about a fifth of the country was in the hands of the partisans, whose numbers were given as 15,000 in 1949. The rebels are depicted as the "broad working masses of Burma." . . . Burma is described as formally a republic since 1948 but in fact still a British colony, while the country's state system is given as one dominated by landowners and capitalists dependent on British monopolistic capital.

Subsequent to the December Bulganin-Khrushchev visit, such critical references were excluded from Soviet accounts of Burma. See, for example, A. N. Uzianov, *Burma Struggles to Strengthen Her Independence*; and V. Vasliev and A. N. Uzianov, *Contemporary Burma*, popular pamphlets (in Russian), published in Moscow in 1956.

23. Cf. *supra*, n. 19. Neither Tinker nor Cady explained whom they meant by the designation "the Socialists"; this ambiguity was also encountered in Washington and London.

24. As an example of such curious speculation, see the undocumented reference to the "day of reckoning" for U Nu who was "ousted" after the 1956 elections, and his "mysterious" return to the office of Prime Minister, in Amry Vandenbosch and Richard Butwell, *Southeast Asia among the World Powers* (Lexington, Ky.: University of Kentucky Press, 1957), pp. 235–36. When the split in the AFPFL finally came in 1958, there was no question but that the self-styled and other Socialists in the Cabinet and leading cadres split on personal and factional lines, not on doctrinal issues (as Chapter 8 has demonstrated).

25. See Trager, "Marxism and Nationalism in Southern Asia," pp. 75–77. The Socialist Party was, until its dissolution after the 1962 coup, an association of leading individuals—a self-styled cadre party. There is no record of formal national party congresses between 1948 and the split in 1958.

26. U Nu, "Political Ideology of the AFPFL," Speech, January 29, 1958. *The Nation*, January 30, 1958, or *Burma Weekly Bulletin*, February 6, 1958; subsequently reprinted as *Towards a Socialist State* (Rangoon: GUB, 1958).

27. William C. Johnstone, *Burma's Foreign Policy: A Study of Neutralism* (Cambridge, Mass.: Harvard University Press, 1963), is generally critical of the policy of neutralism, but argues that Burma's "pioneering" in this respect has turned in a "good" record (p. 256). He is aware of the public record, which supports the view "that the Burma government had become directly involved in discussion with western nations looking toward some sort of agreement, even a defensive alliance as a check to Chinese Communist expansion" (p. 54). But the main thrust of his work is to ignore this admission and to consider Burma as neutralist from the start. See my review of his book in *Journal of Southeast Asian History*, V, No. 1 (March, 1964), 195–98.

28. *From Peace to Stability*, p. 98.

29. *Burma Looks Ahead* (Rangoon: GUB, 1953), "Towards a Welfare State," p. 98. He dropped the word "strict" from his speech at the annual

All-Burma Peasants' Organization Conference, May 24, 1953; see *Forward with the People* (Rangoon: GUB, 1955), p. 40. On one occasion, he defined the "negative" and "positive" aspects of neutrality: see "Burma's Neutral Policy," *Burma, the Seventh Anniversary* (Rangoon: GUB, 1955); shortly thereafter he used only the adjective "positive": see *An Asian Speaks*, p. 18. See also *supra*, n. 5.

30. *Is Trust Vindicated?*, p. 549.

31. See *supra*, n. 5.

32. See, in this connection, Frank N. Trager, "Burma's Foreign Policy, 1948–1956; Neutralism, Third Force and Rice," *Journal of Asian Studies*, XVI (November, 1956), 89–102.

33. See Frank N. Trager, Patricia Wohlgemuth, and Lu-yu Kiang, *Burma's Role in the United Nations, 1948–55*; see also Janet Welsh Brown, "Burmese Policy in the United Nations: An Analysis of Five Selected Political Questions, 1948–1960" (Ph.D. dissertation, American University, 1964) for a summary of Burma's activity and voting record in the U.N. and for comparisons with similar records of India, Indonesia, Thailand, the Philippines, the U.S.S.R., and the United States.

34. *The New York Times*, November 16, 1956.

Chapter 11: Burma and China

1. The data supplied by the Burmese Government in its "brief," *Kuomintang Aggression Against Burma* (Rangoon: GUB, 1953), with illustrations and appendixes, are generally verifiable. See also Brown, *op. cit.*, chap. v, "The Problem of the Nationalist Chinese Troops. . . ." See also O. E. Clubb, *The Effects of Chinese Nationalist Military Activity in Burma on Burmese Foreign Policy*, Hopkins Center Monograph (Rangoon, January 20, 1959). Several armed clashes between Chinese Nationalist "irregulars" and the Burmese Army took place in February, 1961, in the vicinity of a new Chinese-held airstrip at Mong Pai Liao, a Burmese village near the Thai border. The Burmese protested to the United States and to the United Nations. A riot in Rangoon, near the U.S. Embassy, resulted in three deaths. See *The New York Times*, February 15, 18, 22–24, and 26, 1961, and editorial, February 27, 1961.

2. Quoted in U.S. Foreign Service Dispatch, *Review of First Four Years of Burma's Independence*, June 20, 1952.

3. The Chinese Communists had captured Peking at the end of January, 1949. The Nationalists moved the capital south, first to Nanking, then to Canton. The People's Republic was formally established (and immediately recognized by the U.S.S.R.) on September 30, 1949. Burma recognized the People's Republic on December 18, 1949. The Burmese Ambassador U Myint Thein, later Chief Justice of the Supreme Court, had been accredited to the Nationalist Government; he remained in China until October, 1949; was recalled to Rangoon; and was reassigned on June 8, 1950, to Peking, following Burma's recognition of Communist China. There is an Indian account of a Burmese request to Nehru to allow Burma to be the first country in Asia to recognize Communist China. (India recognized the People's Republic on December 30, 1949.) The Indian account of this sequence may have evolved from the brief visit of then Foreign Minister E Maung to New Delhi, December 16–19, to discuss with Nehru "certain subjects of mutual interest." The first Communist Chinese ambassador arrived in Rangoon on August 28, 1950. (The exchange of Burma-U.S.S.R. embassies was announced in August, 1950, and November, 1950, respectively. The Burmese ambassador did not get the opportunity to present his credentials in Moscow until mid-February, 1951. The Russian ambassador arrived in Burma in mid-April, 1951, and presented his credentials five weeks later.)

4. For the text of this "Economic and Technical Cooperation Agreement," which came into force on October 1, 1961, see *Burma Weekly Bulletin*, January 19, 1961.

5. *The Nation*, October 15, 1958.
6. Useful studies (with bibliographical data for further reference) are: Harold J. Wiens, *China's March Toward the Tropics, A Discussion of the Southward Penetration of China's Peoples and Political Control in Relation to Non-Han Peoples of South China and in the Perspective of Historical and Cultural Geography* (Hamden, Conn.: Shoe String Press, 1945), pp. iv, 441; Harold C. Hinton, *China's Relations with Burma and Vietnam* (New York: Institute of Pacific Relations, 1958); J. S. Furnivall, "Historical Setting," and J. K. Musgrave, "The Languages of Burma" and "An Introduction to the Anthropology of Burma," in Trager *et al.*, *Burma*, I, 1–34; II, 544–621; F. M. LeBar, G. C. Hickey, and J. K. Musgrave, *Ethnic Groups of Mainland Southeast Asia* (New Haven, Conn.: Human Relations Area Files, 1965). By far the most important studies of early Burma based on indigenous, Chinese, classical, and European-language sources are those by Gordon H. Luce. A number of his 1918–39 articles that appeared in the *Journal of the Burma Research Society* have now been gathered and republished (along with others) in *Fiftieth Anniversary Publications*, No. 2, pp. 187–403; see also his five reprinted articles in *Journal of the Burma Research Society*, XLII, Part I (June, 1959).
7. Pe Maung Tin and G. H. Luce (trans.), *The Glass Palace Chronicle of the Kings of Burma*; compiled in 1829, during the reign of King Bagyidaw of Burma, it complements the account of Marco Polo of the battle and ultimate fall of Pagan. The Venetian describes the 2,000 elephants, each carrying "twelve to sixteen well-armed fighting men" and the 60,000 horsemen and footmen. "A fine force, as well befitted such a puissant [Burmese] prince . . . The Mongol forces (the Tartars) had only 12,000 well-mounted horsemen" but "had better weapons, and were better archers to boot." *The Book of Ser Marco Polo*, trans. and ed., Sir Henry Yule, rev. Henri Cordier (2 vols.; London: John Murray, 1903), II, 99. In 1920, Cordier added a third volume, *New Light on Ser Marco Polo* (London: John Murray, 1920); see pp. 87–88. The Burmese *Chronicle*, describing the same "invasion," gives the Mongols (called Tarops) "six-million horsemen and two crores [20 million] footmen," and credits King Narathihapate, the *Taroppye*, "the king who fled through fear of the Tarops," with "four hundred thousand soldiers and a great host of elephants and horses." Evidently, a considerable number of soldiers and elephants were involved, but the numbers have been somewhat exaggerated.
8. Harvey, *History of Burma*. See map preceding p. 153, "Burma under the Toungoo Dynasty, 1553–1752." The Burmese also refer to these Shan states as having been formerly under Chinese suzerainty. The transliteration of their names occasionally differs. At times, they will be referred to as Hasha, Lasha, Santa, Mongla, Mongwan, Momgti, Mongwaw, Kenghung, and Kengma. This is the area of *ko shan pye*, "the nine Shan countries," which seesawed between China and Burma obeisance. It is now part of Yunnan, but both the Nationalist and Communist Chinese governments claimed territory west of this area, i.e., in the Burma Shan state area of Hsipaw, Hsenwi, and Maingmaw. See Harvey, p. 323. It is also interesting to note that E. H. Parker, who had been the British Consul at Kiungchow and Officiating Adviser (British) on Chinese Affairs in Burma, wrote a deprecatory history of Burma from "what the Chinese had to say upon the subject," but found "the Chinese annalists [who otherwise are full of details] have been misinformed and . . . go largely by hearsay" on the Toungoo dynasty's successes on the Southeast Asian mainland. *Burma with Special Reference to Her Relations with China* (Rangoon: Gazette Press, 1893), p. 71.
9. Harvey, *History of Burma*, pp. 253; 355–56. J. K. Fairbank and S. Y. Teng, *Ch'ing Administration, Three Studies* (Cambridge, Mass.: Harvard University Press, 1960), pp. 165–70 (pp. 193–98 of former pagination in this reprint from Harvard *Journal of Asiatic Researches*, VI [1941]) confirm Burmese accounts at least between 1662 and 1750, but record from Chinese sources a resumption of tribute missions in 1751 and 1752. See also the

bibliography (Appendix I, pp. 210–14), which in part supplements n. 26 below.

10. See, for example, a popular account of the Burmese hero-general "Maha Thiha Thura," by Tun Tin in *The Burmese Review*, I (February 17, 1947). The author relies heavily on Harvey for specific data. For a scholarly account see G. H. Luce, "Chinese Invasions of Burma in the Eighteenth Century," *Journal of the Burma Research Society*, XV (1925), 115–28.

11. Harvey, *History of Burma*, pp. 253–58, and Phayre, *op. cit.*, pp. 190–203, have brief but useful accounts. Harvey writes: "The Chinese ought to have won . . . [they] threw away the advantage of superior numbers by allowing themselves to be overwhelmed in detail." His anti-Burman bias does not wholly hide the importance of the Burmese victory over the great Manchu Emperor Chien-lung. Incidentally, the Burmese had the benefit of some "heavy artillery," manned, according to Father Sangermano, "by the Christians" (descendants of French, Dutch, and Portuguese captives). (*Op. cit.*, p. 63.)

12. R. K. Douglas, "China and Burmah," *The Asiatic Quarterly Review*, No. 1 (January–April, 1886), p. 151; see also Parker, who gives his characteristically pro-Chinese account of this period: Ming-jui "perished like a noble gentleman and brave soldier that he was." The Chinese, according to Parker, committed a "strategical blunder." The Burmese victory was never actually acknowledged, for the Emperor had "instructed Fu-heng to withdraw his army, and to inform the Burmese that 'out of sheer compassion the Emperor had decided not to annihilate them as they deserved.'" (*Op. cit.*, pp. 82–94.) For an impressive account, freely translated from the Burmese chronicles, including the treaty of 1769, and records of exchanges of three missions in 1787, 1823, and 1833, see Burney, *op. cit.*, pp. 121–49, 405–51, 542–59. Hall has recently called attention to this account in his appreciative article, "Henry Burney, Diplomat and Orientalist," *Journal of the Burma Research Society*, XLI, Parts I and II (December, 1958), pp. 100–10. Hall writes, "In the negotiations of 1886 [see below] the dominant British motive was the appeasement of China, but sheer ignorance of the Burmese case was a factor of no small importance."

13. Hinton, *op. cit.*, p. 32. According to Fairbank and Teng's Ch'ing records, there were Burmese missions in 1776, 1778, 1790–91, 1793, 1795, 1811, 1823, 1825, 1829, 1833–34, 1843, 1853, and 1875 (*op. cit.*, pp. 194–97). However, the authors point out that there were more missions in the period of declining Ch'ing power than at its height. "The most obvious suggestion is that this increase . . . was prompted by commercial motives."

14. Harvey, *History of Burma*, pp. 279–80, 362, indicates that the prior exchange was "sometimes polite . . . sometimes haughty." But he adds that the Burmese "must have made some serious admissions—e.g. the acceptance of the 1792 seal—for the Chinese were able to convince the English Foreign Office that Burma was tributary, so that England, as successor to Burmese liabilities, consented . . . [in] 1886 [after complete annexation of Burma] to send decennial tribute of local produce to China stipulating that the envoys should be of Burmese race." This is discussed further below. See also Hinton, *op. cit.*, pp. 31–33; and Kyaw Thet, "Some Aspects of Sino-Burmese Diplomacy in the Reign of Bodawpaya, 1782–1819, *Burma* (Rangoon), I, No. 4 (July, 1951), 1–6. Dr. Kyaw Thet's Sino-Burmese researches throw considerable doubt on a number of these presumed "missions."

15. Christian, *Burma and the Japanese Invader*, p. 270. But contrary to the visible evidence of the Indian sources of Burma's Buddhist culture, he gratuitously adds that the relationship was "of a dutiful son grateful for the *gifts of culture* rather than that of a politically dependent state [italics added]."

16. *Ibid.*, chap. xii, "The Burma Road," and p. 270. The chapter is a slightly expanded reprint of the author's "Trans-Burma Trade Routes to China," *Pacific Affairs*, XIII, No. 2 (June, 1940), pp. 173–91. For the most

complete study of this subject, see Ma Thaung, "British Interest in Trans-Burma Trade Routes to China, 1826–1876" (Ph.D. dissertation, School for Oriental and African Studies, University of London, 1956).

17. See Furnivall, *Colonial Policy and Practice*, pp. 69–70; "the annexation may be regarded . . . as an episode in the rivalry of Britain and France for supremacy in South-East Asia." Cady, *The Roots of French Imperialism*, amply documents this, although he is inclined, without giving the evidence, to place major responsibility on "the aggressive policies pursued by successive French ministries." (See also Cady, *A History of Modern Burma*, p. 117 and passim.)

18. Christian, *Burma and the Japanese Invader*, p. 270.

19. Maung Maung, *Burma in the Family of Nations*, p. 72. Dr. Maung Maung supplies some interesting quotations from *The Times* (London), February 19 and 26, 1886, which, anticipating the actual terms of the Convention, argued sharply against decennial tributes and territorial claims on the basis of Burmese history. *The Times* was historically accurate. The revival of the tribute mission opened a Pandora's box of Burmese troubles. The February 26 issue pointed out, *inter alia*, that the *ko shan pye* state of Kenhung (or Kiang Hung) had apparently been in Burmese hands in the middle of the nineteenth century. See also Robert K. Douglas, *Europe and the Far East* (Cambridge: Cambridge University Press, 1904), p. 244. Douglas, a former Chinese adviser to British Burma, refers to the "confused notions" of the Foreign Office. See also Hall's comment, *supra*, n. 12.

20. See Hall, *A History of South-East Asia*, "Britain, France and the Siamese Question," pp. 591–612; written from a British point of view.

21. See C. V. Aitchison (compiler), *A Collection of Treaties, Engagements and Sanads Relating to India and Neighboring Countries* (Calcutta: Government of India, 1931), XII, Part IV, 199–283, for a review and compilation of Anglo-Burmese "treaties, engagements and Sanads" since the eighteenth century. All the previously mentioned conventions are listed on pp. 244–60.

22. Girilal Jain, *Chinese "Panchsheela" in Burma* (Bombay: Democratic Research Service, 1956), pp. 23–24. For a careful historico-geographical article on this disputed zone, see Martin R. Norins, "Tribal Boundaries of the Burma-Yunnan Frontier," *Pacific Affairs*, XII, No. 1 (March, 1939), 67–79.

23. The texts appear in Girilal Jain, *op. cit.*, pp. 36–40. They were reprinted during a tense period in the Sino-Burmese border dispute by *The Nation*, August 9, 1956.

24. Martin R. Norins, *op. cit.*, p. 74. See also Hugh Tinker, "Burma's Northeast Borderland Problems," *Pacific Affairs*, XXIX (December, 1956), 324–46.

25. Sun Yat-sen, *San Min Chu I* (*The Three Principles of the People*), trans. Frank W. Price (Chungking: Ministry of Information, 1943), pp. 91–93. Sun Yat-sen formulated these principles while he was in Europe (1896–98) and announced them in 1905. See Li Chien-nung, *op. cit.*, p. 16.

26. For modern references to "The Yunnan-Burma Border Dispute," see Lu-yu Kiang, "Chinese Sources," in Frank N. Trager (ed.), *Japanese and Chinese Language Sources on Burma: An Annotated Bibliography* (New Haven, Conn.: Human Relations Area Files, 1957), pp. 87–106.

27. Hinton, *op. cit.*, p. 35.

28. *The New York Times*, December 7, 1958, carried a story with a New Delhi dateline and an accompanying map showing Peking's encroachments on Indian territory. Prime Minister Nehru is quoted as having told the Parliament that "Communist China has changed many things done by the Kuomintang Government and I do not see any reason why they cannot change the map." Subsequently, *The New York Times*, April 23, 1959, published new maps, showing additional encroachments. Prime Minister Nehru reported

that the Chinese reply to India's representation on this subject "was not very adequate."

29. U Nu, Speech, in Parliament, March 8, 1951, *From Peace to Stability*, p. 197.

30. The McMahon line was presented at the Tripartite Simla Conference of 1913–14, which was attended by representatives of Britain (for India and Burma), Tibet, and China. It delimited some 700 miles of Indian-Tibetan borders eastward to the Talu (Talok) Pass at the junction with Burma. From there, it proceeded in a 120-mile arc along the line of the northern watershed of the Irrawaddy River, except where it crossed the Taron Valley, to Izurazi Pass. Tibet signed the agreement as a sovereign country. China did not sign.

31. "Sino-Burmese Boundary Agreement and Treaty of Friendship and Mutual Non-Aggression," Speech, Chamber of Deputies, April 28, 1960; *Burma Weekly Bulletin*, May 5, 1960. (Hereafter cited as "Speech, April 28, 1960.") The speech is a useful summary of a decade of protracted negotiations. The documents were reprinted by GUB as a thirty-page pamphlet (Rangoon, May 17, 1960). There is a slightly more extensive collection of these and related documents, *A Victory for the Five Principles of Peaceful Coexistence* (Peking: Foreign Language Press, 1960). Hereafter cited as *A Victory*.

32. *The Nation*, July 12, 1953. The story was seemingly ignored in Burma. It was mentioned in the *Christian Science Monitor*, July 13, 1963, but did not otherwise attract attention outside of Burma.

33. *Burma Weekly Bulletin*, December 25, 1954; see also *A Victory*, pp. 3–5.

34. "Report on the Question of the Boundary Line Between China and Burma," Speech, at the fourth session of the First National People's Congress, July 9, 1957. *A Victory*, pp. 17–18. For the full text, see pp. 16–27.

35. Colonel Aung Gyi gave the casualty figures at a press conference held by Prime Minister Ba Swe, August 7, 1956. The clash took place in a strip of the northern Wa state enclosed by the village area of Wamaw, Walun, and Toila. This was about 100 miles east of Lashio, well within the Burmese border. The Burmese armed forces were on a routine flag march (i.e., border patrol) to which the Chinese, already stationed inside Burmese territory, reacted.

36. U Nu, in his "Speech, April 28, 1960," indicated that the Chinese Government, was being so severely criticized in Burma at that time that he "appealed" to the press to "refrain from publishing anything [further] that might jeopardize the negotiations for a peaceful settlement." For typical foreign reactions, see "China, Burma and the Wa," *The Economist* (London), August 19, 1956, p. 571; and Dorothy Woodman, "Three Burmese Villages," *The New Statesman and Nation*, December 29, 1956, pp. 833–34. *The New York Times* coverage is quite useful. See August 1–5, 8, 12, 26; September 4, 7; October 3, 20, 22, 1956.

37. *Burma Weekly Bulletin* November 15, 1956.

38. U Nu, "Speech of April 28, 1960."

39. *The New York Times*, December 11, 15, and 19, 1956. The reception given Chou was compared with that given him during his visit in April, 1955.

40. Speech in Rangoon, *The Nation*, December 12, 1956. Equally encouraging was a remark made on his departure from Rangoon, namely, that the border issue "cannot but be settled peacefully, relations being what they are between Burma and China." See the issue of December 25, 1956. See same speech in *A Victory*, pp. 8–13 (contains minor variations from text in *The Nation*).

41. See, for example, the argument presented by the most prominent newspaper critic for Communist China, U Law Yone, "Why I Favour the 'Package Deal,' " *The Nation*, December 25, 1956.

42. U Nu, "Speech of April 28, 1960."

43. *Ibid*. This is U Nu's figure. See the editorial in *The Nation*, February 2, 1960, which referred to the Chinese demand as "in excess of 500 square miles [which] may have been reduced in later negotiations."

44. For a then current field survey, see Norman D. Palmer, "Chinese Shadow on the Asian Rim," *The New Leader* (New York), May 23, 1960, pp. 16–19.

45. The texts, signed on January 28, were published in *Burma Weekly Bulletin*, February 4, 1960, along with some of the speeches and editorials in leading Burmese newspapers (January 30–February 2, 1960) supporting the agreement. The editorials uniformly approved General Ne Win's accomplishment. *The Nation* congratulates him for "his wise statesmanship . . . which may well prove to be one of the greatest blessings conferred on independent Burma." This is a typical reaction to what elsewhere in Burma was called "the crowning triumph of General Ne Win's Caretaker Government" (*New Times of Burma*, January 30, 1960). See also the Joint Communiqué, texts, and Chou En-lai's "Farewell Speech," all dated January 28, 1960, in *A Victory*, pp. 28–41; for Chinese press and editorial reaction see pp. 45–57.

46. *Burma Weekly Bulletin*, June 30, July 7 and 21, 1960. Vice-Chief of Staff (Army) Brigadier Aung Gyi and Yao Chung-ming, former Ambassador to Burma, then Director of the Treaties and Law Department, headed the Burma and P.R.C. delegations, respectively.

47. *Ibid*., September 1, 1960. See also *ibid*., October 6, 1960, for the announcement of the departure to Peking on September 27 of the Burmese delegation headed by U Nu; and *ibid*., October 13, 1960, for "gifts" and proposed text of the treaty.

48. *Ibid*., with text, January 12, 1961. As indicated (see *supra*, n. 4), the following week's issue contained the text of the Chinese Economic Loan, a bit of icing on the cake.

49. *Ibid*., October 13, 1960.

50. *The Guardian*, VIII, No. 2 (February, 1961), 6.

51. *The Nation*, February 7 and 8, 1958.

52. See S. L. Verma, *The Law Relating to Foreigners and Citizenship in Burma, with a Foreword by Justice U San Maung* (Mandalay: Rishi Raj Verma, 1960), pp. 93–114.

53. See *The Nation*, September 22 and November 26, 1958; see also *The New York Times*, November 27, 1958.

54. *The Nation*, August 30, 1957.

55. *Ibid*., October 5, 1956, January 24, 1958. Hinton, *China's Relations with Burma and Vietnam*, pp. 42–45, summarizes a number of additional references. See also John S. Thomson, "Burma: A Neutral in China's Shadow," *The Review of Politics*, July, 1957, pp. 331–36. When General Ne Win undertook negotiations with the Burma Communist Party in the summer and fall of 1963, one group from the BCP arrived from its base in Kunming, China.

56. A 1960 sample radio survey of "elite group listeners" indicated that within such groups Chinese was either spoken or understood as a second language by eight per cent.

57. For the text and related story, see *Forward*, I, No. 19 (May 7, 1963), 3–4, 11–18. It is interesting to note that Liu Shao-chi's seven-day goodwill visit had been preceded in early April by a seven-day goodwill visit from Marshal R. Y. Malinovski, Minister of Defense, U.S.S.R. See *ibid*., I, No. 18 (April 22, 1963). See also *ibid*., II, No. 4 (September 22, 1963), 4–5, for General Ne Win's pointed reply to Premier Chou En-lai's proposal for a "Heads of Government" conference on complete nuclear and general disarmament. Burma, he indicated, had signed the Nuclear Test Ban Treaty as a proper step toward "gradual and phased agreements," which he believed was "the only method . . . of reaching the ultimate objective of complete and general disarmament."

58. For a relatively recent Chinese Nationalist view, see Yin T'ang Chang, "The 'Kha-khu' Area—A Geographical Study of the Undemarcated Frontier between China, Burma, and India," *Tsing Hua Journal of Chinese Studies* (Taipei), N. S. 1, No. 1 (June, 1956), pp. 122–37. The author primarily uses English postannexation sources to convey the view that the area north of Myitkyina (i.e., from 25° 35' N) is a "no-man's land" or "any-man's land." He indicates that *Kha'khu* is a Kachin word meaning "Upper Reaches" of the Irrawaddy River, but argues that "the Chinese were undoubtedly the first outsiders to have penetrated this area," and that Chinese "frontier officials" exacted tolls "from the natives" and established a political tie to China dating "back to the Ming Dynasty in the 16th Century when Emperor Wan-li sent an expedition . . . to the Triangle area." He ignores, as do most Chinese writers on the subject, the fact that (a) the Tibeto-Burman and Sino-Tibetan people of the area had been incorporated into the first major unified Burmese nation in the eleventh century; (b) the majority of the inhabitants of this area were and are Kachins, Tibeto-Burman in origin like their fellow-citizens in Burma proper; and (c) Emperor Wan-li's expedition was forced to withdraw under sixteenth-century pressure from the second unifying Burmese dynasty, the Toungoo dynasty.

59. *Premier Reports to the People*, pp. 35–36. There have been continuing efforts at peaceful cooperation between Rangoon and Peking. The latter called attention to this at the January 18, 1965, fifth anniversary of the signing of the Sino-Burmese Treaty of Friendship and Mutual Non-Aggression, citing the treaty as a "brilliant example" (*People's Daily* [Peking]). Nevertheless, incidents continue to mar the record. There was, for example, the episode in October, 1964, when the BCP sent a congratulatory message to the Chinese Communist Party on the occasion of the latter's fifteenth anniversary of accession to power. The message included reference to the BCP's aim of establishing "a new Burma of real independence, politically and economically." Peking Radio broadcast the message in English and Burmese. Burma's press reacted sharply. The Burmese-language *Mogyo*, October 10, 1964, said that those who heard the broadcast were "surprised to learn that Red China still has connections with these Burmese insurgents . . . [that the broadcast was] most unjustified." See also *supra*, n. 55.

60. See Frank N. Trager, "The Communist Challenge in Southeast Asia," in William Henderson, *Southeast Asia: Problems of United States Policy* (Cambridge, Mass.: M.I.T. Press, 1963), pp. 134–64.

61. Even during 1959, when the caretaker government renewed what became the successful effort at negotiating the border solution with the People's Republic of China, leading Burmese voiced criticism of Chinese suppressive action in Tibet. See U Nu, *The Guardian*, April 26, 1959, for a cautious expression of such criticism; and for less cautious criticisms, see *The Nation* editorials, March 29, 1959, and June 19, 1959; see also the article by Tillman Durdin, "Asia Deeply Stirred by Tibet Repression," in *The New York Times*, April 19, 1959. Burma, however, abstained on the October 21, 1959, U.N. General Assembly resolution on Tibet.

62. The Chinese made effective use of British offers to reimburse them for various territories; e.g., a letter dated April 10, 1911, in which the British denied claims to the Kachin area but offered a modest payment; also the "rental" of the Namwan Assigned Tract.

Chapter 12: Burma and Her Other Asian Neighbors

1. See George McTurnan Kahin, *The Asian-African Conference, Bandung, Indonesia, April 1955* (Ithaca, N. Y.: Cornell University Press, 1956), pp. 5, 19, 31, 81. For the text of the Final Communiqué see pp. 76–85. Nehru advised the Indian Parliament on April 30, 1955, that Soviet (satellite) colonialism, to which other delegations had referred at Bandung, was not included in the meaning of the above quotation.

2. "To Prefer Is Not to Choose," *Socialist Asia*, III, No. 2 (June, 1954), 9.

3. Statement at the plenary meeting, U.N. General Assembly, December 12, 1956, *Burma Weekly Bulletin*, January 10, 1957. See also the issue of December 13, 1956, for statements made during debate in November, 1956.

4. See, for example, the exchange of letters between U Nu and Nehru when U Nu stepped down from the premiership in 1956, in *The Guardian*, June 22, 1956. See *Burma Weekly Bulletin*, November 17, 1954, for text of an earlier broadcast by U Nu on "Sri Nehru—Architect of South East Asian Solidarity," given on the occasion of Nehru's sixty-fifth birthday.

5. The *Forward*, December 22, 1962, pp. 2–3. The Burmese must wait for a Sino-Indian solution before they can work out with Peking the demarcation of their northwest-corner boundary. See *supra*, Chapter 11.

6. *The Guardian*, February 7 and 9, 1964; *Working People's Daily*, February 10, 1964.

7. "The Joint Communiqué," *The Guardian*, February 19, 1964. See also the editorial, *The Nation*, February 21, 1964. The *Working People's Daily*, February 21, 1964, carried a New Delhi "spokesman" story indicating that India "welcomed" Burma's "consistent" efforts in support of the December, 1962, Colombo proposals. The reference was probably to General Ne Win's meeting with Chairman Liu Shao-chi, in April, 1963. See their joint communiqué on the "Sino-Indian Dispute," *Forward*, May 7, 1963, pp. 3–4.

8. See typical statements of Indian ambassadors to Burma: "India and Burma Encouraged by Each Other's Example," *The Nation*, January 27, 1958; and "Burma and India Are Like-Minded Nations," *The Guardian*, January 27, 1959. Such statements have appeared much less frequently in the 1960's.

9. The *Hanthawaddy*, November 28, 1964, reported that approximately 30,000 Indians had left Burma during the previous twelve months. The first mass departures in the spring of the year occasioned some bitterness between Rangoon and New Delhi, which their respective foreign ministers attempted to dissipate by indicating that the Burmese measures were not discriminatory against Indians, but were directed against all foreigners. See *Working People's Daily*, April 21, 1964; and *The Nation*, April 30, 1964. See also *supra*, Chapter 9, n. 26, and *The Guardian*, February 12, 1965, for an amicable joint Indian-Burmese communiqué on this issue.

10. See, for example, *The Nation*, April 21, and May 15, 1957, for stories of arrests of illegal Pakistani immigrants. In the early days of the rebellions, after 1948, the *mujahids* were frequently but incorrectly regarded as political rebels. They were simply dacoits. See editorial, *The Guardian*, September 8, 1959.

11. *Burma Weekly Bulletin*, May 26, 1960. Note that this took place after Prime Minister Ne Win demitted office in April, 1960, and U Nu had returned to power. However, these negotiations led to a final agreement on Burma's separation (from British-India) debt with Pakistan (Burma had earlier reached agreement on this issue with India). A three-year trade agreement for 600,000 tons of rice included payments in kind which would settle all outstanding financial issues remaining from the time when Burma was a province of British India. See *The Guardian*, January 10, 1960.

12. See *Forward*, January 22, and February 7, 1964. A trade agreement was also signed at this time under which Pakistan agreed to buy 200,000 tons of rice in 1964. For editorial approval, see the *Working People's Daily* and *The Guardian*, January 21, 1964. For the Ne Win–Ayub Khan communiqué, see the *Working People's Daily*, February 19, 1965.

13. January 7, 1965. Fear was expressed in an editorial, *ibid.*, on January 12, that the Malaysian-Indonesian dispute was more dangerous than the Korean War because, if the dispute were "to burn more hot" then "a war between Malaysia and Indonesia, each having her own allies, is most likely to spread to the Indian Ocean and other parts of the Southeast Asian region."

The *Rangoon Daily* kept an interest in this issue through January, 1965.

14. The *Hanthawaddy* and *The New Light of Burma,* January 8 and 11, 1965, respectively.

15. See Kahin, *op. cit.,* pp. 13–14. On February 6, 1965, *The New York Times* quoted an official broadcast from Peking which continued its call for the overthrow of the Thai Government by a "patriotic Front."

16. See, for example, *The New York Times,* October 23, 1954, March 8 and June 26, 1955; *The Nation,* October 15, 1956, May 9 and 17, and September 23, 1957; and the series of articles by U Law Yone, "What Happened in Bangkok, The Story of a Successful Revolution," *The Nation,* September 24–30, 1957. On two occasions in 1959, the Thai Government publicly thanked the Burmese Government for its assistance in 1958. For a time, Burma looked after Thailand's interests in Cambodia, after Thailand and Cambodia had severed relations with each other in December, 1958; Rangoon served as a place of venue for representatives of the Thai and North Vietnamese Red Cross when they helped repatriate some 50,000 refugees to North Vietnam. See *The Nation,* June 5 and September 19, 1959.

17. See *Forward,* I, No. 22 (January 22, 1963), "Special Issue Commemorating Thai-Burmese Friendship," which contains Bohmu Thamain, "Goodwill Journey," an eleven-page story including eight pages of color and black-and-white photographs of the event. To date, this is the only such treatment in the official magazine *Forward.*

18. See *The Nation,* May 20, 1963, which prints, in full, the joint communiqué summarizing the agreement. See also editorial, *The Guardian,* May 20, 1963.

19. See, for example, the *Working People's Daily,* January 24, 1964, and editorial and news, *The Guardian,* January 24, 1964. *Forward* has frequently referred to specific acts implementing the security, economic, and cultural provisions of the agreement. See the following issues of *Forward:* I, No. 17 (April 7, 1963), 3–4; I, No. 20 (May 22, 1963), 2–3; I, No. 22 (June 22, 1963), 4–5; II, No. 13 (February 7, 1964), 2; II, No. 20 (May 22, 1964), 4–5; and II, No. 23 (July 15, 1964), 4.

20. By "restoration," I refer to the series of moves executed by the French, roughly from June 5, 1948 (the Bay of Along Agreement), to June 14, 1949, that in effect ratified the Elysée Agreement. This installed Bao Dai as head of state. See Donald Lancaster, *The Emancipation of French Indo-China* (London: Oxford University Press, 1961), pp. 186–200.

21. *Burma Weekly Bulletin,* November 24, 1954. The following January, the two legations were raised to embassies. At the same time, the Burmese invited the Buddhist leader the Sanga Raja and other notables from ten major monasteries of Laos to the Sixth World Buddhist Council. See also U Nu, *Premier Reports to the People,* pp. 37–38.

22. See P. Talbot and S. L. Poplai, *India and America* (New York: Harper & Bros., 1958), pp. 127–30.

23. "Statement . . . at the Seventh Meeting of the Conference, May 22, 1961," *Burma Weekly Bulletin,* June 15, 1961. Barrington also made an important intervention in which he was critical of the French and Soviet drafts on the International Control Commission that did not allow it to operate effectively and "in close cooperation" with the Lao Government. The Burmese wanted the ICC to have sufficient power to investigate violations and, otherwise, to be able to help the Lao Government keep the peace. See *Burma Weekly Bulletin,* July 20, 1961.

24. *Forward,* September 22, 1962, p. 4.

25. *Forward,* No. 16 (March 22, 1963), pp. 2–3.

26. Editorial, the *Hanthawaddy,* December 23, 1964.

27. Editorial, December 23, 1964. See *supra,* n. 26. The simultaneous appearance of these similar editorials in the two most respected Burmese-language newspapers in Rangoon is not without political significance.

28. Malaysia is the sixth-ranking customer for Burma's rice, following Indonesia, Ceylon, China, India, and Pakistan (though China's position as third-ranking customer may be temporary). In 1964, Burma assigned her ranking and able Ambassador U Pe Kin (a Muslim) to Kuala Lumpur. He had been the Burmese spokesman at the U.N. during the Hungarian crisis in 1956.

29. See Thakin Nu, "Our Achievements," Speech, January 8, 1951, in *From Peace to Stability*, pp. 156–57. U Nu confesses that he knows "what it means to be a puppet," for he had been a "puppet minister" during the Japanese regime. "In those days," he said, "no one dared to speak his mind freely."

30. See, in particular, *Burma Weekly Bulletin*, November 10, 17, 1954, for the exchange by U Kyaw Nyein and Foreign Minister Katsuo Okazaki and the terms of the treaty and agreements.

31. *The Nation*, May 23, 1957.

32. *Forward*, I, No. 13 (February 7, 1963), pp. 2–3. On the whole, the Burmese press was favorably disposed to the reparations settlement of $140 million, although it was $10 million less than the Burmese had expected. But there was an almost unanimous outcry from the press against the commercial loans because of the expected interest rate (around 6 per cent). See, for example, the editorials in the *Hanthawaddy*, January 27, 1963, and *The New Light of Burma*, January 29, 1963.

33. *Forward*, I, No. 20 (May 22, 1963), 3–4; and II, No. 7 (November 7, 1963), 22.

34. *Premier Reports to the People*.

35. The foregoing is not meant to be an exhaustive listing. For a brief, effective review of all such activity in the region see Russell H. Fifield, *The Diplomacy of Southeast Asia: 1945–1958* (New York: Harper & Bros., 1958), chap. x; William Henderson, "The Development of Regionalism in Southeast Asia," *International Organization*, IX, No. 4 (1955), 463–76; B. R. Chatterji, "Southeast Asia in Transition," *India Quarterly*, XII, No. 4 (1956), 388–99, who writes that " '*Bhinneka tunggal ika*' (Different Units Remain One"), the motto of Indonesia, applies also to the whole of Southeast Asia"; and O. H. K. Spate, " 'Region' as a Work of Art," *Orbis*, I, No. 3 (October, 1957), 343–51. Spate, despite the fact that he "hostilely reacts" to "American Academic," which he finds an unpleasant subspecies of English, comments on the possibilities and difficulties in the word "region" from a geographer's point of view.

36. See, for example, a typical speech of Burma's Foreign Minister, U Thi Han, at the Eighteenth General Assembly, September 25, 1963, reprinted in full with supporting editorial in *The Guardian*, September 28, 1963. (The Burmese tend to use the annual opening forum of the U.N. General Assembly to state their general views and specific recommendations.) The Foreign Minister delivered a considered address stressing Burma's nonalignment; her hopes for peaceful coexistence among the powers; her belief in the desirability of universal membership, including Communist China, in the U.N., her satisfaction with any moves toward gradual disarmament; her support for U.N. peace-keeping measures and for more "equitable geographical representation and rotation of membership" in all the organs of the U.N. so as to acknowledge the presence and the responsibilities of "the emerging nations of Asia and Africa."

37. For the full text of their speeches, see U Nu, *The Nation*, September 8, 1961; and U Thi Han, *Working People's Daily*, October 8, 1964; see also the *Working People's Daily*, October 15, 1964.

38. In 1959, SEATO Secretary-General Pote Saresin noted that Burma attended a SEATO air exercise. He publicly expressed the view that the Burmese had "less objection to SEATO." Quoted in *The Nation*, March 6, 1959.

39. Editorials in *The Nation*, January 13, 1960, and *The Guardian*, April

8, 1960, expressed negative views about the proposal, though both papers had been consistently anti-Communist.

40. Editorial, "Burma's International Relations," *Working People's Daily*, October 16, 1964.

Chapter 13: *The United States, Asia, and Burma*

1. S. E. Morrison, *The Maritime History of Massachusetts* (Boston: Houghton Mifflin, 1921), p. 92. Another authority, Seward W. Livermore (see n. 2), relying upon the researches of James D. Phillips, *East Indian Voyages of Salem Vessels before 1800*, Essex Institute Historical Collections (Salem, Mass.: April, 1943), places the date at 1792. The American vessel, presumably the "Astrea," was used in one of the many Burmese wars with Siam. See also Tyler Dennett, *Americans in Eastern Asia* (New York: Macmillan, 1922), Part I, "The East India Trade," pp. 3–65.

2. This paragraph, except where otherwise indicated, is based on Seward W. Livermore, "Early Commercial and Consular Relations with the East Indies," *The Pacific Historical Review*, XV, No. 1 (March, 1946), 31–58.

3. The *Bengal Political Consultations*, No. 6 (December 26, 1811) and No. 1 (March 26, 1812) note the presence of an agent of the American Government in Rangoon, but it is not indicated whether this is Davy or someone else.

4. The first U.S. diplomatic mission to Asia followed the murder of the crew of the Salem ship *Friendship* in Sumatra in 1831. Edmund Roberts of New Hampshire was appointed as the envoy by President Jackson in 1832. He tells his own story in *Embassy to the Eastern Courts of Cochin-China, Siam and Muscat* (New York, 1837). Brief accounts of his mission appear in standard histories of diplomacy. He negotiated a treaty with Siam on March 20, 1833, carried it back to the United States, and returned to Siam to exchange instruments of ratification. He died in 1836, while in the process of executing a subsequent mission to Canton. Roberts did not get to Burma. A second treaty with Siam was negotiated by Townsend Harris in 1856.

5. They were divided among "six Church of England, seven or eight Independents, one or two Presbyterians, fourteen Baptists and others Lutheran. . . . [But] we are all one heart and help each other as much as we can." Letter from Dr. William Carey (the outstanding English Baptist missionary in India, upon whom Brown University conferred a doctorate in March, 1807) to the Reverend Mr. Williams of New York, dated Calcutta, December 18, 1807. The source for this letter and for the American missionary endeavor in Burma can be found in the fascinating accounts which appear in *The Massachusetts Baptist Missionary Magazine* (MBMM), the first volume published in Boston, 1803. After 1817 (Vol. IV), the name was changed to *The American Baptist Magazine and Missionary Intelligencer*, (ABMMI). This journal, in one form or another, has been continued. In addition, the *Annual Reports* of the American Baptist Board of Foreign Missions, created partially as a consequence of Adoniram Judson's conversion and mission to Burma (see his letters to the Reverend Dr. Baldwin and the Reverend Lucius Bolles, August 27 and 31, and September 1, 1812, MBMM, III [1813]), contain valuable data about the arrival of the Americans in Burma. These *Reports* were published separately, but frequently are bound with issues of the journal. See also U Kaung, "The Beginnings of Christian Missionary Education in Burma, 1600–1824," and "1824–1853: Roman Catholic and American Baptist Mission Schools," *Journal of the Burma Research Society*, XX, Part II (1930), 59–75; and XXI, Part I (1931), 1–13. Reprinted in *Burma Research Society, Fiftieth Anniversary Publications*, No. 2, pp. 117–47. The American Baptist mission had been preceded by the Roman Catholic missionaries; they had arrived with the Portuguese at the beginning of the seventeenth century. A young Roman Catholic Burmese foreign-service officer stationed in Europe has recently been adding considerably to our

knowledge of these missionaries. See Vivian Ba, *The Guardian*, IX, No. 8 (August, 1962); XI, No. 5 (May, 1964).

6. Parker Thomas Moon, *Imperialism and World Politics* (New York: Macmillan, 1926), pp. 33ff. See also Tyler Dennett, *op. cit.*, pp. 284–91. He tells the story of the Reverend Peter Parker, M.D., a missionary in China and later a U.S. Commissioner, who, in 1857, proposed that Washington take possession of Formosa, a part of the Empire of China. See also *ibid.*, chap. xxix, "The Missionaries and American Policy in Asia."

7. For a succinct account of these seven Americans during the war and the following period, see John Leroy Christian, "Americans and the First Anglo-Burmese War," *The Pacific Historical Review*, V, No. 4 (December, 1936), 312–24. For the letters quoted, see *ABMMI*, V (January, 1825), 22–23, and IV, No. 7 (January, 1824), 253–54. For a detailed study of the attitudes of missionaries toward the Burmese, see Helen G. Trager, *Burma Through Alien Eyes: Missionary Views of the Burmese in the Nineteenth Century* (Bombay: Asia Publishing House, 1965; New York: Frederick A. Praeger, 1966).

8. Most contemporary British accounts refer to their ability to free the prisoners in Rangoon quickly. See, for example, Captain T. A. Trant, *Two Years in Ava, From May 1824, to May 1826* (London: John Murray, 1827), pp. 24–25.

9. Walter N. Wyeth, *The Wades* (privately printed; Philadelphia, 1891), p. 95. See also William Gammell, *A History of American Baptist Missions* (Boston: Gould, Kendall and Lincoln, 1849), pp. 121–22.

10. This account and the translation of the letter appear in Alfred S. Patton, *The Hero Missionary or a History of the Labors of the Rev. Eugenio Kincaid* (New York: H. Dayton, 1858), pp. 264–79. Patton's dating of these events is confused. January, 1856, should be 1857. According to Christian, *Modern Burma*, p. 31, General Lewis Cass, who in 1852 as Senator from Michigan had denounced Britain's action in seizing Lower Burma, in 1857, as Secretary of State, "received the only diplomatic mission [Kincaid] sent from Burma to the United States."

11. "The kingdoms," etc., would read today, the kingdoms of Sunaparanta (meaning territory west of the Irrawaddy River) and Tampadipa (meaning territory east of this river); in Pali, this would be equivalent to "Burma." Saddan is the name of the cave where the embryo Buddha was made king of the elephants. I am indebted to Dr. E. R. Schmidt, formerly of the South Asia Library, University of Pennsylvania, for the following information: It seems that the State Department held in its archives a "Siamese" copy of the supposed treaty between the United States and Siam that had been negotiated by Edmund Roberts (see *supra*, n. 4). In 1924, the State Department sent it to the Baptists in Burma to be translated. The Baptists discovered that this was the letter from King Mindon to the President. The letter is now back in the National Archives in its original container.

12. *Communications to Foreign Sovereigns and States* (4 vols.), III, 27–28. Manuscript Records of the Department of State (National Archives, Washington, D.C. [R.G. 59]).

13. *Papers Relating to the Foreign Relations of the United States . . . with the Annual Message of the President*, 48th Cong., 1st sess. (Washington, D.C.: Government Printing Office, 1884), Part I, pp. 754–55. Even after the exchange between the President and King Mindon, references to Burma appear most infrequently in these records. See *ibid.* (1873), pp. 318–19, where the U.S. Minister to London, Robert C. Schenck, reports of his friendship with a member of a Burmese delegation in London and indicates that the British received the delegation, not as if it were from a sovereign power, but as if it were under the aegis of the Colonial Office (India). Two years later (*ibid.* [1875], pp. 312–29), there was a dispatch to Washington, together with a number of enclosures from the U.S. legation in Peking, about the Margary Affair, in which Burma was involved since the British regarded

Burma as the southern end of their proposed road to China for the south-western China (Yunnan) trade. The British suspected the Burmese had a hand in the "murder" of Margary and his party. The American legation indicated that the British were "threatening to absorb the whole kingdom [of Burma]."

14. For an interesting account of this, see J. C. Turk, "Building an American Bridge in Burma," *World's Work*, XI (September, 1901), 1148–67.

15. Thomas A. Bailey, *A Diplomatic History of the American People* (5th ed.; New York: F. S. Crofts, 1955), p. 321.

16. The Hawaiian Islands have played a part in American diplomacy, at least from the days when Daniel Webster was Secretary of State (1841–43). While serving in President Tyler's Cabinet, he announced the policy which, in effect, extended the Monroe Doctrine to Hawaii. In 1854, a treaty of annexation was presumably negotiated, but it was not signed by the reigning monarch. He died before he was forced to sign away his independence. From that time on, Washington displayed a continuing political interest, aided by American sugar planters, in the monarchy. In 1893, a revolution "organized by the descendants of American missionaries and traders" dethroned the reigning Queen Liliuokalani. The provisional government, backed by the American Minister and U.S. troops, negotiated an instrument for annexation to the United States, which President Cleveland did not submit for ratification. However, he recognized the Republic of Hawaii in 1894. His successors completed the annexation. See John L. Latane, *A History of American Foreign Policy* (New York: Doubleday, Doran, 1927), pp. 565–68; Julius W. Pratt, *A History of United States Foreign Policy* (New York: Prentice-Hall, 1955), pp. 283–84, 332–35, 391–92.

17. *Progress and Welfare in Southeast Asia* (New York: Institute of Pacific Relations, 1940). It is interesting to note that the monthly *Amerasia*, during the year before the outbreak of World War II (November, 1937, to November, 1938), published but three articles on Southeast Asian topics and in only one of them (John Leroy Christian, "The Kra Canal Fable," February, 1938) is there a reference by name to "southeastern Asia," which he calls "a neglected vineyard by the historian and research worker."

18. This subsequently appeared in *Netherlanders over de zeën* (Utrecht, 1940), and in translation in *Indonesian Trade and Society* (The Hague: Van Hoeve, 1955). Professor Karl J. Pelzer in a book review has recently called attention to a half-dozen scattered references to "Southeast Asia" in the 1920's, *Journal of Asian Studies*, XXV, No. 2 (February, 1965), p. 343.

19. See Vice-Admiral, The Earl Mountbatten of Burma, *op. cit.*

20. In the issue for 1930, p. 79, largely devoted to discussion of United States interests in the Pacific, the Far East, and the Philippines.

21. The lack of popular knowledge about Burma may be illustrated by John Gunther's massive, 600-page *Inside Asia* (New York: Harper & Bros., 1939). In the book, the Philippines receive 19 pages; Singapore, including Malaya, British Borneo, and Sarawak, 17 pages; Indonesia, 10 pages; Siam, 11 pages; and French Indochina and Burma a page each. For Burma, Gunther apparently averaged the years of the three Anglo-Burmese wars, and came up with a complete fiction: "The British detached it [Burma] from the dying body of the Manchu Empire in the 1860's." If we turn to American scholarly work on Burma between the two world wars, using 1942 as a cut-off date, we find that one doctoral dissertation and one expanded M.A. thesis were published: Harry I. Marshall, *op. cit.*; and John Leroy Christian, *Modern Burma* (this is an expanded study of his 1936 M.A. thesis). An edition of this appeared in Shanghai just before Pearl Harbor; most copies were destroyed. It was subsequently reprinted by the University of California Press in 1942; and with two additional concluding chapters (but no other changes) appeared as *Burma and the Japanese Invader* (Bombay: Thacker & Co., 1945). There were four unpublished dissertations: Ray Forest Spear, "The Syncretism of Animism and Buddhism in Burma" (Northwestern University,

1928); Clarence Hendershot, "The Conquest, Pacification and Administration of the Shan States by the British, 1886–1897" (University of Chicago, 1936); Lindsay A. Semmens, "A History of the Development of Education under the British Administration in Burma to 1886" (University of Southern California, 1938); and Cecil C. Hobbs, "Christian Education and the Burmese Family" (Colgate-Rochester Divinity School, 1942). In addition, Burma appears in more than passing reference in only some twelve American works on Southeast Asia, the chief ones being: Paul K. Benedict, "Kinship in Southeastern Asia" (Ph.D. dissertation, Harvard University, 1941), a linguistic study; J. Russell Andrus, *Rural Reconstruction in Burma* (Bombay: Oxford University Press, 1936); Helmut G. Callis, *op. cit.*; Rupert Emerson, Lennox A. Mills, and Virginia Thompson, *Government and Nationalism in Southeast Asia* (New York: Institute of Pacific Relations, 1942); Kenneth S. Latourette, *A History of the Expansion of Christianity* (7 vols.; New York: Harper & Bros., 1937–45); and V. D. Wickizer and M. K. Bennett, *op. cit.* Briefer references will be found in such works as J. B. Pratt, *op. cit.*; Jack Shepherd, *Industry in Southeast Asia* (New York: Institute of Pacific Relations, 1941); and in a limited number of books and articles in the fields of archaelogy and prehistory, anthropology, and linguistics, e.g., W. C. Dodd, *The Tai Race* (Cedar Rapids, Iowa: Torch Press, 1923); Robert Shafer, "The Linguistic Relationship of Mru, Traces of a Lost Tibeto-Burmic Language," *Journal of the Burma Research Society*, XXXI (1940), 58–79; articles in *The Harvard Journal of Asiatic Studies*; and various articles on geology, archaeology, and prehistory by Helmut de Terra and H. L. Movius, Jr. In addition to the foregoing authors who were concerned with Burma and the surrounding area, there were a few American scholars who published material on individual Southeast Asian countries between the world wars (mostly in the 1930's). This material would include (while excluding works concerned with the Philippines): Raymond Kennedy, *The Ageless Indies* (New York: John Day, 1942); Amry Vandenbosch, *The Dutch East Indies* (1st ed., 1933; Los Angeles: University of California Press, 1941); Rupert Emerson, *Malaysia, a Study in Direct and Indirect Rule* (New York: Macmillan, 1937); Lennox A. Mills, *British Rule in Eastern Asia* (London: Oxford University Press, 1942); Virginia Thompson, *French Indo-China* (New York: Macmillan, 1937), and *Thailand the New Siam* (New York: Macmillan, 1941); Kenneth P. Landon, *Siam in Transition* (Chicago: University of Chicago Press, 1939), and *The Chinese in Thailand* (New York: Oxford University Press, 1941); and James M. Andrews, *Siam, Second Rural Economic Survey, 1934–1935*, published in Bangkok, 1935, under the auspices of the Siamese Government and Harvard University. There may be a few others which I have inadvertently omitted.

22. The quotation from Churchill (a speech in the House of Commons) and comment thereon are from Robert E. Sherwood, *Roosevelt and Hopkins, An Intimate History* (New York: Harper & Bros., 1948), pp. 362–63. The eight points of the Atlantic Charter have been widely reprinted. For a convenient source, see U.S. Department of State, *Postwar Foreign Policy Preparation, 1939–1945* (Washington, D.C.: Government Printing Office, 1949), p. 50.

23. *Postwar Foreign Policy Preparation, 1939–1945*, pp. 108–10, 187, 254, 470–72.

24. Sherwood, *op. cit.*, pp. 718–19.

25. *Ibid.*, p. 712. There is little doubt but that Roosevelt envisioned Hong Kong as a "free port," and Indochina being administered as a trust territory. See *ibid.*, p. 777, for an indirect reference: "Roosevelt referred to one of his favorite topics [in the Teheran conversations with Stalin] which was the education of the peoples of the Far Eastern Colonial areas, such as Indo-China, Burma, Malaya and the East Indies, in the arts of self-government; he pointed with pride to the American record in helping the people of the Philippines to prepare themselves for independence. He cautioned Stalin against bringing up the problems of India with Churchill, and Stalin agreed that this was un

doubtedly a sore subject. Roosevelt said that reform in India should begin from the bottom and Stalin said that reform from the bottom would mean revolution." If "education for self-government" was one of Roosevelt's favorite topics, he certainly was ill-informed about the strength of Asian nationalism in the countries he purportedly mentioned.

26. Rupert Emerson, *From Empire to Nation, The Rise to Self-Assertion of Asian and African Peoples* (Cambridge, Mass.: Harvard University Press, 1960), pp. 32–34. Emerson calls attention to Churchill's well-known colonial policy and to the similar position of the Free French (under De Gaulle) at their 1944 Brazzaville Conference.

27. *Postwar Foreign Policy Preparation, 1939–1945*, p. 221.

28. *The United States in World Affairs, 1945–1947* (New York: Harper & Bros., 1947), p. 300.

29. See *Postwar Foreign Policy Preparation, 1939–1945*, pp. 595–606, for general U.N. proposals and arrangements for "territorial trusteeships."

30. *War and Peace in the Pacific* (New York: Institute of Pacific Relations, 1943). The conference had two themes: "(1) What steps can jointly or severally be taken by the United Nations (particularly with those with major interests in the Pacific Area) to aid in the better prosecution of the war and in the establishment of conditions of racial, political and economic justice and welfare? (2) How far and by what means can conclusions drawn from the discussions under point (1) above, be made the basis of a practical program for the United Nations during and after the war?" (p. vi.). The conference was attended by Australia (4 [representatives]), Canada (18), China (17), Free France (4), India (9), Korea (1), Netherlands–Netherlands Indies (12, including 2 Indonesians), New Zealand (4), Philippines (4), Thailand (2), the United Kingdom (20), U.S. (34); and observers from the International Labor Office (6), League of Nations (2), Carnegie Corporation (2), Rockefeller Foundation (2); and 40 members of the International Secretariat, conference staff, and relatives. The conference members came from high positions in the professions, government, and industry. Some seventy papers were prepared by the membership. In addition, about two dozen supplementary papers (reprints, books, etc.) were distributed.

31. Radio address of December 6, 1942, reprinted in H. R. Isaacs, *New Cycle in Asia, Selected Documents* (New York: Macmillan, 1947), pp. 178–81.

32. Harry S. Truman, "Restatement of Foreign Policy of the United States," Department of State *Bulletin*, XIII (October 28, 1945), 653–56. It is interesting to note that, on at least two occasions, Bogyoke Aung San referred hopefully and approvingly to President Truman's "twelve point foreign policy." See *Burma's Challenge*, pp. 64, 169. The references occurred in Presidential addresses before the AFPFL in January and August, 1946.

33. Trager (ed.), *Marxism in Southeast Asia*, chap. vi.

34. John C. Campbell, *The United States in World Affairs, 1948–1949* (New York: Harper & Bros., 1949), p. 6.

35. Department of State *Bulletin*, XIII (October 21, 1945), p. 644. Note that this speech, "The Post-War Period in the Far East," closely paralleled, in substance and in time, President Truman's Navy Day speech, cited in n. 32.

36. Essentially, Vincent did not go beyond the "right of presently dependent Asiatic [sic] peoples to self-government" and preparations for this with timetables. (This is a narrow construction of the 1943 United States "Declaration by the U.N. on National Independence.")

37. *The United States in World Affairs, 1945–1947*, p. 300.

38. *Ibid.*, p. 301. (There were no penalties attached to removing labels.) The warning was issued by Secretary of State Byrnes on October 24, 1945. In December, 1945, the United States urged "all parties to resume conversations [in Indonesia] and to seek a peaceful solution in harmony with the U.N. Charter."

39. The Department of State *Bulletin*, XIII, pp. 261 and 338, announced

that the United States and Thailand had resumed diplomatic relations following a Thai statement on August 19, 1945, "declaring null and void the declaration of war, January 25, 1942 against the United States" and briefly describing the Free Thai Resistance movement against the Japanese. However, on January 16, 1946, the United States announced its refusal to recognize Thailand's occupation of territory claimed by French Indochina. In November, Thailand and France signed an agreement in Washington in which Thailand ceded back the disputed territory while withdrawing her U.N. Security Council complaint against the incursion of French troops.

40. For a concise and useful account, see William Henderson, *Pacific Settlement of Disputes: The Indonesian Question, 1946–1949* (New York: The Woodrow Wilson Foundation, 1954).

41. See "X" (George Kennan), "The Sources of Soviet Conduct," *Foreign Affairs*, XXV (July, 1947), pp. 566–82.

42. Department of State, *United States Relations with China . . . 1944–1949* (Washington, D.C.: Government Printing Office, August 1949), No. 3753, pp. 764–814.

43. This is the "defensive perimeter" speech delivered after the fall of China, on January 12, 1950 (U.S. Department of State *Bulletin*, XXII [January 23, 1950], 111–18). It should be remembered that this speech was given while a new American policy toward Asia was under review by a State Department committee. Philip C. Jessup, Raymond B. Fosdick, President Everett Case of Colgate, and our last Ambassador to China, John Leighton Stuart, were consultants to this committee. Its appointment had been announced in the Department of State *Bulletin*, XXI (August 15, 1949), pp. 236–37.

44. "By the end of 1948 . . . it was agreed among American policy makers that the struggle between the Soviet Union and the United States had reduced the importance of the effort to change Japanese society, and that it was of greater significance to rebuild Japan as a useful base for American power and to reduce the strain on American resources. . . . The United States consequently encouraged the development of a Japanese army—the national police reserve, trained and equipped by the American Army—despite the antiwar provision of the American drafted Japanese Constitution." Quoted from William Reitzel, M. A. Kaplan, and C. G. Coblenz, *United States Foreign Policy, 1945–1955* (Washington, D.C.: The Brookings Institution, 1956), pp. 173–74. It is interesting to note that in this closely written 535-page book, South and Southeast Asian policy is treated rather sketchily on pp. 222–29, 312–18; and always briefly, *passim*.

45. Interview with General Douglas MacArthur, *The New York Times*, March 2, 1949. Quoted in Campbell, *The United States in World Affairs, 1948–1949*, p. 303. Here again are the "fortified islands" of the *Fortune* editors.

46. It is pertinent to note that U.S. assistance to the United Kingdom during the decade of fighting against the Communist rebellion in Malaya was both generous and continuous. In the parallel case of Burma, neither the United Kingdom nor the U.S. was as generous or as understanding. This lack was evident even before Burma abrogated her defense agreement with the United Kingdom, on the grounds of lack of generosity and understanding.

47. On May 18, 1949, Secretary of State Acheson endorsed a statement by Nehru "to the effect that a Pacific Defense Pact would be premature until 'present internal conflicts in Asia' were resolved." Quoted in Richard P. Stebbins, *The United States in World Affairs, 1949* (New York: Harper & Bros., 1950), p. 61. The North Atlantic Treaty had already been signed (April 4, 1949).

48. Department of State *Bulletin*, XIII (November 18, 1945), 814.

49. *Ibid.*, XVI (June 29, 1947), 1314.

50. *Ibid.*, XVII (July 13, 1947), 101.

51. *Ibid.*, XVII (September 28, 1947), 648–49. Chargé d'Affaires E. L. Packer's statement, released to the Burmese press on September 19, 1947,

marked the first time that a United States diplomatic statement addressed to an independent Burmese government appeared in Burma. His statement: "The establishment of diplomatic relations and the exchange of diplomatic representatives between the United States and Burma is a mile-stone in the development of relations between the two countries signifying American recognition of Burma's changed political status. The government of the United States is deeply interested in developments in Burma and west coast Asia and looks forward to Burma's early emergence into full and independent statehood with resulting possibilities for international cooperation in a peaceful world. The United States government is hopeful that cultural and economic relations between Burma and the United States may develop to the mutual benefit of both countries."

52. *Ibid.*, XVII (January 12, 1948), 11. For the quoted messages see p. 61.

53. Ambassador Huddle reached Burma in March, 1948. Within two months, retaining his office in Burma, he was assigned to the Indian-Pakistan Kashmir U.N. Commission. He did not return to Burma until April, 1949, where he remained for six more months. In an interview with this author, Mr. Huddle confirmed the fact that during his ambassadorship, the United Kingdom insisted upon its priority and exclusivity with respect to providing arms for Burma. Obviously, an ambassador who spends thirteen consecutive months of his mission on another assignment outside his mission-post cannot do much for his embassy. He was away from Rangoon during the most critical period of the rebellion in Burma. U.S. Ambassador to Thailand Edwin F. Stanton represented Washington at Burma's Independence Day celebrations in 1948.

54. Department of State *Bulletin*, XVIII (January 4, 1948), 27. It also provided, for United States purposes, local currency equivalent to $3 million. Subsequent issues of the *Bulletin* detail various items (scholarships, teaching appointments, travel, etc.) in the agreement. See, for example, April 18, 1948, p. 487; April 25, 1948, pp. 552–53; June 13, 1948, p. 782, etc.

55. The air-transport agreement was the second one, but it, too, was referred to in the *Bulletin* XXI (October 10, 1949), 557–88, as "the first concluded by the Government of Burma." Obviously, the editors of the *Bulletin* wanted to establish a record of primacy.

56. *Ibid.*, August 29, 1949, p. 313.

57. "Postwar Problems in the Southeast Asia Policy of the United States," in Thayer, *op. cit.*, p. 39.

58. Quoted in Campbell, *The United States in World Affairs, 1948–1949*, p. 6. In 1947, the State Department organized its Policy Planning Staff with George Kennan as chief. He was then, as now, Europe-centered. His successor, Paul Nitze, had some interest in Asia, but (a) Secretary Acheson's interest was not particularly centered on Asia, and (b) after the elections of 1948, the Truman Administration was cautious about Asia because of sensitivity to the Republican criticism of its policy toward China.

59. Richard P. Stebbins, *The United States in World Affairs, 1949* (New York: Harper & Bros., 1950), p. 61.

60. *Ibid.*, p. 439, but see the whole passage for an apologia for the enfeebled American position, pp. 436–48.

61. Hugh Tinker writes that "the first American approach to Burma consisted in reciprocating the sentiments of 1776 but when, during 1948 and 1949, Burma appeared to be heading towards anarchy, American policy planners virtually wrote off the Burma Government as a spent force." (*The Union of Burma*, p. 367.)

Chapter 14: U.S. Policy and Aid to Burma

1. Department of State *Bulletin*, XXII (1950), 502. The above-named committee did not, as such, release any report. However, their general views were expressed by Raymond B. Fosdick in an article in *The New York Times*

Magazine, February 12, 1950, and by Ambassador Jessup in a radio address, "Report to the American People," on April 13, Department of State *Bulletin*, XXII, 627–30. I have treated the development of U.S. policy in Southeast Asia more extensively in "American Foreign Policy in Southeast Asia," R. K. Sakai (ed.), *Studies on Asia* (Lincoln, Neb.: University of Nebraska Press, 1965).

2. Department of State *Bulletin*, XXII (1950), 411; see also 791.

3. *Ibid.*, XXII, 525.

4. *Ibid.*, XXII, 111–18; and *ibid.*, XXII (March 27, 1950). See also Acheson, "Peace Through Strength: A Foreign Policy Objective," *ibid.*, XXII, 1037ff.

5. *Ibid.*, XXII, 334ff. However, McGhee repeated the remarks about Burma found in Acheson's January 12 speech; still assigned Burma's problems of security to the United Kingdom; and otherwise failed to express any sympathetic comment on Burma's plight.

6. *Ibid.*, XXII, 562–67. Rereading this speech once again, fifteen years later, I find it as a whole and in its parts impressive.

7. British Commonwealth Consultative Committee, *The Colombo Plan for Cooperative Economic Development in South and Southeast Asia*, Cmd. 8080 (London, 1950). Burma, Thailand, the Associated States of Indochina, and Indonesia were also present at the first meeting. The United States expressed "complete sympathy" for the effort, and together with the World Bank was expected to furnish funds, for the execution of projects, that fell within the £838 million required from external sources to complete the projected six-year program. U.S. bilateral aid agreements in the area are counted in the total. Burma formally joined the Colombo Plan in 1952. Twenty-two countries comprise the present membership. The *Working People's Daily*, November 15, 1964, carried a three-column excerpt from the *Economic Survey of Burma*, 1964 (Rangoon: GUB, 1964), which reiterated Burma's endorsement of the Colombo Plan.

8. John Foster Dulles, *War or Peace* (New York: Macmillan, 1953), pp. 120–37, 178–84. But see also p. 232 for the absence of "bipartisanship with respect to Far Eastern policies."

9. An Address, San Francisco Commonwealth Club, July 31, 1950. Department of State *Bulletin*, XXIII, 207ff.

10. Department of State *Bulletin*, XXIII, 465–68.

11. Reference to regional security agreements represented a distinct departure from pre-1950 policy. In a later speech, November 15, 1950, Rusk reiterated this interest and indicated that a security pact for Southeast Asia was being "thought" about. *Ibid.*, XXIII, p. 893. This foreshadowing of the Manila (Southeast Asia Treaty Organization) Pact of September, 1954, was again a theme of a speech by Rusk on November 6, 1951. He said then that "initial steps" had been taken toward such a pact and expressed hopes for "further cooperation." *Ibid.*, XXV, 821ff. The Congress, "over the Administration's objections," had written into the 1949 Mutual Defense Assistance Act (P.L. 329, 81st Cong.) a declaration in support of such a regional security organization for free Asia. This may have contributed to the shift in the Department of State's policy on this point.

12. Rusk appears to have recognized the inconsistency. In a speech, "The Underlying Principles of Far Eastern Policy," made before the World Affairs Council, Seattle, November 6, 1951, he said: "Many Americans have been troubled in the past about the issue of colonialism in Indo-China. We believe that that question is well on the way to solution . . . it is not surprising that doubts remain in Indo-China and among other countries of Asia." *Ibid.*, XXV, 821ff. He did not say what kind of solution was on the way.

13. "Foreign Policies Toward Asia," *ibid.*, XXIII (September 18, 1950), 464.

14. *The New York Times*, March 22, 1950.

15. Department of State *Bulletin*, XXIII, 500. For the agreement, see

Department of State, "Economic Cooperation with Burma," *Treaties and Other International Acts Series*, No. 2128 (Washington, D.C.: Government Printing Office, 1950). (Hereafter cited as *TIAS*.) For a full listing of United States–Burma treaties and agreements, see *Treaties in Force* (Washington, D.C.: Government Printing Office, published yearly). The agreement was known in Burma as "the Bilateral."

16. Department of State *Bulletin*, XXII, 856. For the agreement, see *TIAS*, No. 2163.

17. Charles Wolf, Jr., *Foreign Aid, Theory and Practice in Southern Asia* (Princeton, N.J.: Princeton University Press, 1960), p. 82. See "Economic and Program Reference Notes Prepared in Connection with Congressional Hearings on FY 1952 Programs for Southeast Asia, Philippines and Formosa" (mimeographed; September, 1951). This was prepared under the direction of R. Allen Griffin, Director, Far East Program Division, ECA.

18. The author is one of those who made the "longe-range" analysis in the cable traffic between Rangoon and Washington. On my return to the U.S. in 1953, I also prepared a monograph for the 1954 Kyoto Conference of the Institute of Pacific Affairs: "Towards a Welfare State in Burma . . . 1948–54 (New York: Institute of Pacific Relations, 1954; mimeographed). I indicated that Burma was "in for two rude shocks" because of the strain on her thin layers of leadership and because her timetables for development were excessively paced, and the related resources unwisely allocated. I suggested then that a "twenty-year" spread "would not be an unwise time-goal" (pp. 49–60). In the second edition to this work, *Building a Welfare State in Burma*, I again called attention to this problem. With more evidence on hand in 1965 than in 1954, I still believe that the then suggested twenty-year timetable, starting from 1954, was about right. The "two rude shocks"—strain on leadership and the noneconomic factors in economic development—have been felt in Burma and have been partially recognized.

19. An unpublished, unclassified report to the Director of the Foreign Operations Administration, Harold Stassen, itemized:

Number of Projects	Sector	Approximation, in Millions of Dollars
10	Agriculture	$4.1
6	Public health	2.25
12	Education	1.82
To be determined	Industry, transport, and communications	1.14
2	Commodity imports	1.4
1	Engineering and economic planning	1.25
1	Leadership exchange	.2
	Total	$12.16

SOURCE: Frank N. Trager, "Summary Evaluation Report on Burma," August, 1953, typescript with Appendix, 26pp.

20. These are approximate figures; there are minor discrepancies among the sources. See Wolf, *op. cit.*, pp. 90–91; pp. 124–25; pp. 142–43, for funds obligated by total and by sectors for FY '51, '52, and '53. A slightly different approach and totals appear in International Cooperation Administration, *U.S. External Assistance, Obligations and Other Commitments July 1, 1945 through June 30, 1959* (Washington, D.C.: March 16, 1960), p. 23. (Hereafter cited as ICA, *U.S. External Assistance*, 1945–59.) The table in the text is compiled from Wolf, *op. cit.* See also *Burma Weekly Bulletin*, January 13, 1954, for a summary of U.S. aid to Burma, 1950–53.

21. Frank N. Trager and Helen G. Trager, "Exporting and Training Experts," *The Review of Politics*, XXIV (January, 1962), 88–108.

22. See *The Nation*, October 7–9, 14–15, 1951; and editorial, "Thanks for Nothing, Mr. Griffin," December 22, 1951.

23. One of the useful studies of foreign-aid legislation in this period is William Adams Brown, Jr. and Redvers Opie, *American Foreign Assistance* (Washington, D.C.: The Brookings Institution, 1953). The Foreign Assistance Act of 1948—the basic legislation—contained four titles: I, The Economic Cooperation Act of 1948; II, International Children's Emergency Fund; III, Greek-Turkish Aid Act of 1948; IV, China Aid Act of 1948. It was amended and the titles reorganized in succeeding years. In 1950 (P.L. 535, 81st Cong.), Title I remained; II covered the China Area; III, Aid to Palestine Refugees; IV, the new legislation known as the "Act for International Development," or Point IV; and V, International Children's Welfare Work. The 1951 MSA (P.L. 165, 82d Cong.) embraced the former independent agency known as ECA and was renamed the Mutual Security Administration; the Technical Cooperation Administration (Point IV) and the Institute of Inter-American Affairs, which had provided assistance to Latin America, were also placed under it. The several titles of the act were now assigned to areas, e.g., Europe, the Near East and Africa, Asia and the Pacific, American Republics, etc., and to the organization that was to administer the program. After President Eisenhower took office, the MSA was renamed the Foreign Operations Administration and later the International Cooperation Administration. Under Presidents Kennedy and Johnson, it became known as the Agency for International Cooperation. The Mutual Security Act of 1951, as amended and rewritten in 1954, remained the basic legislative authority for all assistance programs since then although, at the beginning of the Kennedy Administration, it was renamed the Foreign Assistance Act. It should be noted, however, that other legislation passed during periods of war, such as the "Buy American" and Battle acts, are Congressional limitations on foreign aid. See also Wolf, *op. cit.*, for documentation of MSA, 1951, and later.

24. Opie, *op. cit.*, pp. 523–24.

25. See *The Mutual Security Program, Second Report to Congress for the Six Months Ending June 30, 1952* (Washington, D.C.: Government Printing Office, 1952), p. 30. These semiannual reports are useful records; so is the annual *Summary Presentation to the Congress* made by the administering agency.

26. "Agreement relating to the assurance required by the Mutual Security Act of 1951," entered into force February 9, 1952. TIAS, No. 2602.

27. These proposals, made to me as Chief of STEM, were subsequently put forward in an unclassified mimeographed document dated June 16, 1952 (in author's possession). It may be noted that U Nu's approach found favor in U.S.–Latin American aid programs after 1960; and was accepted without argument by the Russians when they entered into aid agreements with Burma.

28. Department of State *Bulletin*, XXVII, 864. See TIAS, No. 2888, for the agreement signed in Washington, which came into force on October 24, 1952. These projects totaled $6.58 million, plus U.S. administrative costs for STEM. Between 1950–53, there were almost 100 projects—an excessive number by any yardstick.

29. *The New York Times*, March 30, 1953; and editorial, *New Times of Burma*, March 31, 1953. Rumors had been circulating in Rangoon for some time about such activity. Former U.S. Ambassador to Burma David McK. Key stated: "I had heard persistent reports that Americans were taking part [in KMT attacks] when I was sent there [Burma, in 1950], I found that hard to credit but learned differently later." Quoted in Warren Unna, "CIA: Who Watches the Watchman," *Harper's Magazine*, April, 1958, p. 49.

30. "Address on International Situation," Chamber of Deputies, September 22, 1960, in *Burma Weekly Bulletin*, September 29, 1960.

31. See Trager, Wohlgemuth, and Lu-yu Kiang, *Burma's Role in the United Nations*, pp. 9–13.

32. A token evacuation began in August, 1953; the Burmese renewed their

complaint at the Eighth General Assembly; a more substantial evacuation then took place. Estimates vary, but about 7,000 to 8,000 persons (soldiers and families) were removed from Burma. In 1954, Taiwan "disavowed" those who remained. Pockets of these "bandits" and "guerrillas"—they are thus called by the Burmese press—still remained to create trouble on the borders of Burma, Laos, and Thailand. In March, 1961, U Nu asked the United States or Britain for arms to fight the remnants of these "Nationalist Chinese Irregulars," *The New York Times,* April 1, 1961. *The Nation* April 1, 1961, quoted Colonel Than Sein as saying that there were then 2,500 remaining "Chinese Nationalist Irregulars." Subsequent evacuations removed 4,300 from the Burma–Thai–Laos border area. Since this evacuation in the spring of 1961, the Burmese have estimated officially that only about 800 remain. From a military standpoint, the problem is now manageable. In conversation with any knowledgeable Burmese, the festering KMT issue elicits deeply felt anger toward the Chinese Nationalists and Washington—toward the former because of the danger that it created for all the years since 1950; toward the latter because of its alleged unwillingness to force its client, Chiang Kai-shek, to submit on this issue. In my view, the Burmese assessment—without respect to the larger conflict between the Chinese Nationalists and Communists—is largely justified.

33. *Special Study Mission to Southeast Asia and the Pacific* (Washington, D.C.: Government Printing Office, 1954), p. 65.

34. *The New York Times,* October 15, 16, 19, 23, 1954. These stories referred to Burma's desire for "indirect help," her fear of American "dumping" of rice and other cereals in Asia, her desire to have the Prime Minister visit the U.S. to discuss trilateral rice deals.

35. *Ibid.,* February 27, 1955.

36. Saul Nelson, "Domestic and Foreign Trade," in Trager *et al., Burma,* chap. xxvi, pp. 1393–1449.

37. *Economic Survey of Burma, 1955* (Rangoon: GUB, 1955), p. 2.

38. At this time, U Nu again advanced the view that aid should not be given purely on a grant basis. If the recipient, in some way, repaid the donor, the relationship would not thereby suffer from the "donor" approach. It is interesting to note that in pursuance of this view the Government of Burma sent $10,000 to the American Red Cross in September, 1953, for the relief of tornado victims; and on June 30, 1955, U Nu presented a check for $5,000 to President Eisenhower for the children of veterans of the Burma campaign in World War II. These represented a symbolic reciprocity.

39. TIAS, No. 3498; see also amendments to this agreement, No. 3628 (July 25, 1956); No. 3707 (December 4, 1956); and No. 3846 (June 14, 1957).

40. For the Highway and Facilities Agreement, see Department of State *Bulletin,* XLI (July 27, 1959), 121; and *Burma Weekly Bulletin,* July 16, 1959.

41. See *The New York Times,* July 7, 10, 1959; *The Nation,* July 8 and 11, 1959. The crypto-Communists of the NUF denounced it; see *The Nation,* November 19, 1958; and July 16, 1959. See also the considerate editorials on "Foreign Aid, Its Success and Failure," in *The Guardian,* November 17 and 18, 1959.

42. *Economic Survey of Burma, 1960,* p. 106. See also editorials, *The Guardian,* October 13 and December 18, 1960, for a reasonable criticism of the "wrangle" over the road project and the resolution of the "deadlock."

43. *Economic Survey of Burma, 1964,* quoted in *Working People's Daily,* November 8, 1964.

44. See *Forward,* November 7, 1962, and November 15, 1964, for early progress reports on Namsang. TIAS, No. 5198 covers the P.L. 480 Agreement.

45. See ICA, U.S. *External Assistance, Obligations and Other Commitments July 1, 1945 through June 30, 1959,* p. 23.

46. The IBRD, after almost three years of investigation, 1953–56, made

three successive loans to Burma, totaling $33.35 million, primarily for port of Rangoon and railroad development. In March, 1956, Burma borrowed $15 million from the International Monetary Fund.

47. "A Statistical Summary of Activities from July 1950–June 1965," *Technical Assistance Newsletter* of the U.N. Trade Assistance Board, III, No. 4 (June–July 1965), 11; and *Economic Survey of Burma*, 1963, p. 139. Burma continues to share in the Expanded Technical Assistance Program, receiving approximately $800,000 per year, and has shared, since 1962, in the allocation of the U.N. Special Fund, from which she received an initial grant of approximately $200,000.

48. This paragraph illustrates rather than exhausts the sources and amounts of assistance received by Burma. It does not include, for example, the $200 million in reparations from Japan following the Peace and Reparations Treaty signed in November, 1954, and later amended to include an additional $140 million. Nor does it include private aid from such agencies as the Ford Foundation and the Asia Foundation, both of which were requested to suspend activity in Burma when the RC took power in 1962. General Ne Win preferred only government-to-government aid relationships.

49. *Second Four-Year Plan for the Union of Burma* (*1961–62 to 1964–65*), p. 37ff. This plan, now shelved, was the most sophisticated economic effort yet prepared by official Burmese sources.

Chapter 15: The Burmese Rice Case and Sino-Soviet Aid

1. Union Bank of Burma *Bulletin*, 1962, p. 105; and George T. Beck, *Basic Data on the Economy of Burma* (Washington, D.C.: Department of Commerce, 1958), p. 14. This is an average increase of approximately $2 million of U.S. exports to Burma compared with the previous three years.

2. Several of the following pages are based on an updated section from the author's "Burma's Foreign Policy, 1948–1956; Neutralism, Third Force, and Rice," pp. 99–102. See also Hans Heyman, Jr., "Soviet Foreign Aid as a Problem for U.S. Policy," *World Politics*, XII (July, 1960), 525–40. The literature on this issue, as Heyman points out, has "proliferated." It is among the "most exhaustively reported of all features of contemporary Soviet foreign policy." He supplies some representative references to this literature. Among the more valuable noted therein and since are: Joseph S. Berliner, *Soviet Economic Aid* (New York: Frederick A. Praeger, Inc., 1958); *The Sino-Soviet Economic Offensive in the Less Developed Countries* (Washington, D.C.: Department of State, 1958); Michael Sapir, *The New Role of the Soviets in the World Economy* (Committee for Economic Development, 1958); Charles Wolf, Jr., *Foreign Aid, Theory and Practice in Southern Asia*, chap. xi, "Soviet Economic Aid in Southern Asia," pp. 383–400; and especially, for Burma, Robert L. Allen, "Burma's Clearing Account Agreements," *Pacific Affairs*, XXXI, No. 2 (June, 1958), 147–63.

3. *KTA, Comprehensive Report*, I, 45–48. See also Walinsky, *op. cit.*, p. 118, for what I regard as an apologia for KTA's projections.

4. See Saul Nelson, *op. cit.*, pp. 1415–20; and John H. Badgley, *Burma's Foreign Economic Relations 1948–1958* (Rangoon: The Rangoon-Hopkins Center, 1959), pp. 8–12; and Appendix IV, pp. 1–3. The *Economic Survey of Burma* offers tables made available annually by the State Agricultural Marketing Board on the volume, value, and destination of rice exports.

5. See Union Bank of Burma *Bulletin*, "Foreign Exchange Reserves" (various years). More recently, i.e., 1958–64, these reserves have climbed steadily, reaching approximately $224 million by the end of July, 1965. Some carryover and deteriorated rice was sold as fodder. Not until 1958–59 were all old stocks finally liquidated.

6. As late as December, 1956, the House Committee on Foreign Affairs received a report from its subcommittee charged with an examination and re-

appraisal of foreign policy in relation to Mutual Security and related legislation, in which it was stated that "theoretically it [neutralism] should be opposed by the United States since nations assuming a neutralist stand are, in effect, overlooking and avoiding the moral principles involved in the cold war." However, it was prepared to forego strict application of theory toward uncommitted countries under certain minimum conditions. See H.R. Committee on Foreign Affairs, *Foreign Policy and Mutual Security, Draft Report* (Washington, D.C.: Government Printing Office, 1956), p. 59R.

7. The various Economic Cooperation and Mutual Security acts, generally, or specifically, provided for the use of U.S. agricultural surplus commodities in the granting of aid. See, for example, the Economic Cooperation Act of 1948 (P.L. 472, 80th Cong.) section 112, "Protection of Domestic Economy," which in one form or another was reincorporated in subsequent aid acts; also the Mutual Security Act of 1954 (P.L. 665, 83rd Cong., section 402) which earmarked $300 million to underwrite this export program; and especially P.L. 480, 83rd Cong., devoted exclusively to this issue. These acts are conveniently gathered in the H.R. Committee on Foreign Affairs, *Mutual Security Legislation and Related Documents* (Washington, D.C.: Government Printing Office, 1952); and International Cooperation Administration, *Mutual Security Legislation and Related Documents* (Washington, D.C.: International Cooperation Administration, December, 1955). P.L. 665 repealed previous mutual security legislation but did not substantially change its character.

8. P.L. 480, section 2.

9. The Corporation for Economic and Industrial Research, Inc., *Worldwide and Domestic Economic Problems and Their Impact on the Foreign Policy of the United States* (Washington, D.C.: Government Printing Office, 1959), pp. 8, 69.

10. Between July 1, 1954, and July 1, 1959, the United States entered into more than 150 local-currency sales agreements or supplements to agreements with thirty-eight countries under Title I, P.L. 480. India and Pakistan ranked first and fourth in these arrangements. See the brief, insightful analysis and summary by W. W. Cochrane, "Public Law 480 and Related Programs," *The Annals,* CCCXXXI (September, 1960), 14–19.

11. The quotations are from a Burmese Cabinet Minister as reported in *The New York Times,* October 21, 1954. See also *ibid.,* May 2, 1956; *The Guardian,* November 28, 1959; and *The Nation,* November 27, 1959. The last-named also referred "to the dampening effect that gifts of wheat to India and Pakistan had on the sale of Burmese rice"; but along with other expressions of Burmese opinion, recognizes the propriety of such "humanitarian" gifts.

12. *Foreign Policy and Mutual Security Draft Report,* p. 278.

13. *The New York Times,* October 15 and 24, 1954. See *supra,* Chapter 14, p. 322.

14. *Burma Weekly Bulletin,* April 5, 1956. For a review of these and related arrangements, see Robert L. Allen, *op. cit.;* see also Department of State, *The Sino-Soviet Economic Offensive in the Less Developed Countries,* pp. 70–74; and The Council for Economic and Industry Research, *Foreign Assistance of the Communist Bloc and Their Implications for the United States* (Washington, D.C.: Government Printing Office, March, 1957), pp. 86–87, for a tabular summary of the 1954–56 agreements. This study, with its appendixes and tables, prepared for the U.S. Senate Special Committee to Study the Foreign Aid Program is very helpful. See Appendix B-2 on exports to the bloc, pp. 70–78.

15. A paperback book, *Visit to Burma of N. A. Bulganin . . . and N. S. Khrushchev* (Moscow: Foreign Languages Publishing House, 1956), appeared with extraordinary speed in the bookstalls of Rangoon, priced at approximately ten cents. See pp. 147–48.

16. *The Guardian,* October 25, 1959.

17. The concession obviously conformed to Soviet interests. See Stanley

J. Zyzniewski, "The Soviet Bloc and the Underdeveloped Countries," *World Politics*, XI (April, 1959), 378–98, which analyzes the trade offensive of bloc countries (excluding China) in selected countries of Afro-Asia (Burma included), calling attention, among other things, to the primary role of East Germany, Czechoslovakia, and Poland in this effort. Their continued industrial expansion requires, among other things, the primary products that are available from the Afro-Asian world. Hence the bloc, according to this author, has emphasized trade both as a political weapon and economic necessity. Burma's trade with the U.S.S.R. climbed from zero in 1953 to an average of $15 million per annum in 1955–57. During 1953–57, the total value of its trade with the U.S.S.R. was estimated at $45.1 million, and its trade with the three satellites at $48.2 million. If the other European satellites are added, this latter figure becomes $56.1 million. See *ibid.*, Tables 1–3, pp. 382–83. For these same years, Sino-Burmese trade hovered somewhere between $78 million and $80 million. For the years 1958–61, it climbed to $125 million. See Union Bank of Burma *Bulletin*, various quarters.

18. These figures are taken from the relevant annual editions of the *Economic Survey of Burma. The Nation*, September 15, 1959, reported that General Ne Win's caretaker government had insisted that new barter agreements with the Soviet bloc include payment in sterling for 25 per cent of the total. Only Yugoslavia among the "barter countries" had accepted this condition, but the bloc countries had not yet responded to this new Burmese requirement. The *Economic Survey of Burma*, 1960, p. 42, is silent on this point, although earlier in the year, before U Nu's government was elected, the SAMB had reported forward sales of 77,000 tons of 1959–60 rice to the U.S.S.R. and other "barter countries." In 1960–61, no sales are recorded for these countries. Since 1961, only the U.S.S.R. appears as a buyer. See the 1963 *Economic Survey of Burma*, p. 67. In the three years 1961–64, it purchased 65,000, 80,000, and 100,000 tons, respectively. Since 1960–61, Communist China has become a large buyer of rice, ranging from 355,000 tons in 1960, to 100,-000 tons at the beginning of 1965. See *ibid.*, 1960, 1961, 1962, 1963, 1964, and editorial, "Burma's Rice Trade," *Hanthawaddy*, January 29, 1965.

19. See editions of the Union Bank of Burma *Bulletin* for total trade figures with China. The totals for the Soviet bloc, not including China, are derived from various sources, including the reports to Congress by the International Cooperation Administration made under the terms of the Mutual Defense Assistance Control (Battle) Act of 1951.

20. *Burma Weekly Bulletin*, February 23, 1956.

21. In an interesting examination of the English and Russian texts of a Moscow publication, *Economic Cooperation Between the U.S.S.R. and Underdeveloped Countries* (Moscow: Foreign Languages Publishing House, n.d. [1962]). The Russian text, published in 1963, is longer. Nadia Derkach, *The Differences in Soviet Portrayal of Their Aid to Underdeveloped Countries in English and in Russian* (Santa Monica, Calif.: The RAND Corporation, January, 1964), points out that the English text is bowdlerized. It omits or rephrases the Russian in order to conceal any intent to use Soviet aid as a political weapon in pushing these countries in the direction of "socialism."

22. Ceylon officials made numerous attempts to gain the sympathetic consideration of Western governments when Ceylon faced the necessity of selling its rubber for rice during the Korean War boom period. While serving as Point Four director in Burma, the author was asked to plead Ceylon's case. Obviously, the West did not heed any plea. Ceylon's five-year trade agreement with Communist China was signed on December 18, 1952. For an unpersuasive defense of the U.S. position on this complicated issue, see *Soviet Technical Assistance in Non-Communist Asia*, Staff Study No. 3, Committee on Foreign Relations, 84th Cong. (Washington, D.C.: Government Printing Office, June 10, 1955), p. 21.

23. See Department of State, *The Communist Economic Offensive Through 1963*, Research Memorandum, RSB-43, June 18, 1964. Mimeographed.

24. *The Nation,* November 27, 1959; and *The Guardian,* November 28, 30, 1959.

25. Quoted in *The Nation,* November 28, 1959.

26. John Foster Dulles, "Policy in the Far East," Series 5, No. 76 (Washington, D.C.: Department of State, 1958). Secretary Dulles was addressing the California Chamber of Commerce in San Francisco. His examples of Chinese goods were mainly those of the consumer variety. Additional evidence has since appeared in the case of minerals. The Secretary then said: "This problem as it arises in the Far East is one phase of the economic offensive now being initiated by the Sino-Soviet bloc. Your Government is intensively studying this problem. We have asked business people—some from the group I am addressing—to study it. There is no doubt in my mind but what concrete measures will be needed to assure that in the face of this unfair competition free enterprise will continue to play its full role as a dynamic and expanding force in developing the economies of the free-world nations." Such sensitivity to the problems of "dumping" and "unfair competition" is highly desirable. But it requires a two-way approach.

27. A/Res/1496/XV, October 28, 1960.

28. Essentially, this is the view expressed by *The Economist,* January 7, 1956, pp. 13–14; and again, though less sharply, on March 9, 1957, p. 526.

29. See, for example, Douglas Dillon, "Realities of Soviet Foreign Economic Policies," Address, Mississippi Valley World Trade Council, New Orleans, January 27, 1959, Department of State Publication 6780 (Washington, D.C.) pp. 12–13. Dillon writes: "The short-term objective [of the Sino-Soviet economic offensive] is to provoke and capitalize on tensions between the less developed and the more developed nations of the free world. The long-range aim is to create climates and attitudes in the newly emerging areas which will be conducive to eventual Communist takeover."

30. These credits are reported in the 1964 *Economic Survey of Burma,* "International Assistance Programme," excerpts of which were published in the *Working People's Daily,* November 2, 1964.

31. Union Bank of Burma *Bulletin,* 1962 (latest available statistics), pp. 100, 104–5.

Chapter 16: Burma and the United States: Retrospect and Prospect

1. Pakistan is also a member of the U.S.-supported Central Treaty Organization (the Baghdad Pact); while Thailand, Laos, and the Republic of Vietnam have received special defense commitments from the U.S. which are independent of SEATO. Cambodia has withdrawn from SEATO. The Geneva Agreements of 1962 specifically abrogated the coverage for Laos provided by SEATO.

2. See Frank N. Trager, "Laos and the Defense of Southeast Asia," *Orbis,* VII, No. 3 (Fall, 1963), 550–82; and "Vietnam: The Military Requirements for Victory," *ibid.,* VIII, No. 3 (Fall, 1964), 563–83.

3. *An Asian Speaks,* pp. 13–18. Even the liberal U.S. magazine *The Reporter,* XV (November 15, 1956), 8, 30–32, printed an article that was not too friendly or accurate, "Burma—Parade of Paradoxes," which comments: "Burma has come into the picture lately as one of those so-called uncommitted Asian nations which never commit themselves against Communism." Arthur Bonner, the author, was then CBS correspondent in India. Bonner completely ignored the Second Asian Socialist Conference held in Bombay on November 1–10, 1956, at which time Premier Ba Swe, of whom he was critical, roundly attacked the Soviet invasion and violation of Hungary. Perhaps Bonner's material was written before this event, but he also ignored former Deputy Premier Kyaw Nyein's vigorous denunciation of Soviet imperialism in 1954. He ignored, as did the editors of the magazine—and many others since then—the armed struggle of the Burmese Government against domestic Communist insurrection.

4. The most recent expression of this will be found in the "Joint Communiqué" issued by the Chairman of the Revolutionary Council of Burma and the Indian Prime Minister on the occasion of the former's visit to India. See text, *The Guardian*, February 12, 1965. William C. Johnstone, *op. cit.*, questions whether Ne Win's Revolutionary Council will adhere to the policy of "positive neutralism." He suggests, though he offers no evidence, that Burma's "actions . . . demonstrate that [the] government and the country have come within the sphere of Communist China . . . and the Chinese Communists can exercise a virtual veto on Burma's policy and actions" (p. 294). However, he also states that "at no time since 1948 does it seem that the major nations of either bloc deemed Burma important enough in the furtherance of their interests to make a concerted effort to win the Burma government to their side" (p. 261). Johnstone cannot have it both ways. What is at stake is less the *expressions* of neutralism than the positive ways in which the United States or other countries relate to Burma. This is our burden, as much as it is that of the Burmese. Johnstone, somewhat impatient with neutralism as a policy, nonetheless is forced to admit that Burma's "record . . . has been good."

5. See, for example, *Forward* (August 15, 1964), pp. 11–14, for his first visit to Burma since his election to the post; and the press of the period. The Burmese press, during late February, 1965, immediately echoed U Thant's call for a U.N. Charter revision. See U Yan Gon, "Revising U.N. Charter," *Rangoon Daily* (February 24, 1965).

6. *Burma* (Rangoon), III (July, 1954), 39–45; and "Message," *Forward*, III (November 1, 1964), p. 5.

7. See, for example, U Thant's speech, "A Burmese View of Asian-American Relations," Sixth National Conference, U.S. National Commission for UNESCO, San Francisco, November 8, 1957. The views expressed by U Thant as ambassador have been repeated by every prominent Burmese political figure in and outside the U.N.

8. From an article by Ye Din *Hanthawaddy*, February 1, 1965. The pro-Peking *Ludu* (Mandalay), January 31, 1965, not only supported Indonesia's withdrawal but urged that other nations should get out to join "Red China" and Indonesia and form a new and rival organization. The rival pro-Moscow *Botataung* (Rangoon), February 7, 1965, recommends that the People's Republic of China be admitted and that the U.N. reorganize in such a way as to have "all capitalist, socialist and newly developing nations sitting together on equal status." Earlier, on December 29, 1964, the *Working People's Daily* editorialized that the crisis over U.N. peace-keeping finances should not be allowed to "paralyze" the U.N. and that the smaller nations should seek a way to make the U.N. "continuously effective" by solving both the financial and veto-power issues.

9. Both Burma and India reiterated this in the joint communiqué cited in n. 4 above.

10. There is an essential difference between the U Nu and Ne Win regimes with respect to Buddhism. U Nu, in keeping with the royal tradition, saw the state as a defender of the faith, and constitutionally made Buddhism the state religion. Ne Win, both in his earlier and present administrations, seemingly adopted the view which we would call "separation of church and state"—although it was not adopted without the typical conflict as to where the "wall of separation" should be placed. See, for example, the editorial "Conference of Sanghas of all Sects [of Buddhism]," *Working People's Daily*, February 9, 1965.

11. For text of the pamphlet *Dhammantaraya* [*Dhamma in Danger*], see *Burma Weekly Bulletin*, April 30, 1959. See also Fred von der Mehden, "Burma's Religious Campaign Against Communism," *Pacific Affairs*, XXXIII (September, 1960), 290–99; and Frank N. Trager, "Reflections on Buddhism and the Social Order in Southern Asia," pp. 529–43.

A BIBLIOGRAPHICAL NOTE

Of the making of bibliographies there is no end. Each author reviews the literature of his subject and selects those titles which for various reasons he finds pertinent to it. The reader of this study will find such titles amply cited, usually with the author's comments, in the notes supplied for the chapters. There is little point in reviewing these titles here. However, it may be helpful to the inquiring student to list bibliographical sources should he wish to pursue the subject.

In 1956-57, as an outcrop of the Burma Research Project at New York University, I edited two behavioral-science bibliographies on Burma for the Human Relations Area Files: *Annotated Bibliography on Burma* (New Haven, Conn.: Human Relations Area Files Press, 1956), and *Japanese and Chinese Language Sources on Burma, An Annotated Bibliography* (New Haven, Conn.: Human Relations Areas Files Press, 1957). Whatever their limitations, these two remain the only published bibliographies on the subject. Together they list more than 1,200 entries, all of which are annotated. The first of these bibliographies contains both an alphabetical and topical listing of all cited titles; both refer to thirty-six previously published, more general works with significant bibliographical material on Burma. For references since their publication, the student is best advised to consult the relevant topical sections of the annual bibliographical number of the *Journal of Asian Studies* (formerly the *Far Eastern Quarterly*).

The following items will supplement the foregoing:

BARNETT, L. D. *A Catalogue of the Burmese Books in the British Museum*. London: the British Museum, 1913.

CADY, JOHN F. *A History of Modern Burma*. Ithaca, N. Y.: Cornell University Press, 1958. Bibliography, pp. 651-66.

FISHER, JOSEPH. "Research Bibliography of Books, Documents and

Pamphlets on Burma." Rangoon-Hopkins Center for Southeast Asian Studies. Rangoon, 1953. Mimeographed.

GARD, RICHARD A. "A Select Bibliography for the Study of Buddhism in Burma in Western Languages." Compiled at the request of the International Institute for Advanced Buddhistic Studies, Kaba Aye, Rangoon. Tokyo, 1957. Mimeographed.

HART, D. V. "A Bibliography of Novels about Burma." Syracuse University, August, 1959. Mimeographed.

HLA PE. *Konmara Pya Zat, An Example of Popular Burmese Drama in the XIX Century by U Pok Ni.* Vol. I, Introduction and Translation. London: Luzac and Co., 1952. See footnotes to Introduction and Bibliography.

HOSTEN, H., and THE REVEREND E. LUCE. *Bibliotheca Catholica Birmana.* Rangoon: British Burma Press, 1915. Useful as a start, but the subject warrants further research.

McVEY, RUTH T. *Bibliography of Soviet Publications on Southeast Asia.* Data Paper No. 34, Southeast Asia Program, Cornell University. Ithaca, N. Y., 1959. "Burma," pp. 40-49.

QUIGLY, E. P. *Libraries, Manuscripts and Books of Burma.* London: Arthur Probsthain, 1956. A delightful author-illustrated essay.

STUCKI, CURTIS W. *American Doctoral Dissertations on Asia, 1933-58.* Data Paper, No. 37, Southeast Asia Program, Cornell University. Ithaca, N. Y., August, 1959. Also Supplement, 1963. There is a slowly increasing number of unpublished, completed doctoral dissertations at universities in the United States and England dealing with Burma and related areas; they should be consulted for their special topics.

TRAGER, FRANK N. *Annotated Bibliography of the Works of J. S. Furnivall.* Southeast Asia Studies, Yale University. New Haven, Conn., 1963.

WOODMAN, DOROTHY. *The Making of Burma.* London: Cresset Press, 1962. Bibliography, pp. 577-82. As Dorothy Woodman points out, "the Indian Office Library in London is the main repository of Britain's relations with Burma." Unfortunately, there is, as yet, no bibliography for the unrivaled material in this collection. Nor is there any complete bibliography of the published records of British-Burma relations.

It should be added that there is no bibliography of the many hundreds of works devoted to the World War II period in Burma. (My students and I are in the process of preparing such a work. We hope to cooperate with the Burma Defense Services Historical Research Institute, whose archives I have been privileged to consult.) The Imperial War Museum has compiled an eleven-page mimeographed list, "The Second World War, the Burma Campaign. A List of Selected Titles" (London, 1960)—a meager harvest.

Indigenous Burmese historiography has been the subject of a recent essay by Dr. Than Tun, in the *Working People's Daily Sup-*

plement on the Union Day, February 12, 1965; this has become an increasing concern of Dr. Than Tun and his colleagues Dr. Htin Aung, Dr. Kyaw Thet, and Dr. Yi Yi, among others, who served or are serving as members of the Burma Historical Commission. To these, one must add the wide-ranging publications of the scholar-jurist Chief Justice Dr. Maung Maung. The Commission is responsible, in part, for this post-independence development. Among the retired scholars, Dr. Pe Maung Tin and Professor Gordon H. Luce have contributed the most to our knowledge of Burmese sources. See, for example, the excellent brief account of the Burmese historical chronicles in their Introduction to *The Glass Palace Chronicle of the Kings of Burma* (London: Oxford University Press, 1923), pp. ix-xxii; also their bibliography in " Burma Down to the Fall of Pagan, an Outline," *Journal of the Burmese Research Society,* XXIX, Part I (1939), 274-82. In this connection, the specialized and growing library of the Commission, begun under the leadership of a former director, the late U Kaung, is worthy of notice. And at long last the Burma Government has taken steps to house and catalogue its National Library properly.

INDEX

NOTE: Burmese may have one, two, or three names. Only Christian Burmese have family names. U, Ko, Maung, Thakin, Bo, Mahn, and, for women, Daw and Ma, are usually (although not always) honorifics. Aliases, which some Burmese continue to use throughout life, appear in parentheses.